THIRD EDITION

Understanding Economics
A CONTEMPORARY PERSPECTIVE

Mark Lovewell

Ryerson University
Toronto, Ontario

McGraw-Hill
Ryerson

Toronto   Montreal   Boston   Burr Ridge IL   Dubuque IA   Madison VT
New York   San Francisco   St. Louis   Bangkok   Bogatá   Caracas   Kuala Lumpur   Lisbon   London
Madrid   Mexico City   Milan   New Delhi   Santiago   Seoul   Singapore   Sydney   Taipei

Understanding Economics
A Contemporary Perspective
Third Edition

ISBN: 0-07-091654-3

2 3 4 5 6 7 8 9 10 TCP 0 9 8 7 6 5

Printed and bound in Canada

Statistics Canada information is used with the permission of the Minister of Industry, as Minister responsible for Statistics Canada. Information on the availability of the wide range of data from Statistics Canada can be obtained from Statistics Canada's Regional Offices, its World Wide Web site at <http://www.statcan.ca>, and its toll-free access number 1-800-263-1136.

Care has been taken to trace ownership of copyright material contained in this text; however, the publisher will welcome any information that enables them to rectify any reference or credit for subsequent editions.

Vice President, Editorial and Media Technology: Patrick Ferrier
Executive Sponsoring Editor: Lynn Fisher
Developmental Editor: Maria Chu
Marketing Manager: Kelly Smyth
Supervising Editor: Jaime Duffy
Copy Editor: Erin Moore
Production Coordinator: Mary Pepe
Interior Design and Composition: Lynda Powell
Cover Design: Sharon Lucas
Cover Image Credit: Allsport Concepts/Mike Powell
Printer: Transcontinental Printing Group

National Library of Canada Cataloguing in Publication

Lovewell, Mark A
    Understanding economics: a contemporary perspective/Mark Lovewell.—3rd ed.

Includes index.
ISBN 0-07-091654-3

    1. Economics—Textbooks.   I. Title.

HB171.5.L78 2003a   330   C2003-905491-8

This book is dedicated to the memory of my grandparents:
Cecily Snelson (1901–1987), William Snelson (1899–1980),
Gladys Lovewell (1901–1989), and Ernest Lovewell (1899–1985).

Biography

Mark Lovewell grew up in various communities of his birth province, Newfoundland. He also lived in Bermuda before moving to Alberta as a teenager. He attended high school in the city of Red Deer, and studied undergraduate economics at the University of Alberta in Edmonton. Moving to Ontario, he completed his M.A. in Economics at the University of Toronto. He spent several years at Balliol College, Oxford University, before returning to Toronto. In 1981, he began his career at Ryerson University. His long-time experience teaching Ryerson's introductory Microeconomics and Macroeconomics courses led him to write *Understanding Economics*.

During part of his time at Ryerson, Mark was connected with the University's distance education arm, Open College. He served as Open College's senior tutor and worked intermittently as a broadcaster on Toronto's classical, jazz, and education radio station (now JAZZ-FM). More recently, he helped develop Ryerson's International Economics degree program and for several years served as the program's coordinator. In 2003, he became director of Ryerson's new Arts and Contemporary Studies program, and he currently teaches one of this degree's foundation courses, Ideas that Shape the World. This course gives him a chance to focus on the theories of famous Canadian thinkers such as Marshall McLuhan, Northrop Frye, and Harold Innis.

In addition to his career-related activities, Mark has interests in literature, the arts, and public policy. He is a co-publisher of the national book review magazine, the Literary Review of Canada. Helping administer the magazine and contributing frequent articles to its pages are two of his main leisure activities. For the past twenty years he has lived in the heart of downtown Toronto; he is an avid fan of the city's many cafés and restaurants. He also derives great enjoyment from Toronto's cosmopolitan blend of races and cultures.

Brief Contents

Contents

Preface

This edition has the same purpose as its predecessors, namely, to combine economic theory and application in an up-to-date, accessible, and appealing way. When I first decided to write *Understanding Economics, A Contemporary Perspective*, my aim was to use my years of undergraduate teaching to write a text that could engage first-year students and help them realize the power of economic theory in explaining the practical aspects of their lives. I hope this new edition is as successful as the first two in accomplishing this goal.

What's New in the Third Edition?

The favourable reception of the previous editions led several instructors and students to make valuable criticisms and suggestions for change. I have incorporated many of these suggestions in this new edition. For example, material on the aggregate expenditures model has been divided into two separate appendices, at the end of Chapter 11 and Chapter 12. The first introduces the aggregate expenditures model. The second includes the government sector. This makes it easier for instructors who wish to introduce the model without covering the detailed mechanics involved in incorporating government purchases and taxes. And greater use is made of the Online Learning Centre (www.mcgrawhill.ca/lovewell) that accompanies this book to provide an extended treatment of important economic issues. This online material is written in a style closely allied with the text, making it possible to move seamlessly from one to the other.

These changes have been made without expanding the book's size—a common problem with third editions. Indeed, this new edition is shorter than the second, by 20 pages. This has been achieved by reducing the number of sideline articles dealing with optional theoretical topics such as indifference curves (accompanying Chapter 2) and applied subjects such as the evolution of money (Chapter 13). These articles now appear in the Online Learning Centre. Also, material appearing in the previous edition that was ignored by the vast majority of users has been deleted.

The book's organization is comparable with that of the second edition, with several notable exceptions. The sidelines that accompany Chapter 2 (indifference curves), Chapter 4 (measuring business performance), Chapter 6 (the OPEC cartel), Chapter 7 (labour unions), Chapter 13 (the evolution of money), Chapter 14 (details of current Canadian monetary policy), and Chapter 15 (international finance in Canada) now appear in the Online Learning Centre. Material on the aggregate expenditures model has been divided into two separate appendices, accompanying Chapter 11 and Chapter 12, and Chapter 7 has been shortened.

Specific Changes in the Third Edition

The introductory material at the start of each chapter has been revised to provide a consistent focus on major topics. The sections entitled **Thinking about Economics** appearing in each chapter are now accompanied not just by questions to provoke student thinking and discussion (for example, see Chapter 3, page 53, Chapter 5, page 110,

Chapter 7, page 167), but answers to these questions have been added to the Online Learning Centre.

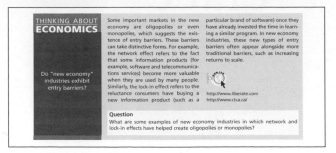

Also, given the importance of hands-on work, Practice Questions have been added following each Brief Review. For example, see Chapter 1, page 19.

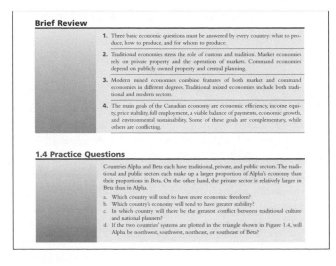

Answers to these Practice Questions appear at the Lovewell Online Learning Centre, www.mcgrawhill.ca/college/lovewell.

Specific chapter-by-chapter changes include:

Part 1

Chapter 1 includes a more detailed description of opportunity cost and its interpretation

The optional Sideline on indifference curves accompanying Chapter 2 has been moved to the Online Learning Centre.

Chapter 3 includes a more detailed description of the mathematical derivation of the numerical value of price elasticities.

Part 2

The optional Sideline on measuring business performance accompanying Chapter 4 has been moved to the Online Learning Centre.

Chapter 5 includes a more detailed description of the profit-maximizing rule and its interpretation.

The optional Sideline on the OPEC cartel accompanying Chapter 6 has been moved to the Online Learning Centre.

Chapter 7's discussion of resource demand for businesses in imperfectly competitive product markets has been moved to the Online Learning Centre. The optional

Sideline on labour unions accompanying this chapter has been moved to the Online Learning Centre.

Part 3

The discussions of the calculation of real GDP in Chapters 9 and 10 have been updated in line with recent reporting changes by Statistics Canada.

Chapter 11 now includes an appendix that deals with the basic aggregate expenditures model.

Chapter 12's appendix now deals with the extension of the aggregate expenditures model to include government.

The optional Sideline on the evolution of money accompanying Chapter 13 has been moved to the Online Learning Centre.

Chapter 14's treatment of Canadian monetary policy tools has been streamlined in line with new Bank of Canada procedures. The optional Sideline on details of current monetary policy in Canada in this chapter has been moved to the Online Learning Centre.

Part 4

Chapter 15's treatment of the balance of payments accounts has been amended to conform to recent reporting changes by Statistics Canada. The optional Sideline on international finance in Canada accompanying this chapter has been moved to the Online Learning Centre.

The Advancing Economic Thought article on John F. Helliwell accompanying Chapter 16 has been shortened.

Current Issues

As did its predecessors, this edition also explores important current issues. After all, economics is part of daily life—in the choices we make, in the decisions of communities, governments, and businesses, and in the media. While developing the theoretical framework of economics, *Understanding Economics* offers real-world examples and explores current economic issues. Articles, essays, and interviews stimulate critical thinking, research, application, and more. By providing a balanced and wide range of perspectives, these elements encourage students to evaluate and debate economic issues for themselves.

The **Sideline** articles, both in the book and at the book's Online Learning Centre, deal with a wide range of economic issues—for example, the debate over the Bank of Canada's zero-inflation policy, and the increasing significance of cross-border financial flows.

Within each chapter, **Advancing Economic Thought** details the ideas of an influential thinker of the past or the present and allows students to judge their contemporary relevance. So, for example, Adam Smith's defence of private markets, Karl Marx's theory of capitalist exploitation, and Thomas Malthus's treatment of population growth are featured, as well as David Foot's treatment of demographic change, Paul Romer's innovative view of economic growth, and Nuala Beck's analysis of the "new economy."

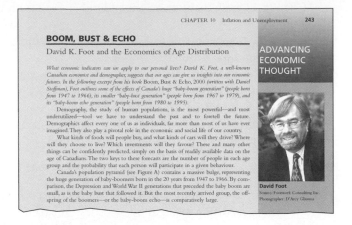

In addition, each chapter includes several points for discussion called **Thinking about Economics**—many with a contemporary focus on new technologies and the Internet—which help students interpret and apply the concepts they are learning through a question-and-answer format.

Emphasis on Skills

Application is the key to effective learning. So that students have ample opportunity to apply the knowledge they acquire, this text emphasizes skills throughout. As an initial review and a resource to return to for direction and hints, the **Skills Resource** focuses on the basics of critical thinking, the use of economic language and visual materials, research, and ways of presenting findings. For example, this resource guides students in evaluating their own work or that of others to see that it is precise, logical, and considered; it reviews interpreting and creating tables and graphs; it illustrates economic forecasting; it lists possible resources; it discusses the use of the Internet as a research tool; and it supports essay-writing and debating.

Skills Resource

Understanding Economics requires that you interpret, analyze, and apply information. Use this general resource first to review the skills you will need and then—as you venture further into *Understanding Economics*—for direction and helpful hints.

The Basics of Critical Thinking

Information, ideas, and opinions abound. Whether you are interpreting and analyzing the work of others or developing your own observations, opinions, and arguments, you must use critical thinking skills. Critical thinking involves precise meaning, logic, and consideration of values and perspectives. Evaluate your work and that of others against these basics.

PRECISE MEANING

The rule "Say what you mean and mean what you say" can be applied to all subjects and topics. Keep in mind these questions: What don't I understand? Can I paraphrase this? What really is the point? What might confuse the audience? Where is the meaning clear? Where is it murky?

See that you're using terminology precisely or define terms in their writing.

In the body of each chapter, issues relating to the use of **Economics as a second language** are highlighted.

> **Marginal Cost**
> "Marginal" has a different interpretation when referring to cost rather than product. While marginal product is defined in terms of each new unit of labour, with cost, the focus switches to new units of output instead.

Questions appear at the end of each chapter, as well as at the end of all supplementary articles. **Policy discussion questions** (at the end of most chapters) deal with practical issues in the application of economic thinking to day-to-day politics. Selected **Internet Application Questions** provide practice in using economics-related resources on the Internet.

Study Aids

To make *Understanding Economics* inviting and engaging for students, care has been taken to present the text in a clear and readable style and to use an appealing design. At the same time, a variety of features make this text user-friendly. Every chapter begins with **Learning Objectives**, which introduce the content students are to learn and which are reinforced with an icon throughout the body of the text where concepts are covered.

Then, each **Brief Review** summarizes key ideas, while margin notes define key terms highlighted in the text. These terms are listed at the end of each chapter under the heading **Key Concepts** for review and are defined again in a consolidated **Glossary** at the end of the book for easy reference. Following each Brief Review are **Practice Questions** whose answers appear in the Online Learning Centre. Because interpreting graphs is a challenge for many students, virtually all graphs are paired with tables so that it is possible to see at a glance how they are plotted. This technique not only makes graphs easier to interpret but also helps students appreciate the usefulness of visual aids in presenting economic information. Lastly, an **Index** helps students access the text in a variety of ways.

Ancillaries

FOR THE INSTRUCTOR

Your Integrated *i*-Learning Sales Specialist is a McGraw-Hill Ryerson representative who has the experience, product knowledge, training, and support to help you assess and integrate any of the below-noted products, technology, and services into your course for optimum teaching and learning performance. Whether it's using our test bank software, helping your students improve their grades, or putting your entire course online, your *i*-Learning Sales Specialist is there to help you do it. Contact your local *i*-Learning Sales Specialist today to learn how to maximize all McGraw-Hill Ryerson resources!

Instructor's Online Learning Centre

The OLC at www.mcgrawhill.ca/college/lovewell includes a password-protected web site for Instructors. The site offers downloadable supplements and **PageOut**, the McGraw-Hill Ryerson course web site development centre.

Instructor's CD-ROM

This CD-ROM contains all the necessary Instructor Supplements, including:

- **Instructor's Manual** Written by the author, this useful manual offers a range of teaching and testing aids.

- **Computerized Test Bank** Written by the author, this test bank contains more than 900 multiple-choice questions categorized by level, type, and topic. The test bank is available in the latest Diploma test-generating software, ensuring maximum flexibility in test preparation, including the reconfiguring of graphing exercises. This Brownstone program is the gold standard of testing programs.

- **PowerPoint® Presentation** Prepared by the author, contains animated illustrations along with a detailed, chapter-by-chapter review of the important concepts presented in the book.

PageOut

This unique point-and-click course web site tool enables you to create a high-quality course web site without knowing HTML coding. With PageOut you can post your syllabus online, assign McGraw-Hill Online Learning Centre or e-Book content, add links to important off-site resources, and maintain student results in the online gradebook. Visit www.mhhe.com/pageout or contact your *i*-Learning Sales Specialist for details.

In addition, content cartridges are also available for course management systems, such as *WebCT* and *Blackboard*, to expand the reach of your course and open up distance-learning options.

i-Learning Services Program

McGraw-Hill Ryerson offers a unique services package designed for Canadian faculty. Our mission is to equip providers of higher education with superior tools and resources required for excellence in teaching. For additional information, contact your local *i*-Learning Sales Specialist.

FOR THE STUDENTS

Study Guide ISBN: 007-092316-7 written by Brenda Gayle-Anyiwe, Seneca College and Mark Lovewell, Ryerson University. This guide, written in conjunction with the text, gives students the opportunity to test their knowledge of text material with questions and answers, as well as helpful hints and summaries, tied to each chapter.

Student Online Learning Centre located at www.mcgrawhill.ca/college/lovewell, offers a wealth of materials, including quizzes, Interactive Graphing Exercises (graphs that can be manipulated to solve exercises like those in the textbook), Internet Application Questions, answers to the text's Practice Questions, answers to the questions following each Thinking About Economics discussion point, Sideline articles, annotated Web links and much more!

Σ-STAT is Statistics Canada's education resource that allows you to view socioeconomic and demographic data in charts, graphs, and maps. Access to Σ-STAT and the CANSIM II database is made available from this web site by special agreement between McGraw-Hill Ryerson and Statistics Canada to purchasers of the Lovewell textbook. Please visit the Online Learning Centre for additional information.

FOR THE INSTRUCTOR

- Want an easy way to test your students prior to an exam that *doesn't* create more work for you?

- Want to access your supplements *without* having to bring them all to class?

- Want an *easy* way to get your course on-line?

- Want to *free up more time* in your day to get more done?

Of course you do!

Then check out your
Online Learning Centre!

- Downloadable Supplements
- PageOut
- Online Resources

Mc Graw Hill **McGraw-Hill Ryerson**

Higher Learning. Forward Thinking.™

Acknowledgements

I am indebted to Maria Chu, Lynn Fisher, and Jaime Duffy for their innumerable editorial contributions in casting this edition in its final form. There are others who have played a significant editorial role in previous editions: Andrea Crozier, Ron Doleman, Laura Edlund, Joan Levack, and Brenda Hutchinson. I am also grateful to the reviewers of this edition for their perceptive comments and criticisms. They include

Doug Beatty, Lambton College
Aurelia Best, Centennial College
Jim Butko, Niagara College
Bruno Fullone, George Brown College
Brenda Gayle-Anyiwe, Seneca College
Sunil Kaplash, University of Victoria
Joan McEachern, Kwantlen College
John Pirrie, St. Lawrence College
Kevin Richter, Douglas College
David Sabiston, Mount Royal College
Martha Spence, Confederation College

Encouragement has come from past and present members of Ryerson's Economics Department, especially Ingrid Bryan, Harry Pope, and Eric Wright, my former associates at CJRT-Open College and my colleagues in Ryerson's Arts and Contemporary Studies program. At the Literary Review of Canada, I would like to thank my associates Bronwyn Drainie, Madeline Koch, Sonali Thakkar, and Helen Walsh for their continuing endeavours to help me improve my writing style. Also, Khoa Nguyen and Pam Fernie have provided me with valuable assistance in a range of areas, some of them directly related to this edition. On a personal note, I wish to thank my parents, Patricia and David Lovewell, my sister Rachael Lovewell, as well as Deborah Brown, Calvin and George Normore, Dorothy Salusbury, Bobbi Speck, and Eva Richter for a wide variety of welcome diversions while this edition was being prepared. Finally, I would like to acknowledge a special debt to my partner Marina Vitkin, without whose support and good-humoured endurance writing this book would not have been possible.

Skills Resource

Understanding Economics requires that you interpret, analyze, and apply information. Use this general resource first to review the skills you will need and then—as you venture further into *Understanding Economics*—for direction and helpful hints.

The Basics of Critical Thinking

Information, ideas, and opinions abound. Whether you are interpreting and analyzing the work of others or developing your own observations, opinions, and arguments, you must use critical thinking skills. Critical thinking involves precise meaning, logic, and consideration of values and perspectives. Evaluate your work and that of others against these basics.

PRECISE MEANING

The rule "Say what you mean and mean what you say" can be applied to all subjects and topics. Keep in mind these questions: What don't I understand? Can I paraphrase this? What really is the point? What might confuse the audience? Where is the meaning clear? Where is it murky?

See that writers are using terminology precisely or define terms in their writing. In your own work, use the standard definition that is appropriate to the subject or discipline. If the meaning might be unclear, clarify it.

Statistics can be a particular trouble-spot. With every statistic you use or come across, ask yourself the following: What information is this giving? What definitions are used? What is the basis of this information (for example, a broad study or a small sample)? How is this relevant to the discussion? How have the numbers been treated? What other factors should be taken into account? What relationships can I see?

See that a statistic means what you think it does and use it with care. For example:

- A **measure** differs from an **indicator**. For example, the *measure* of gross domestic product *indicates* living standards. The *measure* of body temperature *indicates* physical health.

- **Average** differs from **median**. An average (sometimes known as an arithmetic mean) is the sum of all the values divided by the number of values. The median is the middle value in any group of values. For three hourly wages (of $5, $10, and $30), the average wage is $15, but the median wage is $10.

- **Nominal** figures differ from **real** figures. Nominal dollar values make no adjustments for changes in prices over the years. However, real figures are adjusted using a **base year**, which gives a point of comparison. For example, if your nominal income has doubled since the base year at the same time as prices have doubled, your real income has remained the same.

- Percentages sometimes cause confusion. If you are to calculate the percentage difference between two numbers, determine the base from which the percentage is calculated, then divide the difference between the two numbers by the base number and multiply by 100 percent. For example, if a price increases from $1 to $3, it has risen by 200 percent [(($3 − $1) ÷ $1) × 100%]. In this case, $1 is the base number. If, on the other hand, a price decreases from $3 to $1, the base number is now $3. The percentage fall in price therefore, is 67 percent [(($1 − $3) ÷ $3) × 100%].

- Many statistics are **rounded**—for example, to the nearest whole number or nearest thousand.

LOGIC

Logical arguments move from one point to the next in a reasonable and orderly way. Reasons should support each point, and the points should follow some order, often a cause-and-effect order. The **scientific method**, which we outline in Chapter 1, gives one model for a logical approach. In the case of a written or spoken argument, we should be able to answer the following questions: What points does the author make? How does the author support each point? How do the points connect, and are the connections valid? What is the main conclusion?

Read your own work and that of others carefully for the following problems:

- **Personal arguments**. A personal argument attacks an opponent rather than the opponent's reasoning. Personal arguments often appear when economic issues are debated in the political arena. For example, a government's expansionary fiscal policy might be disparaged as being the work of "doctrinaire socialists" rather than being criticized on its own merits.

- **False analogy**. Arguments can often be supported with analogies, or comparisons between two different things. For example, the flow of incomes and spending in an economy is sometimes likened to a circular flow of water. However, one extension of this analogy—that the flow of incomes and spending in an economy would stop unless propelled by some outside force—is false. Each analogy must be checked against the facts.

- **False causation**. Simply because two trends take place at the same time, it does not mean that one trend is causing the other. For example, a trend towards more students staying in school and a trend towards more part-time jobs does not mean that the first necessarily causes the second or vice versa. In each case, examine the situation to see how the factors are related, if at all.

- **Fallacy of composition**. What is true for one component of a group—say, an individual—is not necessarily true for the group as a whole. For example, just because higher saving benefits an individual household, it does not mean that this necessarily helps the entire economy, since a rise in saving can cause spending and production in an economy to fall. Examine each generalization carefully.

CONSIDERATION

Our experiences and background have implications for how we see the world; they inform our perspectives. Because many of the issues explored in *Understanding Economics* deal with how we think things "ought" to be, they bring up questions of values—for example, how you value extra leisure time against more possessions. The key to critical thinking is recognizing and examining our perspectives (including our assumptions) and considering the perspectives of others. A blinkered view of the world—one that does not consider the perspectives of others—makes for a poor, unbalanced argument.

Examine your own work and that of others carefully for the following:

- **Opinions**. Are any opinions stated clearly, explained, and supported? Are any not stated but apparent? Remember that opinions are not the sign of dubious critical thinking. In fact, explicit opinions are preferable to unexamined perspectives in most cases.

- **Statement of specific assumptions.** If assumptions are not clearly identified, can they be inferred? Are the stated assumptions overly simplistic or irrelevant? For example, in an argument about product demand, it is too simplistic to assume that the number of units bought stays constant. In contrast, detailed assumptions concerning how a product is supplied are irrelevant in an argument about product demand.

- **Emotional language.** While emotional language may suit some persuasive arguments (for example, political speeches, letters to the editor, advertising), it can mask lack of evidence or may suggest a biased view. Emotional language—which usually lays blame—is especially common in the popular media. If you are faced with emotional language, try to decide whether an argument would be equally effective without it. Also, keep in mind that emotional language does not always signify that an argument is unreasonable; arguments expressed in reasonable language can also be flawed.

- **Distortions of fact, or faulty logic.** Double-check for misrepresentations and errors in logic in your reading.

Finally, ask yourself whether alternative perspectives have been addressed. If not, why not? Keep in mind that arguments that support the current state of things are not necessarily more objective than those that do not.

To summarize the basics of critical thinking, consider the task of **forecasting**. Suppose you are asked to use a current economic statistic that is in the news to try to forecast future values. To make a prediction concerning the prime interest rate, for example, you must define precisely the problem and terminology, decide which factors affecting interest rates will be most crucial in the near future, and try to weigh the importance of each of these factors in affecting the statistic's current value. Look to economic theory and economists for help; consult newspapers and magazines to see how closely your own hypothesis corresponds to the opinions of professional economic forecasters. Develop an argument, which you will support and check carefully for errors in logic—for example, what factors cause what. Then, present your forecast and evidence precisely, logically, and having considered a range of perspectives. Later, you will likely want to evaluate your forecast against what actually happened. Because forecasting is an extremely difficult task, consider yourself successful if you predicted the right direction of change.

Economics as a Second Language

Because economics involves an extensive vocabulary of specialized terms, it is closely linked to the way we use language. In each chapter, you will find passages highlighted. These passages help you learn the proper use of economics as a "second language" by exploring the following issues:

- **Precise definitions.** With a few exceptions, economic terms—such as "rent" and "aggregate demand"—have precise definitions. But some terms—such as "income equity" and "full employment"—have more than one possible interpretation. When using such potentially ambiguous terms, specify how you are using them.

- **Special meanings.** Terms may have a different meaning in economics than they do in everyday language. For example, in economics the term "investment" typically refers to business purchases of materials, equipment, and buildings rather than to purchases of financial assets, such as stocks and bonds.

- **Descriptive images.** Sometimes economic terms provide a way of describing abstract concepts in a concrete way. Such descriptive images can clarify an argument's underlying logic. For example, the view that education is acquired by individuals to raise their income-earning potential is neatly summarized by the term "human capital."
- **Loaded language.** Descriptive images are not the only way to give language suggestive power. Loaded language, which appears straightforward but subtly colours economic arguments, is common in economics. For example, supporters of a market economy often call it a "free market system," to emphasize the freedom of choice that comes with private markets. Critics of a market economy usually refer to it instead as "capitalism," since this suggests the power of owners of capital in this economic system. Loaded language helps reveal a writer's implicit assumptions. Though loaded language can be misused, arguments that contain this language are not necessarily wrong.

Visual Materials

Because visual materials can present complex information at a glance, they are often used in economics. Whether you are interpreting or creating visual materials, keep the following advice in mind.

TABLES

Tables present *related* information in **columns** (groups of information presented vertically) and **rows** (horizontal lines of information). A **heading** usually appears at the top of each column to describe the information presented; check the column heading to ensure you understand what information is being presented. Tables are "read" left to right—giving the **independent variable** first, at the left. When reading or creating complex tables, use a grid to help you line up information. Double-check at each stage any calculations you must make. Label your table for easy reference and to summarize the relationships it presents. Note that some tables are called **schedules** when they present, for example, the demand and/or supply information for a product.

Often, you will need to examine tables for relationships and trends. Consider the following table. In the left column, the numbers are increasing; in the right column, the numbers are decreasing. On the basis of the hypothetical information in the table, we can say that as the price of compact discs goes up, the quantity sold goes down.

Sales of Compact Discs

Price per CD ($)	CDs Sold (no. of CDs)
$ 4	16
8	12
12	8
16	4

Now, consider this table, which shows hypothetical data for a particular country. It shows that between years 1 and 2, sales of compact discs and cassettes have increased, while sales of long-playing records have decreased.

Sales per Year (millions of units)			
Year	Cassettes	Long-Playing Records	Compact Discs
1	14	11	2
2	17	6	23

Especially when interpreting and analyzing tables that have many columns and rows, you might find it easiest to look at the trend in each column, then start examining the possible relationships among the columns and the trends they demonstrate.

GRAPHS

Related information also can be presented on a graph. Note in the following example how the horizontal line—called the **x-axis**—and the vertical line—called the **y-axis**—form an L-shape to meet at a **point of origin**. The range of values for one variable is indicated on each axis, and each axis is labelled, including the **units**. To graph correctly, the **scale** must be consistent—for example, if the height of the first square on the grid equals $2, the height of each subsequent square must also equal $2. In economics, the **independent variable**, which is the variable that determines the value of the other **dependent variable** is often plotted on the y-axis, while the dependent variable is often plotted on the x-axis. In our example, using the price to give the **y-co-ordinate** and CDs sold to give the **x-co-ordinate**, we can plot the points shown. Joining the points together gives a **curve**. The term "curve" is used even for a straight line.

The resulting curve shows the relationship of the two variables. Note that a graph can relate more than two factors. For example, a third factor—the costs to the CD manufacturer—could be added if the graph's y-axis were changed to represent general dollar amounts.

Curves can depict a variety of relationships and are described in *Understanding Economics* in particular ways. For example, the curve that illustrates prices and CDs sold

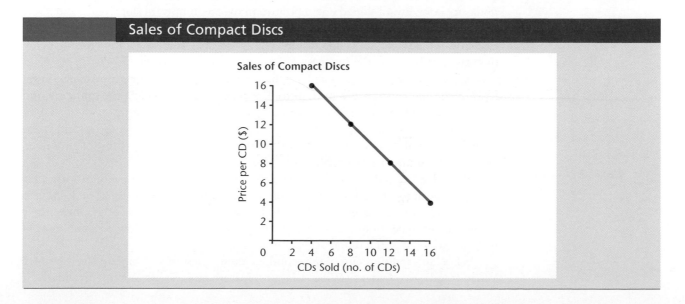

Sales of Compact Discs

shows that as price decreases, the quantity sold increases. In the text, we describe this as having a **negative (downward) slope** ("downward" because graphs, like tables, are "read" left to right and the curve slopes downwards to the right). If, in contrast, the quantity sold increases as price increases, the slope would be described as having a **positive (upward) slope**.

The **slope of a curve** demonstrates another aspect of the relationship—for example, whether the decline in CD sales is the same as the increase in price. In this case, it is, and our graph demonstrates this by showing a curve at a 45-degree angle. Other relationships will be represented by curves that we describe as **horizontal**, **flattened**, **steep**, and **vertical**.

Whenever possible, the terms "steep" and "flattened" should be precisely defined. This is because the slope of a curve depends on the scale used on the x- and y-axes. Take the CD example again. If the scale of the y-axis is reduced or increased, the slope appears to change. This problem is overcome by calculating the numerical value of the slope, which is the change in the variable on the y-axis divided by the related change in the variable on the x-axis. For variables x and y:

$$\text{slope} = \frac{\text{change in y}}{\text{change in x}}$$

In this example, where the decline in CD sales is exactly equal to the increase in price, the slope has a value of -1. Any line whose slope has an absolute value greater than 1 (such as 2 or 3) is described as steep, while lines whose slopes have an absolute value less than 1 (such as 0.5 or 0.25) are said to be flattened.

A line's slope can be used in combination with the line's **vertical intercept**, which is the point where the line intersects its graph's y-axis. Together, the slope and vertical intercept provide an equation for plotting any point on the line. In general terms, this equation can be written as:

$$y = mx + b$$

where m is the value of the line's slope and b is the line's vertical intercept. Both m and b can be either positive, negative, or zero, with each of these possibilities giving lines with different positions relative to the x- and y-axes. For example, a negative slope, m, results in a downward sloped line, a positive m means an upward sloped line, and a zero m gives a horizontal line. In contrast, if a line's vertical intercept, b, is positive, then the line crosses the y-axis above the origin, while a negative b means a line crossing below the origin. If b is zero, the line passes directly through the origin.

When asked to *draw* or *create* a graph, develop and label the graph precisely on the basis of the information given. If, instead, you are asked to sketch a graph, develop a graph with labelled axes and a curve demonstrating the relationship of the variables. When "reading" or developing graphs, use a grid for precision. Label the x- and y-axes carefully, remembering to note units of measurement. Title your graphs for easy reference and to summarize the relationships shown.

Note that depending on the information, graphs can take a variety of forms. For example, the information about sales of cassettes, long-playing records, and compact discs could be presented in a **bar graph**. The same basic principles of graphing apply. When various types of information are shown, as in the graph below, a legend must be included to identify the different types of bars.

When interpreting any graph, consider these questions: What are the variables? What trends are evident? What relationships are suggested? Why? Particularly in

Sales of Compact Discs

Cassette, Record, and Disc Shipments

macroeconomics, you might also ask: What additional factors could have caused this result (for example, a sudden downturn in the economy)?

Research

When you research a topic—for example, to write a research paper—first define your topic and your task carefully so that you do not waste time as you gather information.

Use a range of sources. By doing so, you are more likely to be able to see your topic from different angles, address the relevant factors, and access the best sources. You will also be able to evaluate your sources against one another.

Credit all your sources, both to recognize the debt you owe to others and to allow readers to refer to the sources themselves. As you collect information, note what a direct quotation is, what a paraphrase is, and what a summary is, and note the exact source. For example:

- for articles—author's name, article title, newspaper or magazine title, date of issue, and page number(s)
- for books—author's name, book title, place of publication, publishing company, year of publication, and page number(s)
- for television sources—television station, program name, date, and time of airing
- for CD-ROM (Compact Disc–Read Only Memory) material—author's name, title of article/text portion, date, newspaper/magazine/encyclopedia title, edition, and CD-ROM title

Depending on your topic, you might do primary research, secondary research, or a combination of both. **Primary research**, in such forms as interviews and surveys, involves you in gathering "raw" information. **Secondary research**, which is based on the work of others, allows you to acquaint yourself with a range of opinions and to use data that would be difficult or impossible to collect on your own.

VALUABLE SOURCES

The research sources immediately available to you are probably newspapers (specifically their business sections), news magazines (such as *Maclean's*), business magazines (such as *The Globe and Mail Report on Business Magazine, Forbes, The Economist*), and any collections of news clippings at your library. Some sources, such as *Maclean's*, may be available to you on CD-ROM, while others may be indexed on CD-ROM (for example, within the *Canadian Business and Current Affairs Index* and the *Canadian Index*). Alternatively, most libraries have indices in book form.

In addition, consider the following sources:

- *The Canadian Encyclopedia* and the annual *Canadian Global Almanac* for details on economic institutions in Canada
- E-Stat for Statistics Canada data on the Canadian economy, society, and population in CD-ROM format, as well as Statistics Canada publications, such as the biennial *Canada Year Book*, the monthly *Canadian Economic Observer* and its annual historical supplement, the quarterly *Perspectives on Labour and Income*, plus other more detailed publications on particular topics listed in Statistics Canada's catalogue
- Canadian BusinessDisc and Canadian NewsDisc on CD-ROM
- The Bank of Canada's quarterly *Bank of Canada Review* and the Department of Finance's annual *Fiscal Reference Tables* for recent economic statistics, especially on monetary and government matters
- The World Bank's annual *World Development Report* and the monthly *OECD Main Economic Indicators* for international statistics
- Federal and provincial government bookstores for annual budget papers

Using the Internet

By making millions of documents available with just a few strokes at a computer keyboard, the Internet offers important benefits as a research tool. As more documents become available, the range of this online information will continue to expand rapidly.

Internet documents have their own distinctive features. One is "live" links to other online sources. These links are not as structured as more traditional search techniques, but they often lead to unexpected information. Online sources can also be easily updated or tailored to the demands of users through interactive programs. This may create headaches for the Internet researcher, since information found once may be difficult to retrieve again. But it makes the Internet the perfect vehicle for statistical data and news—topics richly covered in online documents. Shrinking library budgets and rising publishing costs mean that many government documents are now most easily available in online form. Important examples are Statistics Canada's daily reports of newly released information (at http://www.statcan.ca) and summaries of the Bank of Canada's reports on current monetary policy (at http://www.bank-banque-canada.ca). But traditional research methods still have advantages when you are looking for more timeless information. Therefore, keep in mind that online resources are most effective when employed alongside other research methods.

http://www.statcan.ca

http://www.
bank-banque-canada.ca

Always credit Internet documents used in your work. To refer to an online source, include the author's name, article title, title of periodical or journal (where appropriate), date of publication or last update, publication medium (online), computer network (e.g., World Wide Web), the document's electronic address, and the relevant page number (including the document's total number of pages, since this differs depending on the browser used).

Throughout the text, you can practise using the Internet by answering the Internet Application Questions, which are highlighted as shown in the margin. For further information on the Internet, consult the Online Learning Centre that accompanies *Understanding Economics*. It includes links to Internet sources relevant to an introductory Economics course.

Presentation

On the basis of your research, you should be able to present the results in an essay, an oral presentation, or a debate. Once again, evaluate your work against the basics of critical thinking. Whatever the form of your presentation, you should be able to state the thesis or main argument, give support, and address your points in a logical and orderly way. Prepare an outline to ensure that your presentation is well structured and organized.

Essay

An essay should be written in a concise and easy-to-follow style. Remember that your general purpose is to inform and persuade, rather than to overwhelm your reader with complicated concepts and terminology. Keep in mind your specific task and the expectations of readers. Double-check to see that your essay, in fact, does what it is supposed to—for example, "explain," "support or refute," "compare," or "analyze." State your thesis clearly in your introduction, provide any background information your readers will need, support for your thesis, and a conclusion which restates your thesis. Repeatedly revise and edit your writing before handing in the final version.

Class Presentation

Though less formal than an essay, a class presentation requires the same steps of research and preparation. Again, you should structure your discussion using an outline and credit any sources during your presentation.

DEBATE

Usually, when you debate, the thesis is provided for you. In a formal debate, two sides debate a statement or **proposition**. The side arguing for the proposition, called the **affirmative**, and the side arguing against the proposition, called the **negative**, each has a set period of time to make its original arguments, after which each side is allowed time for a **rebuttal** of the other's arguments. Informal debates often include a statement of the argument and support by either side, then discussion and resolution. In both types of debates, research and preparation are key. Consider all sides of the argument. It is also important to remember that the purpose of a debate is to persuade, not to create conflict. Effective debating, therefore, combines logic and tact.

Notes

M. Neil Brown and Stuart Keeley, *Asking the Right Questions* (Englewood Cliffs, NJ: Prentice-Hall, 1990).

Stanley L. Brue and Donald R. Wentworth, *Economic Scenes*, 5th ed. (Englewood Cliffs, NJ: Prentice-Hall, 1992).

Robert Case, *Reading Critically* (Toronto: OISE Press, 1981).

Catherine Harris, "A Guide to Using Statistics," *Canadian Economic Observer* (Ottawa: Statistics Canada, February 1990), pp. 19–33.

Darrell Huff, *How to Lie with Statistics* (New York: W.W. Norton, 1954).

David P. Kreutzer, *Systems Thinking and Dynamic Modeling* (Cambridge, MA: Gould-Kreutzer Associates, 1994).

Donald McCloskey, *If You're So Smart* (Chicago: University of Chicago Press, 1990).

W. Edgar Moore, H. McCann, and J. McCann, *Creative and Critical Thinking*, 2nd ed. (Boston: Houghton Mifflin, 1985).

Questions

1. Calculate each of the following, rounding your answers to one place after the decimal point. In each case, explain your reasoning:
   a. The percentage change when a person's annual income falls from $28 225 to $23 158
   b. The percentage change when a country's exports rise from $20.3 billion to $32.7 billion
   c. A business's profit after a 21.2 percent increase from $402.3 million
   d. An economy's employment level after a 8.2 percent decrease from 12.7 million workers

2. Each statement below contains a logical problem—a personal argument, false analogy, false causation, or fallacy of composition. In each case, identify the problem and briefly explain your answer.
   a. "When a person loses his or her job, total employment in the economy falls."
   b. "Canada's exports to foreign countries have risen because of the accompanying increase in Canadian interest rates."
   c. "Buying shares on the stockmarket is very much like purchasing a lottery ticket—you are making a gamble with a very low chance of success."
   d. "The argument that governments should stay out of the economy is illogical because it is supported only by extreme conservatives."

3. The table below shows how annual CD purchases in a given region are related to the average yearly income of the region's consumers.

CD Purchases

Income ($ thousands)	CDs Purchased (thousands of CDs)
$40	18
30	14
20	10
10	6

a. CD purchases can also be affected by variables other than income. For example, if there is a rise in the price of CDs how will the numbers in the table change? What assumption needs to be made about the price of CDs to analyze the relationship in the table?

b. Draw a graph that shows the curve associated with the numbers in the table.

c. Calculate the slope of the curve you have drawn between the income levels of $30 000 and $40 000. Is this slope positive or negative? Is it constant at all other given values of income and CDs purchased? Explain.

4. The following graph shows the relationship between the hourly wage in the construction industry and the number of construction workers employed.

a. Prepare a table that presents the information shown by the four highlighted points on the graph. Make sure to label your table.

b. Estimate how many construction workers will be employed if the hourly wage falls to $10. Use the table to explain your answer.

c. Your answer in part b above is based on an assumption concerning the relationship you are analyzing. What is this assumption?

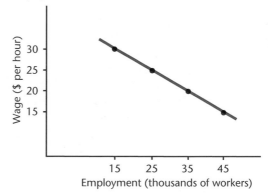

Employment of Construction Workers

5. The equation y = 3x + 4 shows a particular relationship between the variables x and y.

a. Draw a graph that presents the information summarized by the equation as a line.

b. Is this a positively sloped or negatively sloped line?

c. What is the value of y if x is 6? Show your answer using the equation and your graph.

d. What is the value of x if y is 22? Show using both the equation and your graph.

6. The table below shows the lost time (measured in thousands of person-days) due to work stoppages in Canada in various years between 1986 and 2001.

Time Lost in Work Stoppages (thousands of person-days per year)

Year	Manufacturing	Construction	Transportation
1986	2 012	1 374	240
1991	36	556	281
1996	92	757	146
2001	87	531	362

Source: Statistics Canada, "Time Lost in Work Stoppages (thousands of person-days per year)" adapted from the Statistics Canada publication "Canadian economic observer. Historical Statistical Supplement," 2001/02, Catalogue II-210, Vol. 16, July 2002, p. 38.

   a. Convert the data shown in the table into a bar graph.
   b. Which of the three industry groups has experienced the biggest percentage change in time lost to work stoppages between 1987 and 2002? the smallest percentage change?

Internet Application Question

http://www.statcan.ca

Access Statistics Canada's web site (at http://www.statcan.ca). Then use the links to "Canadian Statistics" to find the two most recent annual values for the following variables:
   a. Canada's total population
   b. Canada's unemployment rate, measured as a percentage
   c. Total imports of goods into Canada, valued in Canadian dollars
   d. Total exports of goods from Canada, valued in Canadian dollars
   e. The exchange rate, measured in terms of American dollars per Canadian dollar

Part 1

Working with Economics

The Age of Chivalry is gone—that of sophisters, econo-mists, and calculators has succeeded.

— Edmund Burke, British political writer

Understanding economic principles is important for everyone who votes or participates in the marketplace. How do we go about choosing the products we buy? Do private markets always benefit consumers? What are the best ways to minimize the pollution caused by businesses and households? Can we devise more successful programs to eradicate poverty? Should we expect governments to be doing more to fight unemployment? The next three chapters explore the economic principles that can help us answer such questions.

CHAPTER 1

The Economic Problem

Economy is the art of making the most out of life.

—George Bernard Shaw, Irish playwright

Just as variety adds spice to life, so does choice enliven our everyday existence. Some choices are minor—which pair of shoes to buy and whether to have a pizza or a hamburger for lunch. Others are more important—where to live and what career to pursue. Because our resources are limited, every one of our choices has a price. This is a basic fact of human existence that applies equally to individuals and societies. Individuals must decide how to use their limited time and budgets. Societies, meanwhile, must decide how to employ a fixed supply of resources. Thus, both individuals and societies can use economics to analyze their choices and make the best possible decisions.

LEARNING OBJECTIVES

In this chapter, you will:

1 consider the economic problem—the problem of having unlimited wants, but limited resources—that underlies the definition of economics

2 learn about the way economists specify economic choice

3 examine the production choices an entire economy faces, as demonstrated by the production possibilities model

4 analyze the three basic economic questions and how various economic systems answer them

1.1 What Economists Do

economic problem: the problem of having unlimited wants but limited resources with which to satisfy them

The Economic Problem

Every day, we make choices to meet our wants. Wants vary widely from person to person; we may have a special preference for ice-cream sundaes or chocolate cakes, rock concerts or classical recitals, computer games or comic books. Because we face so many choices, the sum total of wants is virtually unlimited. Our resources, however, are not. Thus, we have the **economic problem**.

THINKING ABOUT ECONOMICS

The famous Indian statesman M.K. (Mahatma) Gandhi once said, "There is enough for the needy, but not for the greedy." What are the implications of this statement for the economic problem?

Gandhi's statement reveals a way the economic problem can be solved without the help of economics—by curbing our selfish wants. Is such a scenario feasible? In some cultures, and for idealistic individuals or small groups, it can be. However, attempts to control the wants of large groups of people have tended to be spectacular failures.

Question
What are some examples of societies that have tried to curb individual wants?

The limited nature of resources—or scarcity—requires that we make choices based on both noneconomic factors, such as the need for security, and economic factors. For many individuals, time and money are most scarce. For societies as a whole, it is the basic items used in all types of production, known as **economic resources**, that are scarce. These resources come not only from nature but also from human effort and ingenuity. Economic resources are often categorized as natural resources, capital resources, and human resources.

economic resources: basic items that are used in all types of production, including natural, capital, and human resources

NATURAL RESOURCES

natural resources: the resources from nature that are used in production, including land, raw materials, and natural processes

Natural resources represent nature's contribution to production. These resources include not only land—used for farms, roads, and buildings—but also raw materials, such as minerals and forests. As well, natural resources include useful natural processes, such as sunlight and water power.

CAPITAL RESOURCES

capital resources: the processed materials, equipment, and buildings used in production; also known as capital

In economics, the term **capital resources**, or capital, refers to the real assets of an economy—the processed materials, equipment, and buildings that are used in production. An example is a newspaper printing plant and its printing presses, as well as the processed inputs—paper and ink—used to make newspapers. Therefore, the term "capital" has a special meaning in economics. As economic resources, capital resources do not include financial capital, such as stocks and bonds. A person's shares in Bombardier, for example, do not add to the economy's stock of real capital. Similarly, the bonds issued by a company, such as Bell Canada, are viewed as financial capital by their holders, but not as real capital by economists.

HUMAN RESOURCES

labour: human effort employed directly in production

entrepreneurship: initiative, risk-taking, and innovation necessary for production

There are two main types of human resources used in production. **Labour** represents human effort employed directly in production, such as the work of a computer programmer, store clerk, factory supervisor, or brain surgeon. On the other hand, **entrepreneurship** is the initiative, risk-taking, and innovation necessary for production. It includes the efforts of the inventor who brings a new product to the market, the head of a multimillion-dollar corporation, the owner of a small variety store, and the student who starts a summer house-painting business. Entrepreneurship is often difficult to pinpoint, but it is this that brings together the natural resources, capital resources, and labour in order to produce a good or service.

RESOURCE INCOMES

Economic resources have corresponding incomes, which reflect their contributions to production. When a natural resource is employed, its owner receives a rent, which is the payment for supplying the resource. Similarly, providers of capital resources (as well as providers of financial capital, such as bonds) receive an income in the form of interest. Finally, people are paid wages for their labour and profit for their entrepreneurship.

Economics Defined

economics: the study of how to distribute scarce resources among alternative ends

Arising from unlimited wants and scarce resources, **economics** is the study of how to distribute limited resources among alternative ends. Economics is divided into two branches, which are studied separately: microeconomics and macroeconomics.

MICROECONOMICS

microeconomics: the branch of economics that focuses on the behaviour of individual participants in various markets

Microeconomics focuses on the behaviour of individual participants in various markets. How do people decide on the quantities of a particular product they will consume? How do businesses decide on the quantities of a particular product they will produce? How are prices set within markets? What determines how incomes are distributed to the various participants in an economy? These are the sorts of questions studied in microeconomics.

MACROECONOMICS

macroeconomics: the branch of economics that takes a wide-ranging view of the economy, studying the behaviour of economic sectors

In contrast, **macroeconomics** takes a more wide-ranging view of the economy. It is concerned with entire economic sectors, which are treated as separate entities. The four important sectors in the economy are households, businesses, government, and foreign markets. How these sectors interact determines a country's unemployment rate, general level of prices, and total economic output. Explaining these larger economic forces is the central task of macroeconomics.

Economic Models

economic models: generalizations about or simplifications of economic reality; also known as laws, principles, or theories

Economists use models to help them understand economic behaviour. **Economic models**—also known as laws, principles, or theories—are generalizations or simplifications of economic reality. As an example, think about the Canadian economy, in which literally millions of separate transactions—sales and purchases—are made each day. Trying to keep track of every sale and purchase for the purpose of understanding economic activity would be impossible. Instead, economists build useful abstractions of reality that allow them to see the basic workings of the economy. In other words, a good economic model allows economists to see the forest instead of the trees.

Without even realizing it, we regularly use models. When driving in unfamiliar territory, for example, we often depend on maps. Although an aerial photograph of our route would be the most realistic representation, it is virtually useless as a driving guide. A road map, however, gives exactly the detail needed to find the way. Similarly, a good economic model can help us understand some facet of economic behaviour without overwhelming us with details.

CAUSE AND EFFECT

How can economic models help explain economic trends and behaviour? Usually, by including two or more **variables**, or factors that have measurable values. For example, the price of an item and the quantity that is purchased of that item are two variables. In a model, variables are connected by a causal relationship, meaning that one variable is assumed to affect another. Suppose a model states that a rise in the price of cellular phones reduces the number of cellular phones purchased. In this case, the variable that is causing the other to change—known as the **independent variable**—is the price of cellular phones. The variable that is being affected—called the **dependent variable**—is the number of cellular phones purchased.

INVERSE AND DIRECT RELATIONSHIPS

A model proposes what effect one variable will have on another. If the value of one variable is expected to increase as the value of another variable decreases, the variables have an **inverse relationship**. An increase in cellular phone prices that reduces the number of phones sold is an example of an inverse relationship. Two variables can have a **direct relationship**, meaning that when the independent variable rises or falls, the dependent variable moves in the same direction. A rise in the hourly wage of bank tellers that causes a corresponding rise in the number of people who wish to work in this occupation is an example of a direct relationship.

THE NEED FOR ASSUMPTIONS

In order to focus on the relationship between two variables, economists must make assumptions to temporarily simplify the real world. Let us return to the relationship that states that the quantity of cellular phones purchased is inversely related to their price. Economists must assume that another factor—such as consumer incomes—is not affecting purchases of cellular phones. Assuming that all other factors affecting a dependent variable remain constant is common in economics. This assumption is known as *ceteris paribus* (pronounced kay'-teh-rees pah'-ri-bus), which is the Latin expression for "all other things remaining the same." The *ceteris paribus* assumption, as well as any other assumptions that are made, should be outlined explicitly in an economic model.

POSITIVE AND NORMATIVE ECONOMICS

In using economic models, we need to distinguish between two types of economic enquiry: positive and normative economics.

Positive economics (sometimes called *descriptive economics*) is the study of economic reality and why the economy operates as it does. It is based purely on economic facts rather than on opinions. This type of economics is made up of positive statements, which can be accepted or rejected through applying the scientific method. "Canadians bought five million CDs last year" is a positive statement—a simple declaration of fact. A positive statement can also take the form of a condition that asserts that if one thing happens, then so will another: "If rent controls are eliminated, then the number of available

variables: factors that have measurable values

independent variable: the variable in a causal relationship that causes change in another variable

dependent variable: the variable in a causal relationship that is affected by another variable

inverse relationship: a relationship in which a change in the independent variable causes a change in the opposite direction of the dependent variable

direct relationship: a relationship in which a change in the independent variable causes a change in the same direction of the dependent variable

ceteris paribus: the assumption that all other things remain the same

positive economics: the study of economic facts and why the economy operates as it does rental units will increase." Both declarations of fact and conditional statements can be verified or disproved using economic data.

normative economics: the study of how the economy ought to operate

In contrast, **normative economics** (also called policy economics) deals with how the world ought to be. In this type of economics, opinions or value judgements—known as normative statements—are common. "We should reduce taxes" is an example of a normative statement. So is "A 1 percent rise in unemployment is worse than a 1 percent rise in inflation." Even people who agree on the facts can have different opinions regarding a normative statement, since the statement relates to questions of ethical values.

Brief Review

1. The basic economic problem faced by both individuals and societies is that while human wants are virtually unlimited, the resources to fulfil them are limited or scarce.

2. Economic resources can be categorized as natural resources, capital resources, and human resources. Each resource has a corresponding income.

3. Whereas microeconomics concentrates on the ways consumers and businesses interact in various markets, macroeconomics takes a broader look at the economy as a whole and highlights such variables as unemployment, inflation, and total output.

4. Economic models contain causal relationships between variables and are based on simplifying assumptions.

1.1 Practice Questions

Analyze the following statement: "The economic welfare of a country's citizens falls if there is a reduction in the quantity of the country's economic resources."

a. The statement refers to two variables. What are they?
b. Which variable is independent and which is dependent?
c. Is the relationship between these variables direct or inverse?
d. Is the statement positive or normative?
e. How is the statement related to the economic problem?

1.2 Economic Choice

LO 1.2

How do people make economic choices? They do so by using effectively the scarce resources they have, which means comparing an action's costs and benefits. This decision-making process, which is at the heart of the economic way of thinking, involves two main factors: utility and cost.

Utility Maximization

utility: the satisfaction gained from any action

self-interest motive: the assumption that people act to maximize their own welfare

Economists assume that whenever you make an economic choice, you are trying to maximize your own utility. **Utility** can be defined as the satisfaction or pleasure you derive from any action. Let us examine utility maximization with the illustration of you and your lunch. Economists assume first the **self-interest motive**, that is, that you are primarily concerned with your own welfare. So, when deciding among lunch options that cost the same amount of money, you pick the one that gives the most utility. For example, suppose someone has $2 to spend at a fast-food restaurant. Two options are available: a pizza slice or a low-calorie veggieburger, each with a price of $2. How does this person make a choice? According to economists, the person decides by making a rational comparison of the utility gained from either product. If the satisfaction from a pizza slice outweighs the pleasures of a veggieburger, they will buy the pizza. If the opposite applies, the veggieburger will win out.

Opportunity Cost

Maximizing utility is only one part of making economic decisions. Acquiring anything prevents someone from pursuing an alternative. Instead of measuring cost in terms of money, economists use a concept that accounts for the tradeoffs resulting from any economic choice: opportunity cost. The **opportunity cost** of any action is the utility that could have been gained by choosing the best possible alternative.

opportunity cost: the utility that could have been gained by choosing an action's best alternative

The notion of opportunity cost involves more than money. To illustrate, the person who spends $2 to buy a pizza slice at the fast-food restaurant faces an opportunity cost equal to the utility that could have been gained by eating a low-calorie veggieburger instead. If the person chooses the veggieburger, the opportunity cost is the sacrificed pleasure of eating a pizza slice. For a weight-conscious consumer, for example, the utility gained from eating the veggieburger probably outweighs the pleasure from eating the pizza slice. This means that the veggieburger's opportunity cost is lower than the opportunity cost of the pizza slice (even though both have the same monetary price), making the veggieburger the preferred choice for this individual.

The concept of opportunity cost also relates to how we spend time, since time passed in one activity means less devoted to another. Suppose a student is deciding whether to spend a free hour watching a TV program or reading a paperback mystery. The opportunity cost of watching the TV program is the pleasure that could have been gained from reading the mystery. Likewise, the opportunity cost of reading the mystery is the benefit sacrificed by not watching the program.

Because utility is subjective and differs for each individual, it is difficult to quantify. Therefore, a simpler method for measuring opportunity cost is often used. Using this more straightforward approach, the opportunity cost of any action is the number of units of the next best alternative that are sacrificed when choosing this action. This approach gives a rough (though not exact) estimate of the utility that could have been gained by choosing an action's best alternative.

1.3 The Production Possibilities Model

LO 1.3

The production possibilities model illustrates the tradeoffs that society faces in using its scarce resources. Like all models, it is an abstraction of the real world based on various simplifications. In this case, the following assumptions are made: only two items are produced, resources and technology are fixed, and all economic resources are employed to their full potential.

Two Products

An immense range of goods and services are produced in the Canadian economy. The production possibilities model, however, narrows the list to only two; for example, computers and hamburgers.

Fixed Resources and Technology

For the model, it is assumed that there is a set amount of available economic resources and that technology remains constant. However, resources can be moved from the production of one good to the other. Workers who make hamburgers, for example, can be shifted to the assembly of computers.

Full Production

In the production possibilities model, all economic resources are employed; that is, there is no excess. Also, resources are used to their greatest capacity, no matter which good they are producing—in this case, computers and hamburgers.

The Production Possibilities Curve

production possibilities schedule: a table that shows the possible output combinations for an economy

production possibilities curve: a graph that illustrates the possible output combinations for an economy

In order to maximize the welfare of its citizens, a society must make economic choices. How much of each good should be produced in a certain year, given the resources at the society's disposal? A choice is necessary because producing more of one item means making do with less of the other. This choice is illustrated in Figure 1.1. On the left is the economy's **production possibilities schedule**—a table outlining, in this case, the possible combinations of computers and hamburgers. Expressing the schedule in a graph gives us the economy's **production possibilities curve**. Because making more of one good means making less of the other, there is an inverse relationship between the quantities of computers and hamburgers produced. Therefore, the curve has a negative slope—from left to right, the curve falls.

As Figure 1.1 demonstrates, it might be possible for the economy to make 900 hamburgers and assemble 1 computer in a given year (point *b*). If the output of hamburgers is reduced to 600, it might also be feasible for the economy to produce 2 computers

---

Figure 1.1	The Production Possibilities Model

A society must choose among possible combinations of two goods. These combinations are shown in the production possibilities schedule and represented by points on the production possibilities curve. Both the schedule and the curve show that more computers can be assembled only if fewer hamburgers are produced. Any points within the curve, as illustrated by *e*, are feasible. Those outside the curve, like *f*, are not.

(point *c*). The extreme cases serve as useful reference points: when all the economy's resources are devoted to the making of hamburgers, a total of 1000 can be produced annually (point *a*), but when the economy devotes all its resources to making only computers, 3 can be made (point *d*).

The Role of Scarcity

As well as depicting the economic choices a society faces, the production possibilities curve highlights the scarcity of economic resources. The curve is a boundary between all those output combinations that are within the reach of an economy and all those combinations that are unattainable. Anywhere inside the curve, such as point *e* in Figure 1.1, represents a feasible combination of the two products. At point *e*, for example, 500 hamburgers and 1 computer can be produced. The production of both hamburgers and computers could be increased by moving towards point *c* on the curve. At any point, such as *e*, some of an economy's resources are not being fully employed or used to their greatest capacity. Hence, all the points inside the curve represent situations where resources are not being fully used.

In contrast, point *f* in Figure 1.1 is outside the curve. In this case, the economy would be producing 800 hamburgers and 3 computers annually. As long as the economy's resources remain constant, this point cannot be reached. More of both hamburgers and computers could be made if point *f* were attainable, but the economy's resources are already being fully utilized at point *c*.

Increasing Opportunity Costs

law of increasing opportunity costs: the concept that as more of one item is produced by an economy, the opportunity cost of additional units of that product rises

The notion of opportunity cost is best seen when moving from one point to another on the production possibilities curve. Notice that the curve in Figure 1.1 bows out to the right. This shape reflects what is called the **law of increasing opportunity costs**, which states that as more of one product is produced, its opportunity cost in terms of the other product increases. This law arises from the fact that economic resources do not transfer perfectly from one use to another. For example, because of training and experience, some workers are better at making hamburgers than assembling computers. When the first computer is assembled, it is made using resources suited to computer assembly rather than to making hamburgers. Hence, the number of hamburgers sacrificed is relatively small. But if further computers are assembled, resources that are not as well suited to this new task must be shifted from making hamburgers. Therefore, more and more hamburgers have to be given up in order to gain each new computer.

The law of increasing opportunity costs is illustrated in Figure 1.2. Assume that society begins by producing only hamburgers (point *a* on the curve) and then decides that 1 computer should be assembled (point *b*). The opportunity cost of this first computer is the number of hamburgers that must be given up. Since hamburger production falls from 1000 to 900, the new computer costs 100 hamburgers. This is shown on the schedule and, on the curve, appears as the height of the triangle connecting points *a* and *b*. The same reasoning can be applied in moving from point *b* to *c*—as a second computer is added, hamburger production drops from 900 to 600. The opportunity cost of this extra computer is, therefore, 300 hamburgers. Finally, in moving from point *c* to *d*, hamburger production drops another 600 to zero, meaning that the opportunity cost of the third computer is 600 hamburgers. The opportunity cost of each new computer, in terms of hamburgers, therefore, rises from 100, to 300, and then to 600.

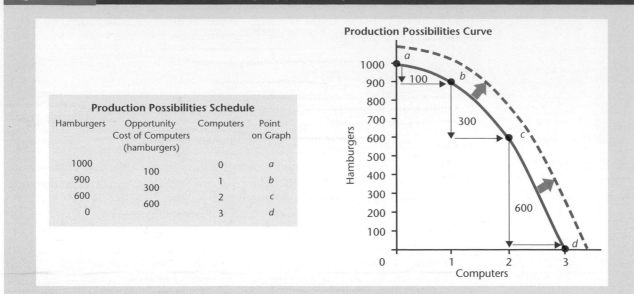

| Figure 1.2 | The Law of Increasing Opportunity Costs |

Production Possibilities Schedule

Hamburgers	Opportunity Cost of Computers (hamburgers)	Computers	Point on Graph
1000		0	a
	100		
900		1	b
	300		
600		2	c
	600		
0		3	d

As the production of computers rises from 0 to 1 unit (from point *a* to *b*), the opportunity cost of the first computer is 100 hamburgers. Further expansion in the output of computers comes at higher opportunity costs: 300 hamburgers for the second computer (from point *b* to *c*), and 600 hamburgers for the third computer (from point *c* to *d*).

Economic Growth

economic growth: an increase in an economy's total output of goods and services

In the long run, this society may experience **economic growth**, or an increase in the total output of goods and services, either due to a rise in the amount of available resources or an improvement in technology. Both trends cause an outward shift in the production possibilities curve, as shown by the dashed curve in Figure 1.2, which means that the area of feasible output combinations expands. As a result, the society can choose output combinations that were previously unattainable—more of both items can now be produced.

By choosing to produce more capital goods, such as computers, and fewer consumption goods, such as hamburgers, a society can increase its amount of available resources, shifting out its future production possibilities curve. Indeed, the focus on capital resources is an important reason why high-income countries—Canada included— have been able to achieve healthy rates of economic growth in comparison with poorer parts of the world.

http://www.oecd.org/statistics

Question
How is the information revolution, including the increased use of computer-based technology, affecting rates of economic growth in such countries as Canada?

Brief Review

1. Economists assume that individuals make economic choices among scarce items by maximizing their own utility while minimizing opportunity cost.

2. The production possibilities curve shows the range of choices faced by an economy. It assumes only two products, fixed resources and technology, and full production.

3. Points inside the production possibilities curve are feasible but indicate that not all resources are being used effectively. Conversely, points outside the curve cannot be reached unless resources increase or technology improves.

4. The fact that economic resources are specialized leads to the law of increasing opportunity costs. As the economy's production of any item is expanded, that item's opportunity cost rises.

1.3 Practice Questions

1. An island castaway spends eight hours each day acquiring two items—coconuts and fish—based on the following production possibilities schedule.

Production Scenario	Coconuts	Fish
a	24	0
b	20	1
c	12	2
d	0	3

   a. From a starting point of production (scenario a), what is the castaway's opportunity of catching the first fish (scenario b)? the second (scenario c)? the third (scenario d)?
   b. Do these results conform to the law of increasing opportunity costs?
   c. If you drew a graph showing the castaway's production possibilities curve, what shape would it have?
   d. What assumptions must be met for the castaway to operate on his production possibilities curve?
   e. What happens to the castaway's production possibility curve if he works for 12 hours, instead of eight hours, each day?
   f. What happens to the castaway's production possibilities curve if he manages to make a fishing rod, which he then uses to catch fish?

2. a. Referring to Figure 1.2, if the economy moves from point *d* to *c*, what is the opportunity cost (in terms of computers) of each of the new hamburgers produced?
   b. What is the opportunity cost of each new hamburger produced when moving from point *c* to *b*?

3. a. Using EconGraphKit (at http://www.mcgrawhill.ca/college/lovewell) draw the production possibilities curve based on the schedule outlined in question 1.
   b. Does the curve you have drawn bow out to the right? How is this shape related to the law of increasing opportunity costs?

1.4 Economic Systems

LO 1.4

Basic Economic Questions

Because of the basic economic problem of scarcity, every country, no matter how it chooses to conduct its economic affairs, must answer three basic economic questions: what to produce, how to produce, and for whom to produce.

WHAT TO PRODUCE

Countries face economic choices when trying to decide what items to produce, as depicted by the production possibilities curve. For example, making more hamburgers means assembling fewer computers. Somehow, a country must decide how much of each possible good and service is to be supplied. Should these decisions be based on past practice, the individual choices of consumers, or government planning?

HOW TO PRODUCE

Once the question of what to produce has been answered, a country must decide how these items should be produced. Which resources should be employed and in what combinations? For example, should farmers use horse-drawn plows and large amounts of labour to produce wheat? Or, should they use sophisticated farm machinery and very little labour? And how should these decisions be made? Should the farmers follow tradition, each choose among their many options, or have their production methods specified by government planners?

FOR WHOM TO PRODUCE

Each country must also determine how its total output of goods and services will be distributed. How output is divided might be based on custom. Alternatively, each person's ownership of economic resources may be the key factor. Or, the government might distribute output in some other fashion.

To answer these three basic economic questions, a country organizes its economy. The result is an **economic system**, which represents the country's distinct set of social customs, political institutions, and economic practices. We will look at three main economic systems: traditional economy, market economy, and command economy. Each of these is a pure or theoretical system; so, few economies come close to them. Most economies today are mixed; that is, they combine aspects of the main economic systems. These systems are all founded on different views of what a society's primary aims should be.

economic system: the organization of an economy, which represents a country's distinct set of social customs, political institutions, and economic practices

Traditional Economy

A **traditional economy** is one in which economic decisions depend on custom, such as a traditional division of work between women and men. The mix of outputs, the organization of production, and the way in which outputs are distributed tend to be passed on relatively unchanged from generation to generation. Religion and culture tend to be considered to be at least as important as material welfare. As recently as a century ago, most people lived in traditional economies, but these economies exist today only in isolated pockets. For example, many farmers in the remote country of Nepal still use traditional methods that have existed for generations. Since they are based on tight social constraints, traditional economies are often resistant to change. Still, the long-term outlook for these economies seems clear: increasingly, they are being broken down by expanding consumer wants and the inability of traditional production methods to meet these wants.

traditional economy: an economic system in which economic decisions are made on the basis of custom

Supporters of traditional economies suggest that they offer the advantage of stability. These economies can also be viewed as beneficial because they emphasize the spiritual and cultural aspects of life. However, critics argue that traditional economies' widespread poverty and social restrictions restrain human potential; people must follow the dictates of custom rather than having the freedom to make their own economic choices.

Market Economy

market economy: an economic system based on private ownership and the use of markets in economic decision-making

In a **market economy**, individuals are free to pursue their own self-interest. This type of economy is based on the private ownership of economic resources and the use of markets in making economic decisions. In this system—often referred to as capitalism—households use incomes earned from their economic resources by saving some and spending the rest on consumer products. Businesses buy resources from households and employ these resources to provide the consumer products demanded by households. Government performs only the political functions of upholding the legal system and maintaining public security.

The transactions between households and businesses in a market economy are illustrated by the circular flow diagram in Figure 1.3. This diagram includes not only households and businesses but also two markets. A **market** is a set of arrangements between buyers and sellers that allows them to trade items for set prices. **Product markets** are those in which consumer products are traded. **Resource markets** are those in which economic resources—natural resources, capital resources, and human resources—are traded.

market: a set of arrangements between buyers and sellers of a certain item

product markets: markets in which consumer products are traded

resource markets: markets in which economic resources are traded

Households and businesses face each other in both sets of markets. In product markets, households are the buyers of consumer products, while businesses are the sellers. In resource markets, the roles are reversed: households sell resources that businesses purchase so that they can produce goods and services. Households and businesses are connected by two circular flows. The inner loop in the diagram shows the circulation of payments—both household incomes and consumer spending. The outer loop shows the circulation of consumer products and economic resources in the opposite direction.

BENEFITS OF A MARKET ECONOMY

Placing markets at the centre of economic activity can have benefits. The main benefits are associated with consumer sovereignty and innovation.

Figure 1.3   The Circular Flow Diagram

Households and businesses are involved in two main markets, one involving consumer products and the other involving economic resources. While the inner loop represents the clockwise flow of incomes and consumer spending, the outer loop indicates the counterclockwise circulation of resources and products.

Consumer Sovereignty

consumer sovereignty: the effect of consumer needs and wants on production decisions

Market economies are characterized by **consumer sovereignty**, meaning that the decision of what to produce is ultimately guided by the needs and wants of households in their role as consumers. In other words, consumers use their dollars to "vote" on what types of goods and services should be produced, based on the role of prices as an important signaling device. Prices play this role by co-ordinating the activities of buyers and sellers to stop either too much or too little of an item from being produced.

For example, if households wish to switch some of their consumption dollars from the purchase of stereos to TVs, a chain reaction will occur in the product and resource markets. In product markets, the extra demand for TVs pushes up TV prices, while the lower demand for stereos pushes down stereo prices. The higher TV prices provide businesses, lured by the chance to make higher profits, with an incentive to supply more TVs. Meanwhile, a price drop for stereos causes businesses to cut their stereo production. These shifts in production also result in changes in the employment of economic resources, with more resources being used to make TVs and fewer being used to make stereos.

Innovation

The incentive to make a profit in a market economy encourages innovation and entrepreneurship, which help foster advances in technology. Consumers benefit through improvements to existing products and the introduction of completely new products.

DRAWBACKS OF A MARKET ECONOMY

The main drawbacks of a market economy are associated with income distribution, possible market problems, and potential instability of total output.

Income Distribution

Without intervention by governments, the distribution of income in a market economy can create significant inequities. If households' incomes are based solely on the ability to supply economic resources, then some individuals in the economy might not earn enough to provide even for their basic needs.

Market Problems

Other deficiencies of market economies arise because private markets do not always operate in a way that benefits society as a whole. Negative external effects of economic activity—for example, pollution—may require intervention by governments to prevent harm to the society. Negative internal effects may also cause governments to step in, for example, when one or a few companies control a certain product market, thus depriving consumers of the advantages of competition.

Instability

Finally, market economies can display considerable instability in the total output produced from year to year. Such fluctuations can harm the economy's participants through substantial variations in prices or employment levels.

As a result of these deficiencies, there are very few real-world examples of pure capitalism. The closest approximations have occurred in the past—in particular, during the first half of the 19th century in Great Britain.

Command Economy

Opposite to a market economy is a **command economy**, in which all productive property—natural resources and capital—is in the hands of government, and markets are largely replaced by central planning. Rather than being based on consumer sovereignty and individual decision-making, command economies rely on planners to decide what should be produced, how production should be carried out, and how the output should be distributed. For example, in a market economy, decisions made by households about how much to consume and how much to save determine the split between consumer and capital products. In a command economy, however, central planners determine the split, on the basis of their judgement of the future needs of the entire economy.

BENEFITS OF A COMMAND ECONOMY

The reliance on planning rather than markets gives command economies some possible benefits related to income distribution and economic growth.

Income Distribution

A country that adopts a command system can choose to distribute income among its citizens on the basis of considerations other than purely economic ones. In these economies, an attempt is usually made to distribute income more equally than would be the case with market economies.

Economic Growth

Central planners can focus on promoting the rate of economic growth by devoting more resources to capital goods than would be the case in a market economy. This strategy can be particularly effective when an economy is first building a manufacturing sector. During this stage of development, economic growth is closely tied to the quantity of capital goods, such as machines and factories, that an economy possesses.

DRAWBACKS OF A COMMAND ECONOMY

Command economies also have serious drawbacks related to planning, efficiency, and individual freedom. Because of these deficiencies, pure command economies are almost as rare as pure market economies; the closest approximation in contemporary times is North Korea.

Planning Difficulties

Trying to plan an entire economy is a difficult task requiring a tremendous amount of information that is unlikely to be at the planners' disposal. Incorrect estimates of future conditions are all too easy to make, leading to overproduction of some items and underproduction of others.

Inefficiencies

Government ownership of productive property can lead to waste and inefficiency, since command economies cannot depend on the lure of profit to promote the efficient use of resources. Without markets to control individual self-interest, corruption of government officials is also a frequent problem. As well, because planners emphasize quantity by setting production quotas, the quality of goods and services can suffer.

Lack of Freedom

Opponents of command economies also suggest that putting so much power into the hands of government stifles individual freedom. Because central planners are responsible for so many economic decisions, people living in command economies have limited economic choices. All too often, critics contend, command economies are associated with a lack of political freedom as well.

Mixed Economy

modern mixed economy: an economic system that combines aspects of a market economy and a command economy; production decisions are made both in private markets and by government

Most countries fall between the extremes of traditional, market, and command economies. A **modern mixed economy** is one that combines both the use of markets and a significant government presence in economic decision-making. Modern mixed economies have proven very popular and take a variety of forms, depending on the relative importance given to private markets and to the economic functions of government. In some countries, such as Canada and the United States, markets play the dominant economic role. In other countries, such as Sweden, the government's economic role is more important. All three examples are illustrated in Figure 1.4, which depicts the range of possible modern mixed economies (along the top edge of the triangle) that exist between the two poles of pure market and command economies.

While modern mixed economies vary widely, they have some common attributes. Each one includes a private sector, in which economic activity is dominated by markets and there is private ownership of productive resources. Each of these economies also includes a public sector, in which governments conduct economic activity—often without the use of markets—and own productive resources.

In most modern mixed economies, the distinction between the private and public sectors is not clear-cut. Governments can intervene in the private sector by levying taxes or providing subsidies to some industries. In Canada, for example, the federal government plays a part in the private sector through personal and corporate taxes and the subsidies it provides to business. Government also intervenes in the private sector by imposing regulations, such as environmental laws, on businesses. In addition, government owns some companies, such as Canada Post.

Figure 1.4	The Range of Economic Systems

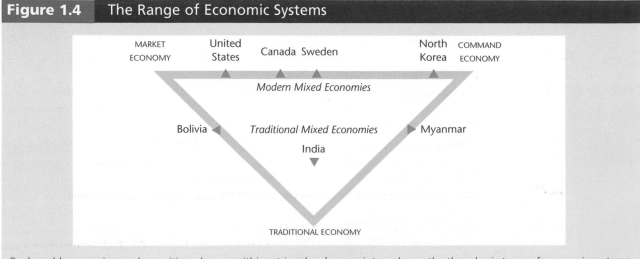

Real-world economies can be positioned on or within a triangle whose points make up the three basic types of economic systems: traditional, market, and command. Countries with surviving traditional sectors combine them with either an emerging private sector (as in Bolivia), public sector (as in Myanmar), or both private and public sectors (as in India).

Countries with entirely traditional economies are rare. However, some countries still possess a significant traditional sector, in which economic activity is based on custom and traditional production methods. Economies that possess a traditional sector alongside more modern sectors are known as **traditional mixed economies**. An example is Bolivia, where market-driven industries, such as mining, co-exist with a traditional sector of peasant farmers. These economies can also involve traditional and public sectors, as in the case of Myanmar (formerly Burma). Finally, all three sectors can co-exist in one economy, as in the case of India. These examples appear in Figure 1.4, in which traditional mixed economies appear below the top of the triangle.

traditional mixed economies: economic systems in which a traditional sector co-exists with modern sectors

CONFLICTS

Mixed economies must deal with the inevitable conflicts among their component sectors. Each sector emphasizes a distinct view of society's underlying aims—the focus on self-interest in a private sector, wider national objectives in a public sector, and continuity in a traditional sector. As the sectors interact, differences in these views are sure to cause friction.

As an example, consider one of Canada's few remaining traditional industries—the Atlantic inshore fishery, which is based on the tradition of small, family-owned business. Canadians view government subsidies to those working in this industry in different ways. Some Canadians resent their taxes being used to prop up an uncompetitive industry. Others see these subsidies as a necessary form of regional aid. Still others view the issue not as an economic one but as a cultural one, since fishing has traditionally been an important part of Atlantic Canada's economy.

Economic Goals

Choosing economic goals is an issue of normative economics and depends on the political and moral constraints set by society. In other words, it requires making value judgements. The economic goals that various countries strive for are often similar. In 1964, the Economic Council of Canada—formerly a federal "think tank" on economic issues—listed what it considered to be the five main goals of the Canadian economy: economic growth, full employment, price stability, income equity, and a viable balance of payments. Many Canadians would add economic efficiency and environmental sustainability to the list. For now, the significance of each of these goals will be briefly summarized.

ECONOMIC EFFICIENCY

economic efficiency: employing scarce resources in such a way as to derive the highest benefit

In general, **economic efficiency** means getting the highest benefit from an economy's scarce resources. In other words, efficiency requires that scarce economic resources be employed in a way that maximizes utility.

INCOME EQUITY

Income equity is achieved when a country's total output is distributed fairly. This begs the question, "What is fair?" Is it fair that the salary of a bank executive is many times higher than the year's wages of a part-time gardener? Because value judgements come into play, defining and satisfying the goal of income equity is controversial.

PRICE STABILITY

inflation: a rise in the general level of prices

Canadian governments try to minimize the country's rate of **inflation**, which is a rise in the general level of prices. As the average price level in the economy increases, households must pay more to buy the same items. In other words, the purchasing power of a single dollar falls. Meanwhile, people's money incomes do not necessarily increase along with these higher prices. Those households whose incomes stay the same or grow only slightly are hurt by inflation because they can buy fewer goods and services than they could before.

FULL EMPLOYMENT

The Canadian government endeavours to minimize involuntary unemployment in the labour force. The labour force can be defined as those people who are working plus those who are involuntarily unemployed and actively seeking employment. The **unemployment rate** is the percentage of the country's labour force that is involuntarily unemployed.

The costs of involuntary unemployment are significant, both to jobless people and to the entire economy. Being without work represents a waste of personal potential and can bring economic hardship to the unemployed and their families. For the Canadian economy, a high unemployment rate means a lower total output than could otherwise be produced. In terms of the country's production possibilities curve, economic activity takes place within the curve, where resources are not used to their full potential.

VIABLE BALANCE OF PAYMENTS

Canadians engage in a constant flow of imports, exports, and financial dealings with other countries. These international flows—including importing, exporting, borrowing, and lending—are of great significance to the Canadian economy. The **balance-of-payments accounts** summarize all transactions between Canadians and foreigners that involve exchanging Canadian dollars for other currencies, such as American dollars or British pounds. Because of Canada's dependence on foreign markets, it is important that Canadian imports and exports roughly balance one another. Similarly, financial flows in and out of the country need to be more or less evenly matched. As long as these conditions are met, then Canada exhibits a viable balance of payments.

ECONOMIC GROWTH

Economic growth, as we have seen, is depicted by an outward shift in the production possibilities curve. Economic growth is an important national goal because it helps to raise the average standard of living for Canadians. Thus, over recent decades, the entire Canadian economy has expanded considerably and individual Canadians are better off than they were in previous decades. For example, an average Canadian worker in the early 2000s can buy over three and a half times as much with his or her income than could an average worker in the early 1920s. Maintaining a healthy rate of growth in the Canadian economy will ensure that future generations will achieve even higher living standards.

ENVIRONMENTAL SUSTAINABILITY

Economic activity must be carried out so that the quality of our physical environment can be sustained without significant harm. Already, the world's air, water, and land resources have seriously deteriorated, so much so that there are signs that irreversible damage has occurred. To eliminate, or at least minimize, these problems in the future requires adjustments in the way economic activity is now conducted, especially in industrialized countries, such as Canada.

COMPLEMENTARY GOALS

In some cases, success in reaching one economic goal makes another goal easier to achieve. Goals that are related in this way simplify the task of those in charge of government economic policy and are said to be complementary. Full employment and

unemployment rate: the percentage of a labour force that is involuntarily unemployed

balance-of-payments accounts: a summary of all transactions between Canadians and foreigners that involve exchanging Canadian dollars for other currencies economic growth, for example, are considered complementary goals, since government policies that help to push up employment levels in an economy also lead to expanded national output.

CONFLICTING GOALS

Some economic goals, however, are bound to conflict so that attaining one goal makes another goal more difficult to achieve. For example, price stability and full employment frequently clash because government measures that bring down the rate of inflation often restrain the level of production in an economy, thus raising the unemployment rate. Similarly, income equity and economic efficiency often clash, since efforts to make the distribution of income fairer can reduce incentives for households to supply their resources. This can mean that an economy's resources are used less efficiently than before. Conflicts like these mean that government policy-makers must set priorities, and this can mean that one goal is achieved at the cost of another.

Brief Review

1. Three basic economic questions must be answered by every country: what to produce, how to produce, and for whom to produce.

2. Traditional economies stress the role of custom and tradition. Market economies rely on private property and the operation of markets. Command economies depend on publicly owned property and central planning.

3. Modern mixed economies combine features of both market and command economies in different degrees. Traditional mixed economies include both traditional and modern sectors.

4. The main goals of the Canadian economy are economic efficiency, income equity, price stability, full employment, a viable balance of payments, economic growth, and environmental sustainability. Some of these goals are complementary, while others are conflicting.

1.4 Practice Questions

Countries Alpha and Beta each have traditional, private, and public sectors. The traditional and public sectors each make up a larger proportion of Alpha's economy than their proportions in Beta. On the other hand, the private sector is relatively larger in Beta than in Alpha.

a. Which country will tend to have more economic freedom?
b. Which country's economy will tend to have greater stability?
c. In which country will there be the greatest conflict between traditional culture and national planners?
d. If the two countries' systems are plotted in the triangle shown in Figure 1.4, will Alpha be northwest, southwest, northeast, or southeast of Beta?

LAST**WORD**

In this chapter, we have seen how individuals make choices on the basis of their calculation of utility and the opportunity cost of scarce personal resources. We have also seen how societies make economic choices on the basis of normative goals and the opportunity cost of scarce social resources. We will return to the ways that individuals make choices in the next two chapters of Part 1. Meanwhile, later parts of the book focus on how society meets its goals: economic efficiency and income equity in Part 2, price stability and full employment in Part 3, and a viable balance of payments and economic growth in Part 4.

Key Concepts

balance-of-payments
  accounts 18
capital resources 3
ceteris paribus 5
command economy 15
consumer sovereignty 14
dependent variable 5
direct relationship 5
economic efficiency 17
economic growth 10
economic models 4
economic problem 3
economic resources 3
economic system 12
economics 4

entrepreneurship 4
independent variable 5
inflation 17
inverse relationship 5
labour 4
law of increasing opportunity costs 9
macroeconomics 4
market 13
market economy 13
microeconomics 4
modern mixed economy 16
natural resources 3
normative economics 6

opportunity cost 7
positive economics 5
product markets 13
production possibilities curve 8
production possibilities schedule 8
resource markets 13
self-interest motive 6
traditional economy 12
traditional mixed economies 17
unemployment rate 18
utility 6
variables 5

Questions

1. Specify whether the following relationships are direct or inverse:
   a. The drop in the price of compact discs reduces the quantity purchased of cassette tapes.
   b. The rise in the average salary of computer programmers increases the number of people seeking a career in computer programming.
   c. The fall in the price of wheat fertilizer increases the amount of wheat planted by farmers.
   d. An increase in the income tax rate paid by households reduces the amount of consumption spending in the economy.

2. Identify the following statements as positive or normative. In each case, explain your answer.
   a. In order to stimulate economic growth, more capital goods and fewer consumer goods should be produced in the Canadian economy.
   b. Inflation in Canada is currently lower than in most other countries.
   c. If a country experiences lower levels of economic efficiency, citizens of the country will experience a decrease in living standards.
   d. The Canadian government should be more concerned with ensuring environmental sustainability and less concerned with achieving low inflation.

3. A consumer would gain more utility from purchasing a TV than from purchasing a stereo, even though both products have the same price of $600. How can the consumer's decision to purchase the TV be explained using the concept of opportunity cost?

4. Below is a production possibilities schedule for a hypothetical economy that produces only two goods—skateboards and bicycles.
    a. Graph this production possibilities schedule, putting skateboard output on the vertical axis and bicycle output on the horizontal axis. (Make sure the numerical scales you choose for each axis are sufficient to plot the points on the curve.) Describe the shape of the curve you have drawn and explain the reason for this shape.

Production Possibilities Schedule

Production Scenario	Skateboards	Bicycles
A	40	0
B	38	1
C	32	2
D	20	3
E	0	4

    b. Calculate the opportunity cost of bicycles in terms of skateboards when the economy moves from point B to C. What is the new opportunity cost for bicycles when the economy moves from point C to D? Do your answers illustrate the law of increasing opportunity costs? How?
    c. Can the economy produce 38 skateboards and 2 bicycles? Why or why not?
    d. If 32 skateboards and 1 bicycle are produced, how would you describe production in this economy?
    e. On your graph, show how a technological improvement in the assembly of bicycles would affect the production possibilities curve.
    f. On your graph, show how an increase in the economy's supply of labour would affect the production possibilities curve.

5. The table below shows the size of the private, public, and traditional sectors in three hypothetical countries.

Sector Sizes in Three Countries (% of country's total economy)

	Private Sector	Public Sector	Traditional Sector
Country A	60%	40%	0%
Country B	30%	0%	70%
Country C	0%	80%	20%

    a. Drawing a diagram based on Figure 1.4, show the approximate position of each of these three countries in the diagram.
    b. Which of these countries likely has the most stable culture? the most equal distribution of income? the greatest economic freedom? Explain.
    c. Traditional sectors in most countries are continually shrinking. On your diagram, portray the movement caused by an increase in the private sector in Country B and an increase in the public sector in Country C.

6. Identify a pair of complementary economic goals and a pair of conflicting economic goals (other than those cited in the chapter). In each case, explain why these goals are related in the way you suggest.

http://www.statcan.ca

7. (Advanced Question)
    a. For the years shown in the table below, calculate Canada's misery index, which is the sum of a country's inflation and unemployment rates, expressed as percentages. Construct a table showing your results.
    b. What was the average value of the misery index during the years 1983–2002? In which years was the index greater than the average value? In which years was it less?
    c. What does the misery index indicate? How are the inflation rate and the unemployment rate weighted in this index? Would everyone agree with this weighting? Explain.

Annual Inflation and Unemployment Rates in Canada, 1983–2002

	Inflation (%)	Unemployment (%)		Inflation (%)	Unemployment (%)
1983	5.8	11.9	1993	1.8	11.4
1984	4.3	11.3	1994	0.2	10.4
1985	4.0	10.7	1995	2.2	9.4
1986	4.1	9.6	1996	1.6	9.6
1987	4.4	8.8	1997	1.6	9.1
1988	4.0	7.8	1998	0.9	8.3
1989	5.0	7.5	1999	1.7	7.6
1990	4.8	8.1	2000	2.7	6.8
1991	5.6	10.3	2001	2.6	7.2
1992	1.5	11.2	2002	2.2	7.7

Source: Statistics Canada, *Historical Statistical Supplement*, 2002/3 (July 2003), cat. no. 11-210-XPB, vol. 17, pp. 36, 48. Reproduced by authority of the Ministry of Industry, 2004. (Visit the Statistics Canada web site at http://www.statcan.ca)

8. (Policy Discussion Question)
    There is currently a debate in Canada over the relative advantages of having health care provided by the public sector or the private sector.
    a. What are the main advantages associated with health care provided by the public sector? by the private sector?
    b. Do you believe more of Canada's health care services should be available privately? Why or why not?

Internet Application Question

http://dc2.chass.utoronto.ca /pwt

Access the Penn World Tables (at http://dc2.chass.utoronto.ca/pwt). Using the most recent year's statistics available, rank the following economies—Canada, United Kingdom, Finland, Hong Kong—by the size of government in each economy. What does your ranking suggest about the systems chosen by each economy?

THE FOUNDER OF MODERN ECONOMICS

Adam Smith and the Invisible Hand

Smith and His Influence

Adam Smith (1723–1790) is known as the father of present-day economics. While he deserves his reputation as a trailblazer, his greatest talent was in combining innovative ideas—many conceived by others—into a theory that had a profound influence on economic thinking, not only in his own time but ever since.

The son of a middle-class Scottish family, he was an avid student, attending universities in both England and Scotland. At the University of Glasgow, he gained a reputation as the classic absent-minded professor, who, when distracted by some difficult theoretical problem, would walk for hours, oblivious to his surroundings.

Smith first made a name for himself through his writings in philosophy. He then turned his attention to economic issues. In 1776, after years of research, he published his classic work, *An Inquiry Into the Nature and Causes of the Wealth of Nations*, which brought him both fame and a modest fortune. For generations, the book was a standard in economics, and it can still be read profitably today.

Adam Smith
Source: ©Bettmann/CORBIS/Magma

The Industrial Revolution

Smith lived at the beginning of the Industrial Revolution. In the latter half of the 1700s and early 1800s, agriculture lost its central role in the British economy. Through a host of technological innovations, a powerful new manufacturing sector based on labour-saving machinery and steam power took its place. By transforming the lives of common people, this revolution had a profound social and economic impact in many countries, but first in Britain:

> The Industrial Revolution marks the most fundamental transformation of human life in the history of the world recorded in written documents. For a brief period, it coincided with the history of a single country, Great Britain. An entire world economy was thus built on, or rather around, Britain, and this country therefore temporarily rose to a position of global influence and power unparalleled by any state of its relative size before or since, and unlikely to be paralleled by any state in the foreseeable future.[1]

The Division of Labour

When Adam Smith was writing *The Wealth of Nations*, these great changes in the British economy were just beginning. As the title of his book suggests, he wished to explain why some countries become more wealthy than others. Smith viewed the division of labour—the degree to which the job of each worker is a specialized task—as the most significant single cause of economic progress. To support this claim, he provided his famous illustration from the trade of pin-making:

> The greatest improvement in the productive powers of labour, and the greater part of the skill, dexterity, and judgement with which it is anywhere directed, or applied, seem to have been the effects of the division of labour....
>
> To take an example,...the trade of the pin-maker; a workman not educated to this business,...nor acquainted with the use of the machinery employed in it,...could scarce, perhaps, with his utmost industry, make one pin in a day, and certainly could not make twenty. But in the way in which this business is now carried on, not only the whole work is a peculiar [i.e., particular] trade, but it is divided into a number of branches, of which

the greater part are likewise peculiar trades. One man draws out the wire, another straight[en]s it, a third cuts it, a fourth points it, a fifth grinds it at the top for receiving the head; to make the head requires three distinct operations; to put it on is a peculiar business, to whiten the pins is another; it is even a trade by itself to put them into the paper; and the important business of making a pin is, in this manner, divided into about eighteen distinct operations, which, in some manufactories, are all performed by distinct hands, though in others the same man will sometimes perform two or three of them.[2]

Smith mentioned that he visited a small factory where, through the division of labour, 10 employees produced a total of 48 000 pins a day—4800 times the estimated product of one pin per worker when the division of labour was not used!

The Invisible Hand

The benefits associated with the division of labour are not the only reason why some nations are better off than others, according to Smith. Economic progress is also spurred by the self-interest motive or the desire individuals have to increase their own happiness. "It is not from the benevolence of the butcher, the brewer, or the baker that we expect our dinner," Smith stated, "but from their regard to their own interest. We address ourselves, not to their humanity but to their self-love, and never talk to them of our own necessities but of their advantages."[3] In other words, if people are free to pursue their own private interests, they act in a way that aids the economy as a whole. What causes this is competition. As long as there are many businesses selling a product, the product's price will be driven down to a point where it covers only the businesses' costs, including a reasonable profit for the owners. If the price of the product were any higher, others would enter the industry in order to gain excess profits. Because consumers can buy the product at the lowest possible price, they reap the ultimate rewards of competition.

In more general terms, the forces of individual self-interest and competition ensure that resources are used in ways that promote economic growth and national prosperity. To explain his theory, Smith used a term that has become part of everyday language. He said that the forces of market competition act like an "invisible hand" so that self-interested behaviour can work to the benefit of all society.

The Principle of *Laissez Faire*

Although Adam Smith pointed out the potential benefits of people's selfish actions, he was not merely acting as a mouthpiece for the business class. As he was quick to point out, individual self-interest ceases to benefit society when competition is lacking. In the case of a monopoly, where a single producer controls an entire market, the business class's selfish motives cause prices to be driven to the highest value that the market will bear, meaning that consumers suffer.

Often, it is governments that cause monopolies to flourish, said Smith, by offering privileges to a chosen firm. In fact, governments themselves can be considered a type of monopoly. All too frequently, Smith argued, public officials engage in political favouritism or misuse their power for private ends. In doing so, they illustrate how selfish behaviour, when unimpeded by private competition, harms rather than helps society.

Given his sceptical view of government actions, Smith asserted the principle of *laissez faire*, the French term for "let things be"—meaning that, in general, governments should interfere as little as possible in the day-to-day operations of private markets.

Relevance for Today

While modern economists, as a rule, express admiration for Smith's achievements, some of them question the suitability of his theories in contemporary times. They suggest that

Smith's "invisible hand" only operates when an economy is made up of many small businesses. However, most modern markets do not meet these requirements. A contemporary American economist named Robert Heilbroner upholds this view:

> Today's market mechanism is characterized by the huge size of its participants: giant corporations and equally giant labor unions obviously do not behave as if they were individual proprietors and workers. Their very bulk enables them to stand out against the pressures of competition, to disregard price signals, and to consider what their self-interest shall be in the long run rather than in the immediate press of each day's buying and selling.[4]

Other economists claim that Smith's conclusions are just as relevant today as they were 200 years ago. Although huge corporations are an important factor in contemporary economies, so are small businesses. And, as various nations become integrated into a single global economy, international competition among companies—both large and small—is playing a greater role than ever before.

Supporters of Smith's relevance also point to the recent growth of private markets in formerly communist and socialist states. They argue that now, even more than before, private competition is preferred over government intervention.

Notes
[1] From *Industry and Empire: From 1750 to the Present Day* by E.J. Hobsbawm (Harmondsworth: Penguin, 1969), p. 13, copyright © E.J. Hobsbawm, 1968, 1969. Reprinted by permission of Simon & Schuster, Inc.
[2] Adam Smith, *The Wealth of Nations* (Harmondsworth: Penguin, 1983), pp. 109–10.
[3] Ibid, p. 119.
[4] *The Worldly Philosophers*, 6th ed. (New York: Simon and Schuster, 1986), p. 59. Copyright © 1953, 1961, 1967, 1972, 1980, 1986, 1992 by Robert L. Heilbroner. Copyright renewed © 1981, 1989 by Robert L. Heilbroner. Reprinted by permission of Simon & Schuster, Inc.

1. The reasons for the output-enhancing effect of the division of labour can be inferred from Adam Smith's illustration of a pin-making factory.
   a. Explain in your own words why the division of labour can lead to increased output in a production process, such as pin-making.
   b. Do you think the use of more specialized machinery in pin-making would also lead to increased output? Why or why not?

2. In each of the following cases, use Adam Smith's concept of the invisible hand to explain the events that occur if the relevant markets are competitive and operate without government intervention. In your answers, identify the self-interested behaviour that causes beneficial results.
   a. Because of Good W's sudden popularity, suppliers of this good presently make exorbitant profits.
   b. A new innovation reduces the cost of producing Good X.
   c. Two neighbouring countries, A and B, agree for the first time to allow goods to flow freely between them.

3. Explain why the absence of the invisible hand of competition in the following situations can lead to harmful results for the consumer.
   a. A catering company wins the exclusive right to sell food in a stadium.
   b. By keeping out potential rivals, a few large corporations control sales of Good Y.
   c. A labour union, which, by law, includes all workers involved in the production of Good Z, manages on the basis of a strike threat to gain a significant wage increase from employers.

SIDELINE

Economics as an Art

The Craft of Economic Thinking

The Role of Assumptions

One of the most common criticisms of economics is summarized by a well-known joke:

> Three hungry castaways—a physicist, a geologist, and an economist—are stranded on a desert island with a single can of beans to eat, and no can-opener.
>
> "I've got the answer," announces the physicist, after thinking about how to extract the beans. "We'll focus sunlight through my eyeglasses to burn a hole in the can."
>
> "Are you crazy?" replies the geologist. "You'll burst it and spill out the beans. Let's punch a hole with a sharp rock."
>
> The economist smiles and shakes his head at their thick-headedness. "No, it's much easier than either of you think. Let's just assume we have a can-opener."

As the joke implies, economists depend extensively on assumptions, some of them rather creative. Scientists, such as physicists and chemists, also make assumptions, but theirs are more often assumptions that can be tested in controlled laboratory experiments. They can duplicate circumstances and isolate the variables they are studying from external factors. Economists rarely have this luxury. When people's economic behaviour is studied in artificial laboratory settings, it does not necessarily match real life. To isolate a relationship between two or more variables requires abstracting from the complexity of the real world and then verifying these economic models by studying transactions in actual markets.

Economics as an Art

Many economists prefer to think of their subject simply as a discipline, rather than as a science like physics or chemistry. They argue that creating models of economic reality requires the talent of being able to represent reality in the most "economical" way possible. A good economic model is, therefore, a little like a sketch by an expert

A good economic model is like an artist's sketch. (Portrait of a Young Woman by Leonardo da Vinci.)
Source: The Royal Collection © 2003. Her Majesty The Queen

artist, such as Leonardo da Vinci; just a few well-chosen lines capture the appearance of the subject, as does da Vinci's sketch above.[1]

The art of model-building in economics is complicated by the fact that economics is a discipline that analyzes human behaviour. The way we behave depends partly on our social surroundings: the political, cultural, and economic aspects of the society we live in. Changes in these social surroundings can affect human behaviour; when this happens, economic models may have to be altered as well. This leads to a complex interaction between economics and the reality it tries to explain:

> Economics is an ever-changing discipline. Partly a product of the great ideological debates about the way human society ought to be organized, it also influences the outcome of those debates. Partly based on a theoretical search for abstract truths, it is also rooted in the realities of public policy and the climate of opinion. Partly an

explanation of how and why an economic system functions, it is affected by the ways in which economic systems change.[2]

Just as a piece of art is a product of the time and place in which the artist lived, so does an economic model reflect the society in which it was developed.

Interestingly, the 20th century's most illustrious economist John Maynard Keynes viewed his subject as science and art. According to Keynes, an economist "must be purposeful and disinterested in a simultaneous mood; as aloof and incorruptible as an artist, yet sometimes as near the earth as a politician."[3] Given such tough requirements, a first-rate economist is a rare creature, indeed. As we will see in later chapters, Keynes himself was someone who possessed the talents necessary to build a simple yet powerful model of the economy. In fact, his theories form the basis of macroeconomics as we know it today.

Notes

[1] This comparison is made by Maurice Levi in *Economics Deciphered: A Layman's Survival Guide* (New York: Basic Books, 1981), p. 10.

[2] From *The Age of the Economist*, 6th ed., by Daniel R. Fusfeld, copyright © 1990 Scott, Foresman and Company. Reprinted by permission of HarperCollins College Publishers.

[3] John Maynard Keynes, *Essays in Biography* (London: Macmillan, 1972) p. 174.

1. For each case below, identify one variable that must be assumed constant to analyze this relationship.
    a. The price of tomatoes affects the amount of tomatoes offered for sale in a farmers' market.
    b. The wage rate paid to gold-miners affects the number of gold-miners that companies choose to employ.
    c. The price of a certain type of machine affects the number of these machines purchased by businesses.

2. Explain whether each of the economic concepts below is equally relevant in all societies. If not, give an example where the concept might not apply.
    a. Opportunity cost
    b. Self-interest motive
    c. Capital resources

SIDELINE

CHAPTER 2

Demand and Supply

Teach a parrot to say demand and supply, and you've created an economist.

— An old joke

Each day, we buy an assortment of goods and services—a meal, a snack, maybe a magazine. What determines the price of the french fries we buy at lunchtime? the selection of chocolate bars we find at our local variety store? the types of articles we see in the magazines we read? The answer to all these questions is demand and supply. In this chapter, we will study the impact of these two forces on our daily lives by analyzing how they operate in individual markets. We will also see how the "invisible hand" of competition coordinates the plans of buyers and sellers through the interaction of demand and supply.

LEARNING OBJECTIVES

In this chapter, you will:

1 consider the nature of demand, changes in quantity demanded, changes in demand, and the factors that affect demand

2 examine the nature of supply, changes in quantity supplied, changes in supply, and the factors that affect supply

3 see how markets reach equilibrium—the point at which demand and supply meet

2.1 The Role of Demand

LO 2.1

demand: the relationship between the various possible prices of a product and the quantities of that product consumers are willing to purchase

quantity demanded: the amount of a product consumers are willing to purchase at each price

A product market exists wherever households and businesses buy and sell consumer products—either face-to-face, or indirectly by mail, telephone, or online. Some markets, such as the market for crude oil, are global in scope. Others, such as the market for hot dogs at a local baseball game, are tiny by comparison.

What Is Demand?

Because households are buyers in product markets, their behaviour can be analyzed using the concept of **demand**, which is the relationship between the various possible prices of a product and the quantities consumers will purchase at each price. In this relationship, price is the independent variable. **Quantity demanded**—the amount of the product that consumers are willing to purchase at each price—is the dependent variable. To isolate the relationship between these two variables, all other factors affecting price and quantity demanded are assumed to remain constant. Recall that this is the assumption of *ceteris paribus*—"all other things remaining the same."

The Law of Demand

Is the relationship between price and quantity demanded direct or inverse? To answer this question, consider the example of strawberries you might eat during a month. As shown in the table in Figure 2.1, you might buy two kilograms per month when each kilogram is priced at $2. If the price rises to $2.50, you will likely purchase fewer strawberries, perhaps one kilogram per month at this new price. Conversely, if the price falls to $1.50, you will probably buy more strawberries per month. At this lower price, strawberries become a better deal in terms of the satisfaction you get from each dollar spent. Thus, you may decide to increase your purchases to three kilograms per month. This inverse relationship between price and quantity demanded, when all other factors are kept constant, is known as the **law of demand**.

law of demand: states that there is an inverse relationship between a product's quantity demanded and its price

---

Figure 2.1   An Individual's Demand Schedule and Curve

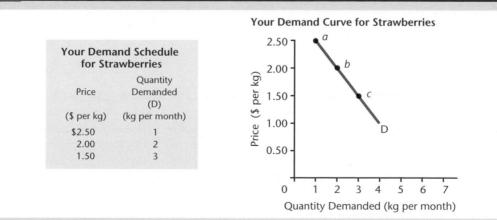

Your Demand Schedule for Strawberries

Price	Quantity Demanded (D)
($ per kg)	(kg per month)
$2.50	1
2.00	2
1.50	3

The demand schedule shows that as the price of strawberries falls, you are willing to purchase more strawberries. The demand curve D depicts this same inverse relationship between price and quantity demanded. For example, a fall in price from $2 to $1.50 causes quantity demanded to rise from 2 kg (point *b*) to 3 kg (point *c*).

The Demand Curve

demand schedule: a table that shows possible combinations of prices and quantities demanded of a product

demand curve: a graph that expresses possible combinations of prices and quantities demanded of a product

change in quantity demanded: the effect of a price change on quantity demanded

The quantities demanded of a product at various prices can be expressed in a **demand schedule** like the one in Figure 2.1. Expressing the schedule on a graph, as shown on the right in Figure 2.1, gives us the consumer's demand curve (D) for strawberries. The **demand curve** is drawn by placing the price of strawberries on the vertical axis and the quantity demanded per month on the horizontal axis. Note that the independent variable (price) is on the vertical axis, while the dependent variable (quantity demanded) is on the horizontal axis. This is a choice economists have made that differs from the convention in mathematics, in which the independent variable (x) is on the horizontal axis and the dependent variable (y) is on the vertical axis.

The demand curve's negative (downward) slope reflects the law of demand: an increase in the product's price decreases the quantity demanded, and vice versa. Changes such as these are examples of a **change in quantity demanded** and produce a movement *along* the demand curve. For example, an increase in the price of strawberries from $1.50 to $2 decreases the quantity demanded per month from three kilograms (point c on the demand curve) to two kilograms (point b)

THINKING ABOUT ECONOMICS

Is the law of demand ever broken?

While extremely rare, the relationship between a product's price and quantity demanded can be direct, in which case the demand curve for the product has a positive (upward) slope. This may happen when a product's high price is seen as a status symbol. For example, the quantity demanded of a designer-shirt may rise when its price rises. Consumers who can afford the shirt are attracted to the item because its high price makes it more fashionable than before. This situation, which can also apply to such products as luxury perfumes and watches, is known as the "Veblen effect." It is named after a famous American economist, Thorstein Veblen (1857–1929), who criticized such purchases and coined the memorable term "conspicuous consumption" to describe them.

Question
What is a specific example of a product that exhibits the "Veblen effect?"

Market Demand

market demand: the sum of all consumers' quantity demanded for a product at each price

Market demand, which can again be shown as a schedule or a curve, is the sum of all consumers' purchases, or quantity demanded, at each price. This is illustrated in Figure 2.2 in the unlikely case that there are just two consumers in the strawberry market—you and a friend—with individual demand curves D_0 (yours) and D_1 (your friend's). While you purchase two kilograms per month at a $2 price, your strawberry-loving friend purchases three kilograms per month at this same price. These amounts are based on what each of you is able and willing to pay for strawberries. The total quantity demanded in the market is, therefore, five kilograms. Repeating this procedure at every possible price gives the market demand curve (D_m) on the lower right in Figure 2.2.

Changes in Demand

demand determinants: factors that can cause an increase or a decrease in a product's demand

Earlier, we stated that to study the relationship between price and quantity demanded, all other factors affecting these variables must be assumed constant. Now, let us examine these other factors, which are known as **demand determinants**. Demand determinants

Figure 2.2   The Market Demand Schedule and Curve

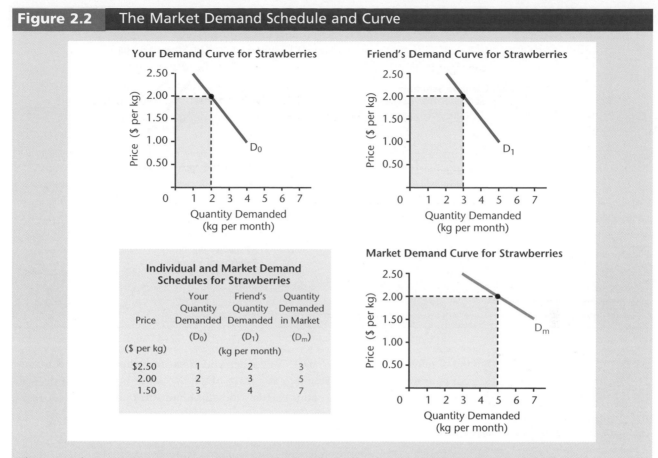

There are only two consumers in the strawberry market: you and a friend, with demand curves D_0 and D_1. The market demand curve (D_m) is found by adding the number of kg purchased by both consumers at each possible price. For example, at a price of $2, you buy 2 kg and your friend buys 3 kg, giving a quantity demanded in the market of 5 kg at this price.

are factors that can cause the entire market demand curve to shift. The five main demand determinants are the number of buyers in a market, their average income, the prices of other products, consumer preferences, and consumer expectations about future prices and incomes. With each determinant, it must be assumed that all other factors remain constant.

NUMBER OF BUYERS

When the number of buyers for a certain product increases, more purchases are made. Thus, the amount of the product demanded increases, whatever its price. The result is called an **increase in demand**. On a graph, an increase in demand is shown as a shift of the *entire* demand curve to the right. When the number of buyers in a market decreases, the amount of the product demanded also decreases at every price, thus causing the entire demand curve to shift to the left. This result is called a **decrease in demand**.

Both cases are illustrated in Figure 2.3 using a hypothetical market for strawberries. The initial amounts demanded per year in the market are shown in the demand schedule under D_0. When demand increases, the amount demanded increases at every possible price. For example, at a price of $2, the amount demanded increases from 9 to 11 million kilograms. Thus, on the graph, the original demand curve (D_0) shifts to the right,

increase in demand: an increase in the quantity demanded of a product at all prices

decrease in demand: a decrease in the quantity demanded of a product at all prices

Figure 2.3 | Changes in Demand

Market Demand Schedule for Strawberries

Price	Quantity Demanded (D₂) (D₀) (D₁)
($ per kg)	(millions of kg)
$2.50	5 ← 7 → 9
2.00	7 ← 9 → 11
1.50	9 ← 11 → 13

Market Demand Curve for Strawberries

When the number of buyers in a market increases, the amount of strawberries demanded increases at every possible price. Each point on the demand curve, therefore, shifts to the right, from D_0 to D_1. Similarly, a decrease in the number of buyers pushes down the amount demanded at every price, shifting the demand curve to the left, from D_0 to D_2.

giving a new demand curve (D_1). When demand decreases, the amount demanded decreases at every price. For example, at a price of $2, the amount demanded decreases from 9 to 7 million kilograms. Thus, the demand curve shifts to the left, from D_0 to D_2.

INCOME

normal products: products whose demand changes directly with income

inferior products: products whose demand changes inversely with income

When consumers' incomes increase, they purchase more luxury products, such as expensive jewellery and caviar. Purchases of more basic items, such as milk and shoes, also rise, but by a smaller proportion. Whether for luxury products or for necessities, demand increases, thus shifting the entire demand curve to the right. Products whose demand changes directly with income are known as **normal products**. There are a few products, known as **inferior products**, for which incomes have the opposite effect. Turnips and second-hand suits are examples. As incomes rise, consumption of these products falls, as buyers switch from turnips to more expensive vegetables and from second-hand suits to new ones. The result is a decrease in demand for these products, reflected in a shift of the entire demand curve to the left.

PRICES OF OTHER PRODUCTS

substitute products: products that can be consumed in place of one another

complementary products: products that are consumed together

Substitute products are products that can be consumed in place of one another. When the price of a product rises, consumers choose to purchase more of any reasonable substitute available, thus shifting the substitute product's demand curve to the right. For example, a higher price for butter causes some consumers to switch to margarine, increasing the demand for margarine. If the price of butter falls, however, there will be a decrease in the demand for margarine.

Complementary products are products that are consumed together, such as cars and gasoline, or compact discs and compact disc players. In the case of complementary products, an increase in the price of one product causes a decrease in demand for its complement. For example, if the prices of cars rise, the demand for gasoline falls. The reverse is also true: a fall in the price of compact discs leads to a rise in demand for compact disc players.

CONSUMER PREFERENCES

People's preferences also affect buying patterns. A significant shift in consumer concerns over nutrition, for example, causes an increase in the demand for nutritious foods. Consumer preferences are also influenced by current fashion or advertising, as in the case of clothing. This is illustrated by a sudden fad for Doc Martens shoes, which increases their demand and shifts this product's demand curve to the right.

CONSUMER EXPECTATIONS

The expectations that consumers have about future changes in prices and their own incomes affect their current purchases. For example, if a majority of consumers expect the price of laptop computers to fall, the current demand for laptops decreases. This is because consumers will delay their purchases of laptops until the expected drop in price occurs. Alternatively, if consumers expect their incomes to grow and the prices of products they buy to remain constant—in other words, if they expect their standard of living to rise—their current demand for normal products will increase, and their current demand for inferior products will decrease.

Change in Quantity Demanded versus Change in Demand

The terms *change in quantity demanded* and *change in demand*, have special meanings in economics. Both types of change are shown in Figure 2.4. As we have seen, a change in quantity demanded results from a change in the product's own price. For example, the number of skis purchased per month will increase when the price of skis decreases, as shown on the graph on the left in Figure 2.4. Here a movement (from point *a* to point *b*) occurs along demand curve D_0, since varying the product's own price does not alter the position of the curve. An increase or decrease in demand, however, results from a change in a demand determinant. For example, a change in consumer preferences or in consumer incomes can cause the entire demand curve to shift. This is because the amount of the product demanded changes at every possible price for the product.

Figure 2.4	Change in Quantity Demanded and Change in Demand

A change in quantity demanded is shown on the left graph as a movement along a single demand curve (D_0) that results from a change in the product's own price. There is a rise in quantity demanded when the price of skis drops, causing a movement from point *a* to point *b*. A change in demand is shown on the right graph as a shift in the entire demand curve to the right, from D_0 to D_1. This shift results from a change in a demand determinant, such as consumer incomes.

The graph on the right shows how an increase in incomes increases the demand for skis, which are a normal product, causing a shift of the entire demand curve for skis from D_0 to D_1.

Brief Review

1. In product markets, demand represents the decisions of households purchasing consumer items.

2. The demand curve for a particular product shows the relationship between its price and the quantity demanded, either by an individual consumer or in the market as a whole. According to the law of demand, price and quantity demanded are inversely related.

3. A change in quantity demanded is shown by a movement along a product's demand curve and is caused by a change in the product's own price.

4. A change in demand is shown by a shift of the entire demand curve and is caused by a change in a demand determinant: the number of buyers, their average income, the prices of other products, consumer preferences, or consumer expectations about future prices and incomes.

2.1 Practice Questions

1. Kate buys 3 milkshakes per week at a price of $1.50, 5 at a price of $1, and 7 at a price of 50 cents. Her friend Carlo buys 5 milkshakes at a price of $1.50, 8 at a price of $1, and 11 at a price of 50 cents.
   a. If these two friends are the only consumers in the market for milkshakes, what are three points on the market demand curve?
   b. Does this market demand curve satisfy the law of demand? Why?
   c. Using EconGraphKit (at http://www.mcgrawhill.ca/college/lovewell), draw the market demand curve for milkshakes.

2. How will the demand for DVDs shift in each of the following situations?
   a. consumer incomes rise
   b. the price of DVD players decreases
   c. there is a sudden expectation by consumers that the price of DVDs will soon drop
   d. the price of movie theatre tickets rises

3. A decrease in the price of DVDs affects both the market for DVDs and the market for videotapes.
   a. Is the change in the DVD market a change in quantity demanded or in demand? Explain.
   b. Is the change in the videotape market a change in quantity demanded or in demand? Explain.

2.2 The Role of Supply

LO 2.2

supply: the relationship between the various possible prices of a product and the quantities of the product that businesses are willing to supply

quantity supplied: the amount of a product businesses are willing to supply at each price

market supply: the sum of all producers' quantities supplied at each price

law of supply: states that there is a direct relationship between a product's quantity supplied and its price

supply schedule: a table that shows possible combinations of prices and quantities supplied of a product

supply curve: a graph that expresses possible combinations of prices and quantities supplied of a product

change in quantity supplied: the effect of a price change on quantity supplied

What Is Supply?

In product markets, supply is related to the selling activity of businesses. The role of supply is most easily analyzed in competitive markets, where the "invisible hand" of competition, identified by Adam Smith, operates. Because the actions of sellers are independent from those of buyers in these markets, the role of supply can be studied separately. In any competitive market, **supply** is the relationship between the various possible prices of a product and the quantities of the product that businesses are willing to put on the market. While the independent variable is again price, the dependent variable is now **quantity supplied**—the amount of the product that businesses are willing to supply at each price. Once again, we can consider both individuals (in this case, individual businesses) and groups (in this case, all businesses producing the same product). **Market supply** is the sum of all producers' quantities supplied at each price. As before, all other factors that affect supply are assumed to be constant.

The Law of Supply

When price changes, quantity supplied changes in the same direction. If the price of strawberries rises, for example, farmers find it desirable to increase the quantity of strawberries they supply because the higher price provides the lure of increased revenue for every unit produced. This direct relationship between price and quantity supplied, when all other factors are kept constant, is called the **law of supply**.

The Supply Curve

The law of supply can be illustrated in a **supply schedule**, such as that for the strawberry market in Figure 2.5. Expressing the schedule on a graph gives us the **supply curve** for the strawberry market. As with the demand curve, a change in a product's price causes a movement *along* the supply curve, thus a **change in quantity supplied**. This is illustrated in Figure 2.5 by the movement from point *f* to point *e* on the supply curve. Because of a drop in the price of strawberries from $2.50 to $2 per kilogram, the

---

Figure 2.5   The Market Supply Schedule and Curve

Market Supply Schedule for Strawberries

Price ($ per kg)	Quantity Supplied (S) (millions of kg)	Point on Graph
$1.50	5	d
2.00	9	e
2.50	13	f

The supply schedule shows that when the price of strawberries falls, as from $2 to $1.50 per kg, then quantity supplied also falls, from 9 million (point *e*) to 5 million kg (point *d*), as farmers find it profitable to produce fewer units. The positively sloped supply curve S indicates a direct relationship between price and quantity supplied.

quantity supplied by farmers per year drops from 13 to 9 million kilograms. The positive (upward) slope of the supply curve illustrates the direct relationship between price and quantity supplied.

Changes in Supply

supply determinants: factors that can cause an increase or a decrease in a product's supply

While price changes will cause changes in quantity supplied, other factors cause supply to change. These factors, which cause the entire supply curve to shift, are known as **supply determinants**. The six main supply determinants are the number of producers, resource prices, the state of technology, changes in nature, the prices of related products, and producer expectations. Once again, with each determinant, we must assume that all other factors remain constant.

NUMBER OF PRODUCERS

increase in supply: an increase in the quantity supplied of a product at all prices

decrease in supply: a decrease in the quantity supplied of a product at all prices

An increase in the number of businesses in an industry causes an **increase in supply**, thus giving a higher quantity supplied at each price and shifting the supply curve to the right. In contrast, a decrease in the number of businesses in the industry creates a **decrease in supply** and a corresponding shift of the supply curve to the left. Both cases are illustrated in Figure 2.6 for the strawberry market. The column marked S_0 in the supply schedule gives the quantity supplied per year by the original number of producers. When the number of producers increases, so does the quantity supplied (indicated by column S_1) at every possible price—for example, from 9 to 11 million kilograms per year at a price of \$2. Thus, the supply curve shifts to the right, from S_0 to S_1. Conversely, a decrease in the supply of the product causes the quantities supplied (indicated by column S_2) to decrease at each possible price, for example, from 9 to 7 million kilograms per year at a price of \$2. The supply curve, therefore, shifts to the left, from S_0 to S_2.

RESOURCE PRICES

As discussed in the previous chapter, businesses buy various resources, such as capital resources and natural resources, to produce goods. If there is a price increase for a resource

Figure 2.6   Changes in Supply

Market Supply Curve for Strawberries

Market Supply Schedule for Strawberries			
Price	Quantity Supplied		
	(S_2)	(S_0)	(S_1)
(\$ per kg)	(millions of kg)		
\$2.50	11 ← 13 → 15		
2.00	7 ← 9 → 11		
1.50	3 ← 5 → 7		

When the number of strawberry producers increases in a market, the quantity supplied of strawberries increases at every possible price. Each point on the supply curve shifts to the right from S_0 to S_1. In contrast, a decrease in the number of producers decreases the quantity supplied of stawberries at every price, shifting the supply curve to the left from S_0 to S_2.

Yes, e-commerce is making at least some markets more competitive. For example, in B2C commerce, it is the supply of computer software, telecommunication services, music, financial services, newspapers, magazines, and information databases that are being most affected, since consumers are able to buy and directly consume these services in digital form over the Internet. Meanwhile, in other B2C markets, such as the book-selling industry, the Internet is being used to order and purchase products, which are then shipped through traditional delivery methods. The basic result in both cases is the same: consumers can access businesses globally rather than just locally, increasing competition.

http://www.amazon.ca

Question
As e-commerce becomes more common, what should happen to the large price spreads currently found for many products when bought in a common currency (i.e., the American dollar) in various national markets?

used in a particular industry, costs for businesses in that industry increase. As a result, fewer units of the product can be produced for the same expenditure. Thus, businesses will tend to cut back on production, causing the supply curve to shift to the left. For example, an increase in the wages of workers in the apple industry causes a decrease in the supply of apples.

STATE OF TECHNOLOGY

Technological progress affects the supply curve by allowing businesses to use more efficient production methods. With increased efficiency, more units can be produced at every price, so supply will increase. Use of a better grain fertilizer, for instance, causes the supply of barley to increase, shifting the supply curve to the right.

CHANGES IN NATURE

Changes in nature—for example, an early frost, record high temperatures, a flood, or an earthquake—can affect the supply of many products, especially agricultural products. A cold, rainy summer in Canada's prairies, for example, will decrease the supply of grains, such as wheat. The market supply curve for wheat will, therefore, shift to the left.

PRICES OF RELATED PRODUCTS

A product's supply can be influenced by changes in the prices of other products. For example, declines in the price of tobacco during the early 1990s caused some Ontario farmers to switch to ginseng, a medicinal root that is popular in east Asia. As a result, the supply for ginseng increased, resulting in a shift to the right of the supply curve.

PRODUCER EXPECTATIONS

If producers expect the price of the item they sell to change in the near future, this affects the product's current supply. For example, barley farmers may anticipate barley prices will soon fall. In this case, they provide the product as much as possible now, raising its current supply. In contrast, an expected rise in the price of beef means beef producers hold back on the amounts they make available to the market, immediately reducing the supply of beef.

Change in Quantity Supplied versus Change in Supply

As in the case of demand, it is important to distinguish between *a change in quantity supplied* and *a change in supply*, both of which are shown in Figure 2.7. An increase or decrease in quantity supplied is the effect of a change in a product's price and is illustrated by a movement along the supply curve. As shown on the graph on the left, a rise in the price of ginseng, which raises the quantity of ginseng produced, is a change in quantity supplied. In contrast, a change in supply is caused by a change in a supply determinant, such as a resource price or a technological innovation. Because the amount of the product supplied is altered at every possible price for the product, a change in supply shifts the *entire* supply curve. As shown on the graph on the right, a decrease in the price of corn increases the supply of ginseng, causing a shift in the entire supply curve to the right.

Figure 2.7	Change in Quantity Supplied and Change in Supply

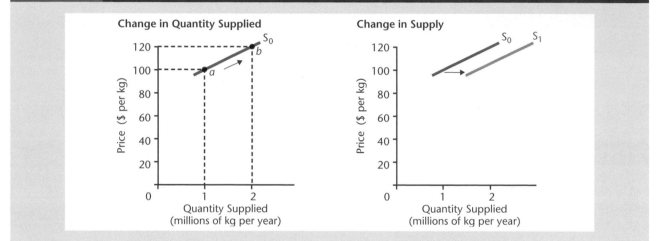

A change in quantity supplied is shown on the left graph as a movement along a single supply curve (S_0) that results from a change in the product's own price. There is a rise in quantity supplied when the price of ginseng rises, causing a movement from point *a* to point *b*. A change in supply is shown on the right graph as a shift in the entire supply curve to the right, from S_0 to S_1. This shift results from a change in a supply determinant—for example, a drop in the price of a related product, such as corn.

Brief Review

1. In product markets, supply is the relationship between the various possible prices of a consumer item and the quantities of the item that businesses are willing to put on the market.

2. The law of supply states that there is a direct relationship between the two variables of price and quantity supplied.

3. A change in quantity supplied is caused by a change in price and is shown as a movement along the supply curve.

4. A change in supply is caused by a change in a supply determinant and is shown as a shift of the *entire* supply curve. The six supply determinants are the number of producers in a market, resource prices, the state of technology, changes in nature, the prices of related products, and producer expectations.

2.2 Practice Questions

1. In a certain tomato market, 5 million kgs are supplied annually at a price per kg of $3, 6 million kgs at a price of $3.50, and 7 million kgs at a price of $4.

   a. Does this supply curve satisfy the law of supply? Explain.

   b. What will happen to the supply of tomatoes if (i) wages paid to farm workers rise; (ii) there is a drop in the price of corn, which can be cultivated instead of tomatoes; (iii) there is a sudden early autumn frost before the tomatoes are harvested; (iv) a new mechanized tomato-picker is introduced that raises efficiency; or (v) producers anticipate that the price of tomatoes will soon fall.

   c. Using EconGraphKit (at http://www.mcgrawhill.ca/college/lovewell), draw the market supply curve for tomatoes.

2. A drop in the price of corn affects both the market for tomatoes and for corn.

   a. Is the change in the corn market a change in quantity supplied or in supply? Explain.

   b. Is the change in the tomato market a change in quantity supplied or in supply? Explain.

2.3 How Competitive Markets Operate

market equilibrium: the stable point at which demand and supply curves intersect

surplus: an excess of quantity supplied over quantity demanded

Market Equilibrium

In competitive markets, demand and supply play a key role in co-ordinating the decisions of consumers and producers. Changes in price drive quantities demanded and supplied to a point of stability, known as **market equilibrium**, where the demand and supply curves intersect. Whenever the market is out of equilibrium—quantity supplied cannot keep up with quantity demanded, for example—the market tries to right itself and achieve equilibrium. To see how equilibrium is reached, consider the example of the strawberry market that appears in Figure 2.8.

EFFECTS OF A SURPLUS

At a price of $2.50 per kilogram, the quantities demanded and supplied of strawberries per year are 7 and 11 million kilograms, respectively. The quantity supplied exceeds the quantity demanded, so there are 4 million more kilograms of strawberries for sale than consumers wish to purchase. This excess is called a **surplus**. As a result of this surplus, producers are holding unwanted inventories.

The pressures produced by a surplus in a competitive market cause the price to fall. As the surplus appears and inventories rise, some producers respond by reducing their prices, and all others soon follow. As the price falls, two adjustments take place. First, consumers buy more at the lower price so that the quantity demanded rises. This increase in quantity demanded is shown as a move down the demand curve in Figure 2.8 (from point *a* to *e*). Second, producers offer less for sale so that the quantity supplied drops. This decrease in quantity supplied is shown as a move down the supply curve in Figure 2.8 (from point *a* to *e*). Both responses reduce the surplus until price comes to rest where quantity supplied matches quantity demanded. Once this happens, the market has reached a stable equilibrium point—at a price of $2 in the case of the strawberry market. At this point, the amount of the product exchanged (9 million kilograms) is simply called "quantity" and can refer to either quantity demanded or quantity supplied.

Figure 2.8   Movement of Price towards Equilibrium

As shown both in the schedule and on the graph, when price (at points *a*) is above its equilibrium level of $2, the quantity of strawberries supplied exceeds the quantity demanded, creating a surplus. This causes price to fall until both quantities demanded and supplied are equal at the equilibrium point (point *e*). If price (at points *b*) is below equilibrium, a shortage results. Price is forced higher until its equilibrium level (point *e*) is again reached.

EFFECTS OF A SHORTAGE

shortage: an excess of quantity demanded over quantity supplied

When price is below equilibrium, the quantity of strawberries that consumers wish to purchase exceeds the quantity supplied. This excess of quantity demanded over quantity supplied is called a **shortage**. Because of this shortage, some consumers are unable to purchase strawberries. For example, at a price of $1.50, the quantities demanded and supplied per year in the strawberry market are 11 and 7 million kilograms, respectively, giving a shortage of 4 million kilograms.

A shortage in a competitive market pushes price higher. Once it becomes apparent that producers do not have enough to satisfy the prevailing quantity demanded, some producers raise their prices, and soon all others do the same. Both consumers and producers respond to the price increase. Consumers purchase less, decreasing quantity demanded from point *b* to *e* on the demand curve. At the same time, producers provide more for sale, raising quantity supplied from point *b* to *e* on the supply curve. As a result of these movements up the demand and supply curves in Figure 2.8, the shortage shrinks until the quantities demanded and supplied are again equal at the equilibrium point.

The Role of Price

Notice that if there is either a shortage or a surplus, the price in a competitive market changes until equilibrium is attained. Only at this point is the pressure for further adjustments eliminated. The market then remains at equilibrium until changes in some demand or supply determinant cause demand or supply to change. Whenever this happens, the shortage or surplus that results will force the market to a new equilibrium point.

Changes in Demand

Consider the case in which the demand for strawberries increases because of a price increase for a substitute product, such as cherries. As a result, as shown in Figure 2.9, the

THINKING ABOUT ECONOMICS

Does a change in demand affect quantity supplied, or does a change in supply affect quantity demanded?

Both situations apply. A shift in the demand curve has an impact on quantity supplied. Notice in Figure 2.9, for example, that an increase in demand causes a rightward movement along the supply curve, meaning that quantity supplied rises as well. Thus, a change in demand pushes quantity supplied in the same direction. With an increase in supply, as depicted in Figure 2.10, there is a rightward movement along the demand curve, which causes an increase in quantity demanded. A change in supply, therefore, drives quantity demanded in the same direction.

Question
How does a decrease in supply affect quantity demanded?

demand curve shifts to the right, from D_0 to D_1. From an equilibrium price of $2 and a quantity of 9 million kilograms, quantity demanded shifts to 13 million kilograms. Quantity supplied lags behind, at 9 million kilograms, thus creating a shortage of 4 million kilograms per year in the market (13 million to 9 million). For the market to right itself, price and quantity supplied both push up to a new equilibrium price of $2.50 and quantity of 11 million kilograms. So, with an increase in demand, the equilibrium values of both price and quantity rise. A decrease in demand would have the opposite effect, causing the equilibrium values of both price and quantity to fall.

Changes in Supply

The effects of a change in supply can be outlined in a similar fashion. For example, the supply of strawberries may increase because new producers enter the industry. As a result, as shown in Figure 2.10, the supply curve shifts to the right, from S_0 to S_1. From an equilibrium price of $2 and quantity of 9 million kilograms, quantity supplied

Figure 2.9   Effects of Changes in Demand on Equilibrium

Market Demand and Supply Schedules for Strawberries

Price	Quantity Demanded		Quantity Supplied
	(D_0)	(D_1)	(S)
($ per kg)			
	(millions of kg)		
$3.00	5 → 9		13
2.50	**7 → 11**		**11**
2.00	**9 → 13**		**9**
1.50	11 → 15		7
1.00	13 → 17		5

When the demand curve shifts to the right, from D_0 to D_1, there is a shortage of 4 million kg at the original equilibrium price (point *a*). As a result, price rises until a new equilibrium point of demand and supply is reached, at point *b*. Both equilibrium price and equilibrium quantity rise from their original values.

Figure 2.10	Effects of Changes in Supply on Equilibrium

Market Demand and Supply Curves for Strawberries

Market Demand and Supply Schedules for Strawberries

Price	Quantity Demanded	Quantity Supplied	
	(D_0)	(S_0)	(S_1)
($ per kg)	(millions of kg)		
$3.00	5	13 → 17	
2.50	7	11 → 15	
2.00	**9**	**9 → 13**	
1.50	**11**	**7 → 11**	
1.00	13	5 → 9	

When the supply curve shifts to the right, from S_0 to S_1, there is a surplus of 4 million kg at the original equilibrium price (point *a*). As a result, price falls until a new equilibrium point of demand and supply is reached at point *b*. In this case, the equilibrium values for price and quantity move in opposite directions, with price falling and quantity rising.

becomes 13 million kilograms. Quantity demanded lags behind at 9 million kilograms, thus causing a surplus of 4 million kilograms per year in the market (13 million to 9 million). For the market to right itself, price is driven down until it reaches a new equilibrium value of $1.50, and quantity demanded is driven up to a new equilibrium value of 11 million kilograms. So, with an increase in supply, the equilibrium values of price and quantity move in opposite directions, with price falling and quantity rising. A decrease in supply would have the opposite effects: price would rise and quantity would fall to reach a new equilibrium point.

Brief Review

1. In a competitive market, the appearance of either surpluses or shortages forces price and quantity towards the intersection of the demand and supply curves. This point represents market equilibrium.

2. An increase in demand—with the demand curve shifting to the right—causes the equilibrium values for both price and quantity to rise. A decrease in demand—with the demand curve shifting to the left—causes the equilibrium values for both price and quantity to fall.

3. An increase in supply—with the supply curve shifting to the right—causes the equilibrium price to decrease and the equilibrium quantity to increase. A decrease in supply—with the supply curve shifting to the left—causes the equilibrium price to increase and the equilibrium quantity to decrease.

2.3 Practice Questions

1. In a particular competitive market, initial equilibrium occurs at a price of $3 and a quantity of 4 million units, until a shift in supply causes equilibrium price to rise.

   a. Which way has supply shifted? Explain.
   b. Will equilibrium quantity increase or decrease?
   c. Will the changes in equilibrium price and quantity be driven by a temporary shortage or temporary surplus?
   d. Using EconGraphKit (at http://www.mcgrawhill.ca/college/lovewell), draw possible demand and supply curves illustrating this change in equilibrium price.

2. In the same competitive market as in question 1, initial equilibrium occurs at a price of $3 and a quantity of 4 million units. Now a shift in demand causes equilibrium price to rise.

   a. Which way has demand shifted? Explain.
   b. Will equilibrium quantity increase or decrease?
   c. Will the changes in equilibrium price and quantity be driven by a temporary shortage or temporary surplus?
   d. Using EconGraphKit (at http://www.mcgrawhill.ca/college/lovewell), draw possible demand and supply curves illustrating this change in equilibrium price.

LAST**WORD**

In this chapter, we have seen how the forces of demand and supply can influence competitive markets and how these markets find an equilibrium through the interplay of buyers and sellers. But our examination of demand and supply is far from over. In the next chapter, we will use what we have learned so far to examine how it is possible to quantify responses of both buyers and sellers to changes in price and the ways in which government policies can influence private markets. Then, repeatedly throughout the rest of the book, demand and supply will reappear, making it clear that they are two of the most basic tools of economic thinking.

Key Concepts

change in quantity demanded 30
change in quantity supplied 35
complementary products 32
decrease in demand 31
decrease in supply 36
demand 29
demand curve 30

demand determinants 30
demand schedule 30
increase in demand 31
increase in supply 36
inferior products 32
law of demand 29
law of supply 35
market demand 30
market equilibrium 39
market supply 35

normal products 32
quantity demanded 29
quantity supplied 35
shortage 40
substitute products 32
supply 35
supply curve 35
supply determinants 36
supply schedule 35
surplus 39

Questions

1. During a given week, Student 1 demands 5 milkshakes at a price per milkshake of $2, 7 at $1.80, 9 at $1.60, and 11 at $1.40. Student 2 demands 4 milkshakes at a price of $2, 5 at $1.80, 6 at $1.60, and 7 at $1.40.
   a. In side-by-side diagrams, graph the demand curves D_1 and D_2 for each student, putting the price of a milkshake on both the vertical axes and the number of milkshakes demanded by one of the students on each horizontal axis. (Make sure that the scales you choose for each axis are sufficient to plot all points on the curves.)
   b. In your own words, explain why the amount of milkshakes demanded by each student rises as the price of milkshakes falls.
   c. Assuming that the two students are the only consumers in the market, construct a table showing the market demand schedule. Draw the market demand curve D_m and explain how it can be derived from the individual students' demand curves.

2. In a certain apple market, 80 000 kilograms are offered for sale each week at a price per kilogram of $2, 160 000 at $3, and 240 000 at $4.
   a. Construct a table showing the market supply schedule for apples, then graph the market supply curve for apples (S_0).
   b. In your own words, explain why the amount of apples offered for sale rises as the price of apples increases.
   c. Using both your table and graph, outline what happens if the amount of apples offered for sale each week increases by 40 000 kilograms at each possible price.

3. For each market whose product is highlighted in italics, sketch a graph (without numbers on the axes) showing the change in either demand or supply. In each case, identify the demand or supply determinant causing the shift.
   a. Medical researchers discover that consumption of *blueberries* reduces the risk of cancer.
   b. New automated equipment is introduced in the production of *silicon chips*.
   c. A significant rise in the price of VCRs affects the market for *videotapes*.
   d. Higher prices for grazing land have an impact on the production of *wool*.
   e. A widespread expectation of higher prices by *potato* farmers affects current quantities supplied of this item.
   f. An influx of new residents into a small town influences *housing* purchases.
   g. A fall in average consumer incomes affects purchases of *bologna*.
   h. A drop in the price of laptop computers influences the consumption of *desktop computers*.
   i. Unusually cold weather in Central America harms the *coffee* harvest.
   j. A rise in the price of wheat affects the production of *barley*.
   k. A widespread expectation by consumers of higher future incomes affects current sales of *automobiles*.
   l. A widespread expectation by consumers of lower prices for *computer games* affects current purchases of this item.

4. Identify one possible cause for each event below:
   a. The demand for electric-powered cars decreases.
   b. The quantity supplied of milk decreases.
   c. The supply of Atlantic cod increases.
   d. The quantity demanded of CDs increases.

Market Demand and Supply Schedules for Baseball Caps

Price ($ per cap)	Quantity Demanded (caps per week)	Quantity Supplied (caps per week)	Surplus (+) or Shortage (–)	Effect on Price (up or down)
$20.00	9 000	15 000	_____	_____
17.50	10 000	13 000	_____	_____
15.00	11 000	11 000	_____	_____
12.50	12 000	9 000	_____	_____
10.00	13 000	7 000	_____	_____

5. a. Copy the table above, which shows demand and supply schedules in a hypo-
        thetical competitive market for baseball caps. Fill in the appropriate numerical
        values for the surplus or shortage of caps in the fourth column and the effect on
        price in the fifth column.
    b. Identify the equilibrium quantity and price. Explain why no other price could
        represent the equilibrium value.
    c. Suppose the demand schedule in this market changes so that 12 000 caps are
        demanded at a price of $20, 13 000 are demanded at $17.50, 14 000 at $15, 15 000
        at $12.50, and 16 000 at $10. Is this an increase or decrease in demand? Explain.
    d. Create a new table like the one you copied in part a. to show the demand and
        supply schedules in this market after the change in demand. Identify the new
        equilibrium price and quantity. Why is the equilibrium price found in part b. no
        longer applicable?
    e. Describe the process that causes the market to move from its initial equilibrium
        to its new one.

Market Demand and Supply Schedules for Inline Skates

Price ($ per pair)	Quantity Demanded (thousands of pairs per week)				Quantity Supplied (thousands of pairs per week)			
	D_0		D_1		S_0		S_1	
$200	45	→	20		95	→	70	
175	55	→	30		80	→	55	
150	65	→	40		65	→	40	
125	75	→	50		50	→	25	
100	85	→	60		35	→	10	

6. a. For the schedules above, draw a graph showing the initial demand and supply
        curves (D_0 and S_0) for inline skates. Identify the original equilibrium price and
        quantity.
    b. Because of heightened concerns over injuries, the demand for inline skates
        changes from D_0 to D_1. On the same graph used in part a., draw the new demand
        curve and indicate the new equilibrium price and quantity associated with D_1
        and S_0. How do these equilibrium values compare with those in part a.?
    c. Now, due to a rise in wages, the supply of inline skates changes from S_0 to S_1.
        On the same graph used in parts a. and b., draw the new supply curve and indi-
        cate the new equilibrium price and quantity associated with D_1 and S_1. How do
        these equilibrium values compare with those found in part b.?

7. How will the following events affect equilibrium price and quantity in a compet-
    itive market? In each case, sketch a graph to help explain your answer.
    a. A drop in consumer incomes influences the demand for drycleaning.
    b. Declining numbers of law school graduates affect the supply of legal services.

      c. An expanding proportion of elderly people in the population has an impact on the demand for chiropractors.

      d. A cost-saving technological innovation influences the supply of computer modems.

8. (Advanced Question)

    Each of the following events affects the demand or supply of the product highlighted in italics. Does the relevant curve shift right, left, or possibly in either direction?

    a. Computer prices fall and at the same time consumer incomes rise, affecting the demand for *software programs*.

    b. The price of coal-mining equipment rises at the same time as the wages paid to coal-miners fall, affecting the supply of *coal*.

    c. The price of frozen dinners drops at the same time as consumer incomes fall, affecting the demand for *instant macaroni-and-cheese dinners*.

    d. Prices of building materials fall at the same time as the prices of residential housing rise, affecting the supply of *commercial buildings*.

    e. A widespread expectation by farmers of a lower price for barley occurs at the same time as the price of wheat falls, affecting the supply of *barley*.

9. (Policy Discussion Question)

    In an attempt to curb the use of illegal drugs, such as marijuana or cocaine, or the use of harmful legal substances, such as tobacco, governments can use two basic options: decreasing demand through public education and decreasing supply through legal restrictions or taxes.

    a. With the aid of two graphs, explain how each type of policy reduces quantity in affected markets. What is the result on the price as seen by consumers for each type of policy?

    b. Which of these two types of policies is likely to have more long-term success? Why?

Internet Application Questions

http://www.canoe.ca

http://www.statcan.ca/english/Estat/licence.htm

1. Access Canoe-Canada's Internet network (at http://canoe.ca). Using the link to "Stock Quotes," find the closing price and total volume for the stock Royal Bank on the Toronto Stock Exchange for the two latest days of trading. What do your results suggest? Has there been a recent dominant trend—an increase or decrease—in the demand or in the supply of Royal Bank shares in the market?

2. Access Statistics Canada's web site (at http://www.statcan.ca/english/Estat/licence.htm).

    a. Using the information found in "Prices and Price Indexes," generate a table showing the percentage changes from the previous period in the farm input price index for Canada since this index was established in 1998.

    b. Based on your table in part a., in which year did supply curves for Canadian agricultural goods shift most? the least?

SPOILT FOR CHOICE

William Stanley Jevons and Utility Maximization

ADVANCING
ECONOMIC
THOUGHT

Jevons and His Influence

Demand can be related to human psychology, if you think of people making purchases to maximize their utility on the basis of their limited budgets. Remember that utility is the satisfaction each individual gains from consuming a variety of goods and services.

William Stanley Jevons (1835–1882), a 19th century English economist, is best known for applying the concept of utility to economics and developing a model of consumption. Jevons found his life turned upside down when, in his teens, his rich family went bankrupt. He was forced to break off his studies to find a job. After working for five years in Australia—during which time Jevons taught himself economics—he had earned enough to return to England and complete his formal education. He went on to become a university professor, a shy man who established his reputation primarily through his writings.

William Stanley Jevons
Source: Stock Montage

The Law of Diminishing Marginal Utility

Jevons based his model of consumption on the utilitarian views of the British philosophers Jeremy Bentham and James Mill. These philosophers assumed that utility can be measured in units, which they called "utils." According to Jevons, a consumer's total utility —or overall satisfaction gained from consuming a particular product—depends on the number of units he or she purchases. Consider the example of a student drinking cups of cappuccino at a sidewalk café on a summer afternoon. As shown in Figure A, the student's total utility increases with every additional cup he drinks, but each new cup gives him less *extra* pleasure than the one before. This is illustrated on the top graph by the increases in total utility between *ab* and *bc*, and then *cd* and *de:* the shaded areas get steadily smaller. These shrinking areas are highlighted on the marginal utility graph. For each extra cup he drinks, the student's marginal—or extra—satisfaction is less.

The fall in marginal utility at higher consumption levels led Jevons to state what has become a general rule in economics. The *law of diminishing marginal utility* states that as a consumer purchases more units of a particular product in a given time period, that consumer's extra satisfaction from each additional unit falls. According to Jevons, common sense suggests that this law applies to the consumption of virtually all products. Other economists developed their own versions of the law of diminishing marginal utility, but Jevons' version has remained the most influential.

Choosing One Product over Another

One of the most important uses of the law of diminishing marginal utility is in helping to understand how much consumers choose to spend on various products. Consider again the student visiting a sidewalk café one afternoon. He arrives with $4 in his pocket and plans to spend it all on $1 cappuccinos and $2 Danish pastries. To get the most out of his $4, the student should use it in a way that gives him the greatest added satisfaction from each new dollar. In other words, he should make each purchase on the basis of which item gives him the highest marginal utility per dollar. These figures can be found by dividing the student's marginal utilities for cappuccinos and pastries by their prices.

When making his first purchase, the student can choose either 12 utils in extra satisfaction from a cappuccino or 16 utils from a pastry, as shown in columns 2 and 5 of the schedule in Figure B. His marginal utilities per dollar are shown in columns 3 and

ADVANCING
ECONOMIC
THOUGHT

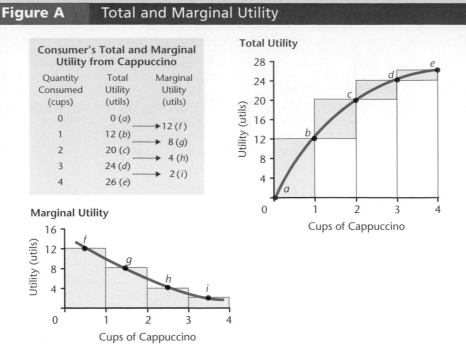

Figure A   Total and Marginal Utility

Consumer's Total and Marginal Utility from Cappuccino

Quantity Consumed (cups)	Total Utility (utils)	Marginal Utility (utils)
0	0 (a)	
1	12 (b)	12 (f)
2	20 (c)	8 (g)
3	24 (d)	4 (h)
4	26 (e)	2 (i)

As illustrated on the top graph, as the student drinks more cups of cappuccino, his total utility continues to rise, but at a decreasing rate. Each new cup provides less added satisfaction than the one before. That each additional cup provides less marginal utility is also illustrated on the lower graph.

6, and on the graphs. Because the 12 utils (12 ÷ $1) per dollar spent on cappuccinos exceeds the 8 utils (16 ÷ $2) per dollar spent on pastries, the student buys a cappuccino. For his second purchase, the student compares the 8 utils (8 ÷ $1) per dollar he could spend on the second cappuccino with the 8 utils per dollar he could spend on his first pastry. Since these marginal utilities per dollar are equal, he buys both items, exhausting his $4.

The Utility-Maximizing Rule

According to the utility-maximizing rule, the student keeps buying both products until the marginal utility per dollar from both cappuccinos and pastries is the same ($MU_1 \div P_1 = MU_2 \div P_2$). This economic law, which Jevons developed, applies no matter how many items are being bought. By following the rule, consumers maximize their overall satisfaction, or total utility, from a whole range of products.

Relevance for Today

Jevons' model rests on the assumption that utility is measurable in set units. While his critics suggested that this assumption is unrealistic, others argued that it is a legitimate way to simplify reality. By assuming that utility could be measured, Jevons made a verifiable conclusion concerning the relationship between two observable variables—the quantity of a product that individuals wish to consume and the price they pay—and the result is unaffected by how this satisfaction is measured. More recently, economists have used the utility theory without assuming measurable units of satisfaction. As long as consumers can say they prefer one set of products to another (without having to state exactly how much more they prefer it), conclusions like those drawn from the law of diminishing marginal utility and the utility-maximizing rule can still be reached.

Figure B   The Utility Maximizing Rule

Cups of Cappuccino (price = $1)			Danish Pastries (price = $2)		
(1) Quantity	(2) Marginal Utility (MU_1) (utils)	(3) Marginal Utility per $ ($MU_1/P_1 = MU_1/\$1$) (utils per $)	(4) Quantity	(5) Marginal Utility (MU_2) (utils)	(6) Marginal Utility per $ ($MU_2/P_2 = MU_2/\$2$) (utils per $)
0			0		
1	12	12	**1**	16	**8**
2	8	**8**	2	12	6
3	4	4	3	8	4
4	2	2	4	4	2

This student buys cappuccinos and pastries until his marginal utility per dollar (MU ÷ P) is the same for both items. Given his $4 budget, he buys 2 cappuccinos and 1 pastry (the highlighted figures in the table and shaded bars on the two graphs). With these purchases, the student's marginal utility per dollar for each product equals 8 utils. The utility-maximizing rule ($MU_1 \div P_1 = MU_2 \div P_2$) is, therefore, satisfied.

Consumer X's Utility Maximization Table

Consumption of A (price = $2)				Consumption of B (price = $4)			
Units of A	Total Utility (utils)	Marginal Utility (utils)	Marginal Utility per $ (utils per $)	Units of B	Total Utility (utils)	Marginal Utility (utils)	Marginal Utility per $ (utils per $)
0	0			0	0		
1	11	—	—	1	10	—	—
2	20	—	—	2	18	—	—
3	27	—	—	3	24	—	—
4	32	—	—	4	28	—	—
5	35	—	—	5	30	—	—

1. a. Copy and complete the table, showing the utility Consumer X gains from products A and B.

b. Find the combination of A and B that maximizes Consumer X's utility if her total expenditure on these two products is $22. Explain your answer using the utility-maximizing rule.

c. If Consumer X's total expenditure on products A and B falls to $12 while the prices of A and B remain unchanged, what is her new utility-maximizing combination of A and B? Again, explain your answer.

2. As a guest at a party, you perceive the price of rootbeer provided by your host as being very close to zero. How will your consumption of rootbeer at the party differ from consumption of your own rootbeer at home? Use the utility-maximizing rule and the law of diminishing utility to explain your answer.

CHAPTER 3

Competitive Dynamics and Government

There is no resting place for an enterprise in a competitive economy.

—Alfred P. Sloan, American businessman

Usually, when we wish to acquire goods and services—a fresh loaf of bread, a pair of shoes in the right size and style, a last-minute holiday package to a Caribbean island—they can be bought quickly and conveniently. In this chapter, we will analyze in more detail the ways in which competitive markets accomplish this task. In particular, we will look at the concept of elasticity and its effect on the interplay of demand and supply. We will also see how governments may choose to intervene in particular markets, by either establishing price controls or dealing with spillover effects. As these examples will show, the dynamics of competitive markets can help or hinder government policies in important ways, and government officials must understand these influences if they are to meet their goals.

LEARNING OBJECTIVES

In this chapter, you will:

1 learn about the price elasticity of demand, its relation to other demand elasticities, and its impact on sellers' revenues

2 learn about the price elasticity of supply and the links between production periods and supply

3 consider how governments use price controls to override the "invisible hand" of competition

4 examine spillover costs and benefits and the ways that government addresses these issues

3.1 Price Elasticity of Demand

price elasticity of demand: the responsiveness of a product's quantity demanded to a change in its price

 LO 3.1

elastic demand: demand for which a percentage change in a product's price causes a larger percentage change in quantity demanded

inelastic demand: demand for which a percentage change in a product's price causes a smaller percentage change in quantity demanded

perfectly elastic demand: demand for which a product's price remains constant regardless of quantity demanded

How can we refine our analysis of the role of demand and its impact in particular markets? One of the most important ways is by studying further the relationship between changes in price and quantity demanded. For example, from Chapter 2 we know that if the price of a video game falls, then the number of games purchased rises. But by how much? If price is reduced by half, will quantity demanded double or triple, or will it rise by a smaller proportion, such as 10 percent or 20 percent? To answer these questions, we need to understand the **price elasticity of demand** (also called demand elasticity). Price elasticity of demand is the extent to which consumers (and the quantity they demand) respond to a change in price.

Elastic and Inelastic Demand

Consumers can be very responsive or very unresponsive to price changes. Consider Figure 3.1, which shows the demand curves for a sidewalk vendor selling ice-cream cones in two seasons. During the winter, the vendor raises her price by 20 percent, from $2 to $2.40. The result is that monthly quantity demanded decreases by 50 percent, from 1000 to 500 cones. If a given percentage change in price causes a *larger* percentage change in a product's quantity demanded, the product has **elastic demand**. Thus, the vendor faces elastic demand in the winter, as shown on the graph on the left. In the summer, greater demand for ice-cream cones pushes demand to the right. In addition, when the vendor increases her price in the summer by 20 percent, from $2 to $2.40, monthly quantity demanded decreases only from 2000 to 1800 cones, or by 10 percent. If a given percentage change in price causes a *smaller* percentage change in quantity demanded, the product has **inelastic demand**. An inelastic demand for ice-cream cones is shown on the graph on the right.

Perfectly Elastic and Perfectly Inelastic Demand

There are two extreme cases of demand elasticity. When a product has **perfectly elastic demand**, its price remains constant whatever quantities are demanded. Because price never varies, the demand curve is horizontal, as shown in Figure 3.2,

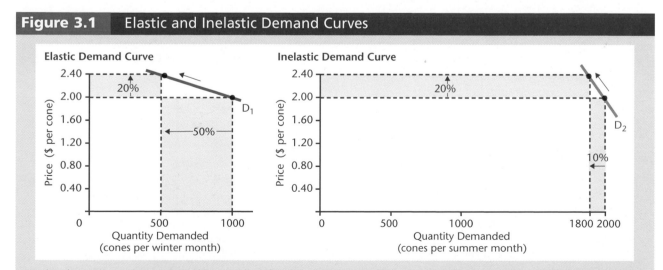

Figure 3.1   Elastic and Inelastic Demand Curves

For the elastic demand curve (D₁) shown on the left graph, a 20 percent increase in price leads to a greater 50 percent decrease in quantity demanded. The graph on the right shows an inelastic demand curve (D₂). The same 20 percent increase in price now leads to a smaller 10 percent decrease in quantity demanded.

perfectly inelastic demand: demand for which a product's quantity demanded remains constant regardless of price

on the left. Consider the example of an individual producer, a soybean farmer, who is a *price-taker.* This means that the farmer has no influence over the market price of soybeans, since the farmer's operations are too insignificant to affect the market. This farmer would face demand as illustrated by the demand curve D_3. Because the same price of $100 per tonne of soybeans applies at all possible amounts demanded, the farmer faces a perfectly elastic demand curve. In contrast, when a product has **perfectly inelastic demand**, its quantity demanded is completely unaffected by price. This situation creates a vertical demand curve, as shown in Figure 3.2, on the right. An example is the demand for insulin: since this product is essential to people who have diabetes, they are willing to pay any price for a certain quantity of insulin. This means that the market demand curve for insulin (D_4) is vertical at a given quantity demanded, such as 1000 L.

Price Elasticity of Demand and Total Revenue

total revenue: the total income earned from a product, calculated by multiplying the product's price by its quantity demanded

Demand elasticity plays a role in determining what effect a price change has on **total revenue** (TR). Total revenue is defined, either for an individual business or for all businesses producing the same product, as the price of a product multiplied by its quantity demanded:

$$TR = P \times Q_d$$

For example, if the price of a certain product is $4 and 1000 units are purchased, then the total revenue generated is $4000 ($4 × 1000).

Consider how a rise in a product's price affects the total revenue of businesses selling the product. The higher price, by itself, increases the revenue pocketed by the sellers, but the accompanying decrease in quantity demanded has the opposite effect. It is the price elasticity of demand that determines which of these two effects—the increase in price or the decrease in quantity demanded—has the greater influence on the sellers' total revenue.

ELASTIC DEMAND

If demand for a product is elastic, price changes cause large variations in quantity demanded. Since a price increase of a certain percentage causes an even bigger percentage

Figure 3.2   Perfectly Elastic and Perfectly Inelastic Demand

A single soybean farmer might face a perfectly elastic demand curve, as shown on the left graph, with a constant price. In contrast, a producer of insulin might face a vertical or perfectly inelastic demand curve, as shown on the right graph, with the quantity demanded constant.

THINKING ABOUT
ECONOMICS

Is the slope of the demand curve related to the price elasticity of demand?

There is no automatic connection between the slope of the demand curve and a product's price elasticity of demand. This is because the slope of the demand curve reflects the change in price divided by the change in quantity demanded, while elasticity is expressed in terms of *percentage* changes in price and quantity demanded. There is a loose connection between the two concepts, however, as shown in Figure 3.1. When two demand curves—one fairly flat and one more steep—are drawn on the same set of axes, the flatter curve (D₁) is more elastic than the steeper curve (D₂) over a given price range. This is because the flatter curve (D₁) is associated with a greater adjustment in quantity demanded and hence a more elastic demand.

Question

Is there an automatic connection between the slope of the demand curve and the price elasticity of demand in the case of perfectly elastic and perfectly inelastic demand curves?

decrease in quantity demanded, the sellers' total revenue is reduced. Likewise, a price decrease of a certain percentage causes an even bigger percentage increase in quantity demanded, thus raising total revenue for the sellers. So, when demand is elastic, total revenue and price have an inverse relationship—total revenue changes in the opposite direction to the change in price.

Let us take a look at an example. All-U-Want Videos faces an elastic demand for video rentals, as shown in Figure 3.3. At a price of $5 per video, 500 videos are rented each day. The store's total revenue at this point on the demand curve is $2500 ($5 × 500 videos). This total revenue is represented by the area of the shaded rectangle AB. At a price of $3 per video, 1500 videos are rented each day, pushing up total revenue to $4500 ($3 × 1500 videos), which is represented by the shaded area BC. Therefore, a decrease in price raises the store's total revenue because the effect of the price decrease is outweighed by the effect of the increased quantity demanded.

Figure 3.3   Revenue Changes with Elastic Demand

With elastic demand, a 40 percent decrease in the rental price from $5 to $3 causes a larger 200 percent increase in daily rentals. Total revenue for the business increases from the area AB to the area BC. Thus, the changes in price and total revenue are in opposite directions. (Note that area C is greater than area A.)

INELASTIC DEMAND

When the demand for a product is inelastic, changes in price have little effect on quantity demanded. Since an increase in price leads to a smaller percentage decrease in quantity demanded, the sellers' total revenue increases. Similarly, a decrease in price causes a smaller percentage increase in quantity demanded, thus causing total revenue to fall. Therefore, when demand is inelastic, price and total revenue have a direct relationship—total revenue shifts in the same direction as the change in price. Take, for example, a ride at an amusement park that has inelastic demand, as shown in Figure 3.4. With a price of $2, there are 10 000 riders a day. Total revenue for the ride's operator, therefore, is $20 000, as shown by the shaded area FG. If price increases to $3, there are 8000 riders a day and a total revenue of $24 000, as shown by the shaded area EF. Therefore, an increase in price adds to the total revenue because the price increase more than compensates for the reduced quantity demanded.

UNIT-ELASTIC DEMAND

unit-elastic demand:
demand for which a percentage change in price causes an equal change in quantity demanded

In the case of **unit-elastic demand**, a percentage change in price causes an *equal* percentage change in quantity demanded. Thus, when demand is unit-elastic, a price change leaves total revenue unchanged. This is because the revenue gain caused by a price increase is precisely offset by the lost revenue due to the decrease in quantity demanded. The effect of a price change on total revenue in this case is summarized, along with all other possible cases, in Figure 3.5.

Factors That Affect Price Elasticity of Demand

Four factors affect a product's price elasticity of demand: the portion of consumer incomes devoted to buying the product, consumer access to substitutes, whether the product is a necessity or a luxury, and the time consumers have to adjust to price changes.

PORTION OF CONSUMER INCOMES

If the price of a product represents a hefty portion of consumer incomes, consumers will be more responsive to price changes. For those consumers who are deciding whether or not to buy a stereo, for example, a price change can determine whether

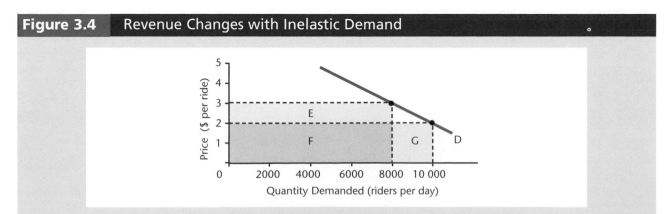

Figure 3.4   Revenue Changes with Inelastic Demand

Because demand is inelastic, a 50 percent rise in the price of the ride causes a smaller 20 percent drop in daily ridership. As a result, total revenue for the ride's operator grows from area FG to area EF. The changes in price and total revenue are, therefore, in the same direction. (Note that area E is greater than area G.)

Figure 3.5	Demand Elasticity and Changes in Total Revenue	
	Price Change	Change in Total Revenue
Elastic Demand	up	down
	down	up
Inelastic Demand	up	up
	down	down
Unit-Elastic Demand	up	unchanged
	down	unchanged

or not they make the purchase. If stereo prices are cut in half, quantity demanded will rise by a considerably higher percentage. In contrast, consumers who are deciding how much sugar to buy pay little attention to price; a 50 percent drop in the price will cause a much smaller percentage increase in the amount of sugar purchased. The demand for big purchases, therefore, tends to be more elastic than the demand for smaller purchases.

ACCESS TO SUBSTITUTES

If there are many close substitutes for a product, consumers will be more responsive to changes in the product's price because they have more options and can easily change their buying patterns. The demand for a particular brand of athletic shoes, for example, will be more elastic than the demand for athletic shoes in general. If only one brand becomes more expensive, its quantity demanded will plummet as consumers substitute cheaper brands. A rise in the price of all athletic shoes, however, will not radically affect quantities purchased. As this example illustrates, the more narrowly a product is defined, the more elastic its demand will be.

NECESSITIES VERSUS LUXURIES

Recall that necessities are essential items—such as bread and milk—that satisfy basic needs rather than wants. Consumers tend to buy similar amounts of necessities, regardless of their price; thus, necessities tend to have inelastic demand. In contrast, such products as tourist travel, expensive sports cars, and yachts are luxuries that buyers can easily live without. Because these items are expendable, their demand tends to be elastic.

TIME

Demand tends to become elastic over time. In the short run, consumers do not generally respond greatly to price. For example, immediately after a price increase, consumers of nachos will not modify their buying habits significantly, and users of furnace oil will continue to purchase furnace oil, regardless of price. Over time, however, consumers change their habits and needs: nacho-eaters might reduce their consumption, and home-owners might change their furnaces so as to use less fuel.

Calculating Price Elasticity of Demand

It is possible to quantify elasticity—that is, give it a numerical value. The larger this numerical value (e_d), the greater the price sensitivity—or price elasticity—of the product's demand. If e_d is greater than 1, then quantity demanded is sensitive to price changes, and demand is elastic. If e_d is less than 1, the quantity demanded is unresponsive to price changes, and demand is inelastic. If e_d is 1, then the product is unit-elastic.

Recall the case of All-U-Want Videos (Figure 3.3), which rents out 500 videos a day at a price of $5 each and 1500 videos when the price drops to $3. All-U-Want Videos can use the following formula to calculate the price elasticity of demand. In the formula, Q_d stands for quantity demanded, and Δ stands for change. (The symbol Δ is the Greek capital letter "delta," which signifies a change in some variable.)

$$
\begin{aligned}
e_d \; &= \; \frac{\Delta\,Q_d \div \text{average } Q_d}{\Delta \text{ price} \div \text{average price}} \\[2mm]
&= \; \frac{(1500 - 500) \div [(1500 + 500) \div 2]}{(\$3 - \$5) \div [(\$3 + \$5) \div 2]} \\[2mm]
&= \; \frac{1000 \div 1000}{-\$2 \div \$4} \\[2mm]
&= \; \frac{1}{{}^{-1}/_2} \\[2mm]
&= \; (-)2
\end{aligned}
$$

In Section 3.1, we identified whether demand curves were elastic or inelastic by comparing percentage changes in quantity demanded and price. To calculate these percentage changes, we divided the absolute changes in both quantity demanded and in price by their respective initial values. While this is the simplest procedure, it is not sufficiently exact when calculating numerical values for elasticity. Instead of using the initial values for quantity demanded and price, we incorporate the average values of these two variables in our formula. Over a given range of a demand curve, these average values are the same no matter whether we are moving up or down the demand curve. This useful property does not apply to the initial values of either quantity demanded or price, which are different depending on where we start on the demand curve.

So, in the numerator and denominator of this formula, the changes in quantity demanded and price, respectively, are divided by each variable's average value. The average quantity demanded is the value at the midpoint between the old and new quantities demanded, and is found by adding together the new and old quantities demanded and then dividing by 2. The same method is used to derive the average price, which is the value at the midpoint between the old and new prices, and is the sum of the new and the old prices divided by 2. Therefore, in the example of All-U-Want Videos, e_d is 2, which means that a certain percentage change in price (calculated using average price) causes twice that percentage change in quantity demanded (calculated using average quantity demanded). Note that the answer is a pure number with no units attached. Also, it always has a negative sign, because its formula's numerator and denominator necessarily have different signs. Because it is customary to define the numerical value of the price elasticity of demand in terms of the number's absolute value, this negative sign is usually cancelled out of the final answer. The negative sign is ignored, so the number is always considered to be positive.

Elasticity and Linear Demand Curves

It is possible to calculate the price elasticity for various ranges along a linear demand curve. A linear demand curve's slope is constant, given the definition of slope as the change in price over change in quantity demanded—the "rise" over the "run." We can see this in Figure 3.6, which shows a hypothetical market demand curve for sodas. Anywhere along this curve, quantity demanded rises by 1 million sodas for each $1 drop in price, giving a slope of −1 millionth. But the curve's elasticity coefficient, which is the ratio of the relative changes in quantity demanded and price, varies as we move along the curve. Between prices $5 and $4, the coefficient has a value of (−)9. Then, for each new lower pair of prices, the coefficient drops—to 2.33 (between $4 and $3), 1 (between $3 and $2), 0.43 (between $2 and $1), and finally 0.11 (between $1 and $0).

The reason for the varying values of price elasticity is that at high prices (such as $5 and $4), the $1 price change is made smaller when dividing by average price ($4.50). At the same time, the change in quantity demanded (1 million sodas) is made larger when compared with average quantity demanded (500 000). The result is an elasticity coefficient greater than 1, with the curve being elastic in its upper range. But further down the demand curve, the relationship between price and quantity is reversed. At low values of price (such as $1 and $0), the same $1 price change is made larger when compared with average price ($0.50), while the high values for quantity demanded (4 million and 5 million sodas) mean the change in quantity demanded of 1 million sodas is made smaller relative to the average quantity (4.5 million sodas). The elasticity coefficient is, therefore, less than 1, and the curve is inelastic in its lower range. Finally, in the curve's middle range, the relative changes in price and quantity demanded just balance one another so that the curve in this range is unit-elastic.

The implication of this illustration is clear: it is best to be careful when referring to a linear demand curve as either elastic or inelastic.

Figure 3.6   Elasticity and a Linear Demand Curve

Market Demand Schedule for Sodas

Price	Quantity Demanded	Price Elasticity of Demand
($ per soda)	(millions of sodas)	(e_d)
5	0	
4	1	9.00
3	2	2.33
2	3	1.00
1	4	0.43
0	5	0.11

The slope of this linear demand curve is always −1 millionth. But at any price range above $3, this linear demand curve is elastic, with a price elasticity (e_d) greater than 1. Between prices $3 and $2, the curve is unit-elastic, given an e_d equal to 1. Finally, at any price range below $2, the curve is inelastic, and e_d is less than 1.

Income and Cross-Price Elasticities

The price elasticity of demand is not the only elasticity concept relating to demand. One can also measure the extent to which a product's quantity demanded varies with changes in consumer income or the price of another product.

Income elasticity (e_i) is defined as the responsiveness of a product's quantity demanded to an adjustment in consumer income and is calculated as the ratio of the changes in quantity demanded and consumer income, with each change divided by its respective average value. The formula for income elasticity is, therefore, similar to the mathematical expression for the price elasticity of demand. It is the ratio of the change in quantity demanded (ΔQ_d) divided by its average value, over the change in consumer income (ΔI) divided by its average value.

$$e_i = \frac{\Delta Q_d \div \text{average } Q_d}{\Delta I \div \text{average } I}$$

Unlike the case of the price elasticity of demand, the income elasticity's sign is important. For an inferior product, this elasticity is negative because changes in consumer incomes and quantity demanded are in opposite directions. To illustrate, lower consumer incomes increase purchases of canned meat, giving a negative denominator and positive numerator in the formula. In contrast, income elasticity is positive for a normal product because changes in consumer income and the product's quantity demanded are in the same direction. For example, higher consumer incomes mean more purchases of normal products, such as television sets, giving both a positive numerator and a positive denominator. While the income elasticity of normal products that are necessities, such as milk and bread, is positive but relatively low (between 0 and 1), for luxuries, such as caviar or expensive jewellery, the income elasticity is high (greater than 1).

Another demand-related elasticity is **cross-price elasticity** (e_{xy}), defined as the responsiveness of quantity demanded of one product (x) to a change in price of another (y). In mathematical terms, the formula for cross-price elasticity is the ratio of the changes in quantity demanded of product x (ΔQ_d) and the price of product y (ΔP_y) with each change divided by the respective average value.

$$e_{xy} = \frac{\Delta Q_d \div \text{average } Q_d}{\Delta P_y \div \text{average } P_y}$$

The cross-price elasticity's sign differs, depending on whether products x and y are substitutes or complementary. When one product is a substitute for the other, the cross-price elasticity is positive. This is because the changes in both x's quantity demanded and y's price are in the same direction—as in the case of a fall in the quantity demanded of cassette tapes caused by a drop in the price of CDs. On the other hand, the cross-price elasticity for complementary products is negative. An increase in the quantity demanded of DVDs, for example, might be caused by a fall in the price of DVD players.

Brief Review

1. Price elasticity of demand is the responsiveness of a product's quantity demanded to changes in the product's price. When demand is elastic, a given percentage change in price causes a larger percentage change in quantity demanded. When demand is inelastic, a given percentage change in price causes a smaller percentage change in quantity demanded.

2. Demand is perfectly elastic when the price of a product is constant at all quantities demanded. Demand is perfectly inelastic when the quantity demanded of a product is constant at all prices. Demand is unit-elastic when a percentage change in price causes an equal percentage change in quantity demanded.

3. Price and total revenue have an inverse relationship when demand is elastic but a direct relationship when demand is inelastic. When demand is unit-elastic, total revenue is constant, regardless of price.

4. Four factors affect the price elasticity of demand of a product: the portion of consumer incomes the product accounts for, access to substitute products, whether the product is a luxury or a necessity, and the amount of time that elapses after a price change.

5. Other demand-related elasticity concepts include income elasticity, which measures the sensitivity of a product's quantity demanded to a change in consumer income, and cross-price elasticity, which measures the sensitivity of a product's quantity demanded to a change in another product's price.

3.1 Practice Questions

1. Annual purchases of laptop computers in a certain market are 10 000 at a price of $3000, 20 000 at a price of $2000, and 30 000 at a price of $1000.

   a. Find producers' total revenue at each price.
   b. On the basis of your answer to part a., is the market demand curve for laptops elastic or inelastic in the price range $3000 to $2000? in the price range $2000 to $1000?
   c. Calculate the numerical values of demand elasticity in the two relevant price ranges.
   d. Are your answers to parts b. and c. consistent?
   e. Using EconGraphKit (at http://www.mcgrawhill.ca/college/lovewell), draw the demand curve for laptops and highlight the rectangles showing total revenue at each of the three prices. Are the changes in these areas consistent with your answers to parts b. and c.? Explain.

2. Calculate the appropriate elasticity coefficient in each of the following cases.

   a. A drop in the price of electric-powered cars from $25 000 to $20 000 causes purchases of gasoline-powered cars to fall from 1 million to 750 000 per year.
   b. Monthly purchases of cellphones rise from 15 000 to 17 500 when the average price of cellphones decreases from $120 to $90.
   c. A fall in average consumer incomes from $80 000 to $50 000 raises weekly purchases of canned sardines from 2000 to 3000 cans.

3.2 Price Elasticity of Supply

price elasticity of supply: the responsiveness of a product's quantity supplied to a change in price

elastic supply: supply for which a percentage change in a product's price causes a larger percentage change in quantity supplied

inelastic supply: supply for which the percentage change in a product's price causes a smaller percentage change in quantity supplied

Just as the price elasticity of demand measures the responsiveness of consumers to a change in a product's price, the **price elasticity of supply** (also called supply elasticity) measures the responsiveness of producers (and the quantities they supply) to changes in the product's own price.

Elastic and Inelastic Supply

In the case of **elastic supply**, a certain percentage change in the product's price leads to a larger percentage change in its quantity supplied. In other words, the quantity that producers are willing to offer for sale is very responsive to price changes. Consider the example of a tomato producer, as in Figure 3.7. As shown on the graph on the left, if the price of tomatoes increases by 50 percent, from $2 to $3 per kilogram, the quantity of tomatoes supplied annually increases from 100 000 to 200 000 kg—a 100 percent increase. If, as shown on the graph on the right, the identical 50 percent price increase for tomatoes causes a much smaller 20 percent increase in quantity supplied—from 100 000 to 120 000 kg—then we have **inelastic supply**. In other words, if a product has inelastic supply, a given percentage change in price results in a smaller percentage change in quantity supplied.

As in the case of the price elasticity of demand, the price elasticity of supply is not the same as the slope of the supply curve. However, when two supply curves are drawn on the same set of axes, as in Figure 3.6, then—over a certain price range—the flatter curve (S_1) is more likely to be elastic than the steeper curve (S_2).

Factors That Affect Price Elasticity of Supply

The main factor that affects the price elasticity of supply is the passage of time. In competitive markets, three production periods can be distinguished: the immediate run, the short run, and the long run. The price elasticity of supply differs in each period. In Figure 3.8, we illustrate elasticity for each of the three production periods in the market for strawberries.

Figure 3.7   Elastic and Inelastic Supply

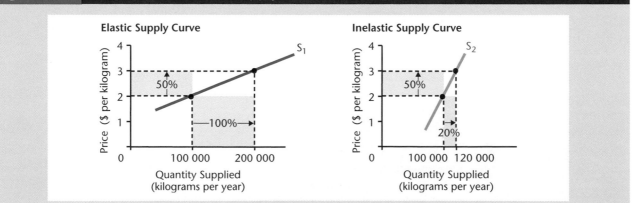

An elastic supply curve (S_1) is shown on the left. A 50 percent increase in price leads to a greater 100 percent increase in quantity supplied. The graph on the right shows an inelastic demand curve (S_2). The same 50 percent increase in price now leads to a smaller 20 percent increase in quantity supplied.

Figure 3.8   Time and Price Elasticity of Supply

The immediate-run supply curve S_1 is perfectly inelastic, since a price change does not affect quantity supplied. The short-run supply curve S_2 is either elastic or inelastic, with quantity supplied varying in the same direction as price. The long-run supply curve S_3 shows the case of a constant-cost industry, where supply is perfectly elastic, since price is constant for every possible quantity supplied. The long-run supply curve S_4 shows the case of an increasing-cost industry, where price rises as quantity supplied expands.

THE IMMEDIATE RUN

immediate run: the production period during which none of the resources required to make a product can be varied

The **immediate run** is the period during which businesses in a certain industry can make no changes in the quantities of resources they use. In the case of strawberry farming, the immediate run may be a month. For example, if the price of strawberries suddenly jumps as a result of an increase in demand, then, during the immediate run, farmers are unable to increase their production. Because quantity supplied is constant, the supply curve (S_1), shown on the left, is vertical at a quantity, such as 750 000 kg. Thus, for the immediate run, the supply is said to be **perfectly inelastic**.

perfectly inelastic supply: supply for which a product's quantity supplied remains constant regardless of price

THE SHORT RUN

short run: the production period during which at least one of the resources required to make a product cannot be varied

The **short run** is the period during which the quantity of at least one of the resources used by businesses in an industry cannot be varied. In the case of strawberry farming, a period of less than a single growing season is bound to be short run. If there is a rise in the price of strawberries from $2 to $2.50, then during the short run, farmers can increase their production by, for example, using more labour and maximizing the crop with mulch or fertilizers, but they cannot bring more land into production until the next growing season. In this case, illustrated on the middle graph, the price rise causes an increase in quantity supplied from 9 to 11 million kilograms. The supply curve (S_2) for the short run may be either elastic or inelastic. This depends on whether a given percentage change in price causes a bigger or smaller percentage variation in quantity supplied.

THE LONG RUN

long run: the production period during which all resources required to make a product can be varied, and businesses may either enter or leave the industry

In the **long run**, the quantities of all resources used in an industry can be varied. Also, businesses may enter or leave the industry. In the case of strawberry farming, the long run is a period longer than a single growing season—perhaps as long as a decade. Over this period, a rise in the price of strawberries will cause a temporary increase in strawberry farmers' profits beyond what they have been in the past. The lure of these greater profits leads to more resources being devoted to strawberry production. Not only will existing farmers expand their operations, but new farmers will enter the market. Both these changes increase the quantity supplied of strawberries. Two results are then possible, depending on what happens to price in the long run at the new, higher production levels.

If strawberry farming is a **constant-cost industry**, the increase in quantity supplied following a short-run rise in the price of strawberries has no effect on resource prices, since strawberry farmers are not major users of any single resource. The lure of extra profits keeps production expanding, and the price of strawberries falling, until this price is finally driven back to its original level. Thus, the price of strawberries always returns to the same level in the long run, regardless of quantity supplied. This means that a constant-cost industry, as shown on the right in Figure 3.8, exhibits a horizontal long-run supply curve (S_3). For the long run, then, supply is said to be **perfectly elastic**.

If strawberry farming is an **increasing-cost industry**, a greater quantity supplied leads to an increase in the price of a single resource, such as land or farm machinery. This increase results because the industry is a major user of this resource. Again, a short-run rise in the price of strawberries causes production to grow as farmers take advantage of extra profits. As long as the lure of profits remains, price is driven down in the long run to its lowest possible level, but price is now above its initial level, since farmers face higher per-unit costs. Hence, the long-run supply curve (S_4) has a positive (upward) slope but is very elastic, showing how quantities supplied are highly sensitive to price changes.

constant-cost industry: an industry that is not a major user of any single resource

perfectly elastic supply: supply for which a product's price remains constant, regardless of quantity supplied

increasing-cost industry: an industry that is a major user of at least one resource

Calculating the Price Elasticity of Supply

The numerical value of the price elasticity of supply (e_s) is calculated in a similar way to the price elasticity of demand. When e_s has a value greater than 1, quantity supplied is sensitive to price changes, and supply is elastic. If e_s is less than 1, quantity supplied is unresponsive to price changes, and supply is inelastic.

Consider the case of the tomato industry with an elastic supply curve (Figure 3.7). When the price of tomatoes rises from \$2 to \$3 a kilogram, the quantity supplied by farmers increases from 100 000 to 200 000 kg. The value of the price elasticity of supply for this industry can be found using the following formula, in which Q_s stands for quantity supplied.

THINKING ABOUT ECONOMICS

Do decreasing-cost industries exist?

Yes, they do. For example, some industries in the information technology sector have witnessed a marked decrease in product costs as the industries have expanded. The case of the computer chips is particularly telling. According to Moore's Law, developed in 1965 by one of the founders of chipmaker Intel, the processing power of computer chips doubles every six months. So far, Moore's Law has been correct, reducing the real price of processing power since the 1960s by 99.9999 percent, and there is no reason why this pace of growth cannot continue. But the problem in extending the analysis of long-run supply elasticity to this scenario is that industries with a pattern of decreasing costs will probably not be perfectly competitive: the advantages of "bigness" for the leading businesses in the industry are simply too large to be ignored.

Question
Presuming a decreasing-cost industry is perfectly competitive, what would the slope of its long-run supply curve be?

$$e_s = \frac{\Delta\, Q_s \div \text{average } Q_s}{\Delta \text{ price} \div \text{average price}}$$

$$= \frac{(200\,000 - 100\,000) \div [(200\,000 + 100\,000) \div 2]}{(\$3 - \$2) \div [(\$3 + \$2) \div 2]}$$

$$= \frac{100\,000 \div 150\,000}{\$1 \div \$2.50}$$

$$= \frac{0.667}{0.4}$$

$$= 1.67$$

Therefore, the tomato suppliers face a price elasticity of supply of 1.67, which means that a certain percentage change in price causes a percentage change in quantity supplied that is 1.67 times as large (when both percentage changes are calculated using average values). Because there is a direct relationship between price and quantity supplied, the changes in these two variables are always in the same direction. Thus, the numerator and the denominator of the supply elasticity formula are either both positive or both negative, giving a final answer that is always positive. Like the numerical value of demand elasticity, this is a pure number with no units attached.

Brief Review

1. Price elasticity of supply is the responsiveness of a product's quantity supplied to changes in the product's price.

2. When supply is elastic, a given percentage change in price causes a larger percentage change in quantity supplied. When supply is inelastic, a given percentage change in price causes a smaller percentage change in quantity supplied.

3. Price elasticity of supply is dependent mainly on the production period. In the immediate run, supply is perfectly inelastic, meaning, a change in price has no effect on quantity supplied. In the short run, supply may be elastic or inelastic.

4. In the long run, price elasticity of supply depends on the industry's use of resources. In a constant-cost industry (not a major user of any one resource), supply in the long run is perfectly elastic, with a constant price at all possible quantities supplied. In an increasing-cost industry (a major user of at least one resource), the long-run supply is very elastic, with price rising gradually at higher quantities supplied.

3.2 Practice Questions

In a certain lettuce market, the price rises from $1 to $1.20 per head. For each case below, determine the value of e_s and describe the shape of the supply curve.

a. In the immediate run, monthly quantity supplied remains constant at 80 000 heads.
b. In the short run, annual quantity supplied rises from 1 million to 1.2 million heads.
c. In the long run, the price of lettuce returns to $1 as quantity supplied continues to expand.
d. Based on your answer to part c., is this a constant-cost or increasing-cost industry?
e. Using EconGraphKit (at http://www.mcgrawhill.ca/college/lovewell), draw the three supply curves.

3.3 Price Controls

price floor: a minimum price set above equilibrium

price ceiling: a maximum price set below equilibrium

Sometimes, governments see fit to control prices, thus overriding the forces of demand and supply and the "invisible hand" of competition. There are two types of price controls. A **price floor** is a minimum price set *above* the level that would exist in equilibrium. An example is agricultural price supports. A **price ceiling** is a maximum price set *below* the equilibrium level. An example is rent controls. Notice that "floor" and "ceiling" have special meanings in economics. A price floor must be higher than equilibrium. Otherwise the floor would have no effect on the price prevailing in the market. Similarly, a price ceiling must be lower than equilibrium. Otherwise, it would be irrelevant.

Demand and supply can be used to analyze the effects of government programs to control prices. Because analyzing price controls also involves weighing one goal against another, the analysis depends on value judgements and so is part of normative economics.

Agricultural Price Supports

Agricultural markets, with their many independent buyers and sellers, are among the most competitive in the Canadian economy. These markets, therefore, provide a useful example of the potential difficulties encountered by competitive producers.

Given the nature of demand and supply for most agricultural products, farmers face product prices that can fluctuate widely. Such products as milk and wheat are viewed as necessities by consumers, so demand curves for these items are inelastic, especially in the short run. Similarly, the short-run supply curves for most agricultural products are inelastic because farmers find it difficult to vary quantity supplied over brief time periods.

Inelastic demand and supply in agricultural markets mean that changes in either demand or supply lead to relatively large price changes. This is illustrated in Figure 3.9, using a hypothetical market for wheat. A decrease in the supply of wheat, due to unfavourable weather, leads to a fairly small decrease in the equilibrium quantity but a considerable rise in price.

Unstable prices, therefore, can cause large fluctuations in farmers' incomes. In the years when prices are high, farmers can make substantial revenues, but low prices cause revenues

Figure 3.9	**Price Fluctuations in Agriculture**

Because both the demand and the supply for wheat are inelastic in the short run, a decrease in supply caused by such a factor as unfavourable weather has a relatively large effect on price, with its equilibrium value rising 20 percent. At the same time, equilibrium quantity adjusts by a smaller percentage.

to plummet. Over the long term, farmers also face pressures from the introduction of more sophisticated and expensive production techniques, which make small producers less able to compete with large agribusinesses. Consequently, many Canadian farmers have decided that the returns from agriculture are no longer worth the effort. The total number of Canadian farms is undergoing a gradual but persistent decline, as shown in Figure 3.10.

To counter these difficulties, farmers often request that governments intervene in markets to stabilize prices at favourable levels. In the past, federal and provincial governments have usually responded positively to these demands, not only out of a desire to stabilize prices and farm incomes but also because the family farm represents a traditional institution that many Canadians wish to see maintained through government intervention.

One type of government program is price supports, illustrated by a hypothetical market for milk in Figure 3.11. Without government intervention, this market would reach an equilibrium price of $1.10 per litre and an associated quantity of 60 million litres sold per year. A government agency pays a minimum or floor price, such as $1.30, which is above the equilibrium level. The floor price has two effects: quantity demanded decreases from 60 to 59 million litres, and quantity supplied increases from 60 to 62 million litres. Both effects lead to a surplus of the commodity of 3 million litres per year (62 million − 59 million), which the government agency purchases.

WINNERS AND LOSERS

Farmers are the obvious winners from price supports. The program causes both price and quantity supplied to increase and also raises farmers' revenues. Consumers lose because of the higher prices they pay, while taxpayers lose because they must foot the bill for the government agency's purchases of surplus products. Finally, by causing economic resources to be devoted to the production of unneeded agricultural surpluses, this program also works to the disadvantage of society as a whole. Are the benefits to

Figure 3.10	Total Number of Farms in Canada (thousands)										
Year	Canada	Nfld	PEI	NS	NB	Que	Ont	Man	Sask	Alta	BC
1931	728.6	n.a.	12.9	39.4	34.0	136.0	192.2	54.2	136.5	97.4	26.1
1941	732.8	n.a.	12.2	33.0	31.9	154.7	178.2	58.0	138.7	99.7	26.4
1951	623.1	3.6	10.1	23.5	26.4	134.3	150.0	52.4	112.0	84.3	26.4
1956	575.0	2.4	9.4	21.1	22.1	122.6	140.6	49.2	103.4	79.4	24.8
1961	480.9	1.8	7.3	12.5	11.8	95.8	121.3	43.3	94.0	73.2	20.0
1966	430.5	1.7	6.4	9.6	8.7	80.3	109.9	39.7	85.6	69.4	19.1
1971	366.1	1.0	4.5	6.0	5.5	61.3	94.7	35.0	77.0	62.7	18.4
1976	338.6	0.9	3.7	5.4	4.6	51.6	88.8	32.1	71.0	61.1	19.4
1981	318.4	0.7	3.2	5.1	4.1	48.1	82.4	29.4	67.3	58.1	20.0
1986	293.1	0.7	2.8	4.2	3.5	41.5	72.7	27.3	63.4	57.8	19.1
1991	280.1	0.7	2.4	3.9	3.2	38.1	68.6	25.7	60.8	57.2	19.2
1996	276.6	0.7	2.2	4.5	3.4	36.0	67.5	24.4	57.0	59.0	21.9
2001	246.9	0.6	1.8	3.9	3.0	32.1	59.7	21.1	50.6	53.7	20.3

The total number of Canadian farms has fallen consistently since 1931. This trend is also reflected in each of the provinces, although there have been several periods during which farm population in some provinces has stayed constant or even increased.

Source: Statistics Canada "Total Number of Farms in Canada (thousands)," adapted from the Statistics Canada publication "Historical Overview of Canadian Agriculture (data and analytical products: 1996 Census of Agriculture)," Catalogue 93-358, August 1997, pp. 2–43 and "Farm Data for the 2001 Census of Agriculture (Initial release)," Catalogue 95F0301, May 15, 2003, Table 3.

Figure 3.11   Effects of Price Supports

Market Demand and Supply Schedules for Milk		
Price	Quantity Demanded (D)	Quantity Supplied (S)
($ per litre)	(millions of litres)	
$1.30	**59**	**62**
1.10	60	60
0.90	61	58

Because the equilibrium price for milk (point *a*) is considered too low, the government agency imposes a price floor. This creates a milk surplus, at points *b*. As long as the demand and supply curves remain the same, this surplus will recur each year, and the government agency's stock of milk will increase.

farmers worth the costs to consumers, taxpayers, and the rest of society? The answer to this question depends on how important you consider the stability and health of the farming sector to be in relation to the costs of supporting the agricultural sector.

Rent Controls

Another way that governments override the "invisible hand" of competition is with price ceilings, which are upper limits to a price, such as rent. For example, a rent-control program was imposed on rental housing in Ontario in the 1970s due to pressure from tenant lobby groups, with capped rent increases kept below the rate of inflation. The effect of rent controls in a hypothetical large community with a competitive rental market is shown in Figure 3.12, assuming that all rental units in this market are identical. Without a rent-control program, equilibrium in the market would occur at a monthly

Figure 3.12   Effects of Rent Controls

Market Demand and Supply Schedules for Units		
Price	Quantity Demanded (D)	Quantity Supplied (S)
($ rent per month)	(units rented per month)	
$700	1700	2500
500	2000	2000
300	**2300**	**1500**

Rent controls force price below the equilibrium level, from point *a* to points *b*. Quantity demanded rises at the new price, while quantity supplied falls. The price ceiling thus causes a shortage.

rent per unit of $500 and a total of 2000 units rented per month. Controls push rents below the equilibrium level, to a value of $300. Consequently, quantity demanded increases from 2000 to 2300 units as more consumers enter the market. At the same time, quantity supplied falls from 2000 to 1500 units as landlords find it profitable to provide fewer units than before.

Quantity supplied is reduced in two ways: new rental construction is cut back, and some existing buildings are demolished or converted to other uses. The result of this artificially low rent is a shortage of 800 (2300 − 1500) rental units. This shortage makes itself felt through a low vacancy rate for units. This means an unusually small percentage of units are available for rent at any given time.

As a rule, shortages foster underground markets. In the case of rental housing, some landlords and tenants who are subletting their apartments to other tenants charge a fee for preference among people on waiting lists. These fees, or bribes, are known as "key money" and are illegal. To get around the law, key money often takes imaginative forms, such as forced purchases of furnishings at exorbitant prices.

WINNERS AND LOSERS

According to critics, rent controls harm society as a whole by driving economic resources away from an important housing market and creating a shortage. Because of the restraints placed on landlords in setting their own price, they are particularly hurt by such controls. Some tenants gain from controls, especially middle-class tenants who have the connections and credentials to acquire the most desirable units. However, the shortage caused by controls pushes many poorer tenants into unregulated units, such as basement flats and rooming houses, with rents that are often higher than for units in the controlled market. Therefore, not only do rent controls lower the stock of rental housing, but they can affect different income groups unfairly.

Brief Review

1. For various reasons, governments sometimes choose to intervene in markets to override the "invisible hand" of competition. Price controls are one form of intervention and take the form of price floors and price ceilings.

2. Setting a price floor, or a minimum allowable price, in a competitive market tends to cause surpluses.

3. Setting a price ceiling, or a maximum allowable price, in a competitive market tends to cause shortages.

3.3 Practice Questions

For each of the following price controls, outline the costs and benefits for consumers and producers.

a. A rent ceiling of $500 per month is imposed in a market where equilibrium rent would otherwise be $650.

b. A price floor of $2 per kg is set in a market for cheddar cheese. Without this program, the equilibrium price for cheddar cheese would be $1.50.

c. A rent ceiling of $700 per month is imposed in a market where the equilibrium rent would otherwise be $600.

3.4 Spillover Effects

spillover effects: external effects of economic activity, which have an impact on outsiders who are not producing or consuming a product

LO 3.4

spillover costs: negative external effects of producing or consuming a product

Besides intervening in particular markets with price controls, governments also play a part in dealing with the external effects of economic activity. These spillover effects arise whenever outsiders are affected by the production or consumption of a particular product. **Spillover effects** occur in even the ideal case of a competitive market, simply because no market exists in isolation. Governments often step in to see that all costs and benefits—private and public—are accounted for. Rather than employing price controls in these cases of market failure, governments usually apply regulations, taxes, or subsidies instead.

Spillover Costs and Benefits

Spillover effects may take the form of either costs or benefits.

SPILLOVER COSTS

Spillover costs are the negative effects of producing or consuming a product that fall on outsiders, not market participants. Environmental pollution is the most common example. Recall that some resources called *free goods*, such as air, can be used free of charge. Still other resources, such as water, have prices that do not reflect the resource's value. Any damage caused to these resources through market activity creates substantial costs for society as a whole.

Producers making products that have negative external effects focus only on their private costs as they make supply decisions. Consequently, the prices of these products are insufficient to cover both private and spillover costs. Figure 3.13 illustrates spillover effects with the example of gasoline used by motor vehicles. Assuming that the market for gasoline is competitive and free of government intervention, equilibrium occurs at point *b*, the intersection of the demand and supply curves D and S_0, with a price per litre of $1.50 and a quantity of 6 million litres.

Because of the environmental damage created by both the production and the consumption of gasoline, spillover costs are associated with this product. If these spillover costs are an extra $1 for each litre of gas, a new supply curve (S_1) can be drawn that incorporates the additional cost per litre. Whereas the old supply curve (S_0) reflects the

Figure 3.13   The Impact of Spillover Costs

Demand and Supply Schedules for Gasoline

Price	Quantity Demanded	Quantity Supplied	
($ per litre)	(D)	(S_0)	(S_1)
	(millions of litres)		
$2.50	4	8 →	6
2.00	5	7 →	5
1.50	6	6 →	4
1.00	7	5 →	3
0.50	8	4 →	2

Without government intervention, equilibrium occurs at point *b*. To account for spillover costs, the government may impose an excise tax of $1 per litre. As a result, the supply curve shifts from S_0 to S_1, moving equilibrium to point *a*.

private costs of producing one more litre of gasoline, the new supply curve (S$_1$) reflects the *private* and *public* costs of each new litre.

Where should the market operate? Price in this market should equal the height of the supply curve, once both private and spillover costs are accounted for. In other words, equilibrium should occur at point *a*, the intersection of D and S$_1$, at a price of $2 and a quantity of 5 million litres. Without government intervention, 1 million too many litres of gasoline is produced and consumed, given the environmental damage associated with both the production and consumption of gasoline. To achieve the preferred outcome, government can impose regulations on the use of gasoline or use its taxing powers. For example, it can levy an excise tax on gasoline equalling $1 per litre. This succeeds in shifting the supply curve from S$_0$ to S$_1$ and ensures that the oversupply of gasoline is corrected.

SPILLOVER BENEFITS

spillover benefits: positive external effects of producing or consuming a product

Spillover benefits are positive external effects of producing or consuming a product. Education is an important example, since society as a whole gains from this service. From an economic perspective alone, education is considered beneficial because of the increased work and income-earning opportunities it affords each individual and because it enriches the nation's human resources. More generally, education is seen as a social good because it helps Canadians to lead more informed, fulfilled, and productive lives.

Suppose that some students are considering an education in engineering. Figure 3.14 gives a hypothetical example. As in any education and career choice, the students would weigh the costs and benefits of obtaining an engineering degree. With the private market for an engineering education being competitive, the demand and supply curves D$_0$ and S have equilibrium point *a*, with a yearly tuition of $4000 per student and an enrolment of 10 000 students.

Society as a whole benefits from having more trained engineers, due to a faster pace of technological change. Hence there are spillover benefits. To see how much

Figure 3.14   The Impact of Spillover Benefits

Without government intervention in the market for engineering education, equilibrium occurs at point *a*. If spillover benefits are determined to be $2000 per student, government can create a subsidy for students pursuing a career in engineering. As a result, the demand curve shifts from D$_0$ to D$_1$, and the new equilibrium is at point *b*, with $2000 of each student's tuition paid by government.

engineering education should be undertaken from society's perspective, we must estimate the spillover benefits of this education. Suppose the result is $2000 per student per year. As a result, a new demand curve (D_1) that incorporates the private and public benefits can be drawn.

Price in this market should equal the height of the demand curve, once both private and spillover benefits are accounted for. In other words, equilibrium should occur at point *b*, at the intersection of S and D_1, with an annual tuition of $5000 and an enrolment of 11 000 students. However, if private benefits alone were accounted for, only 10 000 students (point *a*) would be enrolled, thereby creating a shortfall of 1000 students. To increase enrolment to the desired level, government itself could provide engineering education, or it could subsidize engineering education by giving prospective students vouchers to be turned in to the engineering school. The school would then turn in these vouchers to the government for $2000 per voucher. As a result, the demand curve for engineering education would shift to the right, thereby ensuring that society produces more engineers than would a fully private and competitive market.

PUBLIC GOODS

public good: a product whose benefits cannot be restricted to certain individuals

At the extreme, there are some products for which private benefits and spillover benefits cannot be separated. A **public good** is a product whose benefits cannot be restricted to certain individuals. In other words, while some consumers pay for the product, others get a "free ride." Lighthouses are an example, since any ship that is navigated using a lighthouse benefits whether or not the ship's owners help pay for the lighthouse's upkeep. In this situation, one option is to dispense with markets and have government provide these products. This happens in the case of national defence. Since it is impossible to restrict the benefits of this service only to those citizens who are willing to pay for it, national defence must be financed through compulsory taxation. In other cases, governments can help turn public goods into private goods. For example, increasing elephant populations in African countries can be viewed as a public good. One option is to have governments finance policing measures to stop indiscriminate hunting. Another option that has been tried with some success in several African countries is to make elephants private property so that the owners have an economic interest in maintaining a viable population for commercial hunting. In such cases, a government can prompt the formation of workable private markets.

For most businesses involved in e-commerce, the cost of accessing the Internet is so small as to be virtually negligible. And for many consumers—especially those who access the Internet from their place of work—the effective price is similar. This is because no one owns the Internet. Instead, its operation is overseen by various nonprofit organizations, such as the National Science Foundation. The Internet, therefore, does have the features of a classic public good. As the price of access continues to fall, these features will become more prominent.

Question

Given the ease of access to the Internet, how do the governing bodies that oversee it make sufficient revenues to cover their costs?

Brief Review

1. Spillover effects are the external effects of economic activity that arise because no market exists in isolation.

2. Spillover effects can be negative or positive. Spillover costs, such as pollution, are the harmful effects of producing or consuming a product. Spillover benefits, such as those associated with education, are the positive effects of producing or consuming a product.

3. Governments often step in to see that public as well as private costs and benefits are accounted for. Governments might, for example, intervene with taxes to correct an oversupply in the case of spillover costs or with subsidies to correct a shortfall in the case of spillover benefits.

4. Public goods are products whose benefits cannot be restricted to certain individuals. Governments often step in to provide these goods rather than leave them to private markets. Governments can also attempt to turn such goods into private goods by defining new types of property.

3.4 Practice Questions

In each case below, identify the spillover effect and cite one government policy that could deal with this effect.

a. A late-night dance club in a suburban neighbourhood disturbs nearby residents.
b. A new subway line reduces a city's traffic congestion.
c. The use of throw-away batteries adds to soil pollution.

LASTWORD

This chapter has extended the basics of demand and supply studied in Chapter 2 to examine in more detail how buyers and sellers interact in private markets. The concept of elasticity has allowed us to see how consumer decisions affect the sellers' total revenue and how supply factors affect price and quantity in various production periods. We then looked at some of the ways that government chooses to intervene in private markets—either for reasons of equity (in the case of price controls) or efficiency (in the case of spillover effects). In the following chapters, we will further explore the ways in which businesses and consumers interact in particular markets and how governments focus on the issue of equity to redistribute incomes.

Key Concepts

constant-cost industry 62
cross-price elasticity 58
elastic demand 51
elastic supply 60
immediate run 61
income elasticity 58
increasing-cost industry 62
inelastic demand 51
inelastic supply 60

long run 61
perfectly elastic demand 51
perfectly elastic supply 62
perfectly inelastic demand 52
perfectly inelastic supply 61
price ceiling 64
price elasticity of demand 51

price elasticity of supply 60
price floor 64
public good 70
short run 61
spillover benefits 69
spillover costs 68
spillover effects 68
total revenue 52
unit-elastic demand 54

Questions

1. Explain whether demand for each of the following is likely to be inelastic, elastic, or unit-elastic. Given your answers, outline whether the sellers' total revenue will increase, decrease, or stay constant if each item's price increases.
   a. Milk
   b. A particular computer model
   c. Yachts

2. In each case below, determine the effect on the sellers' total revenue and identify whether the demand curve is elastic, inelastic, or unit-elastic:
   a. Price falls from $2 to $1.50 along the market demand curve for strawberries (D_m) shown in Figure 2.2 in Chapter 2.
   b. Price rises from $150 to $200 along the original demand for skis (D_0) shown in Figure 2.4 in Chapter 2.
   c. Price drops from $12 to $8 along the demand curve for CDs shown on p. xxv of the Skills Resource.

Market Demand and Supply Schedules for Leather Jackets

Price ($ per jacket)	Quantity Demanded (jackets per year)	Quantity Supplied (jackets per year)
$300	69 000	108 000
250	77 000	77 000
200	86 000	53 000
150	94 000	31 000
100	103 000	19 000

3. a. Use the table displayed above to draw a graph showing the market demand curve and supply curve (D_0 and S_0) for a hypothetical market for leather jackets. On your graph, indicate the equilibrium price and quantity.
   b. Due to an increase in the number of producers in this market, the annual quantity supplied in this market increases by 33 000 jackets at every price. On the same graph you have drawn in part a., show the new market supply curve (S_1) and indicate the new equilibrium price and quantity.
   c. Calculate the change in total revenue for producers in this market due to the shift from S_0 to S_1. Is the demand for leather jackets between the old and new equilibrium points inelastic or elastic? Explain.

Market Demand Schedule for Canoes

Price ($ per canoe)	Quantity Demanded (canoes per month)
$800	400
600	800
400	1200
200	1600

4. a. Use the market demand schedule for canoes shown above to find the total revenue at each given price.
   b. On the basis of your answer to part a., state whether the market demand for canoes is elastic, inelastic, or unit-elastic in the three price ranges $800 to $600, $600 to $400, and $400 to $200.
   c. Compute the numerical values of demand elasticity in the three relevant price ranges.
   d. Are your answers to parts b. and c. consistent? Explain.

e. Graph the market demand curve for canoes (D) and calculate the numerical value of its slope. Does a demand curve with a constant slope have a constant numerical elasticity? Explain.

5. Calculate the appropriate elasticity coefficient in each of the following cases:
   a. Annual purchases of computers rise from 200 000 to 300 000 when average consumer incomes increase from $50 000 to $70 000.
   b. Consumer A's monthly magazine purchases fall from 4 to 3 magazines when the price she pays each month for unlimited access to the Internet decreases from $20 to $10.
   c. Weekly purchases of packs of chewing gum rise from 1.2 million to 1.7 million packs when their price declines from $1 to 85 cents.
   d. A fall in the average price of DVDs from $30 to $25 increases purchases of DVD players from 10 000 to 15 000 per month.
   e. A rise in the price of wheat from $110 to $135 per tonne increases the amount supplied by wheat farmers from 8 million to 9 million tonnes.

6. In the silver market, 1 million ounces are offered for sale each month by producers at the initial price of $6 per ounce. The price then rises to $8.
   a. What happens to the quantity supplied of silver in the immediate run at the new $8 price? Sketch the immediate-run supply curve to explain your answer.
   b. In what direction will the quantity supplied of silver change in the short run at the new $8 price? Sketch the short-run supply curve to explain your answer.
   c. How will the price of silver change in the long run if this is a constant-cost industry? an increasing-cost industry? Sketch long-run supply curves to explain your answers.

7. a. Compute the numerical values of supply elasticity for the market supply curve for strawberries (S) shown in Figure 2.5 in the two price ranges $1.50 to $2, and $2 to $2.50.
   b. Is the supply elastic, inelastic, or unit-elastic between prices $1.50 and $2.50?
   c. Must a supply curve with a constant slope have a constant numerical elasticity? Explain.

Market Demand and Supply Schedules for Cream Cheese

Price ($ per kilogram)	Quantity Demanded (thousands of kilograms per year)	Quantity Supplied (thousands of kilograms per year)		
	D_0	S_0		S_1
$4.50	560	1350	→	1890
4.00	590	1130	→	1420
3.50	630	890	→	960
3.00	670	670	→	670
2.50	700	440	→	380

8. a. Using the table above, draw a graph showing the demand curve (D_0) and the short-run supply curve (S_0) for cream cheese. Identify the equilibrium price and quantity in the absence of government intervention and calculate the consumers' total expenditure and the total revenue received by producers.
   b. After lobbying by the dairy industry, government imposes a price support for cream cheese of $4 per kilogram and agrees to purchase any unsold portion of the product at the $4 price. Outline the short-run effect of this program on consumers and producers.

c. In the long run, the annual supply curve for cream cheese becomes S_1. How do the long-run effects of the $4 price support differ from the short-run effects on consumers and producers?

d. Is the price-support program more costly to taxpayers in the short run or in the long run? Explain.

Market Demand and Supply Schedules for Apartments

Price ($ per month)	Quantity Demanded (thousands of units rented per month)			Quantity Supplied (thousands of units rented per month)
	D_0		D_1	S_0
$800	14.5	→	18.4	18.4
700	17.3	→	21.2	17.3
600	19.5	→	23.4	16.4
500	22.0	→	25.9	15.6
400	23.7	→	27.6	14.2

9. For the schedules above, draw a graph showing the original demand curve (D_0) and supply curve (S_0) for apartments in a particular community.

a. Identify the equilibrium price and quantity in the absence of government intervention.

b. Using your graph, outline how a $500 price ceiling imposed by government affects this market. In your answer, make sure to distinguish between tenants who are able to find apartments at the ceiling price and those who are unable to do so.

c. An increase in the price of single-family dwellings in the community causes the demand for apartments to shift from D_0 to D_1. Draw this demand curve on your graph and explain how it influences the impact of the $500 ceiling price on tenants.

Market Demand and Supply Schedules for Cigarettes

Price ($ per pack)	Quantity Demanded (millions of packs per year)	Quantity Supplied (millions of packs per year)	
	(D_0)	(S_0)	(S_1)
$5	7	11	____
4	8	10	____
3	9	9	____
2	10	8	____
1	11	7	____

10. The table above shows hypothetical demand and supply schedules for cigarettes in the absence of government intervention.

a. Draw a diagram showing demand (D_0), supply (S_0), and equilibrium price and quantity in the market before government intervention.

b. Government policy-makers estimate that the spillover costs associated with cigarette smoking are an extra $2 for each pack sold. Outline the nature of these spillover costs in the case of cigarette smoking.

c. On the basis of the estimate in part b., draw a new supply curve (S_1) on your graph that incorporates both private and public costs of producing and consuming cigarettes. Then, using your graph, copy and complete the table accompanying this question. With the aid of your graph and table, identify the preferred equilibrium in this market.

d. Outline the various ways in which government can intervene to achieve the preferred outcome in this market.

11. Identify the spillover effect in each of the following cases and outline a government policy to deal with this effect.
    a. Impaired driving causes numerous accidents on Canadian roads.
    b. Some Canadians get a new vaccine for measles.
    c. Heroin use by pregnant women is hazardous to the health of their offspring.
    d. A mosquito abatement program is established in a particular community.

12. (Advanced Question)
    The total annual revenue for producers of a given product called widgets is always $10 million, regardless of the price.
    a. On the basis of this information, plot the market demand curve for widgets.
    b. How would you describe the elasticity of this demand curve? Explain.

13. (Policy Discussion Question)
    Access the online article *How Rent Control Drives Out Affordable Housing* (at http://www.cato.org/pubs/pas/pa-274.html).
    a. Using the arguments in the article, explain how low-income tenants are often hurt by rent controls,
    b. Outline why rent controls become more difficult to eliminate the longer they have been in existence in a particular community.
    c. Though the article makes a case against rent controls, can you think of any arguments that can be made against abolishing rent controls that are already in place?

http:// www.cato.org/
pubs/pas/pa-274.html

Internet Application Questions

http://www.globalink.org/
tobacco/wb/wb04.shtml

http://www.statcan.ca/
english/Estat/ licence.htm

1. Use the information in *Measures to Reduce the Demand for Tobacco* (at http://www.globalink.org/tobacco/wb/wb04.shtml) to answer the following questions:
   a. What is the range of estimates for the price elasticity of demand for cigarettes in various countries?
   b. Why are demand elasticities for cigarettes higher in low-income countries than in high-income countries?
   c. According to the sources cited in the reading, how many smoking-related deaths would be avoided if there were a worldwide 10 percent price increase for cigarettes? What elasticity assumptions is this estimate based on?

2. Access Statistics Canada's web site (at http://www.statcan.ca/english/Estat/licence.htm).
   a. On the basis of the information found in "Business Enterprises," generate a map showing the average age of farmers in each Canadian province at the time of the last census.
   b. In which province(s) is the average age of farmers the lowest? the highest?

Alfred Marshall
Source: By permission of the Master
and Fellows of St. John's College
Cambridge

GETTING MORE THAN YOU BARGAINED FOR

Alfred Marshall and Consumer Surplus

Marshall and His Influence

The Englishman Alfred Marshall (1842–1924) contributed more to the study of micro-economics and the way it is taught today than any other economist. He was the first to establish the use of demand and supply graphs, for example, and the way we conceive of such tricky notions as equilibrium and elasticity owes much to his clear-headed, logical approach.

Marshall was a student at Cambridge University and went on to spend most of his life there as a professor. Trained as a mathematician, he later switched to economics. Marshall became a model for 20th century economists and taught some of the most famous ones.

Consumer Surplus

One of Marshall's most useful contributions related to the interpretation of demand curves. He realized that an individual's demand for a certain item can be seen in two ways. Figure A shows the demand for pizza by an individual pizza consumer. Recall that an individual's demand curve tells us how much a person is willing to spend on each unit of the product—in other words, what her quantity demanded is at each price. The curve shows that this consumer will buy one pizza at a price of $12, two pizzas at a price of $9 each, and three pizzas at a price of $6 each. According to Marshall, the demand curve can also be viewed in the opposite way. The height of the demand curve at each quantity is the maximum price the consumer is willing to pay for that unit. Therefore, in this example, the consumer is willing to pay up to $12 for her first pizza of the week, $9 for her second, and $6 for her third.

Marginal Benefit

The maximum price a consumer will pay for a certain unit of a product indicates the extra satisfaction, expressed in dollar terms, that he or she receives from consuming that unit. This marginal benefit is closely associated with marginal utility—Jevons' notion of extra satisfaction gained—but is measured in dollars instead of imaginary "utils." While our pizza consumer gains $12 worth of marginal benefit from her first pizza of the week, the second pizza gives her $9 in marginal benefit, and the third only $6, regardless of the actual price.

Total Benefit

Since any total value is simply the sum of all possible marginal values, it is possible to use marginal benefits to find the consumer's total benefit—in this case, the total amount of satisfaction derived from eating pizzas during the entire week. Our consumer receives marginal benefits of $12, $9, and $6 for the first three pizzas she eats each week. The sum of these three numbers—$27—gives the total benefit gained weekly from pizza consumption. This total benefit is shown as area AB under the demand curve, between 0 and 3 pizzas.

Consumer Expenditure

A consumer's expenditure on a product is simply the market price multiplied by the number of units purchased. With a price of $6 and her consumption of three pizzas per week, our consumer faces a weekly bill of $18. This dollar amount, which represents revenue to the seller, is shown as area B on the graph.

Figure A	Consumer Surplus for an Individual

The consumer pays $6 for each of the 3 pizzas but gets more marginal benefit from the first 2 pizzas. At 2 pizzas, for example, the $9 marginal benefit can be split into the $6 market price and the $3 surplus for that pizza. The consumer's total benefit from eating pizzas is area AB, and the total expenditure is area B. So, consumer surplus is area A.

Consumer Surplus

Marshall realized that individuals usually receive more satisfaction from consuming a product than they actually pay for it. This consumer surplus is defined as the net benefit to the consumer from buying a product at its market price and is found by subtracting the consumer's expenditure from the total received benefit. In the case of our pizza-lover, her consumer surplus from pizzas is $9 ($27 − $18). On the graph, consumer surplus is the difference between total benefit (area AB) and expenditure (area B), giving area A.

With the help of the market demand curve, the notion of consumer surplus can be extended to an entire market, as illustrated for the pizza market in Figure B. The market demand curve shows that at a price of $6, consumers buy 100 000 pizzas per week. By adding together the marginal benefits for each consumer, total benefit appears as the entire area AB beneath the demand curve, up to a quantity demanded of 100 000 pizzas. In contrast, total expenditure equals the rectangular area B. Because 100 000 pizzas are purchased at $6, this area equals $600 000 ($6 × 100 000). The consumer surplus for the entire market is the difference between total benefit (area AB) and total expenditure (area B), or the triangular area A. Because this triangle has a height of $10 ($16 − $6) and a width of 100 000, its area equals $500 000 [($10 × 100 000) ÷ 2].

Relevance for Today

Marshall's concept of consumer surplus for an entire market has a wide range of applications.[1] In evaluating a government policy, such as rent controls or price supports, economists often try to calculate the policy's effect on consumer surplus in the affected market. If the consumer surplus is larger with the policy than without it, then the policy is worthwhile, since it increases the net benefit to consumers. Using the notion of consumer surplus in this way assumes that people's satisfaction can be added together in dollar terms, a simplification that is not always appropriate. However, as a rough guide to how different policies affect consumer welfare, the concept is extremely useful.

---

[1] Marshall's notion of consumer surplus was anticipated by the pathbreaking theoretical work of a French engineer, Jules Dupuit. Marshall claimed to have developed his own ideas independently of Dupuit.

**ADVANCING
ECONOMIC
THOUGHT**

Figure B   Consumer Surplus for a Market

Market Demand Curve for Pizzas

**Market Demand Schedule
for Pizzas**

Price	Quantity Demanded (D)
($ per pizza)	(thousands of pizzas)
$16	0
11	50
6	100

A = $500 000

B = $600 000

When consumers in the pizza market are charged a price of $6, they consume 100 000 pizzas. Adding up consumers' marginal benefits for all these pizzas gives a total benefit in the market equal to area AB. At the same time, consumers' total expenditure on pizzas is area B. The total consumer surplus in the market is found by subtracting area B from area AB, so it is equal to area A.

Market Demand Schedule for Water		Market Demand Schedule for Diamonds	
Price ($ per litre)	Quantity Demanded (millions of litres per year)	Price ($ per carat)	Quantity Demanded (thousands of carats per year)
$1000	0	$500	0
800	0.2	400	50
600	0.4	300	100
400	0.6	200	150
200	0.8	100	200
0	1.0	0	250

1. Early economists, including Adam Smith, argued that utility could not be the main determinant of a product's price. To prove this point, they cited a puzzling fact known as the paradox of value. Some of the most useful items, such as water, are very inexpensive, while other items that have little real usefulness, such as diamonds, are very expensive.

a. Define consumer surplus and use the hypothetical demand schedules for water and diamonds in the table above to calculate the consumer surplus for each of these products if water is freely available while diamonds have a price of $100 per carat.

b. On the basis of your answer to part a., outline how the concept of consumer surplus can be used to explain the paradox of value.

2. A market for economics textbooks in a certain country exhibits a linear demand curve, with an annual quantity demanded of 80 000 books at a price of $40, 40 000 at a price of $60, and 0 at $80.

a. Graph the demand curve and calculate the consumer surplus in the market if the price is $40.

b. The government now imposes a tax of $20 per economics textbook sold in the country, which increases the price to $60. What happens to the consumer surplus?

c. The revenues from this tax are used to reduce the price of economics textbooks sold in a distant low-income country. As a result, the consumer surplus for economics students in the foreign country rises by $1 million. Is the loss to domestic students outweighed by the gain for foreign students? Explain.

d. What assumption is this analysis based on?

For the Public Good

The Economic Role of Government

So far, we have looked at some of the ways government intervenes in private markets. But in mixed economies, such as Canada's, government also has an independent economic role. In Canada, this role is a relatively recent creation. Before the 1930s, federal and provincial governments maintained the legal system and provided education up to the secondary school level. But health care and universities were left largely in the hands of the private sector, and unemployment insurance was not available. In comparison to the present, a *laissez faire* attitude characterized the relationship between the public sector and the business sector.

Change began with the Great Depression of the 1930s. Faced with widespread unemployment and deprivation, government officials were forced to attend to the economic welfare of Canadian citizens. From the 1930s to the 1990s, the role of Canadian governments continued to expand. Now, the public sector in Canada provides a host of programs: payments to adults with children, retirement funds for the elderly, insurance for unemployed workers, welfare payments for those who cannot work, subsidies for higher education, free health care, free schooling, and subsidized public housing for low-income families. These programs are provided by all three levels of government, though the federal and provincial governments take the leading role.

Federal Spending Programs

There are four main federal spending programs for households. These are known as transfer payments, since funds are transferred as a way of increasing households' economic welfare rather than in exchange for products or the supply of resources. The Seniors Benefit provides monthly payments to Canadian residents 65 years and over, with higher dollar amounts for those with the lowest incomes. The Child Tax Credit provides payments to low-income parents of children under 18 years old. Employment Insurance (EI) is a federally run insurance program, funded by compulsory contributions from employees and their employers, to aid people unemployed because of layoffs, temporary sickness, or the birth or adoption of a child. Finally, the Quebec and Canada Pension Plans (QPP and CPP) provide workers in Quebec and the rest of Canada with payments after retirement, financed by compulsory contributions from employees and their employers.

Other Spending Programs

Provincial and territorial governments finance the costs of health care, provide subsidies for post-secondary education that translate into reduced tuition fees for students, and (with the help of municipalities) offer welfare services to single-parent families with low incomes, individuals who are unable to find work due to disabilities, and families in crisis. Under the Canada Health and Social Transfer (CHST), the federal government pays for a portion of these costs by providing cash grants and personal income tax revenues to provincial and territorial governments.

Figure A shows the expenditures of the three levels of government. For the federal government, the most important category of expenditure is debt charges, which are interest payments on the government's own debt, followed by transfer payments to persons. The expenditures of provincial and local governments are more heavily weighted towards purchases of goods and services, although transfers to persons are also an important component of total provincial spending.

Taxation

To pay for their spending, Canadian governments use five main types of taxation: personal income taxes, sales taxes, excise taxes, property taxes, and corporate income taxes.

Personal Income Taxes

Personal income taxes are collected by the federal government, proceeds being shared with the provinces and territories (except in Quebec and Alberta, where federal and provincial income taxes are collected separately). Households pay taxes not only on their income from supplying resources but also on any transfer payments they receive. Households also pay income tax on capital gains, which are earnings from selling an asset, such as a bond or a piece of land at a higher price than it was purchased for.

SIDELINE

Figure A   Government Expenditures

Federal (2002–2003) ($ billions)		Provincial (2002) ($ billions)		Local (2002) ($ billions)	
Transfers to persons		Goods and services	133.0	Goods and services	71.0
Benefits to the elderly	25.8	Transfers to		Transfers to	
Employment insurance		Persons	28.7	Persons	3.6
benefits	15.1	Businesses	8.1	Businesses	1.1
Transfers to other levels		Governments	32.4	Provinces	0.9
of government	32.8	Debt charges	26.9	Debt charges	3.1
Direct program			229.1		78.9
spending	65.0				
Debt charges	37.2				
	175.8				

Federal government spending for the budgetary year of 2002–2003 was dominated by transfer payments to persons and debt charges, which together make up almost half of federal spending. The main components of provincial spending are expenditures on goods and services, and transfers to persons and municipalities. Expenditures on goods and services dominate local government spending.

Source: Statistics Canada "Government Expenditures," adapted in part from the Statistics Canada publication "National Income and Expenditures Accounts," Catalogue 13-001, April 2003, pp. 53, 54, 55.

Households may be allowed a variety of deductions (such as contributions to registered retirement savings plans) that reduce the dollar amount on which they are taxed. This amount, known as taxable income, is the basis on which income tax is determined. The tax a household pays rises with taxable income, with tax rates also gradually rising as a household's taxable income increases. These rates are called marginal tax rates, meaning they are calculated as percentages of each extra dollar of taxable income. There are four marginal tax rates in the federal income tax system—16 percent on income up to approximately $30 000, 22 percent on income between $30 000 and approximately $60 000, 26 percent on income between $60 000 and approximately $100 000, and 29 percent on income in excess of $100 000. Once total tax owing has been calculated, households may also claim a variety of tax credits, which directly reduce their tax bill.

Before 2000, all provinces except Quebec levied provincial income taxes as a percentage of the federal tax bill added onto the taxpayer's tax bill. But by 2001, this setup ended, as all provinces moved to levy their own income taxes independently of those set by the federal government. Newfoundland has the highest taxes for high-income earners, with these households paying a combined federal and provincial tax rate of 48.64 percent in 2002. In contrast, residents of Nunavut enjoy the lowest rate for high-income earners, with these households paying a combined rate of 40.5 percent in 2002.

As shown in Figure B, personal income taxes are the most important tax in terms of overall revenue.

Sales and Excise Taxes

Sales and excise taxes are levied by both federal and provincial governments on goods and services. Sales taxes are usually charged on a wide range of goods and services and are calculated as a percentage of the prices of these products. In contrast, excise taxes are charged on particular products, such as gasoline, liquor, and tobacco, and are often expressed as a dollar amount per unit of quantity, rather than in terms of percentages of product price.

Property Taxes

Property taxes are charged by local governments on buildings and land. For taxation purposes, these assets are assigned a value—often not their potential price in the real estate market, but some arbitrary dollar amount set in the past. Then, each year, the local government establishes a tax rate in terms of mills (or thousands) of property value. For example, a mill rate of 80 means that property owners are charged $80 for each $1000 in property value.

Figure B — Tax Revenues for All Levels of Government (2002)

	Percent of Gross Domestic Product	Percent of Total Taxes
Personal income taxes	12.7	41.6
Sales and excise taxes	7.8	25.4
Property taxes	3.6	11.7
Corporate income taxes	3.5	11.0
Miscellaneous taxes	3.2	10.3
	30.8	100.0

Personal income taxes are the most important single source of revenue for the state, followed by sales and excise taxes, property taxes, and corporate taxes.

Source: Karin Treff and David B. Perry, *Finances of the Nation 2002* (Toronto: Canadian Tax Foundation, 2002) A: 4.

Corporate Income Taxes

Corporate income taxes are paid by corporations to governments as a percentage of their annual profits. As with personal income taxes, corporations are allowed to make deductions from their total income in calculating taxable profit. The resulting dollar amount is then taxed at a constant marginal rate by the federal government (27 percent in 2001), with most provincial governments "piggybacking" on this rate.

Debates over Government's Economic Role

As shown in Figure C, taxes by all three levels of government in Canada have increased considerably over the past decades in relation to the size of the entire economy.

Are the amounts we pay in taxes well spent? This is a question subject to perennial debate, not just in Canada but in other countries as well.

Critics of government argue that its economic role suffers from a variety of serious problems. Most importantly, the supply of economic resources can be reduced by government's economic involvement. By reducing the income gained from productive activity, taxes can sometimes discourage employment and business investment. Moreover, spending programs, such as welfare and employment insurance, can have their own effect on the economic decisions we make. For example, welfare recipients may receive more income from welfare than they would upon initially entering the workforce, while habitual claimants of employment insurance may be reluctant to move from occupations and regions of

Figure C — Government Taxes and the Canadian Economy

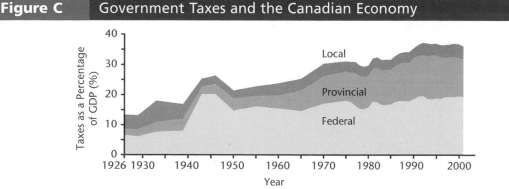

Since the 1920s, the increasing importance of the public sector in the Canadian economy has led to increased taxes (including contributions for such programs as Employment Insurance and CPP/QPP) in relation to the size of the economy. While taxes represented just over 10 percent of Gross Domestic Product (GDP) in 1926, they represented just under 40 percent by 2002.

Sources: Statistics Canada "Government Taxes and the Canadian Economy," data adapted from the Statistics Canada publication "National Income and Expenditure Accounts: Annual Estimates," 1926–1986, Catalogue 13-531, April 1989 and from the Statistics Canada CANSIM II database http://cansim2.statcan.ca, Table 380-0007.

SIDELINE

the country where there is considerable risk of unemployment.

Government spending is criticized for other reasons as well. Some programs, such as employment insurance, are paid both to well-off individuals as well as those in need, making the programs more expensive than necessary. Government programs can also be hampered by overlapping bureaucracies, high administrative costs, and a lack of focus. Critics contend that these inefficiencies mean that government spending is often wasteful and badly managed.

Other observers are willing to admit that Canada's mix of public spending and taxation is not as effective as it could be. But they also argue that we need to see these problems in perspective, especially when we realize that private markets, too, are subject to a variety of flaws. When viewed in this light, government's economic role is something that must be improved rather than necessarily reduced. Regardless of these arguments, there is no doubt that government's role in the economy will continue to be a vital one in the foreseeable future.

1. Which form of taxation do you think has the greatest disincentive effect of productive activity in the economy? Which form of taxation do you think has the least disincentive effect?

2. Provincial tax levels have grown rapidly in the past few decades, as shown in Figure C. Can you make any argument for why provincial governments have needed to increase their spending so rapidly during this period?

SIDELINE

Part 2
Efficiency and Equity

That action is best which procures the greatest happiness for the greatest numbers.

— Francis Hutchinson, British philosopher

All societies must weigh the importance of gaining the most benefits from the economy's scarce resources (efficiency) against the importance of distributing the country's total output fairly (equity). These two goals, which lie at the heart of microeconomics, are often in conflict. In modern mixed economies, such as Canada's, the private sector has traditionally stressed the goal of efficiency, while the public sector—especially in the decades since World War II—has tended to focus on the goal of income equity. In the next five chapters, we will examine the impact of each goal and how they are related. We will also examine the impact of an important third goal—environmental sustainability.

CHAPTER 4

Costs of Production

Knowledge is the only instrument of production that is not subject to diminishing returns.

—J.M. Clark, American economist

There is an old saying: "There's no such thing as a free lunch." In other words, everything has a cost. This chapter highlights one of the most important types of cost—how production creates expenses for businesses. In the future, if not already, most of us will have a close connection with a business as an employee or owner. All of us have a connection to businesses by virtue of being consumers. For now, we will ignore the selling side of business to look at how businesses make decisions about production processes and how they deal with production costs. In later chapters, we will look again at sales revenues to see the crucial role production costs play in determining the profits that companies earn.

LEARNING OBJECTIVES

In this chapter, you will:

1 learn about economic costs (explicit and implicit) of production and economic profit

2 analyze short-run (total, average, and marginal) products and the law of diminishing marginal returns

3 derive short-run (total, average, and marginal) costs

4 examine long-run results of production (increasing returns to scale, constant returns to scale, and decreasing returns to scale) and long-run costs

4.1 Production, Costs, and Profit

business: an enterprise that brings individuals, financial resources, and economic resources together to produce a good or service for economic gain

production: the process of transforming a set of resources into a good or service that has economic value

inputs: the resources used in production

output: the quantity of a good or service that results from production

labour-intensive process: a production process that employs more labour and less capital

capital-intensive process: a production process that employs more capital and less labour

productive efficiency: making a given quantity of output at the lowest cost

A **business** is an enterprise that brings individuals, financial resources, and economic resources together to produce a good or service for economic gain. **Production** is the process of transforming a set of resources into a good or service that has economic value. The resources used in production are known as **inputs**. Recall that natural resources, capital resources, and human resources are the three economic resources used in production. Inputs for most businesses include all three of these *factors of production*. **Output** is the result of this production, the quantity of a good or service that is produced.

Businesses and the industries in which they operate fall into one of three sectors depending on the type of production: primary, secondary, or service (also known as "tertiary"). The primary sector includes industries that extract or cultivate natural resources, such as mining, forestry, fishing, and agriculture. The secondary sector involves fabricating or processing goods and includes, among other industries, manufacturing and construction. Finally, the service sector includes trade industries (both retail and wholesale), such as banking and insurance and the new information industries. Despite the differences among these three sectors, they all follow the same production principles.

Productive Efficiency

In producing a certain good or service, businesses can typically choose from several processes, each using a different combination of inputs. A **labour-intensive process** is one that employs more labour and less capital than do other processes to produce a certain quantity of output. Conversely, a **capital-intensive process** uses more capital and less labour to produce the same quantity of output.

Suppose you have started a small clothing company, Pure 'n' Simple T-Shirts, with a $100 000 inheritance. You rent a building, to use as a factory, and buy a supply of materials. Before you hire workers or buy sewing machines, you discover that you can make 250 T-shirts a day by using one of two possible production processes, each involving a different combination of workers and machines. The combinations of labour and capital employed in each process are shown in Figure 4.1. Process A is labour-intensive, since it requires more workers and fewer machines than does the other process to produce 250 T-shirts per day. Process B is capital-intensive, since it requires more machines and fewer workers than does Process A.

How does a business decide which production process to use? Owners who want to earn as much profit as possible should try to maximize the business's **productive efficiency**, which means making a given quantity of output with the least costly mix of inputs. Selecting the most efficient process, therefore, depends both on the quantity of each input used and on the prices of these inputs. Let us look again at the example

Figure 4.1   Choosing a Production Process

	Workers (labour)	Sewing Machines (capital)
Process A	4	2
Process B	3	3

Pure 'n' Simple T-Shirts can produce a daily output of 250 T-shirts with one of two possible combinations of workers and sewing machines—A, a more labour-intensive process and B, a more capital-intensive process.

of Pure 'n' Simple T-Shirts. As the owner, you can maximize your business's productive
efficiency by using the lowest-priced combination of workers and sewing machines
needed to turn out the daily output of 250 T-shirts. You find that the daily cost of a
worker (an hourly wage, plus employee benefits) is $100, while the daily cost of a
sewing machine (including wear and tear on the machine, use of electricity, and maintenance) is $25. All other costs for the business (for example, rent of the building)
remain constant, no matter which process is used, so they can be ignored in making this
decision. With Process A, the daily costs of employing four workers and two machines
come to $450 [($100 × 4 workers) + ($25 × 2 machines)]. In contrast, the daily costs of
employing three workers and three machines with Process B are $375 [($100 × 3 workers) + ($25 × 3 machines)]. In this case, productive efficiency is maximized by using the
capital–intensive Process B.

LO   4.1

explicit costs: payments
made by a business to businesses or people outside of it

Economic Costs

Businesses face two types of costs: explicit costs and implicit costs. **Explicit costs** are
payments made by a business to businesses or people outside of it. Explicit costs are also
referred to as "accounting costs" because they include all the costs that appear in the
business accounting records. These costs include such items as payments made for
wages, buildings, machinery, and materials. For Pure 'n' Simple T-Shirts, for example, the
explicit costs of producing 250 T-shirts a day using Process B include $375 for labour
and machinery. In addition, the business may face a whole range of other accounting
costs that add up to $675 per day. The daily explicit costs for the business are, therefore,
$1050 ($375 + $675).

implicit costs: the owner's
opportunity costs of being
involved with a business

normal profit: the minimum return necessary for
owners to keep funds and
their entrepreneurial skills
in their business

In contrast, **implicit costs** are estimates of what owners give up by being involved
with a business—the owner's own opportunity cost, in other words, of pursuing this
course of action over another. Implicit costs relate to the resources provided by the owners. One implicit cost is **normal profit**, or the minimum return that owners must
receive to keep their funds and their entrepreneurial skills tied up in their business. To
calculate normal profit, owners must determine the highest possible return they could
have received by using their funds and entrepreneurial skills in another way. Consider
again the T-shirt company. You might estimate that rather than making T-shirts, you
could use your $100 000 to purchase a partnership in your friend's catering business,

which would provide you with a return of $50 a day. Another implicit cost is the wages that owners sacrifice by providing labour to the business. If, for example, you devote labour by working as the manager of Pure 'n' Simple T-Shirts, you might estimate the value of your work as $150 a day, which is what you could earn by working for someone else. The sum of these two costs means that the implicit costs for Pure 'n' Simple T-Shirts are $200 ($50 + $150) per day.

economic costs: a business's total explicit and implicit costs

Recall that economists define "cost" as opportunity cost, which includes any sacrificed opportunity that results from some course of action, even if no outright monetary payment is made. Thus, the **economic costs** encountered by a business are all the opportunity costs involved in production and include both explicit and implicit costs. So, for Pure 'n' Simple T-Shirts, the explicit costs of producing 250 T-shirts per day are $1050, and the implicit costs are $200. The total economic costs faced by the business are, therefore, $1250:

$$\text{Economic costs} = \text{explicit costs} + \text{implicit costs}$$
$$\$1250 = \$1050 + \$200$$

Economic Profit

In accounting, profit is found by deducting explicit costs from total revenue to find **accounting profit**. A different approach is used in economics.

accounting profit: the excess of a business's total revenue over its explicit costs

economic profit: the excess of a business's total revenue over its economic costs

When economic costs are subtracted from total revenue, the excess is known as **economic profit**. If this gives a negative figure, the business faces a negative economic profit or a loss. The daily economic profit of Pure 'n' Simple T-Shirts can be found by calculating total revenue and subtracting economic costs. If 250 T-shirts are sold at a price of $6 each, then the total revenue gained by producing 250 T-shirts is $1500 ($6 × 250 shirts). When the economic costs of $1250 are deducted, we get an economic profit of $250 ($1500 − $1250):

$$\text{Economic profit} = \text{total revenue} - \text{economic costs}$$
$$\$250 = \$1500 - \$1250$$

When a business's economic profit is positive, as it is for Pure 'n' Simple T-Shirts, the business has reason to continue operating, since it is reaping a positive amount after both explicit and implicit costs have been accounted for. But if economic profit is negative over an extended time period, the business's owners should consider closing down, because they are unable to cover all of their explicit and implicit costs.

Brief Review

1. Production processes may be labour-intensive or capital-intensive. To achieve productive efficiency, a business must choose the production process that is the cheapest way to produce a certain quantity of output.

2. Economic costs, as opposed to accounting costs, include both explicit costs (payments to those outside the business) and implicit costs (opportunity costs owners sustain by running the business).

3. Economists measure profitability using economic profit, which is found by deducting both explicit and implicit costs from a business's sales revenue.

4.1 Practice Questions

1. A photocopy shop can produce its daily output of 10 000 copies with either of two processes. Process A uses 2 workers and 6 photocopy machines. Process B uses 3 workers and 3 photocopy machines.

    a. If each worker's daily wage is $80, and the daily rental (as well as wear and tear) of a photocopy machine is $40, will the shop's owner choose Process A or B?
    b. Besides the costs of labour and capital, the owner daily pays $30 in building rent and $10 in business taxes. What are the shop's daily explicit costs?
    c. If the shop's price per photocopy is $0.06, what is the daily accounting profit?
    d. The owner estimates that she could earn $150 a day if she managed another shop instead of her own shop and the $150 000 she invested in her business could earn $30 a day if she put it into her friend's business venture. What are the shop's daily implicit costs? daily economic costs?
    e. What is the shop's daily economic profit?
    f. Should the owner consider closing down her business? Why?

4.2 Production in the Short Run

fixed inputs: inputs whose quantities cannot be adjusted in the short run

variable inputs: inputs whose quantities can be adjusted in the short run

Recall from Chapter 3 that the short run is the period during which quantities of one or more of a business's inputs cannot be varied. In manufacturing, companies usually cannot adjust the quantity of machinery they use or the size of their factories on short notice. In agriculture, there is typically an additional quantity that cannot be varied—the land available for cultivation. Inputs that cannot be adjusted in the short run are known as **fixed inputs**. Inputs that can be adjusted are known as **variable inputs**. Typically, variable inputs in the short run include the labour and materials a business uses in production. For example, as owner of Pure 'n' Simple T-Shirts, you are considering adjusting your current production of 250 shirts a day. You have already bought three sewing machines and cannot acquire more without a considerable delay. Hence, the three machines represent a fixed input for your business in the short run. But you can change the number of workers you employ, so labour represents a variable input in the short run.

 LO 4.2

total product: the overall quantity of output produced with a given workforce

Total, Average, and Marginal Products

To increase production of a certain good or service, a business must employ more of all variable inputs, including workers. The result is a rise in **total product**, which is the overall quantity (q) of output associated with a given workforce. The employment of labour is a convenient measure of a company's scale of production, since labour is a variable input in making virtually all products. But businesses also use other variable inputs, such as natural resources or semi-processed goods.

Once again, let us look at Pure 'n' Simple T-Shirts. Suppose you conduct a few experiments to see what happens to total product for your business when the number of workers employed is changed but the number of sewing machines—three—remains constant. As shown in columns 1 and 2 of Figure 4.2, an increase in workers from three to four, for example, causes an increase in total production from 250 to 270 shirts per day.

average product: the quantity of output produced per worker

In addition to total product, two other concepts are important when analyzing production in the short run. **Average product** is the quantity of output produced per

Figure 4.2　Production in the Short Run

(1) Labour (L) (workers per day)	(2) Total Product (q) (T-shirts per day)	(3) Marginal Product ($\Delta q/\Delta L$) (T-shirts per day)	(4) Average Product (q/L) (T-shirts per day)
0	0		—
		80	
1	80		80
		120	
2	200		100
		50	
3	250		83.3
		20	
4	270		67.5
		10	
5	280		56
		−10	
6	270		45

As the number of workers increases, total product increases when each of the first five workers is hired. Marginal product peaks when the second worker is hired and becomes negative at the same point that total product begins to drop. Average product peaks at two workers.

marginal product: the extra output produced by an additional worker

worker and is found by dividing total product (q) by the quantity of labour (L) employed. **Marginal product**, in contrast, is the extra output produced when an additional worker is hired. Marginal product is calculated by dividing the change in total product (Δq) by the change in the amount of labour employed (ΔL). (The symbol Δ is the Greek capital letter "delta," which signifies a change in some variable.)

Columns 3 and 4 of Figure 4.2 list the marginal and average products for Pure 'n' Simple T-Shirts. When employing three workers, the workforce's average product is 83.3 shirts per day (250 shirts ÷ 3 workers). If a fourth worker is added, the marginal product of this worker is 20 shirts, which comes from subtracting the old total product (250 shirts) from the new total product (270 shirts) and dividing the difference by the change in the workforce from three to four:

$$\text{Average product} = \frac{\text{total product (q)}}{\text{number of workers (L)}}$$

$$83.3 \text{ shirts} = \frac{250}{3}$$

$$\text{Marginal product} = \frac{\text{change in total product } (\Delta q)}{\text{change in workforce } (\Delta L)}$$

$$20 \text{ shirts} = \frac{(270 - 250)}{(4 - 3)}$$

In a table, such as Figure 4.2, marginal product is shown halfway between the values for total and average products. This is because marginal product is defined as a change from one employment level to another. So, for example, in column 3 the marginal product of 20 shirts for the fourth worker is shown between the rows for 3 and 4 workers. The same principle also applies to expressing the marginal product on a graph; the marginal product of 20 shirts for the fourth worker will be plotted halfway between the horizontal co-ordinates for three and four workers.

Diminishing Marginal Returns

**law of diminishing
marginal returns:** at some
point, as more units of a
variable input are added to
a fixed input, the marginal
product will start to
decrease

The marginal product values in Figure 4.2 reflect a law that applies to production in the short run. According to the **law of diminishing marginal returns**, at some point—as more units of a variable input are added to a fixed input—the marginal product will start to decrease, since the new units of the variable input (for example, workers) are being added to an increasingly scarce fixed input (for example, land). It is possible to prove the law of diminishing returns through a type of argument known by the Latin term *reductio ad absurdum* (pronounced *re-dook´-shio ad ab-surd´-um*). This type of argument verifies a statement by showing that its opposite leads to absurdity. For the law of diminishing marginal returns, consider what would happen if you used a flower pot to grow food. If the law of diminishing marginal returns were false, then, as you used more labour, the total product of food grown in the flower pot would rise at a faster and faster rate, until the world's entire food supply could be provided from this single pot. Since this conclusion is obviously absurd, the law of diminishing marginal returns must be true.

In the case of Pure 'n' Simple T-Shirts, where the main fixed input is sewing machines rather than land, the law of diminishing marginal returns can be best understood by thinking of what happens to the use of these machines as the number of workers employed rises. Sooner or later workers find their access to sewing machines lessened as the labour force expands. As a result, after some point each newly hired worker contributes a lower marginal product than the one before.

Three Stages of Production

Pure 'n' Simple T-Shirts' total product is shown on the top graph of Figure 4.3, and its marginal product and average product are shown on the bottom graph. Both graphs can be divided into three ranges. On the bottom graph's first range, marginal product rises as more workers are added. On the top graph's first range, total product rises at a higher and higher rate, giving the curve a positive slope that gets steeper. During the second range, marginal product begins to fall but is still positive. Total product in this second range continues to rise but at a lower rate so that the curve becomes flatter. In the final range, marginal product falls below zero and total product decreases. Points in this last range will never be chosen by the business.

Average versus Marginal Product

The shape of the average product curve reflects an important series of rules governing the relationship between average and marginal values. The average rises if the marginal value is above the average value. The average value stays constant if it equals the corresponding marginal value. Finally, the average value falls if the marginal value is below the average value.

These rules are borne out by the bottom graph in Figure 4.3. At first, marginal product is above average product so that average product must be rising. At two workers, average product crosses the marginal product curve so that values for both must be equal. Here, average product is constant, meaning, it has a zero slope. Beyond this point, marginal product is below average product, causing average product to fall.

The rules that connect marginal and average values apply in a variety of situations. To help explain these rules, we will use an illustration every student is familiar

Figure 4.3   Total, Marginal, and Average Products

Visit the
Web Site

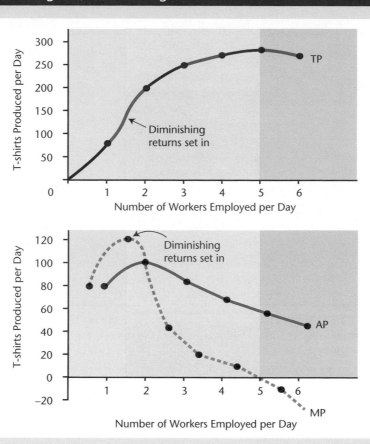

Pure 'n' Simple T-Shirts' total product curve is hill-shaped, with its peak at five workers and its slope dependent on the behaviour of marginal product. The first range, where marginal product rises, applies during the hiring of the first two workers. In the second range, during the hiring of the third, fourth, and fifth workers, marginal product falls and is positive. In the last range, from the sixth worker onwards, marginal product falls and is negative. The shape of the average product curve can be linked to marginal product, since average product reaches a maximum where it crosses the marginal product curve at two workers.

with—marks. Suppose there are two tests in a course, each worth 50 marks, with a student's final grade calculated as the sum of the two marks. A student's *marginal mark* is the mark on each test, while her *average mark* is the total earned so far divided by the number of completed tests. For example, say the student has received a marginal mark of 36 out of 50 on the first test. Her initial average is also 36, which comes from dividing 36 by 1, as shown in Figure 4.4. If the student receives a marginal mark of 34 out of 50 on the second test, her average on the two tests falls to 35 [(36 + 34) ÷ 2]. The student's average mark has declined, because her new marginal mark of 34 is below her previous average of 36. On the other hand, she may get another mark of 36 on the second test. Because her new marginal mark is the same as her previous average, this student's average stays the same at 36 [(36 + 36) ÷ 2]. Finally, if the student receives a mark of 38 on the second test, her average rises to 37 [(36 + 38) ÷ 2]. In this case, her average rises because her new marginal mark is greater than her previous average. All three of these cases are shown in Figure 4.4.

Figure 4.4   A Student's Marginal and Average Marks

		Marginal Mark	Average Mark
Test 1		$\dfrac{36}{50}$	$\dfrac{36}{1} = 36$
Test 2	(Case A)	$\dfrac{34}{50}$	$\dfrac{(36 + 34)}{2} = 35$
	(Case B)	$\dfrac{36}{50}$	$\dfrac{(36 + 36)}{2} = 36$
	(Case C)	$\dfrac{38}{50}$	$\dfrac{(36 + 38)}{2} = 37$

On the first test, the student receives a mark of 36, which represents both her marginal and average marks. In Case A, the marginal mark on the second test is below the previous average, so the average mark falls. In Case B, the marginal mark on the second test equals the previous average, so the average stays the same. In Case C, the marginal mark on the second test is above the previous average, so the average mark rises.

4.3 Costs in the Short Run

fixed costs: economic costs for inputs that remain fixed at all quantities of output

variable costs: economic costs for inputs that vary at each quantity of output

total cost: the sum of all fixed and variable costs at each quantity of output

In the short run, just as businesses use fixed and variable inputs, they face corresponding fixed and variable costs. **Fixed costs** (FC) do not change when a business changes its quantity of output, since these costs relate to fixed inputs, such as machinery and land. **Variable costs** (VC), in contrast, relate to variable inputs, which change when a business adjusts the quantity produced. The most important variable costs are wages and payments for materials used in production. **Total cost** (TC) is the sum of the costs of all inputs, both fixed and variable and is found by adding fixed and variable costs at each quantity of output.

The short-run costs for Pure 'n' Simple T-Shirts are shown in Figure 4.5. The company's fixed costs (column 4) reflect its expenditures on such inputs as factory rent and machinery and are a constant $825, regardless of how many shirts are produced. In contrast, variable costs (column 5) rise along with output. Therefore, at the level of three workers, total cost (column 6) is $1250 ($825 + $425):

$$\text{Total cost (TC)} = \text{fixed cost (FC)} + \text{variable cost (VC)}$$
$$\$1250 = \$825 + \$425$$

Marginal Cost

"Marginal" has a different interpretation when referring to cost rather than product. While marginal product is defined in terms of each new unit of labour, with cost, the focus switches to new units of output instead.

marginal cost: the extra cost of producing an additional unit of output

Marginal cost (MC), or the extra cost of producing an additional unit of output, is the most important cost concept in economics. Marginal cost is found by calculating the change in total cost (ΔTC) that results whenever a new worker is hired and then dividing this change by the change in total product (Δq) that results from employing another worker. So, for example, the marginal costs for Pure 'n' Simple T-Shirts at each output level are shown in column 7 of Figure 4.5. When the fourth worker is hired, total cost in column 6 rises by $110 ($1360 − $1250), and marginal product, in column 3 is 20 shirts (270 − 250). Therefore, the marginal cost of each of these additional 20 shirts is $5.50 ($110.00 ÷ 20 shirts).

Figure 4.5   Short-Run Costs for Pure 'n' Simple T-Shirts

(1) Labour (L)	(2) Total Product (q)	(3) Marginal Product (MP)	(4) Fixed Costs (FC)	(5) Variable Costs (VC)	(6) Total Cost (TC) (FC + VC)	(7) Marginal Cost (MC) (ΔTC/Δq)	(8) Average Fixed Costs (AFC) (FC/q)	(9) Average Variable Costs (AVC) (VC/q)	(10) Average Cost (AC) (AFC + AVC)
0	0		$825	$ 0	$ 825				
		→ 80				→ 140 $1.75			
1	80		825	140	965		$10.31	$1.75	$12.06
		→ 120				→ 160 1.33			
2	200		825	300	1125		4.13	1.50	5.63
		→ 50				→ 125 2.50			
3	250		825	425	1250		3.30	1.70	5.00
		→ 20				→ 110 5.50			
4	270		825	535	1360		3.06	1.98	5.04
		→ 10				→ 105 10.50			
5	280		825	640	1465		2.95	2.29	5.24

Columns 1 and 2 are from Figure 4.2, while columns 4 and 5 represent possible fixed and variable costs for the business. The remaining columns are based on calculations shown in the table. Total cost in column 6 is the sum of the fixed and variable costs. Marginal cost in column 7 is found by dividing the *changes* in total cost by the *changes* in total product. Columns 8 and 9 are derived by dividing fixed and variable costs by total product. Average cost in column 10 is the sum of the average fixed and average variable costs.

$$\text{Marginal cost (MC)} = \frac{\text{change in total cost } (\Delta TC)}{\text{change in total product } (\Delta q)}$$

$$\$5.50 = \frac{\$110.00}{20 \text{ shirts}}$$

Figure 4.6 shows that the marginal cost curve is shaped like the letter "J" (or the Nike "swoosh"). Early in the process of adding labour, the addition of each new worker produces a proportionally greater increase in output than in the existing labour. So, the marginal cost connected with each new worker falls for each extra unit of output as long as marginal product keeps increasing. But at some point, marginal product starts to

Figure 4.6   The Marginal Cost Curve

As illustrated by the case of Pure 'n' Simple T-Shirts, the marginal cost curve (MC) is shaped like the letter "J." At low output levels, the extra cost of each unit produced falls. Marginal cost starts to rise when marginal product begins to fall.

decline. From this point, each new worker contributes fewer extra units of output than the previous worker, and the marginal cost connected with adding a new worker is greater for each extra unit of output. Marginal cost, therefore, rises as long as marginal product continues to fall.

Per-Unit Costs

While marginal cost is based on changes in a business's total product, per-unit costs are expressed in terms of a single level of output. These costs are related to a business's fixed costs, variable costs, and total costs. Hence, there are three separate types of per-unit costs: average fixed cost, average variable cost, and average cost.

AVERAGE FIXED AND AVERAGE VARIABLE COSTS

average fixed cost: the fixed cost per unit of output

average variable cost: the variable cost per unit of output

Average fixed cost (AFC) is the fixed cost per unit of output and is calculated by dividing the business's fixed costs (FC) by its total product (q). Similarly, **average variable cost** (AVC) is the variable cost per unit of output and is calculated by dividing the business's variable costs (VC) by total product (q). For example, for Pure 'n' Simple T-Shirts, the average fixed and average variable costs are found in columns 8 and 9 of Figure 4.5. When three workers are employed, the business's fixed costs of $825 are divided by the total product of 250 shirts, giving an average fixed cost of $3.30. Similarly, the $425 variable costs at this employment level are divided by 250 shirts, resulting in an average variable cost of $1.70.

$$\text{Average fixed cost (AFC)} = \frac{\text{fixed costs (FC)}}{\text{total product (q)}}$$

$$\$3.30 \text{ per shirt} = \frac{\$825}{250 \text{ shirts}}$$

$$\text{Average variable cost (AVC)} = \frac{\text{variable costs (VC)}}{\text{total product (q)}}$$

$$\$1.70 \text{ per shirt} = \frac{\$425}{250 \text{ shirts}}$$

Figure 4.7 shows on a graph the average fixed cost for Pure 'n' Simple T-Shirts. When no shirts are produced, the denominator of the average fixed cost formula is zero, meaning that average fixed cost is an infinitely high number. Average fixed cost then falls as the business's total product increases, since the denominator in the formula rises. Therefore, the average fixed cost curve has a negative (downward) slope, and becomes flatter as output rises.

In contrast, the average variable cost curve shown in Figure 4.7 is saucer-shaped, reflecting its connection with the associated marginal cost curve. At the initial quantities of output, marginal cost is below average variable cost, causing average variable cost to decline. (In terms of our previous example in Section 4.2, this is the case where a student's marginal mark is below her initial average, causing her average mark to fall.) Once the two curves meet (at point *a*)—where the marginal and average values are equal—the average variable cost curve has a zero slope and reaches its minimum. At higher output levels, marginal cost is above average variable cost, causing average variable cost to rise (just as a student's marginal mark that is higher than her initial average leads to a rise in her average mark).

average cost: the sum of average fixed cost and average variable cost at each quantity of output

AVERAGE COST

Average total cost, or simply **average cost** (AC), is the business's total cost per unit of output. Average cost is the sum of average fixed cost and average variable cost at each quantity of output. So, for example, in column 10 of Figure 4.5, when Pure 'n' Simple T-Shirts produces 250 shirts, average fixed cost is $3.30 and average variable cost is $1.70, giving an average cost of $5 ($3.30 + $1.70)

$$\text{Average cost (AC)} = \text{average fixed cost (AFC)} + \text{average variable cost (AVC)}$$
$$\$5 \text{ per shirt} = \$3.30 + \$1.70$$

Like the average variable cost curve, the average cost curve in Figure 4.7 is saucer-shaped. It represents the sum of the values plotted for the average fixed cost curve and the average variable cost curve. At an output level of 250 shirts, for example, the $5 average cost is the sum of the heights of the average fixed cost curve ($3.30) and the average variable cost curve ($1.70). At lower output levels, average cost is high because of average fixed cost. Once average cost has passed its lowest point, its rise is due to the impact of expanding average variable cost. The average cost curve reaches its minimum at point *b*, where it

Figure 4.7	The Family of Short-Run Cost Curves

As Pure 'n' Simple T-Shirts illustrates, when a business's output of a certain product rises, the average fixed cost curve (AFC) falls. The average variable cost curve (AVC) declines until it reaches point *a*, where it meets the marginal cost curve (MC), after which the AVC curve rises. The average cost curve (AC) also falls and then rises. It reaches a minimum at point *b*, where it meets the MC curve.

THINKING ABOUT ECONOMICS

Is production in knowledge-based industries different from that found in more conventional parts of the economy?

The use of knowledge does differ from the use of other inputs, since knowledge is not necessarily used up when employed in production. For example, when a software company produces a new program, it can keep on making it at virtually no marginal cost, especially when software is sold over the Internet.

This means that almost all costs are the fixed ones connected with software development. Variable costs, meanwhile, are virtually zero.

http://shop.microsoft.ca/default.asp

Question
If all costs are fixed, what would a business's average cost curve look like?

intersects the marginal cost curve. This relationship parallels the relationship between average variable cost and marginal cost. Therefore, marginal cost provides the minimum values for both the average variable cost curve and the average cost curve. In each case, an average value remains constant when it equals its associated marginal value.

Brief Review

1. In the short run, production is governed by the law of diminishing marginal returns, which states that as more units of a variable input are added to a fixed input, the marginal product will start to decrease at some point.

2. Because of the law of diminishing marginal returns, the marginal product curve is hill-shaped. The total and average product curves are also hill-shaped because of their connections with changes in marginal product.

3. Marginal cost, or the extra cost of producing another unit of output, is inversely related to marginal product. The marginal cost curve is shaped like the letter "J."

4. Average fixed cost represents fixed costs per unit of output. Its curve has a negative slope and is flatter at higher output levels. Average variable cost, or variable costs per unit of output, has a saucer-shaped curve that reaches its minimum where it crosses the marginal cost curve.

5. Average cost, or total cost per unit of output, is the sum of average fixed and average variable costs at given output levels. The curve for average cost is saucer-shaped and reaches a minimum where it intersects the marginal cost curve.

4.3 Practice Questions

1. Weekly production for a potter varies with the number of workers employed. The potter's total product is 50 pots with 1 worker, 200 pots with 2 workers, 270 pots with 3 workers, 300 pots with 4 workers, and 240 pots with 5 workers.
   a. What is the marginal product for each worker?
   b. Identify the ranges where marginal product rises, where it falls, and where it is negative.
   c. In common sense terms, why does the marginal product of each new worker fall when the third, fourth, and fifth workers are hired?
   d. What is the average product at each employment level?
   e. Explain the relationship between marginal product and average product.
   f. Using EconGraphKit (at http://www.mcgrawhill.ca/college/lovewell), draw the potter's total product curve on one graph, and draw the potter's marginal product and average product curves on another graph.
   g. Explain how the shapes of the three curves you have drawn in part f. are affected by the law of diminishing marginal returns.

2. The potter in question 1 has fixed costs of $100 per week and variable costs of $100 per worker.
   a. What are the potter's variable costs when 0, 50, 200, 270, or 300 pots are produced? What is total cost at each of these outputs?
   b. Calculate the marginal cost when moving from each output to the next.

c. Compute the average fixed cost, average variable cost, and average cost at 50, 200, 270, and 300 pots.

d. Using EconGraphKit (at http://www.mcgrawhill.ca/college/lovewell), draw the potter's average fixed cost curve on one graph, and the potter's marginal cost, average variable cost, and average cost curves on another graph.

e. Do the curves you have drawn in part d. have the shapes you expect? Explain.

4.4 Production and Costs in the Long Run

As we discussed in Chapter 3, the long run is the period in which quantities of all resources used in an industry can be adjusted. So, even those inputs that had been fixed in the short run—such as machinery, buildings, and cultivated land—can be adjusted in the long run. Because all inputs can vary in the long run, the law of diminishing marginal returns no longer applies as in the short run. Instead, new questions arise. If a business expands all inputs used to produce a certain product, how will the output of the product vary, and what effect will these changes have on costs? There are three possible results: increasing, constant, and decreasing returns to scale.

LO 4.4

increasing returns to scale: a situation in which a percentage increase in all inputs causes a larger percentage increase in output

Increasing Returns to Scale

Increasing returns to scale (also known as economies of scale) occur when a business expands all inputs for a certain product by a given percentage and the output rises by an even higher percentage. For example, if a car manufacturer doubles all inputs used to make a certain car model (that is, expands all inputs by 100 percent) and the total output of the car more than doubles (rising by, for example, 150 percent), the manufacturer enjoys increasing returns to scale. Virtually all businesses experience increasing returns to scale over the initial range of output. There are three basic causes: division of labour, specialized capital, and specialized management.

DIVISION OF LABOUR

As Adam Smith illustrated with the pin-making factory over two centuries ago, increases in the scale of production and worker specialization can go hand in hand. Performing fewer tasks allows workers to become more efficient at their jobs. As a result, Smith concluded, quantities of output tend to rise more quickly than the number of workers producing them. The impact of the division of labour is just as prevalent today in labour-intensive production. For example, if a very small restaurant where workers do everything expands, then workers can begin to specialize in either food preparation or service, thus making both sets of workers more efficient in the tasks they do.

SPECIALIZED CAPITAL

In most manufacturing industries, a greater scale of production is associated with the use of specialized machinery. If a car manufacturer raises the quantity of all its inputs, for example, capital equipment can have more specialized functions so that it performs fewer tasks more efficiently than before.

SPECIALIZED MANAGEMENT

The same principle that underlies the division of labour applies to management. When the scale of production is small, there are few managers. Each is forced to deal with a wide range of duties, some of which they are better at performing than others. An accounting expert may need to devise a marketing strategy, or a production manager may have to deal with personnel problems. Along with an enlarged scale of production, more managers are hired, with each assigned to the area in which he or she has the most expertise.

Constant Returns to Scale

constant returns to scale: a situation in which a percentage increase in all inputs results in an equal percentage increase in output

In contrast to increasing returns to scale, in the case of **constant returns to scale**, a business that expands inputs by a given percentage will see output rise by the same percentage. This may be the case for the artisan making pottery; doubling her input also doubles her output. Constant returns to scale usually result when making more of an item requires repeating exactly the same tasks used to produce previous units of output.

Decreasing Returns to Scale

decreasing returns to scale: a situation in which a percentage increase in all inputs causes a smaller percentage increase in output

The last possible case is **decreasing returns to scale**, or diseconomies of scale, in which a business that expands inputs to a product's production by a certain percentage sees output rise by a smaller percentage. For example, a 100 percent expansion in all inputs used by a copy shop may lead to its output rising by only 75 percent. There are two major reasons for decreasing returns to scale: management difficulties and limited natural resources.

MANAGEMENT DIFFICULTIES

Continual expansion in the scale of production will eventually make a business so cumbersome to administer that managers will face problems in co-ordinating operations to ensure efficient production. Virtually all businesses reach an output level above which management difficulties cause decreasing returns to scale to become dominant.

LIMITED NATURAL RESOURCES

In primary industries, such as fishing or forestry, a business may be able to acquire only a limited supply of easily available natural resources, even in the long run. In this case, an output level is reached above which further increases in all inputs lead to a smaller rise in output, resulting in decreasing returns to scale.

Returns to Scale and Long-Run Costs

The concept of returns to scale is useful in analyzing the effect on a business's costs when inputs that are fixed in the short run become variable. Figure 4.8 shows the case of a magazine publishing company that expands its printing plant three times and faces a different short-run average cost curve for each plant size. With each expansion of the plant, the curve shifts to the right, demonstrating the effects of the increased output.

When the plant is first expanded, the short-run average cost curve falls from AC_1 to AC_2. This shift results from increasing returns to scale. Recall that average cost is found by dividing total cost by the quantity of output. With increasing returns to scale, output rises more rapidly than the total cost of inputs so that average cost falls as the scale of production expands.

With the second plant expansion, the shift of the short-run average cost curve (from AC_2 to AC_3) reflects constant returns to scale. Output and the total costs of inputs rise at the same rate when the plant is expanded this second time, so the average cost curve moves horizontally as the output of magazines rises.

Figure 4.8	Long-Run Average Costs

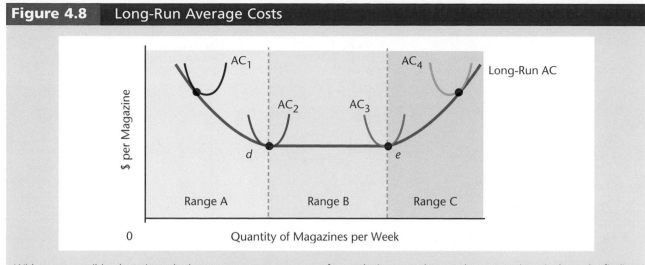

With many possible plant sizes, the long-run average cost curve for producing a product, such as magazines, is drawn by finding the lowest possible short-run average cost at every quantity, which results in a single point being included from each short-run curve. The long-run AC curve has three ranges. Range A has a negative slope, reflecting increasing returns to scale. Range B is horizontal, indicating the constant returns to scale. Range C has a positive slope, showing decreasing returns to scale.

With the final plant expansion, the company's short-run average cost curve not only shifts to the right but also rises (from AC_3 to AC_4). This shift reflects decreasing returns to scale. Since the printing plant's output is rising less rapidly than the total cost of input costs, the average cost curve rises as the production of magazines continues to increase.

Long-Run Average Cost

long-run average cost:
the minimum short-run average cost at each possible level of output

A business's **long-run average cost** in producing a certain product is the lowest short-run average cost curve at each possible level of output. Figure 4.8 shows that the long-run average cost curve is made up of points from the lowest short-run average cost curve at each output level. Given a wide range of possible plant sizes, the long-run AC curve is smooth and saucer-shaped, with only one point represented from each short-run curve. As depicted in Figure 4.8, long-run average cost falls in the initial output Range A because of increasing returns to scale, remains the same in Range B due to constant returns to scale, and rises in Range C because of decreasing returns to scale.

Industry Differences

While virtually all businesses face a saucer-shaped long-run average cost curve, these curves are not necessarily symmetrical for all industries. Often, in an industry, one range (or portion of the curve) will dominate the long-run average cost. Figure 4.9 illustrates long-run average cost curves characteristic of manufacturing industries, craft industries, and primary industries.

MANUFACTURING INDUSTRIES

Manufacturing industries tend to exhibit an extended range of increasing returns to scale due to the degree to which specialization is possible in the use of both labour and capital. This is particularly true of companies in which assembly-line techniques are used. It is not until output is very large that the conditions leading to constant returns

Figure 4.9   Possible Long-Run Average Cost Curves

On the left graph, the long-run AC curve's negative slope dominates, illustrating a wide range of increasing returns to scale, as usually occurs in assembly-line manufacturing. The middle graph shows the long-run AC curve when the horizontal range of constant returns to scale dominates, which is characteristic of craft industries. On the right graph, the positive slope dominates, illustrating the range of decreasing returns to scale, as is common in primary industries.

to scale and decreasing returns to scale become relevant. The long-run average cost curve faced by businesses in most manufacturing industries is shown in Figure 4.9, on the left. In this case, the curve falls over a wide range of output levels before briefly levelling out and then rising.

CRAFT INDUSTRIES

In contrast, craft industries are dominated by constant returns to scale. Because raising output levels of crafts tends to depend on repeating exactly the method of production, an increase in input usually results in an equal increase in output. Hence, except at very low or very high levels of output, the long-run average cost curves for producers of such items as handmade pottery are horizontal, as in the middle graph of Figure 4.9.

PRIMARY INDUSTRIES

Decreasing returns to scale, meanwhile, are most prevalent for businesses in primary industries, as in some types of fishing, where the limits of resource supplies

THINKING ABOUT ECONOMICS

How is technological change affecting returns to scale?

Computers and robotics are making machines "smarter" and more flexible, which means less need for complicated assembly lines and specialized equipment in many manufacturing industries. In these industries, the range of increasing returns to scale ends at comparatively low quantities of output so that businesses can customize their products in small batches—an option that was not available in the past.

http://www.appaut.com
http://www.roboticsworld.com

Question
Do manufacturing businesses that use customized production methods need to be as large as those employing traditional assembly lines?

are particularly acute. In this case, the slope of the long-run average cost curve becomes positive at a relatively low level of output, as shown in Figure 4.9, on the right.

Business Size and Returns to Scale

The predominance of increasing returns to scale in an industry raises the chances that businesses in the industry are large. Because of their lower long-run average costs, big companies have a competitive advantage over smaller rivals. It is increasing returns to scale, for example, that explains the gigantic size of most companies in the automobile industry. In contrast, smaller companies tend to prevail in industries characterized by constant or decreasing returns to scale because there is no cost disadvantage associated with low output levels.

Brief Review

1. When, in the long run, all inputs can be varied, there are three possible results for a business: increasing, constant, and decreasing returns to scale.

2. Increasing returns to scale exist when a given percentage change in inputs causes an even greater percentage change in output. Division of labour, specialized capital, and specialized management are the major causes.

3. Constant returns to scale exist when a given percentage change in inputs causes an equal percentage change in output. When production of any additional product depends on repeating exactly the tasks used to produce the previous product, constant returns prevail.

4. Decreasing returns to scale exist when a given percentage change in inputs causes a lower percentage change in output. Management difficulties and limited natural resources are the major causes.

5. The long-run average cost curve is saucer-shaped, reflecting ranges first of increasing, then constant, and finally decreasing returns to scale.

6. In general, increasing returns to scale dominate in manufacturing industries, constant returns to scale dominate in craft industries, and decreasing returns to scale dominate in primary industries.

4.4 Practice Questions

A business whose only inputs are labour and capital expands its long-run employment level from 6 to 9 workers and its capital from 2 to 3 machines. Assuming that the daily wage is $100 and the daily upkeep (including wear and tear) of each machine is $20, identify the relevant returns to scale and the change in long-run average cost if daily output were to expand in each of the following possible ways:

a. from 120 to 240 units
b. from 120 to 180 units
c. from 120 to 160 units

LAST**WORD**

In this chapter, we have seen how the view of cost in economics differs from that in accounting. This is because economists emphasize productive efficiency, while also recognizing the subjective implicit costs that accountants ignore. The chapter has examined how economic costs for any business fit a set pattern in the short run, due to the law of diminishing marginal returns and its effect on both marginal product and marginal cost. In the long run, a different pattern emerges, based on the variability of all inputs and the three possible returns to scale. In the next two chapters, we will turn our attention from production to the selling side of business activity and see how the revenue conditions that exist in various markets can be combined with the cost concepts outlined in this chapter to determine how businesses maximize economic profit.

Key Concepts

accounting profit 87
average cost 94
average fixed cost 94
average product 88
average variable cost 94
business 85
capital-intensive process 85
constant returns to scale 98
decreasing returns to scale 98
economic costs 87

economic profit 87
explicit costs 86
fixed costs 92
fixed inputs 88
implicit costs 86
increasing returns to scale 97
inputs 85
labour-intensive process 85
law of diminishing marginal returns 90

long-run average cost 99
marginal cost 92
marginal product 89
normal profit 86
output 85
production 85
productive efficiency 85
total cost 92
total product 88
variable costs 92
variable inputs 88

Questions

1. Which production process shown in Figure 4.1 maximizes productive efficiency for Pure 'n' Simple T-Shirts in the following cases? If your answers differ from the case in the text, explain why.
   a. The daily cost of a worker is $20, and the daily cost of a sewing machine is $25.
   b. The daily cost of a worker is $100, and the daily cost of a sewing machine is $150.

2. Rodriguez operates a variety store that provides an annual revenue of $480 000. Each year, he pays $25 000 in rent for the store, $15 000 in business taxes, and $350 000 on products to sell. He estimates he could put the $80 000 he has invested in the store into his friend's restaurant business instead and earn an annual 20 percent profit on his funds. He also estimates that he and his family could earn a total annual wage of $90 000 if they worked somewhere other than the store.
   a. Calculate the total explicit costs and total implicit costs of running the variety store.
   b. What is the accounting profit of the variety store?
   c. What is the economic profit?
   d. In what way is economic profit superior to accounting profit as an indicator of the overall performance of this business? Given the advantages of economic profit as a performance indicator, explain why the concept of economic profit is not often used in accounting.
   e. Should Rodriguez consider closing down this business? Why?

3.   Identify each of the following short-run costs as either variable or fixed:
   a. Depreciation charges for a construction firm
   b. Employee health benefits for an automobile-parts manufacturer
   c. Lumber costs for a pulp-and-paper producer
   d. Property insurance for a restaurant
   e. Gasoline bills for a taxi company

4.   Daily production for Pot-Works, a flowerpot maker, varies with the number of workers employed, as shown in the table below.

Short-Run Production for Pot-Works

(1) Labour	(2) Total Product (pots per day)	(3) Marginal Product (pots per day)	(4) Average Product (pots per day)
0	0		
1	100	—	—
2	280	—	—
3	510	—	—
4	560	—	—
5	540	—	—

   a. Copy and complete the table.
   b. On one graph, draw the total product curve. On another graph, draw the marginal product and average product curves. Explain the relationships between these curves.
   c. On your graphs, identify the ranges where marginal product rises, where marginal product falls and is positive, and where marginal product is negative.

5.   The short-run costs for a parking lot are shown in the table below.

Short-Run Costs for a Parking Lot

(1) Labour (workers employed)	(2) Total Product (cars parked per day)	(3) Marginal Product (cars parked per day)	(4) Fixed Costs	(5) Variable Costs	(6) Total Cost	(7) Marginal Cost	(8) Average Fixed Cost	(9) Average Variable Cost	(10) Average Cost
0	0		$60	$ 0	$___				
1	120	—	60	180	___	$___	$___	$___	$___
2	280	—	60	360	___	—	—	—	—
3	410	—	60	540	___	—	—	—	—
4	520	—	60	720	___	—	—	—	—
5	580	—	60	900	___	—	—	—	—

   a. Copy and complete the table.
   b. At which employment level does marginal product begin to fall? How is this point related to the behaviour of marginal cost in column 7?
   c. On one graph, draw the marginal product curve for this business. On another graph, draw the curves for marginal cost, average variable cost, and average cost.
   d. Using your graph of the business's cost curves, identify the output at which average variable cost and marginal cost have the same value. At what output do average cost and marginal cost have the same value?

6. For the following industries, state whether the long-run average cost curve has an extended range with a negative slope, a positive slope, or a zero slope. In each case, explain how your answer relates to returns to scale.
   a. Handcrafted pottery
   b. Consumer electronics
   c. High-quality wine

7. (Advanced Question)
   Pot-Works, the flowerpot maker in question 4, has $500 in daily fixed costs and a single variable input (labour), with each worker paid a daily wage of $120.

Short-Run Costs for Pot-Works

(1) Labour (workers employed)	(2) Total Product (flowerpots per day)	(3) Fixed Costs	(4) Variable Costs	(5) Total Cost	(6) Marginal Cost
0	0	$___	$___	$___	
1	100	___	___	___	$___
2	280	___	___	___	___
3	510	___	___	___	___
4	560	___	___	___	___

   a. Copy and complete the above table.
   b. On one graph, draw the fixed cost, variable cost, and total cost curves for this business. On another graph, draw this business's marginal cost curve.
   c. Outline the relationship between variable cost, total cost, and marginal cost as this business's output increases.
   d. Referring to the graph accompanying your answer to question 4 above, explain how variable cost and total cost for this business illustrate the law of diminishing marginal returns.

8. If the daily wage paid by Pure 'n' Simple T-Shirts is $100 per worker, while the cost of materials is $0.50 per T-shirt, explain how the values for variable cost are calculated in column 5 of Figure 4.5.

9. (Policy Discussion Question)
   Governments can play a role in promoting knowledge-based industries in which fixed costs are high and marginal costs are close to zero. How?

Internet Application Questions

http://www.statcan.ca

1. Access Statistics Canada's web site (at http://www.statcan.ca). Then use the links to "Canadian Statistics" to find the percentage of Canada's workforce employed in the service-producing sector. Your calculations should be based on the most recent annual statistics available.

2. Use the same source of online information to find the comparable percentage of Canada's workforce employed in the good-producing sector. What percentage of Canada's workforce is employed in primary industries? What percentage is employed in the secondary sector (including utilities and construction)?

CRITIC OF THE MODERN CORPORATION

John Kenneth Galbraith and the Role of Management

Galbraith and His Influence

John Kenneth Galbraith has been one of Canada's most notable intellectual exports. Born in 1908 near Port Talbot, Ontario, he studied agricultural economics at what is now the University of Guelph. He then emigrated to the United States, where, as a professor at Harvard University, he became one of the most widely known economists in the latter half of the twentieth century.

A prolific writer, Galbraith caused considerable debate in the 1960s and 1970s about the role of the modern corporation. He popularized the view that corporate managers possess the real decision-making power in modern capitalist economies. These managers, according to Galbraith, are more interested in their own prestige and income than they are in making profit.

John Kenneth Galbraith
Source: ©Bettmann/CORBIS/Magma

Financing Corporate Activity

To follow Galbraith's argument, we must first consider how corporations finance their operations. Unlike other types of businesses, corporations have a legal status independent of their owners, who have the advantage of limited liability, which means they can lose only what they put into the business. Corporations can acquire funds by issuing stocks and bonds.

Stocks   Corporations sell stocks (also known as shares) through the stock market to buyers, who are known as shareholders. Stockbrokers act as go-betweens in this market, buying and selling stocks on behalf of their customers. People who purchase stocks of a certain corporation do so because they expect to receive dividends, which are periodic payments by the corporation to its shareholders. Shareholders may also expect the price, or resale value, of a company's stock to increase as its profit outlook improves. However, there are no guarantees to shareholders—the company may not perform as expected, and dividends may not be declared (corporations are not required to pay dividends). Also, changing conditions in the stock market can cause price fluctuations for a wide range of stocks.

Bonds   Corporations can also raise funds by selling bonds. A bond is a type of loan that is governed by a formal contract, which sets out when the borrower will provide interest payments and also when the original amount of the loan (known as the principal) will be paid back to the bondholder. Bonds differ from other loan contracts in that they can be bought and sold. If the bondholder wishes to convert a bond into cash, he or she does not return the bond to the borrower but sells it to an interested buyer. Unlike shareholders, bondholders are considered to be lenders to the corporation, rather than its owners. Unless a corporation becomes insolvent, bondholders have no say in the company's operations.

Separation of Ownership and Control

According to Galbraith, the ways that corporations raise funds can cause a separation of ownership and control. Most large corporations have no single shareholder owning a significant portion of the shares but are owned and managed by different groups. On the one hand, the owners are the corporation's shareholders, who receive income through dividends and higher stock prices. On the other hand, the corporation's managers are, strictly speaking, employees. The interests of these two groups, according to Galbraith, do not coincide. A corporation's managers may be more interested in maximizing the company's sales revenue rather than its profit, since as the corporation expands, so will the managers' salaries and power in the organization. Managers may also siphon off profit by providing themselves with generous perks and rewards. While such actions go against shareholder interests, managers do not have to fear reprisals as long as the stake of each shareholder in the company is small enough to rule out a costly examination of management actions.

Relevance for Today

Galbraith's outlook has been influential with the general public and with some economists, although others downplay its relevance. His critics suggest that recent developments in stock markets have tended to increase the power of shareholders over management. Since the 1980s, much attention has been focused on the frequency of corporate takeovers, in which one company buys a sufficiently large portion of another company's shares to control its operations. Corporate takeovers can either be friendly or hostile, depending on how those taking over a company view its current managers. When a takeover is hostile, managers are often turfed out, especially if they have been looking after their own interests rather than maximizing the company's profit. According to Galbraith's critics, the ever-present threat of a hostile takeover helps to ensure that managers act in the shareholders' interests. Critics also cite the growing clout of investment funds, whose administrators often own significant portions of even a large corporation's shares, giving them control over the behaviour of the corporation's managers. In the United States, for example, pension funds and other large institutions own about half the shares of big companies, a rise from just 16 percent in 1965.

1. Outline the advantages and disadvantages of (a) stocks, and (b) bonds, both to corporations and to individual wealthholders.

2. What attributes make a corporation a likely object for a hostile takeover bid? Explain what makes these attributes significant.

CHAPTER 5

Perfect Competition

Under perfect competition, the business dodoes, dinosaurs, and great ground sloths are in for a bad time—as they should be.

—R.H. Bork and W.S. Bowman Jr., American legal scholars

How do the operations of a giant company like Bell Canada differ from those of a small-town restaurant or a single broccoli-farmer? From an economist's perspective, the main distinction is the type of market in which each producer does business. In this chapter, we will introduce the four market structures—perfect competition, monopolistic competition, oligopoly, and monopoly. We will then focus on the first of these structures, perfect competition. We will see that though perfect competition is not the most common market structure, it is an ideal against which all other markets are compared.

LEARNING OBJECTIVES

In this chapter, you will:

1 consider the four market structures and the main differences among them

2 learn about the profit-maximizing output rule and how perfectly competitors use it in the short run

3 examine how perfect competitive markets adjust in the long run and the benefits they provide to consumers

5.1 Market Structures

LO 5.1

perfect competition: a market structure characterized by many buyers and sellers of a standard product and easy entry to and exit from the industry

While product markets come in all shapes and sizes, each has one of four structures: perfect competition, monopolistic competition, oligopoly, or monopoly. The number of businesses involved in the market, whether or not a standard product is being sold, and the ease with which businesses can enter and exit the industry, all determine the market structure.

Perfect Competition

The ideal form of competition, which we will focus on in this chapter, allows for the unobstructed operation of demand and supply forces. **Perfect competition** has three main characteristics: many buyers and sellers, a standard product, and easy entry to and exit from the industry. In a perfectly competitive market, businesses consider the price of the product they sell to be determined by the forces of demand and supply. While common in primary industries, such as agriculture, and in markets for financial assets, such as stocks, bonds, and foreign currencies, perfectly competitive markets are not common in most other sectors of the economy.

MANY BUYERS AND SELLERS

The most important feature of perfectly competitive industries is that there are large numbers of buyers and sellers. For example, in the Canadian broccoli market, there are many consumers and many farmers. As a result, no single participant is large enough to affect the prevailing price in the industry.

STANDARD PRODUCT

In a perfectly competitive market, each business supplies a product that is indistinguishable from that of other businesses. One farmer's crop of broccoli, for example, is not noticeably different from that same variety of broccoli produced by other farmers.

EASY ENTRY AND EXIT

Finally, for a market to be perfectly competitive, businesses must be free to enter or exit the industry. Compared with most other industries, for example, it is relatively easy for farmers to transfer resources from the production of other crops to the growing of broccoli, since agricultural land has a wide variety of uses. Similarly, farmers can leave the broccoli market with little difficulty by devoting resources to alternative agricultural uses.

Monopolistic Competition

monopolistic competition: a market structure characterized by many buyers and sellers of slightly different products and easy entry to and exit from the industry

Monopolistic competition is the structure most prevalent in the service sector and applies, for example, to the restaurant industry. This market structure is characterized by a large number of businesses (though not as many as in a perfectly competitive industry), perceptible differences among the products of competitors, and easy entry and exit of businesses. Product differences can be related to location, quality, or the image consumers have of each business's product.

Oligopoly

oligopoly: a market structure characterized by only a few businesses offering standard or similar products and restricted entry to the industry

An **oligopoly** is a market in which there are only a few businesses, and entry to the industry is restricted. Oligopolies are extremely common in the Canadian economy, as illustrated by the steel, automobile, and insurance industries. The products sold in oligopolies may or may not vary, depending on the particular market. For example, in the steel industry, a standard product is produced, whereas the automobile and insurance industries offer some variety among their products.

Monopoly

monopoly: a market structure characterized by only one business supplying a product with no close substitutes and restricted entry to the industry

A **monopoly** is an industry in which a single business supplies a product with no close substitutes. This market structure is the exact opposite of perfect competition. Monopolies are relatively common in the Canadian economy. Cable TV companies, for example, often have a monopoly in particular regions of the country, and notable Canadian monopolies include Canada Post and Via Rail. Monopoly companies are not always large; small companies, such as a caterer with exclusive rights to sell food at a certain sports stadium, can be monopolies as well.

Entry Barriers

entry barriers: economic or institutional obstacles to businesses entering an industry

Markets that are oligopolies and monopolies require entry barriers to continue as such. **Entry barriers** are economic or institutional obstacles that stop potential competitors from setting up in an industry where economic profits are being made. There are six main entry barriers: increasing returns to scale, market experience, restricted ownership of resources, legal obstacles, market abuses, and advertising.

INCREASING RETURNS TO SCALE

In industries where established companies benefit from increasing returns to scale, and therefore decreasing average costs when output increases in the long run, small companies just entering the market will be unable to charge as low a price.

natural monopoly: a market in which only one business is economically viable because of increasing returns to scale

This is because small companies find it difficult to raise sufficient funds to take full advantage of increasing returns to scale. Such obstacles arise because financial investments are often irreversible, increasing the risks associated with entering an industry. In the extreme case, known as a **natural monopoly**, increasing returns to scale mean that it makes sense to have only one supplier of a product, given the size of the market. This applies to public utilities, which provide such products as water and such services as public transit. Having more than one company would require a large-scale duplication of inputs, thus leading to high per-unit costs and product prices.

While the concept is applicable to some markets, the term "natural monopoly" can be misleading, since there is nothing "natural" about this concept. For example, the telephone industry was once considered a natural monopoly, until recent technological innovations—such as cellular phones and Internet phone services—made it possible to have competition. Similarly, cable TV companies that were once regional monopolies are gradually losing this status because of new forms of satellite delivery.

MARKET EXPERIENCE

Even in cases where increasing returns to scale are not predominant, well-established businesses may have a cost advantage over potential rivals, simply because of their experience. A business can learn from experience how to supply a product more efficiently, thus decreasing its per-unit costs at all possible output levels.

RESTRICTED OWNERSHIP OF RESOURCES

When one or a few businesses control supplies of a resource to make a product, they effectively bar other businesses from entering the industry. One example of such control has been the South African company De Beers, which until recently owned or controlled over 75 percent of the world's supply of diamonds.

LEGAL OBSTACLES

Legislation regarding, for example, patents or licences can act as a barrier to entry. A patent gives the exclusive right to produce, use, or sell an invention for a given period (now 20 years in Canada). This exclusive right allows individuals and companies to reap some rewards of their innovations. Companies can become monopolies with patented products, as did the patent-holder for the artificial sweetener aspartame, known as Nutrasweet. Government licensing, too, can create closed or regulated markets. For instance, only Canada Post has the legal right to provide regular mail service, making it a monopoly in this industry. Similarly, only a certain number of Canadian television or radio stations have broadcast rights within different regions of the country, thus making these broadcasting industries oligopolies.

MARKET ABUSES

predatory pricing: an unfair business practice of temporarily lowering prices to drive out competitors in an industry

Established businesses in an industry may use unfair practices to maintain their dominant positions. A business might, for example, temporarily drop the price of its product below average cost to drive a new competitor out of business. This illegal strategy is known as **predatory pricing**. At one time, predatory pricing was used in the international airline industry; some large companies would cut fares only to increase them once upstart competitors had gone into bankruptcy. Canada's own dominant airline, Air Canada, has also been accused of predatory pricing against some of its small competitors in the domestic market for air travel.

ADVERTISING

The use of advertising as an entry barrier is most common in oligopolies, such as the beer and soft-drink industries. Because consumer preference for these products is so dependent on promotion, established companies with large advertising budgets can often stop small competitors from gaining a significant toehold in these markets. For example, Canada's two largest beer companies, Molson Breweries and John Labatt Ltd.,

THINKING ABOUT ECONOMICS

Do "new economy" industries exhibit entry barriers?

Some important markets in the new economy are oligopolies or even monopolies, which suggests the existence of entry barriers. These barriers can take distinctive forms. For example, the network effect refers to the fact that some information products (for example, software and telecommunications services) become more valuable when they are used by many people. Similarly, the lock-in effect refers to the reluctance consumers have buying a new information product (such as a particular brand of software) once they have already invested the time in learning a similar program. In new economy industries, these new types of entry barriers often appear alongside more traditional barriers, such as increasing returns to scale.

http://www.liberate.com
http://www.ctca.ca/

Question
What are some examples of new economy industries in which network and lock-in effects have helped create oligopolies or monopolies?

use advertising to help them maintain their sales, which represent almost 90 percent of total quantity demanded in the Canadian beer market.

Market Power

Businesses in perfectly competitive markets—or perfect competitors, as they may be called—are price-takers because they are forced to take the price for their product that is set by the market forces of demand and supply. In contrast, businesses in the remaining three types of markets have some influence over a product's price, so they are price-makers. In other words, these businesses have some measure of **market power**, or the ability to affect the price they charge. A business's market power depends on how easy it is for buyers to find substitutes for the business's output.

market power: a business's ability to affect the price of the product it sells

As a rule, a business in a monopoly (a monopolist) has the most market power. It deals with no competitors and has the largest possible size in relation to the industry. Because the monopolist sells a product with no close substitutes, the product's demand curve tends to be less elastic than for other products. A company in an oligopoly (an oligopolist) commonly has substantial market power because of the small number of competitors and the company's large size relative to the industry. A business in a monopolistically competitive market (a monopolistic competitor) has less market power because it faces many competitors and is small in relation to its market. Moreover, because it sells a product with close substitutes, its demand curve is relatively elastic. Finally, a perfect competitor has no market power because of its role as a price-taker. These attributes of different market structures are summarized in Figure 5.1.

One way businesses sometimes use market power is by charging different prices to various consumers. For example, a municipal bus company may offer a discount to students rather than have them not riding the bus at all; a restaurant owner may lower the price of a meal for a lunch special and keep it high for dinner; or an airline will charge lower fares to tourists than to business travellers. This practice, known as "price discrimination," can be used to increase profits by any business with market power, as long

Figure 5.1	Attributes of Market Structures			
	Perfect Competition	**Monopolistic Competition**	**Oligopoly**	**Monopoly**
Number of Businesses	very many	many	few	one
Type of Product	standard	differentiated	standard or differentiated	not applicable
Entry and Exit of New Businesses	very easy	fairly easy	difficult	very difficult
Market Power	none	some	some	great
Example	farming	restaurants	automobile manufacturing	public utilities

While perfect competitors have no market power, due to the large number of businesses selling a standard product, a monopolist has a great deal of market power because it is the only seller of a product with few substitutes. Monopolistic competitors have some market power, due to the differentiated products they sell, and oligopolists have even more, depending on how few the number of businesses in a particular industry.

as the business can stop customers who pay different prices from exchanging the products between themselves, and the business can distinguish between buyers willing to pay high and low prices by using a condition, such as the consumer's age or the time of day when the product is consumed.

Brief Review

1. Product markets have one of four structures: perfect competition, monopolistic competition, oligopoly, or monopoly.

2. Market structure is determined by the number of buyers and sellers in the market, whether or not a standard product is being sold, and the ease with which businesses can enter or exit the market.

3. In monopolies and oligopolies, potential competitors face the entry barriers of increasing returns to scale, market experience, restricted ownership of resources, legal obstacles, market abuses, and advertising.

4. A business's market power, or ability to be a price-maker, tends to be greater for monopolists than for oligopolists and greater for oligopolists than for monopolistic competitors. Perfect competitors possess no market power.

5.1 Practice Questions

1. Identify the market structure in which each of the following sellers operates. Briefly explain each of your answers.
   a. a café in a busy commercial district of a city
   b. a public transit company in a large metropolitan area
   c. a corporation that makes a popular brand of women's perfume
   d. an individual share-owner who sells 100 shares of Bell Canada on the Toronto Stock Exchange

2. A fisherman sells salmon in a perfectly competitive market and faces a price of $5 per kg at possible weekly outputs of 3000 and 4000 kgs.
   a. Identify the fisherman's marginal revenue in this output range.
   b. Explain how the relationship between price and marginal revenue is affected by the fact that this fisherman operates in a perfectly competitive market.
   c. Using EconGraphKit (at http://www.mcgrawhill.ca/college/lovewell), draw the fisherman's marginal revenue curve. Does it have the shape you expect? Explain.

5.2 Perfect Competition in the Short Run

How do businesses make operating decisions? They do so by comparing a range of potential revenues and costs. All businesses—whether they are perfect competitors, monopolistic competitors, oligopolists, or monopolists, and whatever their product—use the same general methods in pursuing maximum profit. However, each business must apply the methods differently, according to the market structure in which it operates. To examine profit-maximizing decisions and actions, we will look first at a perfect competitor in the short run.

Business's Demand Curve

business's demand curve: the demand curve faced by an individual business, as opposed to an entire market

Because a perfect competitor is a price-taker, it must accept the price dictated by the market forces of demand and supply. Thus, the individual **business's demand curve** is different from the market demand curve. Recall that the market demand curve (D_m) has a negative slope, given that price and quantity demanded are inversely related. Because a perfect competitor is one of many businesses in a market, the quantity it chooses to supply has no effect on equilibrium price and quantity in the market. See the graph for the T-shirt market in Figure 5.2. On the left, the intersection of the market demand and supply curves, $(D_m$ and $S_m)$ provides the equilibrium price of $6 per T-shirt. No matter how many shirts Pure 'n' Simple T-Shirts supplies, it will sell all it produces at a price of $6 per shirt. Thus, the individual business's demand curve (D_b) is horizontal, or perfectly elastic, at a price of $6 as shown on the right in Figure 5.2.

Revenue Conditions

On the basis of the horizontal demand curve the business faces, the perfect competitor's total revenue (TR), or the overall earnings from selling a product, is calculated by multiplying the product's price by each potential quantity of output (q). For example, if Pure 'n' Simple T-Shirts sells 250 shirts at a price of $6, then its total revenue is $1500 ($6 × 250). In addition to total revenue, the perfect competitor can examine two other revenue concepts to help make operating decisions: average revenue and marginal revenue.

AVERAGE REVENUE

average revenue: a business's total revenue per unit of output

Average revenue (AR) is the business's total revenue per unit of output (q). When Pure 'n' Simple T-Shirts sells 250 shirts and its total revenue is $1500, its average revenue equals $6 per unit of the product:

$$\text{Average revenue (AR)} = \frac{\text{total revenue (TR)}}{\text{quantity of output (q)}}$$

$$\$6 \text{ per shirt} = \frac{\$1500}{250 \text{ shirts}}$$

Figure 5.2   Demand Faced by a Perfect Competitor

Equilibrium occurs where the market demand and supply curves, $(D_m$ and $S_m)$ meet as shown on the graph on the left. The equilibrium price ($6) sets the position of the business's demand curve (D_b) on the graph on the right.

Note that average revenue for Pure 'n' Simple T-Shirts equals each shirt's $6 price. For all businesses, regardless of the market structure in which they operate, price will equal average revenue. This is because price can be defined in the same way as average revenue—as the business's total revenue per unit of output. The only exception to this rule occurs when a business practises price discrimination (or charges different prices to different customers for exactly the same product).

MARGINAL REVENUE

marginal revenue: the extra total revenue earned from an additional unit of output

Marginal revenue is the extra total revenue (ΔTR) earned when the business sells another unit of output (Δq). For example, if Pure 'n' Simple T-Shirts has an increase in total revenue from $1500 to $1620 when it increases its output from 250 to 270 shirts, then the marginal revenue of each of these last 20 shirts is $6:

$$\text{Marginal revenue (MR)} = \frac{\Delta \text{TR}}{\Delta q}$$

$$\$6 \text{ per shirt} = \frac{\$120}{20 \text{ shirts}}$$

Relationship between Revenue Conditions and Demand

As the case of Pure 'n' Simple T-Shirts illustrates, average and marginal revenues are always equal for a perfectly competitive business. This follows from the fact that average revenue (or price) is constant at each possible quantity of output. Recall that when an average value, such as average revenue, is constant, it equals its related marginal value—which, in this case, is marginal revenue.

Figure 5.3 illustrates the relationships among price, average revenue, and marginal revenue for our example of Pure 'n' Simple T-Shirts. In the table, the values for price (column 1), marginal revenue (column 4), and average revenue (column 5) are identical. The demand curve this perfect competitor faces also represents the business's average revenue and marginal revenue curves. Because the business is a price-taker, this combined curve shows a constant value at all quantities of output. Thus, for a perfectly competitive business:

$$\text{Price (P)} = \text{Average revenue (AR)} = \text{Marginal revenue (MR)}$$

Profit Maximization

profit-maximizing output rule: produce at the level of output where marginal revenue and marginal cost intersect

Regardless of the market it operates in, any business can maximize its profit by following a single **profit-maximizing output rule:** produce the quantity of output (q) at which marginal revenue and marginal cost intersect.

Profit-maximizing rule: Marginal revenue (MR) = Marginal cost (MC)

Of course, this may result in an awkward quantity, such as 5.73 units, in which case, the producer would choose the closest whole number, such as 6 units.

What happens if the condition MR = MC is not met? If each new unit of output is still providing more extra revenue to the business than it adds in cost, output should be increased in order to maximize profit. So, for example, if a business has a marginal revenue of $3 at its current output level, but the marginal cost of producing this unit is $2, the business is wise to increase its output. Recall that profit is the difference between total revenue and total cost. In this case, an additional unit of output is adding more revenue

Figure 5.3   Revenues for a Perfect Competitor

Revenue Schedules for Pure 'n' Simple T-Shirts

(1) Price (P) ($ per T-shirt)	(2) Quantity (q) (T-shirts per day)	(3) Total Revenue (TR) (P × q)	(4) Marginal Revenue (MR) (ΔTR/Δq)	(5) Average Revenue (AR) (TR/q)
$—	$ 0	$ 0		—
6	80	480	480/80 = $6	480/80 = $6
6	200	1200	720/120 = 6	1200/200 = 6
6	250	1500	300/50 = 6	1500/250 = 6
6	270	1620	120/20 = 6	1620/270 = 6
6	280	1680	60/10 = 6	1680/280 = 6

Revenue Curves for Pure 'n' Simple T-Shirts

The business's demand schedule is shown in columns 1 and 2 of the table, which also shows that the constant values of price (P), average revenue (AR), and marginal revenue (MR) are identical. On the graph, the business's horizontal demand curve (D_b) also represents its AR and MR curves.

($3) than it is costing ($2), so the profit added by this unit is $1. Profit-adding units such as these should be produced, no matter how small the contribution to profit. Once output is raised to the level at which marginal revenue and marginal cost are equal, any further increase in output would cause the business's profit to fall. So, for example, if a business produces beyond the output level at which marginal revenue and marginal cost are both $3, the business will soon find the marginal revenue of $3 surpassed by a marginal cost of $4. Hence, each additional unit is subtracting from profit, and output should be returned to the point at which marginal revenue and marginal cost are equal.

So, perfect competitors, like all other businesses, must determine their profit-maximizing output by looking at the business's cost and revenue figures. Pure 'n' Simple T-Shirts, for example, would examine the data in Figure 5.4 and ask: "At what output level does

THINKING ABOUT ECONOMICS

Does the profit-maximizing output rule also apply when a business is making a loss at all possible quantities of output?

Yes. In this case, the profit-maximizing output rule is used to determine the quantity at which the business makes the minimum possible loss. Since a loss is simply a negative profit, this means finding the output level with a negative profit that is closest to zero.

Question

If a loss-making business is choosing between two output levels that provide negative profits of –$100 and –$300, which output level minimizes its loss?

marginal revenue intersect with marginal cost?" If the marginal revenue and marginal cost figures are graphed, as shown, we can see that the profit-maximizing point occurs at point *a*. As the closest associated whole number is 270, Pure 'n' Simple T-Shirts should choose a quantity of 270 T-shirts. Note that, at this point, marginal cost is rising (i.e., upsloping). This condition is essential to make the intersection of the MR and MC curves a profit-maximizing point. If marginal cost were instead falling (i.e., downsloping), then the point would not be a desired one. Units of output to the left of such a point, when seen on a graph would provide a loss. Meanwhile the business would be sacrificing profitable units that could be gained by expanding output.

This point can be checked against the table in Figure 5.4. The figures for marginal revenue (column 3) and marginal cost (column 4) would pass through the same values nearest the output of 270 T-shirts (column 1). As can be seen in both the table and graph of Figure 5.4, the marginal cost of $5.50 falls short of the $6 marginal revenue between the output levels of 250 and 270 T-shirts. In contrast, between 270 and 280 T-shirts, marginal cost (now $10.50) is greater than the constant $6 marginal revenue. (Remember that marginal revenue and marginal cost are defined as changes that occur

---

Figure 5.4   Profit Maximization for a Perfect Competitor

Profit Maximization Table for Pure 'n' Simple T-Shirts

(1) Total Product (q)	(2) Price (P) (=AR)	(3) Marginal Revenue (MR)	(4) Marginal Cost (MC) ($\Delta TC/\Delta q$)	(5) Average Variable Cost (AVC) (VC/q)	(6) Average Cost (AC) (TC/q)	(7) Total Revenue (TR)	(8) Total Cost (TC)	(9) Total Profit (TR – TC)
0	$6					0	$ 825	– $825
80	6	$6	$1.75	$1.75	$12.06	$ 480	965	– 485
200	6	6	1.33	1.50	5.63	1200	1125	75
250	6	6	2.50	1.70	5.00	1500	1250	250
270	**6**	6	5.50	**1.98**	**5.04**	**1620**	**1360**	**260**
280	6	6	10.50	2.29	5.24	1680	1465	215

Profit Maximization Graph for Pure 'n' Simple T-Shirts

The quantity of output at which the business maximizes its short-run profit—or minimizes its short-run loss—is found using either a graph or a table. On the graph, the profit-maximizing output is found where the MR and MC curves intersect at point *a*. Total profit is the area of the shaded rectangle, the width of which is the profit-maximizing output (q) and the height of which is the average revenue (AR) minus average cost (AC) at points *a* and *b*. In the table, this profit-maximizing output occurs where marginal cost (MC) in column 4 passes through the same values as the constant marginal revenue (MR) in column 3. The answer can be verified by calculating total profit at every output level, as in column 9, and then finding the output level at which the highest positive (or lowest negative) profit is possible.

when moving from one output to another.) This means that marginal revenue and marginal cost cross closest to 270 T-shirts. To verify this result, a business's owners might calculate the total profit they would make at every possible quantity of output. The highest positive (or lowest negative) profit figure in this column corresponds to the profit-maximizing quantity. In the case of Pure 'n' Simple T-Shirts, the owner would subtract total cost (column 8) from total revenue (column 7), to get total profit (column 9). So, scanning column 9, it is clear that the best choice is again at 270 shirts, where total profit reaches its highest value of $260 ($1620 − 1360).

While the profit-maximizing point can be verified with the table, using a graph to find this point has a bonus: the graph immediately shows whether or not the business is earning an economic profit. When price (P) exceeds average cost (AC) at the profit-maximizing output, the business enjoys a short-run economic profit. If price is less than average cost, the business suffers a loss, or negative profit. If the business is at a profit-maximizing output where price and average cost are equal, the business is making no economic profit and is said to be at its **breakeven point**. Note, however, that at this point the business is still making a normal profit so that the owners are paid a sufficient amount to keep their funds and entrepreneurial skills tied up in the business.

breakeven point: the profit-maximizing output where price (or average revenue) equals average cost

Business's breakeven point: P = AC at the profit-maximizing output

Because the breakeven point is associated with a profit-maximizing output, this term has a special meaning in economics. Only at a single possible price will a business choose to break even. For a perfect competitor, this price equals minimum average cost. At higher prices, positive profits can be made, while at lower prices, the business can only make a loss.

Using a graph to show the profit-maximizing point has another bonus: with a graph, we can see immediately the relationship of a business's profit to its revenue and costs. The "revenue rectangle" has a height that is equal to price and a width that is equal to the quantity of output. The "cost rectangle" has a height that is equal to average cost and a width that is again equal to the quantity of output. The "profit rectangle" is the area of the revenue rectangle less the area of the cost rectangle. So, for example, in Figure 5.4 the marginal cost curve and marginal revenue curve for Pure 'n' Simple T-Shirts intersect at the profit-maximizing point. As we know from the table also, this point is closest to an output level of 270 shirts and a price of $6 per shirt. Thus, the company's revenue rectangle has an area of $1620 ($6 price × 270 quantity). The cost rectangle has an area of $1360 ($5.04 average cost × 270 quantity). The profit rectangle, then, is the shaded area of $260 profit ($1620 − $1360).

WHEN SHOULD A BUSINESS CLOSE?

Would Pure 'n' Simple T-Shirts remain in business if it were making a loss? In the short run, the business would likely continue to operate as long as it earned sufficient revenue to pay its variable costs. The remaining fixed costs would have to be paid in the short run, whether or not the company stayed in business. As long as a business's total revenue more than covers its variable costs, it is better off remaining in business rather than shutting down and still having to pay its fixed costs. If total revenue were to fall below variable costs, however, the business would not be able to fund even its day-to-day operations, and it would have no choice but to close down.

Recall that total revenue for a business is found by multiplying price by the quantity of output (TR = P × q). Recall also that the sum of variable costs (VC) and fixed costs (FC) equals total cost (TC), so that variable costs can be found by subtracting fixed costs from total cost at any given output level (VC = TC − FC), and average variable cost is variable costs divided by quantity (AVC = VC ÷ q). So that we may consider the question of whether or not a business should continue to operate, let us take a look at average variable cost in another way: variable costs equal average variable cost multiplied by quantity (VC = AVC × q). Now, we can establish a relationship between price and average variable cost by looking at the formula for total revenue (TR = P × q) and the formula for variable costs (VC = AVC × q). Recall that as long as variable costs do not exceed total revenue, the company should stay in business; if the variable costs begin to exceed total revenue, the company should shut down. Cancelling the quantity of output (q)—because it is a common element in both these expressions—means that total revenue exceeds variable costs as long as price is greater than average variable cost. Variable costs exceed total revenue when average variable cost exceeds price. At the profit-maximizing output where total revenue and variable costs (or average variable cost and price) are equal, the business reaches its **shutdown point**, which occurs at the point of minimum average variable cost:

shutdown point: the level of output where price (or average revenue) equals minimum average variable cost

$$
\begin{aligned}
\text{Business's shutdown point:} \quad TR &= VC \\
(P \times q) &= (AVC \times q) \\
P &= \text{minimum AVC}
\end{aligned}
$$

Why does the shutdown point occur where price equals the minimum point on the average variable cost curve? Because at this point the profit-maximizing output rule, MR = MC, is met at the same time as total revenue equals variable costs.

Let us consider our example of Pure 'n' Simple T-Shirts in Figure 5.5. When receiving a price of $6 per T-shirt (at point *a*), the company is maintaining a positive economic profit. If, for some reason, the price drops to $5, the business reaches its breakeven point (point *b*). At the lowest point on the average variable cost curve, at $1.50 (point *c*), average variable cost equals price, thus variable costs equal total revenue.

Pure 'n' Simple T-Shirts' shutdown point:

$$
\begin{aligned}
TR(\$300) &= VC(\$300) \\
P \times q\ (\$1.50 \times 200) &= AVC \times q\ (\$1.50 \times 200) \\
P(\$1.50) &= \text{minimum AVC}(\$1.50)
\end{aligned}
$$

Figure 5.5   Supply Curve for a Perfect Competitor

Supply Curve for Pure 'n' Simple T-Shirts

Supply Schedule for Pure 'n' Simple T-Shirts	
Price (P)	Quantity Supplied (q)
($ per T-shirt)	(T-shirts per day)
$6.00	270
5.00	250
1.50	200
1.40	0

At point *a* on the graph, price exceeds average cost (AC), and positive economic profits are made. Point *b* is the breakeven point, where price equals AC. At lower prices, the business makes a loss. Point *c* is the business's shutdown point, where price equals average variable costs (AVC). Below the shutdown point—for example, at point *d*—average variable costs would exceed price. The marginal cost curve (MC) above point *c* is the business's supply curve (S_b), the highlighted part of the curve.

Point *c* in Figure 5.5 is Pure 'n' Simple T-Shirts' shutdown point. If the price falls further, to a price such as $1.40 (point *d*), the company closes down its operations, since total revenue, which at 200 units of output would now be $280 ($1.40 × 200), no longer covers variable costs ($300).

BUSINESS'S SUPPLY CURVE

business's supply curve: a curve that shows the quantity of output supplied by a business at every possible price

Figure 5.5 also sheds light on how a change in price influences the operations of a perfectly competitive business. For example, if price falls from $6 to $5, the profit-maximizing output for Pure 'n' Simple T-Shirts changes from 270 to 250 shirts. At the same time, the business's economic profit falls to zero, since point *b* is the breakeven point. Notice that the effect of this price change on the business's quantity supplied is shown as a movement along the marginal cost curve (MC). Because the various profit-maximizing points for the business are all on the marginal cost curve, at least a portion of it represents the **business's supply curve** (S_b). The business's supply curve shows the quantity of output supplied by the business at every possible price. If price moves below the shutdown point (point *c*), Pure 'n' Simple T-Shirts will no longer be in business, and its output will fall to zero. Hence, only that part of the marginal cost curve above this point is the business's supply curve (the highlighted part of the MC curve).

MARKET SUPPLY CURVE

The market supply curve (S_m) for a perfectly competitive industry is created using the supply curves for all businesses in the market. So, for the T-shirt market in which Pure 'n' Simple T-Shirts operates, we have the supply curve S_m as illustrated in Figure 5.6. If there are 100 businesses all identical to Pure 'n' Simple T-Shirts in the industry, then the market supply curve for T-shirts is found by adding the profit-maximizing outputs

Figure 5.6   Supply Curves for a Perfectly Competitive Business and Market

Business and Market Supply Schedules for T-shirts

Price (P)	Quantity Supplied	
	(q) (S_b)	(Q) (S_m)
($ per T-shirt)	(T-shirts per day)	
$6.00	270 →	27 000
5.00	250 →	25 000
1.50	200 →	20 000

If the T-shirt industry is made up of 100 identical businesses, then the market supply curve (S_m) is found by multiplying each output level on Pure 'n' Simple T-Shirts' supply curve (S_b) by 100.

produced by all 100 businesses at each possible price. Thus, at a price of $6, the quantity supplied in the market (Q) would be 27 000 shirts (270 shirts × 100 businesses), given that each business's output is 270 shirts.

Brief Review

1. All businesses—whatever market structures they operate in—maximize profits by finding the output level at which marginal revenue intersects marginal cost.

2. At the profit-maximizing output, a business's economic profit is positive if price is greater than average cost. When price and average cost are equal at the profit-maximizing output, the business is at its breakeven point, with economic profit at zero. If price is lower than average cost, then the business is operating at a loss, with negative economic profit.

3. For a perfect competitor, the breakeven point occurs when price equals minimum average cost. At lower prices, a perfect competitor will continue in business until the shutdown point, where price equals minimum average variable cost. A perfectly competitive business's supply curve is only the portion of its marginal cost curve that is above the shutdown point.

4. The supply for the entire perfectly competitive market is found by adding the profit-maximizing outputs of all businesses in the market at each possible price.

5.2 Practice Questions

1. A salmon fisherman who faces a price of $5 per kg produces a weekly output of 4000 kgs. The fisherman's marginal cost is $4.95 between the possible outputs of 3900 and 4000 kgs and $5.05 between the possible outputs of 4000 and 4100 kgs.
   a. Is the fisherman producing at his profit-maximizing point?
   b. If the fisherman's average cost at an output of 4000 kgs is $6, then what is his total profit or loss?
   c. If the fisherman's average variable cost at 4000 kgs is $4, then should he stay in business in the short run?
   d. Using EconGraphKit (at http://www.mcgrawhill.ca/college/lovewell), draw the relevant ranges of the salmon fisherman's marginal revenue, marginal cost, average cost, and average variable cost curves.

2. The salmon fisherman discussed in question 1 has a breakeven point at a price of $5.50 and a weekly output of 5000 kgs.
   a. Is this point on the fisherman's supply curve?
   b. If price is below $5.50, is it possible for the fisherman to make a positive profit?
   c. If price is above $5.50, is it possible for the fisherman to choose a profit-maximizing point where he makes a loss?
   d. Is the fisherman's shutdown point at a price above or below $5.50?
   e. Using EconGraphKit (at http://www.mcgrawhill.ca/college/lovewell), add the relevant information to the graph you drew in question 1.

5.3 Perfect Competition in the Long Run

LO 5.3

In the long run, ease of entry into and exit from a perfectly competitive market becomes a crucial factor. Short-run profits and losses cause perfectly competitive markets to move towards a point of long-run equilibrium. Entrepreneurs enter industries where an economic profit can be expected and leave those industries where there are losses. Movement to and from the industry continues until all the businesses in the market reach long-run equilibrium, at which they are just breaking even, with price equalling average cost and a normal profit being made.

The operation of these long-run competitive forces is illustrated in Figure 5.7 for the T-shirt market. We will assume that this is a constant-cost industry, in which input prices are fixed regardless of the quantity of T-shirts produced. As a representative business in this industry, Pure 'n' Simple T-Shirts is originally in long-run equilibrium at a price of $5 (point a on the left), which is determined by the intersection of the market demand and supply curves (D_0 and S_0) at point c on the graph on the right. At this price, Pure 'n' Simple T-Shirts produces 250 shirts per day. Since price equals average cost, it is breaking even, or making zero economic profit. If the market demand for T-shirts increases from D_0 to D_1, the conditions of long-run equilibrium are temporarily broken. The new price in the market is $6, found at the intersection of D_1 and S_0 (point d). At this new price, Pure 'n' Simple T-Shirts makes a short-run economic profit, as shown on the graph on the left, since price (point b) exceeds average cost. This economic profit acts as a lure to new companies, who enter the industry and cause a shift in the market supply curve to the right, from S_0 to S_1. As a result, price returns to $5. With long-run equilibrium restored (point e), businesses in the market are again breaking even with a price equal to average cost, as exemplified by Pure 'n' Simple T-Shirts.

Figure 5.7   Long-Run Equilibrium for a Perfectly Competitive Business

Long-run equilibrium for a perfectly competitive business, such as Pure 'n' Simple T-Shirts, is shown on the left at point a, where price equals both marginal cost and minimum average cost. Associated with this point is the equilibrium point c for the entire market on the graph on the right. An increase in market demand for T-shirts from D_0 to D_1 shifts equilibrium to point d. At the new profit-maximizing point for the business (point b on the left graph), a positive profit is being made. The lure of economic profit causes new businesses to enter the market. Assuming that this is a constant-cost industry, the market supply curve shifts to the right, from S_0 to S_1, until price is driven back down to its original level at point e. On the left graph, Pure 'n' Simple T-Shirts returns to its long-run equilibrium point a because of these competitive forces.

5.4 Benefits of Perfect Competition

The long-run equilibrium shown in Figure 5.7 illustrates the advantages of perfectly competitive markets for buyers. It also helps explain Adam Smith's assertion that through the "invisible hand" of competition, the self-interest of producers ultimately benefits consumers. Because a perfectly competitive market in long-run equilibrium meets two requirements—known as minimum-cost pricing and marginal-cost pricing—consumers will benefit.

Minimum-Cost Pricing

minimum-cost pricing: the practice of setting price where it equals minimum average cost

By operating at the breakeven point, where price equals minimum average cost, perfectly competitive businesses in long-run equilibrium practise **minimum-cost pricing**. If businesses were not charging the minimum possible average cost as their price, they would change the scale of production and reduce average costs even further in order to maximize profit. By charging the minimum-cost price of $5 when it is in long-run equilibrium, Pure 'n' Simple T-Shirts, for example, is choosing the least costly combination of inputs. Moreover, it is making zero economic profit so that all these cost savings are passed on to the T-shirt buyers. The purchasing power of consumers' incomes when acquiring T-shirts is, therefore, maximized.

Marginal-Cost Pricing

marginal-cost pricing: the practice of setting price where it equals marginal cost

In long-run equilibrium, perfectly competitive businesses also practise **marginal-cost pricing**, meaning they produce at an output level where price equals marginal cost. The fact that they do so follows from the equality of marginal revenue and price for perfectly competitive firms. The profit-maximizing output rule means that perfect competitors choose the quantity of output at which marginal revenue and marginal cost intersect. Since marginal revenue and price are identical for individual businesses, the profit-maximizing output rule can be expressed, also, as the condition that price equals marginal cost.

If each business's marginal cost incorporates all possible costs to society, then a perfectly competitive market in long-run equilibrium operates at a price that fully reflects the product's opportunity cost. Furthermore, if all markets in an economy are close to being perfectly competitive, society's scarce resources are distributed among industries in a way that maximizes the overall satisfaction of consumers. This is because the prices of various products accurately reflect the extra costs of producing them. Considering again the example of T-shirts, if they are priced at $6, while the marginal cost of an additional T-shirt is $3, then more of society's resources should be devoted to T-shirt production. Otherwise, consumers who derive satisfaction (measured in dollar terms) worth less than $6 from an extra unit of this product are not purchasing it, even though many of them would be willing to pay more than the product's marginal cost. Production in this market should, therefore, be increased.

Brief Review

1. In the long run, perfectly competitive markets reach an equilibrium at which businesses are at their breakeven point.

2. In long-run equilibrium, perfectly competitive business operate at the minimum-cost and marginal-cost prices, thereby benefitting consumers.

5.4 Practice Questions

1. A perfectly competitive market is in short-run equilibrium with price at $50 and the average cost of businesses in the market at $40.
   a. Outline the trends that will push this market towards long-run equilibrium.
   b. Once this market reaches its long-run equilibrium, will the minimum-cost pricing rule be met? Explain.
   c. Once this market reaches its long-run equilibrium, will the marginal-cost pricing rule be met? Explain.

LAST**WORD**

In this chapter, we have seen the main ways that market structures differ because of how many businesses there are in each market, whether or not their products are standard, and how easy it is to enter and exit the industry. We have also examined how businesses can maximize economic profit by following the profit-maximizing output rule. We took the case of a perfectly competitive business to analyze how it maximizes profit in the short run and

long run. Because perfect competitors are price-takers, they have to make only one decision when maximizing profit—how much quantity of output to produce. In the next chapter, when we switch our attention to businesses in the other market structures, we will see that they must choose from among various possible quantities *and* prices when maximizing their economic profit.

Key Concepts

average revenue 113
breakeven point 117
business's demand curve 113
business's supply curve 119
entry barriers 109
marginal-cost pricing 122

marginal revenue 114
market power 111
minimum-cost pricing 122
monopolistic competition 108
monopoly 109
natural monopoly 109

oligopoly 108
perfect competition 108
predatory pricing 110
profit-maximizing output rule 114
shutdown point 118

Questions

1. Categorize each seller below on the basis of the type of market it operates in. Explain each of your answers.
   a. A cattle farmer
   b. A computer maker
   c. A picture-framing shop in a large metropolitan area
   d. A seller of Canadian dollars in foreign currency markets
   e. A life insurance company
   f. A liquor store in a remote village
   g. A visual artist
   h. A country that produces a valuable radioactive mineral found in no other part of the world

Profit-Maximization Table for a Vegetable Gardener

(1) Price ($ per kilogram)	(2) Quantity (kilograms per month)	(3) Total Revenue ($)	(4) Total Cost ($)	(5) Marginal Revenue ($ per kilogram)	(6) Marginal Cost ($ per kilogram)	(7) Average Cost ($ per kilogram)	(8) Profit ($)
	0	$ 0	$ 18				$___
				$___	$___		
$___	100	48	41			$___	___
___	200	96	57	___	___	___	___
___	300	144	77	___	___	___	___
___	400	192	106	___	___	___	___
___	500	240	145	___	___	___	___
___	600	288	199	___	___	___	___
___	700	336	294	___	___	___	___
___	800	384	501	___	___	___	___

2. The table above applies to a vegetable gardener who sells carrots at a local farmer's market.
   a. Copy and complete the table. What type of market does the gardener operate in? Explain.
   b. Identify the gardener's profit-maximizing or loss-minimizing quantity of output (rounded to the nearest 100 kilograms) and explain your answer using the profit-maximizing output rule.
   c. On a sheet of graph paper, plot the gardener's marginal revenue, marginal cost, and average cost curves. On your graph, show the profit-maximizing point identified in part b., as well as the area of profit or loss.
   d. At what price and quantity of output (rounded to the nearest 100 kilograms) would the gardener reach the breakeven point? Show this point on your graph.

3. a. On a sheet of graph paper, plot the total revenue and total cost curves for the vegetable gardener in the previous question.
   b. On a separate graph, directly below the one you have drawn in part a., plot the gardener's total profit at the various possible output levels.
   c. On your graphs, highlight the profit-maximizing or loss-minimizing quantity of output and discuss how it can be identified.

4. A fisherman who sells his mackerel catch in a perfectly competitive market faces revenues and costs shown in the table on the next page.
   a. Copy and complete the table, assuming that the fisherman sells his catch at a price of 80 cents per kilogram.
   b. On a sheet of graph paper, carefully plot the fisherman's marginal cost, average fixed cost, average variable cost, and average cost curves.
   c. Which of the output levels in the table represents this fisherman's profit-maximizing or loss-minimizing quantity of output? At this quantity, what is the fisherman's profit or loss? Draw the fisherman's marginal revenue curve on your graph and use this curve to identify the profit-maximizing point as well as the area of profit or loss.

Profit-Maximization Table for a Fisherman

(1) Price ($ per kilogram)	(2) Quantity (kilograms per day)	(3) Total Revenue ($)	(4) Fixed Costs ($)	(5) Variable Costs ($)	(6) Total Cost ($)	(7) Average Fixed Cost ($ per kilogram)	(8) Average Variable Cost ($ per kilogram)	(9) Average Cost ($ per kilogram)	(10) Marginal Cost ($ per kilogram)
	0	$___	$400	$ 0	$___				
$___	90	___	400	55	___	$___	$___	$___	$___
___	220	___	400	110	___	___	___	___	___
___	307	___	400	165	___	___	___	___	___
___	360	___	400	220	___	___	___	___	___
___	385	___	400	275	___	___	___	___	___
___	400	___	400	330	___	___	___	___	___

d. On your graph, identify the business's breakeven point, shutdown point, and supply curve. What is the significance of each of these concepts to the fisherman?

e. If, in the long run, price remains at 80 cents and the total costs shown in the table still apply, what action will this fisherman take? Explain.

5. How do the conditions of minimum-cost and marginal-cost pricing correspond to Adam Smith's notion of the "invisible hand"?

6. Redraw Figure 5.7 assuming an increasing-cost rather than a constant-cost industry.

7. (Advanced Question)
Some cases of price discrimination can be defended as being in the best interests of society while others are indefensible. Give a hypothetical example of each case, and explain the reasoning behind each choice.

8. (Policy Discussion Question)
Does the use of price ceilings and price floors in perfectly competitive markets, as outlined in Chapter 3, help or hinder the achievement of minimum-cost and marginal-cost pricing? Explain.

Internet Application Questions

http://oldfraser.lexi.net /publications/forum/1999/ 12/section_09.html

1. Using the arguments in "Avoiding the Maple Syrup Solution" (at http://oldfraser. lexi.net/publications/forum/1999/12/section_09.html), outline four important barriers to entry that make it difficult for new firms to enter Canada's airline industry.

2. Why is the federal government reluctant to eliminate these entry barriers?

ADVANCING
ECONOMIC
THOUGHT

PROPHET OF CAPITALISM'S DOOM

The Economic Theories of Karl Marx

Marx and His Influence

Karl Marx (1818–1883) is best known as the founder of the international socialist and communist movements. He was born in the German state of Prussia, studied philosophy, and worked as a journalist before beginning his career as a political activist. Exiled from both Germany and France, he moved to England where, with his close friend Friedrich Engels (1820–1895), he applied his revolutionary views to the fields of philosophy, history, and economics.

Of these three subjects, it was what he called "the confounded ramifications of political economy" that gave him the most headaches. In his mammoth three-volume work, *Das Kapital*, Marx developed his theory of economics. He concluded that capitalism, by its very nature, was unjust.

Karl Marx
Source: ©Bettmann/CORBIS/Magma

Marx's View of Capitalism

Marx's years in England allowed him to witness first-hand the effects of the British Industrial Revolution. By the mid-1800s, manufacturing was the mainstay of Britain's economy, and a large portion of the population had moved from rural areas to the burgeoning new cities in the hope of finding jobs in manufacturing. In the long run, the industrial transformation experienced in Britain enhanced the economic well-being of the majority of citizens of industrialized countries. But in Marx's day, the benefits of the Industrial Revolution seemed to be limited to the wealthier members of society. Living conditions were horrendous for the labouring classes in the rapidly expanding urban areas:

> And what cities! It was not merely that smoke hung over them and filth impregnated them, that the elementary public services—water-supply, sanitation, street-cleaning, open spaces, and so on—could not keep pace with the mass migration of men into cities, thus producing, especially after 1830, epidemics of cholera, typhoid and an appalling constant toll [from] air pollution and water pollution...The new city populations...[were] pressed into overcrowded and bleak slums, whose very sight froze the heart of the observer.[1]

Marx's Theory of Capitalism

The Labour Theory of Value   Marx blamed these conditions on capitalism itself. His attack was based on his "labour theory of value," in which prices of products depend on how much labour goes into producing them. According to this theory, only company owners (whom Marx called capitalists) have the financial resources to hire workers and sell the resulting output. By paying wages that are less than the value workers contribute to production, company owners are able to skim off a portion of value for themselves. By doing this, they engage in capitalist exploitation of their workforce.

The Theory of Exploitation   An example will help explain Marx's theory. It may take a worker four hours to make a shirt and eight hours to make a suit. According to Marx, the price of the shirt should then be half that of the suit; say, the prices of the two products are $40 and $80, respectively. If so, workers producing either two shirts or one suit in an eight-hour day create $80 of value. Let us assume that daily wages in the textile trade are $50 and that the cost of materials plus daily wear and tear on the machines each worker uses is $10. The portion of value kept by the capitalist, or each worker's "surplus value," is, therefore, $20 [$80 − ($50 + $10)] as shown in the table below.

ADVANCING
ECONOMIC
THOUGHT

| | | Figure A | | Marx's Theory of Exploitation |

Creation of Surplus Value (when producing 2 shirts or 1 suit)		
	$50 Wage	$30 Wage
Daily wage (W)	$50	$30
Materials and machine wear and tear (M)	$10	$10
Surplus value (SV)	**$20**	**$40**
Total value	$80	$80
Exploitation rate (SV/W)	$\frac{2}{5}$	$\frac{4}{3}$

If daily wages are reduced from $50 to $30, daily surplus value extracted from each worker is increased (the shaded portions on the bar graphs). As a result, surplus value as a proportion of daily wages also increases.

Source: From *Evolution of Economic Thought,* 6th ed. by Brue. © 2000. Reprinted with permission of South-Western, a division of Thomson Learning: www.thomsonrights.com FAX 800-730-2215.

Dynamics of Capitalism

With time, Marx argued, the rate of exploitation by capitalists would worsen, meaning surplus value would increase as a proportion of the daily wage. This could happen either through further decreases in wages or a lengthening of the workday.

Decreased Wages   Capitalists try to slash wages as much as possible. The daily wage in our example could drop from $50 to $30, while the cost of materials, plus the wear and tear on machines, remains constant at $10. As a result, surplus value would rise to $40 [$80 − ($30 + $10)]. Surplus value as a proportion of the daily wage would then increase from $20/$50 to $40/$30.

Lengthening of the Workday   Capitalists also have an incentive to raise the number of hours workers put in each day. This expands the daily value created by each worker. As long as the daily wage remains the same, surplus value as a proportion of this wage would again rise.

Communist Revolution

Marx believed that capitalist exploitation would worsen the living standards of workers until, finally, workers would violently revolt, first in the nations of Western Europe, which were most industrialized at the time Marx was writing, and later in other parts of the world. The overthrow of capitalism would usher in a socialist age based on common ownership of property. Once socialist ownership had been consolidated, true communism would arrive. Governments would disappear and people would be able to live in complete liberty. Society's guiding principle would then be "from each according to his abilities, and to each according to his needs."[2]

Relevance for Today

Marx's theories have been the source of continuing controversy. His detractors challenge the usefulness of the labour theory of value and the notion of surplus value. They argue that other economic resources, such as capital and entrepreneurship, make their own contributions to production and that owners of these resources must receive a payment so that they will keep supplying their resources to businesses.

At the same time, Marx's theories had a significant impact throughout the 20th century. Socialists—who advocate that the community as a whole own and control the means of production, distribution, and exchange—have held power in many parts of the world. Among socialists, communists have accepted the bulk of Marx's theories and applied them in countries subject to communist rule. In most nations, however, Marx's influence has been less direct. Labour movements, for example, owe much to Marx's theories of capitalist exploitation. Through gradual reform, rather than revolution, socialists in such countries as Canada have played a major part in social reform and in creating modern mixed economies in which governments are much more important than they were a century ago.

Notes
[1] Adapted from *Industry and Empire: From 1750 to the Present Day* by E.J. Hobsbawm, (Penguin Books, 1969). Copyright © E.J. Hobsbawm, 1968, 1969. Reprinted by permission.
[2] Karl Marx, *Critique of the Gotha Program*, 1875.

1. For the textile industry example given previously, imagine that each worker's wages are raised from $50 to $60 per day, while other costs remain the same. Create a bar graph to show the resulting change in surplus value per worker. How does surplus value change as a proportion of the daily wage?

2. Imagine that the daily wage of a textile worker remains at $50, but the workday is lengthened to 12 hours, causing each worker to raise production to $120 per day and increasing the other costs (materials and wear on machines) to $15 per worker.
   a. Create a bar graph to show the new surplus value per worker.
   b. Explain how surplus value changes as a proportion of the daily wage.
   c. Explain whether company owners are worse off or better off as a result of the lengthened workday.

3. Average living standards for workers in most capitalist countries have risen significantly since the period when Marx was writing. Outline two reasons why Marx's prediction of falling living standards for workers in these countries has proven to be incorrect.

CHAPTER 6

Monopoly and Imperfect Competition

The biggest things are always the easiest to do because there is no competition.

—Sir William Van Horne, Canadian capitalist

Monopolies can be found in the Canadian economy. Notable examples include public transit systems in Canada's major cities, Canada Post, and Via Rail. More modest firms can be monopolies as well. Pricing decisions by the owner of a town newspaper or a caterer with exclusive rights to sell food at a sports stadium are analyzed with the same tools used in the case of larger companies. Meanwhile, monopolistic competition and oligopoly—often grouped together and called imperfect competition—are even more common. We will see the market forces facing each of these types of firms differ from those facing perfect competitors, and that Adam Smith's invisible hand of competition does not necessarily apply in all real-world markets.

LEARNING OBJECTIVES

In this chapter, you will:

1 consider the demand conditions faced by monopolists, monopolistic competitors, and oligopolists

2 see how monopolists, monopolistic competitors, and oligopolists maximize profits

3 learn about nonprice competition and the arguments over industrial concentration

6.1 Demand Differences

LO 6.1

While perfectly competitive markets do exist, they are by no means the most common market structure. Actual markets are more likely to exhibit features of either monopoly or imperfect competition, which is a category that includes both monopolistic competition and oligopoly. We will look first at the demand conditions faced by businesses in each of these market structures and then at how businesses in each of these markets maximize profit.

Monopoly

As sole supplier of a product, a monopolist faces the same demand curve as that for the entire market—a curve with a negative slope. Therefore, the monopolist has considerable ability to influence price. Figure 6.1 gives the example of Megacomp, the only seller of large supercomputers.

Monopolistic Competition

Because it has some ability to influence the price it charges, a monopolistic competitor faces a different type of demand curve. Consider the example of Jaded Palate, a restaurant that serves highly spiced Cajun food. Customers of this restaurant view its food as distinct from that of nearby restaurants, none of which specializes in this cuisine. If Jaded Palate raises the average price of its meals from $10 to $11, as shown in Figure 6.2, it will lose some, but not all, of its customers. Quantity demanded will fall from 200 to 100 meals a day. If the restaurant lowers the average price of meals from $10 to $9, there will be an increase in quantity demanded, from 200 to 300. Hence, the restaurant faces the demand curve D. Since customers see other restaurants as possible substitutes, a given percentage change in the price of a meal causes an even greater percentage change in quantity demanded. In other words, the monopolistic competitor's demand curve is elastic.

mutual interdependence: the relationship among oligopolists, in which the actions of each business affect the other businesses

Oligopoly

In the case of an oligopoly, the fact that each business makes up a considerable part of the market leads to **mutual interdependence**. This is a situation where businesses in

---

Figure 6.1   Demand Faced by a Monopolist

Demand Schedule for Megacomp

Price ($ millions per computer)	Quantity Demanded (computers per year)
$160	1
120	2
80	3

The demand curve for the individual business is identical to the market demand curve (D). As D shows, if Megacomp increases the price, quantity demanded decreases.

Figure 6.2 Demand Faced by a Monopolistic Competitor

Demand Schedule for Jaded Palate

Price ($ per meal)	Quantity Demanded (meals per day)
$11	100
10	200
9	300
8	400

Demand Curve for Jaded Palate

The restaurant's demand curve (D) has a negative slope so that a change in price causes an opposite change in quantity demanded. Since demand is elastic, the change in quantity demanded is relatively large, compared with the initial change in price.

the industry cannot afford to ignore their competitors' actions that might indirectly affect sales. Because of mutual interdependence, businesses in an oligopoly can operate in either of two ways: as rivals or as fellow players who co-operate to increase combined profits.

RIVALRY AMONG BUSINESSES

Businesses in an oligopoly where rivalry prevails are concerned with maintaining their **market share**, or the proportion of total market sales they control. Because their actions influence their rivals, these businesses must take into account the reactions of competitors whenever they consider a price change. They must then predict how the responses of other businesses will influence their own market share.

Let us consider the hypothetical situation of Universal Motors and its luxury car, the Centaur. If Universal Motors increases its price for the Centaur, competitors will likely keep the prices of their luxury cars constant in order to increase their sales. Thus, Universal Motors will lose some of its market share to its competitors. If, in contrast, Universal Motors lowers its price for the Centaur, its competitors will reduce their prices as well so as not to lose market share. Thus, Universal Motors' market share will remain constant. These actions and reactions among rival companies in an oligopoly are summarized in Figure 6.3.

Now, let us continue the example of Universal Motors in Figure 6.4. If the original price of the Centaur is $30 000, a price increase to $35 000 will cause competitors to keep their prices constant, and the market share for the Centaur will drop from 20 000 to 10 000 cars. The change in quantity demanded (from point *b* to point *a*) causes the demand curve for this price range to be fairly flat. If Universal Motors lowers the price of the Centaur from $30 000 to $20 000, competitors will lower the prices of their cars. Sales of Centaur cars will increase—from 20 000 to 25 000—but not in equal proportion to the price drop. Thus, the demand curve for this price range (from point *b* to point *c*) is steep. As shown on the graph in Figure 6.4, the result is a **kinked demand curve**—a demand curve with two segments, one fairly flat and one steep, with the kink or bend at the original price of $30 000 (point *b*). This kinked demand curve is typical of oligopolies in which businesses jostle one another for profit and market dominance.

market share: a business's proportion of total market sales

kinked demand curve: a demand curve with two segments, one fairly flat and one steep, that is typical of rival oligopolists

Figure 6.3	Actions and Reactions among Rivals in an Oligopoly

Action of Company A	Probable Response of Competitors	Effect on Company A's Market Share	Company A's Quantity Demanded
raise price	keep prices constant	product now high-priced, so market share falls	large decrease as market share lost to competitors
lower price	match price drop	since all companies selling at lower price, Company A's market share stays constant	small increase as lower prices for all companies attract new buyers

CO-OPERATION AMONG BUSINESSES

price leadership: an understanding among oligopolists that one business will initiate all price changes in the market and the others will follow by adjusting their prices and output accordingly

collusion: oligopolists acting together as if they are a monopoly

cartel: a union of oligopolists who have a formal market-sharing agreement

Oligopolists can also co-operate in ways that are against the interests of consumers. In an oligopoly, for example, there may be an unspoken understanding that one company—usually the largest—acts as the price leader. In a case of **price leadership**, other companies will follow any price change initiated by the price leader and adjust their output accordingly. In the past, price leadership has occurred in the automobile and farm-machinery industries. Oligopolies may take their co-operation even further. When oligopolists band together—either secretly or openly—as if they were a monopoly, they are practising **collusion**. In this case, they act jointly to maximize total profits. To do so, the businesses must first estimate the most profitable output level and then agree to maintain this total market output and its associated price. When this sort of agreement among producers is a formal one, the businesses together are known as a **cartel**. The best-known example of a cartel is the Organization of Petroleum Exporting Countries (OPEC).

Figure 6.4	Demand Faced among Rivals in an Oligopoly

The demand curve for Centaur cars is shown as two differently sloped segments. When Universal Motors raises the price above $30 000, competitors keep their prices constant to raise their sales. The results are a substantial drop in the quantity demanded of Centaur cars, and a flat demand curve (from point *b* to point *a*). If price moves below $30 000, competitors are forced to drop their prices as well. Thus, quantity demanded for Centaur cars increases by only a minor amount, producing a steep demand curve (from point *b* to point *c*).

Brief Review

1. Monopolists face the demand curve of the entire market—a downward-sloping curve.

2. A monopolistic competitor faces an elastic demand curve with a negative slope.

3. Oligopolies are characterized by mutual interdependence. Rivalry among oligopolists creates a kinked demand curve because of competitors' responses to price changes.

4. Co-operation among oligopolists may lead to price leadership or collusion. If collusion is formal and explicit, the companies make up a cartel.

6.1 Practice Questions

1. Consider the following demand curves facing a business: (1) relatively inelastic, (2) perfectly elastic, (3) kinked, and (4) relatively elastic. Which one best describes:
   a. a perfect competitor
   b. a monopolistic competitor
   c. a monopolist
   d. an oligopolist in a market where rivalry exists

6.2 Monopoly

LO 6.2

Now let us see how a monopolist chooses to maximize its profit. Because it is a price-maker, the monopolist must establish both a level of output and a price when attempting to maximize profit. Thus, the monopolist applies the profit-maximizing output rule in a different way from that of perfectly competitive businesses.

Revenue Conditions

Figure 6.5 shows the relationships among price, marginal revenue, and average revenue for Megacomp. In the table, price (column 1) and average revenue (column 5) are equal, just as they are for perfect competitors. However, marginal revenue and average revenue are no longer always the same. Recall that if an average value, such as average revenue, declines, then its corresponding marginal value (marginal revenue) is below it. For example, when Megacomp sells its first computer, the business's average and marginal revenues are both equal to $160 million. (Remember that marginal values are graphed halfway between the relevant horizontal coordinates). But once the next computer is added, average revenue falls to $120 million. For this to happen, the second computer must have a lower marginal revenue of $80 million. Selling the second computer requires that the price of *both* computers sold be lowered. Therefore, the extra $120 million from selling the second computer must be adjusted down by the $40 million drop in price on the first computer, giving the marginal revenue of $80 million ($120 million − $40 million)

On the graph shown in Figure 6.5, the demand (D) and average revenue (AR) curves for Megacomp are identical, but the demand and marginal revenue (MR) curves intersect only at their initial points. As the quantity of output for the business rises, marginal revenue drops below price.

Figure 6.5   Revenues for a Monopolist

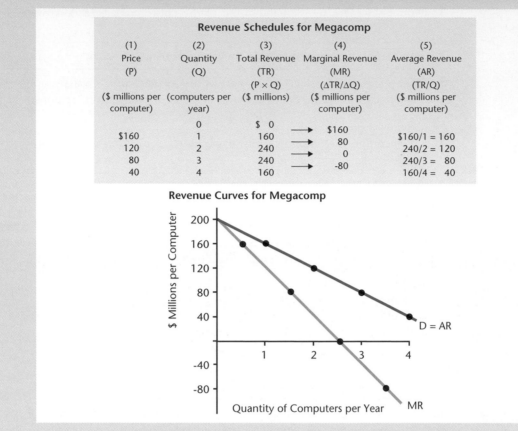

Revenue Schedules for Megacomp

(1) Price (P) ($ millions per computer)	(2) Quantity (Q) (computers per year)	(3) Total Revenue (TR) (P × Q) ($ millions)	(4) Marginal Revenue (MR) (ΔTR/ΔQ) ($ millions per computer)	(5) Average Revenue (AR) (TR/Q) ($ millions per computer)
	0	$ 0		
$160	1	160	$160	$160/1 = 160
120	2	240	80	240/2 = 120
80	3	240	0	240/3 = 80
40	4	160	-80	160/4 = 40

Revenue Curves for Megacomp

Megacomp's demand schedule is shown in columns 1 and 2. Though the values for average revenue (AR) in column 5 are the same as for price (P), Megacomp's marginal revenue (MR) in column 4 equals P and AR only at their initial values. Beyond this point, MR falls more quickly than price when output rises, as shown on the graph.

Profit Maximization

Given its ability to choose price, the monopolist maximizes profit by first finding the appropriate quantity of output, and then, using this quantity level to determine the highest possible price it can charge. This profit-making procedure is illustrated in Figure 6.6. In addition to the business's demand and marginal revenue curves, the graph shows the relevant curves for marginal cost and average cost. To maximize profit, the business must find the point at which marginal revenue and marginal cost intersect. This occurs at point *a*, which is at the profit-maximizing quantity of two computers. Price is then set at $120 million by drawing a vertical line up to the business's demand curve at point *b*, and then across to the price axis.

The table shows the same results: marginal revenue (column 4) and marginal cost (column 5) pass through the same values nearest the quantity of two computers and price of $120 million.

The monopolist may be making an economic profit or a loss, or it may be breaking even, depending on whether the business's average cost is above, below, or equal to price. Because, in our example, Megacomp has an average cost of $90 million (at point *c*) that is below the $120 million price (point *b*), it is making a positive economic profit.

Figure 6.6   Profit Maximization for a Monopolist

Profit Maximization Table for Megacomp

(1) Price (P) (AR)	(2) Quantity (Q)	(3) Total Revenue (TR) (P × Q)	(4) Marginal Revenue (MR) (ΔTR/ΔQ)	(5) Marginal Cost (MC)	(6) Average Cost (AC)
($ millions per computer)	(computers per year)	($ millions)	($ millions per computer)	($ millions per computer)	($ millions per computer)
	0	$ 0			
$ 160	1	160	$160	$60	$140
120	**2**	**240**	80	40	**90**
80	3	240	0	70	83
40	4	160	−80	150	100

Profit Maximization Graph for Megacomp

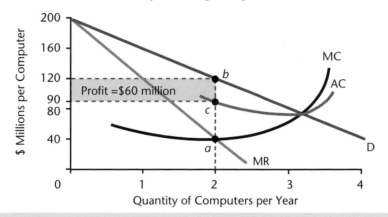

On the graph, the profit-maximizing output is found at the intersection of the marginal revenue (MR) and marginal cost (MC) curves (at point *a*). At this output, the demand curve gives a price (at point *b*) of $120 million (determined by drawing a vertical line to the demand curve, then across to the price axis). The table also shows that marginal revenue and marginal cost pass through the same values around an output of two computers and a price of $120 million. On the graph, Megacomp's profit is the area of the shaded rectangle, with a height equalling the difference between price (point *b*) and average cost (point *c*) and with a width equalling quantity.

THINKING ABOUT ECONOMICS

How easy is it for a monopolist, such as Megacomp, to estimate the profit-maximizing values for price and quantity?

The task requires estimating both demand and costs. Whereas the perfect competitor has an easy time of estimating demand conditions (because market price is the only factor to be determined), monopolists (as well as imperfectly competitive businesses) have a harder task of estimating how much consumers will buy at each possible price. As far as cost estimates are concerned, all businesses must estimate how much the explicit and implicit costs would be at each possible output level. When a business sells more than one item, it must also distribute its costs among these various products.

Question
How easy is it for perfect competitors to estimate costs at each possible output level?

The business's profit rectangle has a height equal to the distance between points *b* and *c* ($30 million = $120 million − $90 million) and a width of two computers, giving a total economic profit of $60 million.

Notice that a monopolist satisfies neither of the conditions for consumer benefit: minimum-cost pricing and marginal-cost pricing. Because the monopolist has no competitors due to entry barriers, it can keep its price constant in the long run. In the case of Megacomp, this price would be $120 million, as shown in Figure 6.6. Since price does not equal the lowest possible average cost, the minimum-cost pricing condition is not met. Similarly, this price is not equal to the business's marginal cost, meaning, the marginal-cost pricing condition is not met either.

Monopoly versus Perfect Competition

To see the impact on price and quantity of a monopoly, let us compare them with price and quantity in a perfectly competitive market. To do this, we will consider what would happen if a perfectly competitive market in long-run equilibrium were transformed into a monopoly.

The market demand and supply curves for the T-shirt industry are shown in Figure 6.7. Equilibrium for a competitive market occurs at the intersection of these curves (point *a*), with a price of $4 and a quantity of 22 000 shirts. If the industry becomes one large company, the market demand curve remains the same, despite the change in the market structure. With the transformation to a monopoly, the demand curve for the entire market becomes the business's demand curve. There is a significant change, however. Now that the business is a monopolist, its price (given by the demand curve) and its marginal revenue are no longer equal. Instead, the marginal revenue curve falls below the demand curve, as was the case for Megacomp.

Next, let us consider supply. Recall that a perfect competitor's supply curve shows the quantity of output supplied by the business at each possible price and is represented by a portion of the marginal cost curve. In turn, the market supply curve is the sum of all the supply curves of the businesses in the market. After the change to a monopoly, production facilities remain the same as before, with inputs originally owned by the perfectly competitive producers now in the hands of one business. When the monopolist combines the cost figures for these various facilities, it finds a marginal cost curve that is merely an extension of the perfectly competitive supply curve, shown in Figure 6.7.

Effects on Price and Quantity

The T-shirt monopoly's profit-maximizing output is 18 000, where the new marginal revenue and marginal cost curves intersect (point *b*). At this output level, the price is $7 (point *c*), as found on the demand curve. Thus, with the transformation from perfect competition to monopoly, T-shirts become more expensive, and fewer of them are produced.

Regulation of Natural Monopolies

When an industry is a natural monopoly, increasing returns to scale mean that the single business can produce a product at a significantly lower per-unit cost than could several companies. To ensure that these cost savings are passed on to the consumer, governments usually intervene in natural monopolies. Either they provide the service through a government-owned corporation (as in the case of Canada Post), or they

Figure 6.7 Monopoly versus Perfect Competition

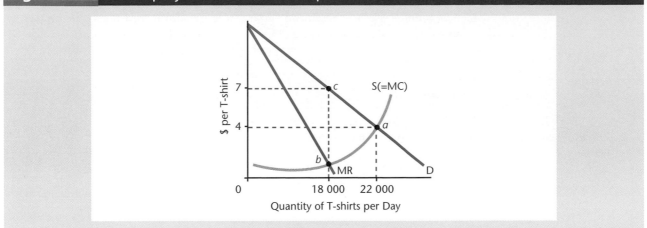

When the T-shirt industry is perfectly competitive, equilibrium occurs at the meeting point (*a*) of the market demand and supply curves (D and S). If the industry becomes a monopoly, the profit-maximizing output for the single seller decreases, where marginal revenue (MR) and marginal cost (MC) meet (point *b*). The new price is found on the demand curve (point *c*).

regulate the single private company in the market (just as the Canadian Radio-television and Telecommunications Commission regulates cable television businesses).

AVERAGE-COST PRICE

average-cost pricing: the practice of setting price where it equals average cost

Public agencies that regulate monopolies have a difficult task. Not only must regulators estimate each business's costs, they must also try to choose the "best" possible price for the monopolist to charge. Usually, regulators use **average-cost pricing** so that the monopolist can break even without public funds. As a practical matter, regulators applying the average-cost price do not undertake the cumbersome task of estimating the cost and demand curves of the regulated business. Instead, they control profits directly. A business's **accounting-profit rate**, or rate of return, is its accounting profit divided by owner's equity and expressed as a percentage:

accounting-profit rate: a measure of a business's profitability, calculated as its accounting profit divided by owner's equity

$$\text{Accounting-profit rate} = \frac{\text{accounting profit}}{\text{owner's equity}} \times 100\%$$

fair rate of return: the maximum accounting-profit rate allowed for a regulated monopoly

The regulating agency imposes a ceiling, such as 8 percent or 9 percent, on the profit rate the business can earn. This **fair rate of return** is arrived at by estimating how much the business needs to cover both explicit costs (such as wages and outlays on materials) and implicit costs (in particular, the business's normal profits).

While it is often the only viable method of regulation, setting a fair rate of return leads to inefficiencies. Because of profit controls, there is little incentive for the company's managers to control costs. Indeed, the easiest way for the business to raise its price is by inflating costs. Generous perks, bloated payrolls, and plush offices are then paid for by consumers in the form of higher prices. Regulators try to overcome such problems by imposing performance standards on the business, but these standards are difficult to implement.

Brief Review

1. The monopolist faces a demand curve that is equal to marginal revenue only at its initial value. Marginal revenue drops more quickly than price as output rises.

2. A monopolist can make a positive economic profit in both the short run and the long run and meets neither of the minimum-cost and marginal-cost pricing conditions.

3. A monopolist necessarily charges a higher price and produces a lower quantity than would a perfectly competitive industry in the same market.

4. Regulators usually force natural monopolies to charge an average-cost price, where the businesses are just breaking even.

6.2 Practice Questions

1. A monopolistic pharmaceuticals company produces a patented drug. In one year, it could sell 400 000 prescriptions at a price of $20, or instead it could sell 500 000 prescriptions at a price of $15.
   a. Identify the marginal revenue associated with this range of the business's demand curve.
   b. Explain the difference between price and marginal revenue given that this company is a monopolist.
   c. Using EconGraphKit (at http://www.mcgrawhill.ca/college/lovewell), draw the relevant ranges of this business's demand and marginal revenue curves.

2. A monopolist produces at a daily output of 100 000 units of output, with marginal cost and marginal revenue at this output both equal to $4 and price equal to $6.
   a. Is the monopolist operating at its profit-maximizing output? Explain.
   b. If the government turns this monopolist into a perfectly competitive market, will output be less than or greater than 100 000 units? Will price be less than or greater than $6?

6.3 Imperfect Competition

Because of the similarities they share, monopolistic competition and oligopoly are often lumped together in a general category, known as imperfect competition. Like monopolists, businesses in both these markets are price-makers, which means that they must decide on both price and quantity when choosing a profit-maximizing point.

LO 6.2

Monopolistic Competition

REVENUE CONDITIONS

Figure 6.8 shows the relationships among price, marginal revenue, and average revenue for a monopolisitic competitor, the Jaded Palate restaurant. As in the case of a monopolist, price and average revenue are the same, but marginal revenue is below average revenue, due to the fact that average revenue is declining. For example, the first 100 meals sold by Jaded Palate have an average and marginal revenue both equal to $11. With the addition of the next 100 meals, however, average revenue declines to $10, while marginal revenue

Figure 6.8   Revenues for a Monopolistic Competitor

Revenue Schedules for Jaded Palate

(1) Price (P) ($ per meal)	(2) Quantity (q) (meals per day)	(3) Total Revenue (TR) (P × q)	(4) Marginal Revenue (MR) (ΔTR/Δq)	(5) Average Revenue (AR) (TR/q)
$—	0	$ 0		
11	100	1100	1100/100 = $11	1100/100 = $11
10	200	2000	900/100 = 9	2000/200 = 10
9	300	2700	700/100 = 7	2700/300 = 9
8	400	3200	500/100 = 5	3200/400 = 8

Revenue Curves for Jaded Palate

The business's demand schedule is shown in columns 1 and 2. The values for price (P) and average revenue (AR) in columns 1 and 5 are equal, while marginal revenue (MR) in column 4 is the same as P and AR only at their initial values. After this, MR falls more quickly than price, as the graph shows.

is lower still at $9. As shown on the accompanying graph in Figure 6.8, Jaded Palate's demand and marginal revenue curves intersect at their initial points, and from then on, the marginal revenue (MR) curve declines more rapidly than the demand (D) curve.

THE SHORT RUN

Given its ability to choose price, the monopolistic competitor maximizes its short-run profit by first finding the appropriate quantity of output and then using this quantity level to determine the highest possible price it can charge. These typical profit-making activities are illustrated on the left in Figure 6.9. In addition to the business's demand and marginal revenue curves, the graph shows the relevant curves for marginal cost and average cost. Once again, in order to maximize profit, the business must find the point at which marginal revenue and marginal cost intersect. This is point *a*, which is at the profit-maximizing quantity of 200 meals. Price is then set at $10 by drawing a vertical line up to the business's demand curve at point *b* and then across to the price axis.

Jaded Palate could be making an economic profit or loss in the short run, or it could be breaking even. As in the case of perfect competitors, the answer can be found by comparing price and average cost at the profit-maximizing quantity. Because the price of $10 is above the $8 average cost at a quantity of 200 meals (point *c*), Jaded Palate is making a positive economic profit. On the graph, the revenue rectangle equals price multiplied by the quantity of output ($10 × 200 meals = $2000), and the cost rectangle equals average cost multiplied by the quantity of output ($8 × 200 meals = $1600). Therefore, the profit rectangle equals $400 ($2000 − $1600) and is shown as the shaded rectangle on the short-run graph.

Figure 6.9   Profit Maximization for a Monopolistic Competitor

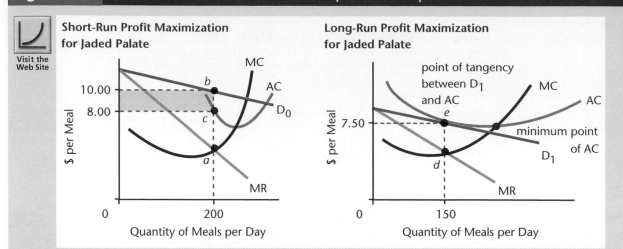

On the left, the business's short-run profit is maximized at point *a*, where the marginal revenue (MR) and marginal cost (MC) curves intersect. The price is found by drawing a vertical line up to point *b* on the business's demand curve (D$_0$) and then across to the price axis. The business's total profit is shown by the shaded rectangle. On the right, the long-run profit-maximizing output of 150 meals occurs at the point where MR and MC are equal (point *d*). The price of $7.50—which equals long-run AC—is point *e* on the business's long-run demand curve (D$_1$).

THE LONG RUN

It is in the long run that the competitive elements of monopolistic competition become evident. Because short-run economic profits are being made in the restaurant industry, new businesses enter the market in the long run. The graph on the right in Figure 6.9 shows how the increase in competition shifts demand (from D$_0$ to the new D$_1$ curve) for established restaurants, such as Jaded Palate. The entry of new competitors causes demand for Jaded Palate to shift leftwards because there are now fewer customers at each possible price that the restaurant can charge. The new demand curve (D$_1$) is also more elastic than D$_0$, since there are more close substitutes available for Jaded Palate's product. Once again, the market adjusts: profits go down, and eventually, long-run equilibrium is reached at point *e*. Besides showing Jaded Palate's demand and marginal revenue curves, the graph on the right shows the marginal cost and average cost curves in the long run. The profit-maximizing point where marginal revenue equals marginal cost now occurs at a quantity of 150 meals (point *d*). The new price is $7.50, which is found at point *e* on the long-run demand curve (D$_1$).

Note that monopolistic competitors reach neither the minimum-cost nor the marginal-cost pricing conditions in long-run equilibrium. Since average cost and price are equal at point *e* in Figure 6.9, the business is breaking even in the long run. However, this price does *not* equal the minimum point on the average cost curve. This minimum-cost price could only be achieved at a higher output for each business. Figure 6.9 also illustrates that in the long run, for monopolistic competitors, price (point *e*) is greater than marginal cost. This means that too few units of output are produced for price to reflect the product's full opportunity cost.

LO 6.2

Oligopoly

We have already seen how an oligopoly that is characterized by rivalry among competitors faces a kinked demand curve. Recall that the kinked demand curve is based on the different responses of competitors when the business either raises or reduces its price. In Figure 6.10, when Universal Motors increases the price of its Centaur car, rivals do not increase their prices. Thus, the quantity demanded of Centaur cars decreases sharply, giving the flatter segment of the demand curve. Were Universal Motors to decrease its price on the Centaur, rivals would follow suit, so the change in quantity demanded would be small, giving the steeper segment of the demand curve.

REVENUE CONDITIONS

The marginal revenue for Centaur cars is shown in the table and on the graph in Figure 6.10. Just as with the demand curve, the marginal revenue curve has two distinct segments. In this case, however, the flatter segment and the steeper segment do not meet but must be joined by a vertical line at the quantity of 20 000 cars, the quantity associated with the $30 000 price.

Figure 6.10   Profit Maximization for an Oligopolist

Profit Maximization Table for Centaur Cars

(1) Price (P) (=AR)	(2) Quantity (q)	(3) Total Revenue (TR) (P × q)	(4) Marginal Revenue (MR) (ΔTR/Δq)	(5) Marginal Cost (MC)	(6) Average Cost (AC)
($ thousands per car)	(thousands of cars per year)	($ millions)	($ thousands per car)	($ thousands per car)	($ thousands per car)
—	0	$ 0			
$35	10	350	$ 35	$15	$30
30	**20**	**600**	25	10	**20**
20	25	500	−20	15	19
10	30	300	−40	25	20

Profit Maximization Graph for Centaur Cars

In an oligopoly characterized by rivalry, a business faces a kinked demand curve (D) with two segments. The marginal revenue curve also has two segments; however, the segments are separate, so they must be joined with a vertical line. On the graph, the marginal revenue (MR) and marginal cost (MC) curves meet at point *a*, giving the profit-maximizing output level. To determine price, we must look to the demand curve; at the relevent quantity, the price should be $30 000 (point *b*). According to the table also, the values of marginal revenue (column 4) and marginal cost (column 5) pass through the same values around the same output as on the graph.

PROFIT MAXIMIZATION

To maximize profit, the oligopolist, like all businesses, must follow the profit-maximizing output rule. Therefore, Universal Motors should produce at the output level where the marginal revenue and marginal cost curves intersect, at point *a* in Figure 6.10, or 20 000 cars. According to the demand curve, this quantity of cars should be sold at a price of $30 000 (found by extending a vertical line from a quantity of 20 000 to the demand curve, at point *b*, which aligns on the price axis with a $30 000 price). Looking at the table in Figure 6.10, we can see that marginal cost and marginal revenue pass through the same values closest to an output of 20 000 cars.

At the profit-maximizing point, an oligopolist may make a positive, negative, or zero economic profit in the short run. When average cost is below price at the business's profit-maximizing output, the business makes a positive economic profit. When average cost is above price at the profit-maximizing output, the business makes an economic loss. When average cost and price are equal at the profit-maximizing output, the business breaks even. In the case of Universal Motors, at the output level of 20 000 cars and the price of $30 000 (point *b* in Figure 6.10), the average cost is $20 000 (point *c*). Therefore, the company makes an economic profit on Centaur cars equal to quantity multiplied by the difference between price and average cost, or $200 million [20 000 × ($30 000 − $20 000)].

The kinked demand curve—which applies equally in both the short run and the long run—explains why rival oligopolists tend to keep prices constant even as costs change. In the case of the Centaur illustrated in Figure 6.10, as long as the marginal cost and marginal revenue curves intersect at a quantity of 20 000, Universal Motors will not change its price. Only if marginal cost changed so dramatically that its curve and the marginal revenue curve no longer intersected at 20 000 (the vertical connection between the two segments) would Universal Motors change its price.

As in the case of monopolistic competitors, oligopolists achieve neither the minimum-cost nor the marginal-cost pricing conditions. Because of limited competition created by entry barriers, an oligopolist that faces rivals can remain indefinitely at one price, such as $30 000 in Figure 6.10. At this price, the business is making a positive economic profit and fails to reach the output level where average cost is at its lowest value. So, the minimum-cost pricing condition is broken. The condition of marginal-cost pricing is also broken; as Figure 6.10 shows, the price of $30 000 is greater than marginal cost. The same conclusions apply for colluding oligopolists, as the prices they charge are even higher.

THINKING ABOUT ECONOMICS

Why are there no supply curves for businesses in imperfectly competitive markets?

A supply curve is relevant only when a business plans how much output to produce at various prices. Perfect competitors do this, but not the sellers in other types of markets. Given its demand curve, a monopolistic competitor or oligopolist chooses one output level and then charges the highest possible price the demand allows at that quantity. It is, therefore, impossible for an imperfectly competitive business to devise a supply curve that is independent of the demand conditions it faces.

Question
Is it possible for a monopolist to derive a supply curve?

ANTI-COMBINES LEGISLATION IN CANADA

anti-combines legislation:
laws aimed at preventing
industrial concentration and
abuses of market power

Because of the inefficiencies that oligopolies can cause, their activities are subject to laws aimed at preventing industrial concentration and abuses of market power, which are known as **anti-combines legislation**. Canada's anti-combines laws date back to 1889 but, until recently, were largely unsuccessful.

That violations were considered criminal offences was one reason for the lack of success. Criminal cases require that guilt be established beyond a reasonable doubt. This requirement does not easily make use of economic analysis—analysis that is so vital to considering anti-competitive behaviour. A second reason is that Canadian governments have traditionally been less opposed to industrial concentration than those in other countries, the United States in particular. Many Canadians have argued that domestic businesses need to be large in order to be internationally competitive, especially in sectors with significant increasing returns to scale. Canada's lawmakers, therefore, have typically given the goal of international competitiveness and efficiency greater weight than they have domestic competition.

The Competition Act of 1986 was a major reform of Canada's anti-combines legislation. It offered a combination of criminal and civil provisions, strengthened penalties, and built on the almost century-long experience of anti-combines legislation and prosecution. The Act covers business practices that prevent or lessen competition, including the practices described in the following sections. Of these, the first three are still criminal offences, with penalties ranging from fines to possible imprisonment of company executives, while the last two are considered civil matters, which are reviewed by a government-administered panel known as the Competition Tribunal.

Conspiracy

Businesses that conspire or agree to fix prices, allocate markets, or restrict entry to markets can be charged under the Competition Act. In order for a business to be found guilty, its actions must be proven to unduly restrain competition. Violators can face fines of up to $10 million or prison terms of up to five years. One case of conspiracy involved nine real estate boards in five provinces. After complaints from customers and some industry members about commissions, services, and other practices, an investigation began. The Canadian Real Estate Association came forward to settle the matter, which was resolved out of court.

Bid-Rigging

Companies that bid on contracts may arrange among themselves who will win each contract and at what price. By taking turns at winning bids and by inflating prices, all conspirators are winners. Unlike the more general conspiracy charge, bid-rigging is considered an automatic offence; undue restraint does not have to be proven. In a recent case, three heating equipment suppliers were convicted on six counts of sharing out the market, in part by rigging bids; each company was fined $1000 on each count. Penalties are at the courts' discretion, but reflect the seriousness with which the courts view the crime and so can include, for example, $1 million fines and five-year prison terms.

Predatory Pricing

The policy and practice of temporarily dropping a price for a product below its average cost to drive a new competitor out of business is a criminal offence. In one case, a company provided free supplies of a drug to hospitals. Because the company's goal was to generate long-term sales after eliminating competition, the company was fined $50 000.

Abuse of Dominant Position

Companies that control most of the sales in a market are not allowed to use their dominant position to engage in anti-competitive behaviour. One case of abuse involved the Canadian maker of (and former patent-holder for) the artificial sweetener aspartame, known as NutraSweet. According to the findings of the Competition Tribunal, the company had used its power to have several major purchasers of aspartame sign long-term contracts to buy NutraSweet exclusively, rather than the products of the competition. The company was not allowed to enforce these old contracts or to negotiate new ones of the same sort. Typically, the Tribunal requires that the guilty company cease its anti-competitive behaviour. The Tribunal can also use stronger measures to restore competition in the market; for example, by requiring partial break-up of a business into smaller units.

Mergers

A merger is the combining of two companies into one. The Competition Tribunal has the power to prohibit a merger in Canada—no matter what the size or nationality of the companies involved—if the merger could prevent or substantially reduce competition. Exceptions are often made if a merger will increase efficiency and pass on savings to consumers. In practice, it is uncommon for the Tribunal to disallow a merger. Mergers can be of three sorts, depending on the connection between the companies involved.

horizontal merger: a combination of former rivals

A **horizontal merger** combines former competitors. One example of a horizontal merger was the purchase several years ago of Canadian Airlines International by its rival, Air Canada. Horizontal mergers allow businesses to take advantage of the increasing returns to scale that arise from combining production. Horizontal mergers can also reduce the level of competition in the market, thereby giving the new, combined company more market power and potential profit.

vertical merger: a combination of a business and its supplier

A **vertical merger** combines a business and its supplier. A steelmaker that purchases an iron ore mine is one example, as is a fashion design company merging with a clothing wholesaler. Vertical mergers can guarantee a supply of needed inputs or can ensure distribution of the product. For example, the Canadian restaurant company Cara has taken over many of its food suppliers, and PepsiCo's acquisition of Pizza Hut ensured that PepsiCo soft drinks are sold in these restaurants.

conglomerate merger: a combination of businesses in unrelated industries

A **conglomerate merger** combines businesses in unrelated industries. The main reason for such mergers is to help companies smooth out fluctuations in profit that occur during booms and recessions. A company whose profit plummets during a downturn in the economy—a manufacturer of luxury yachts, for example—might decide to purchase a chain of discount hardware stores, which are not affected in the same way.

Brief Review

1. A monopolistic competitor faces a marginal revenue curve that intersects with its corresponding demand curve only at their initial values. From that point, the marginal revenue curve falls faster than does the demand curve.

2. In the short run, a monopolistic competitor can make an economic profit or loss. In the long run, however, competitive forces drive monopolistic competitors to a breakeven point.

3. An oligopolist in a market that is characterized by rivalry faces a marginal revenue curve of two disconnected segments, one steeper than the other. These segments are associated with the two portions of the kinked demand curve.

4. Because of limited competition, oligopolists can make an economic profit even in the long run.

5. Imperfectly competitive businesses satisfy neither the minimum-cost nor the marginal-cost pricing conditions met by perfectly competitive businesses in the long run.

6. Governments in such countries as Canada use anti-combines legislation to prevent industrial concentration and abuses of market power.

6.3 Practice Questions

1. A photocopy shop in a monopolistically competitive market could daily sell 10 000 copies at a price of 4 cents, or it could sell 15 000 copies at a price of 3 cents.
   a. Identify the marginal revenue associated with this range of the business's demand curve.
   b. Explain the difference between price and marginal revenue given that this business is a monopolistic competitor.
   c. Using EconGraphKit (at http://www.mcgrawhill.ca/college/lovewell), draw the relevant ranges of this business's demand and marginal revenue curves.

2. A monopolistic competitor operates at its short run profit-maximizing point, with a weekly output of 100 000 units and a price of $5.
   a. If the business's average cost is initially $6, what happens in the long run if it stays in operation?
   b. If the business's average cost is initially $4 instead, then how will the long run trends for this business differ?

3. An oligopolist in a market where rivalry prevails is operating at the kink in its demand curve, with a daily output of 400 units and a price of $5.
   a. At this output level, what is the shape of the business's marginal revenue curve? Why?
   b. If costs for this business were to undergo a rise at every output level, would this business necessarily raise its price? What is the significance of this result?

6.4 Traits of Imperfect Competition

nonprice competition: efforts to increase demand through product differentiation, advertising, or both

product differentiation: efforts to make a product distinct from that of competitors

LO 6.3

Nonprice Competition

In addition to changing product prices, imperfectly competitive firms can compete in another way. **Nonprice competition** refers to the efforts of imperfectly competitive producers to increase demand for their products by swaying consumer preferences. The two strategies used are product differentiation and advertising.

PRODUCT DIFFERENTIATION

Product differentiation is a company's attempt to distinguish its product from that of competitors. Designer labels on a clothing manufacturer's jeans and an "exclusive" set of toppings on a pizza restaurant's product are examples of product differentiation. The changes made to a product may be cosmetic—slick packaging, for example—or they may be substantial, such as providing the product at a more convenient location. Product differentiation has two goals: to increase demand (thus raising the quantity demanded at every price) and to decrease demand elasticity (so that prices can be increased without losing customers to competitors). Meeting both goals increases a business's profit and market power.

ADVERTISING

Advertising can play two roles in imperfectly competitive markets. It can provide the consumer with information, as with newspaper classified ads, and it can promote consumer preferences for a product, as is commonly the case for radio and television ads. Advertising has the same two goals as product differentiation: to increase demand for the product and to make the demand more inelastic. For example, a producer of athletic shoes, such as Nike, advertises in order to raise the quantity demanded of its shoes at every possible price. The producer also aims to make consumers less likely to switch brands if Nike shoes go up in price. Again, the company's profit and market power are increased if its advertising strategy meets the two goals.

NONPRICE COMPETITION AND BUSINESS

For a single imperfectly competitive business, product differentiation and advertising increase both revenues and costs. Total revenue increases when the demand for the business's product increases and the demand becomes more inelastic. However, the business's total costs increase because of the extra costs of undertaking nonprice competition. If the gain in total revenues outweighs the extra costs of product differentiation and advertising, profits are increased. Whether or not this extra profit can be made depends on how easy it is to influence consumer preferences. Businesses in oligopolies typically find advertising a profitable strategy, especially when large advertising budgets serve as an entry barrier.

NONPRICE COMPETITION AND THE CONSUMER

For the consumer, product differentiation leads to higher prices by raising per-unit costs and enhancing an individual business's market power. However, consumers will likely have more choices because of businesses' efforts to differentiate their products. So, for example, the fact that TVs produced by competing companies are distinctive raises the average price of TVs but gives consumers a wider selection of possible features than they would otherwise have had.

The impact of advertising on the consumer is also mixed. In some cases, advertising is anti-competitive, leading to more market power for established firms. However, advertising can also increase competition. By giving new companies the chance to familiarize buyers with their products, advertising can offer consumers more choice. In this case, advertising lessens the market power of established businesses and leads to more industry flexibility. An example that portrays both possible effects is the Canadian soft-drink industry. This market is an oligopoly that for decades was dominated by two giant businesses, Coca-Cola and PepsiCo, whose market power was enhanced by their high levels of advertising. However, partly through the effects of advertising, smaller private-label producers (usually connected with supermarket chains) have been able to become major players in the Canadian market.

THINKING ABOUT ECONOMICS

Can imperfectly competitive businesses use their market power to charge different prices to different consumers?

Yes. For example, a municipal bus company may offer a discount to students rather than have them not riding the bus at all, a restaurant owner may lower the price of a meal for a lunch special and keep it high for dinner, or an airline will charge lower fares to tourists than to business travellers. This practice, known as "price discrimination," can be used to increase profits by any business with market power (including imperfectly competitive businesses and monopolists), as long as the business can stop customers who pay different prices from exchanging the products between themselves, and the business can distinguish between buyers willing to pay high and low prices by using a condition such as the consumer's age or the time of day when the product is consumed.

Question
Are all consumers hurt when a business adopts a policy of price discrimination?

Industrial Concentration

It is usually fairly obvious that an industry is either perfectly competitive or monopolistic. Most industries, however, fall between the two extremes, and, therefore, represent some form of imperfect competition. It is not always easy to establish whether an imperfectly competitive industry is monopolistically competitive or an oligopoly. The most common indicator is a **concentration ratio**, which is the percentage of total sales revenue in a market earned by the largest business firms.

concentration ratio: the percentage of total sales revenue earned by the largest businesses in the market

Concentration ratios are commonly measured for the four largest business firms in any market, in which case they are known as four-firm ratios. An industry might be considered to be monopolistically competitive if its four-firm ratio is below 50 percent. If the four-firm ratio is above 50 percent, the industry is considered to be an oligopoly. So, for example, if a certain market has total annual sales revenues of $100 million—with the four largest companies having sales of $42 million, $27 million, $14 million, and $8 million—the four-firm ratio is 91 percent ($\frac{42 + 27 + 14 + 8}{100} \times 100\%$). In this case, the industry is considered an oligopoly. Concentration ratios for selected Canadian industries are shown in Figure 6.11.

Because of rapidly expanding foreign trade, Canadian manufacturing markets are in a state of flux. Before these changes began in the late 1980s, about half of Canada's manufacturing industries had four-firm ratios of over 50 percent and could, therefore, be classified as oligopolies. Many Canadian service industries are concentrated as well. Compared with the United States, Canada has relatively small markets, each of which

Figure 6.11	Concentration Ratios in Selected Canadian Industries (1988)

	Share of Industry Sales by Four Largest Businesses
Tobacco products	98.9
Petroleum and coal products	74.5
Transportation	68.4
Beverages	59.2
Metal mining	58.9
Paper and allied industries	38.9
Electrical products	32.1
Printing, publishing, and allied industries	25.7
Food	19.6
Finance	16.4
Machinery	11.3
Retail trade	9.7
Clothing industries	6.6
Construction	2.2

Sales in such industries as tobacco products, beverages, and transportation equipment are dominated by the four top businesses in each industry, indicating high levels of concentration. Meanwhile, in such industries as retail trade, clothing, and construction, the four top businesses in each industry have a much smaller proportion of industry sales, indicating low levels of concentration.

Source: Statistics Canada "Concentration Ratios in Selected Canadian Industries (1998)" adapted from the Statistics Canada publication "Annual Report of the Minister of Industry, Science and Technology Under the Corporations and Labour Unions Returns Act, Part I, Corporations," 1988, Catalogue 61-210, October 1991, p. 94.

is more likely to be dominated by just one or a few businesses. It has been estimated that, overall, about three-fifths of Canadian economic activity takes place in concentrated markets that are either monopolies or oligopolies. In the American economy, the corresponding estimate is just over one-fifth.

Although Statistics Canada has not published industry concentration ratios since 1988, it does calculate the proportion of operating revenue from all sources (not just sales) received by the largest five firms in a variety of Canadian industries. In 1999, for example, these proportions ranged from a high of over 60 percent in banking to less than 10 percent in construction as well as in agriculture, forestry, fishing, and hunting. These proportions, though only rough indicators of market power, give a sense of the extent to which large businesses (both Canadian and foreign) dominate some Canadian markets.

THE DEBATE OVER INDUSTRIAL CONCENTRATION

industrial concentration:
market domination by one or a few large businesses

The effect of market power on the economy can be studied in the context of **industrial concentration**, which refers to the domination of a market by one or a few large companies. Because of their small numbers and great sizes, these companies possess significant market power. Figure 6.12 gives an indication of how large some individual Canadian companies are in relation to Canadian business as a whole.

Can industrial concentration work to the advantage of consumers? To answer this question, we must weigh the costs and the benefits of huge companies dominating a given market.

Increasing Returns to Scale versus Market Power

Defenders of industrial concentration emphasize the role of increasing returns to scale. They say this is especially important in a time when businesses are more likely than

Figure 6.12	Concentration in the Canadian Economy (1999)

**Share of Assets and Share of Revenues
for Enterprises with $75 million or more in Revenues**

	Assets	Revenues
Foreign	$18.9	$26.2
Canadian	57.8	30.5
	$76.7	$56.7

Enterprises with revenues of $75 million or more control over three-quarters of total assets in Canadian industries. Of this, the bulk is controlled by Canadian enterprises. In terms of sales revenue, these enterprises have a less significant share.

Source: Statistics Canada "Concentration in the Canadian Economy (1999)," adapted from the Statistics Canada publication "Corporations Returns Act (CRA)," 1999, Catalogue 61-220, June 2002, pp. 24–25.

ever to compete in huge global markets. In many industries, only large businesses with a substantial market share can produce the quantity of output necessary to take advantage of increasing returns to scale. As a result, these big businesses have lower per-unit costs than would competitive businesses in the same market. These cost savings may then be passed on to consumers in the form of lower prices. Critics of industrial concentration say that the benefits of increasing returns to scale must be weighed against the market power held by large monopolists and oligopolists. This market power allows big companies to charge a higher price than would occur with more competition in the market.

Technical Innovation

Some people have argued that "big business" is needed to promote innovation and technological advances. However, recent evidence points to the opposite conclusion. Companies in highly concentrated industries—either monopolies or oligopolies—tend not to innovate as rapidly as those in more competitive markets, where the continual jockeying for profit encourages improvements in products and production processes.

THINKING ABOUT ECONOMICS

What is happening to concentration ratios as a result of increasing international trade flows throughout the world, as well as the expanded use of the Internet for commercial transactions?

Concentration ratios are becoming less useful indicators of market structure, since Statistics Canada includes only domestic businesses in its calculations. National concentration ratios can overestimate the level of competition in markets that are highly localized, with one or two businesses dominating certain regions. For example, while the many radio broadcasters in Canada would result in low official concentration ratios, the fact that most broadcasters operate in highly concentrated regional markets would not be reflected. But in markets where there is a significant international presence, official concentration ratios underestimate competition by ignoring the role of imports. So, for example, Canada's motor vehicle industry would appear less concentrated if foreign imports were taken into account.

Question

Do official concentration ratios overestimate or underestimate competition in Canada's bookselling industry?

Brief Review

1. Product differentiation and advertising are forms of nonprice competition common in imperfectly competitive markets. Their effect on the consumer is mixed.

2. Concentration ratios are measures of the percentage of total sales revenue in a market as earned by the biggest companies within the industry. These ratios suggest the degree of competition in an industry, although they do have some deficiencies.

3. Industrial concentration has its supporters and its critics. The arguments for and against concentration centre around increasing returns to scale, excess market power, and technical innovation.

6.4 Practice Questions

1. An industry is composed of 12 businesses, each with annual sales of $2 million.
   a. Calculate the industry's four-firm concentration ratio.
   b. How would you categorize this industry?
   c. Could a business in this industry have an incentive to use non-price competition? Explain.
   d. Is non-price competition an offence against Canada's anti-combines laws?
   e. If two of the businesses in this market merged, what type of merger would it be classified as?

2. Big businesses in concentrated industries may be able to take advantage of the lower average costs that come from large outputs. Does this mean that industrial concentration is always good for consumers? Explain.

LAST**WORD**

In this chapter, we have seen how the profit-maximizing procedure for businesses that operate as monopolists, monopolistic competitors, or oligopolists differs from that used by perfect competitors. At their profit-maximizing points, we found that inefficiencies exist in all three market structures, since they break the minimum-cost and marginal-cost rules that regulate social efficiency. Given the possible extent of these inefficiencies in monopolies and oligopolies, regulation and anti-combines legislation is applied in these markets. But these government controls are subject to debate, depending on how one views the potential costs and benefits of industrial concentration.

Key Concepts

accounting-profit rate 137
anti-combines legislation 143
average-cost pricing 137
cartel 132
collusion 132
concentration ratio 147
conglomerate merger 144
fair rate of return 137
horizontal merger 144
industrial concentration 148
kinked demand curve 131
market share 131
mutual interdependence 130
nonprice competition 146
price leadership 132
product differentiation 146
vertical merger 144

Questions

1. For each of the following cases, (i) create a table showing the business's revenue schedules, (ii) plot the business's demand and marginal revenue curves on a sheet of graph paper, and (iii) explain how the relationship between demand and marginal revenue is affected by the type of market in which this business operates.

   a. A dairy farmer, who sells milk in a perfectly competitive market, faces a price of $2 per litre at possible outputs of 1000, 2000, 3000, or 4000 litres per week.

   b. Biodata Software is the sole seller of a programming language with unique scientific applications. The company finds that each month, it can sell 60 copies of the language at a price of $400 and 60 extra copies for each $100 reduction in price.

   c. Stan's Coffee Shop operates in a monopolistically competitive market. It sells 100 cups of coffee daily at a price of 95 cents per cup. For each 5-cent reduction in price, it sells 100 extra cups, until a minimum possible price of 80 cents is reached.

   d. The Big Hair Company sells shampoo in an oligopoly characterized by rivalry. The business's daily sales are 2000 bottles at a price of $3, 4000 at $2.50, 5000 at $2, and 6000 at $1.50.

Profit-Maximization Table for Presto Cleaners

(1) Price ($ per shirt)	(2) Quantity (shirts per month)	(3) Total Revenue ($)	(4) Total Cost ($)	(5) Marginal Revenue ($ per shirt)	(6) Marginal Cost ($ per shirt)	(7) Average Cost ($ per shirt)
	0	$___	$ 3000			
				$___	$___	
$4.50	1000	___	5000			$___
				___	___	
4.00	2000	___	6000			___
				___	___	
3.50	3000	___	7500			___
				___	___	
3.00	4000	___	12000			___
				___	___	
2.50	5000	___	20000			___

2. Presto Cleaners, a small drycleaning shop, operates in a monopolistically competitive market, with revenues and costs as shown in the table above.

   a. Copy and complete the table, and on a sheet of graph paper, plot Presto's demand, marginal-revenue, marginal-cost, and average-cost curves.

   b. Using your graph, identify Presto's profit-maximizing or loss-minimizing quantity of output (rounded to the nearest 1000 shirts) and price and calculate the area of profit or loss. Explain how these values can be derived using the table.

   c. What will happen to Presto's profit or loss in the long run? Explain.

Profit-Maximization Table for Citrus Delight

(1) Price ($ per carton)	(2) Quantity (thousands of cartons per day)	(3) Total Revenue ($ thousands)	(4) Total Cost ($ thousands)	(5) Marginal Revenue ($ per carton)	(6) Marginal Cost ($ per carton)	(7) Average Cost ($ per carton)
	0	$___	$50			
				$___	$___	
$2.10	30	___	90			$___
2.00	60	___	110	___	___	___
1.90	90	___	126	___	___	___
1.70	100	___	139	___	___	___
1.50	110	___	169	___	___	___

3. A producer of fresh orange juice, Citrus Delight, operates in an oligopoly and has revenues and costs as shown in the table above.
   a. Copy and complete the table, and on a sheet of graph paper, plot Citrus Delight's demand, marginal-revenue, marginal-cost, and average-cost curves. Explain the shapes of the demand and marginal revenue curves.
   b. Using your graph, identify Citrus Delight's profit-maximizing or loss-minimizing quantity of output (rounded to the nearest 30 000 cartons) and price and calculate the area of profit or loss.
   c. Will Citrus Delight's profit or loss necessarily disappear in the long run? Explain.

Profit-Maximization Table for True North Railways

(1) Price ($ per passenger	(2) Quantity (passengers per day)	(3) Total Revenue ($)	(4) Total Cost ($)	(5) Marginal Revenue ($ per passenger)	(6) Marginal Cost ($ per passenger)	(7) Average Cost ($ per passenger)
	0	$___	$24 750			
				$___	$___	
$350	50	___	26 750			$___
280	100	___	27 750	___	___	___
210	150	___	27 900	___	___	___
140	200	___	28 000	___	___	___
70	250	___	29 000	___	___	___
0	300	___	34 500	___	___	___

4. True North Railways, which is the sole provider of passenger rail service to a remote community, has revenues and costs shown in the table above.
   a. Copy and complete the table. On a sheet of graph paper, plot True North's demand, marginal-revenue, marginal-cost, and average-cost curves. Would the

business ever freely choose to operate in the output range where marginal revenue is negative? Explain.

b. Using your graph, identify True North's profit-maximizing quantity of output (rounded to the nearest 50 passengers) and price and calculate the area of profit.

c. Government officials decide to regulate True North's operations. Use your graph to identify the average-cost price and associated quantity of output (rounded to the nearest 50 passengers) that regulators could choose. Outline one problem connected with this regulated price.

5. Which of the three sorts of mergers is least likely to lead to a reduction of competition in an industry? Why?

6. An industry is made up of six firms with sales of $50 million, $55 million, $80 million, $30 million, $65 million, and $100 million.
   a. Calculate the industry's four-firm concentration ratio.
   b. How would you categorize this industry?

7. Identify whether official concentration ratios for the following products will tend to overestimate or underestimate the level of competition.
   a. Magazines
   b. Telephone services

8. (Advanced Question)
   For each of the following cases of nonprice competition, outline the likely effects on (i) the business undertaking the strategy, (ii) other businesses in the market, and (iii) consumers.
   a. A recording company is the first to produce recordings of a new style of popular music.
   b. A major corporation that makes laundry soap increases the amount it spends on advertising.
   c. A cosmetics firm changes the brand name of one of its perfumes to give it greater appeal to young buyers.
   d. A lawyer starting her practice decides to break with tradition by advertising the prices she charges.

Internet Application Question

http://www.ct-tc.gc.ca/index.html

Using either media reports or the information provided in the Competition Tribunal's web site (at http://www.ct-tc.gc.ca/index.html), summarize a recent case before the Competition Tribunal involving (a) a merger that could lessen competition, and (b) abuse of dominant position.

CAN CAPITALISM SURVIVE?

Joseph Schumpeter and the Prospects for Capitalism

Joseph Schumpeter (1883–1950) is one of the most famous economists of the 20th century, and the originality of his ideas and the breadth of his learning have been matched by few others. Born in a middle-class business family, he enjoyed an aristocratic upbringing after his father died and his mother married a high-ranking military commander in the Austrian army. Schumpeter studied law and economics at the prestigious University of Vienna. After working as a lawyer, he took up a career as a professor of economics. For a brief period after World War I, he served as the Minister of Finance in the Austrian government. In the 1930s, the political turmoil surrounding the rise of the Nazis in Germany caused him to move to the United States, where he taught for many years at Harvard University.

Joseph Schumpeter
Source: ©Bettmann/CORBIS/Magma

Schumpeter and His Influence

Schumpeter's work is fascinating because of his ability to combine seemingly contradictory ideas. While a strong supporter of capitalism and private markets, he devised a theory of capitalist development that has interesting parallels with the work of Karl Marx. Like Marx, Schumpeter used not only the tools of economics but also the other social sciences. He was, therefore, able to highlight the role played by politics and culture in affecting economic conditions.

The crucial player in Schumpeter's theory of capitalism is the entrepreneur. For Schumpeter, entrepreneurs are much more than risk-takers—they are innovators who, through imagination and creativity, supply new products or adopt new types of technology. While not necessarily inventors, they are able to bring fresh ideas to the marketplace. As Schumpeter noted:

> To carry any improvement into effect is a task entirely different from the inventing of it, and a task, moreover, requiring entirely different kinds of aptitudes. Although entrepreneurs, of course, may be inventors just as they may be capitalists, they are inventors not by nature of their function but by coincidence and vice versa.[1]

Schumpeter saw entrepreneurs as the driving forces of economic progress. He believed that a capitalist system would ensure the fastest possible pace of technological change because capitalism allows entrepreneurs to keep the profits resulting from their innovations.

According to Schumpeter, the importance of perfectly competitive markets is overrated in economic theory. In real capitalist economies, he said, competition usually takes place between a few rivals in oligopolistic markets. In pursuit of profit and market power, the rivals introduce new products and production methods, which, in turn, lead to economic growth and revitalize the capitalist system. Schumpeter called this process "creative destruction," since it destroys parts of the economy at the same time as it creates new industries and products.

Predictions for the Future

Given Schumpeter's opposition to socialism and his strong support for capitalism, we might expect that he would predict the downfall of socialism and the final victory of capitalism throughout the world. On the contrary, he believed that in the long run, capitalism was doomed, not because of its internal economic contradictions but because of cultural and political trends flowing from its success. Hence, in answer to the question, "Can capitalism survive?" he gave the straightforward answer, "No. I do not think it can."[2]

ADVANCING ECONOMIC THOUGHT

According to Schumpeter, because of the advantages they possess, giant companies will gradually take over most industries. In the process, the innovative spirit that once guided them will be crushed, as the imaginative entrepreneur is replaced by the cautious professional manager at the helm of business. Without the entrepreneur, there will no longer be a force in society to support the institution of private property.

At the same time, the growing class of intellectuals—professors, writers, and journalists—who live well off the prosperity provided by the capitalist system, will use their persuasive powers to turn others against capitalism. Therefore, a majority of people will also become opposed to property rights. Why are so many intellectuals hostile to capitalism? Because, stated Schumpeter, most of them are outsiders who are much more competent at criticizing the system than they are at working within it.

Schumpeter predicted that the elimination of the entrepreneur and the new popular hostility towards capitalism would lead to more government involvement in the economy. Attempts would be made by government bureaucrats to smooth out economic fluctuations as well as reduce inequalities in the distribution of incomes. Gradually, the role of private property would shrink, and capitalist societies would turn towards socialism—of either the democratic or the authoritarian variety.

Relevance for Today

It is important to note that Schumpeter developed his theories before and during World War II, before the massive expansion in government activity that took place in developed capitalist countries, such as Canada. In the 1960s and 1970s, as criticism of capitalist institutions became common in Canada and other countries, many commentators suggested that Schumpeter's forecasts contained a good deal of truth. Are his predictions still as applicable in the 2000s as they were in previous decades? Some would argue that there has been a resurgence in entrepreneurship and popular support for capitalism that now makes Schumpeter's theories less relevant than they once were.

> During the late 1960s...Schumpeter's predictions seemed to be coming true. Third World nations, newly liberated from Europe, turned to socialism. By the early 1970s, Ph.D.s were driving taxicabs and blasting the establishment. But what did the 1980s bring us? Yuppies, short hair, striped shirts, and a parade of underdeveloped nations trading Das Kapital in for Dress for Success. ...Nobody urges centralized planning anymore.... Even if a return to market mechanisms does not magically turn poverty into wealth, at least governments have jettisoned rigid, ideological abhorrence of market economic systems.[3]

But, right or wrong, Schumpeter's work provides a classic example of how economic theorizing can be made to include not only economic factors but also political and social trends.

Notes
[1] Joseph A. Schumpeter, *The Theory of Economic Development* (New York: Oxford University Press, 1961), pp. 88–89.
[2] Joseph A. Schumpeter, *Capitalism, Socialism and Democracy* (New York: Harper & Row, 1976), p. 61, as quoted in *New Ideas From Dead Economists* by Todd G. Buchholz. Copyright © 1989 by Todd G. Buchholz. Used by permission of Dutton Signet, a division of Penguin Books USA Inc.
[3] From *New Ideas From Dead Economists* by Todd G. Buchholz. Copyright © 1989 by Todd G. Buchholz. Used by permission of Dutton Signet, a division of Penguin Books USA Inc.

1. Outline one possible reason why Schumpeter's predictions about capitalism have not been borne out in the 1980s and 1990s.

CHAPTER 7

Wages, Rent, Interest, and Profit

We have only one asset, and that is people!
—Sylvia Ostry, Canadian economist

Two activities unite all businesses: they sell products, and they hire resources. So far, we have concentrated on the selling. Now, we will focus on the way businesses use economic resources. How many workers should a particular company hire? Is it worthwhile for the business to purchase and use another machine? Should a farmer use more land to grow a crop? In this chapter, we will examine how businesses make choices about the economic resources they employ. We will also explore the factors that affect incomes from labour and look at other resource incomes—rent, interest, and profit.

LEARNING OBJECTIVES

In this chapter, you will:

1 consider how businesses choose the profit-maximizing amount of a resource they use when they are price-takers in the product markets in which they sell their products

2 learn about the factors that affect wages, including productivity, education, experience, job conditions, regional disparities, market power, and discrimination

3 look at the incomes from other resources—rent, interest, and profit

7.1 How Resource Markets Operate

LO 7.1

In earlier chapters, we have concentrated on product markets—the markets in which consumer goods and services are traded. Now, we will take a look at the other half of the picture—resource markets, in which economic resources are traded. Recall that in resource markets households sell economic resources to businesses, and households receive incomes in return. So, for their contribution of natural resources (including land), capital resources, and human resources (in particular labour and entrepreneurship), households receive incomes in the form of rent, interest, wages, and profit.

When analyzing resource markets, economists are especially interested in the way that resource prices are set, since these prices play a crucial role in determining people's incomes. For example, the relevant price in a labour market is the wage, which is the amount earned by a worker for providing labour for a certain period. While a wage is usually thought of as a worker's income paid on an hourly basis, the term is used more broadly in economics to include workers' incomes (often known as salaries) paid by the day, month, or year. It is important to remember that resource markets are affected by a wide array of factors. While social customs, governments, and labour unions play a part in determining resource prices, the interaction of demand and supply remains the central feature in these markets. Indeed, demand and supply conditions often influence resource markets *despite* outside intervention.

The Demand for Resources

Unlike the demand for consumer items, the demand for resources is determined indirectly. Since resources are used to produce final goods and services, it is the demand for these products that ultimately determines how much of the resources are demanded. For example, the number of printing presses demanded by a newspaper publishing company depends on the demand for the company's product. If the newspaper attracts more readers, the company will respond by increasing production and, therefore, buying more printing presses. Similarly, the number of workers hired by a car manufacturer depends on demand in the car market. A drop in the demand for cars will lower the demand for workers, resulting in hiring freezes and, perhaps, even layoffs.

marginal productivity theory: the theory that businesses use resources on the basis of how much extra profit these resources provide

To calculate resource demand, economists use **marginal productivity theory**, which states that businesses use resources on the basis of how much extra profit these resources provide. Therefore, when deciding whether or not it is profitable to buy one more unit of a resource, businesses consider three factors: the resource's marginal cost, its marginal product, and the marginal revenue provided by each new unit of output produced. To illustrate the resource choices a business makes, we will look at businesses with varying powers in product markets.

Product and Resource Price-Taker

Let us first consider the example of a strawberry farm. We will assume that the strawberry market is perfectly competitive, that the farmer hires labour in a perfectly competitive resource market, and that the factors other than output and labour remain constant. So, the farmer hires workers in a market with many buyers and sellers, each of them having no effect on the prevailing price of the resource—namely, the hourly wage for farm workers. Therefore, the strawberry farm is a price-taker in both its product and resource markets.

According to the marginal productivity theory, a business decides how much of a resource to use on the basis of the resource's marginal product and marginal revenue, in addition to the resource's marginal cost to the business.

MARGINAL PRODUCT

The strawberry farmer must first estimate how much output will be added by hiring each new worker, while all other factors remain constant. In other words, the farmer must determine each worker's marginal product. Columns 1, 2, and 3 of the table in Figure 7.1 show the results. For the sake of simplicity, we assume that the marginal product of labour starts to decline with the very first worker. At harvest time, the farmer hires more labour, and the total quantity of strawberries picked per hour increases, as shown in column 2. However, the marginal product of labour, shown in column 3, declines. For example, when the second worker is hired, the total product of strawberries rises from 10 to 18 kg, giving a marginal product for the second worker of 8 kg (18 − 10). With the third worker, the total product rises from 18 to 24 kg, giving a marginal product for the third worker of only 6 kg (24 − 18).

Marginal Revenue

Once the marginal product of each worker is determined, the farmer must calculate the marginal revenue gained by selling the additional strawberries. Because the farmer is a price-taker in the perfectly competitive strawberry market, the price of strawberries is constant, and the price and marginal revenue for strawberries are equal. Hence, the

---

Figure 7.1   Labour Demand and Supply for a Product and Resource Price-Taker

Labour Demand and Supply Schedules for a Strawberry Farm

(1) Labour (L) (no. of workers)	(2) Total Product (q) (kilograms)	(3) Marginal Product (MP) ($\Delta q/\Delta L$) (kilograms)	(4) Output Price (P) ($ per kilogram)	(5) Total Revenue (TR) (P × q)	(6) Marginal Revenue Product (MRP = $\Delta TR/\Delta L$)	(7) Marginal Resource Cost (MRC = W) ($ per hour)
0	0		$2	$ 0		
1	10	10	2	20	$20 (a)	$10
2	18	8	2	36	16 (b)	10
3	24	6	2	48	12 (c)	10
4	28	4	2	56	8 (e)	10 ⟩(d)
5	30	2	2	60	4 (f)	10

Labour Demand and Supply Curves for a Strawberry Farm

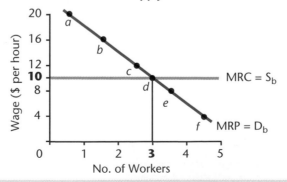

The price-taking business's demand for labour (D_b) is found by calculating the marginal revenue product (MRP), or the change in the business's total revenue from hiring each new worker. The business's supply curve (S_b) is the marginal resource cost (MRC) of each new worker. Since the business can hire workers at a constant wage, S_b is a horizontal line, and the business's profit-maximizing employment level of labour is at point d.

farmer needs to know only the price of strawberries to find marginal revenue. Figure 7.1 shows the price of strawberries in column 4 as $2 per kilogram.

MARGINAL REVENUE PRODUCT

marginal revenue product: the change in total revenue associated with employing each new unit of a resource

The effects of marginal product and marginal revenue on the business's demand for labour are summarized by the concept of **marginal revenue product** (MRP), which is the change in total revenue associated with employing each new unit of a resource—in this case, each new worker. Because it represents the *extra* revenue provided by the *extra* units of output produced by each new worker, marginal revenue product incorporates both marginal revenue and marginal product. The table in Figure 7.1 shows total revenue in column 5 (found by multiplying each total product value by price), and the marginal revenue product (the change in total revenue) in column 6. Expressing the marginal revenue product on the graph gives us the marginal revenue product curve. So, in the strawberry farm example, total revenue is $20 (10 × $2) when employing one worker and $36 (18 × $2) when employing two workers. Therefore, the marginal revenue product of the second worker is the difference between the two amounts, or $16 ($36 − $20), shown on the graph at point *b*.

LABOUR DEMAND AND SUPPLY

marginal resource cost: the extra cost of each additional unit of a resource

Given this information, it is a straightforward task for the strawberry farmer to find the profit-maximizing employment of labour. The extra cost of each additional unit of a resource for the business is referred to as **marginal resource cost** (MRC). In the case of the strawberry farmer, who is a price-taker in the labour market and, therefore, a "wage-taker," marginal resource cost is simply the prevailing wage paid to farm workers. In our example, the wage is $10 per hour. According to the marginal productivity theory, the employer will use additional resources as long as marginal resource cost does not exceed marginal revenue product. Therefore, our strawberry farmer will hire three workers because each of the first three workers adds revenue ($20, $16, and $12, respectively) greater than the $10 cost per worker. Beyond this point, it is not profitable to hire more workers, since the extra revenue that each worker will provide the business will be less than the extra cost of that worker.

business's labour demand curve: a graph showing the possible combinations of workers demanded by a business at each possible wage

business's labour supply curve: a graph showing the possible combinations of workers supplied to a business at each possible wage

Expressed on the graph in Figure 7.1, the marginal revenue product curve represents the **business's labour demand curve** (D_b). The business's labour demand curve shows how many workers are demanded by a business at each possible wage. The demand curve has a negative (downward) slope because businesses find it profitable to employ more workers at lower wages. The marginal resource cost curve represents the **business's labour supply curve** (S_b). This curve shows how many workers are supplied to a business at each possible wage. Because the business is a price-taker in the resource market, this curve is horizontal. No matter what action the strawberry farmer takes, the wage is fixed at the equilibrium wage determined by the entire market.

PROFIT-MAXIMIZING EMPLOYMENT RULE

profit-maximizing employment rule: a business should use a resource up to the point where the resource's marginal revenue product equals its marginal resource cost

The profit-maximizing point for the business occurs at the intersection of its demand and supply curves for labour (D_b and S_b). In other words, the business will hire workers up to the point where marginal revenue product and marginal resource cost are the same. This result provides a general **profit-maximizing employment rule** for resources. No matter what market a business operates in, it should use a resource up to the point where the resource's marginal revenue product equals its marginal resource cost.

Profit-maximizing employment rule:

$$\begin{array}{ccc} \text{Marginal revenue} & & \text{Marginal resource} \\ \text{product} & = & \text{cost} \\ \text{(MRP)} & & \text{(MRC)} \end{array}$$

Note that the profit-maximizing employment rule parallels the profit-maximizing output rule (outlined in Chapter 5), which is used by businesses to decide levels of output. Recall that the profit-maximizing output rule states that in order to maximize profits, a business should produce the quantity of output at which marginal revenue and marginal cost intersect, since up to this point, every unit of output has a marginal revenue that exceeds its marginal cost. Similarly, a business can maximize its profits by using a resource up to the point at which marginal revenue product equals marginal resource cost. By doing so, the business employs all units that give more *extra* revenue than they add to the business's costs.

THINKING ABOUT ECONOMICS

Is marginal productivity theory equally applicable to economic resources other than labour?

In theory, a business should make choices about all economic resources on the basis of each resource's marginal revenue product and marginal resource cost. In practice, however, marginal revenue product tends to be calculated for labour and for natural resources but not for the other economic resources. This is because both labour and natural resources can be measured in standardized units—for example, an hour of a certain type of labour or a hectare of a certain grade of land.

In contrast, it is usually harder to calculate marginal revenue product for capital goods. While it is possible to calculate the marginal revenue product of a particular material or type of machine used by a business, this cannot be done for an entire investment project—when a business contemplates building a factory, for example. One investment project differs so much from another that it is impossible to measure them in standardized units. Because they are physically indivisible, they must be counted in monetary terms—the number of dollars a business needs to undertake a certain investment project.

Question
Entrepreneurship is also difficult to measure. Why?

MARKET DEMAND AND SUPPLY

labour market demand curve: a graph showing the possible combinations of workers demanded in a certain labour market at each possible wage

labour market supply curve: a graph showing the possible combinations of workers supplying their labour in a certain labour market at each possible wage

Now, if we assume that all 1000 employers of farm workers in the region have marginal revenue product curves identical to the one shown in Figure 7.1, we can derive the **labour market demand curve** (D_m). The labour market demand curve shows how many workers are demanded in a competitive labour market at each possible wage. By adding the labour demand curves of all businesses in this market, we have the labour market demand schedule and curve shown in Figure 7.2. For example, at an hourly wage of $14, each of the 1000 farmers demands two workers, which gives a total labour demand of 2000. If the wage were to drop to $10, each farmer would demand three workers, raising total labour demanded in the market to 3000.

Corresponding to this market demand for farm workers is a **labour market supply curve** (S_m), which shows the total supply of workers offering their services in a

Figure 7.2 Demand and Supply in a Competitive Labour Market

The market demand curve for strawberry farm workers (D$_m$) is found by adding together the workers demanded by each farm at various wages. In a competitive labour market, this demand curve and the market supply curve (S$_m$) intersect at equilibrium point e.

certain labour market at each wage. This curve has a positive (upward) slope because, in general, higher wages in a given market encourage more workers to offer their labour in that market. Suppose that for our strawberry market, wages increase from $10 per hour to $14 per hour. Figure 7.2 shows that this wage increase would increase the quantity of farm workers supplied from 3000 to 4000. Figure 7.2 also demonstrates another feature of resource markets that is similar to that in product markets: equilibrium occurs at the intersection of the labour market supply and demand curves.

Changes in Resource Demand

Resource demand can change for a variety of reasons. There are three main resource demand determinants: changes in product demand, changes in other resource prices, and technological innovation. Each demand determinant affects the business's marginal revenue product, which, in turn, causes a change in resource demand.

PRODUCT DEMAND

Recall that the demand for resources depends on the demand for the consumer products these resources help to produce. Therefore, when the demand for a certain product changes, the demand for resources used to produce the product changes in the same direction. As more people use computers in their leisure time, for example, the demand for computer programmers will increase. Meanwhile, if skiing becomes less popular as a pastime, the demand for ski-lift operators will decline.

Changes in product demand affect the demand for resources through changes in product prices. For example, if the demand for strawberries increases, their price increases, and each strawberry farm worker's marginal revenue product increases as well. Each strawberry farmer's marginal revenue product curve shifts to the right, as does the business's demand curve for labour. Therefore, the entire market demand curve for farm workers shifts to the right. In the same way, a decrease in the demand for cushions decreases the price Nirvana Cushions can charge, which, in turn, decreases each worker's marginal revenue product and reduces the business's demand for labour.

OTHER RESOURCE PRICES

complementary resources: resources that are used together

Resources used in a particular production process can be related in two ways. **Complementary resources** are used together, as in the case of steam shovels and steam-shovel operators. When two resources are complementary, the price for one resource and the demand for the other resource have an inverse relationship. So, for example, if steam shovels drop in price, the number of these machines will increase, and the demand for the labour of steam-shovel operators will increase as well.

substitute resources: resources that can be used in place of one another without affecting output

Substitute resources, in contrast, are resources that can be used in place of one another without affecting the business's or industry's output. The price for one resource and the demand for the substitute resource have a direct relationship. So, for example, if steam shovels drop in price, use of these machines will increase, and demand for manual labour will decrease.

TECHNOLOGICAL INNOVATION

labour productivity: the quantity of output produced per worker in a given period of time; the average product of labour

A third resource demand determinant is technological innovation. Suppose a new cushion-producing machine is introduced at Nirvana Cushions. If labour and the new machinery are complementary resources, each worker's marginal product will rise and Nirvana Cushions' demand for labour will increase. In this case, there will also likely be an increase in **labour productivity**, which is the quantity of output produced per worker in a given period of time—in other words, the average product of labour.

THINKING ABOUT ECONOMICS

How does the increased use of capital resources in the Canadian economy affect Canadian workers?

Recall that businesses producing a certain product can usually choose from among production processes that combine different proportions of inputs. For a given quantity of output, a labour-intensive process employs more labour and less capital resources, while a capital-intensive process employs less labour and more capital resources. The use of more capital-intensive methods of production by Canadian businesses affects parts of Canada's workforce in different ways. As a rule, highly skilled labour benefits when more capital-intensive forms of production are used. Since this labour is usually a complementary resource to new forms of machinery, the employment of more capital by Canadian businesses tends to raise the productivity as well as the demand for skilled labour.

The effects of capital-intensive production processes on semiskilled and unskilled labour are more indefinite. In the past, automated production processes in manufacturing industries often called for workers to perform simplified and highly repetitive tasks. In these cases, labour was a complementary resource to machinery: continued automation increased labour demand and raised both wages and employment levels. However, with the growth of the new economy, new types of capital resources have increasingly been substituted for semiskilled and unskilled labour. As the use of capital resources increases, therefore, the demand for semiskilled or unskilled labour decreases.

http://www.hrdc.gc.ca/menu/jobs.html

Question
Some types of semiskilled and unskilled labour are complementary with the capital resources used in the new economy. What is an example?

However, if Nirvana Cushions' workers and the new machinery are substitute resources, the use of this new machine will reduce the marginal product of each worker, and Nirvana's demand for labour in this industry will decrease.

Brief Review

1. Resource markets, like product markets, are governed by the forces of demand and supply. However, the demand for resources is determined indirectly.

2. On the basis of the profit-maximizing employment rule, businesses decide how much of a resource to use by equating the resource's MRP (the change in total revenue associated with each new unit of resource) and MRC (the extra cost to the business of employing each additional unit of resource).

3. In a perfectly competitive resource market, the business is a price-taker; therefore, the business's resource supply (or MRC) curve is a horizontal line. In this market, the profit-maximizing employment level occurs where the business's resource demand (or MRP) curve and its resource supply curve intersect.

4. In a perfectly competitive resource market, the market's resource demand is the sum of the individual businesses' resource demand. The market's resource supply is the sum of all the individual resource owners' resource supply. Equilibrium is the point at which the market demand and market supply curves for the resource intersect.

5. Resource demand can be affected by changes in product demand, changes in other resource prices, and technological innovation.

7.1 Practice Questions

1. A farmer sells pumpkins in a perfectly competitive product market at a price of $1 per kg and hires workers in a perfectly competitive labour market at an hourly wage of $15. The farmer's hourly total product is 30 kgs when employing one worker, 54 kgs with two workers, 72 kgs with three workers, 84 kgs with four workers, and 90 kgs with five workers.

   a. Construct a table similar to the one in Figure 7.1 to calculate the marginal revenue product of each worker this farmer could hire.
   b. Compare these values for marginal revenue product with the farmer's marginal resource cost, and identify how many workers the farmer will choose to hire. Explain your answer using the profit-maximizing employment rule.
   c. Using EconGraphKit (at http://www.mcgrawhill.ca/college/lovewell), draw the farmer's marginal revenue product and marginal resource cost curves, and show the farmer's profit-maximizing employment level.
   d. If there are 10 000 identical employers of farm workers in this region, then how many farm workers will be demanded at a wage of $15?
   e. Using EconGraphKit (at http://www.mcgrawhill.ca/college/lovewell), draw the labour demand curve for this market, as well as a possible labour supply curve that gives an equilibrium wage of $15.

2. Identify how each of the following situations in the fruit-growing industry affects the demand for unskilled farm labour.

   a. Nutrition-conscious consumers increase their demand for fruit.
   b. New fruit-picking machines are introduced.
   c. The growth of urban areas in fruit-growing areas causes the rents for fruit-growing farmland to undergo a significant increase.

7.2 Wages and their Determinants

LO 7.2

So far, we have examined how the forces of demand and supply determine the wage in a given labour market. Now, let us study the big picture of many markets and of various jobs and the factors that determine wages for Canadian workers.

Looking at the wider national labour market highlights the tremendous differences among Canadians' incomes gained from labour. Figure 7.3 shows the distribution of earnings (defined as wages and self-employed income) in the Canadian economy. In 2000, about three out of 10 Canadian earners made less than $15 000 annually. At the other end of the scale, over one in four Canadian earners made $40 000 or more. (These figures are earnings before taxes.)

There are seven main determinants of wage levels in labour markets: labour productivity, education, experience, job conditions, regional disparities, market power, and discrimination.

LABOUR PRODUCTIVITY

As seen earlier in this chapter, in a given job market, the level of labour productivity, or the output per worker in a given time, determines the wage of that worker. Among the

Figure 7.3   Distribution of Earnings (2000)

Earnings	Percentage of All Earners
Under $5000	13.4
$5000–$9999	11.4
$10 000–$14 999	9.2
$15 000–$19 999	8.4
$20 000–$24 999	7.8
$25 000–$29 999	8.1
$30 000–$34 999	7.2
$35 000–$39 999	6.3
$40 000–$44 999	5.5
$45 000–$49 999	4.5
$50 000–$59 999	6.7
$60 000 and over	11.5
	100.0

Earnings of Canadians varied widely, with over 3 out of 10 Canadian earners making less than $15 000 annually. In contrast, 1 in 4 Canadian earners made $40 000 or more annually.

Source: Statistics Canada "Distribution of Earnings (2000)," adapted from the Statistics Canada publication "Income Trends in Canada," October 2002, Catalogue 13F0022, June 2003, Table 101.

determinants of labour income, productivity is the most important. The output of each worker varies because of such factors as the worker's ability to do the job, the use of complementary resources, and the state of technology. With more capable workers, additional complementary resources, or a technological innovation, the marginal revenue product of each worker rises, pushing up the demand for labour as well as the prevailing wage.

Education

In general, the more education a worker needs to perform a job, the higher is the pay. As Figure 7.4 shows, using the example of income earners in managerial occupations, those with a university degree earn considerably more annual income than those with only up to eight years of school. The most significant differences in average annual incomes are between those with eight or less years of schooling and those with some high school education ($22 385 compared with $41 033, or an 83 percent increase for the person with some high school education), and for those with post-secondary diplomas and those with university degrees ($49 657 compared with $76 238, or a 54 percent increase for the university graduate). Work that requires job-related training tends to have a higher marginal revenue product than does work that requires very little job-related training, so education is linked to labour productivity. Therefore, education has an impact on labour demand.

Education also has an impact on labour supply. As every student knows, education is costly and time-consuming. For example, students who undertake a full-time post-secondary program have not only out-of-pocket costs, such as tuition and books, but also an important opportunity cost: the income that could have been earned by entering the workforce immediately. Of course, students who attend public post-secondary institutions do not bear the entire cost of their education (taxpayers, through government programs, pick up the remainder). Education provides benefits; acquiring skills and knowledge may itself be a reward for the work and effort involved. Just the same, a worker entering the labour force with a higher education tends to expect a return on his or her education investment.

human capital: the income-earning potential of a person's skills and knowledge

Economists view work-related education as an investment in **human capital**, which is the income-earning potential of a person's skills and knowledge. According to this perspective, an educational program is only worthwhile if the expected rise in the

Figure 7.4	Education and Average Income (2000)

Education	Average Incomes (Managerial Occupations)
University degree	$76 238
Post-secondary diploma	49 657
Some post-secondary	43 805
High school graduate	39 571
Some high school	41 033
0 to 8 years of school	22 385

In general, incomes rise with the educational level achieved by the income earner. Average earnings for those with a university degree are much higher than those for income earners who have completed the eighth grade or less of schooling.

Source: Statistics Canada "Education and Average Family Income (2000)," adapted from the Statistics Canada publication "Income Trends in Canada," October 2002, Catalogue 13F0022, June 2003, Table 106.

individual's lifetime income outweighs the sum of that education's direct and indirect costs. "Human capital" expresses the ways in which an individual's education choices correspond to businesses' investment decisions, but it is important not to let this term mask education's distinctive features. Education often has a consumption component, which is the pleasure associated with learning. This component may be especially significant in subject areas with little income-earning potential.

Experience

seniority rights: the workplace privileges provided to workers who have the longest experience with their employer

Experience is another determining factor of income levels. On-the-job experience increases a worker's productivity, pushing up the demand for the worker's labour and the wage rate. In many industries, workers gain certain privileges the longer they work for a single employer. Because of these **seniority rights**, older workers are often paid higher wages and can apply first for promotions and overtime work, allowing them to earn higher incomes than their younger colleagues.

The positive effect of workplace experience on earnings is one of the main reasons why average incomes rise with age during the first part of a person's working life. Figure 7.5 shows the relationship between age and average incomes using the case of those in managerial occupations. As the age of the income earner rises to the 45 to 54 age range, average family income increases; thereafter, incomes tend to decrease as workers retire.

Job Conditions

Often, two occupations provide very different earnings even when productivity and education levels in each occupation are the same. One reason for this discrepancy is that working conditions in the two occupations can make one less appealing than the other. In order to attract workers to less-appealing occupations, employers must offer higher wages. For example, garbage collectors receive higher wages than most other unskilled workers, in part because of their unattractive working conditions.

Figure 7.5   Age and Average Income (2000)

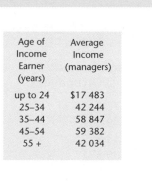

Age of Income Earner (years)	Average Income (managers)
up to 24	$17 483
25–34	42 244
35–44	58 847
45–54	59 382
55 +	42 034

As shown by the case of those in managerial occupations, average incomes generally rise and then fall with the age of the income earner, peaking at the 45 to 54 age bracket.

Source: Statistics Canada "Age and Average Family Income (2000)," adapted from the Statistics Canada publication "Income Trends in Canada," October 2002, Catalogue 13F0022, June 2003, Table 106.

THINKING ABOUT
ECONOMICS

Suppose three friends graduating from high school choose different career paths: the first enters the workforce directly as a clerical worker, the second enrolls in a university arts program for a major in English literature with a focus on medieval poetry, and the third pursues a degree in computer science. What do these decisions suggest about the friends' economic choices?

According to the economic view of human capital, by not making a further investment in education, the first friend sacrifices possible income gains later in life for immediate earnings. In other words, receiving a dollar in purchasing power now is worth much more to this individual than receiving greater purchasing power in the future. The English major is willing to give up immediate income for future benefit and will likely have a future income greater than the first friend's but perhaps not as much as he would if he pursued another type of post-

secondary education. From this economic viewpoint, this friend sees the knowledge he will gain from his post-secondary education primarily as a consumption item rather than as an investment in human capital. The third friend is also willing to give up immediate income for future increases in welfare. She views education as an investment in her human capital to increase future earning power and, hopefully, as a source of pleasure as well.

Question
Is any one of these economic choices more rational than the others?

Regional Disparities

Wage differences often have a geographic dimension. In Canada, workers in the same occupation earn different incomes, depending on the region they live in. For example, a fishplant worker in British Columbia may earn more than a worker doing the identical job in Newfoundland. In a perfectly functioning labour market, workers in a single occupation would move from one part of the country to another until wage disparities in this occupation were eliminated. However, labour tends to be immobile. Even when workers find moving to be economically feasible, they and their families may be reluctant to adjust to new jobs, schools, and surroundings. Labour immobility is especially pronounced for multiple-income families because of the added difficulty of two or more people changing jobs. Immobility is also common among older workers, who tend to be more settled in their jobs and communities.

Market Power

The market power workers have also affects their wages. As a rule, earnings in labour markets that are unionized tend to be higher than in non-unionized markets. Professional organizations for such groups as doctors and lawyers can also play a similar role in providing their members with market power. There are two main methods that unionized workers can use to increase their market power—industrial unions and craft unions—each of which influences labour markets in different ways.

INDUSTRIAL UNIONS

industrial union: a labour union of workers in a certain industry, no matter what their occupations

An **industrial union** includes workers in a certain industry, no matter what their occupations. Hence, these unions are also referred to as inclusive unions and are most common in sectors that primarily use unskilled and semiskilled labour. The automobile, steel, and forestry industries are examples.

CRAFT UNIONS

craft union: a labour union of workers in a particular occupation

A **craft union** includes workers in a particular occupation. Craft unions restrict whom they allow to be members, so they are also referred to as exclusive unions. They are common in skilled trades, such as printing, as well as in some parts of the construction industry, such as carpentry and bricklaying. Some professional organizations, which limit numbers of newcomers in a particular occupation, can also be viewed as being similar to craft unions. In any labour market dominated by a craft union, acquiring a union card is an essential first step in being allowed to work. To become a member of such a union, a worker often must complete an apprenticeship program and write a licensing examination. While craft unions' requirements attempt to ensure craft standards, they also allow unions to determine the supply of workers in the market and to negotiate higher wages for their members.

Discrimination

job discrimination: hiring, wage, and promotion decisions based on criteria other than a worker's credentials or performance

Discrimination, too, can play a role in determining wages. **Job discrimination** occurs when decisions regarding hiring, wages, or promotion are based on some trait of the worker other than credentials or performance. Job discrimination stems from the prejudices of employers and may be based on a variety of factors, for example, gender, race, age, or physical ability. While job discrimination in a variety of forms is illegal, it still exists.

Job discrimination is an important factor in explaining the wage gap between men and women, which in 2000 meant that women on average earned 71.7 percent of the average wage for men. Canadian studies suggest that while 40 percent of this gap is related to differences in hours worked by men and women, a third is due to a discriminatory division of jobs, and another 10 percent to direct job discrimination, which involves paying men and women different amounts for substantially the same work. The remainder of the gap is explained by a variety of factors, such as differing average levels of experience, education, and unionization for men and women.

Brief Review

1. Wages vary significantly in the Canadian labour market. Factors that determine wage levels are labour productivity, education, experience, job conditions, regional disparities, market power, and discrimination.

2. Work-related education and training can be viewed as an investment in human capital, or an individual's earning power. Ignoring the consumption aspect of knowledge, an education is worthwhile when its returns, in the form of future income gains, exceed its direct and indirect costs.

3. The positive effect of experience and seniority rights on earnings is one of the main reasons why family income tends to rise with age.

4. Industrial unions represent all workers in a certain industry, so they negotiate wages across an industry; craft unions represent workers in a particular occupation; and they can both affect the supply of labour in the market and negotiate wages.

7.2 Practice Questions

1. In each of the following cases, which worker is likely to be paid a higher wage? Identify the primary wage determinant that is relevant in each case.

   a. a carpenter residing in Alberta or a carpenter residing in Quebec
   b. a truck driver or a janitor
   c. a postal worker or an employee of a courier company
   d. a waitress or a warehouse clerk
   e. a lawyer or a paralegal consultant

7.3 Other Resource Incomes

rent: the payment for use of a productive resource that is available only in a fixed amount

LO 7.3

Rent

So far, we have concentrated on the income from labour. Now, let us turn to the other resource incomes. The first, **rent**, is defined very precisely in economics as the payment for use of a productive resource that is available in only a fixed amount. Note that it is distinct from the term "rent" in more general use. For example, the total monthly payment to a landowner by a tenant often includes not only economic rent (payment for a resource in fixed supply) but also payment for utilities, maintenance, and administration, plus a normal profit for the owners. Land is the most significant resource that provides rent. With few exceptions (for example, when landfilling or drainage systems create more land), land is available in only a fixed supply.

THE MARKET FOR LAND

To see how the rent for land is determined, we must make a number of assumptions. We will assume that we can separate economic rent from payments for any buildings or improvements made on the land; we will assume that the market for land is competitive, with many buyers and sellers; and we will assume that each unit of land is of the same quality.

The Equilibrium Value of Rent

Figure 7.6 shows demand and supply for land in a particular region. Because there is a fixed supply of land, the supply curve is perfectly inelastic, or vertical at its fixed amount. Demand, however, is variable; quantity demanded decreases at higher rents and increases at lower rents. Therefore, the demand curve for land has a negative (downward) slope. Market equilibrium occurs at a rent of $10, where the two curves intersect. Since we have assumed that we can separate economic rent from other payments, this $10 is entirely payment for the land.

Changes in Demand

Because the supply of land is fixed, only a change in demand can vary the equilibrium value of rent. Recall that the demand for resources is determined indirectly because it is derived from demand for other products. Therefore, the main factor that can change demand for land is a change in the price for the products the land is used to produce. Suppose that the land in the region we are considering is devoted entirely to cattle ranching and that all cattle ranchers are renting land from landowners. In

Figure 7.6	Equilibrium in the Market for Land

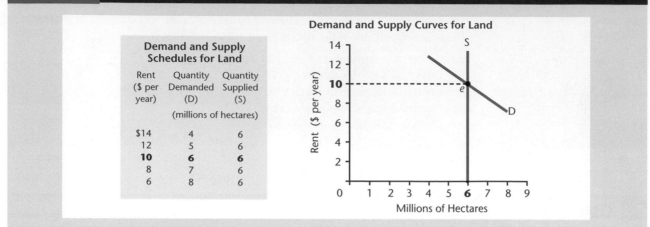

Demand and Supply Schedules for Land

Rent ($ per year)	Quantity Demanded (D)	Quantity Supplied (S)
	(millions of hectares)	
$14	4	6
12	5	6
10	**6**	**6**
8	7	6
6	8	6

The demand curve for land shows the total quantities of land demanded at each rent. Given that the region has a fixed supply of land (6 million hectares), the supply curve for land is a vertical line. Equilibrium occurs at point *e*, giving a rent of $10 for each hectare of land.

Figure 7.7, the initial demand is shown as D_0, and point *a* is the original equilibrium. If the price of beef rises, cattle ranchers will find they can increase their revenue for each unit of land. As a result, cattle ranchers will demand more land at every possible price, thus shifting the demand curve to the right, to D_1. The change in the demand will cause the equilibrium value of rent to rise to $12 (point *b*).

LO	7.3

Interest

Another form of income that contributes to the overall incomes of Canadians is interest. While related to the supply of capital resources, interest can also be viewed as a

Figure 7.7	Changes in the Demand for Land

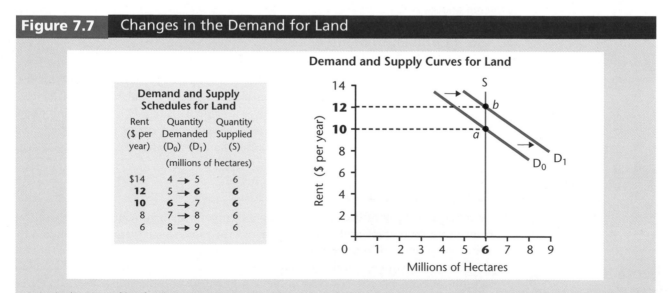

Demand and Supply Schedules for Land

Rent ($ per year)	Quantity Demanded (D_0) (D_1)		Quantity Supplied (S)
	(millions of hectares)		
$14	4 → 5		6
12	5 → **6**		6
10	**6** → 7		6
8	7 → 8		6
6	8 → 9		6

A rise in the price of beef will increase the quantity demanded of ranch land at every possible rent, as shown by the shift from D_0 to D_1. As a result, equilibrium moves from point *a* to point *b*, and rent increases from $10 to $12 per hectare.

THINKING ABOUT ECONOMICS

Does the economic analysis for land apply to other types of productive resources?

It does only if the other resources have a fixed supply. Consider a natural resource, such as minerals or water. If the known supply is limited (and therefore fixed), payments over and above the costs for extracting, processing, and distributing the resource can be called economic rents.

There is another interesting application of the economic theory of rent. A few lucky individuals, such as star athletes or entertainers, owe their success to the talents they possess. We might consider their talents as having a fixed supply. Therefore, much of the income earned by these people is really an economic rent that pays them for making their talents available in the market. Consider, for example, the hockey star Paul Kariya. We could consider a portion of his multimillion-dollar yearly salary to be a wage, but most of it is an economic rent paid by team owners who want to reap the rewards of having a future superstar on their team.

Question
Does all of Paul Kariya's salary represent an economic rent? Why not?

---

principal: the amount of a loan, excluding interest

interest: the payment to a lender by the borrower for use of money loaned

financial income. When money is lent to a consumer or business, the lender requires that not only the **principal** (the loan amount) be paid back but also that **interest** (a payment for use of the money) be paid. Interest, in effect, is payment by the borrower to the lender for the opportunity cost of the money being used in one way over another. In other words, interest is the price of borrowing money.

Interest is determined as a percentage of the principal, which is known as the interest rate. The interest rate, or rate of return on loanable funds, is one of the key prices in the economy.

Consider the example of a travel agency, Mariposa Vacations, which decides to borrow $2000 from a bank. The bank agrees to lend the money for a year and sets the interest rate at 7 percent *per annum*. Interest rates are typically given as *per annum*, or per year. Therefore, at the end of the year, Mariposa Vacations will pay back the principal ($2000) plus interest at a rate of 7 percent (0.07 × $2000 = $140), for a total of $2140 ($2000 + $140).

RANGE OF INTEREST RATES

Not all loans have the same interest rate. The interest rate charged on a particular loan depends on four factors: the borrower's credit risk, the loan period, whether or not collateral is provided, and the size of the loan.

Credit Risk

credit risk: the assessed likelihood of a borrower not repaying a loan

When deciding whether to lend funds to a borrower, a lender tries to establish the borrower's **credit risk**, which is the assessed likelihood of the borrower not repaying the loan. In the case of a business, if the business has healthy profits, a solid history and a strong future in the industry, a small existing debt, and a record of repaying loans on time, the credit risk is low. So, for example, Bell Canada would pay a lower interest rate than would a new goldmining business with no track record.

Loan Period

In general, the shorter the time before the loan must be repaid, the lower is the interest rate; the longer the time, the higher is the interest rate. In effect, the borrower pays for the added time the lender will not have that money available and for the added risk of an extended loan period. For example, a lender might be willing to lend funds for a single year at an annual interest rate of 8 percent, but the same borrower would be charged an annual rate of 10 percent for a two-year period.

Collateral

collateral: assets pledged by a borrower as security against a loan; these assets can be seized by the lender if the loan is not repaid

Lenders often have the security of **collateral**, which are assets pledged by a borrower as security. If a loan is not repaid, the lender acquires these assets. Collateral can take a variety of forms. For example, a mortgage is a loan whose collateral is in the form of land and buildings. As a rule, lenders demand a higher interest rate on loans that are not secured with collateral than on those that are secured with collateral.

Size of the Loan

The larger the loan, the lower is its interest rate. Because lending involves certain administration charges—for example, for paperwork and collections—that do not change substantially with the size of the loan, it is cheaper for the lender to make one loan for $1 million rather than 50 loans for $20 000 each.

LO 7.3

Profit and Entrepreneurship

Profit is the last resource income. Recall that economic profit is a business's total revenue minus total implicit and explicit costs. In other words, a positive economic profit is the income paid to owners of a business after all other resource payments have been made. Critics of the capitalist system attribute profit to the power of business owners rather than to their contributions to the economy. While it is true that profits can be excessive, profit serves an important positive function in private markets by acting as a return to entrepreneurs for their risk-taking. In a private-market economy, no one will take on the risks of owning a business unless they can expect to make at least a normal profit return. Profit, therefore, provides an essential private incentive for people to take these risks.

Brief Review

1. In economics, rent is the payment for use of a productive resource that is available in only a fixed quantity, such as land.

2. Because the supply of land is fixed, only changes in the demand for land can affect the equilibrium value of its rent. The fact that resource demands are derived demands means that the major factor that can change the demand for land is a change in the price of the products that the land is used to produce.

3. Interest is income earned on money that is lent. The interest rate an individual borrower pays depends on the borrower's credit risk, the loan period, whether or not collateral is provided, and the size of the loan.

4. Profit is the income paid to owners of a business after all other resource payments have been made. At least a normal profit is essential if individuals are to engage in entrepreneurial activity in a private market economy.

7.3 Practice Questions

1. In each of the following cases, identify the relevant change in demand or supply and the direction of the trend in the price of the resource.

   a. A major oil spill causes land rents to change in a certain coastal resort area.

   b. The economic rent a visual artist receives from each piece of art she sells changes due to the decision by a major art gallery to showcase her work.

   c. The economic rents gained by professional Canadian hockey players are affected by the influx of European hockey players into North American professional leagues.

   d. Global warming causes the level of the world's oceans to rise, affecting land rents in a small island-based country

2. In each of the following cases, which loan is likely to have a higher interest rate? Why?

   a. a $250 000 loan to a new high-tech business or a $250 000 loan to an established small-town hardware store

   b. a $100 000 loan to a business that is repaid either over three years or five years

   c. a five-year loan to a business that is either for $10 000 or for $250 000

   d. a five-year $50 000 residential mortgage or a five-year $50 000 personal loan

LAST**WORD**

In this chapter, we have seen how marginal productivity theory can be used to explain the demand for resources and how this theory can be applied to the determination of various resource incomes. In particular, we have examined the causes for differences in wage rates in different occupations.

In the next chapter, we apply this analysis by examining the distribution of income for households in Canada. And we will see the large extent to which governments intervene to reduce the disparities that exist in resource earnings.

Key Concepts

business's labour demand curve 159
business's labour supply curve 159
collateral 172
complementary resources 162
craft union 168
credit risk 171
human capital 165

industrial union 167
interest 171
job discrimination 168
labour market demand curve 160
labour market supply curve 160
labour productivity 162
marginal productivity theory 157

marginal resource cost 159
marginal revenue product 159
principal 171
profit-maximizing employment rule 159
rent 169
seniority rights 166
substitute resources 162

Questions

Production Conditions for Ham-It-Up Radios

Labour (number of workers)	Total Product (radios per week)	Marginal Product (radios per worker)	Average Product (radios per worker)
0	0		
1	120	_____	_____
2	200	_____	_____
3	270	_____	_____
4	320	_____	_____
5	340	_____	_____
6	350	_____	_____
7	340	_____	_____

1. The table above gives short-run production conditions for a company that makes radios.
   a. Copy and complete the table and identify the ranges where marginal product is positive and where it is negative.
   b. Explain the relationships between marginal product and total product, and between marginal product and average product.
   c. On one graph, draw the total product curve. On another graph, draw the marginal product and average product curves. Why do the curves in these graphs differ from the corresponding curves portrayed in Figure 4.3 (in Chapter 4) of the text?

Labour Demand and Supply Schedules for a Salmon Fisherman

(1) Labour (no. of workers)	(2) Total Product (kilograms per hour)	(3) Marginal Product (kilograms per hour)	(4) Product Price ($ per kilogram)	(5) Total Revenue ($ per hour)	(6) Marginal Revenue Product ($ per hour)
0	0		$3	$____	
1	16	_____	3	_____	$____
2	28	_____	3	_____	_____
3	37	_____	3	_____	_____
4	44	_____	3	_____	_____
5	47	_____	3	_____	_____

2. The table above shows cost and revenue data for a salmon fisherman who sells his catch for $3 per kilogram in a perfectly competitive product market and hires boat-hands in a perfectly competitive labour market at an hourly wage of $15.
   a. Copy and complete the table, and on a sheet of graph paper, plot the fisherman's labour demand and labour supply curves.
   b. What explains the shapes of the curves you have drawn in part a.?
   c. How many full-time boat-hands will the fisherman employ? Explain using the profit-maximizing employment rule and your graph.

    d. If the wage rate rises to $24 per hour, how many full-time boat-hands will the fisherman now employ? Again, explain using the profit-maximizing employment rule and your graph.

3. Outline the effect of each of the following situations on the demand for labour in the production of computer chips.
    a. There is a fall in the price of silicon, which is used to make computer chips.
    b. There is a rise in the price of machinery which can be substituted for labour in the production of computer chips.
    c. The demand for computer chips falls.

4. Identify how each of the following trends will affect demand or supply in the market for unskilled labour within Canada. Also identify how the equilibrium wage and employment level for this labour will change in each case.
    a. There are a greater number of dropouts from the Canadian educational system.
    b. The equilibrium wage for unskilled labour in Mexico increases.
    c. To fund a new government pension scheme, employers must start paying a tax for each unskilled worker they employ.

5. Identify the direction of each of the following trends as well as the changes in demand and/or supply that cause them.
    a. An influx of immigrants causes land rents to vary in a major metropolitan area.
    b. Widespread environmental damage alters the economic rent received by owners of drinkable water.
    c. The expansion of a professional basketball league leads to an adjustment in the economic rent received by the league's star player.
    d. A major oil discovery in the Middle East influences the rent on oil-drilling properties in Alberta.

6. The ratio of wages for university graduates versus high-school graduates has recently increased much more rapidly in the United States than it has in Canada. Using the concepts you have learned from this chapter, give two possible reasons why.

7. (Advanced Question)
Taking into account labour productivity, education, and job conditions, outline some of the problems that would arise if all workers in the Canadian economy received a uniform wage.

8. (Policy Discussion Question)
    a. Summarize the treatment of minimum wage laws in the online article *The Economics of Minimum Wage Laws* (at http://oldfraser.lexi.net/publications/pps/14/summary.html).
    b. Explain the economic theory on which this treatment is based.
    c. Compare this perspective with the viewpoint found in the online article *The Case for Increasing the Minimum Wage* (at http://www.policyalternatives.ca/bc/bcminwageqf.html).
    d. What accounts for the radically different conclusions that these two articles come to?

http://oldfraser.lexi.net/publications/pps/14/summary.html

http://www.policyalternatives.ca/bc/bcminwageqf.html

Internet Application Questions

http://stats.bls.gov:80/oco/oco2003.htm

http://www.aflcio.org/corporateamerica/paywatch/

1. Access the online version of the *Occupational Outlook Handbook* prepared by the United States Government's Bureau of Labour Statistics (available at http://stats.bls.gov:80/oco/oco2003.htm). Use the search options accompanying this handbook to find (i) the three occupations projected to grow the fastest, and (ii) the three occupations with the largest projected numerical increases in total employment during 1998-2008 in the United States. For each occupation, outline one factor that could explain its appearance on one of these lists.

2. a. According to the information in *CEO Pay and Global Unfairness* (at http://www.aflcio.org/corporateamerica/paywatch/), is the average American corporate executive paid a salary equalling the executive's marginal revenue product? Why or why not?

   b. What sort of argument could be made against the conclusions drawn in this article?

REAPING THE REWARDS

David Ricardo and the Theory of Rent

Ricardo and His Influence

In the generation after Adam Smith, several influential thinkers worked to extend his theories. Of this group, now known as the classical economists, David Ricardo (1772–1823) left the greatest mark. Unlike most who have made a study of economic questions, Ricardo had practical experience in business.

Born in London, Ricardo spent part of his childhood in Holland, then moved back to England with his parents, where he went on to amass such a great fortune on the London stock market that he retired to the country in his early 40s. There, he turned his attention to the subject known as "political economy."

Like others of his time, Ricardo wanted to understand the questions of who gets what in an economy, and why. To do this, he needed a theory of rent. The issue of land rent was especially important in 19th century Britain because most farmers did not own the land they cultivated but leased it from a small group of landowners, mostly members of the aristocracy. By coincidence, in February of 1815, four British writers published pamphlets outlining theories of rent; of those theories, Ricardo's became the standard.

David Ricardo
Source: ©Bettmann/CORBIS/Magma

Ricardo's Theory of Rent

According to Ricardo's theory, the rent to a landowner for a certain piece of farmland equals the excess revenue that remains after paying all other costs, including the farmer's normal profit. Why do landowners receive all this surplus revenue? They do so because the quantity of the land is fixed. Farmers bid against one another to rent each parcel of land; this bidding process raises the rent for each parcel to its maximum possible value.

Suppose, for example, that wheat farmers lease four different grades of land. The table and graph in Figure A on the next page show the output of wheat per hectare on each grade of land. While grade A land provides an annual crop of 50 kg per hectare, the other grades each produce, respectively, 40, 20, and 10 kg. For all grades of land, farmers have a cost of $100 per hectare for all other inputs. This figure includes not only explicit production costs, such as wages, but also implicit costs, such as the farmer's normal profit.

So, with the output and costs now established, we can determine rent according to Ricardo's theory. For each hectare of land, rent equals the farmer's revenue minus the production costs of $100. If the price of wheat is $5, the 50 kg output from a hectare of grade A land gives the farmer a total revenue of $250 per hectare. Therefore, rent for this particular grade of land is the total revenue minus the production costs, or $150 ($250 − $100). Because lower-quality land produces a lower output, and therefore lower revenue, the lower grades of land have lower rents. For example, a hectare of grade C land produces an output of 20 kg of wheat, giving the farmer a revenue of $100 (20 kg × $5 per kg); after the costs of $100 are paid from the revenue, the rent stands at zero ($100 − $100). The lowest grade of land, grade D, would not be cultivated, since the production costs ($100) exceed its revenues (10 kg × $5 per kg = $50).

In Ricardo's theory, the rent of a hectare of agricultural land depends on the price of the product it produces. So, in our example, an increase in the price of wheat to $10 would increase the rents on each grade of land. For example, the rent of a hectare of grade A land would rise to $400, or the difference between the farmer's new revenue ($10 × 50 kg = $500) and the constant production costs ($100). Similarly, the rents for grades B and C land rise to $300 and $100 per hectare, respectively, and grade D land

ADVANCING ECONOMIC THOUGHT

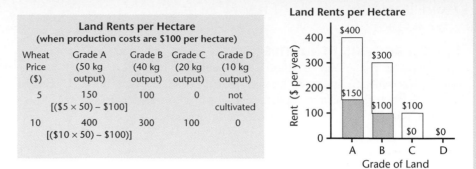

Figure A   Ricardo's Theory of Rent

Land Rents per Hectare
(when production costs are $100 per hectare)

Wheat Price ($)	Grade A (50 kg output)	Grade B (40 kg output)	Grade C (20 kg output)	Grade D (10 kg output)
5	150 [($5 × 50) – $100]	100	0	not cultivated
10	400 [($10 × 50) – $100)]	300	100	0

The production costs are constant at $100 per hectare with different grades of land, but the output of wheat per hectare varies from 10 to 50 kg. The table and bar graph show the resulting land rents given two wheat prices. If the price of wheat is $5 per kg, the rents for the three highest grades of land would be $150, $100, and $0, respectively. On the bar graph, the shaded areas indicate the rent at the $5 price. If the price of wheat increased to $10 per kg, the rents on the highest grades of land would rise, and the fourth grade (D) would enter production, as indicated by the unshaded areas on the bar graph.

Source: From *Evolution of Economic Thought,* 5th ed. by Brue. © 1994. Reprinted with permission of South-Western, a division of Thomson Learning: www.thomsonrights.com FAX 800-730-2215.

would be brought into production with a rent of zero, since its revenue now matches production costs. Grade D land, therefore, represents the new margin of cultivation.

Rent and Population Growth Ricardo's explanation of rent played an important part in his predictions for the future, which he outlined in *Principles of Political Economy and Taxation*, first published in 1817. As population increased, said Ricardo, less productive land would have to be brought into production once premium-quality land became fully utilized. Wheat output per worker would, therefore, decline, meaning the price of wheat would gradually rise. Because bread was such an important staple in the diets of workers and their families, higher wheat prices would push up the wages that employers would have to pay. And these higher wages, said Ricardo, would lower businesses' profits.

Who would benefit from these trends? It would not be the employers, whose profits would shrink, nor the workers, whose higher wages would only keep up with costs. It would be the well-off landowners who would reap the rewards as higher food prices forced up rents. Unlike other classes in society, said Ricardo, these landowners provided no productive service themselves but were simply fortunate enough—probably through inheritance—to have gained ownership of an essential economic resource.

The Corn Laws Already renowned for his theories, Ricardo became famous for applying them when he served as a representative in Britain's parliament. One of the most contentious issues facing the British government in Ricardo's time was whether or not to abolish the country's Corn Laws. These laws restricted the purchase of foreign wheat (or "corn" as it was then called) through a system of tariffs, or taxes on imports. The tariffs, which were meant to aid British farmers, raised average wheat prices. Therefore, Ricardo argued, the tariffs helped no one but the wealthy landowners who benefitted from increased rents. While the Corn Laws were not repealed until after Ricardo's death, his theories and political involvement were both important in the struggle against these laws.

Henry George and the Single Tax Movement

While Ricardo did not draw any radical conclusions from his theory of rent, others did. In later decades of the 19th century, the privileged position of landowners, both in Europe and North America, increasingly came under attack. One of the most zealous critics of landowners was the American journalist and economist Henry George (1839–1897).

Should those lucky enough to own land be able to make often lavish unearned incomes from this ownership at the expense of productive capitalist employers and workers? Like many reformers, George thought not, and in his well-known book *Progress and Poverty* (1879), he set out his solution: all taxes should be replaced by a 100 percent tax on land rent.

According to George and his many supporters, this tax would have far-reaching benefits. Because the amount of land is fixed by nature, imposing a land rent tax would not reduce the supply of land. Moreover, the revenues from this tax would be so great that all other taxes could be repealed. Repealing all other taxes would stimulate greater production.

George's proposal was so popular that at the end of the 19th century, his name was almost a household word in Britain and North America. However, no government ever adopted the single tax. Most economists criticized it, stating that such a tax would harm many poor people (for example, elderly widows) and might cause huge social upheavals as all landowners found the return on their investments completely wiped out. Critics also pointed out that much of what was classified as land rent, in fact, represented the landowner's payment for other items, such as interest payments and the depreciation of buildings on the land. Recent critics point to the increase in government spending, which would mean that 100 percent land rent taxes could no longer provide sufficient revenues to replace all other taxes.

ADVANCING ECONOMIC THOUGHT

1. a. According to David Ricardo's theory of rent, what would happen to the rent per hectare paid on grades A, B, C, and D land if the price of wheat increased to $30?
   b. In Ricardo's theory, what causes the price of wheat to rise gradually over time?
   c. According to Ricardo, which groups in society benefit, which lose, and which are relatively unaffected by the trends that accompany increasing wheat prices? Why?

2. Food prices have not continually risen as predicted by Ricardo's theory. Why not?

CHAPTER 8

Income Distribution

A decent provision for the poor is the true test of civilization.

—Samuel Johnson, English writer

Imagine that one person enjoys all the luxuries of a consumer culture, while another barely scrapes by. Is this fair? What could and should be done, and how? In mixed market economies, such as Canada's, governments deal not only with competition in the market and with spillover effects, as we have seen in previous chapters, but also with the distribution of income. In this chapter, we examine the distribution of income among Canadian households and the problem of poverty. We also look at how Canadian governments promote income equity, through transfer payments and taxation.

LEARNING OBJECTIVES

In this chapter, you will:

1 learn about the distribution of income among Canadian households, how this distribution is measured, and the factors underlying the distribution

2 consider the causes of poverty and the way poverty is measured

3 analyze the effectiveness of government intervention to change the distribution of income

8.1 The Distribution of Income

LO 8.1

In the last chapter, we examined the incomes from resources and the factors that affect these incomes. Now, we will look at who gets what and why.

Income Shares

To get an overview of who gets what in the economy, economists typically rank Canadian households by income and then categorize households into five groups on the basis of their income levels. Each group, therefore, represents 20 percent, or one-fifth, of the total number of Canadian households. Figure 8.1 shows the pre-taxation income levels of the five groups for various years. In 2000, the fifth of Canadian households with the lowest incomes received a small proportion—a mere 4.5 percent—of all households' total pre-tax income, while the fifth of Canadian households with the highest incomes received 45.2 percent. The groups in-between the extremes received 10.1 percent, 16.1 percent, and 24.2 percent, respectively.

Looking at the figures for selected years, one can see that there has been surprisingly little change in income distribution since the 1950s. For example, in 1951, the fifth of Canadian households with the lowest incomes received 4.4 percent of all households' total pre-tax income, whereas the fifth with the highest incomes received 42.8 percent.

The Lorenz Curve

Lorenz curve: a graph showing the cumulative distribution of income among a country's households

Comparing distributions of income for different years can be a cumbersome task, given the amount of information included in Figure 8.1. Therefore, economists simplify matters by summarizing the results on a graph. However, rather than simply presenting the shares of each one-fifth of households, economists present the *cumulative* distribution of income. The **Lorenz curve**, as this graph is known, conveniently summarizes how equally or unequally income is distributed.

Figure 8.1 Income Distribution in Selected Years

	Percentage of Total Pre-Tax Income Received by Each Fifth of Households						Average Income (2000)
	1951	1961	1971	1981	1991	2000	
Lowest 20%	4.4	4.2	3.6	4.5	4.7	4.5	$ 12 421
Second 20%	11.2	11.9	10.6	10.9	10.4	10.1	27 846
Third 20%	18.3	18.3	17.6	17.6	16.7	16.1	44 483
Fourth 20%	23.3	24.5	24.9	25.2	24.7	24.2	66 867
Highest 20%	42.8	41.1	43.3	41.8	43.5	45.2	124 851
Average of total							55 292

Proportionally, income shares have not changed considerably since 1951. Consistently, the group of households with the highest income received over 40 percent of the total income, while the group of households with the lowest income received less than 5 percent.

Sources: Statistics Canada "Income Distribution in Selected Years," adapted from the Statistics Canada publications "Incomes of non-farm families and individuals in Canada" 1951–65, 1969, p. 78, "Income distribution by size in Canada," 1983, Catalogue 13-2307, March 1985, and "Income in Canada," 2000, Catalogue 75-2002, November 2002, p. 80.

To see how the Lorenz curve does this, take another look at the income distribution for 2000 given in Figure 8.1. Seen as separate shares of total pre-tax income, the figures—4.5 percent, 10.1 percent, 16.1 percent, 24.2 percent, and 45.2 percent—do not seem to say a lot. However, we can look at the first and second groups together; then the first, second, and third groups together; and so on. The results are shown in Figure 8.2. For example, whereas the 20 percent of Canadian households with the lowest incomes receive 4.5 percent of the total income, the 40 percent of households with the lowest incomes receive 14.6 percent, and the 60 percent of households with the lowest incomes receive 30.7 percent. Plotted on a graph—with the variables being the percentage of households and the percentage of income—these figures give the Lorenz curve. The points *a, b, c, d,* and *e* represent the cumulative income shares.

Interpreting the Lorenz Curve

To see what this curve tells us about the distribution of income among Canadian households, it can be compared with Lorenz curves for two hypothetical economies with income distributions at the extremes: perfectly equal and perfectly unequal.

PERFECT EQUALITY

The first hypothetical Lorenz curve represents the case of *perfect equality*, where each household earns an identical amount. Therefore, 20 percent of households receive 20 percent of the total income (as shown at point *f* in Figure 8.2), 40 percent receive 40 percent, 60 percent receive 60 percent, and so on. The result is the 45-degree line shown in Figure 8.2. The closer the actual Lorenz curve is to this hypothetical case—in other words, the less bow-shaped it is—the more equal is the distribution of incomes in the economy.

Figure 8.2	The Lorenz Curve

Distribution of Household Income		Cumulative Distribution of Household Income		
Share of Income in 2000 (%)		Cumulative Share of Income in 2000 (%)		
Lowest	4.5	Lowest 20%	4.5	(a)
Second	10.1	Lowest 40%	14.6 = 4.5 + 10.1	(b)
Third	16.1	Lowest 60%	30.7 = 16.1 + 14.6	(c)
Fourth	24.2	Lowest 80%	54.9 = 30.7 + 24.2	(d)
Highest	45.2	100%	100.0 = 54.9 + 45.2	(e)

Point *a* on the graph shows that the group with the lowest income received 4.5 percent of the total pre-tax income in 2000. Point *b* shows that the groups receiving the lowest 40 percent of pre-tax income in 2000 received 14.6 percent (4.5 + 10.1). Each subsequent point shows the cumulative income distribution; therefore, point *e* shows that 100 percent of households earned 100 percent of total incomes (the numbers do not add exactly due to rounding). Connecting all the points gives the Lorenz curve. To contrast, the extremes of perfect equality and perfect inequality are shown. The closer the Lorenz curve is to the curve representing perfect equality (and the farther from the curve of perfect inequality), the more equally incomes are distributed.

PERFECT INEQUALITY

At the other extreme of income distribution is *perfect inequality*, with only one household receiving all of the economy's income, while all other households receive nothing. The hypothetical Lorenz curve in this circumstance would follow the horizontal and vertical axes of the graph, as shown by the two thick lines in Figure 8.2 forming a right angle at the bottom right-hand corner. The closer the Lorenz curve is to this hypothetical case—meaning, the more bow-shaped it is—the more unequal is the distribution of income.

Reasons for Income Inequality

The differences in incomes of individual households can be attributed to a variety of causes. Wages and salaries make up about 70 percent of income earned in Canada. Hence, the factors that determine wages outlined in Chapter 7—labour productivity, education, experience, job conditions, regional disparities, market power, and discrimination—play an important role in income inequality. However, not all income inequalities are related to these factors. Profit, rent, and interest also play a part. Three main factors determine these other types of income and can sometimes affect wages as well: risk-taking, ability, and wealth.

RISK-TAKING

Risk-taking in an economy can take a variety of forms. For example, workers in some occupations earn unstable incomes. More importantly, the risks that entrepreneurs take mean that their profit earnings fluctuate widely. While unsuccessful risk-takers often face the threat of hardship and bankruptcy, successful risk-takers reap significant rewards in the form of high profits.

ABILITY

Because of different abilities, some individuals may pursue careers in high-paying areas, while others make no earnings at all. Those individuals who find their talents in short supply—star athletes or gifted computer programmers, for instance—can sometimes earn extravagantly high incomes due to their special abilities.

THINKING ABOUT ECONOMICS

Is income inequality necessarily a bad thing?

While gross inequalities in income are undesirable, a perfect equality of incomes is not necessarily desirable because of the tradeoff between equity and efficiency. Without differences in incomes, the incentive to undertake further education, to take unpleasant jobs for greater pay, to save one's earnings, and to take risks would be severely hampered. Without some degree of income inequality, an economy's total output would be below its highest possible level. The goal of income equity is, therefore, usually interpreted as reducing, rather than eliminating, the inequalities that would exist in a pure market economy.

Question
Sometimes, extremely unequal distributions of income can hamper rather than promote efficiency. Why?

WEALTH

wealth: ownership of financial assets, such as stocks and bonds, or real assets, such as buildings and land

Most rent and interest incomes flow from the ownership of **wealth**. Wealth takes the form of financial assets, such as stocks and bonds, or real assets, such as buildings and land. There are two main ways to acquire wealth: through one's own saving, or by inheriting wealth from others.

Interestingly, wealth tends to be much more unequally distributed than income. Figure 8.3 shows the share of wealth held by the top 1 percent, 5 percent, and 20 percent of households in various years for four countries: Sweden, Canada, France, and the United States. In Canada, the top 1 percent owned 16.8 percent of the country's total wealth, while the top 5 percent owned 37.5 percent, and the top 20 percent owned 68.8 percent. This last figure is significantly higher than the 40.8 percent share for the top one-fifth income group after transfer payments and taxes. While less equally distributed than in Sweden, wealth in Canada is distributed more evenly among households than it is in either France or the United States.

Figure 8.3   Distribution of Wealth in Selected Countries

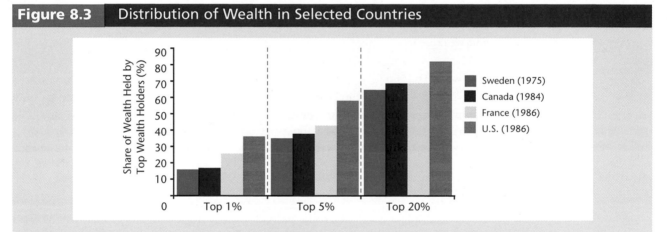

In 1984, the top 1 percent of Canadian households held 16.8 percent of Canada's wealth, the top 5 percent held 37.5 percent, and the top 20 percent held 68.8 percent. In Canada, the distribution of wealth among households is more equal than it is in France or the United States, but less so than in Sweden.

Source: Ontario Fair Tax Commission, *Wealth Tax Working Group Final Report* (Toronto, March 1993), p. A20.

8.2 Poverty

poverty: a situation in which a person's income is inadequate to provide the necessities of life

One of the main reasons behind the economic goal of income equity is the desire to minimize poverty. **Poverty** is a situation in which a person's income is inadequate to provide the necessities of life, such as food, clothing, and shelter. In practical terms, any precise definition of poverty is open to debate. All would agree that food is a necessity of life, but what sort of food should a person be able to afford? Also, should such products as TVs and radios be considered necessities in a rich industrialized country, such as Canada, when they are luxuries in other countries? These are examples of questions governments must address when trying to define and minimize poverty.

The Poverty Line

In Canada, poverty is defined in relation to the average Canadian income and expenditures. The average Canadian family spends 44 percent of its household after-tax income on food, clothing, and shelter. Statistics Canada defines as poor any household that spends an additional 20 percent, or a total of 64 percent, on these items. For simplicity, Statistics Canada uses this relationship to identify a **poverty line**, or income level below which a household is classified as poor.

poverty line: an income level below which a household is classified as poor

In dollar terms, the poverty line—which is also known as the low-income cut-off (LICO)—depends on the number of household members and the size of the community they live in, since people in rural areas or small towns can live more cheaply than those in urban centres. Figure 8.4 shows the poverty lines as determined for 2000. For example, the poverty line would be a yearly income of $29 163 for a household of four persons living in a large city, or a yearly income of $9947 for an unattached individual living in a rural area.

LO 8.2

Incidence of Poverty

How common is poverty among different groups in Canadian society? Using Statistics Canada's LICO poverty line, an estimated 3.3 million Canadians lived in poverty in 2000, of which 870 000 were children under the age of 18 years. As a proportion of Canada's total population, the number of poor Canadians has been falling in the last few decades. While 27.9 percent of families and 49.2 percent of unattached individuals were classified as poor in 1961, 7.9 percent of families and 28.6 percent of unattached individuals were classified as poor in 2000.

Figure 8.5 shows how the incidence of poverty among households (defined by LICO) is classified by certain characteristics: the gender of the household head, his or her age, and education.

GENDER AND HOUSEHOLD TYPE

In general, poverty rates are considerably higher among unattached individuals of either gender than among families, with 28.6 percent of all unattached individuals being poor, as opposed to 7.9 percent of all families. Unattached females are more

Figure 8.4 | The Poverty Line for Various Households (2000)

Size of Household Unit	Urban Areas (categorized by size)				Rural Areas
	500 000 and over	100 000 to 499 999	30 000 to 99 999	Less than 30 000	
1 person	$15 172	$12 780	$12 583	$11 498	$ 9 947
2 persons	18 513	15 594	15 353	14 030	12 138
3 persons	23 415	19 723	19 419	17 745	15 352
4 persons	29 163	24 565	24 186	22 101	19 120
5 persons	32 595	27 456	27 031	24 701	21 371
6 persons	36 027	30 346	29 877	27 301	23 622
7 or more persons	39 459	33 237	32 722	29 902	25 872

The poverty line varies among household sizes and the households' community size. Within a given household category, a household would be considered poor if its after-tax income were below the income listed.

Source: Statistics Canada "The Poverty Line for Various Households (2000)," adapted from the Statistics Canada publication "Income in Canada," 2000, Catalogue 75-202, November 2002, p. 121.

Figure 8.5	The Incidence of Poverty (2000)

	Percentage of Households Below the Poverty Line in 2000
Families	7.9
Unattached Individuals	28.6
Gender and Household Type	
Married couples with children	7.4
Single-parent families (female head)	33.9
Elderly unattached males	16.8
Nonelderly unattached males	27.0
Elderly unattached females	21.0
Nonelderly unattached females	38.2
Age of Household Head (years)	
Less than 18	28.5
18–24	35.8
25–54	20.1
55–64	21.3
65+	15.5
Education of Household Head	
Less than high school	28.0
Graduated from high school	21.1
Some post-secondary	28.2
Post-secondary certificate or diploma	17.8
University degree	11.3

The greatest incidence of poverty is among unattached individuals, women, single-parent families, families with a household head under 25 years in age, and those with minimal education.

Source: Statistics Canada "The Incidence of Poverty (2000)," adapted from the Statistics Canada publication "Income in Canada," 2000, Catalogue 75-202, November 2002, pp. 115, 118.

likely to be poor than unattached males, while single-parent families tend to be poorer than two-parent families.

AGE

Households headed by the youngest group (24 and under) and the second oldest group (54–64) are more heavily represented among the ranks of the poor than are other households.

EDUCATION

Those households headed by a person with less education (no high school diploma) have the highest poverty rates. As we saw in Chapter 7, education affects wage levels. As a result, education level attained is a factor of poverty for the working poor.

EMPLOYMENT

While poverty is more common among the unemployed, a notably high proportion of the employed are poor as well. Indeed, for nonelderly unattached individuals classified as poor, over half—54.4 percent in 1998—were employed for at least part of the year. This group, known as the "working poor," is often found in primary industries, such as fishing, where wages are low and seasonal employment is common.

REGION

Poverty also varies from region to region. Historically, poor households tend to be concentrated in certain regions, particularly the Atlantic provinces and parts of Quebec. However, poverty exists throughout Canada. For example, a third of Canada's poor live in Ontario.

Debates over the Measurement of Poverty

Poverty is a fuzzy concept. When we call someone poor, should we use a relative measure of poverty, such as Statistics Canada's LICO as a poverty line, or is it more appropriate to use some absolute measure which is applicable to a wide range of countries? In recent years, there has been considerable criticism of the use of Statistics Canada's LICO measure. Its relative definition of poverty is one reason. In 1959, for example, a Canadian household was considered poor if it spent more than 70 percent of its before-tax income on food, clothing, and shelter. By 2000, this figure had fallen to 55 percent. So, as Canadians become better off, the LICO measure of poverty would include more people, even if no one's living standards fell. There are also other serious problems with this measure, connected with the way that benefits in kind (such as subsidized housing) are treated. Given these drawbacks, even Statistics Canada refuses to endorse the application of LICO as an accurate measure of poverty.

Recently, the federal government has introduced an alternative measure of poverty, known as the Market Basket Measure (MBM), which is based on an absolute definition of those items considered as necessities. A household making an income lower than the amount needed to buy these items is then considered poor using this new MBM measure. This new measure produces a stated poverty rate lower than the one associated with Canada's current LICO poverty line—in 1996, for example, the poverty rate would have fallen from 17 percent of the total Canadian population (both families and unattached individuals) using LICO to 12 percent with the MBM

Yes. One attempt, by the International Labour Organization (the ILO), applied the American income cut-off (a daily income equivalent of US$14.40 per person) to countries around the world, as an estimate of what percentage of each country's population lives below this constant poverty line. Using the ILO's measure, in the early 1990s Canada had the second lowest poverty rate (6 percent) of any major industrial country, with only Japan's rate being lower at 4 percent. Rates in other major industrial countries include 12 percent in France, 13 percent in the United Kingdom, and 14 percent in the United States. The American income cut-offs are equivalent to about half the income values used by Statistics Canada in its LICO measure of the poverty line.

Question
Would most Canadians view the ILO's poverty line (about $20 Canadian a day per person) as a fair indication of which households in Canada are poor?

approach. Supporters of this new approach say it will give us a clearer picture of the incidence of poverty in Canada—one which is directly comparable with other countries. Those who criticize this initiative say it is a way for governments to "define away" the problems that many Canadians face because of the extent to which they fall short of average incomes in the Canadian economy.

Brief Review

1. The pre-tax income share of each fifth of households in Canada, as shown using the cumulative distribution known as the Lorenz curve, has not changed significantly in the last 50 years. Factors that determine wages, as well as risk-taking, ability, and wealth, play a part in determining this income distribution.

2. In Canada, poverty is usually defined in relation to the average Canadian income and expenditures on necessities. The poverty line, which depends on household type, is the income level below which a household is classified as poor.

3. Poverty is most prevalent among unattached individuals (especially women), single-parent families (especially those headed by women), and those under 25 and between 55 and 64 years old.

4. In recent years, Statistics Canada's relative measure of poverty has come under increasing criticism, and other possible measures based on absolute definitions of poverty have been proposed by Canadian governments but have yet to be officially adopted.

8.2 Practice Questions

1. In a hypothetical country called Libra, there are five households with annual incomes of $5000, $10 000, $15 000, $30 000, and $40 000.

   a. Calculate the shares of total income earned by each household.
   b. What are the cumulative shares of income earned by each household that would be used to draw this country's Lorenz curve?
   c. Using EconGraphKit (at http://www.mcgrawhill.ca/college/lovewell), draw Libra's Lorenz curve.

2 a. Summarize how Statistics Canada's low-income cut-off (LICO) measure is calculated.
   b. Explain why this measure is a relative rather than an absolute measure of poverty.

8.3 The Canadian Welfare Society

welfare society: a society in which the government plays a major role in attempting to ensure the economic well-being of its citizens

universality: the principle applied to transfer payments, whereby benefits are provided to all, regardless of income

means testing: a procedure whereby transfer payments vary according to a recipient's income

LO 8.3

A mixed economy, such as Canada's, can be described as a **welfare society**, in which the government plays a major role in attempting to ensure the well-being of its citizens. In Canada, it is both government transfer payments, such as the Canada Pension Plan and Employment Insurance, and personal income taxes that most significantly address the specific goal of income equity.

Transfer Payments and Income Equity

UNIVERSALITY VERSUS MEANS TESTING

In the past, transfer payments to households were often based on the principle of **universality**. The principle of universality means that benefits apply to all individuals, no matter what their incomes. Universal programs had the advantage of treating everyone in the same way. However, universal programs also had drawbacks. Their main weakness was their expense: in order to provide substantial help to those who needed it most, a large sum of money had to be paid to *all* recipients.

In recent years, there has been a move towards **means testing**, whereby transfer payments vary according to a recipient's income. The main advantage of these programs is that benefits can be directed to those who need them most, so poor households receive the highest payments. However, governments may use means testing to limit spending by narrowing qualifications.

IMPACT ON INCOME DISTRIBUTION

Government transfer payments to individual households from all three levels of government are an average of between 10 and 20 percent of households' income, with payments to unattached individuals representing a larger proportion, as a rule, than for families. As shown in Figure 8.6, these payments make up over 50 percent of total income for the poorest 20 percent of households, whereas for the richest 20 percent of households, they represent under 5 percent of total income. These payments, therefore,

Figure 8.6	Transfer Payments and Income Equity (2000)		
	Average Transfer Payments Received	Transfer Payments as a Percent of Total Income	Share Received of Total Transfer Payments
Lowest 20%	$6 767	54.5	22.2
Second 20%	8 345	30.0	27.4
Third 20%	6 447	14.5	21.1
Fourth 20%	4 955	7.4	16.3
Highest 20%	3 968	3.2	13.0
Average of Total	6 096	11.0	

At higher household incomes, transfer payments make up a progressively smaller percentage of total income. In general, transfer payments fall in dollar terms for household in higher income brackets, but there is an exception for the poorest 20 percent of households who receive a smaller dollar amount (and share of total transfer payments) than does the second poorest 20 percent of households.

Source: Statistics Canada "Transfer Payments and Income Equity," adapted from the Statistics Canada publication "Income in Canada," 2000, Catalogue 75-202, November 2002, p. 26.

do have some impact on equalizing the distribution of income—although not as much as they possibly could, as shown by the fact that transfer payments to the second poorest 20 percent of income earners tend to be higher (an average of $8345) than for the poorest 20 percent (an average of $6767).

Taxes and Income Equity

As for taxes, two principles can be applied in deciding whether or not the burden of a tax is distributed in a manner that is fair to all taxpayers: the principle of benefits received and the principle of ability to pay.

BENEFITS RECEIVED

benefits received: the principle applied to taxation, whereby taxes are geared to the benefits each taxpayer gains from government activity

The principle of **benefits received** suggests that taxes should be geared to the benefits each taxpayer gains from government activity. In this case, government services are paid for in the same ways that products are bought and sold in the private sector. The benefits-received principle is the guiding philosophy behind some taxes. The proceeds from a tax on gasoline, for example, are often earmarked for road construction and maintenance, thereby allowing governments to have drivers who use the most gasoline—and use the roads the most—pay the most for road upkeep.

ABILITY TO PAY

ability to pay: the principle applied to taxation, whereby taxes vary in proportion to a taxpayer's financial resources

A tax philosophy more closely tied to the goal of income equity is based on the principle of **ability to pay**. According to this principle, taxes should vary in proportion to a taxpayer's financial resources—in particular, income. As sensible as the principle may be, it is difficult to measure ability to pay. For example, do all individuals earning $40 000 have the same ability to pay taxes, or does their taxpaying capacity also depend on other factors, such as the number of dependent children they support? Suppose a person's income rises by 50 percent, from $40 000 to $60 000. Should his or her tax bill also rise by 50 percent, or by some larger or smaller percentage?

Taxes and Income

Taxes are related to income in three possible ways, with a certain type of tax being progressive, regressive, or proportional.

PROGRESSIVE TAXES

progressive tax: a tax that increases as a proportion of income as income increases

A **progressive tax** is one that increases as a proportion of income as the income increases. In other words, well-off taxpayers are taxed more in both dollar terms *and* percentage terms. For example, someone making an annual income of $10 000 might pay 10 percent of total income, or $1000, for a certain tax, but a person making $20 000 a year might pay 15 percent of total income, or $3000, for that same tax.

REGRESSIVE TAXES

regressive tax: a tax that decreases as a proportion of income as income increases

In contrast, a **regressive tax** is one that decreases as a proportion of income as income increases. In other words, taxpayers with low incomes pay proportionately more of their incomes for the tax than do well-off taxpayers, even though the well-off taxpayer may pay more as a dollar amount. For example, one taxpayer making $10 000 a year might pay 8 percent in tax, or $800, while another taxpayer with an annual income of $20 000 might pay 6 percent, or $1200, for the same tax.

PROPORTIONAL TAXES

proportional tax: a tax that remains constant as a proportion of income for all incomes

Finally, a **proportional tax** is one that remains constant as a proportion of income for all incomes. Therefore, while taxpayers with different incomes pay proportionately the same tax, the well-off taxpayer pays a higher dollar amount. For example, with a 6 percent tax rate, one taxpayer with an annual income of $10 000 would pay $600 in tax, while another taxpayer with an annual income of $20 000 would pay $1200.

TAXES AND INCOME EQUITY

Not all of Canada's taxes promote income equity. For example, sales and excise taxes tend to be regressive (unless combined with a system of tax credits), since the poor spend a higher proportion of their incomes on consumption items than do the rich, who are more likely to save part of their incomes. Property taxes (at least those on buildings rather than those on land) are also often regressive, largely because the poor devote a higher proportion of their incomes to housing than do the rich. Corporate income taxes are more difficult to classify as either progressive or regressive. To the extent that these taxes reduce the income of shareholders—a rich group in Canadian society—they are progressive. However, corporations that have considerable market power may succeed in passing on the burden of the tax to consumers in the form of higher prices for their products. In this case, the corporate tax is regressive in a similar way to a sales tax.

In contrast, personal income taxes are progressive, as detailed in Figure 8.7. The poorest fifth of income earners pay just 10.3 percent of their incomes in this tax, while the richest pay almost a quarter of their incomes. In dollar terms, the greater payments by high income households is even more pronounced: an average of almost $30 000 for the richest fifth of households in contrast to $1300 for the poorest fifth. Thanks to the effect of personal income taxes, therefore, post-tax incomes in Canada are much more equally distributed than they would otherwise be.

Figure 8.7	Personal Income Taxes and Income Equity (2000)		
	Average Personal Income Taxes Paid	Personal Income Taxes as a Percent of Total Income	Share Paid of Total Personal Income Taxes
Lowest 20%	$ 1 281	10.3	1.3
Second 20%	3 173	11.4	5.5
Third 20%	7 166	16.1	13.2
Fourth 20%	12 881	19.3	23.8
Highest 20%	29 814	23.9	56.1
Average of Total	10 862	19.6	

At higher household incomes, personal income taxes make up a progressively higher percentage of total income. In general, personal income taxes rise in dollar terms for households in higher income brackets, and they also rise sharply as a share of total personal income taxes.

Source: Statistics Canada "Personal Income Taxes and Income Equity (2000)," adapted from the Statistics Canada publication "Income in Canada," 2000, Catalogue 75-202, November 2002, p. 51.

THINKING ABOUT ECONOMICS

Are there any signs that the distribution of incomes in Canada is becoming more unequal?

While the overall distribution of total incomes has not shown a significant perceptible change, beneath the surface, worrisome trends can be discerned. Between 1993 and 2000, for example, the after-tax incomes of the poorest fifth of Canadian households rose in inflation-adjusted terms by 7.7 percent. In contrast, the after-tax incomes of the richest fifth of Canadians rose by 18.7 percent during the same period. This rising gap was most prevalent up to 1998. But the overall difference in income movements between 1993 and 2000 is still significant.

Question
What factors can be used to explain the growing gap between the rich and the poor in the Canadian economy?

Brief Review

1. Canadian governments promote the goal of income equity primarily through transfer payments and personal income taxes.

2. Transfer payments may be either universal, with all Canadians receiving the same payment, or means-tested, with benefits determined by the recipient's income. During the past few decades, there has been a shift from universality to means-testing by Canadian governments.

3. Government transfer payments in Canada play a part in reducing the disparities in the distribution of private earnings, though not consistently since the poorest fifth of Canadians do not receive the greatest benefit.

4. Taxes may be based on benefits received by a taxpayer from government activity, or on the taxpayer's ability to pay. Canada's personal income tax system is progressive, with the proportion of income paid in tax rising significantly as household income increases.

8.3 Practice Questions

1. In the hypothetical country Libra, where five households earn $5000, $10 000, $15 000, $30 000, and $40 000, each household receives a $5000 government transfer payment and pays a 25 percent income tax.

   a. Find the income of each household after receiving transfer payments and paying taxes.
   b. Calculate the new shares of total income received by each household.
   c. What are the new cumulative shares of income received by each household?
   d. Using EconGraphKit (at http://www.mcgrawhill.ca/college/lovewell) draw the new Lorenz curve.
   e. Is the new income distribution more or less equal than before transfer payments and taxes? Explain.

LAST**WORD**

In this chapter, we have seen how the factors affecting various resource incomes impact the distribution of income in Canada. We have also seen the extent to which government transfer payments and taxes affect this distribution. Analyzing the distribution of income allowed us to see the extent of poverty in Canada, using Statistics Canada's own measure of low income. We then explored some of the controversies that surround the definition of poverty, which makes this a topic in normative economics. Having dealt with the microeconomic functions of government, in the next part of the text, we will turn to government's actions in the macroeconomy as it attempts to stabilize the business cycle. In doing so, we will see that some of the government programs discussed in this chapter, which promote income equity, also have a role to play in stabilizing the economy over time.

Key Concepts

ability to pay 190	poverty 184	regressive tax 190
benefits received 190	poverty line 185	universality 189
Lorenz curve 181	progressive tax 190	wealth 184
means testing 189	proportional tax 191	welfare society 189

Questions

Distribution of Household Income (2000)

	Income before Transfer Payments and Taxes (1)		Income before Taxes (2)		Income after Transfer Payments and Taxes (3)	
	Income Share	Average Income	Income Share	Average Income	Income Share	Average Income
Lowest 20%	2.3	$ 5 655	4.5	$ 12 421	5.0	$11 141
Second 20%	7.9	19 501	10.1	27 846	11.1	24 673
Third 20%	15.5	38 036	16.1	44 483	16.8	37 317
Fourth 20%	25.2	61 912	24.2	66 867	24.3	53 986
Highest 20%	49.1	120 883	45.2	124 851	42.8	95 036
	100.0%	49 196	100.0%	55 292	100.0%	44 429

Source: Statistics Canada "Distribution of Household Income (2000)," adapted from the Statistics Canada publication "Income in Canada," 2000, Catalogue 75-202, pp. 75, 80, 82.

1. The table above shows the income shares going to each one-fifth of Canadian households before government transfer payments (column 1), after the receipt of transfer payments (column 2), and after the receipt of transfer payments and the payment of personal income taxes (column 3). Using the data in this table, do the following:

    a. For each of the five income groups, calculate the changes in average income from income before transfer payments and personal income taxes, to pre-tax income, to income after transfer payments and personal income taxes.

    b. Comment on the results, noting and explaining the most significant changes.

2   a. Figure 8.2 gives the Lorenz curve based on incomes prior to taxation but after transfer payments. Using the data from the previous question, create a graph giving two Lorenz curves: one using income shares prior to transfer payments and personal income taxes and another after both transfer payments and personal income taxes.

  b. Compare the results. Given that one of the main goals of transfer payments and personal income taxes is income equity, how effective do you think these forms of government intervention are?

Income Shares in Selected Countries

Country	Share of Income Received by Each Fifth of Income Earners				
	1 (lowest)	2	3	4	5 (highest)
Canada	7.5	12.9	17.2	23.0	39.3
China	5.9	10.2	15.1	22.2	46.3
Sweden	9.6	14.5	18.1	23.2	34.5

Source: Adapted from *World Development Indicators 2002*, by the World Bank. Copyright 2002 by The International Bank for Reconstruction and Development/The World Bank. Table 5 "Distribution of Income or Consumption," pp. 74, 76.

3. The table above shows the share of income received by each fifth of income earners, from lowest to highest, in selected countries for various years.
  a. Construct a table showing the cumulative distribution of income among the five groups of income earners in each country.
  b. On the basis of your table in part a., draw and label a Lorenz curve for each country on the same large graph. Then, rank the countries from the most equal to the least equal income distribution.

4. Why is the distribution of wealth in most countries more unequal than the distribution of income?

5. Outline four common causes of poverty in Canada.

6. Identify the following taxes as progressive, regressive, or proportional and explain your answers:
  a. A tax on inherited wealth
  b. A 7 percent sales tax on all goods and services (with no accompanying tax credit)
  c. A personal income tax with a constant marginal tax rate (and no deductions from income)
  d. A tax on residential housing

7. (Advanced Question)
  The Gini coefficient provides a single numerical measure of income distribution and is defined as the area between a Lorenz curve and the 45-degree line of perfect equality divided by the entire triangular area under this same 45-degree line. The result is a value between 0 and 1.
  a. The Gini coefficient for the distribution of total pre-tax income in Canada has risen from .336 to .354 between 1991 and 2000. What does this suggest has happened to the equality of income distribution during this period?
  b Standardized Gini coefficients for the distribution of income are .408 in the United States, .249 in Japan, .300 in Germany, .327 in France, .361 in the United Kingdom, .273 in Italy, and .315 in Canada. What do these figures suggest about the comparative equality of income distribution in these seven countries?

http://www.oldfraser.lexi.net
/publications/forum/1999
/10/section_02.html

http://www.ccsd.ca/pubs/inc
kids/2.html

8. (Policy Discussion Question)

Compare the views of the child poverty and its proper measurement, as presented in *Measuring Child Poverty* (at http://www.oldfraser.lexi.net/publications/forum/1999/10/section_02.html) and *Income and Child Well-being* (at http://www.ccsd.ca/pubs/inckids/2.html).

a. Which of these two perspectives do you find more convincing?

b. How does the debate over the proper measurement of child poverty affect the sorts of policies that are suggested to deal with this problem?

Internet Application Question

http://www.ccsd.ca/facts.
html

Using the information provided in Chapter 2 of Canadian Council on Social Development's 'Working Definitions of Poverty' at http://www.ccsd.ca/facts.html (Adobe Acrobat required), outline two possible measures of Canadian poverty besides Statistics Canada's LICO. What are the advantages and disadvantages of these two measures in relation to LICO?

Thomas Malthus
Source: National Portrait Gallery

THE DOOMSDAY PROPHET

Thomas Malthus and Population Growth

Malthus and His Influence

Known as the "doomsday prophet" for his gloomy predictions of the economic and social future, Thomas Malthus (1766–1834) was an economist as well as a clergyman. Malthus's theories and predictions sprang from an unlikely source: a reform-minded writer named William Godwin (1756–1836), who believed that future society would be transformed by science and human reason. Wars, disease, and crime would finally come to an end, Godwin thought, and the need for government would vanish. Malthus's *Essay on Population* (1798), in which he published his arguments against Godwin's vision, was destined to be one of the most influential economic works of the 19th century.

Malthus's basic point was that utopian visions of the future ignore the negative effects of population growth. According to Malthus, food production and population levels expand at different rates. At best, he said, food increases in what mathematicians call an algebraic progression (1, 2, 3, 4...) as more variable inputs are devoted to a certain amount of usable land. In contrast, population increases in a geometric progression (1, 2, 4, 8...), with levels doubling again and again in a set period. Malthus estimated this period to be 25 years.

Given these assumptions, it was easy for Malthus to predict a discrepancy between food production and the needs of the population. The following time chart shows numbers taken from Malthus's *Essay*. For convenience, population and food stocks in Year 1 are set equal to 1 unit. Food production expands by 1 unit every 25 years as population doubles in the same period. After 225 years, population will have outstripped food by a factor of just over 50 (512 ÷ 10) to 1.

A Malthusian Time Chart

Year	1	25	50	75	100	125	150	175	200	225
Food	1	2	3	4	5	6	7	8	9	10
Population	1	2	4	8	16	32	64	128	256	512

If food grows by 1 unit every 25 years but population doubles over the same period, then after 225 years, food production will be 10 times higher, but population will be 512 times higher.

Source: Henry William Spiegel, *The Growth of Economic Thought* (Durham, NC: Duke University Press, 1971), p. 272.

Malthus warned of desperate circumstances if his predictions came true. He also outlined how population growth could be slowed by either a decrease in the birth rate or an increase in the mortality rate. He had little faith that the number of births would decrease; however, he did feel that at some point, if birth rates did not fall, a limited food supply would bring on misery, famine, plagues, or war, thereby decreasing the population.

Implications and Influence of Malthus's Theory

On the basis of his assumptions, Malthus believed that aid to those in need would be self-defeating, as it would encourage larger families and therefore more population growth. In the long run, he said, this population growth would result in starvation. During the 19th century, Malthus's views had a powerful effect on government policies. In Britain, for example, aid to people who were physically able to work was restricted to those willing to give up their possessions and move into a workhouse, where prolonged labour brought them virtually no pay—only room and board.

Social reformers attacked this "Malthusian" policy, calling it misguided and cruel. The appalling conditions in British workhouses were exposed in many books and pamphlets, Charles Dickens' fictional account *Oliver Twist* being the most famous. Not surprisingly, it was because of Malthus's work that economics was dubbed "the dismal science" by its critics.

Relevance for Today

Fortunately, Malthus's dire predictions have proven to be wrong, at least in those countries with which he was directly concerned. While he later refined the logic of his arguments, their foundations were shaky. Malthus implied that the state of technology would remain fixed; however, the dramatic changes in technology since his day have increased food production in most countries. Malthus also overlooked the extent to which large families were the result of economic necessity. In his own day, high infant mortality rates and the lack of old age pensions meant that large families provided parents with security in old age. Also, during his time, child labour provided extra income to a family. Today, with social welfare programs, child labour laws, and the means to limit population growth, population growth rates in industrialized countries have been far below what Malthus imagined. Indeed, in some of these nations, the rate is close to zero.

While population growth continues to be a *global* concern, the history of Malthus's theory has a valuable lesson: care must be taken in applying economic models to the real world and to government policy.

1. a. Briefly explain why Thomas Malthus believed the growth in living standards in such countries as Britain could eventually stagnate.

   b. Summarize two main reasons why the pessimistic warnings of Malthus proved to be unwarranted.

2. Critics of Malthus suggested that by assuming a set ratio between the growth rates of food and population, he was ignoring the role of food prices. Explain how this argument could be used against Malthus's theory.

Part 3

Economic Stability

In the long run, we are all dead. Economists set themselves too easy, too useless a task if in tempestuous seasons they can only tell us that when the storm is long past the ocean is flat again.

— John Maynard Keynes, English economist

So far, we have concentrated on the microeconomic issues associated with efficiency, income equity, and the environment. In this section, we turn to macroeconomics, with its emphasis on ensuring economic stability. All of us feel the impact of fluctuations in the Canadian economy. Particularly to those Canadians who lose their jobs or see the purchasing power of their incomes drop, economic instability is more than an abstraction. The next six chapters investigate the measurements of economic health, the nature and causes of fluctuations in the Canadian economy, and the ways in which these fluctuations can be reduced through government policy.

CHAPTER 9

Measures of Economic Activity

All progress is precarious, and the solution of one problem brings us face to face with another problem.

—Martin Luther King Jr., American civil rights and religious leader

How much activity is occurring in the Canadian economy? Are the incomes of Canadians rising or falling? How do living standards in Canada compare with those in other countries? Just as you use a thermometer to check your temperature, nations must diagnose and understand their economic health before they can respond to questions such as these ones. This chapter examines various indicators of Canadian economic activity, especially the most prominent measure—Gross Domestic Product (GDP). In later chapters, we will consider GDP further and examine additional measures, what they indicate, and the economic realities of stability and instability.

LEARNING OBJECTIVES

In this chapter, you will:

1 learn about Gross Domestic Product (GDP) and the two approaches to calculating it

2 consider real GDP and per capita GDP and their possible uses and limitations when comparing living standards in different years or different countries

3 analyze other economic measures developed from the national income accounts

9.1 **Gross Domestic Product**

LO 9.1

national income accounts: accounts showing the levels of total income and spending in the Canadian economy

Gross Domestic Product: the total dollar value at current prices of all final goods and services produced in Canada over a given period

income approach: a method of calculating Gross Domestic Product by adding together all incomes in the economy

expenditure approach: a method of calculating Gross Domestic Product by adding together all spending in the economy

National Income Accounts

Keeping track of the Canadian economy is the task of Statistics Canada, a federal agency. This agency prepares the country's **national income accounts**, which give various measures of total income and spending in the Canadian economy. National income accounts play a role for the economy as a whole, comparable with the role of income statements in an individual business. They allow us to evaluate the performance of the Canadian economy and to compare it with other nations' economies.

Measuring Gross Domestic Product

A variety of measures of economic activity can be developed from the national income accounts. Of these, the most common measure in Canada is **Gross Domestic Product**, or GDP. GDP is the total dollar value of all final goods and services produced in the economy over a given period. The dollar value is calculated at current prices, and the period is typically a year. As Figure 9.1 shows, GDP uses dollar value because it effectively simplifies the picture; dollar value is a way to quantify and combine a wide range of goods and services.

TWO VIEWS OF GDP

Canada's GDP is calculated using two approaches, one measuring income and the other measuring spending. Figure 9.2, which illustrates the circular flow for a simple economdroy, where only consumer products are sold, shows both approaches. The diagram shows two economic sectors: households and businesses. Recall that whereas the inner (clockwise) loop represents the flow of payments, the outer (counterclockwise) loop represents the flow of products and resources. The upper portion of the diagram shows the economy's resource markets, in which natural and capital resources as well as human resources (labour and entrepreneurship) are sold by households for incomes. The **income approach** to GDP involves adding together all the incomes in the economy to give GDP. The lower portion of the diagram shows the economy's product markets, in which final consumer products are sold by businesses to households. The **expenditure approach** to GDP involves adding together all spending in the economy to give GDP.

THE GDP IDENTITY

In the simple economy shown in Figure 9.2, because all spending on final consumer products ends up as some form of household income, annual income equals annual

Figure 9.1	Calculating Gross Domestic Product		
Product	Current Price (P)	Annual Output (Q)	Total Dollar Value (P × Q)
Surgical lasers	$1000	3	$3000
Milkshakes	2	1000	2000
			GDP = $5000

It is impossible to add together the economy's annual output of surgical lasers and milkshakes without taking into account money values. If three surgical lasers and 1000 milkshakes are produced, then GDP is the sum of both outputs valued at their current prices.

Figure 9.2	Circular Flow in a Simple Economy

Households and businesses meet in both resource and product markets. The inner (clockwise) loop represents the flow of money. The outer (counterclockwise) loop represents the flow of products and resources. The income approach to GDP measures the flow of incomes in the upper portion; the expenditure approach measures the flow of spending in the lower portion.

GDP identity: Gross Domestic Product calculated as total income is identical to Gross Domestic Product calculated as total spending

spending. As a result, GDP found using the income approach and GDP found using the expenditure approach are the same. This relationship between the two approaches is known as the **GDP identity**:

$$\text{GDP expressed as total income} \equiv \text{GDP expressed as total spending}$$

The triple-lined identity sign in this formula—a stronger version of the equals sign (=)—indicates that the expressions on both sides are always identical.

The GDP identity applies not only to the simplified economy shown in Figure 9.2 but also to the entire Canadian economy. Statistics Canada, therefore, uses both approaches—the income approach and the expenditure approach—to calculate GDP. As will be seen later in the chapter, the circular flows of income and spending in the Canadian economy incorporate not only the interaction of households and businesses in product and resource markets but also flows relating to financial markets, government, and the rest of the world. This involves a wide range of goods and services. Therefore, Statistics Canada does not restrict itself to consumer products; instead, it considers incomes from and expenditures on all goods and services in Canada.

The Income Approach

INCOME COMPONENTS OF GDP

As discussed in Chapter 1, wages, rent, profit, and interest make up Canadian incomes. These four payments form the basis of GDP calculated using the income approach. Because of practical difficulties in distinguishing resource earnings, Statistics Canada applies its own classification system: wages and salaries, corporate profits, interest income, and proprietors' incomes (including rent).

To these four classes of income, Statistics Canada adds three other classifications: indirect taxes, depreciation, and a statistical discrepancy account. These three categories help balance GDP that is calculated using the income approach with GDP that is calculated using the expenditure approach. Using the income approach, GDP is the sum of all seven categories.

Wages and Salaries

Wages and salaries are the largest income category, representing about 52 percent of GDP. This category includes direct payments to workers in both business and government, as well as employee benefits, such as contributions to employee pension funds.

Corporate Profits

In theory, all corporate profits are a payment to share-owning households. This category includes all corporate profits declared to government, including the profits paid as corporate income tax, the profits paid out to corporate shareholders as dividends, and the profits put back into the business. The final subcategory of profits put back into the business, or **retained earnings**, represents the funds that corporations keep for new investment. Also included in the category of corporate profits are adjustments to the value of businesses' unsold products.

retained earnings: profits kept by businesses for new investment

Interest Income

Interest income includes interest paid on business loans and bonds and, to a lesser extent, such income as royalty payments. This category does not, however, include interest payments made by consumers and government, since consumer loans and government debt are viewed simply as transfers of purchasing power.

Proprietors' Incomes and Rents

Proprietors' incomes include the earnings of sole proprietorships and partnerships, including self-employed professionals and farmers. These incomes are received by owners for supplying various types of resources to their businesses. The income to landlords from renting property is also included in this category.

Indirect Taxes

Indirect taxes, such as provincial sales taxes, are charged on products rather than levied against households or businesses. Because of this, their monetary value is not included in the main income components of GDP using the income approach. But this value is included in the expenditure approach. To balance the results from the two approaches, taxes (minus any subsidies businesses receive) are added to income-based GDP.

Depreciation

Durable assets—such as buildings, equipment, and tools—wear out and need to be replaced. This is considered a cost of doing business and, therefore, shows up in product prices as well as the expenditure approach to GDP. To balance the two approaches to calculating GDP, the income approach must also include depreciation.

Statistical Discrepancy

Because businesses' and individuals' records might be faulty or missing, GDP figures for the two approaches do differ. Therefore, the GDP figures are actually estimates, and any discrepancy between them is known as a *statistical discrepancy*. To balance the two figures, Statistics Canada divides the difference between the two approaches. As shown in Figure 9.3, the discrepancy was 1 billion in 2002. Half the amount (0.5 billion) is added to the lower estimate of GDP, and half (0.5 billion) is deducted from the higher GDP estimate.

Figure 9.3	Canada's Gross Domestic Product (2002)

Income Approach ($ billions)		Expenditure Approach ($ billion)	
Wages and salaries	597.3	Personal consumption (C)	656.2
Corporate profits	143.4	Gross investment (I)	218.9
Interest income	49.4	Government purchases (G)	230.0
Proprietors' incomes and rents	71.1	Net exports (X – M)	50.3
Indirect taxes	138.2	Statistical discrepancy	–0.5
Depreciation	155.0		
Statistical discrepancy	0.5		
Gross Domestic Product	1154.9	Gross Domestic Product	1154.9

With the income approach, GDP is the sum of incomes and balancing items, as shown on the left. With the expenditure approach, GDP is the sum of expenditures, as shown on the right. Both totals are reconciled with an equal amount for statistical discrepancy.

Source: Statistics Canada "Canada's Gross Domestic Product (2002)," adapted from the Statistics Canada publication, "Canadian economic accounts quarterly review, First Quarter 2003" Catalogue 13-010, Vol. 2, No. 1, May 2003, pp. 12–13.

The Expenditure Approach

GDP found using the expenditure approach is the sum of purchases in product markets. In order to explore this in greater detail, we must first distinguish between categories of products. Later, we will examine the categories of expenditures.

CATEGORIES OF PRODUCTS

final products: products that will not be processed further and will not be resold

intermediate products: products that will be processed further or will be resold

Final products are those that will not be processed further and will not be resold. How much the ultimate user pays for the product determines the value of a final product. An example might be a pad of paper bought at the corner store. In contrast, **intermediate products** are those that will be processed further or will be resold. Advertising services bought by a soft-drink manufacturer or clothing bought by a wholesaler are examples. Something is a final product or an intermediate product on the basis of how it is used. For example, flour that is bought by a household for home baking is a final product; however, flour that is bought by a bakery to make bread to be sold is an intermediate product.

To understand why the distinction matters, consider that some products will be sold many times in product markets—first as intermediate products and then as final products. The products to make a pad of paper, for example, may be sold once by the logging company to the paper producer, a second time by the paper producer to the retailer, and a third time by the retailer to you. Since the cost of the wood may be $1 out of the retail price of $4, the value of the final product covers the value of the wood used to make it.

double-counting: the problem of adding to GDP the same item at different stages in its production

value added: the extra worth of a product at each stage in its production; a concept used to avoid double-counting in calculating GDP

If the values of all products—final and intermediate—were included in the GDP calculations, we might have the problem of **double-counting**. Double-counting would cause estimates of GDP to be too high and not reflect the real activity in the economy. To avoid this problem, the concept of **value added** is applied to GDP. This concept helps quantify the extra worth of the product at each stage in its production. Figure 9.4 uses the example of the pad of paper to show the results of double-counting and how the concept of value added deals with it. Statistics Canada subtracts the value of all purchases of

Figure 9.4   Value Added in Making Paper

Production Stage	Total Value Paid/Received	Value Added	Business That Adds Value
1. Wood is cut and transported to paper mill	$1.00	$1.00	logging company
2. Paper is processed and sold to retailer	2.75	1.75 (2.75 – 1.00)	paper company
3. Paper is sold by retailer to consumer	4.00	1.25 (4.00 – 2.75)	retailer
	$7.75	$4.00	

The value added by each business at each production stage is the value of the business's output, minus its cost of intermediate products. The sum of the values added at all stages of production represents the price of the pad of paper when it is finally sold.

intermediate goods and services by businesses from the value for which intermediate and final products are sold.

EXCLUDED PURCHASES

Expenditure-based GDP is calculated on the basis of almost all purchases in the Canadian economy. Note, once again, that figures for GDP calculated using this approach are adjusted for any statistical discrepancy. But before we examine the categories of purchases included in GDP, let us examine those that are excluded because they are not related to current production. There are two types: financial exchanges and second-hand purchases.

Financial Exchanges

A gift of money—between family members, for example—is not a transaction included in GDP for the simple reason that the transaction just shifts purchasing power from one party to another. Similarly, bank deposits and purchases of stocks are not included; however, payments for any financial service—bank service charges or a commission to a stockbroker—are included.

Second-Hand Purchases

Purchases of second-hand, or used, goods are also excluded from GDP because these products have already been counted at their first sale to a consumer. In other words, including second-hand purchases in GDP would double-count, or overestimate, the value of products sold.

INCLUDED PURCHASES

expenditure equation: the equation that states that GDP is the sum of personal consumption (C), gross investment (I), government purchases (G), and net exports (X – M)

Purchases included in GDP calculations fall into four categories: personal consumption (C), gross investment (I), government purchases (G), and net exports (X – M). Each of these categories contributes to the circular flow of payments in the Canadian economy. The following **expenditure equation** shows that GDP is simply the sum of these four types of spending.

$$GDP = C + I + G + (X - M)$$

Personal Consumption

Personal consumption (C) is household spending on goods and services. These purchases make up the largest component, about 60 percent, of GDP. Of the goods and
services consumed, **nondurable goods**, such as food, are consumed just once. **Durable
goods**—such as automobiles—are consumed over time.

Gross Investment

The second component of expenditure in GDP is **gross investment** (I). This category includes purchases of assets that are intended to produce revenue. Gross investment
varies—usually from between 15 and 25 percent of GDP—from year to year. The most
important spending in this category is on equipment and machines used by businesses—for example, a carpenter's purchase of a lathe or a newspaper publisher's purchase
of a printing press. Expenditures by government agencies on equipment and machines
also fall into this category.

In addition, gross investment includes changes in the money value of unsold goods
and materials, known as **inventories**. So that businesses can meet unexpected
demand for particular products without stopping production to wait for deliveries of
inputs, they often keep inventories of inputs on hand. Because these inventories are
income-producing assets, an increase in an economy's inventories over a given year is
seen as positive investment spending. In contrast, a decrease in inventories is seen as negative investment spending.

The construction of all buildings, including houses and apartments, is considered
another part of gross investment. Owner-occupied housing is added here, rather than as
part of personal consumption, because owner-occupied dwellings *could* be rented out
by the owner to make an income. From an economic perspective, homeowners make
an investment when they purchase their properties and then rent to themselves.

Gross investment is related to the economy's **capital stock**, which is the total
value of productive assets that provide a flow of revenue. Recall that capital assets,
such as machinery and equipment, wear out over time. The accompanying decrease
in the value of these capital assets is known as **depreciation**. Subtracting annual
depreciation of an entire economy's capital assets from new gross investment gives **net
investment**. Net investment, therefore, represents the yearly change in the economy's
stock of capital.

Consider the example in Figure 9.5. An economy has $200 billion of capital stock
at the beginning of a year and depreciation of $40 billion during the year. If gross
investment over the same period is $100 billion, then net investment equals $60 billion
(= $100 billion − $40 billion). This $60 billion represents the amount by which the cap-
ital stock expands during the year. So, by the year's end, the value of the economy's capital stock is $260 billion (= $200 billion + $60 billion).

While they cannot be included in GDP, it is interesting to highlight the sources of
funds for investment. The funds used for capital investment come not only from businesses' retained earnings but also from households' **personal saving** (S). By depositing
funds in banks and by investing in stocks and bonds, households provide a flow of personal savings to businesses. Figure 9.6 shows this flow of funds for investment, as well as
the flows of incomes and spending between businesses and households.

Government Purchases

Government purchases (G) include current spending by all levels of government
on goods and services, and typically make up about 20 percent of GDP. The federal

Figure 9.5   Net Investment and Capital Stock

In a growing economy, the decline in the economy's capital stock during a year due to depreciation is outweighed by gross investment over the same period. The year-end capital stock is greater than the capital stock at the start of the year by the amount that gross investment exceeds depreciation. This increase, shown by the dark rectangle, represents the economy's net investment during the year.

THINKING ABOUT ECONOMICS

Does gross investment include spending on education and training?

As discussed in Chapter 7, education can be considered an investment in human capital, with knowledge and skills representing a vital part of an economy's productive assets. Some economists argue that Statistics Canada should include at least some spending on education as part of gross investment and add human capital to its estimate of Canada's total capital stock. Statistics Canada does not do this because of the difficulty in separating out the investment component of education. Instead, education appears either as part of personal consumption or government purchases.

Question

If spending on education were incorporated in Canada's gross investment, then how would the definition of Canada's total capital stock have to be adjusted?

Figure 9.6   Financial Markets and the Circular Flow

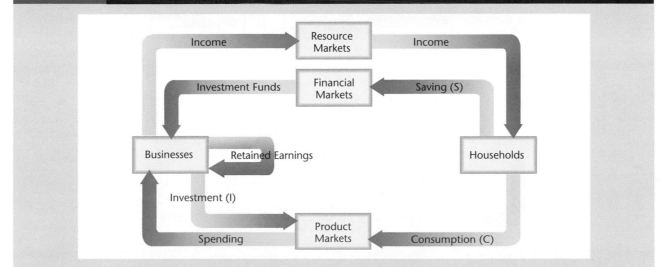

Personal saving is transformed into investment funds for businesses by financial markets. Businesses then use these funds, plus their retained earnings, to make investment. Investment and personal consumption form part of total spending.

government buying a battleship for the armed forces and a municipality hiring a paving company to do road repairs are two examples of government spending.

transfer payments: government payments to household or other levels of governments

Some types of government spending are not included in this category. **Transfer payments** are payments from one level of government to another or to households. These are excluded from government purchases, since they are simply a redistribution of purchasing power. For the same reason, government subsidies to businesses are also excluded. Both transfer payments and government subsidies are viewed, instead, as negative taxes, meaning, they are tax payments in reverse. Expenditures by government-owned agencies on income-producing assets—for instance, hydro-electric dams built by Ontario Power Generation, or post offices built by Canada Post—are also excluded from government purchases because these amounts are considered part of gross investment.

Government spending is partly financed through taxes from both households and businesses. Governments also finance their spending through borrowing, which takes place in financial markets. Figure 9.7 shows the role of government in the economy's circular flow of incomes and spending.

Net Exports

exports: foreign purchases of Canadian goods and services

This final category of purchase includes purchases of Canadian goods and services by the rest of the world, or **exports** (X). Suppose, for example, that a British consumer buys a Canadian cellular phone, or an American tourist spends a night in a Canadian hotel. Because payments for these transactions remain in the Canadian circular flow of incomes and spending, exports contribute to GDP. This expenditure category also accounts for **imports** (M), or Canadian purchases of goods and services from the rest of the world. Such spending includes, for example, a Canadian cheese-lover buying French cheese, a Canadian steelmaker buying a Japanese-made casting machine, or a Canadian police force buying an American radar device. Because payments for these

imports: Canadian purchases of goods and services from the rest of the world

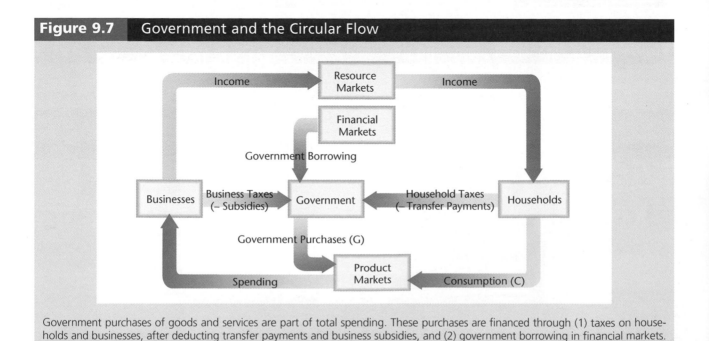

Figure 9.7   Government and the Circular Flow

Government purchases of goods and services are part of total spending. These purchases are financed through (1) taxes on households and businesses, after deducting transfer payments and business subsidies, and (2) government borrowing in financial markets.

transactions leave the Canadian circular flow of incomes and spending, imports are subtracted from GDP.

net exports: exports minus imports

To reconcile spending inside and outside the Canadian economy in calculating GDP, Statistics Canada uses the category of **net exports** (X − M), or exports minus imports. When represented as net exports, these purchases represent a small fraction of GDP; however, the values of exports and imports, viewed separately, each accounts for over 35 percent of GDP.

Figure 9.8 shows the roles of exports and imports in the circular flow of the Canadian economy. Note that the rest of the world also plays a part in the Canadian economy by lending to and borrowing from financial markets. Loans from the rest of the world to the Canadian economy are flows into the economy, while Canadian loans to the rest of the world are flows out of the economy.

Figure 9.8	The Rest of the World and the Circular Flow

Whereas exports are part of total spending in product markets, imports are deductions from total spending. Lending by the rest of the world, after subtracting borrowing by the rest of the world, represents an inflow to Canadian financial markets.

Brief Review

1. Statistics Canada prepares national income accounts to track various measures of income and spending in Canada.

2. The most prominent measure of economic activity is Gross Domestic Product (GDP), which is the total money value of all final goods and services produced in the economy over a given period.

3. GDP can be calculated by adding all incomes in resource markets or all expenditures in product markets. After taking account of several balancing items, including a statistical discrepancy, the two approaches give the same figure.

4. Using the income approach, GDP is the sum of four main income items—wages and salaries, corporate profits, interest income, and proprietors' incomes (including rent)—plus indirect taxes and depreciation.

5. The expenditure approach depends on the concept of value added to avoid double-counting of purchases.

6. Using the expenditure approach, GDP is the sum of personal consumption, gross investment, government purchases, and net exports but neither financial exchanges nor second-hand purchases.

9.1 Practice Questions

1. Identify whether or not each of the following transactions would be included in GDP. In each case explain which expenditure or income component of GDP the transaction represents, if it is included in GDP.

   a. a consumer purchases a used television
   b. a toy store adds to its stock of inventories
   c. a consumer buys a new car
   d. a Canadian corporation pays interest to owners of its bonds
   e. a provincial government repaves a highway
   f. a wealth holder places $1000 in her bank account
   g. an unemployed worker receives an employment insurance payment from the government
   h. a French farmer purchases a Canadian-made piece of farm machinery

2.

	($ billions)
Government purchases	43
Proprietors' incomes and rents	29
Exports	14
Indirect taxes	25
Gross investment	35
Wages and salaries	76
Corporate profits	38
Interest income	17
Imports	15
Net investment	26
Personal consumption	85
Statistical discrepancy	?

   The national accounts for a hypothetical economy are shown in the above table.

   a. What is the expenditure-based estimate of this economy's GDP?
   b. What is the income-based estimate of GDP?
   c. What is the value of the statistical discrepancy? Explain.
   d. What is this economy's GDP?
   e. What is the value of this economy's depreciation? How did you find this figure?

9.2 GDP and Living Standards

per capita GDP: GDP per person, calculated as GDP divided by population

real GDP: GDP expressed in constant dollars from a given year

per capita real GDP: GDP per person, expressed in constant dollars from a given year

How do living standards in Canada today compare with past living standards? And how does Canadian economic performance compare with that of other countries? **Per capita GDP**, or GDP per person, is frequently used in answering these questions.

A country's GDP is divided by its population to find its per capita GDP. So, for example, in 2002, Canada's GDP was $1 154 949 million and its population was 31.414 million. Hence, per capita GDP was $36 765 per person:

$$\text{Per capita GDP} = \frac{\text{GDP}}{\text{population}}$$

$$\$36\ 765 = \frac{\$1\ 154\ 949\ 000\ 000}{31\ 414\ 000}$$

Adjustments to Per Capita GDP

Depending on how per capita GDP is to be used, either of two adjustments can be made to it: an inflation adjustment or an exchange-rate adjustment.

INFLATION ADJUSTMENT

Because prices change over the years, per capita GDP must be adjusted when comparing economic well-being in the same country in different years. This is done by using **real GDP**, which is GDP expressed in constant dollars from a given year (currently, 1997 is the reference year). When a country's real GDP is divided by its population, the result is **per capita real GDP**, or real GDP per person. This adjustment allows comparisons to be made between per capita GDP despite changes in price. For example, Canada's 2002 real GDP, expressed in 1997 dollars, was $1 074 516 million. Given Canada's 2002 population of 31.414 million, per capita real GDP in 2002 was $34 205. In contrast, the per capita real GDP for 1992 was $26 636 (= $755 848 million ÷ 28.377 million).

$$\text{Per capita real GDP} = \frac{\text{real GDP}}{\text{population}}$$

$$\$34\ 205 = \frac{\$1\ 074\ 516\ 000\ 000}{31\ 414\ 000}$$

EXCHANGE-RATE ADJUSTMENT

To compare various countries' per capita GDP for a given year, we must adjust for the different currencies. This is done by expressing all countries' GDPs in one currency, the standard being the American dollar. For example, per capita GDP for 2001 in the United States was $35 398 in American dollars, while Canada's per capita GDP for 2001 in American dollars was $22 982. When expressed in a common currency, Canada's GDP is significantly lower than that of the United States.

Limitations of GDP

As with any economic indicator, it is important to distinguish what specifically is being *measured* by GDP and what GDP *indicates*. Recall that GDP is a *measure* of the total money value of all final goods and services produced in an economy over a given period. Also, GDP indicates, to some extent, living standards. However, like all indicators, it has quantitative and qualitative limitations.

Not necessarily. As experienced travellers know, converting a US$1 into local currencies can buy significantly more in one country than another. So that incomes can be compared more effectively, a concept known as purchasing-power parity (PPP) has been developed to adjust for these differences in domestic prices. Such PPP-adjustment is now becoming common when comparing per capita GDP in different countries. In 2001, for example, Canada's per capita GDP in PPP-adjusted US$ was $30 258, whereas it was $22 982 without this adjustment.

Question

What does the PPP-adjustment of Canada's per capita GDP suggest about prices in Canada versus those in the United States?

EXCLUDED ACTIVITIES

Because GDP represents the market value of goods and services produced in an economy, it does not include some types of productive activities. Excluding these activities means that GDP can understate economic activity and living standards.

nonmarket activities: productive activities that take place outside the marketplace

Nonmarket activities—such as housework, unpaid child care, and the work of "do-it-yourselfers"—take place outside the marketplace, so they are excluded from GDP. However, these productive activities have a vital impact on the living standards of Canadians.

underground economy: all the market transactions that go unreported

The **underground economy** includes all the market transactions that are unreported and, therefore, also left out of GDP. One example of a transaction in the underground economy is smuggling, which is an illegal activity. In contrast, other "under-the-table" transactions may be for legal purchases—for example, gardening services that are paid for by cash or barter so that taxes on these transactions can be avoided.

Estimates of the size of Canada's underground economy vary widely. Some economists have tried to measure the underground economy by studying how much cash is held by the public, since underground transactions are commonly paid for with cash to escape detection. Using this method, it has been estimated that Canada's underground economy is equal to anywhere from 10 to 25 percent of GDP, meaning that it has an annual value of $100 billion or more. Statistics Canada's own studies suggest that Canada's underground economy is much smaller—between 1 and 5 percent of GDP. Because of the difficulty in gathering data, these are only "guesstimates."

PRODUCT QUALITY

Today's GDP includes purchases of products not available a few decades ago—personal computers, fax machines, and VCRs, to name only a few. As well, many other products, such as cars and photocopiers, have increased substantially in quality with little or no rise in price. GDP, which can only add up selling prices, cannot fully capture these quality improvements.

COMPOSITION OF OUTPUT

Another limitation related to the money-value basis of GDP is that it tells us nothing about what is produced and purchased. Suppose one country dedicates most of its GDP to military uses, but another country dedicates the same GDP to health care and education for its citizens. While the GDPs may be the same, the countries' living standards would differ considerably.

INCOME DISTRIBUTION

The fact that incomes may be distributed in a range of ways can have profound effects on the living standards of individuals. But GDP does not reflect how output is distributed among a country's citizens. So, for example, citizens in two countries with the same per capita GDP may have very different living standards if one country's income is widely distributed, while most of the other country's income is in the hands of a few.

LEISURE

Although we might be able to work every waking hour, most of us consider leisure a requirement for a satisfactory standard of living. However, leisure is not bought and sold in the market, so it cannot be accounted for by GDP. Thus, although the average Canadian work week has gradually become shorter—to almost half of what it was a century ago—GDP has no way of representing this change. Because of this, GDP understates economic well-being.

THE ENVIRONMENT

Since GDP quantifies economic activity in terms of its money value, it does not adequately represent another factor: the environment. GDP does not differentiate between economic activities that are harmful to the environment and those that are not, and it may not effectively represent spillover costs and benefits. So, for example, while the clean-up following an oil spill would be added to GDP, the creation of a new nature preserve would likely not be added.

THINKING ABOUT ECONOMICS

Is it possible to overcome the problems associated with using GDP as an indicator of living standards by using broader measures that include non-economic variables?

Some economists think so. One measure of living standard is the Human Development Index (HDI) outlined in the article on Mahbub ul Haq at the end of the chapter. Another is the Genuine Progress Index (GPI), a relatively new indicator of sustainable development and well-being. In Nova Scotia, a value for the province's GPI will soon be calculated annually by a research group known as GPI Atlantic. This index contains social, economic, and environmental components, including estimates of the value of unpaid work (both voluntary and housework), the value of natural capital, such as forests and the marine environment, and social indicators, such as income distribution and the level of health care.

Question

Not all economists would agree with the philosophy behind the GPI. Why not?

9.3 Other Economic Measures

Statistics Canada uses the national income accounts to calculate other measures, which are employed in various ways.

Gross National Product

Gross National Product (GNP) is the total income acquired by Canadians both within Canada and elsewhere. Note that while GDP focuses on incomes made in *Canada*, GNP focuses on the earnings of *Canadians*.

LO 9.3

To calculate GNP, two adjustments to GDP must be made. Income earned from Canadian financial investments by the rest of the world—interest payments on a Canadian government bond held in Japan, for example—is deducted from GDP to find GNP. Although included in GDP, such earnings are not part of the earnings of Canadians. Also, income earned from financial investments by Canadians in the rest of the world—a stock dividend from an American company paid to a Canadian share-holder, for example—is added to GDP to find GNP. While not included in GDP, this income is part of Canadians' earnings.

These two adjustments can be made in an investment income account. Because, traditionally, financial investment by the rest of the world in Canada has been higher than financial investment by Canadians in the rest of the world, the account gives *net* investment income to the rest of the world, and is subtracted from GDP to give GNP. As Figure 9.9 shows, Canadian GNP is less than Canadian GDP.

This is the case in all countries, such as Canada, in which large parts of the nations' financial assets are owned by foreigners so that each year there is a net outflow of finan-cial investment income. But in other countires, such as the United Kingdom, the nation's citizens' foreign financial investments are greater than the amounts of the nation's assets owned by foreigners. For these countries, GNP is greater than GDP. In Canada, GNP is now used only when comparisons are being made with countries that stress GNP rather than GDP in their national accounts.

Disposable Income

One other income measure that derives from the national accounts, and which we will make use of often in the chapters that follow, is **disposable income**, or DI, which is income, after the payment of income taxes, that households can either consume or save. As shown in Figure 9.10, this income measure is significantly lower than GDP and GNP.

Figure 9.9	Deriving Gross National Product (2002)

	($ billions)
Gross Domestic Product (GDP)	1154.9
Deduct: Net investment income to the rest of the world	(–) 27.4
Gross National Product (GNP)	1127.6

GNP is less than GDP because foreign financial investments in Canada exceed Canadian financial investment in the rest of the world.

Source: Statistics Canada "Deriving Gross National Product (2002)," adapted from the Statistics Canada CANSIM II database http://cansim2.statcan.ca Table 380-0030.

Figure 9.10 Deriving Other Income Measures (2000)

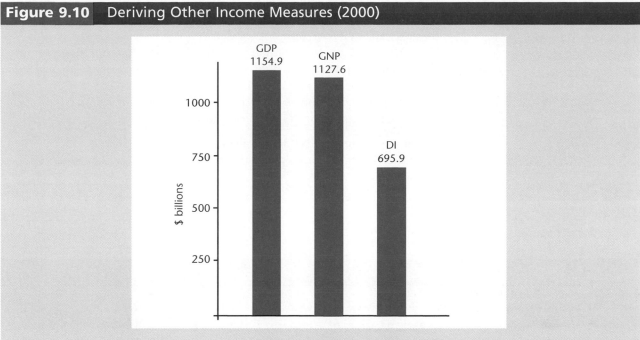

GNP is less than GDP, due to the importance of foreign financial investments in Canada. Disposable income is less than both GDP and GNP.

Source: Statistics Canada "Other Income Measures (2002)," adapted from the Statistics Canada publication "National income and expenditure accounts, quarterly estimates, Fourth Quarter 2002," Catalogue 13-001, Vol. 50, No. 4, April 2003, pp. 32–33.

Brief Review

1. To make comparisons among years and countries, GDP is expressed per capita, or per person. To compare GDP for different years, it is adjusted for inflation to derive real GDP, and then expressed per capita. To compare GDP among countries, a common currency must be used, usually American dollars.

2. GDP has its limitations as an indicator of living standards: it excludes nonmarket activities and the underground economy; it does not reflect changes in product quality or what specific products a country is producing; it cannot account for income distribution or leisure; and it cannot adequately account for environmental spillover costs and benefits.

3. Other measures of economic activity and income include Gross National Product and disposable income.

9.3 Practice Questions

1. In a given year, a country's GDP in terms of the country's own dollars is $235 billion.

    a. If the country's population is 6 million, then what is per capita GDP?

b. If each of the country's own dollars is worth US$0.56, then what is the country's per capita GDP in terms of US dollars?

c. If each of the country's dollars is worth US$0.60, after adjusting for purchasing power parity, then what is the country's per capita GDP in PPP-adjusted US dollars?

d. Explain why the country's per capita GDP in PPP-adjusted US dollars is higher than its per capita GDP in unadjusted US dollars.

2 a. When is a country's GNP higher than its GDP?

b. Do citizens of a country benefit when GNP is higher than GDP? Explain.

LAST**WORD**

In this chapter, we have examined how economists measure economic activity using a variety of statistics—in particular, GDP. And we have seen how GDP—adjusted for such factors as population, price changes, and differences in foreign currencies —has often been used as an indicator of national well-being. In the following chapters, GDP will reappear as one of the main measures of economic fluctuations used by government as they attempt to stabilize levels of economic activity. But first, we will analyze the importance of two related statistics: the rates of inflation and unemployment.

Key Concepts

capital stock 206
depreciation 206
disposable income 214
double-counting 204
durable goods 206
expenditure approach 201
expenditure equation 205
exports 208
final products 204
GDP identity 202
government purchases 206
Gross Domestic Product 201

gross investment 206
Gross National Product 214
imports 208
income approach 201
intermediate products 204
inventories 206
national income accounts 201
net exports 209
net investment 206
nondurable goods 206
nonmarket activities 212
per capita GDP 211

per capita real GDP 211
personal consumption 206
personal saving 206
real GDP 211
retained earnings 203
transfer payments 208
underground economy 212
value added 204

Questions

Metrica's National Accounts (2004)

	($ billions)
Corporate profits	55
Exports	68
Wages and salaries	546
Gross investment	157
Government purchases	184
Indirect taxes	75
Personal consumption	490
Interest income	43
Imports	27
Depreciation	79
Proprietors' incomes and rents	56
Statistical discrepancy	?

1. The data in the table above apply to a hypothetical country, Metrica, during 2004.
    a. Use the data to find income-based and expenditure-based estimates of Metrica's GDP.
    b. Outline how the statistical discrepancy between the two estimates in part a. can be used to find a single GDP value.
    c. By how much is Metrica's capital stock expanding or contracting in 2004? Explain.

2. The production of a kilogram of smoked salmon requires a fisherman to catch salmon worth $1.40, which is prepared by a food processor and sold to a retailer for $2.20, who then sells it to a consumer for $2.75. With the aid of a table similar to Figure 9.4, explain how this product appears in GDP, using the concept of added value.

3. For each of following cases, give a possible example. Explain each of your answers.
    a. A product that is always a final product
    b. A product that is always an intermediate product
    c. A product that, depending on how it is used, is sometimes a final product and sometimes an intermediate product

4. For each of the following transactions, identify whether or not it would be included in GDP:
    a. An accountant receives payment for preparing a client's personal income tax return.
    b. An owner of a Canada Savings Bond is paid interest on this bond.
    c. A business buys a new piece of production equipment.
    d. A student is paid for shovelling a neighbour's sidewalk.
    e. An unemployed carpenter receives an employment insurance payment.
    f. A town council hires a contractor to do paving work on the town's roads.
    g. A newspaper publisher buys newsprint to add to its inventories of supplies.
    h. An electronic hobbyist sells a used computer to a friend.
    i. A fisherman receives a government subsidy to help relocate to a larger community.

j. A Canadian business sells medical equipment to a Japanese hospital.

k. A wealth-holder sells 1000 shares issued by a Canadian corporation.

l. A home-owner repairs his own leaking roof.

5. Each of the following cases applies to a country whose per capita real GDP has been steadily rising at 1 percent a year. In each case, explain whether GDP overstates or understates the change in living standards.

a. The average amount of leisure time for workers has decreased.

b. The relative importance of the nonmarket sector has risen.

c. Incomes have become less equitably distributed.

d. A larger proportion of the economy's resources are devoted to recycling and the introduction of environmentally sustainable production techniques.

6. (Advanced Question)

On a single diagram, show how financial markets, government, and the rest of the world can be integrated in the circular flow.

Internet Application Questions

http://www.statcan.ca

http://www.statcan.ca/
english/Estat/licence.htm

http://www.statcan.ca

1. Access Statistics Canada's web site (at http://www.statcan.ca).

a. Use the links to "Postsecondary Resources" to find the value in the most recent year available for expenditure-based GDP at market prices.

b. Also find the values for the most recent year available for the components of expenditure-based GDP at market prices: (i) personal consumption, (ii) gross investment, (iii) government purchases, (iv) net exports, and (v) the statistical discrepancy.

2. Access Statistics Canada's E-Stat site (at http://www.statcan.ca/english/Estat/licence.htm).

a. On the basis of the information found in *National Accounts*, generate a two-dimensional graph showing the purchasing power parity for the Canadian dollar in terms of the American dollar for Gross Domestic Product since 1981.

b. If the Canadian dollar were trading at its purchasing power parity, would it be lower or higher than it is today? Explain.

3. Access Statistics Canada's web site (at http://www.statcan.ca).

a. Use the links to "Postsecondary Resources" to find the most recent figures in Statistics Canada's *Income-Based GDP Table*.

b. Use this data to update the income-based statistics in Figure 9.3 of the text.

4. Access the United Nations Development Programme's web site (at http://hdr.undp.org/).

a. Use the links to the latest Human Development Indicators to find the countries with the 10 highest PPP-adjusted per capita GDP levels.

b. What global ranking does Canada have based on PPP-adjusted per capita GDP?

c. Using these links, also find the countries with the 10 highest GDP levels in terms of US dollars.

d. What global ranking does Canada have based on $US GDP?

Adding the Human Dimension

Mahbub ul Haq and the Human Development Index

ADVANCING
ECONOMIC
THOUGHT

Is the use of per capita GDP to compare national living standards inherently flawed? Some economists say it is. They point to such factors as access to education and to health care, which they argue are as vital as income in determining the quality of life. In recent decades, this view has led to the creation of more inclusive measures of national well-being. Most successful is the Human Development Index (HDI), published annually by the United Nations Development Programme, and the brainchild of economist Mahbub ul Haq (1934-1998), a leading figure in the field of development economics.

Haq grew up in Pakistan when it and neighbouring India were being established at the end of the British colonial period. The economic difficulties faced by both countries in their early years left Haq with an abiding interest in the issue of development. During his study of economics—first at Cambridge University in the United Kingdom, then at Yale and Harvard in the United States—he came to disagree with what was then the prevailing view of development, which stressed economic growth to the exclusion of all other factors. Instead, he saw development as a general process of providing people with new choices, rather than simply expanding their incomes. This perspective is now the dominant one in economics, in part due to Haq's own contributions. He describes the change this way:

> Only 30 years ago, it would have been heresy to challenge the economic growth school's tacit assumption that the purpose of development is to increase national income. Today, it is widely accepted that the real purpose of development is to enlarge people's choices in all fields—economic, political, cultural. Seeking increases in income is one of many choices people make, but it is not the only one.[1]

Mahbub ul Haq
Source: Courtesy of United Nations Development Program

Most of Haq's early career as an economist was spent working for the Pakistan government. In 1982, he was appointed the country's Planning and Finance Minister and used this powerful position to try to curtail the power of Pakistan's wealthy feudal elite, a small group of 22 landowning families whose political influence had allowed them to maintain a favoured position in the country's tax system. But Haq's attempted reforms met with limited success, and by 1988, his growing disillusionment with Pakistan's regime (led by military general Zia ul Haq) and his wish to influence policy-making at a global level spurred him to move to the United States to work for the United Nations Development Programme (the UNDP).

The HDI and Its Calculation

A charismatic figure, who managed to mix idealism with powers of persuasion, Haq soon played a leadership role at the UNDP. It was due to his inspiration that, in 1990, the UNDP began publishing an annual Human Development Report, with detailed statistical estimates of the Human Development Index for countries across the globe. This index combines four separate statistics—each country's per capita GDP adjusted for purchasing power parity (PPP), its rate of adult literacy, the average years of schooling, and its citizens' life expectancy at birth—to give an indicator of well-being that stresses the satisfaction of basic human needs.

The national rankings based on the HDI have some important differences from those based on per capita GDP alone. For example, in 2002, Canada had the third highest HDI ranking for any country in the world, largely due to its high average length of schooling and life expectancy. But in terms of PPP-adjusted per capita GDP, Canada's position in recent years has gradually fallen so that the country is now in the seventh place—not only behind traditionally rich countries, such as Switzerland and the United States, but also fast-growing upstarts, such as Kuwait and Singapore.

The Debate over the HDI

How good is the HDI as a measure of living standards? While its inclusion of education and health-care indicators are easy to defend, some economists question the statistic's usefulness. In particular, the HDI rankings for rich countries are complicated by a close clustering of scores. For example, in 2002, top-ranked Norway had an HDI ranking of 0.942, while runner-up Sweden's score was 0.941. With such a small numerical difference, is it that meaningful to rank Norwegians' living standards as being significantly different from those of Swedes?

The clustering of scores is especially problematic, given the bias in some of HDI's component statistics. Most suspect are the rates of adult literacy reported by various countries. In 2003, for example, all the top 20 nations in the HDI ranks (including Canada) reported a literacy rate of 90 percent or above. The legitimacy of these figures is subject to doubt. In the case of Canada, some studies suggest there is a significant minority of the population whose literacy skills are minimal at best. If so, then Canada's high ranking could be illusory.

There is also controversy over the way income differences are treated in the HDI. Haq's insistence that human development is primarily an issue of satisfying basic human needs led him to downplay the importance of per capita GDP as a component in the index. For countries with per capita GDPs above the global average, extra income is discounted at higher and higher rates. To illustrate, the United States' per capita GDP is about 23 percent higher than the comparable Canadian figure in Canada. But in calculating the HDI, this translates into a difference of just 3 percent—a level of discounting that some economists find excessive.

Another criticism relates to the HDI's use of life expectancy as a component. Changes in this statistic for any country are very gradual and difficult to estimate. Canada's current life expectancy of 78.8 years, for example, is one of the highest in the world. But is this statistic relevant for young Canadians today? Breakthroughs in medical research will probably mean that young people in Canada, as well as other rich industrialized countries, can expect to live much longer lives, and it is unclear in which countries this trend will be most pronounced.

Refining the HDI

Haq was aware of these objections: "The HDI is neither perfect nor fully developed," he admitted. "It requires continuous analysis and further refinement."[2] And there is no doubt that the index will be modified in the future. Indeed, refinements of the index are already under way. Haq was opposed to adding further components to the existing index because, "[m]ore variables will not necessarily improve the HDI," he argued. "They may confuse the picture and blur the main trends."[3] But in recent years, each new Human Development Report has included adjusted HDIs that highlight income disparities within particular countries as well as disparities between men and women. The result has been a growing attention by economists on the crucial links between the distribution of incomes and economic development.

Despite debates over its composition, the HDI has gained ever greater prominence, and there is every indication that its importance will increase further. By helping to make governments more accountable for the human dimensions of development, Haq has played an important role in broadening the conception of development to include notions of social justice and a practical concern for the world's poor.

Notes
[1] Mahbub ul Haq, *Reflections on Human Development* (Oxford: Oxford University Press, 1995), p. xvii.
[2] *Ibid*, p. 61
[3] *Ibid*, p. 58

1. Outline a possible problem with each of the four statistics—purchasing-power-adjusted GDP, the rate of literacy, average years of schooling, and life expectancy—included in the Human Development Index as a guide to living standards.

2. The United Nations Development Programme calculates additional statistics to help compare living standards in various countries. Access the UNDP's web site (at http://www.undp.org) to learn about these measures. Choosing one, explain its usefulness as an indicator of living standards.

http://www.undp.org

3. Using the information at *Measuring Human Development* (at p. 14 at http://www.hdr.undp.org/reports/global/2001/en/pdf/chapterone.pdf), outline how each of the statistics included in the Human Development Index are measured, as they appear in the HDI.

http://www.undp.org

ADVANCING ECONOMIC THOUGHT

CHAPTER 10

Inflation and Unemployment

Unemployment and inflation still preoccupy and perplex economists...and everyone else.

—James Tobin, American economist

Ask working Canadians what economic prospect concerns them most, and the answer will likely be unemployment. Ask a pensioner the same question, and chances are the answer will be inflation. Our anxiety over these two economic evils is not misplaced; in fact, price stability and full employment are among Canada's most important economic goals. This chapter explores the effects of a trend of rising prices, how the trend is measured, and how it often hurts most those who can afford it least. We will also examine unemployment: how it is measured, its causes, and its costs, not only for individuals but for the entire economy.

LEARNING OBJECTIVES

In this chapter, you will:

1 learn about inflation, how it is measured, and its effect on nominal and real incomes

2 examine the official unemployment rate, the different types of unemployment, and the definition of full employment

10.1 Inflation

LO 10.1

deflation: a general
decrease in the level of
prices

consumer price index: a
measure of price changes for
a typical basket of consumer
products

item weights: the proportions of each good in the
total cost of the basket of
consumer goods used to
calculate CPI

base year: the survey year
used as a point of comparison in subsequent years

Inflation, as introduced in Chapter 1, is a general increase in the prices of goods and services in an entire economy over time. Suppose, for example, that Canada has an annual inflation rate of 3 percent this year. Inflation does not mean that all prices are rising. Some prices are rising, others are remaining constant, while still others may be falling; however, the *overall* rise in prices is 3 percent. In exceptional cases—most notably during the 1930s—prices may remain constant, in which case the inflation rate is zero, or there may be a general decline in prices. A general decrease in the level of prices is called **deflation.** To explain why Canadian governments stress the goal of price stability, let us first examine inflation in detail, how it is measured, and its implications for the economy.

The Consumer Price Index

The tool most commonly used to measure overall changes in prices is the **consumer price index** (CPI). This index monitors price changes in a representative "shopping basket" of consumer products. So that it can determine what typical Canadian households buy, Statistics Canada surveys their buying habits every few years.

A simple illustration, as given by Figure 10.1, allows us to see how the consumer price index indicates price changes. Suppose the shopping basket includes only two items—hamburgers and milkshakes. An investigator conducting a survey in 2003 finds that each month an average consumer buys 10 hamburgers at $2 each and 30 milkshakes at $1 each. In other words, the typical consumer spends $20 on hamburgers and $30 on milkshakes, for a total of $50 per month. Therefore, two-fifths (0.4) of the consumer's total budget is spent on hamburgers and three-fifths (0.6) on milkshakes. These fractions represent the **item weights**, or proportions of each good in the total cost of the shopping basket.

To give a point of comparison for prices in subsequent years, the year in which the survey is conducted acts as the **base year**. The combined price of the representative

Figure 10.1   Simple Consumer Price Index

	Prices	Quantity Consumed per Month	Expenditure per Month	Weights
		Results of 2003 Survey		
Hamburgers	$2.00	10	$20	$20 ÷ $50 = 0.4
Milkshakes	$1.00	30	$30	$30 ÷ $50 = 0.6
			$50	

	Prices	2004 Price 2003 Quantity
		Prices in 2004
Hamburgers	$2.20	$2.20 × 10 = $22.00
Milkshakes	$1.05	$1.05 × 30 = $31.50
		$53.50

In this simplified economy, 10 hamburgers and 30 milkshakes fill the monthly shopping basket of an average consumer. If the value of this basket rises from $50 to $53.50 during the course of a year, the annual inflation rate is 7 percent, with the consumer price index moving from 100 to 107.

products in the base year is considered the reference point, and the index in the base year is set at 100. Suppose, in our example, that the prices of hamburgers and milkshakes rise to $2.20 and $1.05 in 2004. On the basis of the quantities determined by the 2003 survey, the amount spent each month on hamburgers and milkshakes can be calculated. In other words, the same quantity of hamburgers at the new hamburger price (= 10 × $2.20) and the same quantity of milkshakes at the new milkshake price (= 30 × $1.05) give a total cost of $53.50 (= $22 + $31.50). Compared with the 2003 total cost ($50) of the same products, prices have risen by $3.50 (= $53.50 − $50.00) or 7 percent from the base year [=($3.50 ÷ $50) × 100]. Hence, the 2004 consumer price index is 107.

While it includes many more items, the actual CPI is calculated by Statistics Canada in the same way. Figure 10.2 shows the item weights for the major components of the CPI. Every month, the prices of about 600 representative products included in the CPI shopping basket are researched in a variety of Canadian communities. The index is calculated from the results. In the typical case of rising prices, the percentage increase in the consumer price index represents the inflation rate. For example, if the CPI has a value of 100 at the end of one year and a value of 110 at the end of the next year, the inflation rate over the year has been 10 percent. In other words, the change in the index (110 − 100), expressed as a percentage [=(10 ÷ 100) × 100], is the inflation rate (10 percent).

NOMINAL VERSUS REAL INCOME

cost of living: the amount consumers must spend on the entire range of goods and services they buy

The consumer price index is useful in helping consumers determine the **cost of living**, or the amount they must spend on the entire range of goods and services they buy. In particular, the CPI allows consumers to judge how much better or worse off they are as a result of inflation. Suppose, for example, a consumer's monthly income increases from $1000 to $1050 during a year when the CPI rises from 100 to 110. If the consumer's own monthly purchases roughly correspond to those in the representative

---

Figure 10.2 Consumer Price Index Weights (1992)

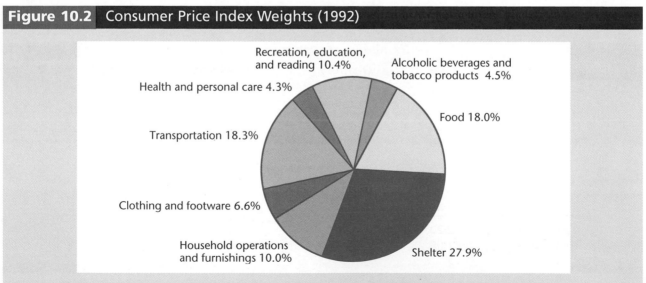

According to Statistics Canada's 1992 survey, a typical urban household's expenditures had the above weights. As shown, housing was the biggest expenditure, followed by food and transportation.

Source: Statistics Canada "Consumer Price Index Weights (1992)," adapted from the Statistics Canada publication, "Your guide to the consumer price index," Catalogue 62-577, December 1996, p. 6.

nominal income: income expressed in current dollars

real income: income expressed in constant base-year dollars

"shopping basket," he can evaluate the personal impact of inflation. To see how this consumer's purchasing power is affected by inflation, we can express his **nominal income**, or income valued in current dollars, as a **real income**, or income expressed in constant base-year dollars. To determine real income for a given year, the consumer's nominal income ($1050) is divided by the value of the consumer price index for that year expressed in hundredths (1.10):

$$\text{Real income} = \frac{\text{nominal income}}{\text{CPI (in hundredths)}}$$
$$\$954.55 = \frac{\$1050}{1.10}$$

In other words, the consumer's monthly income of $1050 has a purchasing power of $954.55 when valued in constant base-year dollars. His income has not increased proportionally with the cost of living. For the consumer's purchasing power to keep up with inflation, his income would have to increase by the same percentage as the increase in prices—that is, by 10 percent, or $100 (= $1000 × 0.10), to $1100 (= $1000 + $100).

As our example shows, the purchasing power of a current dollar is inversely related to the consumer price index: the lower the CPI, the higher is the purchasing power of nominal income; and the higher the CPI, the lower is the purchasing power of nominal income. Therefore, those whose incomes increase at a higher rate than the rise in prices have a higher standard of living. On the other hand, those whose incomes increase at a lower rate than the rise in prices are worse off than before.

Limitations of the CPI

As with any economic indicator, the consumer price index has a number of limitations. In this case, they are: consumer differences, changes in spending patterns, and product quality. In some circumstances, these limitations can severely reduce the index's usefulness.

CONSUMER DIFFERENCES

Individual consumption patterns do not always match those of the typical urban household. Hence, the consumer price index may not apply to many consumers' individual cost of living. Consider, for example, a fashion-conscious reader. This person tends to spend a larger proportion of her budget on clothing and books than the typical consumer and, consequently, might travel less than the average consumer. For this individual consumer, the official index understates the impact of price changes in clothing and books but overstates the impact of price changes in travel fares.

CHANGES IN SPENDING PATTERNS

Statistics Canada periodically surveys households to update both the contents and the item weights of the "shopping basket." But these statistical changes occur relatively infrequently, while the changes in actual consumption patterns are ongoing and gradual. This can lead to an important bias in the stated inflation rate using the CPI. In the case of items whose prices rise very little, or even decrease, consumers will likely choose to buy more. For example, more cellular phones and DVD players were steadily purchased in the late 1990s and early 2000s, as their prices fell. Over time, these products have too low a weight in the CPI basket, so that the index overstates the rate of inflation. In contrast, consumers tend to buy less of items whose prices rise the most. Over time, these products have too high a weight in the CPI basket, meaning the index again overstates the rate of inflation.

PRODUCT QUALITY

The index cannot reflect changes in quality that are unmatched by changes in price. For example, items in the CPI shopping basket, such as medicines and stereos, may improve tremendously in quality, yet their prices may not increase proportionally with quality and may even fall. So, while the standard of living may increase because of the increased quality, this will not be reflected in the CPI.

Over time, Statistics Canada tries to adjust the items in the index to account for these quality improvements, but it is difficult to do so completely. As with changes in spending patterns, the result is that the CPI overstates the rate of inflation—by a total amount of about 0.5 percent a year, according to recent Canadian estimates.

The GDP Deflator

GDP deflator: an indicator of price changes for all goods and services produced in the economy

Another indicator of price changes is the **GDP deflator**. Unlike the CPI, which focuses on a small number of consumer items, the GDP deflator measures price changes for all goods and services produced in the economy and weights them in terms of the economy's total output. The item weights in this index are altered yearly, depending on how goods and services are represented in current GDP. While this frequent updating increases the accuracy of the GDP deflator, it means that values for this index are not as quickly available as values for the consumer price index. Because of this drawback, the GDP deflator receives less publicity than the CPI. Given the difference in the way they are calculated, the two indicators give similar but not identical estimates of inflation.

Figure 10.3 shows how a GDP deflator can be calculated in a simplified economy that produces only computer microchips. In 2003, which is the reference year, the GDP deflator is equal to 100. In order to calculate the value of the GDP deflator in each subsequent year, the output of each year is multiplied by the current price per microchip, divided by the same output in reference year prices and then multiplied by 100. For example, the 2004 output of microchips is 2000 and the price is 30 cents. This $600 value of output (2000 × $0.30) is divided by the same output in 2003 prices (= 2000 × $0.20), or $400, to give a GDP deflator of 150 [=($600 ÷ $400) × 100]. The result shows that the general price level has risen by one-half between 2003 and 2004. In other words, the inflation rate was 50 percent.

NOMINAL VERSUS REAL GDP

Just as nominal incomes for an individual household can be adjusted to take account of price changes, so the value of the economy's entire output can be adjusted for inflation.

Figure 10.3	Simple GDP Deflator				
(1) Year	(2) Output of Microchips	(3) Current Price	(4) Output at Current Price (2) × (3)	(5) Output at 2003 Price (2) × $0.20	(6) GDP Deflator [(4) ÷ (5)] × 100
2003	1000	$0.20	$200	$200	100
2004	2000	0.30	600	400	150
2005	2500	0.40	1000	500	200

The GDP deflator in any year is calculated by taking the economy's annual output at current prices (column 4), dividing by this same output valued in reference-year prices (column 5) and then multiplying the result by 100. While the GDP deflator has a value of 100 in 2003, which is the reference year, it rises in proportion with the prices of the economy's output.

nominal GDP: Gross Domestic Product expressed in current dollars

Recall that real GDP (or real output) is GDP expressed in constant dollars from a chosen reference year. In contrast, **nominal GDP** (or nominal output) is GDP expressed in current dollars. Recall that real income for the individual household measures the purchasing power of that household over time. In the same way, real GDP gives an indication of the purchasing power of an entire economy. To find real GDP, economists and statisticians divide nominal GDP by the GDP deflator expressed in hundredths:

$$\text{Real GDP} = \frac{\text{nominal GDP}}{\text{GDP deflator (in hundredths)}}$$

This formula can be applied to Canada's GDP in Figure 10.4 to give GDP in constant reference-year (1997) dollars. Canada's nominal GDP was $1154.9 billion in 2002. This amount divided by the GDP deflator expressed in hundredths, which was 1.0748 (107.48 ÷ 100), gives a real GDP of $1074.5 billion (= 1154.9 billion ÷ 1.0748). The same approach can be used for years prior to the reference year. For example, Canada's 1992 nominal GDP was $700.5 billion. This amount divided by the GDP deflator expressed in hundredths, which is 0.9268 (= 92.68 ÷ 100), gives a real GDP for 1992, expressed in 1997 dollars, of $755.8 billion (= $700.5 billion ÷ 0.9268). Notice that when the adjusting number is more than 100, as in 2002, nominal GDP is reduced or deflated to find real GDP. In the opposite case, where the index falls short of 100, as in 1992, nominal GDP is expanded or inflated when this adjustment is made.

Figure 10.4   Finding Real Gross Domestic Product

(1) Year	(2) Nominal GDP (current $ billions)	(3) GDP Deflator (1997 = 100)	(4) Real GDP (1997 $ billions) [(2) ÷ (3)] × 100
1992	$700.5	92.68	$755.8
1997	882.7	100.00	882.7
2002	1154.9	107.48	1074.5

Canada's real GDP in any year is found by dividing the economy's nominal GDP, which is expressed in current dollars, by the value of the GDP deflator. While Canada's nominal output rose from $700.5 to $1154.9 billion between 1992 and 2002, the nation's real output in 1997 dollars increased by a much smaller amount, from $755.8 to $1074.5 billion.

Sources: Statistics Canada "Finding Real Gross Domestic Product," adapted from the Statistics Canada publication, "Canadian economic accounts quarterly review, First Quarter 2003," Catalogue 13-010, Vol. 2, No. 1, May 2003, pp. 12, 14.

Inflation's Effects

Figure 10.5 shows Canada's inflation record since 1926. After a period of deflation during the Great Depression of the 1930s, significant inflation occurred during and immediately after World War II. Relatively low rates of inflation during the 1950s and 1960s were then followed by gradually rising rates during the 1960s and 1970s. Since the mid-1980s, inflation rates have again gradually fallen to low levels.

Why are high inflation rates, such as those experienced by Canadians during the 1970s and early 1980s, such a serious problem? Inflation redistributes purchasing power among different groups in ways that can be both economically harmful and unjust; in other words, purchasing power keeps pace with inflation for some individuals but not

Figure 10.5   The Inflation Rate

The graph shows annual inflation rates as measured by changes in the GDP price deflator. While deflation occurred during the early 1930s, inflation has been the dominant trend ever since. Inflation was most pronounced after World War II, during the 1970s, and in the early 1980s. In the late 1980s and early 1990s, the inflation rate dropped significantly and it has remained low up until the early 2000s.

Sources: Statistics Canada "The Inflation Rate," adapted from the Statistics Canada publication, "Canadian economic observer. Historical statistical supplement," 2001/02, Catalogue 11-210, Vol. 16, July 2002 and "National Income and Expenditure Accounts," Catalogue 13-001, Vol. 50, No. 4, April 2003, pp. 106, 107.

for others. To see the effects of inflation, we will look at its effects on household incomes and on borrowing and lending.

INCOMES

Inflation means not only increasing prices but expanding nominal incomes as well. The effect on households' purchasing power depends on which is greater—inflation or the increase in nominal income. If a household's nominal income increases steadily every year but inflation is at a higher rate, the household loses purchasing power. So, for example, this year's dollars buy fewer groceries than did last year's dollars, even with the expanding nominal income. If, in contrast, the same household has a nominal income that increases at roughly the same rate as inflation, the household maintains its purchasing power. In other words, each year's dollars buy about the same amount of groceries. Therefore, whereas some households may feel the full impact of inflation on their living standards, others may have the impact cushioned by income adjustments, and there are others who may even benefit from inflation because their nominal incomes rise more quickly than inflation. One of the most costly aspects of inflation for society is that this redistribution of purchasing power occurs in an arbitrary way. The winners are often those with substantial economic resources, while the losers are commonly those least able to withstand a drop in purchasing power.

Many labour unions negotiate income adjustments for their members. As a result, workers' wages are adjusted using the consumer price index, or cost of living, as it is popularly known. In the collective agreement, provisions for these adjustments are called **cost-of-living-adjustment** (COLA) **clauses**. When workers' incomes automatically increase by the rate of inflation, they are called **fully indexed incomes**. In this case, nominal income rises at the same rate as prices, so real income stays the same. For example, if the inflation rate between 2003 and 2004 is 10 percent, a worker originally earning a monthly income of $1000 receives a new monthly income of $1100, thereby maintaining purchasing power. The worker's real income in 2003, using 2003

cost-of-living-adjustment clauses: provisions for income adjustments to accommodate changes in price levels, which are included in wage contracts

fully indexed incomes: nominal incomes that automatically increase by the rate of inflation as the base year, is $1000 (= $1000 ÷ 1). In 2004, the same worker's real income, expressed in 2003 dollars, is again $1000 (= $1100 ÷ 1.10).

Other people may receive incomes that are only partially indexed or are fixed. These are the people—including, for example, pensioners, unskilled and nonunionized workers, and recipients of government transfer payments—who lose the most from inflation. **Partially indexed incomes** rise more slowly than the inflation rate, causing real incomes to fall. Suppose, for example, that a single parent has only welfare payments of $1000 per month as income. If the inflation rate is 10 percent between 2003 and 2004, the household needs a 10 percent rise, or an extra $100, in nominal income to maintain its purchasing power. If the payments increase by only 7 percent, they rise by $70, for a total of $1070 per month. Using 2003 as the base year, the household's real income falls from $1000 in 2003 to $972.73 (= $1070 ÷ 1.10) in 2004.

In contrast to indexed and partially indexed incomes, **fixed incomes** are incomes that stay at the same nominal dollar amount. In other words, these incomes do not change at all in response to inflation. Suppose, for example, that a pensioner receives a set monthly payment of $1000. Any increase in prices will cause purchasing power to decrease and, thereby, the pensioner's real income will be reduced. So, with the same hypothetical 10 percent inflation rate between 2003 and 2004, the pensioner's real income, expressed in 2003 dollars, drops from $1000 in 2003 to $909.09 (= $1000 ÷ 1.10) in 2004.

BORROWING AND LENDING

Whatever interest rate is established in financial markets, if the lender lends funds at an interest rate that is not adjusted for inflation, the lender may lose out.

To illustrate, we have to distinguish between two types of interest rates. The **nominal interest rate** is the interest rate expressed in money terms. For example, Mariposa Vacations borrows $2000 at 7 percent per annum. At the end of the year, Mariposa Vacations will pay back the principal ($2000), plus interest (0.07 × $2000 = 140), for a total of $2140 (= $2000 + $140).

In contrast, the **real interest rate** is the nominal interest rate minus the rate of inflation.

$$\text{Real interest rate} = \text{nominal interest rate} - \text{inflation rate}$$

If the inflation rate is 3 percent in the year that Mariposa Vacations takes out the loan, then the loan's real interest rate is 4 percent—the 7 percent nominal interest rate minus the 3 percent rate of inflation. The real interest rate reflects the fact that because of inflation, the funds lent (the principal) have less purchasing power at the end of the one-year term than they did at the time the loan was made. Thus, the bank lending to Mariposa Vacations receives $140 (7 percent) in nominal interest at the end of the year, but only $80 (4 percent) in real interest.

Once the nominal interest rate has been agreed upon, it is fixed. So, lenders try to anticipate the rate of inflation for the loan period and build it into the nominal interest rate. This rate built into the nominal interest rate is known as the **inflation premium.** Lenders, therefore, determine what real interest rate they desire and add an inflation premium to determine the nominal interest rate:

$$\text{Nominal interest rate} = \text{desired real interest rate} + \text{inflation premium}$$

For example, the manager at Mariposa Vacations' bank may have anticipated a 2 percent inflation rate and wanted a real interest rate of 5 percent. So, on the $2000 one-year loan, she expected the bank would receive real interest of $100 (= $2000 × 0.05)

partially indexed incomes: nominal incomes that increase by less than the rate of inflation

fixed incomes: nominal incomes that remain fixed at some dollar amount regardless of the rate of inflation

nominal interest rate: the interest rate expressed in money terms

real interest rate: the nominal interest rate minus the rate of inflation

inflation premium: a percentage built into a nominal interest rate to anticipate the rate of inflation for the loan period and an inflation premium of $40 (= $2000 × 0.02) to compensate for the reduced purchasing power of the original $2000 principal.

What happens if the inflation rate turns out to be higher than lenders anticipated? Suppose, in our example, the inflation rate is actually 4 percent instead of 2 percent. As a result, the bank actually receives only 3 percent real interest—that is, the 7 percent nominal rate minus the 4 percent inflation rate. This is substantially less than the 5 percent real interest rate the bank manager anticipated. Because the inflation rate is higher than anticipated, the real interest rate is lower than the desired real interest rate, and lenders are worse off, while borrowers are better off. On the other hand, if the inflation rate is less than anticipated, the real interest rate is higher than the desired real interest rate, and lenders are better off, while borrowers are worse off. Only when the inflation rate is exactly as anticipated will the real interest be the same as the desired real interest rate, so that lenders and borrowers are unaffected by inflation.

THINKING ABOUT
ECONOMICS

Why is inflation much more common than deflation?

Like inflation, deflation arbitrarily redistributes purchasing power—though in ways opposite to inflation. More importantly, deflation can feed on itself. When the general price level falls, households may delay purchases as they expect further price declines. With less spending in the economy, prices do tend to fall an extra amount. As a result, households postpone spending even longer. To forestall such self-building cycles of delayed spending, government policy-makers generally do all they can to avoid even small amounts of deflation.

Question
Who is helped and who is harmed by deflation?

Brief Review

1. Inflation is a general increase in the prices of goods and services in the entire economy. A general fall in prices is known as deflation.

2. The consumer price index (CPI) is one indicator of inflation, or changes in the cost of living. The CPI measures price changes in a typical "shopping basket" of consumer products.

3. Whereas nominal income is expressed in current dollars, real income is expressed in constant base-year dollars. Real income equals nominal income divided by the current value of the CPI (expressed in hundredths).

4. The GDP deflator measures price changes for all goods and services produced in the economy and weights them in terms of the economy's total output. Nominal GDP divided by the current value of the GDP deflator (expressed in hundredths) gives the economy's real GDP, or real output in terms of dollars from some reference year.

5. The extent to which inflation affects individuals' purchasing power varies. Those people whose incomes are fully indexed to inflation rates maintain purchasing power. However, those with partially indexed or fixed incomes lose purchasing power.

6. Lenders also lose from inflation if inflation is higher than they anticipated with the inflation premium.

10.1 Practice Questions

1. The following table shows a consumer's weekly purchases during 2003 and 2004.

	Prices		Quantities Consumed per Week	
	(2003)	**(2004)**	**(2003)**	**(2004)**
Hamburgers	$2.50	$2.75	5	4
Bottles of cola	1.25	1.30	10	11

   a. Calculate the value of the consumer's 2003 shopping basket using first 2003 and then 2004 prices.
   b. If 2003 is used as the base year, what is the 2003 value of the consumer's price index? the 2004 value?
   c. Using 2003 as the base year, what is the inflation rate between 2003 and 2004?

2. Fill in the blanks in the following table for a hypothetical economy.

Year	Nominal GDP (current $ billion)	GDP Deflator	Real GDP (2002 $ billions)
2001	$____	97.458	$210.7
2002	234.3		
2003	245.9	101.340	
2004	258.7	____	251.3
2005	____	105.438	261.4

10.2

Unemployment

LO 10.2

labour force population: the population, with specific exclusions, from which Statistics Canada takes a random sample for the labour force survey

Recall from Chapter 1 that another economic goal of Canada is full employment. Of all economic statistics, the unemployment rate is the one most often highlighted in the media, discussed by politicians, and noticed by Canadians. For most people, the prospect of involuntary unemployment provokes considerable anxiety. To see why, we must understand unemployment, how it is measured, and its implications for individuals and for the economy as a whole.

The Labour Force Survey

Statistics Canada keeps track of the Canadian workforce through a monthly survey of about 53 000 households. These households are a random sample of the **labour force population**, which includes all residents of Canada 15 years of age and over, except those living in the Northwest, Nunavut, and Yukon Territories, on First Nations reserves, and in institutions (for example, jails and psychiatric hospitals), and full-time members of the armed forces. The **labour force** is made up of those people in the labour force population who either have jobs or are actively seeking employment. By its definition, the labour force leaves out such groups as pensioners who do not have jobs and are not looking for work. It also excludes those who have given up looking for a job, as well as full-time homemakers who, while they work, do not do so in the formal job market.

labour force: all people who either have a job or are actively seeking employment

The **participation rate** is the percentage of the entire labour force population that makes up the labour force. For example, in 2002, Canada's labour force was 16.6894 million, and the labour force population was 24.9451 million, so the participation rate was about 67 percent. In other words, of the defined labour force population, about 67 percent is participating in the labour market:

participation rate: the percentage of the entire labour force population that makes up the labour force

$$\text{Participation rate} = \frac{\text{labour force}}{\text{labour force population}} \times 100$$

$$66.9\% = \frac{16\ 689\ 400}{24\ 945\ 100} \times 100$$

Statistics Canada also examines the participation rates of specific groups of people. Figure 10.6 shows recent trends in labour force participation for women and men as well as two age groups. As shown, the participation rate for women has increased steadily until the early 1990s and has remained relatively stable since. In contrast, the participation rate for men has decreased. This decline is largely due to the growing popularity of early retirement. Overall, the participation of young people in the labour force is somewhat higher than it was in 1975, and it has increased in recent years, as young people are more likely to work part-time while in school, college, or university.

The Official Unemployment Rate

Once the labour force has been defined, its members can be divided into those who are employed and those who are unemployed. The official unemployment rate is the number of unemployed people in the labour force as a percentage of the entire labour force. For example, Canada's 2002 labour force of 16.6894 million people was composed of 15.4118 million people who were employed and 1.2776 million who were not. Therefore, the unemployment rate was 7.7 percent:

$$\text{Unemployment rate} = \frac{\text{unemployment in labour force}}{\text{labour force}} \times 100$$

$$7.7\% = \frac{1\ 277\ 600}{16\ 689\ 400} \times 100$$

Figure 10.7 summarizes the relationships among Canada's population, labour force, labour force population, and unemployed labour force.

Drawbacks of the Official Unemployment Rate

Because of the way the official unemployment rate is calculated, it may either understate or overstate the true level of unemployment in the Canadian economy. Critics of this official rate point to the following factors: underemployment, discouraged workers, and dishonesty.

Figure 10.6 Participation Rates

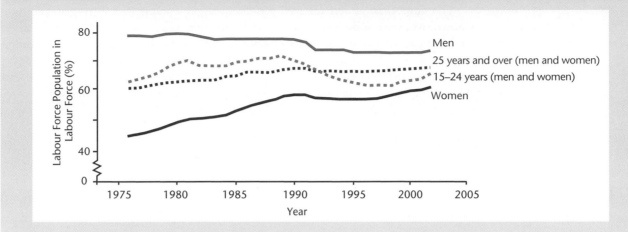

Since the 1970s, participation in the labour force by women has increased. In contrast, participation rates for men has fallen. Participation rates for young people have fluctuated widely.

Sources: Statistics Canada "Participation Rates," adapted from the Statistics Canada publication, "Canadian economic observer. Historical statistical supplement," 2001/02, Catalogue 11-210, Vol. 16, July 2002, p. 28.

UNDEREMPLOYMENT

The official unemployment rate makes no distinction between part-time and full-time employment, nor docs it reflect the appropriateness of the work. While some part-time workers prefer part-time work, others would want full-time work if it were available. Also, in hard times, some workers may have to work at jobs that do not fully utilize their skills and education. Thus, we have the problem of **underemployment**. It is sometimes argued that the official rate understates unemployment by ignoring underemployed workers.

underemployment: the problem of workers being underutilized, either as part-time workers or by working at jobs not appropriate to their skills or education

DISCOURAGED WORKERS

Unemployment statistics also do not take into account people who, after searching for a job without luck, give up looking. Because they are not actively seeking employment,

Figure 10.7 The Canadian Labour Force (2002)

$$\text{Participation rate} = \frac{\text{labour force}}{\text{labour force population}} \times 100 = \frac{16\ 689\ 400}{24\ 945\ 100} \times 100 = 66.9\%$$

$$\text{Unemployment rate (\%)} = \frac{\text{unemployed in labour force}}{\text{labour force}} \times 100 = \frac{1\ 277\ 600}{16\ 689\ 400} \times 100 = 7.7\%$$

In 2002, Canada's total population was about 31 million. Of this number, 24.9451 million were considered part of the labour force population. The labour force constituted 66.9 percent of the labour force population, or 16.6894 million. Of this labour force, 92.3 percent, or 15.4118 million, were employed. The remaining 1.2776 million in the labour force were unemployed, giving an unemployment rate of 7.7 percent.

Source: Statistics Canada "The Unemployment Rate," adapted from the Statistics Canada publication, "Canadian economic observer. Historical statistical supplement," 1999/00, Catalogue 11-210, Vol. 14, July 2000, p. 36, "National Income and Expenditure Accounts: Annual Estimates," 1926–1986, Catalogue 13-351, April 1989, pp. 214–215, and from the Statistics Canada web site http://www.statcan.ca/english/Pgdb/econ10.htm.

discouraged workers:
unemployed workers who
have given up looking for
work

these **discouraged workers** are not considered part of the labour force. Again, it is sometimes argued that this causes the official rate to understate unemployment.

The number of underemployed and discouraged workers rises during an economic downturn, since job prospects—especially for full-time work—are at their bleakest. During the recession of the early 1990s, for example, estimates suggested that the numbers of underemployed and discouraged workers would have added up to 10 percent to the official unemployment rate. In recent years, this increase above the official rate would have been smaller—about 3 percent for underemployment and discouraged workers combined.

DISHONESTY

People responding to Statistics Canada's labour market survey may state that they are actively looking for work when, in fact, they are not. While the extent to which such dishonesty affects the unemployment rate is difficult to measure, it does make it possible for the official rate to overstate unemployment.

Types of Unemployment

When examining unemployment, we should distinguish among four types: frictional, structural, cyclical, and seasonal unemployment.

FRICTIONAL UNEMPLOYMENT

frictional unemployment:
unemployment due to being
temporarily between jobs or
looking for a first job

Workers who are temporarily between jobs or have begun looking for their first jobs are experiencing **frictional unemployment**. A dental assistant who has left one job voluntarily to look for another and a recent college graduate looking for career-related work are examples. Frictional unemployment is a permanent feature of labour markets and represents about 3 percent of the labour force at any given time.

STRUCTURAL UNEMPLOYMENT

structural unemployment:
unemployment due to a mismatch between people and
jobs

Another type of unemployment arises largely from structural changes in the economy. **Structural unemployment** is due to a mismatch between people and jobs—unemployed workers cannot fill the sorts of jobs that are available. This type of unemployment occurs primarily because of gradual changes in the economy. Long-term adjustments in what items are produced (for example, the current shift from goods to services), how they are produced (largely due to technological change), and where they are produced cause such unemployment.

Because of these changes, workers lose out; they are displaced. Consider a worker who loses her job in manufacturing because of automation. She might not yet have the skills for the expanding service sector. In the same way, an unemployed fisherman living in a remote village cannot easily take advantage of employment opportunities elsewhere. Because gaining new skills, moving to obtain work elsewhere, and developing new industries in a region all take time, structural unemployment can persist for long periods.

CYCLICAL UNEMPLOYMENT

cyclical unemployment:
unemployment due to fluc-
tuations in output and
spending

Economies and businesses must cope with fluctuations in output and spending, causing unemployment to rise and fall. This type of unemployment is called **cyclical unemployment**. An auto worker, for example, may work overtime in periods of strong consumer demand for cars but be laid off in leaner times.

SEASONAL UNEMPLOYMENT

seasonal unemployment: unemployment due to the seasonal nature of some occupations and industries

In some Canadian industries—agriculture, construction, and tourism, for example—work is seasonal, with lower employment in the winter months. As a result, some workers experience **seasonal unemployment**. Compared with many other countries, seasonal unemployment is particularly significant in Canada, given its climate and the importance of its primary resource industries. So that month-to-month comparisons can be made without the influence of seasonal unemployment, Statistics Canada calculates seasonal changes and adjusts the official unemployment rate accordingly.

Full Employment

full employment: the highest reasonable expectation of employment for the economy as a whole

natural unemployment rate: the unemployment rate that defines full employment

Defining **full employment** is a tricky task. In effect, full employment is the highest reasonable expectation of employment for the economy as a whole and is defined in terms of a **natural unemployment rate**. This rate includes frictional unemployment but traditionally excludes cyclical unemployment. This rate also excludes seasonal unemployment, which is already omitted from the official unemployment rate using seasonal adjustment.

In the 1950s and 1960s, full employment in the Canadian economy was defined by the Economic Council of Canada as a natural unemployment rate of 3 percent. In other words, full employment was 100 percent labour force employment minus 3 percent frictional unemployment. As Figure 10.8 shows, the unemployment rate, which reached almost 20 percent during the Great Depression of the 1930s, decreased considerably over the following decades. However, full employment—as it was defined—was only occasionally achieved.

Since the 1970s, the unemployment rate has been well over 3 percent. In light of recent economic trends and thinking, many economists argue that in addition to frictional unemployment—which will always exist—the definition of full employment should also accommodate at least some structural unemployment. This, they say, is because structural unemployment *can* be reduced, but only very gradually. While definitions of full employment in the 2000s vary, most include a natural unemployment rate

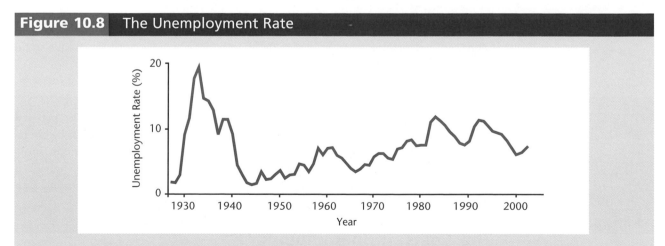

Figure 10.8   The Unemployment Rate

After rising significantly in the 1930s, the unemployment rate fell to 2 to 4 percent for much of the 1940s and 1950s. Since the late 1950s, the rate has gradually risen. Much of this increase can be attributed to a rise in natural unemployment.

Sources: Statistics Canada "Unemployment Rates by Province, Gender, and Age (2002)," adapted from the Statistics Canada CANSIM II database http://cansim2.statcan.ca Table 282-0002.

of between 6 and 7 percent. Because of this, full employment does not mean what it would seem to—that everyone who wants a job has one. Indeed, a significant proportion of the labour force (6 to 7 percent) is unemployed.

Increases over the past few decades in both the actual and the natural unemployment rates represent worrisome trends. Several factors are often highlighted in explaining these trends.

STRUCTURAL CHANGE

Recall that structural adjustments in an economy occur whenever there are changes regarding what products are produced as well as in how and where they are produced. Over the past few decades, the pace of structural change in the Canadian economy has accelerated. The growth of the service sector and shrinking of the traditional manufacturing sector, the rise of the new economy, and the removal of many international trade barriers have each led to the displacement of workers and, therefore, caused increases in long-term structural unemployment.

UNEMPLOYMENT INSURANCE

Most unemployed workers today have a significant advantage over those in previous generations. The financial cushion provided by unemployment insurance has allowed job seekers to devote more time and effort to searching for employment than in the past, which increases frictional unemployment. Reforms to unemployment insurance in the early 1970s also made it easier for those experiencing seasonal and structural unemployment to claim benefits. Thus, unemployment insurance can be a factor in increasing the unemployment rate. Overall, it is estimated that this factor added between 0.5 percent and 2 percent to the unemployment rate since the 1970s. However changes to the unemployment insurance system (now called Employment Insurance) in the 1990s have made it more difficult to claim benefit, reducing this effect.

CHANGING PARTICIPATION RATES

Recall from Figure 10.6 that, over the last few decades, young people have added to the labour force. Not only do they add to the supply of unskilled labour when they first enter the labour force, but as they acquire skills and work experience, they also suffer greater frictional unemployment than more experienced workers. As a result, the increased participation rates among young Canadians (which declined for a while in the 1990s) swelled the ranks of the unemployed.

MINIMUM WAGES

Minimum wage levels set by the provinces have increased a great deal in the past few decades. For young people in particular—who are more likely than others to be affected by minimum wage laws—this has meant an increase in the number of people looking for work. For example, one Canadian study suggested that a 10 percent increase in the minimum wage reduces employment by 1 percent for male teenagers and 2.7 percent for female teenagers.

The Costs of Unemployment

High unemployment rates hurt both individuals and the Canadian economy as a whole. As Figure 10.9 shows, the rates vary from province to province and among groups of people. To jobless workers and their families, unemployment, especially for extended

THINKING ABOUT ECONOMICS

How do minimum wages cause unemployment?

A minimum wage has an effect on the market for unskilled labour by creating a wage floor above equilibrium. The minimum wage, therefore, creates a surplus, with a greater supply of workers than there are available jobs at that wage. In evaluating the effectiveness of minimum wages, the higher wages received by employed workers must be weighed against the unemployment caused for others.

Question
Why does a minimum wage have virtually no effect for skilled workers?

periods, can create stress and discouragement, disrupt family life, lower self-esteem, and cause financial hardship. The economy as a whole loses the output the worker could have produced.

potential output: the real output, or Gross Domestic Product, associated with full employment

One way to measure the cost of unemployment for the entire economy is by calculating the extent to which **potential output**, or the real output associated with full employment, exceeds actual output. According to Okun's Law—named after the American economist Arthur Okun—for every percentage point that the unemployment rate exceeds the natural unemployment rate, the gap between potential output and actual output is 2.5 percent.

In 2002, for example, real GDP in (constant) 1997 dollars was $1074.5 billion, while the unemployment rate was 7.7 percent, or 1.2 percent above an assumed natural

| **Figure 10.9** | Unemployment Rates by Province, Gender, and Age (2002) |

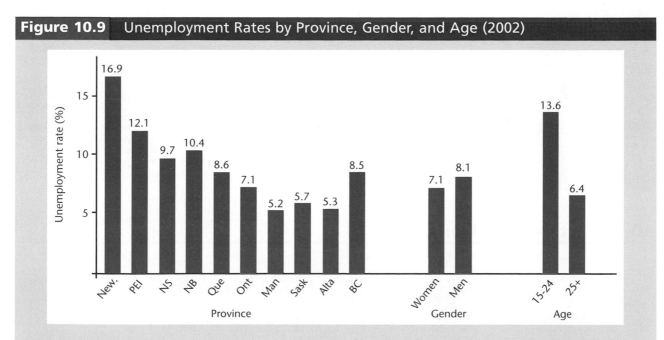

Unemployment rates vary from province to province. The 2002 rates were highest among the Atlantic provinces and Québec, and lowest in Manitoba. Rates for women were slightly lower than for men, and young people were more likely to be unemployed than those 25 years or over.

Source: Statistics Canada "Unemployment Rates by Province, Gender, and Age (2002)," adapted from the Statistics Canada, CANSIM II database http://cansim2.statcan.ca, Table 282-0002.

unemployment rate of 6.5 percent. According to Okun's Law, real output could have been 3.0 percent (= 1.2 × 2.5) higher if unemployment equalled the natural rate. In other words, in 1997 dollars, 2002 real GDP could have been $32.2 billion (= $1074.5 billion × 0.03) higher.

This method of measuring the costs of unemployment is difficult to apply, both because of disagreements over the natural unemployment rate and because it can be argued that these are costs of unemployment even if actual output equals or exceeds potential output. But it gives a good indication of the substantial cost of unemployment, not just to those workers who are directly affected but to the economy as a whole.

Brief Review

1. The labour force population is Canada's population age 15 years and over, with some exclusions.

2. The participation rate is the percentage of those in the labour force population who make up the labour force, which includes all those people who are employed or who are actively seeking work within the formal economy. Participation rates for women have risen considerably in the last few decades.

3. The official unemployment rate is the percentage of the labour force that is unemployed.

4. The official unemployment rate, which has risen significantly in the last few decades, does not take into account underemployment, discouraged workers, and dishonest answers given in labour market surveys.

5. Unemployment can be categorized as frictional, structural, cyclical, or seasonal.

6. Full employment is the highest reasonable expectation of employment for the economy as a whole and is defined in terms of a natural unemployment rate. Traditionally, the natural unemployment rate only accommodated frictional unemployment; now, however, many economists believe it should include at least some structural unemployment.

7. The costs of unemployment are profound and numerous for unemployed workers and their families. Unemployment costs to the economy as a whole are indicated by the extent to which potential output exceeds actual output.

10.2 Practice Questions

1.
Unemployed members of the labour force	2.3 million
Total population 15 years of age and over	58.9 million
Participation rate	64 percent
Workers with full-time jobs	21.4 million
Part-time workers who do not wish to have full-time jobs	4.2 million
Part-time workers who wish to have full-time jobs	3.5 million
Total population less than 15 years of age	14.6 million

Use the information for a hypothetical economy in the above table to find the following:

a. the labour force
b. the labour force population
c. the official unemployment rate

2. Using the information in the table shown in question 1, derive an estimate of this hypothetical economy's unemployment rate that includes underemployment.

LAST**WORD**

In this chapter, we have seen how inflation and unemployment are measured and examined the economic problems caused by each. While we have looked at some of the causes of both problems, it is necessary to build a model of macroeconomic activity to fully understand the factors that determine them and to analyze the relationship that exists between them. In the next chapter, we devise such a model that serves this role.

Key Concepts

base year 223
consumer price index 223
cost-of-living-adjustment clauses 228
cost of living 224
cyclical unemployment 234
deflation 223
discouraged workers 234
fixed incomes 229
frictional unemployment 234
full employment 235

fully indexed incomes 228
GDP deflator 226
inflation premium 229
item weights 223
labour force 232
labour force population 231
natural unemployment rate 235
nominal GDP 227
nominal income 225
nominal interest rate 229

partially indexed incomes 229
participation rate 232
potential output 237
real income 225
real interest rate 229
seasonal unemployment 235
structural unemployment 234
underemployment 233

Questions

1. The table below gives data on Student A's monthly purchases during 2003 and 2004.

Student A's Monthly Purchases

	Prices		Quantities Consumed per month	
	(2003)	**(2004)**	**(2003)**	**(2004)**
Hotdogs	$1.50	$1.60	3	2
Cans of cola	.75	.70	16	18
Chocolate bars	1.00	1.00	7	7
Magazines	3.50	4.50	3	2
DVD rentals	3.00	2.75	2	3

a. Calculate the value of Student A's 2003 shopping basket using 2003 prices. What are the item weights associated with this shopping basket?

b. Calculate the value of Student A's 2003 shopping basket using 2004 prices. If 2003 is used as the base year, what is the 2004 value of Student A's price index? What is the 2003 value of this index? By what percentage has this index changed between 2003 and 2004?

Finding the GDP Deflator

	Output in 2004	Prices in 2004	Prices in 2003
CDs	4	$22.00	$16.00
Bags of chips	50	1.80	1.50

2. The table above shows output and prices during 2004 in an economy that produces only two goods—CDs and bags of chips.
   a. What is the total value of the economy's output in 2004 valued in 2004 prices?
   b. What is the total value of the economy's output in 2004 valued in 2003 prices?
   c. On the basis of your answers to parts a. and b., calculate the value of the GDP deflator in 2004 if 2003 is treated as the reference year.
   d. In what ways does the calculation of the GDP deflator differ from the calculation of the consumer price index?

Finding Real Gross Domestic Product

Year	Nominal GDP (current $ billions)	GDP Deflator	Real GDP (1997 $ billions)
1993	$____	94.014	$773.5
1995	810.4	97.229	____
1997	882.7	____	____
1999	980.5	101.239	____
2001	1092.2	____	1027.5

3. a. Copy and complete the table above.
   b. Explain why real GDP is less than nominal GDP in some years and greater than nominal GDP in other years.

4. Outline how each of the following individuals is influenced by unexpected inflation:
   a. A lawyer whose costs and revenues both rise by the inflation rate
   b. The owner of a heavily indebted restaurant
   c. A worker with a union contract that includes a COLA clause
   d. An injured worker who lives on a partially indexed pension

5. For each of the following years, determine the real interest rate. Find the difference between this rate and the desired real interest rate and explain how any difference affects borrowers and lenders.
   a. In year 1, the nominal interest rate is 9 percent, the inflation premium on loans is 3 percent, and actual rate of inflation is 4 percent.
   b. In year 2, the nominal interest rate is 10 percent, the inflation premium is 4 percent, and the actual rate of inflation is 2 percent.
   c. In year 3, the nominal interest rate is 8 percent, the inflation premium is 2 percent, and the actual rate of inflation is 2 percent.

Finding Participation and Unemployment Rates

Total population 15 years of age and over	4.2 million
Those 15 years of age and over not in the labour force population	1.4 million
Part-time workers who wish to have full-time jobs	100 000
Part-time workers who do not wish to have full-time jobs	300 000
Discouraged workers	400 000
Workers with full-time jobs	1.2 million
Unemployed members of the labour force	150 000

6. Use the hypothetical data in the table above to calculate the following variables:
   a. The labour force population
   b. The labour force
   c. The participation rate
   d. The official unemployment rate
   e. The unemployment rate, including underemployment and discouraged workers.

7. Outline how the employment conditions of the following individuals can be explained using the concepts introduced in the chapter. In each case, state whether or not the individual is included in the official unemployment rate.
   a. A laid-off typesetter who so far has had no success finding a similar job, due to the replacement of typesetters by computers
   b. A former cod fisherman who gives up looking for work and goes on welfare
   c. A farm labourer who is unemployed during the winter months
   d. A graphic artist who loses her job during an economic downturn
   e. A part-time store clerk who looks for a full-time position in the same occupation
   f. A bricklayer receiving employment insurance who works for a renovation company that operates in the underground economy
   g. A recent business school graduate who searches for her first career-related position

8. Using Okun's Law, calculate the gap between potential output and actual output in the Canadian economy in 2000 and 2001. In your answers, assume a natural unemployment rate of 6.5 percent.
   a. In 2000, the unemployment rate was 6.8 percent and real GDP in 1997 dollars was $1012.3 billion.
   b. In 2001, the unemployment rate was 7.2 percent and real GDP in 1997 dollars was $1027.5 billion.

9. (Advanced Question)
   a. Using the table accompanying Question 1, calculate the value of Student A's 2004 shopping basket using 2004 prices as well as the item weights associated with this basket. What would the value of this 2004 shopping basket have been in 2003? If 2004 is used as the base year, what is the 2003 value of Student A's price index? What is the 2004 value? By what percentage has this index changed between 2003 and 2004?
   b. Why do the percentage changes in Student A's price index differ depending on which year is chosen as the base year?

Internet Application Questions

http://www.statcan.ca

1. Access Statistics Canada's web site (at http://www.statcan.ca).

   a. Use the links to "Postsecondary Resources" to find the annual changes in Canada's consumer price index for the last four years for which data are available. Which component of the CPI has risen most quickly over this four-year period? Which component has fallen the most (or risen the least)?

   b. Use the links to "Postsecondary Resources" to find (i) the unemployment rate, (ii) the participation rate, and (iii) the proportion of the labour force population that is employed (known as the employment/population ratio) for Canada during the last four years for which data are available. Explain how movements in these three variables have been related over the relevant four-year period.

http://www.oecd.org

2. Refer to the most recent issue of the OECD's *Key Economic Indicators* (at http://www.oecd.org).

   a. Find the latest monthly unemployment rates in the seven large industrial economies in the OECD (the United States, Japan, Germany, the United Kingdom, France, Italy, and Canada). Which of these countries has the highest unemployment rate? Which has the lowest? Where does Canada rank in this list?

   b. Find the latest annual CPI inflation rates in the same seven economies. Which of these countries has the highest inflation rate? the lowest? Where does Canada rank?

http://www.bankofcanada.ca/english/inflation_calc.htm

3. Employ the Bank of Canada's online *Inflation Calculator* (at http://www.bankofcanada.ca/english/inflation_calc.htm) to calculate the overall changes in the CPI, and the average inflation rates between:

   a. 1995 and 2004
   b. 1985 and 1994
   c. 1975 and 1984

http://www.statcan.ca/english/Estat/licence.htm

4. Access Statistics Canada's E-Stat site (at http://www.statcan.ca/english/Estat/licence.htm).

   a. On the basis of the information in "Labour," generate a table showing the annual unemployment rates for men 15 years and over and women 15 years and over since 1976.

   b. Historically, the unemployment rate for women in Canada was higher than for men, but now the two rates are related in the opposite fashion. In which years did this switch take place? What arguments can you make to explain this switch?

BOOM, BUST & ECHO

David K. Foot and the Economics of Age Distribution

What economic indicators can we apply to our personal lives? David K. Foot, a well-known Canadian economist and demographer, suggests that our ages can give us insights into our economic futures. In the following excerpt from his book Boom, Bust & Echo, 2000 *(written with Daniel Stoffman), Foot outlines some of the effects of Canada's huge "baby-boom generation" (people born from 1947 to 1966), its smaller "baby-bust generation" (people born from 1967 to 1979), and its "baby-boom echo generation" (people born from 1980 to 1995).*

Demography, the study of human populations, is the most powerful—and most underutilized—tool we have to understand the past and to foretell the future. Demographics affect every one of us as individuals, far more than most of us have ever imagined. They also play a pivotal role in the economic and social life of our country.

What kinds of foods will people buy, and what kinds of cars will they drive? Where will they choose to live? Which investments will they favour? These and many other things can be confidently predicted, simply on the basis of readily available data on the age of Canadians. The two keys to these forecasts are the number of people in each age group and the probability that each person will participate in a given behaviour.

Canada's population pyramid (see Figure A) contains a massive bulge, representing the huge generation of baby-boomers born in the 20 years from 1947 to 1966. By comparison, the Depression and World War II generations that preceded the baby boom are small, as is the baby bust that followed it. But the most recently arrived group, the offspring of the boomers—or the baby-boom echo—is comparatively large.

David Foot
Source: Footwork Consulting Inc.
Photographer: D'Arcy Glionna

The Baby Boom (1947 to 1966)

The baby boom, both those born in Canada and those born elsewhere, totals 9.9 million people in 1998, or 32.4 percent of the Canadian population.

Why did the baby boom happen? A likely explanation is that during these 20 years, Canadians knew they could afford large families. The postwar economy was robust, the future seemed full of promise, and young couples wanted to share that bright future with a big family. The second reason was the high immigration levels that prevailed during the 1950s; immigrants tend to be people of childbearing age, and they made an important contribution to the boom.

The front-end boomers have done pretty well for themselves. There are a lot of them, so they had to compete for jobs when they entered the workforce in the 1960s. But the entry of vast numbers of young baby-boomers into the marketplace through the 1970s and 1980s created wonderful opportunities for the front-enders already entrenched in business and government.

Those born towards the end of the 1950s also understand the baby boom but, unlike the front-enders, they are less well positioned to profit from that knowledge. Most members of this boomer subgroup have a house and are in a career, but that career seems to be going nowhere because the rungs ahead of them are clogged with older boomers who are still 15 to 20 years from retirement.

Things are tough for the late-1950s group, but not nearly as bad as they are for the back end that arrived just after them. These are the 3.1 million people born from 1961 to 1966. They are the same age as the characters in Douglas Coupland's novel *Generation X,* which gave the early-1960s group its name. Many of them were still living at home with their parents at their 30th birthday because, faced with horrendous obstacles in the labour market, they have not been able to get their careers on track. That is why, while

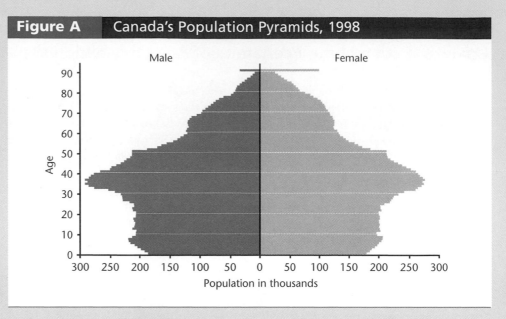

Figure A   Canada's Population Pyramids, 1998

front-end boomers were earning 30 percent more than their fathers by age 30, back-enders were making 10 percent less than their fathers at the same age.

One of the worst things the Gen-Xers have to cope with is their parents—the Depression generation. These are the 60-year-olds sitting at the top of the corporate ladder, approaching the end of very successful careers, and unable to fathom why their 30-year-old offspring are living at home. Tension is tremendous in these families. Often, the father is certain that his own success is based solely on his own merit, while he sees his son's failure as a result of lack of drive and ambition.

The Baby Bust (1967 to 1979)

The commercial introduction of the birth control pill in 1961 and the rising participation of women in the labour market led to declining fertility over the 1960s. The result was a decline in births and a smaller cohort, often called the baby bust. In 1998, 5.6 million Canadians were in this cohort. The baby-busters have done pretty well so far, especially the younger ones. They had no difficulty finding part-time jobs in high school, unlike their older brothers and sisters, who had less opportunity to earn money in high school because they had so many competitors. During the 1990s, university entry standards have been falling, making it easier for busters to get into the school of their choice.

The Baby-Boom Echo (1980 to 1995)

As of 1998, there were 6.5 million members of the echo generation. What is the outlook for the echo kids? It will not be quite as smooth sailing as the baby-busters have had, but it will not be as disastrous as for Generation X either. Like the baby boom, the echo has a front end, born in the 1980s, that will have an easier ride than its back end, born in the first half of the 1990s. The latter group, Generation X-II, will experience the familiar disadvantages of arriving at the rear of a large cohort. Generation X-II will have a life experience similar to that of its parents, the first Generation X. Just as the first Gen-Xers have done, Gen X-II will have to scramble.

However, Gen X-II should be better prepared than its parents were to cope with high youth unemployment and other difficulties associated with a large cohort. That is because these kids have their Gen-X parents to teach them. By contrast, the original Generation X was the offspring of a small cohort that was not equipped to prepare them for the difficult world they encountered when they left home in the early 1980s.

Note
Abridged from *Boom, Bust & Echo 2000* by David K. Foot with Daniel Stoffman. Published by Macfarlane Walter & Ross, Toronto, 1998, pp. 8, 13, 15, 16, 24-31.

1. On the basis of the demographic factors outlined in this article, predict whether (*ceteris paribus*) the following variables will rise or fall between 2002 and 2010. In each case, explain your answer.
   a. Unemployment rates for youth aged 15 - 24
   b. Interest rates
   c. Sales of housing
   d. Stock market prices

Internet Application Question

Access Statistics Canada's web site (at http://www.statcan.ca). Then use the links to "Postsecondary Resources" to access population projections for various age groups in 2011 and 2026.
   a. Calculate the projected percentages of the population in the 0-24, 25-39, 40-64, and 65 + age groups, both in 2011 and 2026.
   b. Using the concepts introduced in Foot's article, explain the projected changes in the relative sizes of each of these age groups between 2011 and 2026.

http://www.statcan.ca

ADVANCING
ECONOMIC
THOUGHT

CHAPTER 11

Economic Fluctuations

It's a recession when your neighbor loses his job; it's a depression when you lose yours.

—Harry Truman, American president

For decades, real output and average living standards in Canada have gradually increased, but the economy rarely grows steadily. Sometimes, production and incomes increase sharply; at other times, they inch up or even fall. Such fluctuations occur in all free-market economies, with occasionally devastating results. During the Great Depression of the 1930s, for example, real output in Canada dropped by over 25 percent, while unemployment soared. In the late 1960s, the opposite happened: an overheated economy led to accelerating inflation, which significantly reduced some Canadians' living standards. More recently, the recession of the early 1990s led to layoffs and plant closings throughout Canada, leaving a legacy of displaced workers and lost production that took years to overcome. This chapter analyzes the causes of these types of instability.

LEARNING OBJECTIVES

In this chapter, you will:

1 learn about aggregate demand and the factors that affect it

2 analyze aggregate supply and the factors that influence it

3 study the economy's equilibrium and how it differs from its potential

4 examine Canada's historical record of economic growth

11.1 Aggregate Demand

aggregate demand: the relationship between the general price level and total spending in the economy

real expenditures: total spending in an economy, adjusted for changes in the general price level

What determines the connections among inflation, unemployment, and levels of spending and real output in the Canadian economy? As in the case of individual markets, the explanation can be given in terms of demand and supply. First, we will look at how the concept of demand can be applied to the economy as a whole to see the relationship between the general price level and total spending in the economy, which is known as **aggregate demand** (AD).

Recall that total spending on an economy's goods and services is the sum of four components: consumption, investment, government purchases, and net exports. The primary groups responsible for this spending are households, businesses, governments, and foreigners. Total spending in an economy, adjusted for changes in the general price level, is referred to as **real expenditures** and is calculated using the GDP price deflator. Suppose, for example, that $1080 billion in nominal dollars are spent in Canada in a year in which the GDP deflator has a value of 120. Therefore, real expenditures, or total output purchases, equal $900 billion ($1080 billion ÷ 1.2) in constant dollars.

Economists attempt to identify the factors that influence real expenditures. One of the most important factors is the price level, since changes in prices cause changes in spending. In other words, not only is the price level used to calculate real expenditures, it also affects real expenditures.

The Aggregate Demand Curve

aggregate demand schedule: the relationship between the general price level and total spending in the economy expressed in a table

aggregate demand curve: the relationship between the general price level and total spending in the economy expressed on a graph

Aggregate demand can be expressed in a table, known as the **aggregate demand schedule**, or on a graph, known as the **aggregate demand curve** (AD). Figure 11.1 shows an aggregate demand schedule and an aggregate demand curve. Just as with a demand curve for a single product, the price variable is placed on the vertical axis of the graph, and the output variable is placed on the horizontal axis.

Recall that price and quantity demanded of a single product almost always have an inverse relationship: as price rises, quantity demanded decreases, and vice versa. The same can be said for the general price level and real expenditures, although for different reasons. Whereas quantity demanded of a certain product can be explained by the

Figure 11.1   Aggregate Demand

Aggregate Demand Schedule

Price Level	Real GDP (1997 $ billions)	Point on Graph
200	650	a
160	700	b
120	750	c

As the general level of prices increases, less real output is bought for two reasons. (1) The real value of financial assets, such as bank accounts and bonds, decreases. As a result, households feel less wealthy, so they reduce their consumption spending. (2) Net export spending is reduced, as both foreigners spend less on Canadian exports and Canadian residents spend more on imports.

law of diminishing marginal utility, the amount spent in the entire economy is determined by two entirely different factors: the wealth and foreign trade effects. Note that the response to a change in the price level is a movement along the aggregate demand curve. For example, if the GDP price deflator rises from 160 to 200, then real expenditures on this particular AD curve fall from $700 billion to $650 billion in terms of 1997 dollars.

WEALTH EFFECT

A household may have wealth in the form of financial assets as well as real assets. The nominal values of these financial assets—such as bank accounts and retirement savings plans—stay the same, no matter what the price level; however, their real values change with any rise or fall in the price level. To find the real value of financial assets, their nominal value must be divided by the price level:

$$\text{Real value of financial assets} = \frac{\text{nominal value of financial assets}}{\text{price level}}$$

When the price level rises, the real value of households' financial assets decreases. Because consumers feel they have less wealth, they spend less on consumption items. As a result of this **wealth effect**, real expenditures drop.

FOREIGN TRADE EFFECT

Changes in the price level also influence foreign trade. When the price level in Canada rises, Canadian exports become more expensive for foreigners. As a result, sales in foreign markets fall, causing a decrease in export expenditures. At the same time, products imported into Canada become cheaper relative to higher-priced domestic products. Therefore, import expenditures by Canadians rise. The **foreign trade effect**—as this combination of effects is known—involves a decrease in net exports $(X - M)$ and, thus, a decline in real expenditures.

Changes in Aggregate Demand

In addition to the price level, other factors can influence total spending. However, these factors, called **aggregate demand factors**, change total spending at all price levels. In other words, they shift the aggregate demand curve. Recall that spending has four components—consumption, investment, government purchases, and net exports. When factors other than price level affect any of these components, they, in turn, affect total real expenditures.

Suppose, for example, that due to an increase in government purchases, the aggregate demand curve shifts to the right by $50 billion, as shown in Figure 11.2, from AD_0 to AD_1. This change is known as an **increase in aggregate demand**. Similarly, a decrease in another component of real expenditures, such as consumption spending, would cause a decrease in total expenditures. This **decrease in aggregate demand** would be represented by a shift in the aggregate demand curve to the left.

Aggregate demand factors can be categorized by the spending component they immediately affect. As we consider each in turn, we must assume that all other aggregate demand factors and the price level remain constant.

CONSUMPTION

Recall that personal consumption and saving are the two uses of disposable income. Thus, consumer spending is decided when households determine how much to spend

wealth effect: with changes in the price level, the real value of households' financial assets changes, causing households to adjust their spending

foreign trade effect: with changes in the price level, expenditures on imports change in the same direction, while expenditures on exports change in the opposite direction

aggregate demand factors: variables that cause changes in total expenditures at all price levels

increase in aggregate demand: an increase in total expenditures at all price levels

decrease in aggregate demand: a decrease in total expenditures at all price levels

| **Figure 11.2** | Changes in Aggregate Demand |

Aggregate Demand Schedule

Price Level	Real GDP	
	AD_0	AD_1
	(1997 $ billions)	
200	650 $\longrightarrow$	700
160	700 $\longrightarrow$	750
120	750 $\longrightarrow$	800

An increase in government purchases causes an increase in real expenditures at every price level. Thus, aggregate demand increases, and the AD curve shifts to the right from AD_0 to AD_1.

or save. Changes in disposable income, wealth, consumer expectations, and interest rates can all affect consumer spending. With any change in consumer spending, total expenditure changes also, thereby shifting the aggregate demand curve.

Disposable Income

The most significant determinant of consumer spending is the level of disposable income (DI) in the entire economy. The economy's total disposable income may change as a result of changes in population or changes in disposable income per household. Higher income taxes, for example, decrease household disposable income. Disposable income and consumer spending have a direct relationship. So, when disposable income rises, there is a rise in consumer spending, thereby adding to total expenditures and shifting the aggregate demand curve to the right.

Wealth

Wealth and income are quite different. Whereas income consists of earnings received over time, wealth is made up of financial and real assets. Real assets (such as houses and appliances) and financial assets (such as stocks and bonds) are measured at a particular point in time. We have already considered the wealth effect—the effect of the price level on the value of wealth, which then influences consumer spending. Factors other than price level can affect wealth, however, and, in turn, affect consumer spending. For example, if stock prices jump, households owning stocks enjoy increased wealth; as a result, these households will likely spend more of their disposable income. Aggregate demand will increase, and the aggregate demand curve will shift to the right. Conversely, an increase in consumer debt means that households lose wealth. Households reduce their spending as a result, and aggregate demand decreases.

Consumer Expectations

Consumer expectations influence the demand for a single product. Similarly, these expectations can affect aggregate demand by changing general consumption patterns. If consumers expect prices to rise—for example, because of a calamity, such as war or a flood—they will spend more now and save less. As a result of this higher consumer spending, aggregate demand increases, and the aggregate demand curve shifts to the right. In the same way, if consumers expect their incomes to rise soon, they again spend more and save less, causing an increase in aggregate demand.

Interest Rates

Because households often borrow to purchase durable goods, such as cars and furniture, changes in real interest rates can affect their purchasing decisions. If the real interest rate falls, consumers are more likely to borrow in order to buy big-ticket items. Consumer spending rises, and the aggregate demand curve shifts to the right. Conversely, a jump in the real interest rate has the opposite effect: because consumer spending falls, aggregate demand decreases, and the aggregate demand curve shifts to the left.

INVESTMENT

Investment represents spending on projects where earning a profit is anticipated. The investment component of aggregate demand is limited to planned investment, which excludes unintended changes in inventories.

real rate of return: constant-dollar extra profit provided by a project each year, stated as a percentage of the project's initial cost

How does a business decide whether or not to make an investment? The business first calculates all the expected revenues and costs of the project in constant dollars. Then it calculates the project's **real rate of return**, which is the constant-dollar extra profit provided by the project each year, stated as a percentage of the project's initial cost. Let us consider a T-shirt maker, Pure 'n' Simple T-Shirts. As its owner, you are deciding whether to buy a $100 sewing machine, which is expected to last for one year. After its effects on day-to-day operating costs are taken into account, the machine is expected to add $112 in constant dollars to your business's net revenue. The extra profit gained from purchasing the machine is, therefore, $12 ($112 − $100). Thus, the machine's real rate of return, as a percentage of its $100 price, is 12 percent [($12 ÷ $100) × 100%].

Because most businesses borrow money to finance their investment projects, they will pursue projects for which the return on the project exceeds, or at least equals, the real interest rates they will be charged. In other words, any project is undertaken if its annual benefit is greater than or at least equal to its annual cost.

We have focused on a single business; now let us turn our attention to the entire economy. Suppose that businesses in the economy are considering four possible investment projects. Projects A, B, C, and D each have a cost of $15 billion. However, their real rates of return differ. Project A has a real rate of return of 10 percent, B a rate of 8 percent, C a rate of 6 percent, and D a rate of 4 percent. Figure 11.3 shows the projects' respective profits as rectangles. While each rectangle has the same width, representing the projects' uniform $15 billion cost, the heights differ to reflect the different rates of return.

To see how interest rates affect investment in the economy, let us place the real interest rate on Figure 11.3 also on the vertical axis. Recall that only investment projects with a real rate of return equal to or greater than the prevailing real interest rate will be undertaken. So, if the real interest rate is 12 percent, businesses in the economy would not invest in any project, since none provides a sufficient real rate of return to cover the cost of borrowing. This is shown as point *a* in Figure 11.3. If the real interest rate falls to 8 percent, businesses in the economy will invest in Projects A and B, as shown by point *b*, because their real rates of return equal or exceed the costs of borrowing. As a result, investment in the economy rises to $30 billion. Finally, if interest rates drop even further, to 4 percent, businesses in the economy will invest in Projects A, B, C, and D, as shown by point *c*, thereby increasing investment in the economy to

Figure 11.3   Investment Demand

Investment Demand Schedule

Real Interest Rate (%)	Total Investment	Point on Graph	Projects Undertaken
	(1997 $ billions)		
12	0	a	—
8	30	b	A, B
4	60	c	A, B, C, D

Investment Demand Curve

As the real interest rate decreases, more investment projects are undertaken. When the interest rate is 8 percent, only Projects A and B are carried out, since their estimated real rates of return are greater or equal. If the interest rate falls to 4 percent, Projects C and D can be pursued as well.

investment demand: the relationship between interest rates and investment

investment demand schedule: the relationship between interest rates and investment expressed in a table

investment demand curve: the relationship between interest rates and investment expressed on a graph

$60 billion. This relationship between interest rates and investment is known as **investment demand**. Investment demand can be expressed in a table, called the **investment demand schedule**, or on a graph, called the **investment demand curve** (D_I).

Now that we have seen how total investment in the economy is determined, it is easier to recognize the various aggregate demand factors related to investment. A rise in investment causes an increase in aggregate demand, thereby shifting the aggregate demand curve to the right. Conversely, a fall in investment causes a decrease in aggregate demand, thereby shifting the aggregate demand curve to the left. Investment not only changes because of interest rates, as we have seen, but also because of business expectations.

Interest Rates

As shown by the investment demand curve in Figure 11.3, real interest rates and investment have an inverse relationship. Hence, a rise in real interest rates causes a decrease in aggregate demand, and a fall in real interest rates causes an increase in aggregate demand.

Business Expectations

Business expectations—whether optimistic or pessimistic—can affect the position of the investment demand curve. If businesses anticipate that profits will increase, the investment demand curve shifts to the right, thereby causing an increase in aggregate demand. Conversely, if businesses anticipate that profits will drop, the investment demand curve shifts to the left, leading to a decrease in aggregate demand.

GOVERNMENT PURCHASES

A rise in government purchases—such as highway construction, for example—causes an increase in aggregate demand, while a fall in government purchases causes a decrease in aggregate demand. Recall that this component of spending does not include government transfer payments. Seniors' Benefit payments, for example, are classified as negative taxes, which flow *from* rather than *to* governments.

NET EXPORTS

As seen earlier, net exports can vary due to changes in the price level. For example, a drop in the Canadian price level increases net exports because Canadian exports are cheaper in the rest of the world and imports are made more expensive in Canada. As a result of this foreign trade effect, a change in the price level influences total spending in the economy, which is expressed as a movement along the aggregate demand curve.

Other factors that affect net exports—and that cause a *change* in aggregate demand—include incomes in foreign countries and foreign exchange rates. The effect of changes in these factors is represented by a shift in the aggregate demand curve.

Foreign Incomes

Suppose incomes rise in a foreign country, such as France. French citizens will be able to buy more products as a result. Not only will they purchase French products but also those of other countries. As a result, Canadian net exports to France will likely rise, thereby increasing Canada's aggregate demand. Conversely, a fall in foreign incomes will likely reduce Canadian net exports, thereby decreasing Canada's aggregate demand.

Exchange Rates

exchange rate: the value of one nation's currency in terms of another currency

An **exchange rate** is the value of one nation's currency in terms of another currency. The value of the Canadian dollar can be expressed in any other currency but is usually compared with American dollars. One way to express the exchange rate is to state how many American cents are needed to buy one Canadian dollar. A rise in the value of the Canadian dollar—for example, from 75 to 80 cents—means more American currency is needed to purchase Canadian funds. In this example, Canada's currency becomes more expensive for Americans to purchase. At the same time, American currency becomes cheaper for Canadians to purchase, since we get more of it—80 cents as opposed to 75 cents—in exchange for one Canadian dollar.

If the Canadian dollar goes up in value, exports from Canada become more expensive for Americans. So, a product priced at $1 in Canada costs not 75 cents in American funds but 80 cents. At the same time, American products imported into Canada fall in price when expressed in Canadian currency. One Canadian dollar now buys American products with an American price of 80 cents, whereas earlier the same dollar could buy American products with an American price of only 75 cents.

Because of the impact of exchange rates on prices, net exports fall when the Canadian dollar goes up in value, causing aggregate demand to decrease. A drop in the value of the Canadian dollar has the opposite effect: net exports rise, thereby increasing aggregate demand. The effects of this and other aggregate demand factors are summarized in Figure 11.4.

THINKING ABOUT ECONOMICS

Which of the components of aggregate demand is most likely to vary?

While consumption, government purchases, and net exports all vary substantially, investment is the most unstable element in aggregate demand. This is because investment depends so heavily on business expectations, which can be subject to volatile swings as perceptions of the future change.

Question
Which of the components of aggregate demand is the most stable?

Figure 11.4   Shifts in the Aggregate Demand Curve

Aggregate demand increases and the AD curve shifts to the right, with the following:	Aggregate demand decreases and the AD curve shifts to the left, with the following:

(1) An increase in consumption due to
  (a) a rise in disposable income
  (b) a rise in wealth unrelated to a change in price level
  (c) an expected rise in prices or incomes
  (d) a fall in interest rates
	(1) A decrease in consumption due to
	  (a) a fall in disposable incomes
	  (b) a fall in wealth unrelated to a change in the price level
	  (c) an expected fall in prices or incomes
	  (d) a rise in interest rates

(2) An increase in investment due to
  (a) a fall in interest rates
  (b) an expected rise in profits
	(2) A decrease in investment due to
	  (a) a rise in interest rates
	  (b) an expected fall in profits

(3) An increase in government purchases	(3) A decrease in government purchases

(4) An increase in net exports due to
  (a) a rise in foreign incomes
  (b) a fall in value of the Canadian dollar
	(4) A decrease in net exports due to
	  (a) a fall in foreign incomes
	  (b) a rise in the value of the Canadian dollar

Brief Review

1. Aggregate demand is the relationship between the price level and total spending in the economy. This relationship can be expressed in an aggregate demand schedule or on an aggregate demand curve (AD).

2. Total spending in the economy, adjusted for inflation, is known as real expenditures, and includes the spending of households, businesses, governments, and foreigners.

3. The general price level and total spending in the economy have an inverse relationship, thereby giving the aggregate demand curve a negative slope.

4. Both the wealth effect and the foreign trade effect, which arise from price level changes, cause movements *along* the aggregate demand curve.

5. In contrast, aggregate demand factors cause a change in total spending at all price levels, thereby *shifting* the aggregate demand curve. Anything other than the price level that changes consumption spending, investment, government purchases, or net exports shifts the aggregate demand curve.

11.1 Practice Questions

1. Identify the impact of each of the following trends on the aggregate demand curve. In each case where there is a shift, explain which component(s) of aggregate demand cause the shift.
   a. The federal government cuts taxes for low-income households.
   b. There is a slump in share prices on Canadian stock markets.

c. The price level in Canada rises.

d. Canadian interest rates fall.

e. The Canadian dollar rises in value against the US dollar.

f. Canadian businesses become less confident about the future.

2. Using EconGraphKit (at www.mcgrawhill.ca/college/lovewell), show the difference between an increase and a decrease in aggregate demand.

11.2 Aggregate Supply

LO 11.2

aggregate supply: the relationship between the general price level and real output produced in the economy

aggregate supply schedule: the relationship between the general price level and real output expressed in a table

aggregate supply curve: the relationship between the general price level and real output expressed on a graph

So far in this chapter, we have focused on the role of spending in the economy. Now, let us turn our attention to the role of production. **Aggregate supply** is the relationship between the general price level and real output produced in the economy. Figure 11.5 shows aggregate supply expressed in a table, called the **aggregate supply schedule**, and on a graph, called the **aggregate supply curve** (AS).

The Aggregate Supply Curve

As Figure 11.5 shows, the price level and real output are directly related, giving the aggregate supply curve a positive slope. At higher price levels in the economy, businesses are encouraged to produce more; at lower price levels, businesses may not be able to make a profit or break even in the short run, so they reduce output. Variations in an economy's output caused by changes in the price level result in movements *along* the aggregate supply curve.

Recall from Chapter 10 that unemployment reduces real output from what it could be. If full employment were achieved—in other words, if only natural unemployment occurred—the economy would reach its potential output. If, as sometimes happens, the unemployment rate temporarily falls below the natural unemployment rate, real output rises temporarily above potential output.

Figure 11.5 Aggregate Supply

Businesses respond to increasing prices by producing more real output. At low output levels (such as point a), businesses produce significantly below capacity, and the AS curve is relatively flat. As output increases above the potential output level of $725 billion (point c), businesses produce above their normal capacity, and the AS curve is steep.

Let us consider the hypothetical example in Figure 11.5. Potential output—the real output associated with full employment—has a value of $725 billion. The real output level, as shown by the aggregate supply curve (AS), is much lower than its potential at point *a* but greater than the potential output at point *d*. Note that above the potential output level, the aggregate supply curve becomes very steep. This shows that businesses are producing above their normal capacity, which is possible in the short run only if businesses employ overtime labour and temporarily rent new machinery. These temporary measures mean that any expansion in real output—for example, from $725 billion (point *c*) to $730 billion (point *d*)—requires a relatively large increase in the price level to cover businesses' additional per-unit costs. Conversely, at real output levels below the potential output, the production capacity of businesses is under-utilized, with some labour and capital equipment either working part-time or sitting idle. A rise in real output, as from $650 billion (point *a*) to $700 billion (point *b*), can be made with a relatively small increase in the price level to cover additional per-unit costs.

Changes in Aggregate Supply

Of course, other factors in addition to the price level can influence real output. However, these factors, known as **aggregate supply factors**, change real output at *all* price levels. In other words, they *shift* the aggregate supply curve. Once again, as we examine each in turn, we must assume that all other aggregate supply factors and the price level remain constant.

INPUT PRICES

Aggregate supply assumes steady input prices for the businesses that are producing the output. Changes in input prices—an increase in wages, for example, or decreased prices for imported raw materials due to a rise in the value of the Canadian dollar—alter production costs. These changes can occur frequently over brief periods of time. When a rise in the price of an input pushes up production costs, businesses reduce their real output and the aggregate supply curve shifts to the left. Note, however, that nothing happens to change the economy's potential output. Conversely, if the price of an input decreases, production costs fall. Businesses then raise their real output, causing the aggregate supply curve to shift to the right, while the economy's potential output stays the same. These changes apply to the short run, so they are called a **short-run decrease in aggregate supply** and a **short-run increase in aggregate supply**, respectively. Figure 11.6 shows an example.

RESOURCE SUPPLIES

Over the long term, supplies of resources in an economy—especially human and capital resources—tend to grow. With any such increase, businesses produce more real output at every price level. In other words, more inputs over the long run increase aggregate supply, as well as the economy's potential output. Figure 11.7 shows the outcome—a **long-run increase in aggregate supply**. The reverse is also possible. With a long-run reduction in the amounts of any resource, businesses will produce lower real output at all prices, thereby causing a **long-run decrease in aggregate supply**, which is accompanied by a reduction in the economy's potential output.

Because production tends to adjust less rapidly than spending, changes in aggregate supply tend to be slower to occur than changes in aggregate demand. Input

aggregate supply factors: variables that change total output at all price levels

short-run decrease in aggregate supply: a decrease in total output at all price levels, with no change in potential output

short-run increase in aggregate supply: an increase in total output at all price levels, with no change in potential output

long-run increase in aggregate supply: an increase in total and potential output at all price levels

long-run decrease in aggregate supply: a decrease in total and potential output at all price levels

Figure 11.6   A Short-Run Change in Aggregate Supply

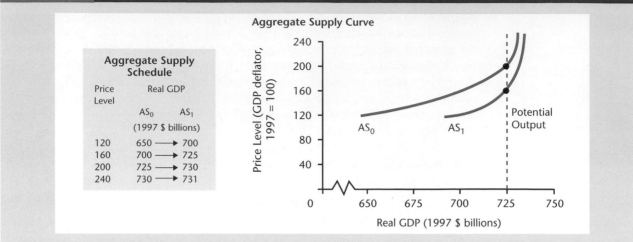

Aggregate Supply Schedule

Price Level	Real GDP	
	AS_0	AS_1
	(1997 $ billions)	
120	650 ⟶ 700	
160	700 ⟶ 725	
200	725 ⟶ 730	
240	730 ⟶ 731	

A drop in the wage rate results in an increase in real output at every price level, from AS_0 to AS_1. The movement is greatest at low price levels where substantial excess capacity exists. Because a decrease in wages does not affect long-run production trends, potential output stays constant.

prices, which may change quickly, often take time to affect real output. Changes in resource supplies and the other long-run determinants of aggregate supply tend to occur even more gradually. Though aggregate supply is more stable than aggregate demand over the short run, the long-run effect of aggregate supply on the economy can be profound.

PRODUCTIVITY

Productivity is the real output produced per unit of input over a given period of time. In particular, labour productivity is found by dividing a nation's real output by the total number of hours worked by its labour force:

Figure 11.7   A Long-Run Change in Aggregate Supply

Aggregate Supply Schedule

Price Level	Real GDP	
	AS_0	AS_1
	(1997 $ billions)	
120	650 ⟶ 700	
160	700 ⟶ 750	
200	725 ⟶ 775	
240	730 ⟶ 780	

An increase in a country's supplies of economic resources causes both aggregate supply and potential output to increase, thereby shifting the AS curve from AS_0 to AS_1 and raising potential output.

$$\text{Labour productivity} \ = \ \frac{\text{real output}}{\text{total hours worked}}$$

Increases in productivity are due largely to technological progress. A technological innovation raises productivity, when the same amount of economic resources can produce more real output at every price level, causing a long-run increase in aggregate supply similar to that shown in Figure 11.7. Likewise, a technological decline reduces the real output produced with the same resources, resulting in a long-run decrease in aggregate supply.

GOVERNMENT POLICIES

Government policies can also influence aggregate supply through their effects on the business environment in an economy. For example, suppose that taxes rise for businesses and households. Because the after-tax returns on supplying economic resources are reduced, businesses and households may reduce the resources they supply at every price level. As a result, real output falls, causing a long-run decrease in aggregate supply. Conversely, lower taxes may encourage businesses and households to increase their supply of economic resources, leading to a rise in real output and a long-run increase in aggregate supply.

Government regulations, such as environmental and safety standards, typically raise per-unit costs for businesses. Hence, more regulation causes businesses to produce less real output at every price level, causing a long-run decrease in aggregate supply. Similarly, less regulation stimulates production, leading to a long-run increase in aggregate supply. The effects of these and other aggregate supply factors are summarized in Figure 11.8.

Figure 11.8 Shifts in the Aggregate Supply Curve

Aggregate supply increases, with the AS curve shifting to the right, and potential output staying the same with the following:	Aggregate supply decreases, with the AS curve shifting to the left, and potential output staying the same with the following:
(1) A decrease in input prices due to (a) a fall in wages (b) a fall in raw material prices	(1) An increase in input prices due to (a) a rise in wages (b) a rise in raw material prices

Aggregate supply increases, with the AS curve shifting to the right, and potential output increasing with the following:	Aggregate supply decreases, with the AS curve shifting to the left, and potential output decreasing with the following:
(2) An increase in supplies of economic resources due to (a) more labour supply (b) more capital stock (c) more land (d) more entrepreneurship	(2) A decrease in supplies of economic resources due to (a) less labour supply (b) less capital stock (c) less land (d) less entrepreneurship
(3) An increase in productivity due to technological progress	(3) A decrease in productivity due to technological decline
(4) A change in government policies: (a) lower taxes (b) less government regulation	(4) A change in government policies: (a) higher taxes (b) more government regulation

THINKING ABOUT ECONOMICS

Is the information revolution having a significant effect on the position of Canada's aggregate supply curve?

According to some economists, the aggregate supply curve in such countries as Canada is being significantly affected by the advances in information technology (IT)—not so much because of the rise of the new economy but due to the way that IT is improving efficiency in the old economy. According to these economists, the result is a improvement in labour productivity and a gradual rightward shift in the aggregate supply curve. There is a good deal of evidence that this trend occurred in the American economy during the late 1990s, given its high growth rates in labour productivity. The evidence for this trend in Canada, however, is less compelling.

Question
How does the information revolution improve efficiency among old-economy businesses?

Brief Review

1. Aggregate supply is the relationship between the price level and real output produced in the economy. This relationship can be expressed in an aggregate supply schedule or on an aggregate supply curve.

2. Because higher prices encourage increased real output and vice versa, the price level and real output have a direct relationship, thereby giving the aggregate supply curve a positive slope.

3. Since real output may not reflect the full use of all resources—for example, labour—an economy may not reach its potential output.

4. While changes in the price level cause movement *along* the aggregate supply curve, aggregate supply factors—changes in input prices, supplies of economic resources, productivity, and government policies—*shift* the curve and so change real output of an economy and aggregate supply.

5. Short-run changes in aggregate supply, caused by varying input prices, do not change an economy's potential output. However, long-run changes in aggregate supply do change an economy's potential output in the same direction.

11.2 Practice Questions

1. Identify the impact of each of the following trends on aggregate supply. In each case, specify whether the change in aggregate supply is a short-run or a long-run change.
   a. The capital stock available to the Canadian economy undergoes a significant expansion.
   b. The federal government introduces tough new environmental regulations on Canadian business.
   c. The price of electricity increases.

d. Wages for Canadian workers are reduced.
e. Global warming causes a rise in ocean levels, affecting Canadian coastal areas.
f. Due to a fall in immigration, the size of the Canadian labour force declines.
g. The rate of adoption of new technologies by Canadian firms increases.

2. Using EconGraphKit (at www.mcgrawhill.ca/college/lovewell), show the difference between a short-run increase and a long-run increase in aggregate supply

11.3 Equilibrium Aggregate Demand and Supply

LO 11.3

So far, we have been looking at aggregate demand and aggregate supply separately. Now we will consider them together. What happens if real output at a certain price level exceeds real expenditures? Alternatively, what happens if real output at a certain price level falls short of what participants in the economy wish to spend? Figure 11.9 presents the answers to these questions. As with demand and supply in a competitive market for an individual product, the forces underlying aggregate demand and aggregate supply push the economy to an equilibrium point. An economy's equilibrium price level and real output occur at the intersection of the aggregate demand and aggregate supply curves.

Inventory Changes

Unintended changes in inventories cause price levels and real outputs to reach equilibrium. We will look at the two possibilities: the results of an inventory increase and of an inventory decrease.

Figure 11.9   An Economy in Equilibrium

If the price level, at points *a*, is above its equilibrium level, real output exceeds expenditures. An unintended rise in inventories causes businesses to lower prices until output and expenditures are the same (point *b*). When the price level is below its equilibrium value (points *c*), there is an unintended fall in inventories. Businesses increase prices until equilibrium is reached (point *b*).

RESULTS OF AN INVENTORY INCREASE

Suppose the general price level is above the equilibrium price level, at 200 (points *a*). At this price level, real output exceeds real expenditures, meaning more is produced than is purchased in the economy. Businesses have an unintended increase in inventories—in other words, a surplus—which represents **positive unplanned investment**. As a result of this surplus, prices of individual products decrease, pushing down the general price level.

The general decrease in prices influences both households and businesses. Because of the wealth and foreign trade effects, the response of buyers is to increase spending. So, real expenditures in our example increase towards point *b*. Meanwhile, lower prices cause businesses to decrease real output, and since real output and unemployment are inversely related, this causes a rise in the unemployment rate. These trends continue until real output and real expenditures are equal at the equilibrium point (point *b*).

RESULTS OF AN INVENTORY DECREASE

Suppose, on the other hand, that the price level is below its equilibrium value, at 120 (points *c*). Expenditures exceed production, creating a shortage. This leads to an unintended decrease in inventories, known as a **negative unplanned investment**. Because particular products are in short supply, prices rise. The response of buyers is to decrease spending. Meanwhile, the higher price level causes businesses to raise real output, causing unemployment to fall. These trends continue until real output and real expenditures are equal at the equilibrium point (point *b*).

THE ROLE OF UNPLANNED INVESTMENT

Note that in the case of either an unintended increase or decrease in inventories, unplanned investment plays a central role in stabilizing the economy. Unplanned investment is positive when the price level is above its equilibrium value and negative when the price level is below its equilibrium value, and in each case, unplanned investment is identical to the discrepancy between aggregate demand and aggregate supply.

This is illustrated by the aggregate demand and supply schedules in Figure 11.9. The $75 billion discrepancy between aggregate demand and aggregate supply at a price level of 200 means there is an unintended $75 billion increase in inventories. Hence, there is unplanned investment of $75 billion. Likewise, the shortage of $100 billion that appears at the 120 price level translates into an unintended $100 billion drop in inventories. Unplanned investment is, therefore, –$100 billion.

Injections and Withdrawals

The tendency of an economy to move towards equilibrium can also be outlined by looking at the flows of income payments and purchases that connect resource and product markets. There are three flows, known as **injections**, that add to the main income-spending stream in any economy: investment (I), government purchases (G), and exports (X). Corresponding to these injections are three outward flows of funds, known as **withdrawals**. Withdrawals, which divert funds from the income-spending stream in any economy, are saving (S), taxes (T), and imports (M).

There is no need for these individual injections and withdrawals to be equal. Even those injections and withdrawals related to the same sector can have different values. To see why, we will look at each related pair of injections and withdrawals in turn.

INVESTMENT AND SAVING

Recall that personal savings from households provide the bulk of funds in financial markets. Most funds are borrowed by businesses for investment. However, the amount saved and the amount invested in an economy are not equal for three reasons. First, recall that companies keep a portion of their profits to reinvest. These retained earnings supplement personal savings in financing investment. Second, governments also borrow money. The more governments borrow, the less personal savings end up in the hands of businesses. Third, we must also consider the foreign flows we have already discussed. Because lending by the rest of the world has usually exceeded borrowing by the rest of the world, foreign funds have typically added to Canadian savings available for investment.

GOVERNMENT PURCHASES AND TAXES

Recall that transfer payments and business subsidies are viewed as negative taxes. In the past, government purchases usually exceeded taxes. To make up for the discrepancy, governments have borrowed funds in financial markets. In recent years, taxes have usually exceeded government purchases. Governments have used these excess revenues to pay off some of their outstanding debt.

EXPORTS AND IMPORTS

In the past, Canada's imports of both goods and services have typically been greater than its exports. In other words, Canadians spent more on products from the rest of the world than they received in revenues from selling products to the rest of the world. At the same time, foreign lenders have typically provided funds to Canadian financial markets, with lending by foreigners being greater than borrowing by foreigners. So, the surplus of lending by foreigners has helped make up for the shortfall in net exports.

TOTAL INJECTIONS AND WITHDRAWALS

While individual injections and withdrawals are not necessarily equal, there is an important connection between them that applies when an economy is at equilibrium. If the circular income-spending stream is thought of as a flow of water—a water-ride at an amusement park, for example—then it is easy to see what will happen if the amount of water flowing into this stream is more or less than the water flowing out. If inward flows exceed outward flows, the amount of water circulating in the stream must be increasing. Conversely, if inward flows are less than outward flows, the amount of water must be decreasing. Only if inward and outward flows are equal will the water-ride function well. Viewed in this way, comparing total injections and withdrawals provides a way of explaining macroeconomic equilibrium that complements the approach using aggregate demand and aggregate supply.

Total injections are the sum of investment, government purchases, and exports $(I + G + X)$. Total withdrawals are the sum of saving, taxes, and imports $(S + T + M)$. Just as only the planned portion of investment is included in real expenditures to find aggregate demand, only planned investment is included in total injections.

Total injections $(I + G + X)$ and total withdrawals $(S + T + M)$ may be equal or unequal. When total injections exceed total withdrawals, flows into the income-spending stream are greater than flows out. Hence, the income-spending stream rises and speeds up. In other words, real output and spending in the economy expand. On the other hand, if total withdrawals exceed total injections, flows into the income-spending stream are less than outflows. Hence, the income-spending stream falls and slows down. In other words, real output and spending in the economy contract. Finally, in the case of equilibrium, total injections equal total withdrawals. Because inward and outward flows match, the income-spending stream circulates at a steady rate so that real output and spending in the economy stay constant.

Equilibrium versus Potential Output

An economy's equilibrium point can occur at its potential output, as illustrated in Figure 11.10. If so, then, unemployment at equilibrium equals the natural unemployment rate.

RECESSIONARY GAPS

recessionary gap: the amount by which equilibrium output falls short of potential output

While the situation shown in Figure 11.10 is possible, an economy's real output rarely equals its potential output. If equilibrium output is below its potential level, unemployment is above the natural unemployment rate. In this case, the difference between equilibrium output and potential output is known as a **recessionary gap**. Figure 11.11 shows on the left an economy with a recessionary gap of $25 billion. This is the amount by which real output would have to increase from its equilibrium value of $700 billion in order to attain its potential level of $725 billion.

INFLATIONARY GAPS

inflationary gap: the amount by which equilibrium output exceeds potential output

If equilibrium output is above its potential output, unemployment is temporarily below the natural unemployment rate. Inflation will accelerate if this situation persists. When equilibrium output exceeds potential output, therefore, the discrepancy is called an **inflationary gap**. Figure 11.11 shows, on the right, an economy with an inflationary gap of $5 billion. In this case, the equilibrium output of $730 billion would have to fall by $5 billion to achieve the potential output of $725 billion.

A recession differs from the notion of a recessionary gap. As we will soon see, during a recession, real output moves from above to below its potential level, with an inflationary gap transformed into a recessionary gap. On the other hand, a recessionary gap occurs whenever real output is below its potential level—in the latter stage of a recession as well as the first stage of an expansion or recovery.

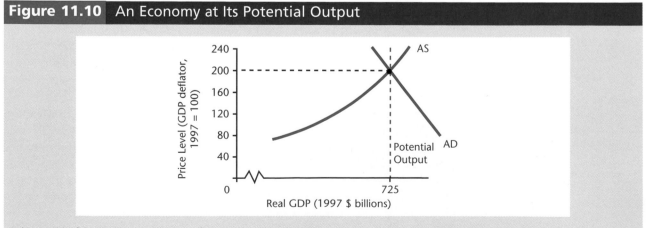

Figure 11.10   An Economy at Its Potential Output

It is possible for equilibrium to occur at the economy's potential output. In this case, actual unemployment equals the natural unemployment rate.

Figure 11.11 | Recessionary and Inflationary Gaps

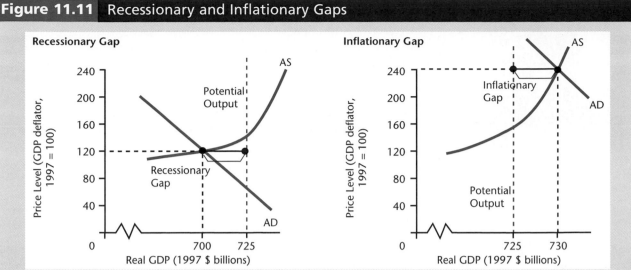

When real output falls short of potential output, the difference between the two is a recessionary gap, as shown on the left. In contrast, when real output temporarily exceeds its potential level, the difference between the two is an inflationary gap, as shown on the right.

Brief Review

1. An economy's equilibrium price level and real output occur at the intersection of the aggregate demand and aggregate supply curves.

2. The economy moves towards equilibrium through the workings of positive and negative unplanned investment—in other words, surpluses and shortages.

3. When an economy is at equilibrium, total injections (I + G + X) equal total withdrawals (S + T + M). If total injections exceed total withdrawals, real output rises, and the economy expands. If the reverse is true, real output falls, and the economy contracts.

4. If equilibrium output is less than potential output, the difference between the two is a recessionary gap. When equilibrium output exceeds potential output, the discrepancy in the output levels is an inflationary gap.

11.3 Practice Questions

1 a. Outline the trends that occur in an economy if the initial price level is above its equilibrium level.
   b. Now outline the opposite case where the initial price level is below its equilibrium level.

2 a. In the case of each injection (I, G, X) there is a related withdrawal. Identify the three pairs of related injections and withdrawals.
   b. Does each injection have to be in balance with its related withdrawal when the economy is in equilibrium? Why or why not?

3 a. When there is a recessionary gap, is the actual unemployment rate above or below its natural rate? Explain.

b. In the opposite case of an inflationary gap, how is unemployment related to its natural rate?

c. How are the levels of frictional, structural, and cyclical unemployment each affected by a protracted recessionary gap?

d. Using EconGraphKit (at www.mcgrawhill.ca/college/lovewell), draw an aggregate demand/aggregate supply graph showing an economy that is facing a recessionary gap.

11.4 Economic Growth and Business Cycles

LO 11.4

Economic Growth in Canada

Recall from Chapter 1 that economic growth is an increase in the total output of goods and services. The term can refer to the percentage increase in an economy's total output, usually measured by real GDP, or it can refer to a percentage increase in the per capita real GDP. For example, Canada's real GDP, valued in 1997 dollars, was $1040.388 billion in 2001 and $1074.516 billion in 2002, while the country's population expanded from 31 110.6 to 31 414.0 million during the same period. Using the first definition, Canada's annual rate of economic growth was 3.3 percent [=($1074.5 billion − $1040.4 billion) ÷ 1040.4 billion]. Since per capita real GDP rose from $33 442 (= $1040.388 billion ÷ 31 110.6 million) to $34 205 (= $1074.516 billion ÷ 31 414.0 million), economic growth using the second definition was 2.3 percent. Use of each definition depends on the context. The first definition of economic growth is most appropriate when measuring an economy's overall productive capacity, while the second definition better indicates long-term changes in living standards, since more output per capita means an average individual is better off than before.

Historically, Canada has had high rates of economic growth. As a result, Canada had the seventh highest per-capita output of the rich industrialized countries (after adjusting for purchasing power differences) in 2000. However, while Canada's long-term growth has been impressive, Figure 11.12 shows that increases in per-capita real output have varied widely since the Confederation.

BEFORE WORLD WAR I (1870-1914)

In the 44 years from just after the Confederation to World War I, Canada's per-capita output, measured in 1997 dollars, rose from $2312 to $5283. The economy's lacklustre growth record in the 1870s was followed by a more rapid rise in per-capita real output in the 1880s and 1890s—sometimes attributed to Prime Minister John A. Macdonald's National Policy, which stimulated Canadian manufacturing through high tariffs on imports. The gradual increase in growth rates during these decades was also a part of the worldwide trend towards greater prosperity as well as a rapid expansion of staple exports, such as wheat, that accompanied the settlement of the Canadian West.

THE INTERWAR PERIOD (1914–1945)

World War I ushered in a period of more unstable growth, with a lower long-term growth trend than in the previous period. After a period of negative growth just after World War I, Canada's per-capita real output rose and then fell sharply during the 1920s and early 1930s, before increasing rapidly during the latter part of the 1930s and World

Figure 11.12   Canada's Economic Growth

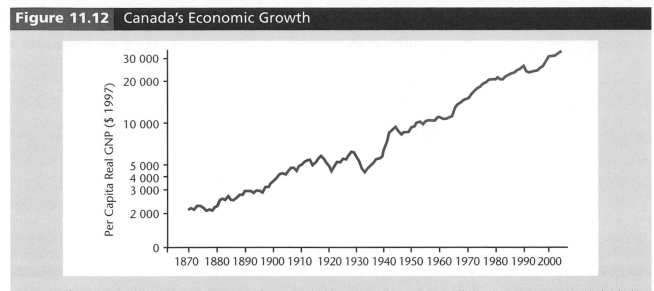

In terms of real output per capita, Canada's growth was gradual between 1870 and 1914. There were steep upswings in both the 1920s and early 1940s but an abrupt decline in the early 1930s. Until 1973, there was steady growth in per-capita income, averaging about 2 percent per year. Since then, the average rate of growth has been less. Note that the scale on the vertical axis is *logarithmic* to highlight change.

Sources: Adapted from A.G. Green and M.C. Urquhart, "New Estimates of Output Growth in Canada: Measurement and Interpretation," in Douglas McCalla and Michael Huberman (eds.), *Perspectives on Canadian Economic History* (Toronto: Copp Clark Longman, 1994), pp. 160–61; Statistics Canada "Canada's Economic Growth," adapted from the Statistics Canada publications, "Canadian economic observer. Historical statistical supplement," 2001/02, Catalogue 11-210, Vol. 16, July 2002, pp. 6, 7, 42, "Canadian Economic Accounts Quarterly Review," First Quarter 2003, Catalogue 13-010, Vol. 2, No. 1, May 2003, p. 17, and from the Statistics Canada CANSIM II database http://cansim2. statcan.ca Tables 380-0030 and 051-0001.

War II. Overall, between 1914 and 1945, per-capita real output almost doubled from $5283 to $9660.

THE POSTWAR PERIOD (1945–)

Between 1945 and 1973, Canada shared in the worldwide rise in prosperity, achieving a fairly steady growth in living standards of about 2 percent annually. Since the OPEC-spurred oil crisis of 1973, however, there has been a worrisome decrease in the rate of Canadian growth, except between 1983 and 1989 and between 1997 and 1999, when growth in per-capita real output again exceeded 2 percent. Overall, since 1945, per-capita real output in Canada has increased over three times to $33 389 by 2002.

Economic Growth and Productivity

What are the main factors determining economic growth? Changes in per-capita real output are determined by labour productivity, or the quantity of output produced per worker in a certain time period. Labour productivity can be applied not only to businesses and industries but also to countries' economies. Consider, for example, a hypothetical economy with a labour force of five workers who are employed for 2000 hours annually. In other words, the economy uses 10 000 hours of labour per year (= 5 × 2000). If real GDP in the economy is $200 000, labour productivity is $20 (= $200 000 ÷ 10 000):

$$\text{Labour productivity} = \frac{\text{real output}}{\text{total hours worked}}$$

$$\$20 = \frac{\$200\ 000}{10\ 000}$$

If real GDP in this economy rises to $202 000 in the following year and the number of labour hours remains constant, then the new level of labour productivity is $20.20 (= $202 000 ÷ 10 000), representing an increase of 1 percent [(= $20.20 − $20.00) ÷ 20) × 100%]. Such growth in labour productivity depends on long-run trends, such as changes in the quantity of capital and quality of labour in an economy, as well as the pace of technological progress.

Business Cycles

In terms of aggregate demand and aggregate supply, economic growth can be caused by a long-run increase in aggregate supply (which is accompanied by a rise in an economy's potential output) or by short-run changes in aggregate demand and aggregate supply. As we can see from Figure 11.12, rarely does the growth of actual output follow the gradually rising long-run trend in the economy's potential output. Usually, the growth in actual real output is accompanied by recessionary and inflationary gaps, and these gaps do not happen at random. Instead, they occur on the basis of a pattern of short-run changes in aggregate demand and aggregate supply.

As a rule, a sustained rise in real output, known as a period of **expansion** or recovery, is followed by an extended period of falling real output, known as a **contraction**. These rises and falls in real output constitute a pattern known as the **business cycle**.

Figure 11.13 shows the business cycle in a simplified form. The long-run trend of potential output to rise is shown by a dashed line. Actual output moves towards and away from this potential output in a cycle of successive contractions and expansions.

expansion: a sustained rise in the real output of an economy

contraction: a sustained fall in the real output of an economy

business cycle: the cycle of expansions and contractions in the economy

ACTUAL VERSUS POTENTIAL OUTPUT

When actual output exceeds potential output, the resulting inflationary gap is the difference between real output (point *a*) and potential output (point *b*). Real output then falls below its potential level shown by the trend line. In this case, the recessionary gap is the amount by which real output falls short of its potential—in other words, the difference between potential output (point *c*) and real output (point *d*).

Figure 11.13   The Business Cycle

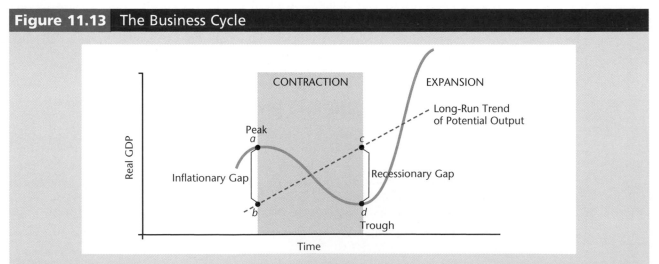

Real GDP rises and falls in a cycle of expansion and contraction. These fluctuations can be compared with a trend line that represents long-run growth potential. The distance between actual output and the trend line represents the size of either the economy's inflationary gap (as in the case of points *a* and *b*) or the economy's recessionary gap (as in the case of points *c* and *d*).

Contraction

peak: the point in the business cycle at which real output is at its highest

Consider the case of an economy that has reached its **peak**. At this point (point *a*), the economy is said to be experiencing a boom, which occurs when real GDP is at its highest value in the business cycle. The inflationary gap has reached its maximum width, unemployment is at its lowest possible level, and real output can grow no larger in the short run. From this point, the economy contracts.

THE ROLE OF EXPECTATIONS

Any decrease in aggregate demand can be magnified by the reactions of both households and businesses to initial reductions in spending and output. To understand how this occurs, recall that spending by both households and businesses is influenced by expectations of the future. Households vary consumption expenditures depending on their anticipation of future prices and incomes, while businesses decide how much to invest on the basis of estimates of future profit.

Expectations of the future are often made simply by extending current trends. Sometimes this can create a self-fulfilling prophecy, that is, if the economy is experiencing reductions in real output and spending, then many households and businesses assume that income and spending will drop further. As a result, there will likely be decreases in three types of spending: consumption, investment, and exports. The prospect of lower future incomes causes households to spend less, especially on durable items. Similarly, the decline in spending that businesses expect causes a drop in real rates of return for investment projects, leading to further declines in investment. The effect on exports occurs because periods of contraction usually arrive in various countries simultaneously. Therefore, it is probable that foreign consumers and businesses are reacting in the same way as their domestic counterparts, thus reducing exports. In other words, the expectations of businesses and households create a downward spiral in which declines in real output lead to further declines in spending and in output. Enough pessimism creates the very economic conditions people fear.

EFFECTS OF A CONTRACTION

Figure 11.14 shows the effects of a decrease in aggregate demand from AD_0 to AD_1. Equilibrium output declines from its initial value of $730 billion (point *f*) to a final value of $700 billion (point *e*). As a result, unemployment gradually rises above its natural rate, with the initial inflationary gap of $5 billion turning into a recessionary gap of $25 billion. At the same time, there is downward pressure on prices. If inflation is originally zero, as in Figure 11.13, then the price level falls from 240 to 160, causing deflation.

RECESSIONS AND DEPRESSIONS

recession: a decline in real output that lasts for six months or more

depression: a particularly long and harsh period of reduced real output

trough: the point in the business cycle at which real output is at its lowest

In general, the longer the period of declining real output, the more serious are its effects. A decline in real output that lasts for six months or more is known as a **recession**. A **depression** occurs if the reduction in real output is particularly long and harsh, as happened during the early 1930s.

Expansion

The spiral of worsening expectations and declining real output does not last indefinitely. Sooner or later, the economy reaches a **trough**, where real output is at its lowest possible value in the business cycle. In Figure 11.13, this occurs at point *d*. At this point, not only is the economy's recessionary gap at its widest, but unemployment

Figure 11.14   Expansion and Contraction

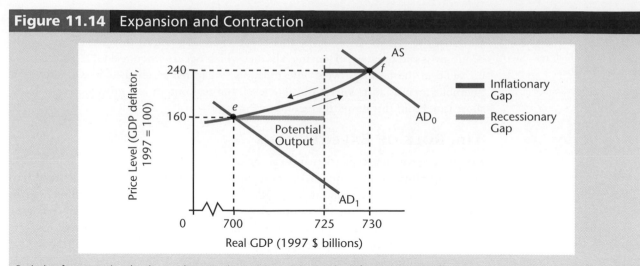

Periods of contraction lead to a decrease in aggregate demand, shifting the curve from AD_0 to AD_1. This leads to a fall in equilibrium output from $730 to $700 billion (points f to e). As a result, the initial inflationary gap of $5 billion turns into a recessionary gap of $25 billion. Periods of expansion reverse the change, causing the curve to shift from AD_1 to AD_0 and increasing equilibrium output (points e to f).

is at its highest level. After this turning point, the dampening effect of expectations is counteracted by other factors, and the economy enters a phase of expansion.

THE ROLE OF EXPECTATIONS

As in periods of contraction, expectations play a role in maintaining a recovery. Initial increases in real output and spending lead to optimistic forecasts of continuing growth. Therefore, consumption, investment, and exports all increase. Consumers react to the prospect of higher incomes by spending more, especially on durable goods. At the same time, businesses increase their investment because optimism causes further rises in estimated real rates of return. Finally, in the case where other countries are experiencing similar trends, foreign buyers also increase their spending and buy more exports. Increased consumer spending, business investment, and exports lead to continual increases in aggregate demand, until a new peak is reached and the stage is set for another period of contraction.

EFFECTS OF AN EXPANSION

Figure 11.14 also shows the effects of an expansion. In this case, the aggregate demand curve shifts to the right, from AD_1 to AD_0. Because of the rise in equilibrium output,

THINKING ABOUT ECONOMICS

Which sectors of the economy are most affected by a downturn?

While a recession or a depression is felt in every sector, those industries that make capital goods or durable consumer goods, such as automobiles and appliances, are the hardest hit. This is because purchases of these products can be postponed until after the downturn has ended.

Question
What sectors are least affected by a downturn?

the original recessionary gap is turned into an inflationary gap. Corresponding to this movement, the unemployment rate goes from above to below its natural rate, while the accompanying rise in the general price level causes inflation.

Brief Review

1. Economic growth refers to either increases in an economy's real output or increases in its real output per capita.

2. Overall, Canada's rate of economic growth has been high, giving Canada the seventh highest per-capita output of the rich industrialized countries in 2000.

3. Real output rarely equals potential output. Instead, output and expenditures generally follow a cycle of expansions and contractions, which together make up the business cycle.

4. The highest output occurs at a peak in the business cycle. From this point, the economy contracts, so aggregate demand decreases. Consumer and business expectations magnify the downward trend.

5. The lowest output occurs in a trough in a business cycle. From this point, the economy expands, so aggregate demand increases. Again, expectations magnify the upward trend.

11.4 Practice Questions

1 a. Business cycles are rarely symmetric; in other words, the durations of expansions and contractions are not as equal as they appear in Figure 11.13. By studying the actual pattern of Canada's economic growth, as shown in Figure 11.12, which phases tend to have a longer duration—expansions or contractions?

   b. Based again on Figure 11.12, in which period did the Canadian economy experience the most dramatic contraction? the most dramatic expansion?

2. "If enough people believe times are going to get better, they will." Analyze this statement based on the role of expectations in determining movements in the business cycle.

LAST**WORD**

In this chapter, we have developed a model to show how an economy's real output is determined, and we have examined the factors that cause the growth in real output to veer from the long-run trend of potential output. In the next chapter, we begin our discussion of how government policymakers can intervene in this process to reduce the instability of economic growth—first by focusing on the use of fiscal policy and then on money and the application of monetary policy. We will see that the macroeconomic role of governments in conducting stabilization policy is an area in which disagreement is quite common—not just in the political sphere, but among different groups of economists as well.

Key Concepts

aggregate demand 247
aggregate demand curve
  247
aggregate demand factors
  248
aggregate demand schedule
  247
aggregate supply 254
aggregate supply curve 254
aggregate supply factors
  255
aggregate supply schedule
  254
business cycle 266
contraction 266
decrease in aggregate
  demand 248

depression 267
exchange rate 252
expansion 266
foreign trade effect 248
increase in aggregate
  demand 248
inflationary gap 262
injections 260
investment demand 251
investment demand curve
  251
investment demand
  schedule 251
long-run decrease in
  aggregate supply 255
long-run increase in
  aggregate supply 255

negative unplanned
  investment 260
peak 267
positive unplanned investment 260
recession 267
recessionary gap 262
real expenditures 247
real rate of return 250
short-run decrease in
  aggregate supply 255
short-run increase in
  aggregate supply 255
trough 267
wealth effect 248
withdrawals 260

Questions

1. In a hypothetical economy, 100 investment projects worth $1 million each are undertaken when the real interest rate is 11 percent, and 50 more projects worth $1 million each are undertaken every time the real interest rate falls by 2 percent.
   a. On the basis of this information, construct a table showing the investment demand schedule.
   b. Draw a graph showing the investment demand curve.
   c. How much investment will be undertaken in this economy if the real interest rate is 5 percent? Explain.

2. Identify the impact of each of the following trends on aggregate demand. In each case, draw a graph to show the effect on the aggregate demand curve as well as on the equilibrium price level and real output.
   a. Consumers become more confident about the prospects for output growth in the Canadian economy.
   b. Canadian interest rates rise.
   c. Political pressure causes an increase in tax rates on households earning high incomes.
   d. A newly elected federal government increases its purchases of goods and services.
   e. The American economy experiences a boom.
   f. The Canadian dollar falls in value against the American dollar.

3. Identify the impact of each of the following trends on aggregate supply. In each case, draw a graph to show the effect on the aggregate supply curve as well as on the equilibrium price level and real output.
   a. Canadian workers receive higher wages.
   b. A cheap new source of energy raises labour productivity in the Canadian economy.
   c. The federal government reduces corporate income tax rates.
   d. Due to a global environmental crisis, there is a reduction in the amount of available land.
   e. The price of oil decreases.
   f. The Canadian dollar rises in value against the American dollar.

Hypothetical Aggregate Demand and Aggregate Supply Schedules

Price Level (1997=100)	AD_0	AD_1	AS_0	AS_1
		(1997 $ billions)		
140	200	160	270	310
130	220	180	260	300
120	240	200	240	280
110	260	220	220	260
100	280	240	180	220

4. The table above shows aggregate demand and aggregate supply schedules in a hypothetical economy.

a. Draw a graph to identify the equilibrium price level and real output in this economy, if the relevant schedules are AD_0 and AS_0.

b. With AD_0 and AS_0 as the relevant schedules, what happens if the price level is 140? 110?

c. Draw a new graph to show the effects on equilibrium if aggregate demand shifts from AD_0 to AD_1, while aggregate supply remains at AS_0. Describe this change in aggregate demand and outline two possible trends that could have caused the change.

d. On the same graph you have drawn in part c., show the effects on equilibrium if aggregate supply shifts from AS_0 to AS_1, while aggregate demand remains at AD_0. Describe this change in aggregate supply and outline two possible trends that could have caused the change.

5. Outline how a fall in injections will affect the income-spending stream and equilibrium real output. Discuss how the same result can be found using aggregate demand and aggregate supply.

6. "Over time, long-run changes in aggregate supply are the key determinants of changes in real output." Evaluate this statement using evidence from the chapter.

7. Why does a $100 million decrease in aggregate demand have a greater impact on real output when the economy is below its potential output than when it is above its potential output?

Year	Annual Percentage Change in Real GDP (1997 $)	Year	Annual Percentage Change in Real GDP (1997 $)
1982	–2.9	1993	2.3
1983	2.7	1994	4.8
1984	5.8	1995	2.8
1985	4.8	1996	1.6
1986	2.4	1997	4.2
1987	4.3	1998	4.1
1988	5.0	1999	5.4
1989	2.6	2000	4.5
1990	0.2	2001	1.5
1991	–2.1	2002	3.3
1992	0.9		

Source: Adapted from the Statistics Canada publications, "Canadian economic observer. Historical statistical supplement," 2001/02, Catalogue 11-210, Vol. 16, July 2002, p. 6 and "Canadian Economic Accounts Quarterly Review," First Quarter 2003, Catalogue 13-010, Vol. 2, No. 1, May 2003, p. 14.

8. Study the table above. Identify the following and give support for your answer:
a. Years in which the economy expanded

b. Years in which the economy contracted

c. Peaks

d. Troughs

9. Predict how each of the following will tend to move during (i) economic expansions, and (ii) economic contractions:

a. Consumption of durable goods

b. Consumption of nondurable items

c. Planned investment

d. Exports

e. Imports

f. Wage rates

g. Unplanned investment

10. Give examples of industries that will perform well during (i) contractions, and (ii) expansions.

11. (Advanced Question)

Discuss how changes in the following variables could affect aggregate demand in order to reduce (i) an inflationary gap, or (ii) a recessionary gap:

a. Government purchases

b. Personal and corporate tax rates

c. Interest rates

d. The Canadian dollar's value in American dollars

Internet Application Questions

http://www.fin.gc.ca/

1. a. Refer to the most recent issue of Finance Canada's publication The Economy in Brief (at http://www.fin.gc.ca/access Link to Publications) to find the latest quarterly growth rates in consumption, government expenditures, exports, imports, and the various components of investment spending.

b. Which of these categories increased the most? Which increased the least, or declined the most?

c. On the basis of the above answers, which of the four main elements of aggregate demand had the most positive effect on real output? Which element had the least positive (or negative) effect on real output?

http://www.statcan.ca/

2. Access Statistics Canada's web site (at http://www.statcan.ca/) and use the links in "Postsecondary Resources" to find the base-year values for GDP, C, I (leaving out investment in inventories), G, and (X–M) during the four most recent years available.

a. Compute annual percentage rates of change for each of these variables.

b. On the basis of your answers to a., discuss how each of the four components of aggregate demand tend to move in relation to total real expenditures.

http://www.statcan.ca/english/Estat/ licence. htm

3. Access Statistics Canada's E-Stat site (at http://www.statcan.ca/english/Estat/licence.htm).

a. On the basis of the information in "National Accounts," generate a two-dimensional graph showing Canada's expenditure-based real GDP since 1961.

b. In which years since 1961 did Canada experience peaks and troughs in the business cycle?

APPENDIX

The Aggregate Expenditures Model

The aggregate demand and aggregate supply approach that we have employed so far highlights the impact of price changes on both spending and output, but it downplays fluctuations in the individual components of total spending. In contrast, the aggregate expenditures model focuses on these individual spending components, on the basis of the assumption that prices are constant. It, therefore, provides an alternative tool for analyzing how stabilization policies affect various parts of the economy.

Consumption and Saving

To see this alternative approach, let us start by looking at how households choose to divide their disposable income (DI) between consumption (C) and saving (S) in an economy in which imports (including that portion consumed by households) are constant, regardless of income. This means that when DI changes, the only consumption adjustment made by households is in the purchases of domestically produced items. Such consumption spending tends to change proportionally with any change in the economy's disposable income. For example, if DI increases by $200 billion, C may always rise by $150 billion, which means S must rise by the remaining $50 billion.

The effect on domestic consumption of a change in income is known as the economy's marginal propensity to consume, or MPC, and it is calculated by taking the ratio of the change in the consumption of domestic items over the initial change in income. Likewise, the economy's **marginal propensity to save**, or MPS, is the effect of a change in income on saving. It can be calculated by taking the ratio of the change in saving over the initial change in income. Note that because disposable income is either consumed or saved, the MPC and MPS must sum to equal 1. For example, if a $200 billion increase in DI raises C by $150 billion and S by $50 billion, MPC is 0.75 (= $150 billion ÷ $200 billion) and MPS is 0.25 (= $50 billion ÷ $200 billion), which together equal 1. And, because C and S always vary proportionally when DI changes, both MPC and MPS are constant at each level of disposable income.

Figure A shows how the values for consumption and saving in a hypothetical economy depend on disposable income. As portrayed on the graph and accompanying table, consumption and saving always sum to equal DI. For example, if DI is $800 billion, then C is $800 billion, and S is zero. At this breakeven point, all DI is consumed, and none is saved. In contrast, if DI is $1400 billion, then C is $1250 billion, and S equals $150 billion so that saving is positive. But if DI is at zero, then C is $200 billion, and S is -$200 billion. Even with a zero DI, consumers must satisfy their basic needs by spending $200 billion. They do so by borrowing this amount, which means they engage in negative saving of -$200 billion. Again, C and S sum to equal DI.

The slope of the C line in Figure A equals the economy's MPC (0.75) because this ratio shows the change in C (the "rise") over the change in DI (the "run"). Similarly, the slope of the S line equals the MPS (0.25), given that it portrays the change in S over the change in DI.

A Private Economy

This specification of consumption and saving can be extended to show equilibrium in the entire economy. We will look first at an economy in which there is no government and, thus, no government purchases or taxes. For the sake of simplicity, we will assume DI and GDP are equal. We will also assume that not just imports (M) but also investment (I) and exports (X) are constant amounts at all income levels—for example, I is $25 billion, X is

marginal propensity to save (MPS): the effect on saving of a change in income

Figure A   Consumption and Saving

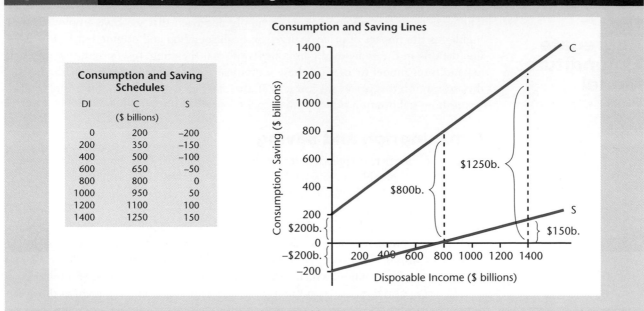

Consumption and Saving Lines

Consumption and Saving Schedules

DI	C	S
	($ billions)	
0	200	−200
200	350	−150
400	500	−100
600	650	−50
800	800	0
1000	950	50
1200	1100	100
1400	1250	150

C and S levels always sum to equal DI. For example, at a DI of $1 trillion, C and S sum to this amount (= $950 billion + $50 billion). The slope of the C line is the marginal propensity to consume (MPC), and the slope of the S line is the marginal propensity to save (MPS).

$375 billion, and M is $350 billion. So, in this economy, there are only two injections (investment and exports) and only two withdrawals (saving and imports). Moreover, the marginal propensity to save (MPS) is the same as the marginal propensity to withdraw (MPW), since saving in this private economy is the only withdrawal that varies with income.

The aggregate expenditures model incorporates two approaches to derive the economy's equilibrium. The first focuses on spending and output levels and is known as the **spending-output approach**. The second concentrates on total levels of injections and withdrawals and is known as the **injections-withdrawals approach**.

spending-output approach: an approach to deriving equilibrium GDP that focuses on total expenditures and total output

injections-withdrawals approach: an approach to deriving equilibrium GDP that focuses on total injections and total withdrawals

THE SPENDING-OUTPUT APPROACH

With just three spending components—consumption (C), investment (I), and net exports (X-M)—in a private economy, the aggregate expenditures (AE_0) line can be found by combining the $25 billion in investment and the $25 billion (= $375 billion − $350 billion) in net exports with consumption at every income level. This is portrayed in the top table and on the graph of Figure B, where the initial consumption line is shifted upwards by a total of $50 billion (= $25 billion + $25 billion) at each GDP to find aggregate expenditures. Because the AE_0 line and the original consumption line are parallel, they both have the same slope, which equals MPC, or 0.75.

On the basis of the spending-output approach, equilibrium GDP occurs where aggregate expenditures equal the amount of output actually produced. Given the double interpretation of GDP—which represents both income and output—the amount of output actually produced is shown by the level of GDP. In terms of the graph, this is the distance shown on the horizontal axis. To translate this same distance onto the vertical axis, a line can be drawn emanating from the origin at a 45-degree angle, since all

Figure B   Equilibrium with No Government

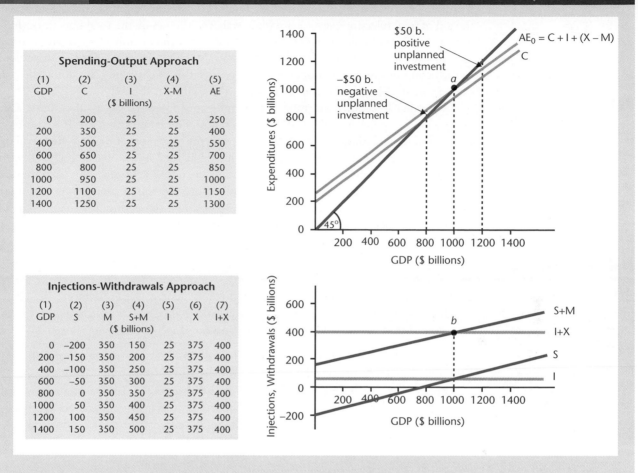

Spending-Output Approach

(1) GDP	(2) C	(3) I	(4) X-M	(5) AE
		($ billions)		
0	200	25	25	250
200	350	25	25	400
400	500	25	25	550
600	650	25	25	700
800	800	25	25	850
1000	950	25	25	1000
1200	1100	25	25	1150
1400	1250	25	25	1300

Injections-Withdrawals Approach

(1) GDP	(2) S	(3) M	(4) S+M	(5) I	(6) X	(7) I+X
			($ billions)			
0	-200	350	150	25	375	400
200	-150	350	200	25	375	400
400	-100	350	250	25	375	400
600	-50	350	300	25	375	400
800	0	350	350	25	375	400
1000	50	350	400	25	375	400
1200	100	350	450	25	375	400
1400	150	350	500	25	375	400

On the top graph, equilibrium occurs at point *a*, where the AE line crosses the 45-degree line emanating from the origin, since, here, total expenditures (the vertical distance) equal the GDP produced (the horizontal distance). On the bottom graph, the same GDP is found at point *b*, where injections (I +X) and withdrawals (S+M) are equal.

points on this line have the same vertical and horizontal coordinates. The equilibrium condition is, therefore, met at point *a*, with a GDP of $1 trillion, where the AE line intersects the 45-degree line. At this point, aggregate expenditures—the sum of consumption ($950 billion), investment ($25 billion), and net exports ($25 billion)—equals the $1 trillion in GDP that is actually produced.

At any GDP below this equilibrium level, aggregate expenditures exceed the amount of output actually produced. For example, at a GDP of $800 billion, aggregate expenditures are $850 billion. This leads to a $50 billion unintended decrease in inventories and, therefore, a negative unplanned investment of -$50 billion. As a result of this negative unplanned investment, businesses increase production, pushing up GDP towards its equilibrium level. In contrast, at a GDP of $1200 billion, aggregate expenditures are $1150 billion, which is less than the amount of output actually produced. The result is a $50 billion unintended increase in inventories, which means a positive unplanned investment of $50 billion. In this case, businesses react by cutting production, pushing down GDP towards its equilibrium value.

THE INJECTIONS-WITHDRAWALS APPROACH

In the lower table and on the graph of Figure B, the same equilibrium is found with the aid of total injections and total withdrawals. On the graph, the total injections (I+X) line is horizontal, reflecting the fact that both investment and exports are constant amounts at each GDP level. The total withdrawals (S+M) line has a positive slope equal to the economy's marginal propensity to save, since this line is found by adding the constant amount of imports to the saving line, whose slope is the MPS.

The total injections and total withdrawals lines intersect where they both equal $400 billion at point *b*, with a GDP of $1 trillion. The equilibrium GDP found using the injections-withdrawals approach is, therefore, the same as found using the spending-output approach. At any GDP level below this value, total injections exceed total withdrawals, which speeds up the economy's income-spending stream, raising GDP towards its equilibrium level. In contrast, at GDP levels above the equilibrium value, total injections fall short of total withdrawals, which slows down the economy's income-spending stream, reducing GDP towards its equilibrium value.

Brief Review

1. Households either consume or save disposable income (DI). Therefore, any related points on the economy's consumption and savings line sum to equal DI. The slope of the consumption line is MPC, and the slope of the saving line is MPS.

2. In a private economy where I, M, and X are all constant amounts regardless of income, equilibrium GDP is found in two ways. Using the spending-output approach, equilibrium occurs where aggregate expenditures equal the amount of output actually produced. On the basis of the injection-withdrawals approach, equilibrium occurs where total injections and total withdrawals are equal.

Questions

1. In an economy with consumption and saving schedules shown in Figure A, what would happen to the saving schedule if the consumption schedule at every possible income level rose by $100 billion?

2. Explain how the economy shown in Figure B reaches its equilibrium level if:
   a. it is initially at a GDP of $600 billion.
   b. it is initially at a GDP of $1400 billion.

Key Concepts

injections-withdrawals
approach 274

marginal propensity to
save (MPS) 273

spending-output approach
274

MAKING AN ECONOMY GROW

Paul Romer and New Growth Theory

Recently, the role of knowledge has been highlighted in theories of economic growth. Part of this new emphasis is due to the contemporary American economist Paul Romer.

The knowledge economy. Knowledge workers. Knowledge-based industries. Ideas-driven growth. The words trip off the tongue with ease, not just in academic circles but in the mainstream population as well.

These new economic buzzwords reflect the fact that knowledge and ideas have become the vital engines of economic growth. The boom in such fields as computer software, telecommunications, pharmaceuticals, and bio-technology clearly shows that the jobs of the future, and Canada's overall prosperity, depend on wise investments in the new knowledge-based economy.

The brain behind the buzzwords is Paul Romer, an intense, 46-year-old economist who has had a revolutionary impact on economic thinking and, in the process, upset the apple cart of traditional economic theories of growth.

Romer is a professor of economics at the University of California at Berkeley, a visiting fellow at the Hoover Institution, and the Royal Bank Fellow at the Canadian Institute for Advanced Research (CIAR). The praise for Romer's work is lavish and, to him, slightly embarrassing. *The Economist* has said that historians will date the revival of growth theory in economics to Romer. The effect of his work has been likened to the intellectual upheavals caused by Adam Smith and John Maynard Keynes.

Romer's New Growth Theory is now widely accepted, but back in 1979, when he was a 25-year-old graduate student at Queen's University in Kingston, Ontario, it was tantamount to claiming that the emperor had no clothes. Romer was at Queen's because his wife, Virginia Langmuir of Toronto, was returning to complete her residency as a physician there.

Left alone, with little academic supervision, Romer began to ponder the question that has intrigued economists for decades: what are the causes of long-term growth?

> "One of the features of that year at Queen's was that there was no one to tell me that this is how you have to think about growth," Romer recalls. "So I started, in a sense, from a clean piece of paper and said: 'Gee! How should I try to go about understanding this really interesting phenomenon?'
>
> "Economists had built up a relatively sophisticated and productive way of thinking about growth, but we weren't learning much more from that framework. So, as much by trial and error as by chance, I started out on a new path."

Traditional economic theory held that growth was the result of two factors of production: labour and capital. But there was a nagging problem with this so-called neoclassical theory: it could not explain why the developing countries, given liberal amounts of labour and capital, failed to grow as fast as the developed nations.

Romer had the answer: knowledge. He made it the third—and most important—factor of production. By knowledge, he meant new and better ways of doing things, as well as ideas, innovation, invention, and discovery. Knowledge entails taking objects that are relatively worthless and rearranging them in new combinations to create value. For example, the sand on a beach has little value, but turn it into a silicon chip, and it becomes immensely valuable.

Paul Romer
Source: Courtesy of Paul Romer

Another compelling example is Bill Gates. He can walk through a customs barrier anywhere in the world and swear he has nothing to declare when, in fact, his brain carries the multi-billion-dollar secrets of Microsoft, which have made him the wealthiest man on earth.

"The key issue is to understand knowledge or ideas as economic goods." Romer explains. "Ideas are very different from things. When you're dealing with things, the best institutions to use are prices, free markets, and strong property rights."

But you cannot just transfer these same governing principles to the market-place of ideas, Romer says. Objects tend to have relatively fixed costs per unit, while ideas have high upfront costs but low reproduction costs. Developing an idea—say a new piece of software—might take $100 million, while producing a copy of it on a floppy disk can cost less than 50 cents.

This raises the question of how to set the right price for the discovery of an idea. Romer cites the example of polymerase chain reaction (PCR)—a way of getting tiny amounts of DNA to multiply—which won the Nobel Prize in chemistry for Kary Mullis in 1993.

"At the start, we put a very high price on PCR because it's extremely valuable," Romer says. "But after the idea has been produced, the most efficient thing for society as a whole is to let that idea be freely used by other scientists and researchers in the hope that it will lead to the discovery of more new ideas."

Romer's New Growth Theory seems to have struck a chord with academia and the general public alike because it carries with it the message of optimism. Traditional economic theory held that since the way of doing things was relatively constant, no matter the capital and labour expended, over time, society would get smaller and smaller returns. This was known as the law of diminishing returns. New Growth Theory, by contrast, embraces a law of increasing returns.

To illustrate the mind-boggling opportunities that ideas can generate, Romer uses the example of a manufacturing process in which 20 different parts must be attached to a frame. You could attach them in a given order: part one first, part two second, part three third, and so on. Or you may attach them in another order: part one first, then part 20, then part seven, and so on. If you calculate all the possible sequences for attaching those parts, you get 10 to the 18th power, a number that is larger than the total number of seconds that have elapsed since the Big Bang created the universe. So the possibilities out there are virtually limitless.

What lies ahead for Paul Romer? Plenty of different things. At the CIAR, he is descending from the ivory tower and examining practical policy questions about restructuring financial incentives for universities so that graduates can find better niches in the knowledge economy.

But this influential economist is, at heart, a loner: "People like me don't work very well in structured environments. A colleague of mine says that trying to work with us (economists) is like trying to herd cats."

Asked about leisure time, he replies with a laugh, "What's that?" And the future? "Oh, more of the same," Romer says. "I'll continue to be an intellectual bomb-thrower."

Indeed.

Source: Gillian Cosgrove, "Knowing about Growing," *Canadian Banker*, (May/June, 1996), pp. 20-22.

1. a. Give an example of a Canadian idea that has been subject to the increasing returns associated with knowledge.

   b. Summarize how the company can benefit from these increasing returns.

2. Does Romer's theory provide an argument for or against strong patent protection for new ideas? Explain.

ADVANCING ECONOMIC THOUGHT

CHAPTER 12

Fiscal Policy

Democracy will defeat the economist at every turn at its own game.

—Harold Innis, Canadian economist and historian

Should governments sit idly through the upheavals caused by the business cycle? Certainly not, according to John Maynard Keynes, the founder of modern macroeconomics. Governments can do plenty to stabilize the economy—not only during downturns when unemployment is high but also during inflationary upswings. Governments can use certain policies to achieve economic stability; for example, they can spend more money or reduce taxes to cause changes in total spending and aggregate demand. This chapter examines the theory behind such policies and their outcomes.

LEARNING OBJECTIVES

In this chapter, you will:

1 learn about expansionary and contractionary fiscal policies, which are used by governments seeking economic stability

2 analyze the multiplier effect of fiscal policy, as determined by the marginal propensities to consume and withdraw

3 consider budget surpluses and deficits and their impact on public debt and public debt charges

12.1 Fiscal Policy

stabilization policy: government policy designed to lessen the effects of the business cycle

LO 12.1

expansionary policies: government policies designed to reduce unemployment and stimulate output

contractionary policies: government policies designed to stabilize prices and reduce output

fiscal policy: government stabilization policy that uses taxes and government purchases as its tools; budgetary policy

fiscal year: the 12-month period to which a budget applies

monetary policy: government stabilization policy that uses interest rates and the money supply as its tools

The Goal of Stabilization

To lessen the effects of ups and downs in the business cycle—particularly inflation and unemployment—governments use stabilization policies. A **stabilization policy** attempts to influence the amounts spent and produced in an economy. The goal of such a policy is to keep the economy as close as possible to its potential output. At this point, only natural unemployment exists, and inflation is restrained.

Stabililization policies fall into two categories, depending on the state of the economy and the effect the policy is meant to have on the economy. When total output is below its potential, policy-makers want to eliminate the recessionary gap—in other words, reduce unemployment and stimulate total output. Policies with these goals are called **expansionary policies**.

In contrast, if the economy is booming, policy-makers want to cut the inflationary gap—in other words, stabilize prices and bring the economy back down to its potential output. Policies with these goals are called **contractionary policies**.

STABILIZING THE BUSINESS CYCLE

Assuming that it can be applied quickly and effectively, stabilization policy may be used to smooth out the business cycle. Figure 12.1 shows how stabilization policy can reduce the severity of economic troughs and peaks and the recessionary and inflationary gaps associated with them. The closer the economy stays to the long-run trend of potential output, the lower will be the social costs of unemployment and inflation to the country's citizens.

In general, governments can affect spending and output levels in an economy through two sets of instruments. First, recall that governments have an extensive impact on the economy through taxation and government purchases. Because a government's annual budget sets out what the government will tax and spend, the budget becomes an instrument of stabilization policy. Such a policy is called **fiscal policy**, "fiscal" meaning "budgetary." The 12-month period to which the budget applies is called the **fiscal year**. Governments can also exert their influence on interest rates and the economy's money supply. A policy that uses these tools is called monetary policy. We will focus on fiscal policy in this chapter and turn our attention to **monetary policy** in later chapters.

Figure 12.1   Stabilization Policy and the Business Cycle

Effective stabilization policy minimizes the severity of the peaks and troughs in the business cycle. Differences between actual output and the long-run trend of potential output are, therefore, smaller, thus reducing recessionary and inflationary gaps.

Use of Fiscal Policy

Governments apply fiscal policy during any part of the business cycle. So, during a recession or depression, government action is geared towards increasing spending and output in the economy. Such **expansionary fiscal policy** involves increasing government purchases, decreasing taxes, or both. In contrast, during an inflationary boom, government policy-makers concentrate on restraining output and spending. Such **contractionary fiscal policy** involves decreasing government spending, increasing taxes, or both.

INJECTIONS AND WITHDRAWALS

One way to see how fiscal policy works is to look at injections and withdrawals. Recall from Chapter 11 that investment, government purchases, and exports make up injections to the income-spending stream; saving, taxes, and imports are withdrawals from the stream.

With expansionary fiscal policy, governments increase their purchases and, thus, raise injections to the circular flow. As a result, injections rise relative to withdrawals, and the total flow increases. Reducing taxes has the same effect. By withdrawing less from the income-spending stream, withdrawals decrease relative to injections, and the total flow increases. As the total flow rises, equilibrium output is pushed up.

Contractionary fiscal policies have the opposite effect. Governments that decrease their purchases reduce injections to the circular flow. As a result, injections fall relative to withdrawals, and the total flow decreases. Raising taxes has the same effect; withdrawals rise relative to injections, and the total flow decreases. As the total flow falls, equilibrium output is pushed down.

AGGREGATE DEMAND

Another way to look at fiscal policy is through its effects on aggregate demand and aggregate supply. To increase aggregate demand so that the economy expands to its potential, policy-makers raise government purchases, cut taxes, or both. Increasing government purchases has an immediate effect on aggregate demand since government purchases are a component of real expenditures. As Figure 12.2 demonstrates, the equilibrium price level and output are pushed up as a result.

expansionary fiscal policy: government policy that involves increasing government purchases, decreasing taxes, or both to stimulate spending and output

contractionary fiscal policy: government policy that involves decreasing government purchases, increasing taxes, or both to restrain spending and output

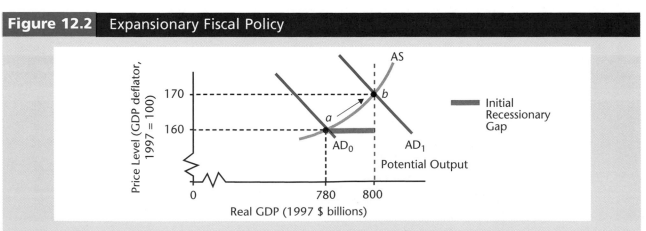

Figure 12.2   Expansionary Fiscal Policy

A rise in government purchases or a cut in taxes increase aggregate demand, shifting the aggregate demand curve from AD_0 to AD_1. This causes a rise in the equilibrium price level, and output rises to its potential level (from point a to point b). As a result, the economy's $20 billion recessionary gap is eliminated.

The effect of tax cuts is less immediate because there is no guarantee that households and businesses will alter spending in response to a tax change. Cutting taxes enables households and businesses to spend more, so both consumption and investment should increase, thereby shifting the aggregate demand curve to the right. Again, Figure 12.2 illustrates the results.

If a government has a contractionary fiscal policy—in other words, if it wants to decrease aggregate demand so that the economy contracts to its potential—policy-makers will reduce government purchases, raise taxes, or both. As with expansionary fiscal policy, the effect of decreasing government purchases is immediate, while the effect of increasing taxes is less so. Figure 12.3 illustrates both cases. A fall in government purchases reduces aggregate demand, thereby shifting the aggregate demand curve to the left. Higher taxes reduce households' disposable income and businesses' profits. Consumption and investment both decline, thereby reducing aggregate demand and shifting the aggregate demand curve to the left.

AUTOMATIC STABILIZERS

As we have seen, fiscal policy involves adjusting government purchases or taxes. These actions are intentional; laws must be passed and budgets brought down. Because it is up to a government's discretion to take these actions, fiscal policy is known as **discretionary policy**. In contrast, some stabilizing forces are automatic—that is, they do not involve the direct involvement of government decision-makers.

Established taxation and transfer payment programs, such as progressive income taxes, Employment Insurance, and welfare payments, act as **automatic stabilizers** in the business cycle. In a period of contraction, **net tax revenues** (taxes minus transfers and subsidies) decrease; during a period of expansion, net tax revenues increase. As a result, spending and aggregate demand are stimulated in a downturn and suppressed in an upswing, thereby helping to smooth out the business cycle.

To see how automatic stabilizers work, let us first consider an economy that is contracting. Because household incomes and business profits fall, the taxes that a government can collect from households and businesses also fall. As jobs are lost and businesses suffer, government transfer payments and subsidies are increased. Both trends cause a decline in net tax revenues. Because incomes are bolstered by one program

discretionary policy: intentional government intervention in the economy, such as budgeted changes in spending or taxation

automatic stabilizers: built-in measures, such as taxation and transfer payment programs, that lessen the effects of the business cycle

net tax revenues: taxes collected minus transfers and subsidies

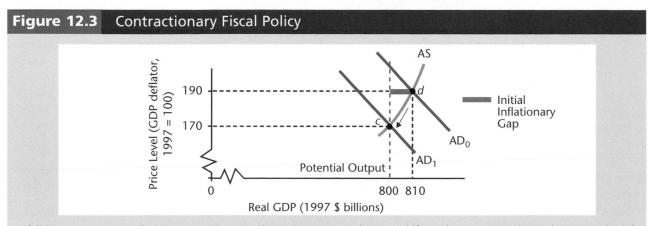

Figure 12.3   Contractionary Fiscal Policy

A fall in government purchases or a rise in taxes decrease aggregate demand, shifting the aggregate demand curve to the left from AD_0 to AD_1. This causes a fall in the equilibrium price level, and output falls to potential level (from point *d* to point *c*). As a result, the economy's inflationary gap is eliminated.

and taxes are reduced by the other, spending increases over what it would have been, helping to push the economy towards its potential output.

When the economy expands, the opposite happens. Personal incomes and business profits increase. As a result, governments collect more in taxes. Because the nation is more prosperous and the employment rate is high, transfer payments and subsidies are reduced. Both trends cause a rise in net tax revenues. Because taxes have risen, spending and aggregate demand decrease, helping to push the economy back down to its potential output.

THINKING ABOUT ECONOMICS

How significant are automatic stabilizers in the Canadian economy?

The expanding role of Canadian governments since World War II has led to a substantial increase in rates of taxation as well as rising expenditures on transfer payments. Higher tax rates and more generous transfer payments have both served as important automatic stabilizers in the Canadian economy during recent decades—a point that is stressed by economists who support greater government involvement in the economy.

Question
How will the recent tax cuts by federal and provincial governments affect the significance of automatic stabilizers?

Brief Review

1. Governments use stabilization policies to minimize ups and downs in the business cycle. Such policies are categorized as expansionary or contractionary policies, depending on the state of the economy and the effect of the policy on the economy.

2. Fiscal policy affects spending and output through taxes and government purchases. Monetary policy affects spending and output through interest rates and the economy's money supply.

3. Expansionary fiscal policy involves increasing government purchases, decreasing taxes, or both. Such a policy increases aggregate demand and pushes up the equilibrium price level and output.

4. Contractionary fiscal policy involves decreasing government purchases, increasing taxes, or both. Such a policy decreases aggregate demand and pushes down the equilibrium price level and output.

5. In contrast to discretionary policies, automatic stabilizers are built-in factors that affect aggregate demand and minimize the impact of inflationary and recessionary gaps.

12.1 Practice Questions

1. In each of the following cases, state whether policy-makers should raise or reduce government purchases. If an action is being taken, explain the policy-makers' rationale for taking this action.
   a. Real output is less than its potential level.
   b. Unemployment is below its natural rate.
   c. Real output equals its potential level and unemployment is at its natural rate.

2. Explain how automatic stabilizers work during the following periods.
   a. The economy is experiencing a recession, with shrinking incomes and spending.
   b. The economy is in an expansionary phase, with rising incomes and spending.

12.2 The Spending Multiplier

LO 12.2

multiplier effect: the magnified impact of a spending change on aggregate demand

Government decision-makers must have some way of estimating, in terms of money values, the impact that their policies will have on the economy. In general, a certain money change in government purchases or taxation does not cause the same money change in total real output. Like a pebble dropped in a pond causes ripples, fiscal policy has a multiplier effect.

The Multiplier Effect

The **multiplier effect** is the magnified impact of any spending change on aggregate demand. It assumes that the price level stays constant. So, the multiplier effect is the change in spending at one price level, multiplied by a certain value to give the resulting change in aggregate demand.

Let us consider an example. Suppose government institutes an expansionary fiscal policy. As part of this policy, government pays Spender A, a trade consultant, $1000 for her services. The economy's output rises by $1000, and the consultant's revenues rise by $1000. (We will assume that the consultant incurs only negligible costs.) This consultant spends half the amount she earns on a Canadian product and uses the rest for saving, imports, and taxes. In other words, she pays $500 to the supplier of a Canadian product, Spender B, thereby increasing Spender B's income (assuming that B also has negligible costs). The economy's total output has been expanded again by $500, with the remaining $500 withdrawn from the income-spending stream by Spender A in the form of saving, imports, and taxes. Spender B, with his $500 in new income, spends $250 on Canadian products and uses the other $250 on saving, imports, and taxes. His $250 purchase also has an impact on the Canadian economy and provides income to someone else. And it goes on. Any given purchase made by government has an initial effect, a secondary effect, and so on.

As the example illustrates, the inclination to spend and the inclination to save or otherwise withdraw funds from the economy both determine the multiplier effect. These factors are summarized by the concepts of marginal propensity to consume and marginal propensity to withdraw.

Marginal Propensity to Consume

marginal propensity to
consume: the effect on
domestic consumption of a
change in income

The **marginal propensity to consume** (MPC) is the effect on domestic consumption of a change in income and applies to individual households and the economy as a whole. In effect, MPC answers the question: "If income increases this amount, how much extra will be spent on domestic goods and services?" MPC is defined as the change in consumption on domestic products as a proportion of the change in income.

$$MPC = \frac{\text{change in consumption on domestic items}}{\text{change in income}}$$

Marginal Propensity to Withdraw

As the earlier example illustrated, not all income is spent, and what is may not be spent on domestic products. As a result, some income does not reappear in the circular flow. Recall from Chapter 11 that there are three types of withdrawals: saving, taxes, and imports. Part of income is saved, part is paid out in taxes, and part is used to buy imports. The **marginal propensity to withdraw** (MPW) is the effect of a change in income on withdrawals. It is defined as the change in total withdrawals as a proportion of the change in income.

**marginal propensity to
withdraw:** the effect on
withdrawals—saving,
imports, and taxes—of a
change in income

$$MPW = \frac{\text{change in total withdrawals}}{\text{change in income}}$$

Let us consider the concepts of MPC and MPW together. Suppose a person's income rises by $1000. Of that, the consumer spends $300 on domestic products but uses the rest on savings, taxes, and imports. In this case, the marginal propensity to consume is 0.3 ($300 ÷ $1000), while the marginal propensity to withdraw is 0.7 ($700 ÷ $1000). Note the relationship between the values of the marginal propensities to consume and withdraw: their sum equals 1. This is always the case because income is either spent on domestic consumption or withdrawn from the circular flow as saving, imports, or taxes.

$$1 = MPC + MPW$$
$$1 = 0.3 + 0.7$$

To see in detail how the multiplier effect works, let us consider our example of the trade consultant again. The marginal propensities to consume and withdraw in each round, or stage, of spending help to determine the multiplier effect. Figure 12.4 illustrates the example.

FIRST ROUND

Recall that the government pays Spender A, the trade consultant, $1000. Not only does her income rise, but the economy's output also rises by $1000. The effect is illustrated on the left in Figure 12.4.

SECOND ROUND

Spender A starts the second round of spending by using the extra $1000 in income. Because her marginal propensity to consume is 0.5 (= $500 ÷ $1000) and her marginal propensity to withdraw is also 0.5 (= $500 ÷ $1000), she puts an extra $500 into the circular flow but withdraws $500 in the form of saving, imports, and taxes. As a result, the economy's real output undergoes a further rise of $500.

| Figure 12.4 | The Effect of a Rise in Government Purchases |

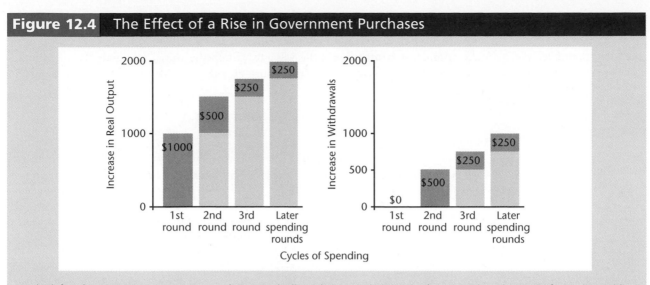

On the left, a $1000 rise in government purchases gradually pushes up real output by $2000, with each round of spending adding successively smaller amounts (as indicated by the darker rectangles). On the right, each successive round of spending involves greater amounts of withdrawals, until new withdrawals equal the initial rise in spending.

THIRD ROUND

Recall that Spender B spends $250 of his $500 in income on domestic products and an equal amount on saving, imports, and taxes. Therefore, Spender B's marginal propensity to consume is 0.5 (= $250 ÷ $500), and his marginal propensity to withdraw is also 0.5 (= $250 ÷ $500). Figure 12.4 shows that he adds another $250 to the economy's real output.

LATER SPENDING ROUNDS

The same process of spending providing income, which is then spent domestically or withdrawn, repeats, with expenditures and withdrawals getting smaller in each round. For example, if the spender in the fourth round also has a marginal propensity to consume of 0.5, another $125 (= $250 × 0.5) will be added to the economy's real output. This process finally ends when real output has risen by a total of $2000.

INJECTIONS AND WITHDRAWALS

To see why total output grows by $2000, let us turn our attention to the withdrawals that have occurred with each spending round, shown on the right in Figure 12.4. Note that with each subsequent round of spending, there are new withdrawals. Eventually, total withdrawals equal $1000. This result can be interpreted in terms of injections and withdrawals, or leakages.

Before the expansionary fiscal policy, the economy was in equilibrium, with injections and withdrawals being equal. As a result of the government's discretionary policy—that is, its $1000 planned increase in government purchases—total injections exceed total withdrawals, causing output to rise. In each round of spending, withdrawals increase. This expansion continues until withdrawals equal the initial discretionary injection. At this point, injections and withdrawals are both $1000 higher than they were before government purchases were increased.

The Spending Multiplier

Now that we have seen the multiplier effect in action, we will give it a numerical value. The **spending multiplier** is the value by which the initial spending change is multiplied to give the total change in output—in other words, the shift in the aggregate demand curve.

$$\text{Total change in output} \atop \text{(shift in AD curve)} = {\text{initial change} \atop \text{in spending}} \times {\text{spending} \atop \text{multiplier}}$$

In our example, because initial spending rose by \$1000 and total output increased by \$2000, the spending multiplier equals 2. This figure can be found by rearranging the above equation to isolate the multiplier:

$$\text{Spending multiplier} = \frac{\text{total change in output (shift in AD curve)}}{\text{initial change in spending}}$$

$$2 = \frac{\$2000}{\$1000}$$

If total output increased instead by \$3000 as a result of a \$1000 rise in government purchases, then the multiplier would be 3 (= \$3000 ÷ \$1000).

To see what determines the value of the spending multiplier, recall that the economy's total output expands until new withdrawals equal the initial government purchase—the new injection. In our original example, the marginal propensity to withdraw was 0.5, meaning that 50 cents were withdrawn for every \$1 of new output in the economy. Output, therefore, had to expand by \$2000 to create the needed \$1000 in new withdrawals, giving a spending multiplier of 2. If the marginal propensity to withdraw had been 0.33, then 33 cents would have been withdrawn for each dollar of new output. Hence, output would have had to increase by \$3000 to create \$1000 in extra withdrawals, giving a spending multiplier equal to 3.

These examples point to the inverse relationship between the marginal propensity to withdraw and the spending multiplier. If MPW is 0.5, the multiplier equals 2. If MPW is 0.33, the multiplier is 3. Therefore, the spending multiplier is the reciprocal of the marginal propensity to withdraw.

$$\text{Spending multiplier} = \frac{1}{\text{MPW}}$$

$$2 = \frac{1}{0.5}$$

EFFECT OF A TAX CUT

The multiplier effect can be applied to the other stimulus that governments use: tax cuts. Recall that tax cuts can be used to expand the economy. Lower taxes leave households and businesses with more funds to spend and invest. In this case, the initial spending stimulus of the tax cut is multiplied by the spending multiplier, or the reciprocal of MPW. The result is an increase in total output, shown as a shift in the aggregate demand curve.

In contrast to government purchases, however, a tax adjustment has a smaller initial effect on spending. Recall our example of a \$1000 government purchase from Spender A. Spender A's initial transaction with the government was added directly to real output before taking into account further rounds of spending. In contrast, if a reduction in taxes increases Spender A's disposable income by \$1000, some of this amount would be withdrawn from the circular flow before its first effect on real output. Only that amount used to buy domestic products represents the initial spending increase. For example, if the marginal propensity to consume is 0.5, then the initial change in spending on domestic items is $500 (= $1000 × 0.5). This $500 spending increase is then multiplied by the spending multiplier, or 2 (1 ÷ 0.5). As a result, the aggregate demand increases by $1000 (= $500 × 2), which is less than the $2000 increase caused by an initial $1000 government purchase.

The effect of a tax change can be summarized in mathematical terms. The initial change in spending on domestic items that results from a change in taxes (T) is found by multiplying the economy's marginal propensity to consume by the size of the tax change, and this product is then multiplied by the economy's spending multiplier (1 ÷ MPW) to derive the overall shift in the aggregate demand curve. And since this spending change is in the opposite direction to the tax change itself, the expression is preceded by a minus sign.

$$
\begin{array}{c}
\text{Total change in output} \\
\text{(shift in AD curve)}
\end{array}
=
\begin{array}{c}
\text{initial change} \\
\text{in spending}
\end{array}
\times
\begin{array}{c}
\text{spending} \\
\text{multiplier}
\end{array}
$$

$$\$1000 = -(\text{MPC} \times \text{change in T}) \times \frac{1}{\text{MPW}}$$

$$\$1000 = -(0.5 \times -\$1000) \times \frac{1}{.05}$$

$$\$1000 = \$500 \times 2$$

RELEVANCE OF THE SPENDING MULTIPLIER

Recall that throughout our discussion of the multiplier effect, we have assumed that the price level is constant. However, what happens to the spending multiplier if price levels vary?

As shown in Figure 12.5, fiscal policy affects the price level as well as output. Recall from Chapter 11 that the slope of the aggregate supply curve is steep as it reaches or surpasses the potential output level. So, as shown in Figure 12.5, when the aggregate demand curve shifts to the right from AD_0 to AD_1, it moves to a steep portion of the aggregate supply curve. In this case, the change in the equilibrium point, from point a to point c, means that while both price levels and output rise, the price level rises proportionally more than output does. So, in general, when the economy is close to its

Figure 12.5   The Multiplier Effect and Price Changes

If spending affected output alone, with a spending multiplier of 1.5, a $20 billion rise in government purchases would push the output from point a to point b. However, since price level is also affected, the shift from AD_0 to AD_1 causes equilibrium to move to point c. Because of the slope of the AS curve, the closer an economy is to its potential, the greater will be the impact of a change in aggregate demand on the price level instead of output.

potential level, the increase in aggregate demand translates into higher price levels more than into expanded production. In other words, with the stated goal being a stable economy and expanded output, expansionary fiscal policy is less effective the closer the economy is to its potential. Similar reasoning applies to contractionary fiscal policy. When the economy is above its potential, a decrease in aggregate demand means that both price level and total output fall. However, price level falls proportionally more than total output does.

In summary, because of possible changes in the price level, the multiplier effect is less definite than the use of a simple formula would indicate. The multiplier calculation is, nonetheless, useful in indicating the *maximum* change in equilibrium output following a certain fiscal policy.

Benefits of Fiscal Policy

Fiscal policy has two benefits as a stabilization tool: its regional focus and its direct impact on spending.

REGIONAL FOCUS

Some parts of Canada may be more affected than others by the business cycle. Fortunately, discretionary fiscal policy can focus on particular regions. For example, during a recession, new government purchases or programs to reduce the amount of tax paid can be targeted to regions where unemployment rates are highest. In a boom, spending cuts and tax hikes can be concentrated on the regions where inflation is at its worst. Similarly, automatic stabilizers have the greatest effect in regions that need them the most. During recessions, net tax revenues drop most in regions hardest hit by unemployment and falling output. For example, the greatest rise in Employment Insurance payments is in areas with the highest growth in unemployment. During booms, the largest increase in net tax revenues occurs in regions where the economy is most overheated. For example, revenues from personal income tax expand most quickly in areas where employment and incomes are most buoyant.

IMPACT ON SPENDING

As indicated by the previous discussion of the multiplier effect, the influence of a stabilization policy is tied to its initial effect on spending. Monetary policy influences spending through a fairly elaborate chain of events. In contrast, fiscal policy has a more straightforward impact—at least when altering government purchases. The first spending adjustment is then assured, since the government itself initiates the change.

THINKING ABOUT ECONOMICS

How large is the spending multiplier in the Canadian economy?

Several estimates of the Canadian spending multiplier have been made. The average value is about 1.5. If this figure is correct, then, as Figure 12.5 illustrates, a $20 billion jump in government purchases shifts the aggregate demand curve to the right by $30 billion. However, given the positive slope of the aggregate supply curve, this change means a rise in the price level as well as in total output. In this case, output would rise by $25 billion.

Question
Why has the value of Canada's spending multiplier fallen in recent decades?

Drawbacks of Fiscal Policy

Offsetting the benefits of fiscal policy are three main drawbacks: policy delays, the political visibility of this policy, and its effects on public debt.

DELAYS

While automatic stabilizers work promptly to stabilize the economy, discretionary measures are sometimes delayed. Three time lags can slow down fiscal policy-makers: the recognition lag, the decision lag, and the impact lag.

The **recognition lag** is the amount of time it takes policy-makers to realize that a policy is needed. Suppose that economic growth suddenly slows. A few months may pass before statistical evidence of this becomes available. It may then take several more months for policy-makers to decide whether this represents a minor fluctuation or the start of a recession.

The **decision lag** is the period that passes while an appropriate response is formulated and implemented. Suppose policy-makers have decided that, indeed, the economy is entering a recession. They must then decide what to do about it. Should they increase government purchases, reduce taxes, or use some combination of the two measures? Once they have decided, the policy must be passed into law and included in a budget.

Finally, once the policy is implemented, there is an **impact lag**—the time that elapses between implementing the policy and its having an effect on the economy. In the case of government spending to combat a recession, for example, many rounds of spending must take place before the full multiplier effect is felt in the economy.

As a result of these time lags, a year or more may pass between the cause and the effect of a fiscal policy. Meanwhile, the economy may already have moved to a completely different point in the business cycle. In the extreme case, the use of fiscal policy may worsen the business cycle by stimulating output during upswings and suppressing it during downturns.

POLITICAL VISIBILITY

Discretionary fiscal policy is a highly visible element of government activity. Not surprisingly, therefore, it is often affected by political as well as economic considerations. Voters are likely to respond more favourably to increases in government purchases and cuts in taxes than they are to spending decreases and tax hikes, regardless of the appropriateness of these policies for the economy. As a result, political parties understandably favour expansionary fiscal policy, especially when an election is coming up.

PUBLIC DEBT

While there remains a political bias towards expansionary policy, the federal government has used stimulative measures more sparingly in recent recessions. This reluctance to increase government purchases or decrease taxes is related to Canada's **public debt**, which is the total amount owed by the federal government as a result of its past borrowing. This differs from total government debt, which includes the debts of individual provinces and territories—and sometimes incorporates local governments and hospitals as well. Given the recent growth in provincial debt, this distinction can be important. Public debt, which is owed by Canadian taxpayers to owners of Canadian government bonds, totalled $507.7 billion at the start of 2002.

The federal government spends large sums related to its debt. **Public debt charges** are the amounts paid out each year by the federal government to cover the interest charges on its public debt. Just as payments of interest on a bank loan do not

---

recognition lag: the amount of time it takes policy-makers to realize that a policy is needed

decision lag: the amount of time needed to formulate and implement an appropriate policy

impact lag: the amount of time between a policy's implementation and its having an effect on the economy

public debt: the total amount owed by the federal government as a result of its past borrowing

public debt charges: the amounts paid out each year by the federal government to cover the interest charges on its public debt reduce the principal of the loan, public debt charges do not reduce the overall size of the public debt.

In 2002–2003, for example, the federal government's public debt charges were $37.2 billion. This figure represented an average interest rate of about 7 percent [($37.2 billion ÷ $507.7 billion) × 100%] that the federal government paid to the bondholders who owned its $507.7 billion debt.

Public debt grew rapidly in recent decades so that now public debt charges are by far the largest single expenditure made by the federal government. In 2002–2003, for example, over a fifth of every federal tax dollar went to pay interest on Canada's public debt. Because the government has not yet been able to significantly reduce the public debt, when an individual bondholder cashes in a Canadian government bond, the government replaces the funds by selling more bonds. Starting in the 1990s, worries over this trend have constrained the use of expansionary fiscal policy. As a result, such a policy—which has the potential to increase Canada's public debt further—has been used less.

Brief Review

1. The multiplier effect—the magnified impact of fiscal policy on aggregate demand—is determined by the marginal propensity to consume and the marginal propensity to withdraw.

2. Assuming a constant price level, the spending multiplier is the value by which an initial spending change is multiplied to give the total change in real output.

3. Because a new injection brings about new withdrawals that equal the initial injection, the spending multiplier is the reciprocal of the marginal propensity to withdraw.

4. In the case of a tax cut, the initial spending adjustment is less than the change in taxes because a portion of the tax cut represents withdrawals from the circular flow of spending and income.

5. While fiscal policy can target certain regions and have a direct impact on spending, it also suffers from delays, problems associated with political visibility, and its impact on public debt.

12.2 Practice Questions

1   a.   If an economy is initially in equilibrium and injections rise by $1 million, then by how much will withdrawals have to rise in order to bring injections and withdrawals back in balance?
    b.   If the economy's MPW is 0.67 then by how much will incomes and output have to rise to create the required additional expenditures?
    c.   Explain how your answer to part b. is based on the formula for the spending multiplier.

2.   For each of the following cases, calculate the spending multiplier and state the direction and size of the shift in the AD curve.
    a.   Government purchases fall by $10 billion in an economy with an MPW of 0.60.
    b.   A tax cut causes an initial $25 billion rise in spending in an economy with an MPW of 0.80.
    c.   Government purchases rise by $15 billion in an economy with an MPC of 0.25.
    d.   A $30 billion tax rise occurs in an economy with an MPC of 0.45.

Impact of Fiscal Policy

LO 12.3

balanced budget: the situation where a government's expenditures and revenues are equal

budget surplus: the situation where a government's revenues exceed its expenditures

budget deficit: the situation where a government's expenditures exceed its revenues

Budget Surpluses and Deficits

Government expenditures and revenues are affected both by discretionary fiscal policy and by the workings of automatic stabilizers. In the rare case where a government's expenditures and revenues are equal, the government is running a **balanced budget**.

In general, government expenditures and revenues are not equal. When a government's revenues exceed its expenditures, there is a **budget surplus**. For example, in 2002-2003, the federal government's total expenditures were $175.8 billion, and its total revenues were $178.7 billion. Therefore, the budget surplus was $3.0 billion.

$$\text{Budget surplus} = \text{government revenues} - \text{government expenditures}$$
$$\$3.0 \text{ billion} = \$178.7 \text{ billion} - \$175.8 \text{ billion}$$

In contrast, when a government's expenditures exceed its revenues, there is a **budget deficit**. For example, in 1996–1997, the federal government's total expenditures were $149.8 billion, and its total revenues were $140.9 billion. Therefore, the budget deficit was $8.9 billion:

$$\text{Budget deficit} = \text{government expenditures} - \text{government revenues}$$
$$\$8.9 \text{ billion} = \$149.8 \text{ billion} - \$140.9 \text{ billion}$$

The size of a government's surplus or deficit in relation to the economy's overall GDP gives an indication of what type of discretionary fiscal policy is in operation, as well as the built-in effects of automatic stabilizers.

For example, the federal government's $3.0 billion budget surplus in the 2002-2003 fiscal year was 0.3 percent (= $3.0 billion ÷ $1154.9 billion) of the 2002 nominal GDP of $1154.9 billion. In contrast, the $8.9 billion budget deficit in the 1996–1997 fiscal year was 1.1 percent (= $8.9 billion ÷ $833.1 billion) of the 1996 nominal GDP of $833.1 billion.

A government's deficit should not be confused with its debt. A budget deficit occurs when a government's expenditures exceed its revenue during a given period. The government's debt, on the other hand, represents the sum of all its past budget deficits minus any budget surpluses.

SURPLUSES

In some unusual cases, budget surpluses are related to discretionary fiscal policy. For example, a government might decide to suppress the inflationary effects of an economic boom by cutting defence spending and raising income taxes. However, it is more likely that budget surpluses are the result of built-in factors. During a boom, for example, rising tax revenues that outweigh transfer payments can cause provincial budgets to show a surplus.

DEFICITS

Budget deficits sometimes indicate active expansionary policies that increase government expenditures or reduce revenues. During an economic downturn, for example, the federal government may increase its spending on roads and bridges, or it may institute a temporary sales-tax cut to stimulate household spending. Budget deficits more often come about as a result of automatic stabilizers. For instance, fewer jobs and less spending during a recession lead to rising Employment Insurance benefits and sagging income tax revenues. Both these trends push the federal budget into a deficit position.

IMPACT ON PUBLIC DEBT

Because federal surpluses and deficits have not balanced each other in the long run, they have had a tremendous impact on the size of Canada's public debt. When the federal government has a budget deficit, which in the past has been most common, the public debt increases by the same amount. For example, Canada's public debt at the start of the 1996-1997 fiscal year was $574.3 billion. Because the federal government ran a budget deficit of $8.9 billion in 1996–1997, its public debt at the start of the 1997–1998 fiscal year increased to $583.2 billion (= $574.3 billion + $8.9 billion). In the case of a federal budget surplus, the public debt can be reduced by the same amount. For example, when the federal government ran a $3.0 billion budget surplus in 2002–2003, its public debt was reduced from $507.7 billion at the beginning of the fiscal year to $504.7 billion (= $507.7 billion − $3.0 billion) at the beginning of the next fiscal year.

Fiscal Policy Guidelines

There are three principles that guide government fiscal policy: annually balanced budgets, cyclically balanced budgets, and functional finance.

ANNUALLY BALANCED BUDGETS

Those who criticize government intervention in the economy tend not to support fiscal policy. In general, these critics suggest that any fiscal policy that is used must be guided by the principle of an **annually balanced budget**. In other words, revenues and expenditures should balance every year. So, for example, new spending programs must be matched with higher taxes. In essence, by advocating an annually balanced budget, these critics dismiss active fiscal policy as an option.

Opponents of this principle suggest that it is based on faulty reasoning. While an annually balanced budget might make sense for a particular household, it is not necessarily appropriate for society as a whole. After all, the business cycle does not span one year, but many. During an economic contraction, for example, tax revenues decrease. To balance the budget, a government would have to reduce government purchases, thereby worsening the slump in spending. This problem occurred during the early years of the Great Depression in Canada.

annually balanced budget: the principle that government revenues and expenditures should balance each year

CYCLICALLY BALANCED BUDGETS

A less stringent principle—and one that has more supporters—is that of a **cyclically balanced budget**. In other words, government revenues and expenditures need not be balanced every year, but they should balance over one business cycle. The deficits from periods of contraction should roughly equal the surpluses from periods of expansion.

cyclically balanced budget: the principle that government revenues and expenditures should balance over the course of one business cycle

FUNCTIONAL FINANCE

The principle of **functional finance** stems from the view that policy-makers should concern themselves primarily with correcting fluctuations caused by the business cycle. Rather than trying to balance budgets either annually or over the business cycle, governments should base a year's fiscal policy on the needs of the economy.

functional finance: the principle that government budgets should be geared to the yearly needs of the economy

In practice, the choice of fiscal policy guidelines depends on the government's belief in fiscal policy as an effective tool for stabilizing the economy. The defenders of functional finance are those who see fiscal policy as a powerful stabilization tool, while economists who back a cyclically or annually balanced budget tend to be less convinced of fiscal policy's effectiveness.

Recent Fiscal Policy

The predominant view of fiscal policy in Canada has undergone a profound change since the mid-1980s. Similar changes have taken place in other developed economies. In the 1970s and early 1980s, functional finance was the guiding principle behind fiscal policy in Canada and many other countries. Since then, there have been attempts to move towards cyclically balanced budgets.

In Canada, this change in view relates primarily to past budget deficits and their impact on the economy as a whole. Figure 12.6 shows the combined budget balance of the federal, provincial, and territorial governments as a proportion of Canada's nominal GDP for the years 1980–1981 to 2000–2001. For example, in relation to Canada's 2000 nominal GDP of $1065.0 billion, the federal government's $18.1 billion budget surplus in 2000–2001 was 1.7 percent [(= $18.1 billion ÷ $1065.0 billion) × 100%]. Similarly, the provincial and territorial governments, when viewed as a single unit, had a combined budget surplus in 2000–2001 of $12.0 billion, which as a share of nominal GDP was 1.1 percent [(= $12.0 billion ÷ $1065.0 billion) × 100%]. Therefore, the sum for both levels of government was 2.8 percent of nominal GDP. Because this period spans two recessions and two periods of expansion, it illustrates the changing view of fiscal policy.

Total government deficits were highest during the periods corresponding to the recessions of the early 1980s and early 1990s. However, there were significant differences in fiscal policy. During and just after the slump of the early 1980s, the overall budget deficits of Canadian governments were about 10 percent of Canada's nominal GDP. The budget deficits of the lower levels of government, which were relatively small, came about largely because of automatic stabilizers as tax revenues fell with slumping output and incomes. The large federal deficits were due not only to automatic stabilizers but also to the use of discretionary expansionary policy by government policy-makers. In particular, the federal government increased purchases of goods and services to counteract the effects of sagging output and incomes.

Figure 12.6   Budget Balances Relative to GDP

The budget balances for the federal, provincial, and territorial governments combined are shown as percentages of Canada's nominal GDP. Recessions in the early 1980s and early 1990s each caused an increase in combined budget deficits. During the long economic expansion of the 1990s, these deficits gradually declined and turned to a combined surplus.

Source: Department of Finance, *Fiscal Reference Tables* (October 2002), pp. 10, 36. Reproduced by authority of the Ministry of Industry, 2004.

Following the recession of the early 1980s, the Canadian economy experienced a prolonged period of economic growth, with first a recovery and then a boom occurring in the later years of the decade. By 1988, when the unemployment rate was under 8 percent, the Canadian economy was near its potential output. Despite these boom conditions, budgets did not show an overall surplus. In fact, the combined deficits of the federal, provincial, and territorial governments were still about 5 percent of nominal GDP in 1988 and 1989.

During and just after the downturn of the early 1990s, the combined deficits of the lower levels of government were much more significant in comparison with the size of the federal deficit. As a result, the overall budget deficits of all levels of government were again nearly 10 percent of Canada's nominal GDP. However, these deficits were less a result of discretionary policy than of automatic stabilizers. This difference resulted from worry over the increased public debt and reduced confidence in the effectiveness of discretionary fiscal policies to counteract a recession. As the economy expanded during another long expansion in the mid- and late 1990s, the impact of automatic stabilizers, falling interest rates, and spending cuts by all levels of government led to the emergence of an overall budget surplus for Canadian governments. Not even the faltering economic growth rates of the early 2000s could eradicate this surplus.

THINKING ABOUT
ECONOMICS

Why, until recently, have budget deficits been so common for Canadian governments through all phases of the business cycle?

Many observers believe that in the early 1990s Canada entered a harmful deficit–debt spiral. Large federal budget deficits expanded Canada's public debt, which, in turn, raised annual interest payments on the public debt. The same trend was also noticeable for provincial governments. Greater debt charges for all levels of government increased their spending, which, in turn, raised deficits even more. Without the deficit-cutting measures pursued by all levels of government in the mid-1990s, this trend could have led to even higher government deficits and debt levels in the future.

Question
What benefits can arise from a protracted period of budget surpluses?

Brief Review

1. When government expenditures equal revenues, the budget is balanced. Budget surpluses occur when revenues exceed expenditures. When expenditures exceed revenues, there is a budget deficit.

2. Fiscal policy may be based on three possible guidelines: annually balanced budgets, cyclically balanced budgets, or functional finance. At the federal level, functional finance had been the guiding principle in Canada since the 1970s, although cyclically balanced budgets are increasingly favoured.

3. Between the early 1980s and late 1990s repeated budget deficits—in periods of both expansion and contraction—caused Canada's government debt to balloon.

12.3 Practice Questions

1. A government has an outstanding debt of $100 billion.
   a. If, in a given year, the government spends $10 billion and brings in $15 billion in taxes, then what is the government's budget deficit or surplus, and what happens to its debt?
   b. If, instead, the government's expenditures are $12.5 billion and its tax revenues are $10 billion, then what is the government's budget deficit or surplus, and what happens to its debt?

2. Outline a potential advantage and a potential problem with each of the three fiscal policy guidelines:
   a. annually balanced budgets
   b. cyclically balanced budgets
   c. functional finance

LAST**WORD**

In this chapter, we have seen how governments can use their own spending and taxation decisions to affect the price level or real output in the entire economy. We have seen how such discretionary actions can have an amplified impact through the workings of the spending multiplier and how established government spending and taxation programs, such as Employment Insurance and welfare, help stabilize economic activity, even without the use of discretionary fiscal policy. In the next chapter, we begin our analysis of the monetary and financial components of the economy in order to see how these elements offer government policy-makers another set of tools in pursuing stabilization policy.

Key Concepts

annually balanced budget 294
automatic stabilizers 283
balanced budget 293
budget deficit 293
budget surplus 293
contractionary fiscal policy 282
contractionary policies 281
cyclically balanced budget 294

decision lag 291
discretionary policy 283
expansionary fiscal policy 282
expansionary policies 281
fiscal policy 281
fiscal year 281
functional finance 294
impact lag 291
marginal propensity to consume 286

marginal propensity to withdraw 286
monetary policy 281
multiplier effect 285
net tax revenues 283
public debt 291
public debt charges 291
recognition lag 291
spending multiplier 288
stabilization policy 281

Questions

1. In each of the following cases, state whether the economy faces a recessionary or inflationary gap, outline possible fiscal policies, and explain how each of these policies affect aggregate demand:
   a. The unemployment rate is 5.5 percent, and inflation is rising.
   b. Real output is falling, and unemployment is 9.5 percent.
   c. The unemployment rate is 6.5 percent, and prices are stable.

2. In each of the following cases, calculate the values of MPC, MPW, and the spending multiplier:
   a. A $1 million increase in income leads to a $350 000 rise in consumption on domestic items.
   b. A $4 million decrease in income results in a $1 million drop in consumption on domestic items.
   c. A $5 million decrease in income causes a $3 million drop in withdrawals.

3. "The more regressive Canada's tax system, the less effective automatic stabilizers become." Discuss.

4. Assume that Canadian governments tax away 40 cents of each dollar of new income, that 30 percent of the remaining 60 cents of disposable income is spent on imports, and that 5 percent of disposable income is saved.
   a. What is the value of the marginal propensity to withdraw?
   b. How much of each new dollar of income is spent on domestic consumption items?
   c. What is the value of the Canadian spending multiplier?

5. Draw charts similar to those in Figure 12.4 to show the changes in real output and withdrawals that occur in the first three spending rounds when there is a $810 increase in government purchases in an economy with an MPC of 0.33.

6. For each of the following cases, calculate the spending multiplier and find the direction and size of the shift in the AD curve:
   a. Government purchases increase by $2 billion in an economy with an MPW of 0.65.
   b. Government purchases decrease by $5 billion in an economy with an MPC of 0.45.
   c. A $3 billion tax rise occurs in an economy with an MPW of 0.7.
   d. A $4 billion tax cut causes an initial $1.5 billion increase in spending on domestic items.

7. A decrease in government purchases of $8 billion leads to an initial $4.4 billion decrease in withdrawals.
   a. Find the values of MPW, MPC, and the spending multiplier in this economy.
   b. State the direction and size of the shift in the AD curve.
   c. Draw a graph showing the policy's possible effects, given an initial equilibrium price level and real output of 130 and $650 billion.

8. Explain the effects of a rise in personal and corporate tax rates on (a) the equilibrium real output and price level, (b) the spending multiplier, and (c) the effectiveness of automatic stabilizers in smoothing out the business cycle.

9. Provincial governments sometimes pursue discretionary fiscal policies. How does the spending multiplier for this type of policy within a provincial economy differ from the corresponding multiplier for federal fiscal policy within the entire Canadian economy? Explain.

10. With the aid of aggregate demand/aggregate supply graphs, outline how the principle of an annually balanced budget can increase the severity of recessionary and inflationary gaps through the business cycle.

11. Explain how a series of federal budget surpluses can lead to a spiral of larger surpluses and rapidly decreasing public debt.

12. (Advanced Question)
    Using two aggregate demand/aggregate supply graphs, show why the estimate of potential output is so crucial in determining the size of an economy's recessionary and inflationary gaps.

Internet Application Questions

http://www.fin.gc.ca/

http://www.statcan.ca/english/Estat/licence. htm

1. Access the Department of Finance's website (at http://www.fin.gc.ca/) and use the links provided to find the most recent budget documents for the federal government.
    a. Explain how the annual federal deficit or surplus is related to changes forecast in net public debt in the current fiscal year.
    b. Is net public debt expected to rise or fall relative to GDP in the current year? Explain.

2. Access Statistics Canada's E-Stat site (at http://www.statcan.ca/english/Estat/licence. htm).
    a. Using the information found in "National Accounts," generate a two-dimensional graph showing net current government expenditure on goods and services as a percentage of expenditure-based GDP (each expressed as an adjusted annual average) in the years starting in 1981.
    b. What does your graph in part a say about the shifts in fiscal policy by Canadian governments in the 1980s and 1990s?

APPENDIX

The Aggregate Expenditures Model and Government

The Impact of Government

Government is incorporated in the aggregate expenditures model by including both government purchases and taxes. We will assume that government purchases (G) are $200 billion at every GDP level. Likewise, taxes (T) are a lump-sum amount of $200 billion—which remains constant regardless of GDP.

THE SPENDING-OUTPUT APPROACH

Using the spending-output approach, government purchases have a direct effect on aggregate expenditures, as portrayed on the top graph and in the table in Figure A, with the AE line raised by $200 billion from AE_0 to AE_1. Taxes have an indirect impact on aggregate expenditures, through their impact on disposable income. The $200 billion lump-sum tax reduces disposable income at each GDP level by $200 billion. With an MPC of 0.75, consumption at every GDP level drops by $150 billion (–$200 billion multiplied by 0.75). Therefore, the AE line shifts down by $150 billion from AE_1 to AE_2.

The impact of government purchases and taxes can be combined to derive the overall effect on the AE line. Given the line's $200 billion upward shift due to government purchases from AE_0 to AE_1, and its $150 billion downward shift with the tax-induced drop in consumption from AE_1 to AE_2, its overall shift is upward by $50 billion ($200 billion – $150 billion), from AE_0 to AE_2. The effect on equilibrium GDP, as shown in the graph, is an expansion from $1.0 trillion to $1200 billion (from points *a* to *c*).

THE INJECTIONS-WITHDRAWALS APPROACH

The change in equilibrium GDP using the injections-withdrawals approach is shown on the lower graph and in the table of Figure A. The addition of government purchases shifts total injections (now the I+G+X line) upwards by $200 billion. Meanwhile, taxes have a double effect on withdrawals. First, total withdrawals shift upwards by $200 billion from S_0+M to S_0+T+M due to the incorporation of the $200 billion in taxes at every GDP level. But total withdrawals also shift down by $50 billion, from S_0+T+M to S_1+T+M, because the $200 billion drop in the economy's disposable income causes saving at every GDP level to fall by $50 billion (–$200 billion multiplied by the MPS of 0.25). Overall, there is a $150 billion upward shift in total withdrawals, from S_0+M to S_1+T+M, producing an equality of total injections and total withdrawals at point *d*, corresponding to the new equilibrium GDP level of $1200 billion.

The Balanced Budget Multiplier

The $200 billion increase in total output from $1 trillion to $1200 billion illustrates what happens when a government moves from one balanced budget to another—in this case, from a position where G and T both equal zero, to a position where G and T equal $200 billion. With the aid of the aggregate expenditures model, we can see that the change in equilibrium GDP is the very same amount as the change in the balanced budget: with the increase in G and T of $200 billion, equilibrium GDP rises by $200 billion as well.

This relationship is captured by the **balanced budget multiplier**, or the value by which the change in G (or the equivalent change in T) is multiplied to find the resulting change in equilibrium GDP. The balanced budget multiplier can be derived by

balanced-budget multiplier: the value by which an identical change in G and T is multiplied to find the resulting change in equilibrium GDP

Figure A The Impact of Government

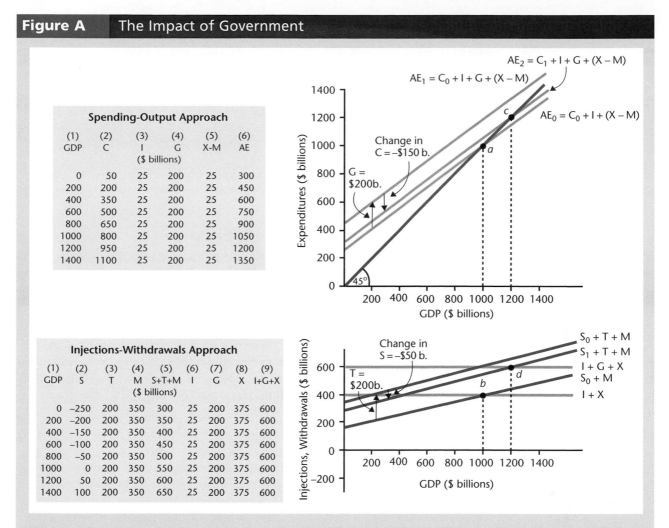

Spending-Output Approach

(1) GDP	(2) C	(3) I	(4) G	(5) X-M	(6) AE
		($ billions)			
0	50	25	200	25	300
200	200	25	200	25	450
400	350	25	200	25	600
600	500	25	200	25	750
800	650	25	200	25	900
1000	800	25	200	25	1050
1200	950	25	200	25	1200
1400	1100	25	200	25	1350

Injections-Withdrawals Approach

(1) GDP	(2) S	(3) T	(4) M	(5) S+T+M	(6) I	(7) G	(8) X	(9) I+G+X
				($ billions)				
0	-250	200	350	300	25	200	375	600
200	-200	200	350	350	25	200	375	600
400	-150	200	350	400	25	200	375	600
600	-100	200	350	450	25	200	375	600
800	-50	200	350	500	25	200	375	600
1000	0	200	350	550	25	200	375	600
1200	50	200	350	600	25	200	375	600
1400	100	200	350	650	25	200	375	600

With $200 billion in G and T, the AE line shifts up by an overall amount of $50 billion, raising equilibrium GDP to $1200 billion (at point c) using the spending-output approach in the top diagram. Using the injection-withdrawals approach, as shown in the lower diagram, total injections shift up by $200 billion, while total withdrawals shift up by an overall amount of $150 billion. Again equilibrium GDP rises to $1200 billion (at point d).

analyzing the output effects of the change in government purchases and the change in taxes. The impact of the change in government purchases is found by multiplying the initial change in spending (the change in G) by the spending multiplier (1 ÷ MPW):

$$\text{Total change in output} = \text{change in G} \times (1 \div \text{MPW})$$

In contrast, the initial change in spending caused by the tax change is in the opposite direction to the tax change itself. For example, a tax increase causes disposable income to fall. The resulting drop in consumption spending is found by multiplying the economy's marginal propensity to consume by the size of the tax increase. This expression is preceded by a minus sign, to show that the tax increase causes a reduction in spending, and is then multiplied by the spending multiplier (1 ÷ MPW).

$$\text{Total change in output} = -(\text{MPC} \times \text{change in T}) \times (1 \div \text{MPW})$$

Combining these two formulas, and keeping in mind that the change in G equals the change in T, the balanced budget multiplier is derived by adding the two right-hand sides of the formulas to find the combined total change in output.

Total change in output = [change in G × (1 ÷ MPW)] + [−(MPC × change in T) × (1 ÷ MPW)]

The spending multiplier (1 ÷ MPW) can be factored out of both expressions on the right-hand side of the expression.

Total change in output = [(1 − MPC)(change in G or T)] × (1 ÷ MPW)

Finally, the spending multiplier (1 ÷ MPW) can be combined with the first bracketed expression (1 − MPC) on the right-hand side of the expression.

Total change in output = [(1 − MPC) ÷ MPW] × (change in G or T)
= [(1 − 0.75) ÷ 0.25] × ($200 billion)

Because MPC and MPW sum to equal 1, (1 − MPC) is identical with MPW. The expression can, therefore, be simplified further:

Total change in output = balanced budget multiplier (1) × (change in G or T)

As shown by this last formula, the value of the balanced budget multiplier is always 1, which means that an identical change in government purchases and taxes need merely be multiplied by 1 to find the overall change in output.

Aggregate Demand and Aggregate Supply

How can this analysis be interpreted using the model of aggregate demand and aggregate supply? So far we have been assuming that the price level is constant. But when seen in terms of the more complete model of aggregate demand and aggregate supply, the balanced budget multiplier allows us to calculate the shift in the AD curve that results from an identical change in government purchases and lump-sum taxes.

Once changes in the price level are taken into account, the overall change in equilibrium real GDP in an economy with flexible prices will depend on the nature of the economy's AS curve. Only if the AS curve is horizontal does the aggregate expenditures model give a complete answer, as shown in Figure B. Otherwise, the actual change in equilibrium real GDP will be less than the change using the aggregate expenditures model. This includes any output changes found using the balanced budget multiplier. But as long as this limitation is kept in mind, the aggregate expenditures model provides a useful tool for analyzing the impact of fiscal policy.

Brief Review

1. When government is introduced, government purchases shift up the AE line, but at the same time, the AE line shifts down as taxes cause a reduction in disposable income and consumption. Using the injections-withdrawals approach, government purchases shift up total injections. At the same time, taxes shift up total withdrawals directly, but indirectly shift down withdrawals due to the reduction in disposable income and saving.

2. According to the balanced budget multiplier, an identical change in both government purchases and taxes will cause the very same change in equilibrium GDP. The value of the balanced budget multiplier, therefore, is 1.

Figure B   Aggregate Demand and Aggregate Supply

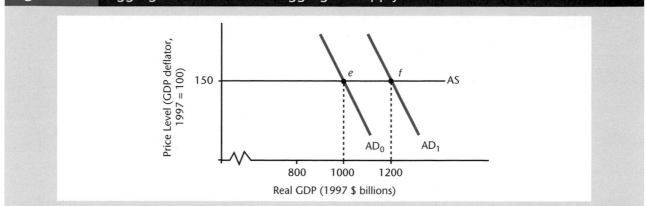

When seen in terms of the model of aggregate demand and aggregate supply, in which the price level is flexible, the impact of incorporating $200 billion in both government purchases and taxes will be a $200 billion rightward shift in the AD curve from AD_0 to AD_1. The resulting change in equilibrium real GDP will also be $200 billion only if the AS curve is horizontal, as shown by the movement from points *e* to *f*.

Questions

1. a.   Using both the spending-output and injections-withdrawals approaches, show what would happen to the hypothetical economy outlined in this appendix if the levels of government purchases and taxes both rose from $200 billion to $400 billion.

    b.   Can your answer to part a. be found using the balanced budget multiplier? Explain.

    c.   In what way must your answer to part a. be adjusted once changes in the price level are taken into account? Explain using a graph of aggregate demand and aggregate supply.

2. John Maynard Keynes used the analysis found in the aggregate expenditures model to argue that an increase in saving might be harmful, given its effect on equilibrium GDP.

    a.   Taking the case of a private economy with no government purchases or taxes, use the injections-withdrawals approach to illustrate his argument.

    b.   Is it reasonable, on the basis of this analysis, to argue that an increase in saving is always harmful to the economy? Explain.

Key Concepts   balanced-budget multiplier 300

ECONOMIST EXTRAORDINAIRE

John Maynard Keynes and the Transformation of Macroeconomics

John Maynard Keynes
Source: ©Bettmann/CORBIS/Magma

Keynes and His Influence

The best blueprint for a model economist comes from the past century's most illustrious one—John Maynard Keynes (1883–1946). An Englishman, he was a well-rounded and energetic individual who wrote on mathematics, formulated economic policy as an adviser to the British government and a director of its central bank, and served as a representative at international conferences, such as the Paris Peace Conference that ended World War I. On top of all this, Keynes found time to be a college administrator, edit a major economics journal, produce theatre, chair an insurance company, and serve as an investment trust manager, while accumulating a considerable personal fortune through his own investments.[1]

Keynes came from a privileged background—his father was an economist, and his mother was a city politician. After attending the exclusive boarding school Eton, Keynes studied mathematics at Cambridge University, where he began a lifelong association with the Bloomsbury Group, an influential circle of English writers and artists with a shared taste for the unconventional and a reputation for snobbery.

In response to the Great Depression plaguing North America and Europe, Keynes published his book *The General Theory of Employment, Interest, and Money*. By 1936, when the book was published, millions of jobless people had given up hopes of finding work, and capitalism seemed to many to be on the verge of self-destruction, just as Karl Marx had predicted decades earlier. There was a widespread call for government intervention to combat the Depression. Keynes, however, went one step further: he supported the call for government intervention with a coherent theory, which stressed the role played by aggregate demand in determining output in the macroeconomy.

Keynes and his followers were able to convince most politicians and economists that action was needed. The government programs they advocated were later viewed as crucial in hastening the end of the Depression. Keynesian ideas dominated macroeconomics from after World War II to the 1970s, when events brought about a new period of questioning and debate.

Neoclassical Theory

Prior to Keynes' influence, most economists held the opinion that economic slow-downs—even those as severe as the Great Depression—were self-correcting. This view of the economy, referred to as neoclassical theory, is based on two major assumptions: flexible labour markets and Say's Law.

Flexible Labour Markets   According to neoclassical economists, both the demand and supply of labour depend on the real wage rate, or wages expressed in constant base-year dollars, rather than the nominal wage rate, which is valued in current dollars. Neither workers nor employers are fooled by price changes; therefore, they adjust their behaviour only when the purchasing power of wages changes. Employers demand less labour at higher real wage rates, while workers choose to supply more. As Figure A illustrates, the labour market can be shown using the demand and supply curves D_L and S_L.

Neoclassical economists distinguished between two types of unemployment: voluntary and involuntary. Voluntary unemployment exists whenever workers decide that real

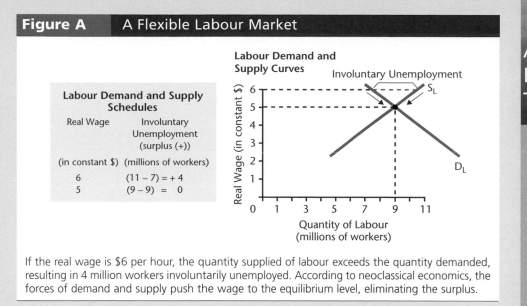

Figure A	A Flexible Labour Market

Labour Demand and Supply Schedules

Real Wage	Involuntary Unemployment (surplus (+))
(in constant $)	(millions of workers)
6	(11 − 7) = + 4
5	(9 − 9) = 0

If the real wage is $6 per hour, the quantity supplied of labour exceeds the quantity demanded, resulting in 4 million workers involuntarily unemployed. According to neoclassical economics, the forces of demand and supply push the wage to the equilibrium level, eliminating the surplus.

wages are not high enough to make work worthwhile. In contrast, involuntary unemployment—when someone wants to work at the current real wage rate but cannot find a job—is of much greater concern to policy-makers. According to neoclassical economics, involuntary unemployment occurs when market demand and supply create a surplus—for example, at a $6 real wage rate, as shown in Figure A. As long as labour markets are flexible, the market forces of demand and supply eradicate the surplus—for example, when market forces push wages towards an equilibrium point of $5. Because markets are flexible, involuntary unemployment is no more than a short-run problem.

Say's Law   Neoclassical economists also assumed that periods of underspending in the economy are short-lived. Their view was based on a principle known as Say's Law, first outlined by the French economist Jean-Baptiste Say. Using the circular flow of money in the economy, Say argued that supply automatically creates its own demand; that is, we produce goods and services in order to purchase others. A tailor makes clothes, for example, in order to have funds to buy other products.

Even if some of these funds are withdrawn from the circular flow, the production of goods and services generates enough funds to purchase them, as long as total withdrawals and total injections are equal. Neoclassical economists believed that this occurred because total withdrawals and injections can be equal *at any output*. According to their view, interest rates charged in financial markets will vary until withdrawals leaving the circular flow are matched by injections. Therefore, reduced spending is only temporary; total expenditures and production soon balance each other out.

Keynesian Theory

Keynes challenged both assumptions of the neoclassical economists. Having done so, he provided a theory that explained how involuntary unemployment and underspending had become chronic problems during the Depression.

Challenge to Flexible Labour Markets   Keynes believed, unlike the neoclassical economists, that workers are influenced by *money illusion*. By this, he meant that workers respond to changes in nominal wages rather than in real wages and purchasing power.

ADVANCING
ECONOMIC
THOUGHT

Consider a case in which prices fall, as they did during the Great Depression. If the price level drops by 10 percent, workers should not mind if their nominal wages are cut by 10 percent as well because real wages and purchasing power are not affected. However, workers *do* mind, according to Keynes. Workers see a decrease in nominal income as a drop in living standards, and trade unions tend to reject nominal wage cuts. Therefore, the nominal wage rate does not move despite downward pressure.

Figure B illustrates Keynes' view of labour markets. The quantity demanded and supplied of labour both vary with the nominal wage rate. Because the nominal wage will not decrease despite market pressure, the involuntary unemployment caused by a nominal wage, such as $8, can last indefinitely. Only if there is an increase in spending, shifting demand to the right, will this unemployment be reduced.

Figure B	An Inflexible Labour Market

Labour Demand and Supply Schedules

Nominal Wage	Involuntary Unemployment
(in current $)	(surplus(+)) (millions of workers)
8	(12 − 8) = +4
7	(10 − 10) = 0

At a nominal wage of $8 per hour, 4 million workers are involuntarily unemployed. According to Keynesian economics, because these nominal wages will not respond to downward pressure, the market does not move towards the equilibrium wage of $/ per hour. Instead, involuntary unemployment persists.

Challenge to Say's Law   Keynes proved that despite its superficial appeal, Say's Law is not always valid. Output levels—not interest rates—adjust to bring about a balance between total injections and withdrawals. When injections are less than withdrawals, output falls until a new equilibrium level is reached. It is only *at this equilibrium output* that Say's Law is true, with injections and withdrawals the same. Also, this output is quite possibly associated with high unemployment. Hence, Keynes concluded that underspending is not necessarily self-correcting. So, governments must step in to create the needed jobs.

Note
[1] D.E. Moggridge, *Keynes* (London: Macmillan, 1976), p. 12.

1. Outline how the neoclassical economists and Keynes would differ in their interpretation of the following trends:
   a. A fall in wages (measured in both real and nominal terms)
   b. An increase in injections

2. a. Why did neoclassical economists believe government intervention to be unnecessary during periods of low output and high unemployment?
   b. Why did Keynes disagree with neoclassical economists on this issue?

Mountain or Mirage

The Debate over Public Debt

At first sight, the figures are astounding. From 1982, when public debt was under $5000 per Canadian, by 2001 the federal government's debt rose to about $17 200 per capita. And supplementing this 2001 figure is another amount over $7600 that each Canadian owes because of the debts of the provincial and territorial governments—making a total of almost $25 000 a head.

Is public debt too high? Are the potential costs of this debt exaggerated by those who want less government involvement in the economy? Or does the truth lie somewhere in-between? Because the costs are great, whatever the truth—huge debt at one extreme, potentially reduced government programs at the other—this is a question not only for economists and policy-makers but also for the public as a whole. Let us take a look at the opposing perceptions.

Debt Problems Are Overemphasized

People who believe that the negative aspects of public debt have been exaggerated give four main arguments: public debt can increase current output, most of this debt is owed to ourselves, we should take into account the assets created by this debt, and as a percentage of GDP, the debt is still lower than it has sometimes been in the past.

Benefits of Public Debt As discussed in Chapter 10, the amount by which real output falls short of its potential level represents the permanent loss of output due to high unemployment. To the extent that expansionary fiscal policy minimizes this gap, it provides a significant benefit—both by supplementing the economy's output and by reducing the human costs of unemployment. According to this argument, any disadvantages caused by the increases in federal debt are minor, compared with its positive contribution to economic growth.

Debt to Ourselves The federal government issues bonds to deal with the debt. However, most bonds—over 70 percent of the total value—are actually a liability Canada owes to Canadian bondholders. Supporters of fiscal policy stress this number's significance. They argue that when interest is paid on Canadian-owned public debt, funds are simply taken from one group of Canadians in the form of taxes or new borrowing and given to another group of Canadians. In other words, the total "economic pie" does not get bigger or smaller—just the sizes of the slices.

Assets versus Liabilities When debt is used to create productive assets, it can be defended in the same way as the debt acquired by businesses for investment purposes. While Canadian government investment in capital goods—at least as defined in the national accounts—has fallen in recent decades as a percentage of GDP, supporters of fiscal policy suggest that the problem lies in the definitions. They believe that we should define productive assets more widely to include the country's human resources, whose worth is promoted through such expenditures as education. Unfortunately, it is difficult to put a value on a country's stock of productive assets when they are broadly defined in this way.

Comparisons with the Past Because of substantial inflation and economic growth over the years, debt trends expressed in current-year dollars are inadequate. A much better indication of the economy's ability to bear public debt is to express the debt as a percentage of nominal GDP, as shown in Figure A. For example, the $507.7 billion public debt at the end of the 2001–2002 year equalled 46 percent of the 2001 nominal GDP of $1092.2 billion [($507.7 ÷ $1092.2) × 100%]. In contrast, the federal government's debt charges of $39.3 billion equalled 3.6 percent [$39.3 ÷ $1092.2) × 100%]. It is interesting to note that, when measured in this way (column 3), public debt has sometimes been at higher levels in the past. For example, Canada's public debt in 1936–1937, while only $3.1 billion in nominal dollars, was 67 percent of that year's GDP. By 1946–1947, after federal borrowing to help finance Canada's involvement in World War II, public debt was over 100 percent of that year's GDP—a figure much higher than the 1996–1997 level of 74 percent.

Public Debt Is a Major Problem

People who are concerned about present levels of public debt concentrate on a different set of arguments: the growth of public debt charges in relation to the size of the economy, the recent

SIDELINE

Figure A   Public Debt and GDP (billions of current dollars)

(1) Year	(2) Public Debt (billions of current-year $)	(3) Public Debt (% of nominal GDP)	(4) Public Debt Charges (% of nominal GDP)
1926-1927	2.3	46	2.5
1936-1937	3.1	67	3.0
1946-1947	12.7	107	3.9
1956-1957	11.4	35	1.5
1966-1967	17.2	27	1.8
1976-1977	39.9	20	2.4
1986-1987	271.7	54	5.3
1996-1997	593.3	74	5.7
2001-2002	507.7	46	3.6

As a percentage of nominal GDP, public debt rose between the 1920s and 1940s, and then fell until the 1970s. However, high interest rates during the 1980s and the first part of the 1990s meant that as a percentage of nominal GDP, public debt charges were higher than ever before.

Source: Department of Finance, Quarterly Economic Review: Special Report (March 1992), pp. 33–34, and Economic Statement and Budget Plan 2003, p. 294.

significance of provincial and territorial government debts, the apparent limits to future tax increases, and the potential future burdens that government debt may place on Canadians.

Public Debt Charges Although public debt as a proportion of GDP is lower today than during some other periods in Canada's history, public debt charges—or the annual interest payments on this debt—rose substantially until recent years. As shown in column 4 of Figure A, public debt charges as a percentage of GDP were much higher in the 1980s and 1990s than in any previous decade since the 1920s, with public debt charges reaching almost 6 percent of nominal GDP in the mid-1990s. This trend was due to high real interest rates during the 1980s and the first part of the 1990s. A subsequent drop in real interest rates has eased the problem, but public debt charges remain high, compared with the past.

Provincial and Territorial Debts The comparison of public debt and nominal GDP shown in Figure A underestimates the overall expansion of debt for all levels of government in Canada. In former decades, the debts of the provincial and territorial governments in Canada tended to be relatively minor. At the end of the 1981–1982 fiscal year, for example, the combined net debts of the provincial and territorial governments

represented only 4 percent of Canada's GDP. By the end of the 2001–2002 fiscal year, however, this combined debt stood at about $239 billion, or 22 percent of the country's GDP. Adding this debt to the federal debt means that the total debt of all levels of government was almost 70 percent of GDP.

Tax Limits When total government debt charges rise, Canadian governments can keep their budget deficits in check, either by increasing taxes or by reducing other expenditures, known as program spending. In the past, tax increases have commonly been used as a way of limiting budget deficits. However, in recent years, Canadians have grown more reluctant to shoulder further tax burdens, making it unlikely that tax rates can rise much beyond present levels. As a result, governments have been forced to engage in unpopular cuts in program spending.

Potential Future Burdens Many economists argue that public debt imposes future burdens on the entire Canadian economy. According to the crowding-out effect, higher levels of government borrowing raise the demand for loans. This leads to an increase in interest rates, causing businesses to reduce their investment spending. The result is a lower future stock of real capital in the economy and hence a lower rate of economic growth.

Another potential burden of public debt is the portion owed to foreigners. Over one-quarter of Canada's combined federal and provincial/territorial debt is now foreign-held, and this proportion has risen considerably in recent decades. Unlike the case of domestically held debt, the interest payments on this debt represent a transfer of purchasing power from Canadians to foreigners. The higher the proportion of public debt owed to foreigners, therefore, the greater this transfer will be in the future.

1. During a certain fiscal year, the interest rate is 6 percent, federal spending (excluding public debt charges) is $180 billion, and federal tax revenues are $200 billion.

    a. What is the federal government's budget deficit if public debt at the start of the year is $500 billion? $600 billion? What conclusions can you draw concerning the relationship between budget deficits and the size of the public debt?

    b. How would your answers in part a. differ if the average interest rate on the public debt were 5 percent instead of 6 percent? What conclusions can you draw concerning the relationship between budget deficits and interest rates?

2. "A reduction in public debt should cause an increase in investment." Evaluate this statement using arguments provided in the article.

3. (Policy Discussion Question)
    Read the article on Canadian debt (at http://oldfraser.lexi.net/publications/forum/ 2000/01/section_08.html).

    a. Based on the information in this article, summarize how direct debt plus other liabilities of Canadian governments changed from 1996–97 to 1997–8.

    b. Which programs caused the rise in Canadian governments' total liabilities? There is an important difference between Canadian governments' direct debt and their other liabilities, in terms of the burden they impose on taxpayers. What is it?

    c. Provide one possible policy change that could significantly reduce Canadian governments' total liabilities and explain whether or not you believe this policy change to be warranted.

http://oldfraser.lexi.net/publications/
forum/2000/01/section_08.html

CHAPTER 13

Money

The two greatest inventions of the human mind are writing and money—the common language of intelligence and the common language of self-interest.

—Honoré-Gabriel Mirabeau, French statesman and orator

Money talks, and, depending on who is listening, it can say a variety of things. Money's allure is undeniable. However, it is neither static nor easy to define; it has taken many forms and continues to evolve today. This chapter highlights three main issues: the functions money performs in modern economies, the connection between money and interest rates, and how banks help create money.

LEARNING OBJECTIVES

In this chapter, you will:

1 examine the functions of money, its components, and the various definitions of money

2 learn about the demand for and supply of money and about equilibrium in the money market

3 see how money is created and consider the money multiplier

13.1 Money and Its Uses

barter: a system of trading one product for another

coincidence of wants: the situation where someone purchasing an item finds a seller who wants what the purchaser is offering in return

liquidity: the ease with which an asset can be converted into a means of payment

unit of account: a pricing standard that allows all products to be valued consistently

The Functions of Money

Money serves three separate functions in any economy. It provides a means of exchange, a store of purchasing power, and a measure of value.

MEANS OF EXCHANGE

The most important function of money is that it acts as a means of payment whenever items are bought and sold. Without money, market participants must trade one product for another product, a transaction known as **barter**.

Barter is an unwieldy method of exchanging products. Someone purchasing an item must find a seller who wants what the purchaser is offering in return. In other words, there must be a **coincidence of wants** between both parties. For example, a barber who wants to buy a clock must find a clockmaker who wants a haircut. Because a coincidence of wants is usually difficult to achieve, trade is discouraged, so most people living in a barter system produce many items for themselves.

Money overcomes these problems. The barber can deal with any clockmaker and pay in money, which the clockmaker can then use to purchase a wide range of items.

The benefits of money as a means of exchange are far-reaching. People can minimize the time they spend finding others with whom they can buy and sell. They can also focus their productive activity by devoting themselves to economic pursuits in which they are most adept. The barber can stick to cutting hair and the clockmaker to making clocks. Specialization promotes the division of labour and allows an economy to achieve higher levels of output. Therefore, the use of money not only facilitates transactions of goods and services—it also raises living standards.

STORE OF PURCHASING POWER

Money's second function is providing a safe and accessible store of wealth. Money is an attractive store of purchasing power during the period between the time it is earned and the time it is spent.

There are both benefits and drawbacks associated with holding wealth as money. Money's major advantage is its **liquidity**, or the ease with which it can be turned into a means of payment. Assets are most liquid when they can be quickly turned into money with little loss in value. All financial assets are liquid to some degree, but none as much as money, which is perfectly liquid by its very nature.

Recall, however, that for any economic choice, there is an opportunity cost. In this case, the cost of holding wealth in the form of money is the income sacrificed by not holding it in some other form. For example, someone who holds wealth by stashing a thousand-dollar bill in a cookie jar is sacrificing the income the wealth could earn if it were converted into a stock or bond. As a result, people hold wealth as money when the benefits of liquidity outweigh the income that could be earned by holding it in another form.

MEASURE OF VALUE

Money also provides buyers and sellers with a **unit of account**, or pricing standard. The unit of account allows all products to be valued consistently against a common measure—in other words, it provides a point of comparison between, for example, apples and oranges. So, if apples cost $2 per kilogram and oranges cost $4 per kilogram, it is easy to see that oranges cost twice as much as apples. Recall from Chapter 9 that the unit of account does the same on a grander scale; expressing Gross Domestic

Product (GDP) as a money value simplifies the picture by allowing a wide range of products to be quantified and combined.

In contrast, a barter economy requires many measures of value. The question, "How much does this cost?" would bring the inevitable reply, "It depends on what you've got." A clock, for example, might be exchanged for 100 apples, 50 oranges, 20 loaves of bread, 2 haircuts, or some number of any other product a market participant is offering. As well as creating a confusion of prices, a barter economy is difficult to measure.

THE CANADIAN FINANCIAL SYSTEM

Now that we have defined the functions money serves, we will consider the system in which it operates as well as the supply of money. The supply of money is closely associated with institutions known as **deposit-takers**, which accept funds provided by savers and lend these funds to borrowers. For the deposit-taker, the deposits it accepts and owes back to savers are its liabilities; the funds it lends to borrowers, and which borrowers owe the deposit-taker, are its assets. These institutions make a profit by paying lower interest rates on deposits than they charge on loans.

Not all funds flowing into the institution flow out. Deposit-takers also keep on hand some amount, known as **cash reserves**, so that depositors can withdraw funds when they request them. Because deposit-takers make little or no income from cash reserves, they hold only the minimum of their assets in this form.

Deposit-takers fall into two categories: chartered banks and near banks.

CHARTERED BANKS

Chartered banks form the backbone of Canada's financial system. Unlike other deposit-takers, these institutions are allowed, through a charter they receive from the federal government, to sell a wide range of financial services.

While there are about 50 chartered banks in Canada, six big banks dominate the sector—RBC (Royal Bank), the Canadian Imperial Bank of Commerce, BMO (Bank of Montreal), Scotiabank, the TD (Toronto-Dominion) Bank, and the National Bank. Each of these banks has many branches, following what is known as a branch banking system. Together, the "big six" control about 90 percent of Canada's chartered bank deposits and assets, as shown in Figure 13-1. Most of the remaining chartered banks are relatively small foreign-owned banks. Apart from American and Mexican banks, which are exempt because of recent trade agreements, these banks are limited by law to 12 percent of Canadian chartered bank assets.

The Canadian chartered banking system is, therefore, an oligopoly. While the reduced competition may lead to some market inefficiencies, it also enhances the financial soundness of the Canadian system. By comparison, in the United States, there are over 8000 commercial banks. About a third of them operate under federal law and are known as national banks. The others, called state banks, are controlled by state governments. Many of these state banks are relatively small and have few branches. While competition is enhanced by the number of players, the modest size of each bank can increase the chance of financial difficulties.

NEAR BANKS

In contrast to chartered banks, **near banks** are not chartered and have more specialized services. The most important are trust companies, mortgage loan companies, and credit unions.

deposit-takers: institutions or businesses that accept funds provided by savers and lend these funds to borrowers

cash reserves: funds kept on hand by deposit-takers to meet the needs of depositors withdrawing funds

chartered banks: deposit-takers allowed by federal charter to offer a wide range of financial services

near banks: deposit-takers that are not chartered and have more specialized services; mainly trust companies, mortgage loan companies, and credit unions

Figure 13.1 — Chartered Banks and Near Banks in Canada

(total assets, $ billions, 2002)			
Chartered Banks		**Near Banks**	
RBC	$ 377.7	Trust and mortgage	
Scotiabank	296.4	loan companies	$ 10.2
TD	278.0	Credit unions and	
CIBC	273.3	caisses populaires	134.1
BMO	252.9	Total	$144.3
National	74.6		
Others	135.6		
Total	$1688.5		

The "big six" chartered banks dominate the financial services market. These banks hold about 90 percent of all chartered bank assets, and their combined assets are more than 10 times those of near banks.

Sources: Bank of Canada, Bank of Canada Banking and Financial Statistics (January 2003), Tables D1–D2; Canadian Bankers Association, Bank Financial Results, Fourth Quarter Results January 2003.

Trust companies administer various types of accounts, including estates and trust funds. They also compete with chartered banks by taking deposits and granting loans, mainly to households.

As their name suggests, mortgage loan companies specialize in granting mortgages and raise some of their funds through deposit-taking. A mortgage is a loan whose collateral is in the form of land and buildings.

Credit unions (called *caisses populaires* in Québec, where they are particularly prevalent) are nonprofit institutions that take deposits and grant loans to their members.

OTHER FINANCIAL INSTITUTIONS

In addition to deposit-takers—especially chartered banks—there are other types of financial institutions: insurance companies and investment dealers. Insurance companies offer insurance policies to their clients and use the funds to buy various types of income-producing financial assets. Investment dealers buy and sell financial securities, such as stocks and bonds, for their customers.

THE FINANCIAL SYSTEM

Traditionally, chartered banks, trust companies, insurance companies, and investment dealers formed the four pillars of the financial system. Each group had its specialized functions. Now, however, regulations governing financial institutions in Canada and in other countries have been loosened. Financial deregulation, as it is called, has allowed each institution to perform a wider range of functions.

For example, chartered banks have taken on some of the functions of other financial institutions. "Financial supermarkets" have sprung up to give a complete range of financial services under one corporate roof. While deregulation has promoted competition and efficiency, some critics fear it is leading to several giant companies controlling most of the Canadian financial system.

The Supply of Money

The supply of money is made up of currency and some deposits.

CURRENCY

currency: paper money and coins

Currency includes paper notes, such as 20-dollar bills, issued by Canada's central bank, the Bank of Canada. It also includes coinage produced by the Royal Mint.

DEPOSITS

Recall that deposits are given to deposit-takers and lent out to borrowers, who pay interest. In this way, chartered banks and near banks make their profits. Deposits can be classified according to the conditions of their use. In general, the access the depositor has to his or her funds determines the interest rates paid on deposits. The longer a deposit-taker can make use of the funds and the fewer the services the deposit-taker provides, the higher will be the interest rate.

Demand Deposits

demand deposits: accounts of funds to which depositors have immediate access

In some cases, depositors can demand immediate access to their money. Such deposits are called **demand deposits** and take the form of current and personal chequing accounts. Depositors can withdraw money directly from the bank or can write cheques, which are a convenient way for depositors to authorize banks to pay a certain sum to a named person or institution. In return for easy access to their deposits and because processing cheques is a relatively expensive operation, depositors receive a lower interest rate, or no interest, on their money.

Notice Deposits

notice deposits: accounts of funds for which deposit-takers may require notice before withdrawals can be made

Deposit-takers can require notice before depositors withdraw funds in certain cases. **Notice deposits**, as these are called, pay substantial rates of interest but limit or exclude cheque-writing. Traditionally, both chartered banks and near banks accept notice deposits.

Term Deposits

term deposits: accounts of funds to which depositors have no access for a fixed period of time

When depositors guarantee that they will not withdraw their funds for a fixed period of time, deposit-takers can pay a higher interest rate. **Term deposits**, as these are called, are traditionally accepted by chartered banks and near banks. Term deposits made by households are called personal term deposits, and those made by businesses are known as nonpersonal term deposits.

Foreign Currency Deposits

foreign currency deposits: accounts of funds held by Canadian residents that are valued in foreign currency

Some deposits provided by chartered banks in Canada are valued in terms of a foreign currency—usually the American dollar. These **foreign currency deposits**, which are held by Canadian residents, are treated as a separate class of deposit.

Money Defined

What *is* money? The definitions range from the very narrow to the broad. In the following sections and in Figure 13.2, we will examine the four most common definitions used by economists and government decision-makers: M1, M2, M3, and M2+.

Figure 13.2   The Canadian Money Supply

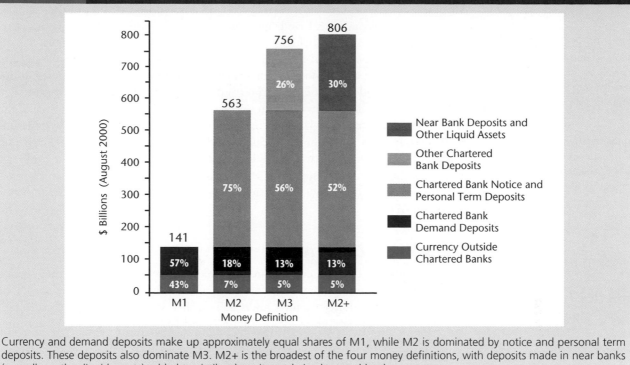

Currency and demand deposits make up approximately equal shares of M1, while M2 is dominated by notice and personal term deposits. These deposits also dominate M3. M2+ is the broadest of the four money definitions, with deposits made in near banks (as well as other liquid assets) added to similar deposits made in chartered banks.

Source: Bank of Canada, Banking and Financial Statistics, (January 2003), Table E1, S50, S51.

M1

M1: the narrowest definition of money, consisting of currency outside chartered banks and publicly held demand deposits at chartered banks

The narrowest definition of money is **M1**. Its two components—publicly held currency and publicly held demand deposits at chartered banks—are the two most intensively used forms of money. Note that only currency circulating outside chartered banks is part of M1; cash reserves held by chartered banks are not included. Also note that only demand deposits held by the public at chartered banks are included; government-owned deposits are left out. Because of their importance, currency outside chartered banks and demand deposits appear in all other money definitions also.

M2

M2: a broader definition of money, consisting of M1 plus notice deposits and personal term deposits at chartered banks

M2 is a broader definition of money that includes not only currency outside chartered banks and demand deposits at chartered banks (M1) but also funds from notice deposits and personal term deposits at chartered banks. While currency and demand deposits are perfectly liquid, notice deposits and personal term deposits are often converted into another form before being used as a means of payment.

M3

M3: the definition of money consisting of M2 plus non-personal term deposits and foreign currency deposits at chartered banks

An even broader definition of the money supply is **M3**. M3 includes the components of M2 (currency outside chartered banks plus demand deposits, notice deposits and personal term deposits at chartered banks) as well as nonpersonal term deposits and foreign currency deposits at chartered banks. These additional types of deposits are relatively liquid, although less so than those included in M2.

M2+

With the growing similarity between chartered banks and near banks in the Canadian financial system, economists have been paying more attention to a fourth definition of the money supply. **M2+** includes currency outside chartered banks plus demand deposits, notice deposits, and personal term deposits at both chartered banks and near banks. Some similar assets issued by other financial institutions are also included. It does not, however, include any nonpersonal term deposits or foreign currency deposits.

Note how the definitions build on one another, all including the most narrow definition M1. In contrast to M1, other definitions of money include what is sometimes called **near money**. Near money includes all deposits at chartered banks except publicly held demand deposits (which are included in M1), all deposits at near banks, and some other highly liquid assets, such as Canada Savings Bonds. While relatively easily converted to a means of payment, near money is less frequently used than money as defined by M1.

Choosing a Definition

Since currency and demand deposits are used solely as means of payment, they seem to fit best the definition of money. Therefore, many economists view M1 as the most accurate measure of the money supply. Others believe that M1 is too narrow; these economists prefer broader definitions—especially M2 and M2+. They point to recent innovations in payment methods that have made the accounts included in M2 and M2+ more liquid.

THE ROLE OF CREDIT CARDS

One of the main causes of the increasing liquidity of M2 and M2+ is the ability many consumers now have to pay with "plastic." A **credit card** provides its holder with the opportunity to buy goods and services with instantly borrowed funds. When a credit card is used for a purchase, the lending institution makes a loan or "credit" to the user equal to the amount of the sale. This loan lasts as long as it takes the credit card user to pay off the monthly bill.

Contrary to popular perception, credit cards are not money. They are simply an easy way for buyers to borrow funds for short periods. However, credit cards do have an indirect effect on the money supply by altering the way depositors use their deposit accounts.

Well-timed purchases made with credit cards do not have to be settled for over a month. So, for example, a person making a $50 purchase with a credit card is essentially taking out a short-term loan for the same amount. As long as this loan is paid back promptly, the purchaser is charged no interest. If credit card balances are not cleared monthly, however, the interest rate charged is higher than on most other consumer loans.

About half of all credit card users pay off their outstanding balances each month. Rather than paying currency for purchases throughout a month, card users can keep their funds in their deposit accounts until credit card payments are due. Because they can maintain their deposit accounts longer, they can accumulate more interest. If card users pay off their balance monthly (and so incur no interest charges), they can profit by using credit cards effectively. This trend to use deposit accounts in combination with credit cards has led some economists to suggest that M2 and M2+ are increasingly the accurate measures of the money supply.

THE INTRODUCTION OF DEBIT CARDS

debit card: a means of payment that instantaneously transfers funds from buyer to seller

Buyers now have a new way of paying with plastic. A **debit card** allows a payment to be made through an instantaneous transfer of funds. While similar in appearance to credit cards, debit cards represent a different type of transaction because the buyer's account is instantly reduced or "debited" by the amount of the purchase.

Unlike credit cards, which are issued only to people who have an acceptable credit history, debit cards can be employed by virtually any depositor. They can be of particular benefit to people who are tempted to overuse the instant spending power provided by credit cards. There are costs associated with debit cards, however. In the short term, the retail sector must pay for a sophisticated computer system. In some cases, this is leading to higher prices for the consumer. However, in the long term, there will be a downward pressure on prices as business costs associated with handling cash are reduced.

THINKING ABOUT ECONOMICS

Will cash eventually disappear?

Because everyone with a deposit account can use a debit card, it is possible that paper currency may be phased out. A cashless society would bring with it some significant benefits. Conceivably, consumers would face lower prices as the costs associated with handling cash fall, while the problems of theft would be reduced. Also, since records would exist for all transactions, it would be easier for governments to collect taxes and stamp out illegal activities.

However, a cashless society has potential drawbacks. Critics point out that governments may intervene unduly, that computer records of citizens' transactions and activities would mean a loss of privacy, and that the expense and complexities of cashless business would shut down some businesses and deter others from starting. And, of course, those involved in the underground economy, which depends on cash, would not welcome its demise.

In the future, a widespread desire for the benefits associated with traditional cash might lead to new forms of electronic currency. This "e-currency," whose worth will be measured in digital value units (DVUs) will likely use encryption technology and digital signatures to make anonymous payments possible. And it is probable that it will be private institutions, rather than governments, which will issue these new forms of currency.

Question

How will the creation of new e-currencies affect the ability of national governments to control the money supply?

Brief Review

1. Money serves as a means of exchange, a store of purchasing power, and a measure of value. In contrast, barter is a cumbersome system of exchange.

2. Canada's financial system includes chartered banks, near banks, insurance companies, and investment dealers. Increasing deregulation is changing the functions of financial institutions.

3. Deposit-takers accept deposits and grant loans. Deposits vary according to their conditions.

4. Money may be defined narrowly as currency outside chartered banks and demand deposits at chartered banks (M1), or it may be defined more broadly to include less liquid assets sometimes known as near money.

5. Credit and debit cards are not directly part of the money supply but are gradually changing the use of money.

13.1 Practice Questions

1. Explain why a barter economy cannot effectively perform money's three main functions.

2.
Currency outside chartered banks	$20 billion
Notice and personal term deposits at chartered banks	$157 billion
Publicly held demand deposits at chartered banks	$34 billion
Notice and personal term deposits at near banks	$164 billion
Total value of insurance policies	$215 billion
Currency inside chartered banks	$15 billion

The table above provides data for a hypothetical economy. Use this data to find:
a. M1.
b. M2.

13.2 The Money Market

LO 13.2

transactions demand: the demand for money that is related to its use as a means of exchange

asset demand: the demand for money that is related to its use as a store of purchasing power

The Demand for Money

Recall that money functions as a means of exchange, a store of purchasing power, and a measure of value. In the economy as a whole, money is demanded for reasons related to the first two functions.

TRANSACTIONS DEMAND

If there is a rise in an economy's real output or price level, the total value of transactions expands. This increases the demand for money. Conversely, a fall in real output or the price level decreases the total value of transactions and the demand for money. In other words, changes in the total value of transactions affect the **transactions demand** for money, which is connected to money's use as a means of exchange.

ASSET DEMAND

In contrast, the **asset demand** for money is associated with money's function as a store of purchasing power. As discussed earlier, the main cost of holding money is the added income that could have been earned by converting it into a higher-paying asset, such as a bond.

Bonds are formal contracts that set out the amount borrowed, by whom, for what period of time, and at what interest rate. Most bonds can be bought and sold among lenders on the open market. When bonds "mature," or reach the end of their term, the bond issuer pays the principal to the bondholder.

On the bond market, prices for bonds are inversely related to the prevailing interest rate. To see why, suppose you purchased a $1000 bond with an interest rate specified as 6 percent per annum. In other words, you are guaranteed an annual interest payment of $60 until the bond matures, at which time you, or whoever else holds the bond, will be repaid the $1000 principal. Two years later, you want to sell the bond, but the prevailing interest rate is 12 percent. In other words, newly issued $1000 bonds are promising annual interest payments of $120, while the bond you own promises only a $60 annual interest payment. Because its annual payment is half that of new bonds, your bond will fall in price to about $500, or half the value of a newly issued $1000 bond. Similarly, if the interest rate declines from its initial value of 6 percent to 3 percent, the price of your bond will double from its original value of $1000 to about $2000, since it provides twice the annual interest payment ($60) than the payment found on a newly issued $1000 bond ($30).

Bonds are the most popular way for governments and large businesses to raise funds. They are also attractive assets. Because they can be easily bought and sold before their term has ended, they offer liquidity as well as relatively high rates of return in exchange for the risk associated with changes in bond prices. For individuals who hold wealth, therefore, bonds offer the likeliest alternative to holding money—depending on how individuals view the tradeoff between bonds' higher rates of return and higher risk.

For these reasons, the asset demand for money is inversely related to the nominal interest rate on bonds. When this interest rate increases, the prices of bonds fall. Lower bond prices cause some individuals to convert their money into bonds, reducing the asset demand for money. Similarly, a reduction in the nominal interest rate means that the prices of bonds rise. Higher-priced bonds become a less attractive option for wealthholders, causing more of them to hold money rather than bonds, thus pushing up the asset demand for money.

money demand: the amounts of money demanded at all possible interest rates

Money demand represents the amounts of money demanded, unadjusted for inflation, at all possible interest rates. Money demand expressed in a table gives the **money demand schedule**; expressed on a graph, it gives the **money demand curve** (D_m). As Figure 13.3 shows, the money demand curve has a negative slope. This slope is determined by the asset demand for money, which is inversely related to interest rates. As we have just seen, a rise in the nominal interest rate on bonds reduces the asset demand for money, while a fall in the nominal interest rate increases the asset demand. Therefore, a change in the asset demand causes a change in the quantity of money demanded, or a movement along the money demand curve.

money demand schedule: money demand expressed in a table

money demand curve: money demand expressed on a graph

In contrast, a change in transactions demand changes the amounts demanded at all interest rates—that is, it causes a shift in the money demand curve. An increase in either real output or the price level raises the transactions demand for money at every possible interest rate. Hence, the money demand curve shifts to the right, from D_{m0} to D_{m1}, as shown in Figure 13.3. Conversely, a decrease in either real output or the price level shifts the money demand curve to the left.

The Supply of Money

money supply: a set amount of money in the economy, as determined by government decision-makers

While money demanded is inversely related to interest rates, the **money supply** is a set amount (unadjusted for inflation) determined by government decision-makers. As Figure 13.4 shows, money supply can be expressed in a table, giving the **money supply schedule**, or on a graph, giving the **money supply curve** (S_m). No matter

money supply schedule: money supply expressed in a table

money supply curve: money supply expressed on a graph

Figure 13.3 | The Demand for Money

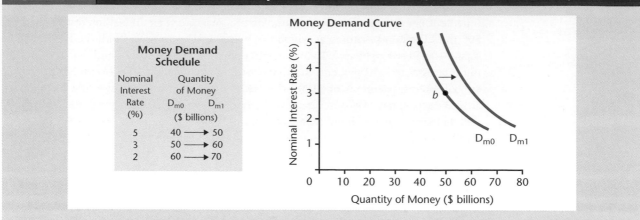

Because a greater quantity of money is demanded at lower nominal interest rates, the money demand curve has a negative slope. A change in the interest rate causes a change in the asset demand for money, which is shown as a movement along the money demand curve. For example, a rise in the interest rate causes a decrease in the quantity of money demanded (from point *b* to point *a*). An increase in real output or the price level causes money demand to increase at all interest rates, as shown by the shift from D_{m0} to D_{m1}.

what the nominal interest rate, the amount of money supplied is a constant value, as depicted by the vertical supply curve (S_{m0}). Only when government decision-makers decide to change the money supply does the supply curve shift. Therefore, the supply curve shifts to the right, from S_{m0} to S_{m1}, only when the government increases the money supply. Likewise, the money supply curve shifts to the left only when the government decreases the money supply.

Equilibrium in the Money Market

The demand and supply of money interact in the money market to bring about a state of equilibrium. As shown in Figure 13.5, the equilibrium level of the nominal interest

Figure 13.4 | The Supply of Money

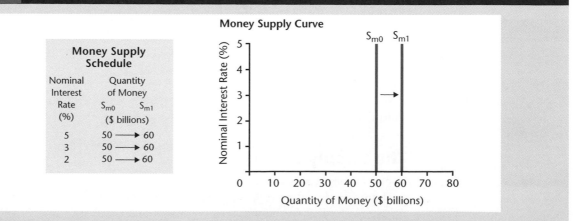

Because government policy-makers determine the supply of money at any given time, the money supply curve is a vertical line at that amount. Any change in the money supply results in a shift of the vertical line, as shown, for example, by the shift from S_{m0} to S_{m1}.

Figure 13.5   Equilibrium in the Money Market

Money Demand and Supply Schedules

Nominal Interest Rate (%)	Quantity Supplied	Quantity Demanded	
		($ billions)	
	(surplus (+) or shortage (−))		
↓5	(50 − 40) = +10 ↓		
3	(50 − 50) = 0		
↑2	(50 − 60) = −10 ↑		

Money Demand and Supply Curves

When the nominal interest rate exceeds its equilibrium value, the quantity of money supplied exceeds quantity demanded. This surplus leads to more buying of bonds, forcing bond prices up and the nominal interest rate down, until the quantity of money demanded and supplied are the same. When the nominal interest rate is below its equilibrium value, the opposite occurs. A shortage of money pushes the interest rate up until the equilibrium point is reached.

rate is found at the intersection of the money demand and money supply curves. As usual, surpluses and shortages help bring about equilibrium in the market.

When the interest rate is above its equilibrium level—for example, at 5 percent as opposed to 3 percent in Figure 13.5—there is a surplus of money. In other words, more money is supplied than is demanded. As people try to rid themselves of money and buy assets that will provide high earnings, the demand for these assets rises, pushing up their price and causing the nominal interest rate to fall. This trend of falling interest rates continues until the discrepancy between the demand and supply of money is eliminated.

In the opposite case, the interest rate falls short of the equilibrium value, as at 2 percent on the graph, causing a shortage of money. In other words, more money is demanded than is supplied. As people try to sell assets, such as bonds, in order to acquire money, the price of these assets falls, causing the nominal interest rate to rise until the equilibrium point is attained.

Brief Review

1. Demand for money is of two types, each of which is related to a function of money. Transactions demand relates to the function of money as a means of exchange; asset demand relates to the function of money as a store of purchasing power.

2. Money demand is the amounts of money demanded at all possible interest rates, which can be expressed in a table or on a graph. The money demand curve has a negative slope because of the inverse relationship of money demanded to interest rates.

3. Money supply is a set amount that is determined by government decision-makers. As a result, the money supply curve is a vertical line at this set amount.

4. The economy's equilibrium interest rate and money supply occur at the intersection of the money demand and money supply curves.

13.2 Practice Questions

1. Explain what happens in the money market in the following situations:
   a. The nominal interest rate is above its equilibrium level.
   b. The nominal interest rate is below its equilibrium level.

2. A $20 000 bond provides an interest rate specified as 5 percent of the bond's initial face value per annum.
   a. What is the annual interest payment on this bond?
   b. What would happen to the price of this bond if the prevailing interest rate moves to 2 percent?
   c. What would happen to the price of this bond if the prevailing interest rate moves to 10 percent?

13.3 Money Creation

LO 13.3

When setting the money supply, government policy-makers must take into account the actions of deposit-takers. This is because a substantial portion of money in the economy is held in the form of deposits.

Recall that deposit-takers receive deposits from savers and lend to borrowers, while keeping some cash reserves on hand for withdrawals by depositors. By charging higher interest rates to borrowers than they pay to depositors, deposit-takers make profits. In a sense, through this process of receiving deposits and lending funds, chartered banks and near banks create deposit money. This is not by some trick of magic but by the roles played by cash reserves and the profit motive.

Desired Reserves

desired reserves: minimum cash reserves that deposit-takers hold to satisfy anticipated withdrawal demands

Until 1994, chartered banks were legally required to hold certain levels of cash reserves, more than near banks were required to hold. Since then, both chartered banks and near banks have kept only **desired reserves**, which are the minimum amounts of cash necessary to satisfy anticipated withdrawal demands.

The Reserve Ratio

reserve ratio: desired reserves expressed as a percentage of deposits or as a decimal

In general, the more money a deposit-taker holds in deposits, the greater the withdrawals it can expect. Therefore, the best way to deal with anticipated withdrawals is for the deposit-taker to hold a certain portion of deposits in the form of cash reserves. This portion, which can be expressed as a percentage or in decimal terms, is the **reserve ratio**. Suppose, for example, that a bank has a reserve ratio of 0.10. If the bank has deposits of $100 million, then it will hold 10 percent of this dollar value as desired reserves ($100 million × 0.10):

$$\text{Reserve ratio} = \frac{\text{desired reserves}}{\text{deposits}}$$

$$0.10 = \frac{\$10 \text{ million}}{\$100 \text{ million}}$$

Different types of deposits have different reserve ratios. For example, demand deposits require a higher reserve ratio than do other types of deposits. However, to examine the process of money creation, we will simplify matters by assuming a uniform reserve ratio.

Excess Reserves

excess reserves: cash reserves that are in excess of desired reserves

At times, deposit-takers find that their cash reserves exceed desired levels, or they have **excess reserves**. For example, a chartered bank with deposits of $100 million and desired reserves of $10 million may find itself holding $14 million in actual cash reserves:

$$\text{Excess reserves} = \text{cash reserves} - \text{desired reserves}$$

$$\$4 \text{ million} = \$14 \text{ million} - \$10 \text{ million}$$

Because idle cash reserves earn no profit, deposit-takers will try to transform any excess reserves into income-producing assets as quickly as possible. They, therefore, lend out the full amount of excess reserves. In our example, the bank will lend out the $4 million excess to borrowers.

The Money Creation Process

To see how lending out excess reserves "creates" money, let us consider an example. For the time being, we will make two key assumptions. First, the public holds money in the form of deposits and uses only cheques for transactions. Second, all deposits are made to one sort of deposit-taker, which we will simply call banks, and all deposits are of one type, which allows cheques to be written against them. We will also assume the banks' reserve ratio for their deposits to be 0.10, or 10 percent.

FIRST TRANSACTION

At the outset, Cabot Bank has cash reserves equal to desired reserves. However, Saver A receives $1000 in currency and immediately deposits it in Cabot Bank. As shown in Figure 13.6, Cabot Bank has a new cash asset as well as a new deposit liability to Saver A, each equalling $1000. So far, there has been no change in the amount of money in the economy, only in who holds it. Because the $1000 in currency is transformed into $1000 held in a deposit, no money is added to the money supply. (Recall that the $1000 in currency sitting in the vault of Cabot Bank is not considered part of the money supply.)

Figure 13.6	Opening a Deposit		
	Cabot Bank		
Assets		**Liabilities**	
Cash Reserves	+*$1000*	Saver A's Deposit	+*$1000*

Saver A deposits $1000 at Cabot Bank. As a result, Cabot Bank has new cash assets and deposit liabilities of $1000.

SECOND TRANSACTION

Because of Saver A's deposit, Cabot Bank's total deposits increase by $1000. At the same time, the actual cash reserves increase by $1000 as well. However, with a reserve ratio of 0.10, Cabot Bank really only wants to keep $100 of the newly deposited $1000 on hand as desired reserves ($1000 × 0.10). As a result of this new deposit, Cabot Bank has excess reserves of $900 ($1000 − $100).

The bank responds by lending $900 to Borrower X. As Figure 13.7 demonstrates, the new loan increases Cabot Bank's deposit liabilities by $900. In other words, by lending out its excess reserves, Cabot Bank creates $900 in new money.

Figure 13.7	Granting a Loan

Cabot Bank			
Assets		**Liabilities**	
Cash Reserves	$1000	Saver A's Deposit	$1000
Loan to Borrower X	+*$900*	Borrowers X's Deposit	+*$900*

Cabot Bank lends out its $900 in excess reserves to Borrower X, creating new loan assets and deposit liabilities of $900. Since Borrower X's new deposit is money, the money supply has risen by $900.

THIRD TRANSACTION

Now that he has the money, Borrower X uses his $900 loan to purchase goods or services. Figure 13.8 shows the resulting changes in both Cabot Bank's cash assets and the new deposit to Borrower X—they are both reduced by $900.

Figure 13.8	Withdrawing a Deposit

Cabot Bank			
Assets		**Liabilities**	
Cash Reserves	$100 ($1000 − *$900*)	Saver A's Deposit	$1000
Loan to Borrower X	$900	Borrower X's Deposit	$0 ($900 − *$900*)

When Borrower X withdraws the $900 from his deposit, Cabot Bank's cash assets and deposit liabilities each fall by $900.

FOURTH TRANSACTION

So, does reducing Cabot Bank's deposits mean the newly created money suddenly disappears? It does not, if we take Borrower X's $900 purchase into account. Suppose Borrower X bought something for $900 from Saver B. Saver B, in turn, deposits the $900 from the sale in her account at Fraser Bank. As a result, Fraser Bank's cash assets and deposit liabilities increase by $900, as shown in Figure 13.9. This means that the $900 deposit originally created by Cabot Bank has simply moved to Fraser Bank. As a result of this transaction, there is no change in the money supply.

Figure 13.9   Accepting Deposit Funds

	Fraser Bank	
Assets		**Liabilities**
Cash Reserves +$900	Saver B's Deposit +$900

Saver B deposits the $900 from Borrower X's purchase in her account at Fraser Bank. The bank's cash assets and deposit liabilities both rise by $900.

FIFTH TRANSACTION

Now, let us consider Fraser Bank. Because Saver B's deposit to Fraser Bank increases the total deposits of the bank, desired reserves should increase by $90 (= $900 × 0.10). Once again, however, the deposit of $900 also increases the cash reserves, thereby giving excess reserves of $810 (= $900 − $90).

Because the excess reserves can be put to use to earn profits, Fraser Bank lends the $810 to Borrower Y. As a result, Fraser Bank's loan assets and deposit liabilities have jumped by $810, as shown in Figure 13.10. Because of this rise in deposits, more new money has been created, so the money supply has been boosted by another $810.

Figure 13.10   Granting a Loan

	Fraser Bank	
Assets		**Liabilities**
Cash Reserves +$900	Saver B's Deposit +$900
Loan to Borrower Y +$810	Borrower Y's Deposit +$810

Fraser Bank lends out its $810 in excess reserves to Borrower Y. This creates added loan assets and deposit liabilities of $810. Since Borrower Y's new deposit is money, the money supply increases by $810.

The Money Multiplier

The possible transactions are endless. However, we can see the process of money creation in the few transactions outlined. Recall that the quantity of money increased once, when Cabot Bank lent out its $900 in excess reserves to Borrower X, and again, when Fraser Bank lent out its excess reserves of $810 to Borrower Y. In other words, the money supply increases by $1710 in these few transactions. Money will continue to be created as long as banks find they have excess cash reserves to lend out.

Note how the process of money creation is similar to the process of the spending multiplier, as outlined in Chapter 12. In this money creation process, an initial change in money has a magnified effect on the money supply. The **money multiplier** is the value by which the initial change is multiplied to give the maximum total change in money supply. Suppose, for example, that the initial change in excess reserves is $900 and the final change in the money supply is $4500; the money multiplier, therefore, has a value of 5:

money multiplier: the value by which the amount of excess reserves is multiplied to give the maximum total change in money supply

$$\text{Change in money supply} = \text{change in excess reserves} \times \text{money multiplier}$$
$$\$4500 = \$900 \times 5$$

The Multiplier Formula

The value of the money multiplier is determined in the same way as the size of the spending multiplier. Recall that the spending multiplier is the reciprocal of the marginal propensity to withdraw (MPW), which indicates how much is taken out of the income-spending stream with each spending cycle.

In the case of the money creation process, deposit-takers hold back a certain portion of the funds in each lending cycle. As we have seen, this portion is determined by the reserve ratio. So, in money creation, the multiplier is the reciprocal of the reserve ratio. In our example, with banks reserving 10 percent (or 0.10) of deposits, the money multiplier is 10 (1.00 ÷ 0.10). In other words, the initial change in excess reserves ($900) eventually causes an increase in the money supply of $9000:

$$\text{Money multiplier} = \frac{1}{\text{reserve ratio}}$$

$$10 = \frac{1}{0.10}$$

$$\text{Change in money supply} = \text{change in excess reserves} \times \text{money multiplier}$$

$$\$9000 = \$900 \times 10$$

Therefore, when government decision-makers wish to change the money supply by a given amount, as seen earlier in Figure 13.4, they cause a change in excess reserves which, when multiplied by the money multiplier, creates the desired change. For example, if they wish the money supply to change by $10 billion, and the money multiplier has a value of 10, then the initial change in excess reserves is $1 billion ($10 billion ÷ 10).

Adjustments to the Money Multiplier

In order to see how money is created, we temporarily assumed that all money is in the form of deposits, and all deposits are made to one sort of deposit-taker offering only a single type of deposit. However, these assumptions do not hold true in reality. Let us consider the implications in turn.

THINKING ABOUT
ECONOMICS

How relevant is the money multiplier in the Canadian monetary system?

The money multiplier represents the maximum possible effect of money creation. Returning to our example, the money multiplier formula allows us to specify the maximum amount ($9000) by which the quantity of money rises as a result of the infusion of $900 in new excess cash reserves into the economy. Because of the various factors that influence this increase, the exact size of the money multiplier can vary significantly.

Question
Given Canada's move to voluntary rather than legally required cash reserves, what has happened to the size of the money multiplier?

PUBLICLY HELD CURRENCY

The public, of course, does use currency, and currency is a part of all definitions of money. So, rather than all money going to deposit-takers, who then keep some as reserves and lend the rest, some money does circulate and is unaffected by the money multiplier. Thus, in our example, the money supply would not increase by $9000 but by a lesser amount.

DIFFERENCES IN DEPOSITS

As we have noted, there is a wide range of deposit types, and not all types are represented in the narrowest definition of money M1. Therefore, as deposit money expands in the succession of transactions, not all of it will be reflected as an increase in money supply defined as M1. So, the money supply in our example would increase by an amount less than $9000.

Brief Review

1. Deposit-takers reserve a certain percentage of deposits to satisfy withdrawal requests from depositors. This percentage is known as the reserve ratio, and the resulting dollar amount equals the desired reserves.

2. Cash reserves in excess of desired reserves are lent out to borrowers in order to create profit.

3. In the same way that spending is magnified, lending excess reserves magnifies deposits.

4. The money multiplier is the reciprocal of the reserve ratio and the maximum value by which an initial change in excess reserves changes the money supply.

13.3 Practice Questions

1. A chartered bank has $1 million in deposits and $40 000 in desired reserves. Its excess reserves are initially zero.
   a. What is this bank's reserve ratio?
   b. If a further $100 000 is deposited in the bank, by how much do the bank's desired reserves increase? the bank's excess reserves?
   c. With the aid of a chart similar to Figure 13.7, identify by how much can this bank increase the money supply.

2. A depositor places $200 in cash in her bank. The reserve ratio in the banking system is 6 percent.
   a. By how much do excess reserves initially change in the depositor's own bank?
   b. What is the maximum amount by which the money supply changes once the process of money creation in the banking system is complete?

LAST**WORD**

In this chapter, we have examined the relationship between the money supply and the financial system and the factors that affect the demand and supply of money. While money demand results from the public's desire to hold money for transactions and as an asset, the money supply is determined by government decision-makers, who can change the amount of excess reserves in the banking system, which then has an amplified effect on the money supply through the workings of the money multiplier. In the next chapter, we analyze the monetary role of government decision-makers in more detail, by focusing on the Bank of Canada and the way it conducts monetary policy to stabilize the economy.

Key Concepts

asset demand 318
barter 311
cash reserves 312
chartered banks 312
coincidence of wants 311
credit card 316
currency 314
debit card 317
demand deposits 314
deposit-takers 312
desired reserves 322
excess reserves 323

foreign currency deposits 314
liquidity 311
M1 315
M2 315
M2+ 316
M3 315
money demand 319
money demand curve 319
money demand schedule 319
money multiplier 325

money supply 319
money supply curve 319
money supply schedule 319
near banks 312
near money 316
notice deposits 314
reserve ratio 322
term deposits 314
transactions demand 318
unit of account 311

Questions

1. Identify which of the three functions of money is most relevant in the following situations:
   a. A consumer compares prices on various brands of clothing.
   b. A restaurant-owner writes a cheque to pay for food purchases.
   c. A wealth-holder temporarily keeps part of her financial assets in a chartered bank deposit.
   d. A borrower deposits currency in his chartered bank to pay off a loan.

Total value of corporate shares	$500 billion
Currency outside chartered banks	$28 billion
Notice and personal term deposits at chartered banks	$288 billion
Publicly held demand deposits at chartered banks	$31 billion
Federal government bonds	$623 billion
Notice and personal term deposits at near banks	$235 billion
Other liquid assets included in M2+	$18 billion
Nonpersonal term and foreign-currency deposits at chartered banks	$254 billion

2. Use the hypothetical data provided in the table above to calculate (a) M1, (b) M2, (c) M3, and (d) M2+.

Money Demand and Supply Schedules

Nominal Interest Rate (%)	Money Demanded (D_m) ($ billions)	Money Supplied (S_m)
5.0	$ 90	$130
4.0	110	130
3.0	130	130
2.0	150	130
1.0	170	130

3.   a. Use the schedules in the above table to draw a graph showing the money demand and money supply curves. Identify the equilibrium point.
   b. What happens in this market if the prevailing interest rate is initially 5 percent? 1 percent?
   c. With the aid of your graph, outline the effects of a $20 billion decrease in the money supply.
   d. In which direction will the equilibrium interest rate move if real output in the economy increases? if the price level decreases? Why?

4.   A bond is initially worth $10 000 and provides an interest rate of 4 percent.
   a. Explain how this bond's price changes if the prevailing interest rate falls to 2 percent.
   b. What happens to the bond's price if the prevailing interest rate rises to 6 percent?

5.   Hudson Bank has a reserve ratio of 5 percent and $10 million issued in deposits.
   a. If the bank's actual reserves are $600 000, then what are its excess reserves?
   b. By how much can this bank increase the money supply?

6.   Champlain Bank has a reserve ratio of 4 percent, $5 million issued in deposits, and $200 000 in actual reserves. What is the effect on the bank's excess reserves if $15 000 in currency is deposited in the bank?

7.   A wealth-holder withdraws $200 from her bank and stashes this currency in a cookie jar. Assume that other economic participants hold their money in one type of deposit in a financial system with a single type of deposit-taker with a reserve ratio of 5 percent.
   a. Outline the first two transactions that occur as a result of this withdrawal.
   b. What is the final change in the money supply? Explain.

8.   (Advanced Question)
   a. How can the value of deposit-takers' assets be negatively affected during economic downturns?
   b. How might the reactions of depositors intensify the problems outlined in part a.?
   c. Suggest some ways these financial risks faced by deposit-takers can be minimized either by government policy-makers or by deposit-takers themselves.

9.   (Policy Discussion Question)
   Read *Competition in the Canadian Financial Services Sector* (at http://www.cba.ca) from the Canadian Bankers Association's *Fast Facts*. Based on points raised in this article, outline the new forms of competition faced by Canada's chartered banks due to legal changes and technological trends.

http://www.cba.ca

1. Access the *Weekly Financial Statistics* at the Bank of Canada's web site (at http://www. bankofcanada.ca/) and use the data in this report to find seasonally adjusted values for M1, M2, and M3 for the most recent month available.

2. Access Statistics Canada's E-Stat site (at http://www.statcan.ca/english/Estat/licence. htm).
    a. Using the information found in "Business Enterprises," generate a two-dimensional graph showing gross M1, M2, and M2+ (each expressed as adjusted annual averages) for Canada since 1968.
    b. On the basis of your graph in part a., which of these three definitions of the money supply has increased at the quickest rate? the slowest rate?

WE ARE WHAT WE MAKE

The Theories of Harold Innis

Money is not the only commodity whose attributes have a wider economic significance. The physical aspects of commodities and their production played a central role in the theories of the innovative Canadian economist Harold Innis (1894-1952). Raised in rural Ontario, he planned to become a lawyer, but his legal studies were waylaid by his growing interest in economics, which he studied at the University of Chicago—a well-known centre of economic research. He then taught for many years at the University of Toronto, while his writings exerted a growing influence not only on the study of Canadian economic history but also on other related areas.

Harold Innis
Source: University of Toronto Libraries

Staples Thesis

Innis's researches took him far beyond the usual domain of economics. His first aim was to explain the guiding forces of Canada's economic history. Why has development been concentrated in certain regions and during particular eras?

His answer was an intriguing one. Innis focused on what he called staple products—natural resources that could be exploited by Canadians and sold in foreign markets for export revenues. According to Innis's staples thesis, several natural resources have played crucial roles in the evolution of the Canadian economy. In each case, development has been shaped by where and how the resource has been extracted and used. Innis's emphasis on staple products led him to highlight geographical aspects of development, as well as the linkages between staple industries and other parts of the economy.

Innis's own work concentrated on the role of fish and furs in encouraging European settlement in Canada. Cod fish provided the first impetus to this settlement, and fishing continued to serve as the primary staple industry on much of Canada's east coast until recent times. In central Canada, development centred on the lucrative fur industry, where high European prices allowed for a high markup and generous export revenues.

Furs remained central Canada's dominant staple item until early in the 19th century, when the growing demands of ship-building and construction industries in both the United States and Europe meant that forestry took over as Canada's major staple industry. After the 1860s, however, lumber exports declined, and there was no staple item to take its place. Not surprisingly, this was a time of economic stagnation in Canada. Then, in the two decades leading up to World War I, wheat prices rose, encouraging the large-scale agriculture expansion that accompanied the settlement of the Prairie provinces.

After World War I, new natural resources—minerals, oil and gas, and hydroelectric power—have served as staple goods, but none with the same dominance as in previous eras. The Canadian economy's current shift from manufacturing to services and knowledge is difficult to interpret using Innis's theory. Nonetheless, the staples thesis offers insights into Canada's economic history and is still applicable in some regions of the country.

Communications Theory

In his later years, Innis turned to a more basic and wide-ranging question. What is the central factor determining the type of society we live in? Nothing less than the way we communicate. This was later popularized by the famous Canadian thinker Marshall McLuhan—who was heavily influenced by Innis's ideas—as "the medium is the message."

Some types of communication exhibit a space bias, meaning they are well suited for conveying messages across geographical distances. An example is a lightweight paper letter. Other ways of communicating show a time bias, working best when communication spans time, as with a message carved on a stone monument.

Innis divided history into periods on the basis of the dominant medium of communication. Time-biased communication in a society leads to an emphasis on tradition and religious belief. A space-biased medium causes an interest in short-lived worldly matters and aids in the formation of geographical empires.

For example, Innis believed that early pre-literate cultures exhibited a vitality that matched their dominant form of communication. Speech is more effective in passing on information from one generation to another than it is in bridging space. Cultures depending on the spoken word were therefore time-biased, with custom playing an important role.

In about 3000 BCE, writing was invented in ancient Mesopotamia (present-day Iraq). Early writing was preserved in clay and stone. These materials are durable but cumbersome to transport. Hence the societies that used them were time-biased, stressing the supernatural and tradition. As Innis pointed out, both the yearly calendar and the pseudo-science of astrology were developed in these early time-centred cultures.

Papyrus is a portable but fragile plant material. It was first used for writing in Egypt and became popular throughout the Mediterranean. A space-biased means of communication, it made possible the expansion of the Roman Empire and the flowering of secular culture.

Parchment, also known as vellum, is made from animal skins. From about the 8th century CE, it became the dominant writing medium in Europe. Durable but difficult to move, it represented a return to time-biased means of communication. Using Innis's theory, this accounts for the renewed emphasis on tradition and religious faith during the Middle Ages.

Paper—light, portable, and space-biased—was invented in China during the 2nd century CE, and by the 12th century CE, it had arrived in Europe. Its use made feasible the development of printing and, according to Innis, encouraged an interest in commerce and worldly culture that, at about 1500 CE, ushered in the modern era in Europe. Paper-based communication also facilitated the empire-building of such countries as Spain, Portugal, and, later, France and Britain.

What of today's communications revolution that has accompanied the introduction of TV, radio, telephones, and computers? If anything, our culture's bias towards space has been intensified. While political empires have gone out of fashion, the entire world is fast becoming one vast "information empire" in which geographical distance has lost its significance. And how is this new global order held together? Not by sea-power or trade routes, but by optical-fibre cables, radio waves, and satellites. If anything, the continuing development of instantaneous forms of communication makes the space-biased aspects of our culture ever more powerful.

1. Using one of the staple resources from Canada's past as an example, explain some possible ways that the extraction or use of this resource affected the development of Canada and its economy.

2. How would Innis explain the fact that contemporary societies are so consumed by passing fads and the present moment?

CHAPTER 14

Monetary Policy

There were warnings of apprehension from economists.
There always are: apprehension is their business.

—Stephen Leacock, Canadian writer and economist

According to an old joke, ask two economists the same question, and you will get three answers. Economists—like any social scientists—do disagree, and very often, their disagreements revolve around stabilization policy—especially monetary policy. In this chapter, we explore the workings of monetary policy and then study some of the issues that are key to the use of both fiscal and monetary policies.

◼ LEARNING OBJECTIVES

In this chapter, you will:

1 learn about the Bank of Canada and its functions

2 analyze the tools the Bank of Canada uses to conduct monetary policy

3 examine the tradeoff between inflation and unemployment

14.1 The Bank of Canada

LO 14.1

The moving force behind Canada's monetary policy is the Bank of Canada, which has served as Canada's central bank since 1935. A wholly government-owned institution, the "Bank," as it is known, has been given a mandate to perform four basic functions relating to money and the financial system: managing the money supply, acting as "the bankers' bank," acting as the federal government's fiscal agent, and ensuring the stable operation of financial markets.

Managing the Money Supply

The most important role of the Bank of Canada is to conduct monetary policy by controlling the amount of money circulating in the economy. Not only does it issue paper currency, but more importantly, it affects the activities of chartered banks and near banks so that it can vary the supply of money and interest rates. In managing the money supply, the Bank is concerned with three goals: minimizing inflation in order to preserve the purchasing power of the dollar; maintaining real output as close as possible to its potential level; and regulating the external value of the Canadian dollar on foreign exchange markets.

Acting as the Bankers' Bank

The Bank of Canada holds the deposits of financial institutions that are members of the Canadian Payments Association (CPA). The association includes the chartered banks and some near banks—in particular, the larger trust companies and representatives of credit unions and *caisses populaires*.

The CPA acts as a clearing house for cheques of both chartered banks and near banks. Suppose, for example, that Depositor A has a chequing account with Tecumseh Trust. He writes a $50 cheque to Depositor B, who deposits this cheque in her account at Elgin Bank, increasing her deposit balance by $50. Elgin Bank delivers the cheque to Tecumseh Trust and receives $50 in return. This payment between the two banks is actually made by using the accounts kept by both institutions (or larger banks acting as their representatives) at the Bank of Canada. The $50 is transferred from Tecumseh Trust's account to Elgin Bank's account at the Bank of Canada. To complete the entire exchange, Tecumseh then cancels the cheque it has received and reduces Depositor A's deposit account by $50. Each day, every cheque transaction like this is added up, and the accounts of CPA members are all "cleared" at once. This procedure vastly simplifies the transactions that are made necessary by the use of cheques among various deposit-takers.

The accounts of CPA members at the Bank of Canada, which are known as settlement balances and are part of the CPA members' cash reserves, are kept so that funds are available to meet the daily clearing of payments. When a CPA member finds that its account is too low, it can borrow from the Bank of Canada. The Bank provides an overnight loan, or an "advance," as it is usually known, by depositing the required funds in the CPA member's account. The interest rate charged on these advances is called the **bank rate**. Because the bank rate is higher than interest rates on other overnight loans, CPA members try to minimize their advances from the Bank of Canada. Nonetheless, they are a necessary backup to guarantee that CPA members always have sufficient funds in their accounts at the Bank of Canada.

bank rate: the interest rate CPA members are charged on advances from the Bank of Canada

Acting as the Federal Government's Fiscal Agent

In Chapter 12, we discussed the fiscal, or budgetary, policy that Canadian governments institute in order to level out the business cycle. In order to conduct the business of spending, taxing, and so on, the federal government needs a bank to manage its transactions and financial assets. In its role as the government's fiscal agent, the Bank of Canada engages in three main tasks: the Bank holds some of the government's bank deposits and decides where the other deposits should be held; it acts as the government's banker by clearing federal government cheques; and it handles the financing of the federal government's debt by issuing bonds. Government bonds fall into various categories, the most notable being Canada Savings Bonds and treasury bills.

Canada Savings Bonds:
federal government bonds that have a set value throughout their term

Canada Savings Bonds are popular with household savers. These bonds differ from others in that they are not bought and sold after they have first been issued. Instead, holders of Canada Savings Bonds who want their funds back before the bonds have matured must "cash in" the bonds with the Bank of Canada at a set price. Since savers know exactly how much they will receive for the bond during its entire term, this feature of Canada Savings Bonds increases their attractiveness. Recall that ordinary bonds, in contrast, fluctuate in price before their maturity date depending on the value of interest rates in the economy. Hence, they are somewhat riskier than Canada Savings Bonds.

treasury bills: short-term federal government bonds that provide no interest, but are sold at a discount

Treasury bills are an important type of short-term federal government bond. They have terms of three months to a year and are usually issued in large denominations. Unlike other government bonds, treasury bills provide no interest payments. Rather, they are sold at a marked down price. For example, a one-year treasury bill worth $100 000 might be bought—usually by banks and other financial institutions—for $95 000. Once the treasury bill matures, the holder receives the face value of $100 000, thereby earning an income of $5000 (= $100 000 − $95 000). Viewed in another way, the $5000 earned at maturity can be seen as interest on the original purchase price, or as a nominal rate of interest of 5.3 percent [= ($5000 ÷ $95 000) × 100%]. The price for federal treasury bills is decided at an auction conducted every second Tuesday by the Bank of Canada.

Ensuring the Stability of Financial Markets

In tandem with other agencies, the Bank of Canada supervises the operation of financial markets to ensure their stability. The Bank has a particular responsibility in overseeing the activity of chartered banks. By doing so, it helps protect the safety of depositors' funds and the soundness of the financial system.

THINKING ABOUT ECONOMICS

How is the auction of treasury bills conducted?

The main buyers in the treasury bill market are the chartered banks, the large near banks, and investment dealers. The Bank of Canada also buys treasury bills to become part of its bond holdings. Buyers provide written bids, which outline the price they are willing to pay and the number of bills they want. As in any auction, the bills go to the highest bidders; those who bid highest have their orders filled first.

Question
What are the main factors that determine the average price of treasury bills at each auction?

14.2 Monetary Policy

LO 14.2

expansionary monetary policy: a policy of increasing the money supply and reducing interest rates to stimulate the economy

Recall that monetary policy involves the Bank of Canada changing interest rates, altering the money supply, or both, in order to stabilize the economy. Our analysis of money and deposit-takers allows us to examine the way in which monetary policy is conducted.

Expansionary Monetary Policy

When real output falls short of its potential level, a recessionary gap is created. To stimulate output and increase employment, the Bank of Canada can use **expansionary monetary policy**. Such action is referred to informally as "easy money policy."

The Bank of Canada applies easy money policy by expanding the money supply. As shown on the left in Figure 14.1, increasing the money supply shifts the money supply curve (S_m) to the right, causing a drop in the equilibrium interest rate.

To see how this lower interest rate affects aggregate demand, remember that a fall in interest rates makes borrowing funds cheaper. With a decline in the nominal interest rate, the real rate of interest falls as well. Businesses respond by increasing their investment spending, and households purchase more durable goods, raising consumption. Both adjustments spur an initial increase in spending that is then magnified by the same successive cycles of new spending, as seen in the case of an expansionary fiscal policy, as discussed in Chapter 12.

The effect is the same as when government purchases increase. The change in aggregate demand, or total spending, is found by calculating the product of the spending multiplier and the initial spending change. Suppose, for example, that the initial increase in investment and consumption totalled $9 billion and the value of the economy's spending multiplier is 1.67. The total change in aggregate demand is then $15 billion:

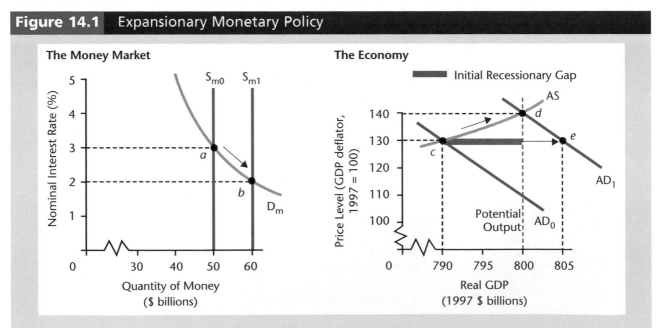

Figure 14.1   Expansionary Monetary Policy

When the economy is in a recession, the Bank of Canada can increase the supply of money, shown by the shift from S_{m0} to S_{m1} on the left, thereby pushing down the interest rate (point *a* to point *b*). Because of the initial spending increase and the spending multiplier, the result in the economy as a whole is an increase in aggregate demand, as shown on the right as the $15 billion shift from AD_0 to AD_1. Output does not rise by $15 billion (from point *c* to point *e*); rather, the price level and output both rise to give a new equilibrium at point *d*, with output at the potential level of $800 billion and the recessionary gap eliminated.

Total change in output (shift in AD curve)	=	initial change in spending	×	spending multiplier
$15 billion	=	$9 billion	×	1.67

As shown on the right in Figure 14.1, the $15 billion shift in the aggregate demand curve causes equilibrium output to rise by a smaller amount—$10 billion—because of the accompanying price level rise.

Contractionary Monetary Policy

contractionary monetary policy: a policy of decreasing the money supply and increasing interest rates to dampen the economy

Conversely, during an economic boom, the Bank of Canada can inhibit spending and inflation with **contractionary monetary policy**. Such action, also known as "tight money policy," decreases the money supply. The result, as shown on the left in Figure 14.2, is that the money supply curve (S_m) shifts to the left, driving up the equilibrium interest rate.

The higher nominal interest rate results in a higher real interest rate as well. This discourages investment spending by businesses as well as consumption spending on durable items by households, so it influences aggregate demand. Both trends cause an initial reduction of spending that is then magnified by the spending multiplier. Suppose, for example, that investment and consumption spending decline initially by $9 billion, and the spending multiplier is 1.67. As a result, the total decrease in aggregate demand is $15 billion.

Once again, the change in output causes a lesser change in actual spending because of the change in price level at the same time. In this case, as shown on the right in Figure 14.2, the $15 billion decrease in aggregate demand causes a $5 billion decrease in equilibrium output.

Figure 14.2   Contractionary Monetary Policy

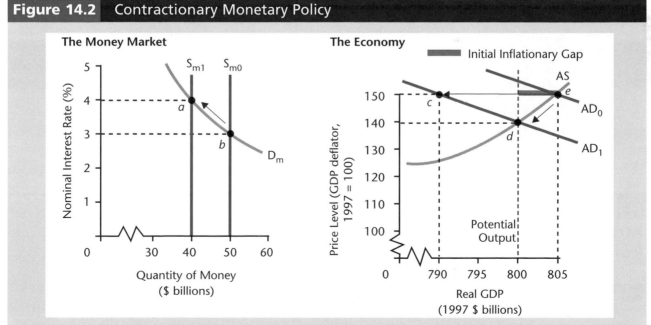

During an economic boom, the Bank of Canada can decrease the supply of money, shown by the shift from S_{m0} to S_{m1} on the left, thereby pushing up the interest rate (point b to point a). Because of the initial spending decrease and the spending multiplier, the result in the economy as a whole is a decrease in aggregate demand, as shown on the right as the $15 billion shift from AD_0 to AD_1. Output does not fall by $15 billion (from point e to point c); rather, the price level and output both fall to give a new equilibrium at point d, with output at the potential level of $800 billion and the inflationary gap eliminated.

Brief Review

1. Canada's central bank—the Bank of Canada—manages the money supply, serves as a bank for chartered banks and some near banks, acts as the federal government's fiscal agent, and helps to ensure the stability of financial markets.

2. Expansionary monetary policy raises real output towards its potential level by increasing the money supply and decreasing interest rates. The resulting increase in investment and consumption is magnified by the spending multiplier to give an even greater increase in aggregate demand.

3. Contractionary monetary policy reduces real output towards its potential level by decreasing the money supply and increasing interest rates. The resulting decrease in investment and consumption is magnified by the spending multiplier to give an even greater decrease in aggregate demand.

14.2 Practice Questions

1. Suppose the Canadian economy is facing an unemployment rate of 8.5 percent, and a declining rate of inflation.
   a. Should the Bank of Canada use a contractionary or expansionary monetary policy?
   b. Carefully explain the steps by which the monetary policy you identified in part a. will affect the economy.
   c. With the aid of EconGraphKit (at http://www.mcgrawhill.ca/college/lovewell), draw two graphs (one of the money market and the other showing the economy's aggregate demand and aggregate supply) to show how monetary policy might operate to stabilize the economy.

2. a. What is the nominal interest rate on a one-year treasury bill with a face value of $1 million if its purchase price is $980 000?
   b. If the Bank of Canada wishes to move the nominal interest rate on one-year treasury bills to 3 percent, should the Bank increase or decrease the supply of these bills it sells in its auction? Explain.

14.3 Tools of Monetary Policy

LO 14.3

open market operations: the buying and selling of bonds by the Bank of Canada in the open market

The Bank of Canada has two different tools it can use to conduct monetary policy: open market operations and (as a signal of its intentions) the target overnight rate.

Open Market Operations

Recall that the Bank of Canada sells and buys back federal government bonds. Its role in the bond market is a major tool with which the Bank of Canada conducts monetary policy. Through selling and buying back federal and other bonds, the Bank of Canada can use deposit-takers' cash reserves as a lever to influence both the money supply and interest rates. Because these transactions take place in the open bond market, they are called **open market operations**.

BOND SALES

Consider the sale by the Bank of Canada of a $1000 bond to Bondholder A. When the sale takes place, Bondholder A pays for the bond with a cheque written against his deposit account at Cartier Bank. The Bank of Canada sends the cheque to Cartier Bank, which then cancels the cheque and reduces Bondholder A's account by $1000. Most importantly, Cartier Bank pays the Bank of Canada for the cheque by having $1000 taken out of its Bank of Canada account, as shown in Figure 14.3.

The money supply immediately falls by $1000 due to the loss of the deposit previously held by Bondholder A. Assuming that the reserve ratio is 0.10, Cartier Bank's excess reserves are cut by $900, causing a multiple reduction of the money supply. Cartier Bank has less money available to lend. With a reserve ratio of 0.10 and a maximum money multiplier of 10, the further decline in the supply of money could be as much as $9000 (= $900 × 10).

Therefore, the sale of bonds reduces the cash reserves of deposit-takers, which, in turn, cuts back on lending and finally decreases the supply of money. By selling bonds, the Bank of Canada engages in contractionary monetary policy.

BOND PURCHASES

Now, consider the implications of the Bank of Canada buying back bonds from members of the public in the open market. Suppose the Bank of Canada buys back a $1000 bond from Bondholder B. Bondholder B receives a cheque from the Bank of Canada, which she deposits in her account at Cartier Bank. On acquiring the cheque, Cartier Bank delivers it to the Bank of Canada and receives in return a $1000 addition to its Bank of Canada deposit.

As Figure 14.4 shows, both the money supply and Cartier Bank's cash reserves increase by $1000 due to the new deposit held by Bondholder B. However, the bank, with a reserve ratio of 0.10, need only hold back $100. Therefore, the bank has excess reserves of $900 (= $1000 − $100). Cartier Bank will lend this money, which, in turn, will increase the money supply in a series of transactions similar to those outlined earlier in this chapter. Assuming a uniform reserve ratio of 0.10, we can see that the

---

Figure 14.3   A Bond Sale

Bank of Canada

Assets		Liabilities	
Bonds	−$1000	Cartier Bank's Deposit	−$1000

Cartier Bank

Assets		Liabilities	
Reserves at Bank of Canada	−$1000	Bondholder A's Deposit	−$1000

When the Bank of Canada sells a bond to Bondholder A, its bond assets fall, as do its deposit liabilities to Cartier Bank. Meanwhile, Cartier Bank's cash assets at the Bank of Canada decrease, as do its deposit liabilities to Bondholder A. The drop in Bondholder A's deposit immediately reduces the money supply by $1000. With a reserve ratio of 10 percent, Cartier Bank's excess reserves fall by $900 and the money multiplier has a value of 10. Because reductions to deposits are magnified, the money supply drops by as much as an extra $9000 (the $900 decrease in excess reserves multiplied by the money multiplier).

Figure 14.4	A Bond Purchase

Bank of Canada

Assets		Liabilities	
Bonds	+$1000	Cartier Bank's Deposit	+$1000

Cartier Bank

Assets		Liabilities	
Reserves at Bank of Canada	+$1000	Bondholder A's Deposit	+$1000

If the Bank of Canada purchases a bond from Bondholder B, its bond assets rise, as do its deposit liabilities to Cartier Bank. From Cartier Bank's perspective, its cash assets at the Bank of Canada increase, as do its deposit liabilities to Bondholder B. The new deposit from Bondholder B immediately adds $1000 to the money supply. With a reserve ratio of 0.10, Cartier Bank's excess reserves increase by $900, while the money multiplier has a value of 10. Because deposits expand, the money supply increases by as much as an extra $9000 (the $900 increase in excess reserves multiplied by the money multiplier).

money multiplier (10, or the reciprocal of 0.10), creates a further increase in the money supply of up to $9000 (= $900 × 10).

Therefore, buying back bonds allows the Bank of Canada to practise expansionary monetary policy. Cash reserves increase, resulting in increased lending, which causes the money supply to expand.

The Target Overnight Rate

overnight rate: the interest rate on overnight loans between chartered banks and other financial institutions

The **overnight rate** is the interest rate on overnight loans between chartered banks and other financial institutions. At any given time, the Bank makes sure that the overnight rate stays within a publicized range of 50 basis points (a basis point is one-hundredth of a percentage point, with the target overnight rate at the midpoint of this range). The Bank keeps the overnight rate near the target overnight rate by using its main monetary policy tool. When the Bank buys bonds on the open market, the accounts of CPA members at the Bank increase in value, which reduces the need for overnight borrowing and pushes down the overnight rate. On the other hand, when the Bank engages in an open-market sale of bonds, the accounts of CPA members at the Bank are reduced, raising the need for overnight borrowing as well as the overnight rate.

Since 1996, the bank rate has been set at the ceiling of the 50-basis-point range for the overnight rate. Whenever the Bank changes the target overnight rate, the 50-basis-point range and the bank rate change as well. This signifies where monetary policy is heading in the near future.

prime rate: the lowest possible interest rate charged by deposit-takers on loans to their best corporate customers

If the change in the target overnight rate is substantial, deposit-takers may decide to alter their own interest rates in the same direction. In particular, they adjust their **prime rate**, which is the lowest possible rate charged by deposit-takers on loans to their best corporate customers. When the prime rate varies, so do all other rates for depositors and borrowers.

Benefits of Monetary Policy

Monetary policy has two main benefits: its separation from politics, and the speed with which it can be applied. These benefits have made monetary policy the most important stabilization tool in recent years.

SEPARATION FROM DAY-TO-DAY POLITICS

Unlike fiscal policy, which is a well-publicized element of the political process, monetary policy is detached from immediate political influence. While the Bank of Canada is under the control of parliament, as represented by the prime minister and cabinet, in practice, the Bank of Canada is controlled by appointed officials—the most important being its governor, who serves a seven-year term—and its operations are veiled from public view. Thus, monetary policy tends to be focused on economic rather than political goals.

SPEED

Recall that fiscal policy suffers from recognition, decision, and impact lags. While recognizing a problem can also cause a delay in monetary policy and the impact of any policy may also be delayed (by anywhere between 12 and 18 months), decisions regarding monetary policy can be made speedily.

Drawbacks of Monetary Policy

Monetary policy does have two major drawbacks: its relative weakness as an expansionary tool, and its broad impact.

WEAKNESS AS AN EXPANSIONARY TOOL

The Bank of Canada is quite capable of restraining an overheated economy during a boom period. By squeezing deposit-takers' excess reserves through open-market sales of bonds, it can be assured that the money supply will fall, pushing up interest rates and reducing spending and output.

However, matters are not necessarily so straightforward during a severe recession or depression. While the Bank can increase deposit-takers' cash reserves through open-market purchases of bonds, there is no guarantee that this will translate into more bank loans and an expansion of the money supply. If deposit-takers hold on to their extra cash reserves, the desired increase in the money supply will not occur, which can make the use of expansionary monetary policy seem like "pushing a string."

BROAD IMPACT

Unlike fiscal policy, which can be focused on particular regions, monetary policy affects every region of the country uniformly. When the Bank of Canada raises interest rates during a boom, for example, the impact is felt not only in those areas with overheated economies but also in areas that have been relatively unaffected by the upswing. As a result, regions already enduring high rates of unemployment experience even more.

Brief Review

1. One major way the Bank of Canada pursues monetary policy is through open-market operations. Buying bonds from the public is expansionary policy that increases chartered bank reserves, leading to a magnified increase in the money supply. In contrast, selling bonds reduces the money supply.

2. The Bank of Canada signals its intentions by setting the target overnight rate, which, in turn, influences the prime rate. A rise in the target overnight rate signals contractionary policy. A fall in the target overnight rate signals expansionary policy.

3. While monetary policy has the benefits of its isolation from politics and the speed with which decisions can be made, it is less effective for expansion than for contraction, and it cannot be focused on particular regions as can fiscal policy.

14.3 Practice Questions

1. The Bank of Canada buys a $10 000 bond from a member of the public. With the aid of a chart similar to Figure 14.4, outline the effects of this bond purchase on each of the following variables if the reserve ratio in the banking system is 5 percent.
    a. the bond seller's bank deposit
    b. desired reserves at the bond seller's bank
    c. excess reserves at the bond seller's bank
    d. the maximum change in the money supply

2. The Bank of Canada sells a $2000 bond to a member of the public. With the aid of a chart similar to Figure 14.3, outline the effects of this bond sale on each of the following variables if the reserve ratio in the banking system is 10 percent.
    a. the bond buyer's bank deposit
    b. desired reserves at the bond buyer's bank
    c. excess reserves at the bond buyer's bank
    d. the maximum change in the money supply

14.4 Inflation and Unemployment

LO 14.3

demand-pull inflation:
inflation that occurs as increased aggregate demand pulls up prices

Stabilization policies—both fiscal and monetary—are usually applied to affect inflation and unemployment. The task of policy-makers is complicated by the fact that the relationship between inflation and unemployment is usually an inverse one. So, for example, an increase in aggregate demand during an economic expansion means that equilibrium between aggregate demand and aggregate supply is found at a higher price level and higher output, as shown in Figure 14.5. The increase in price level translates into inflation, and the increase in output translates into lower unemployment. In other words, there is a tradeoff—higher prices for more jobs. Because increased demand pulls up prices, economic expansion that causes inflation is known as **demand-pull inflation**.

Figure 14.5 Demand-Pull Inflation

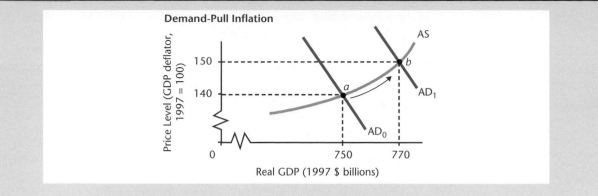

During expansionary times, aggregate demand increases, shifting the aggregate demand curve from AD_0 to AD_1. The result is that the price level rises from point *a* to point *b*. In other words, increased demand *pulls* up prices.

The Phillips Curve

Recall from Chapters 11 and 12 that Keynesian economics stresses the inverse relationship between inflation and unemployment as found in demand-pull inflation. On the basis of the assumption that there is a fixed and predictable inverse relationship between unemployment and inflation, one Keynesian economist—A.W.H. Phillips—created a curve that expresses this relationship. This **Phillips curve** is shown in Figure 14.6.

According to the Keynesian perspective, if an economy with an inflation rate of 2 percent and an unemployment rate of 8 percent (point *b* in Figure 14.6) experiences demand-pull inflation, the inflation rate will rise at the same time that unemployment decreases to, for example, point *a*. Increased aggregate demand creates shortages in labour markets, which put upward pressure on wages, thereby boosting inflation. In the same way, decreased aggregate demand increases unemployment, which puts downward

Phillips curve: a curve expressing the assumed fixed and predictable inverse relationship between unemployment and inflation

Figure 14.6 The Phillips Curve

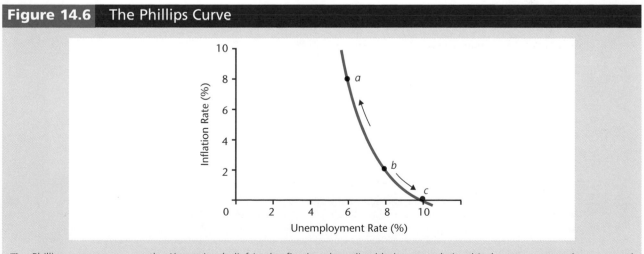

The Phillips curve expresses the Keynesian belief in the fixed and predictable inverse relationship between unemployment and inflation that occurs with demand-pull inflation. When the economy moves from point *b* to point *a*—which may happen as a result of expansionary stabilization policies—inflation increases, and unemployment decreases. In contrast, contractionary policies cause the economy to move from point *b* to point *c*.

pressure on wages, thereby reducing the rate of inflation. We see this in the shift from point *b* to point *c*.

In the past, the Phillips curve was often treated by governments as a "policy menu." Governments using expansionary fiscal or monetary policies would anticipate a move up the curve, for example, from point *b* to point *a*; governments using contractionary fiscal or monetary policies would expect a move down the curve, for example, from point *b* to point *c*.

The extent to which Phillips curves are applicable can be seen using historical data for Canada. Figure 14.7 plots annual unemployment and inflation rates for 1960 to 2002. Let us consider the relevance of the Phillips curve to three periods.

FROM 1960 TO 1972

For the years 1960 to 1972, in general, higher inflation accompanied lower unemployment, and vice versa. In other words, inflation during this period was of the demand-pull variety. Therefore, the points indicating inflation and unemployment rates fall in a broad band from which we can draw a Phillips curve, shown in Figure 14.7 with a solid line. Because inflation and unemployment had a predictable inverse relationship, Canadian federal governments were able to use the curve when trying to predict how their stabilization policies would affect the economy.

Figure 14.7	**Shifts in the Phillips Curve**

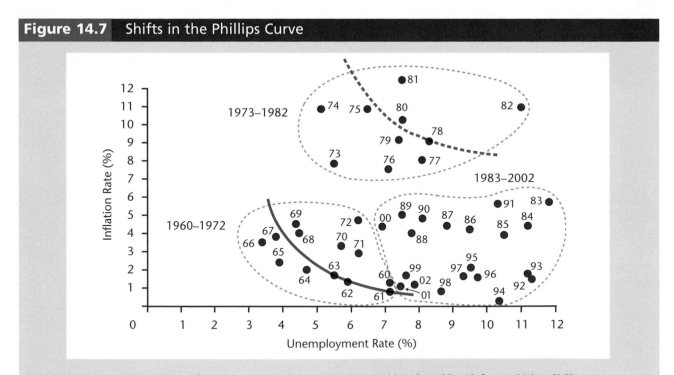

During the years 1960 to 1972, inflation and unemployment rates stayed in a broad band, from which a Phillips curve can be drawn (shown as a solid line). In the period from 1973 to 1982, the predictable relationship broke down. However, it seems that the Phillips curve moved to the right (shown as a dashed line) as both inflation rates and unemployment rates were above those in the previous period. In the period from 1983 to 2002, the trend was to lower inflation, but unemployment rates remained high. As a result, the new position of the Phillips curve was not clear for this period.

Sources: Statistics Canada "Shifts in the Phillips Curve," adapted from the Statistics Canada publication "National income and expenditure accounts: annual estimates," 1926–1986, Catalogue 13-531, April 1989, pp. 214–215 and from the Statistics Canada CANSIM II database http://cansim2.statcan.ca Tables 282-0002 and 380-0056.

FROM 1973 TO 1982

In the years between 1973 and 1982, the previously predictable relationship between inflation and unemployment in Canada broke down. Most notably, inflation rose from 1973 to 1974, while unemployment remained about the same. This trend was repeated in the years 1979 to 1981. The Phillips curve for the Canadian economy during this period, shown as a dashed line in Figure 14.7, demonstrates that inflation and unemployment overall were greater in this period than in the last.

As this period illustrates, sometimes unemployment and inflation have a direct relationship rather than an inverse relationship. A rising rate of inflation associated with constant or expanding unemployment—that is, consistently low output—is known as **stagflation**. This name refers to the combination of *stag*nation and in*flation*.

Stagflation can be caused by a decrease in aggregate supply. During the period from 1973 to 1982, for example, businesses faced rising prices for inputs, largely due to rising oil prices. Oil prices were 10 times higher in 1981 than they were at the start of 1973 because of the cartel behaviour of OPEC—the Organization of Petroleum Exporting Countries. In response to increases in input prices, businesses decrease their output, thus reducing aggregate supply. The result, shown in Figure 14.8, is a fall in equilibrium output and a rise in the price level. Because the increased costs push price levels up, this situation is known as **cost-push inflation**. During the 1970s, demands for increased wages further decreased aggregate supply and worsened cost-push inflation.

stagflation: a combination of consistently low output (and so constant or expanding unemployment) and rising inflation

cost-push inflation: inflation that occurs as increased production costs decrease aggregate supply, which then pushes up prices

FROM 1983 TO 2002

From 1983 to 2002, the stagflation of the previous period was partly reversed. While unemployment rates remained stubbornly high in Canada through most of the 1980s and 1990s, by the mid-1990s inflation had fallen to levels not seen since the early 1970s. Note, however, that there was no consistent relationship between inflation and unemployment during this period. While the new Phillips curve was presumably below the Phillips curve for the previous period, its position was not apparent from the behaviour of the economy between 1983 and 2002, as illustrated in Figure 14.7.

Figure 14.8   Cost-Push Inflation

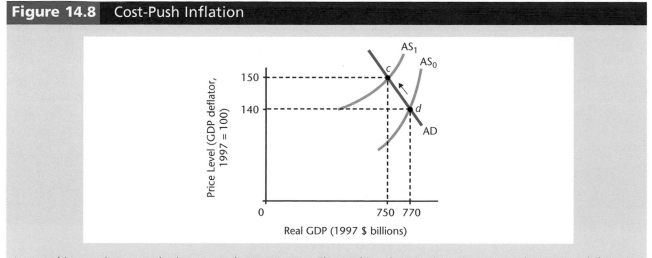

Increased input prices cause businesses to decrease output. The resulting decrease in aggregate supply means a shift in the aggregate supply curve from AS_0 to AS_1. The result is that the price level is pushed up from point *d* to point *c*. In other words, increased costs *push* up prices.

Three main factors account for Canada's lower inflation since 1983. Oil prices fell dramatically in the mid-1980s and the pace of technological change accelerated after the mid-1990s, increasing aggregate supply and restraining increases in the price level. In addition, the recessions of 1981–1982 and 1990–1991 had a major impact on reducing inflation rates by decreasing aggregate demand. This impact was especially strong, given the contractionary monetary policies conducted by the Bank of Canada during both recessions.

THE ECONOMY'S SELF-STABILIZING TENDENCY

Another reason for shifts in the AS curve relates to the economy's capacity to stabilize itself in the long run, as forces push the economy towards its potential output, where unemployment is at its natural level. While the economy may rarely reach this long-run equilibrium, economic fluctuations can be fully understood only if this self-stabilizing tendency is taken into account.

Figure 14.9 illustrates a simplified version of this process for a hypothetical economy. The short-run tradeoff between output and the price level is shown by the aggregate supply curve. But only at point *b*, which is associated with the economy's potential output, is the economy stationary in the long run. At any other point on the curve, the economy will sooner or later display its built-in tendency to stabilize.

During an economic boom, the economy's equilibrium may be at a point, such as *c*, where output is above its potential level. Because unemployment is below its natural rate, tight labour markets allow workers to bargain for higher nominal wages. These wage hikes raise business costs, leading to a decrease in aggregate supply. Equilibrium, therefore, moves back towards the economy's potential output, and unemployment rises towards its natural rate.

The opposite occurs when an economy's equilibrium is below its potential output, as at point *a* on the graph, with a high unemployment rate. Workers initially resist any attempts to reduce their nominal wages, as was pointed out originally by Keynes. However, over time, unemployment puts downward pressure on nominal wages. This causes an increase in aggregate supply, boosting output back towards its potential level and lowering unemployment towards its natural rate.

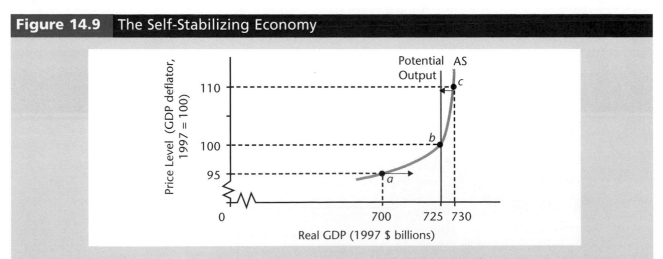

Figure 14.9   The Self-Stabilizing Economy

At point *b*, the economy could remain indefinitely at its potential output. However, when equilibrium is at point *c* in a boom, the economy's self-stabilizing tendency will push the aggregate supply curve to the left, so that the potential output can be resumed. The same is true if the economy's equilibrium is at point *a* in a recession. The self-stabilizing tendency will push the aggregate supply curve to the right.

The Long-Run Supply Curve

long-run aggregate supply curve: the vertical AS curve at the potential output level

In either case, the vertical line shown on the graph at the potential output level can be interpreted as this hypothetical economy's **long-run aggregate supply curve**, since it shows all those points consistent with stable equilibrium in the long run.

The existence of this curve, and the self-stabilizing process that underlies it, represents a partial return to the perspective of neoclassical economics before John Maynard Keynes. It is now accepted by most economists, though its importance is disputed. Those economists who see little need for government stabilization policy believe the economy adjusts quickly by itself towards its potential output level. In contrast, many economists see the self-adjusting process as a slow one, which means that government stabilization policy can still play an important role in reducing the severity of the ups and downs in the business cycle.

Brief Review

1. Inflation and unemployment have often had an inverse relationship. In periods of expansion, the result is demand-pull inflation.

2. The Phillips curve represents the Keynesian assumption of an inverse and predictable relationship between inflation and unemployment. While the Phillips curve applied to Canada in the period from 1960 to 1972, it has been less relevant since.

3. Since the 1970s, inflation and unemployment in Canada have frequently had a direct relationship. Stagflation has been caused largely by decreases in aggregate supply due to price increases of inputs. The result is cost-push inflation.

4. Overall inflation and unemployment rates in Canada increased in the period from 1973 to 1982, shifting the Phillips curve to the right. From 1983 to 2002, unemployment continued to be high but inflation declined.

5. In the long run, changes in wage rates and the resulting movement in the aggregate supply curve mean that equilibrium is driven towards the long-run aggregate supply curve which is at the economy's potential output.

14.4 Practice Questions

1. Outline the effect of the following trends on an economy's Phillips curve.
   a. cost-push inflation
   b. demand-pull inflation
   c. a contractionary monetary policy

2 a. If an economy is initially at an equilibrium point to the right of its long-run aggregate supply curve, then what will be the long-run process whereby the economy will reach this curve?
   b. In the opposite case where an economy is initially at an equilibrium point to the left of its long-run aggregate supply curve, then how will the economy reach this curve in the long run?

LastWORD

In this chapter, we have seen how the Bank of Canada uses its available tools of monetary policy to affect inflation and unemployment, as well as to stabilize the economy over the business cycle. Now, we turn to the Bank of Canada's possible influence on the international value of the Canadian dollar, as well as examining the balance of payments accounts that help determine it. This discussion introduces the topic of Canada's role in the global economy, which is the theme of Part IV. In this final section, we examine not only the foreign sector, but also international trade, as well as some of the contentious issues connected with economic growth and Canada's role in the global economy.

Key Concepts

bank rate 334
Canada Savings Bonds 335
contractionary monetary policy 337
cost-push inflation 345
demand-pull inflation 342

expansionary monetary policy 336
long-run aggregate supply curve 347
open market operations 338

overnight rate 340
Phillips curve 343
prime rate 340
stagflation 345
treasury bills 335

Questions

1. Changes in real output and the price level caused by monetary policy have their own effect on interest rates.
   a. Using graphs like those shown in Figure 14.1, explain whether this effect intensifies or partly counteracts the initial impact of an expansionary monetary policy on the equilibrium interest rate.
   b. What does your analysis in part a. suggest about the effectiveness of monetary policy?

2. a. What is the nominal rate of interest on a one-year $1 million treasury bill if its purchase price is $975 000? if its purchase price is $960 000?
   b. Given your answers to part a., how can the Bank of Canada adjust supply in the auction of treasury bills to increase the nominal rate of interest on treasury bills?
   c. How can the Bank of Canada adjust its own purchases in the auction of treasury bills to decrease the nominal rate of interest on treasury bills?

3. When would it be more advantageous to hold Canada Savings Bonds than to hold regular bonds? when nominal interest rates are rising or falling? Explain.

4. Using T-accounts like those in Figure 14.4, show how a $1 million purchase of government bonds by the Bank of Canada from Bondholder X, who has a deposit at Frontenac Bank, will affect Frontenac Bank's excess reserves, given a reserve ratio of 5 percent. What is the maximum final effect on the money supply? Explain.

5. Calculate the maximum amount by which the following policies will change the money supply:
   a. $100 million of bonds are bought by the Bank of Canada when the reserve ratio is 5 percent.
   b. $50 million of bonds are sold by the Bank of Canada when the reserve ratio is 7.5 percent.

6. "Changes in the target overnight rate can affect the money supply only if backed up by the use of open market operations." Discuss, using either expansionary or contractionary monetary policy as an example.

Inflation and Unemployment in Macronia

Year	Inflation Rate	Unemployment Rate
2002	4	5
2003	2	8
2004	3	6

7. a. Draw a Phillips curve on the basis of the hypothetical information in the above table.
   b. What types of stabilization policies could have caused the change that takes place between 2002 and 2003? between 2003 and 2004?
   c. What are the benefits and costs of the changes that take place between 2002 and 2003?
   d. What are the benefits and costs of the changes that take place between 2003 and 2004?
   e. Suppose that in 2005 the inflation rate is 5 percent and the unemployment rate is 10 percent. What has happened to the Phillips curve? What could explain this change?

8. Given the economy's self-stabilizing trends that determine the long-run aggregate supply curve, what shape does the Phillips curve have in the long run? Explain.

9. (Advanced Question)
   American economist Alan Blinder has popularized what he calls Murphy's Law of Economic Policy: "Economists have the least influence where they know the most and are most agreed; they have the most influence on policy where they know the least and disagree most vehemently." Using evidence from this chapter, state whether you agree or disagree with Blinder's statement.

Internet Application Questions

1. Using the information available at the Bank of Canada's web site (at www.bankofcanada.ca/), draw a chart showing any changes in the target overnight rate, as well as the upper and lower limits of the overnight rate's 50 basis-point range, from month to month during the current calendar year.

2. Access the summary of the most recent Monetary Policy Report at the Bank of Canada's web site (at http://www.bankofcanada.ca/).
   a. On the basis of this summary, state whether monetary policy during the relevant time period covered by the report has been expansionary or contractionary.
   b. Summarize the reasons why the Bank believes such a policy was needed.

http://www.bankofcanada.ca/

http://www.statcan.ca/english/Estat/licence.htm

3. Access Statistics Canada's E-Stat site (at http://www.statcan.ca/english/Estat/licence.htm).
   a. Using the information found in "Business Enterprises," generate a two-dimensional graph showing the daily bank rate in Canada since 1997.
   b. What does your graph in part a say about shifts in Canadian monetary policy in the years since 1997?

Money Matters

Milton Friedman and Monetarism

Friedman and His Influence

One of the most influential figures in the discipline of economics during recent decades has been the American economist Milton Friedman (born in 1912). He was both a student and a long-time professor at the University of Chicago, an institution where the ideas of the neoclassical economists lived on, despite the Keynesian revolution of the 1930s and 1940s.

Friedman is perhaps most famous as a promoter of *laissez-faire* capitalism in the tradition of Adam Smith. He has popularized his views in his books *Capitalism and Freedom* (1962) and *Free to Choose* (1980) as well as in numerous magazine articles and TV appearances. Friedman's pro-market outlook stems from his belief that wages and prices in private markets are fairly close to their most efficient, perfectly competitive values, while such externalities as pollution can best be dealt with through private lobbying and negotiation, rather than through government intervention. Since governments are inefficient by their very nature, says Friedman, and because they hinder individual freedom, their intervention in private markets should be minimized.

Friedman would replace income-support programs, such as welfare and Employment Insurance, with a single, guaranteed annual income system. He also argues that many functions currently performed by governments could be performed more efficiently by the private sector, if businesses are chosen to fulfill each specified task at the lowest possible cost.

The Role of Money

Friedman has contributed to various aspects of economics, but his most wide-ranging work is associated with the economic perspective known as "monetarism," which emphasizes the influence of money in the economy.

Monetarism is a recent extension of theories that dominated macroeconomics before John Maynard Keynes. Like neoclassical economists, such as William Stanley Jevons and Alfred Marshall, monetarists believe that the economy is able to adjust to shocks without government intervention. While admitting that the economy can be temporarily set off course, monetarists argue that misguided government intervention usually just makes economic fluctuations worse. Because they stress the importance of money, monetarists blame unwise use of monetary policies in particular.

Central to monetarism is the concept known as the velocity of money (V), or the number of times, on average, that money is spent on final goods and services during a given year. For the economy as a whole, the velocity of money can be calculated by dividing nominal GDP by the money supply (M). Suppose, for example, that Canada's nominal GDP is $1 trillion and M1 (recalling the definitions of money from Chapter 13) is $50 billion. Each of the dollars in the stock of money must then have been used 20 times to finance this level of activity:

Milton Friedman
Source: ©Bettmann/CORBIS/Magma

$$\text{Velocity of money (V)} = \frac{\text{nominal GDP}}{\text{M}}$$

$$20 = \frac{\$1 \text{ trillion}}{\$50 \text{ billion}}$$

These calculations lead us to another cornerstone of monetarism. Recall that nominal GDP is the total money value of all final goods and services produced in the economy over a given period. So, GDP expresses both the price level (P) and real output (Q). In other words, the $1 trillion in nominal GDP may be broken down into a price level of 2.0 and a real output of $500 billion:

$$\text{Nominal GDP} = P \times Q$$
$$\$1 \text{ trillion} = 2.0 \times \$500 \text{ billion}$$

The two formulas above can be combined to derive the equation of exchange, which is central to Friedman's theory. The equation states that the money supply multiplied by the velocity of money (M × V) equals the price level multiplied by real output (P × Q):

$$M \times V = P \times Q$$
$$\$50 \text{ billion} \times 20 = 2.0 \times \$500 \text{ billion}$$

The Quantity Theory of Money

According to the quantity of theory of money, which is accepted by Friedman and other monetarists, both the velocity of money and real output are relatively stable. Changes in velocity, they say, are primarily due to long-run factors, such as the move to credit and debit cards, while real output varies only slightly from its potential level. Friedman has accommodated Keynesian theory by recognizing that wages can be inflexible, but he believes that this inflexibility is short-lived, with economic participants soon adjusting to any changes in prices or unemployment.

If both the velocity of money and real output are fairly stable, as is assumed in the quantity theory of money, then there is a straightforward relationship between money and prices. This is shown by the equation of exchange, when both velocity and real output are set at constant values, $V^\star$ and $Q^\star$:

$$M \times V^\star = P \times Q^\star$$

Adjustments in the price level (P) must then be due to changes in the money supply (M). In other words, according to Friedman, inflation is primarily caused by too much money chasing the products available for purchase in an economy.

Monetarist Policies

Unlike other economists, who treat money as only one element that determines output and inflation levels, Friedman considers variations in the money supply the most significant factor in the economy. In mainstream theory, the process through which money influences the economy is a lengthy one. An expansion in the money supply, for example, must first reduce interest rates, then boost investment and consumer spending on durable goods, and finally change aggregate demand, thereby shifting the aggregate demand curve to the right. If any of these links in the chain is weak, then the process of change breaks down. In contrast, Friedman and other monetarists view the impact of monetary changes as being more straightforward and predictable. In this perspective, an assumed stable velocity of money means that adjustments in the money supply translate immediately into higher nominal GDP and increased prices.

Because monetarists consider monetary policy to be a powerful instrument, most judge it too strong for central banks to apply wisely. Fluctuations in real output will be lessened, they suggest, if no discretionary policy is used at all. Instead, governments should impose a monetary rule that forces the central bank to increase the money

ADVANCING
ECONOMIC
THOUGHT

supply by a constant rate each year. The rate that monetarists recommend—usually in the range of 3 percent—is based on long-term real growth in the economy.

But the experience in Canada and other countries during the 1970s and 1980s has not provided convincing evidence for the overriding importance of money in influencing the economy or in the usefulness of a set monetary rule. As a result, most economists do not support monetarist theory and its recommendations in its entirety. However, monetarist thinking has certainly caused an increased focus in contemporary macroeconomics on the possible links between money and other central economic variables, such as the price level and real output.

1. In a hypothetical economy, the annual velocity of money is 10, and level of real output is $800 billion. In year 1, the economy's money supply is $100 billion and in year 2 is $112 billion. Calculate the rate of inflation between years 1 and 2 in each of the following cases:
   a. The velocity of money and the economy's real output stay constant.
   b. The velocity of money in year 2 rises to 12, and the level of real output stays constant.
   c. The velocity of money stays constant at 10, and the level of real output rises 3 percent.

2. If the pace of technological change in an economy increases—as many economists suggest it did in the American economy in the mid-1990s—then, what problems does this create for central banks following the monetary rule?

Part 4

Canada in the Global Economy

Like other animals, we find and pick up what we can use, and appropriate territories. But unlike the other animals, we also trade and produce for trade.

—Jane Jacobs, American urban affairs expert and author

Products used to move relatively slowly in the world—Canadian lumber was transported by sailing ships to Britain, for example. Now goods are often flown by aircraft, and services are delivered by satellite or optical cable. Just as innovations in telecommunications have broken down barriers of geographical distance to create a "global village"—a term coined by Canadian communications theorist Marshall McLuhan—a unified world marketplace is coming into being. These last three chapters consider Canada in the global economy, first looking at the foreign sector in Canada, then examining international trade, and finally exploring some of the contentious issues connected with economic growth and Canada's role in the global economy.

CHAPTER 15

The Foreign Sector

That knowledge has become the key resource means that there is a world economy, and that the world economy, rather than the national economy, is in control.

—Peter F. Drucker, American social philosopher

For all nations, including Canada, the move towards a global economy is bringing about changes in living standards, employment patterns, and prospects for growth. In this chapter, we examine how foreign transactions are summarized in the balance-of-payments accounts, and we study the influence of currency exchange rates. We will also see how international financial investment has affected Canada's external debt and levels of foreign ownership in the Canadian economy.

LEARNING OBJECTIVES

In this chapter, you will:

1 be introduced to the balance-of-payments accounts, which include the current account and the capital and financial accounts

2 learn about exchange rates and how they are determined

3 examine exchange rate systems and their evolution

<table>
<tr><td>

15.1 The Balance of Payments

LO 15.1

</td></tr>
</table>

As seen in earlier chapters, the rest of the world is linked with the Canadian economy through trade. Foreigners enter Canadian product markets by buying Canadian exports. In turn, Canadians buy foreign imports. Foreign spending on Canadian exports represents a monetary inflow for Canada's product markets, while Canadian spending on imports represents a monetary outflow from the Canadian economy.

Recall also that the same principles apply to trading financial assets, such as stocks and bonds. Foreigners enter Canadian financial markets by buying Canadian stocks and bonds, thereby creating an inflow of funds to Canadian financial markets. Of course, foreigners also sell foreign stocks and bonds to Canadians, thereby creating an outflow of funds from Canadian financial markets.

The Balance-of-Payments Accounts

The connections between the Canadian economy and the rest of the world are shown in detail using Canada's balance-of-payments accounts. Recall from Chapter 1 that these accounts provide a summary of all transactions between residents of Canada and those of foreign countries that involve exchanging Canadian dollars for some other international currency. At any given time, a statement of the accounts will show how the inflows and outflows "balance."

RECEIPTS AND PAYMENTS

Transactions in the accounts are divided into receipts and payments. The receipts represent monetary inflows to the Canadian economy, including both foreign purchases of Canadian exports and inflows from foreigners when they buy Canadian financial assets. Receipts are considered positive, so they are given a plus sign (+) in the accounts.

Payments, on the other hand, represent monetary outflows from the Canadian economy. They include outlays by Canadians for foreign imports and foreign financial assets. Payments are considered negative, so they are given a minus sign (–) in the accounts.

The Current Account

current account: the summary of all foreign transactions associated with current economic activity in Canada and involving Canadian dollars

Figure 15.1 shows the portion of the balance-of-payments statement that is called the **current account**. This account summarizes all foreign transactions associated with current economic activity in Canada and involving Canadian dollars. The current account includes four types of transactions: trade in merchandise (in other words, tangible goods) as well as in three "invisible" items—trade in services, flows of investment income, and transfers.

TRADE IN MERCHANDISE

merchandise balance of trade: merchandise export receipts minus merchandise import payments

The most significant and obvious components of the current account are Canadian exports and imports of goods, or "visibles," as they are known. Canadians sell a broad range of merchandise exports and buy an equally broad range of merchandise imports. In years when the dollar value of Canadian exports of visibles outweighs that of Canadian imports of visibles, the current account shows a positive **merchandise balance of trade**. For example, in 2002, payments for Canadian exports of merchandise were \$410.3 billion and payments for Canadian imports of merchandise were \$356.1 billion, giving a positive merchandise balance of trade of \$54.2 billion. In contrast, in years when imports of goods outweigh exports, the current account shows a negative merchandise balance of trade.

Figure 15.1   Canada's Current Account (2002)

| | (Canadian $ billions) | | | | | |
	Receipts (+) (Canadian $ inflows)		Payments (–) (Canadian $ outflows)		Balance (net) (Canadian $ inflows – outflows)
Merchandise trade	410.3	–	356.1	=	+54.2
Trade in services	58.2	–	66.1	=	–7.9
Balance of trade (net exports)				=	+46.3
Investment income	29.9	–	60.3	=	–30.4
Transfers	6.7	–	5.3	=	+1.4
Current account surplus (+) or deficit (–)					+17.3

The current account details receipts (Canadian dollar inflows) and payments (Canadian dollar outflows) for merchandise trade and nonmerchandise transactions (trade in services, investment income, and transfers). In contrast to the large surplus in the 2002 merchandise balance of trade, Canada had a smaller surplus in its 2002 balance of trade (net exports). Overall, for 2002, the difference between total receipts and total payments gave a current account surplus of $17.3 billion.

Source: Statistics Canada "Canada's Current Account," adapted from the Statistics Canada CANSIM II database http://cansim2.statcan.ca Tables 376-0001 and 376-0002 and from the Statistics Canada publication "Canada's balance of international payments," Fourth Quarter 2002, Catalogue 67-0001, Vol. 50, No. 4, March 2003, pp. 54–55.

$$\text{Merchandise balance of trade} = \text{merchandise export receipts} - \text{merchandise import payments}$$

$$+\$54.2 \text{ billion} = +\$410.3 \text{ billion} - \$356.1 \text{ billion}$$

NONMERCHANDISE TRANSACTIONS

The three remaining "invisible" components of the current account—trade in services, investment income, and transfers—are known collectively as nonmerchandise transactions.

Services

Not only do Canadians import and export goods, but they also exchange services with foreigners. One important type of traded service is tourism. Spending by foreign tourists travelling in Canada represents a service export that creates an inflow of funds from foreign countries. Conversely, when Canadians travel outside Canada, their spending in foreign countries is considered a service import that causes an outflow of Canadian funds to foreign hands.

Canadians also import services when they pay foreigners to provide freight and shipping for goods. Likewise, Canadians export services when they transport goods on behalf of foreigners. In addition, a host of other invisible service items, such as insurance and telecommunications, are traded between Canadians and other countries. In 2000, the service account had a net balance of –$7.9 billion, showing that more services were imported by Canadians than were exported.

Investment Income

Dividends to owners of company stocks appear as investment income in the current account, as do interest payments to owners of bonds. An American company's dividends received by a Canadian stockholder, for example, are treated as a receipt in the current account, or a positive figure. In contrast, payments to a German owner of a Canadian government bond are shown as a payment in the accounts, or a negative figure.

Because of extensive foreign ownership of Canadian stocks and bonds, payments of investment income usually overwhelm receipts, giving Canada a large negative balance on its investment income account. This is illustrated by the 2002 balance of −$30.4 billion.

Transfers

Transfers are funds entering and leaving Canada through payments, either by individuals or government that do not involve shifts in financial assets. Private gifts that involve cash rather than financial assets and which are either to or from Canada, pension payments to and from Canada, as well as government foreign aid to low-income countries are all considered to be transfers. When new immigrants to Canada bring funds with them, these funds are considered an inflow to the Canadian economy. In contrast, federal government spending on foreign aid is considered an outflow. In 2002, transfers showed a net balance of +1.4 billion.

Current Account Balance

current account deficit: a negative net balance in the current account resulting from lower receipts than payments for merchandise and nonmerchandise transactions

current account surplus: a positive net balance in the current account resulting from higher receipts than payments for merchandise and nonmerchandise transactions

balance of trade: for both goods and services, receipts (inflows of Canadian dollars) less payments (outflows of Canadian dollars)

capital account: the summary of transfers of ownership of savings and intangible assets

financial account: the summary of all foreign transactions of financial assets involving Canadian dollars

When the receipts represented in Canada's current account are lower than the payments, this results in a negative net balance, which is known as a **current account deficit**. On the other hand, when receipts on the current account outweigh payments, Canada has a **current account surplus**. In 2002, this surplus totalled $17.3 billion.

The Balance of Trade

Two of the four components of the current accounts can be viewed in another way. Canada's **balance of trade** represents both goods *and* services, so it is identical to net exports (X − M), which was discussed in previous chapters. In recent years, Canada's surplus in merchandise trade has been greater than the deficit in trade in services, giving a surplus in the balance of trade of all products. Note that the two terms "balance of trade" and "merchandise balance of trade" are quite different; despite this, the terms are frequently and inaccurately interchanged by the media, leading to some confusion.

The Capital and Financial Accounts

Figure 15.2 shows another portion of the balance-of-payments statement called the capital and financial accounts. The **capital account** summarizes transfers of ownership of savings and intangible assets such as patents or trademarks. For example, if a U.S. company buys a patent owned by a Canadian, this purchase is considered to be an inflow on the capital account. In contrast, when a resident of China receives part of a Canadian's bequest, this is an outflow on the capital account.

The **financial account** summarizes all foreign transactions of financial assets involving Canadian dollars. Suppose a foreigner buys a Canadian government bond and holds bank deposits valued in Canadian dollars. This ownership of financial assets is being *exported* from Canada, so an inflow of receipts is shown on the capital account. Note, however, that the interest paid on bonds or deposits appears as an outflow on the current account.

Suppose also that a Canadian purchases stock in a foreign company. In this case, the Canadian's ownership is seen as an import of ownership, so the transaction is considered to be an outflow from the capital account. Once again, note that any payment

Figure 15.2	Canada's Capital and Financial Accounts (2002)					
	(Canadian $ billions)					
	Receipts (+) **(Canadian** **$ inflows)**		**Payments (–)** **(Canadian** **$ outflows)**		**Balance (net)** **(Canadian** **$ inflows –** **outflows)**	
Capital Account	5.6	–	0.8	=	+4.8	
Financial Account						
Portfolio investment	17.9	–	43.9	=	–26.0	
Direct investment	33.6	–	24.7	=	+8.9	
Other financial investments	12.6	–	7.2	=	+5.4	
Total capital and financial account surplus (+) or deficit (–) (excl. official reserves)	64.1	–	75.8	=	–11.7	

The capital account details receipts and payments for financial investment (portfolio and direct investment) and other capital flows. In 2002, there was a large negative balance for each portfolio investment, which more than offset the positive balance in direct investment, giving a capital account deficit.

Source: Statistics Canada "Canada's Capital and Financial Accounts (2002)," adapted from the Statistics Canada CANSIM II database http://cansim2.statcan.ca Tables 376-0001 and 376-0002 and from the Statistics Canada publication "Canada's balance of international payments," Fourth Quarter 2002, Catalogue 67-0001, Vol. 50, No. 4, March 2003, pp. 54–55.

on the financial asset—in this case, a dividend—would appear as an inflow on the current account.

PORTFOLIO AND DIRECT INVESTMENT

The most significant transactions on the financial account are associated with the buying and selling of stocks and bonds. These flows are often referred to as financial investment and can be divided into portfolio investment and direct investment. Note that financial investment differs from investment, as defined by economists. While investment refers to businesses' purchases of real assets, financial investment refers to the buying of stocks and bonds.

portfolio investment: financial investment (purchases of stocks and bonds) that does not give the buyer a controlling interest in the institution issuing the assets

When the financial investment does not give the buyer a controlling interest in the institution issuing the assets, it is called **portfolio investment**. Suppose, for example, a Japanese resident buys a Canadian federal government bond. This would be shown as a receipt, or positive entry, on the financial account. Conversely, if a Canadian purchases a few hundred shares in a large American corporation that trades on the New York Stock Exchange, the transaction would be shown as a payment, or negative entry, on the financial account. Portfolio investment in and out of Canada may produce either a positive or negative balance. In 2002, for example, there was a net balance of –$26.0 billion.

direct investment: financial investment (purchases of stocks) that gives the buyer of the financial assets a controlling interest in the institution issuing the assets

In contrast to portfolio investment, **direct investment** is financial investment that gives the buyer of the financial assets a controlling interest in a company. In the case of a corporation, this may be 50 percent of the company's voting shares, or even less if ownership of the other shares is widely scattered. For example, an inflow of direct investment would occur if an Australian financier gained control of a Canadian gold-mining company. An outflow would arise if a Canadian retailer acquired majority ownership of a British competitor.

Canada's net balance of direct investment varies widely from year to year. If Canada is viewed as an attractive place in which to do business, heavy inflows of direct investment lead to an overall positive balance as was the case in 2002, when direct investment totalled +$8.9 billion. If other countries seem more appealing to foreign and Canadian investors, there can be an overall negative balance.

OTHER FINANCIAL INVESTMENTS

Most of the remaining transactions on the financial account are connected with day-to-day fluctuations in bank deposits. If, for example, a foreigner puts funds into a Canadian-dollar bank account, a positive receipt is created in Canada's financial account. Likewise, a negative payment on the account can be caused by a Canadian adding more to a US-dollar bank account.

CAPITAL AND FINANCIAL ACCOUNT BALANCES

When receipts on Canada's capital and financial accounts exceed payments, this results in a positive net balance known as a **capital and financial accounts surplus**. Such a surplus means that there are lower investments by Canadians in foreign markets than by foreigners in the Canadian market. It is also possible to show a **capital and financial accounts deficit**, with a negative net balance and outflows exceeding inflows. In 2002, for example, this balance was −$11.7 billion. Such a deficit means that there are higher investments by Canadians in foreign markets than by foreigners in the Canadian market.

Balance-of-Payments Surpluses and Deficits

Adding Canada's current and capital and financial accounts balances (as well as a statistical discrepancy, which accounts for hidden transactions that are impossible to measure) gives a relatively small figure known as a **balance-of-payments surplus** if it is positive and a **balance-of-payments deficit** if it is negative. This surplus or deficit shows whether or not inflows are higher than outflows on all foreign transactions involving trade and financial assets. In 2002, for example, Canada had a balance-of-payments deficit of $0.3 billion, as shown by the negative balance in Figure 15.3. In other words, for that year, outflows exceeded inflows on the combined current and capital and financial accounts.

capital and financial accounts surplus: a positive net balance in the capital and financial accounts, demonstrating lower investments by Canadians in foreign markets than by foreigners in the Canadian economy

capital and financial accounts deficit: a negative net balance in the capital and financial accounts, demonstrating higher investments by Canadians in foreign markets than by foreigners in the Canadian economy

balance-of-payments surplus: a positive net balance on the balance-of-payments statement, demonstrating greater receipts than payments for the current and capital and financial accounts combined; balanced with changes in official reserves

balance-of-payments deficit: a negative net balance on the balance-of-payments statement, demonstrating lower receipts than payments for the current and capital and financial accounts combined; balanced with changes in official reserves

THINKING ABOUT ECONOMICS

In the past, Canada has habitually run current account deficits and capital and financial account surpluses. Why?

The frequency of deficits in Canada's current account has been closely tied to the high degree of foreign ownership in the Canadian economy. To compensate for this outflow of interest and dividend payments, there has had to be a sizable inflow of investment funds from foreigners on the financial account, which means more foreign ownership of Canadian financial assets and higher investment outflows in the future. Financial account inflows are achieved by making Canadian bonds especially attractive to foreign buyers. Traditionally, this has been accomplished through higher real interest rates than in other countries—particularly the United States.

Question
As Canadian interest rates move closer to American rates, what effect has this had on the balance of payments?

change in official reserves: use of government's reserves of foreign currency to influence the international value of the Canadian dollar, as shown on the balance-of-payments statement

CHANGES IN OFFICIAL RESERVES

To influence the international value of the Canadian dollar (as we will discuss later), the Bank of Canada sometimes buys and sells foreign currencies, using government's reserves of foreign currency. The effect of these operations on the flow of Canadian dollars is known as the **change in official reserves**. As shown in Figure 15.3, the change in official reserves is equal in value (and opposite in sign) to the surplus or deficit noted in the balance of payments. In 2002, for example, the +$0.3 billion change in reserves matches the −$0.3 billion balance-of-payments deficit. This positive change in official reserves indicates that the Bank of Canada bought Canadian dollars (creating an inflow) by selling foreign currency for the government's official reserves. In the same way, if there were a balance-of-payments surplus, there would be a negative change in official reserves equal to that amount. This negative change in official reserves would indicate that the Bank of Canada sold Canadian dollars (causing an outflow) and bought foreign currency.

Once the change in official reserves is added to the balance-of-payments surplus or deficit, the balance-of-payments accounts sum to zero. In other words, the inflow of funds from foreigners matches the outflow of funds from Canadians, ensuring that the accounts balance. This balance occurs because holders of Canadian dollars who buy foreign currency must engage in transactions of equal value with holders of foreign currency buying Canadian dollars. For example, $1 in Canadian currency can be sold for Japanese yen only if someone is willing to purchase this Canadian dollar in return for yen.

The fact that the balance of payments account sum to zero provides Statistics Canada with the means of estimating the size of the statistical discrepancy. As seen in Figure 15.3, this discrepancy is relatively large. The large size of the statistical discrepancy relates to the fact that there are considerable international flows which government authorities are unable to directly measure. Funds that either enter or leave the country due to the smuggling of goods or because of undeclared financial investments are the largest part of these unrecorded foreign transactions.

Figure 15.3	Canada's Balance of Payments (2002)

(Canadian $ billions)	Balance (net)
1. Current account	+17.3
2. Capital and financial accounts	−11.7
3. Statistical discrepancy	−10.6
Balance-of-payments surplus (+) or deficit (−)	−0.3
4. Change in official reserves	+0.3

The sum of the current and capital and financial accounts, adjusted for the statistical discrepancy, gives Canada's balance of payments. In 2002, the result was a balance-of-payments deficit of −$0.3 billion. Because there must be change in the official reserves of foreign currency to balance any deficit or surplus, the 2002 balance of payments shows a positive change in reserves.

Source: Statistics Canada "Canada's Balance of Payments (2002)," adapted from the Statistics Canada CANSIM II database http://cansim2.statcan.ca Tables 376-0001 and 376-0002.

Brief Review

1. Because products and financial assets are exchanged between Canadians and foreigners, foreigners participate in the Canadian economy.

2. The current account summarizes all receipts and payments from international trade in merchandise, trade in services, flows of investment income, and transfers of funds. In the past, the current account has typically shown payments exceeding receipts, giving a current account deficit.

3. Because Canada's balance of trade is the exports of goods and services less imports of goods and services, it is the same as net exports (X – M).

4. The capital and financial accounts summarize all foreign transactions related to the buying and selling of assets. Large inflows of funds from foreigners buying Canadian bonds mean that in the past Canada typically has shown a capital and financial accounts surplus.

5. The current account (which has usually shown a deficit) and the capital and financial accounts (which have usually shown a surplus) are adjusted for statistical discrepancy but balanced by changes in the official reserves. The Bank of Canada either sells or buys Canadian dollars to adjust the monetary flows.

15.1 Practice Questions

1. For each of the following transactions, identify where it appears on Canada's current account and whether it is classified as a receipt or a payment.
   a. A Canadian movie chain purchases the rights to screen an Italian film in Canada.
   b. An American family purchases a Canadian-made trailer for their summer vacation.
   c. A Canadian sends a monetary gift to relatives in India.
   d. A Canadian shareholder receives dividends from a Japanese corporation.

2. For each of the following transactions, identify where it appears on Canada's capital and financial accounts and whether it is classified as a receipt or a payment.
   a. A British wealth-holder purchases bonds issued by a Canadian provincial government.
   b. An Australian mining company is purchased by a Canadian-owned corporation.
   c. A Canadian receives a cash bequest from a Spanish relative.
   d. A Norwegian shipping company opens a deposit in Canada.

3. For each of the transactions in Question 2 that appears on Canada's financial account, identify whether it is a portfolio, direct, or other investment, and explain why.

15.2 Exchange Rates

LO 15.2

foreign exchange market:
the global market in which national currencies are traded

Any transaction that appears in the balance-of-payments accounts involves trading Canadian dollars for another currency. Transactions that are classified as receipts involve foreign currency being sold to buy Canadian dollars. For example, a company that purchases Canadian paper sold in France trades European euros for Canadian dollars to pay the Canadian paper company. In contrast, transactions that are classified as payments involve Canadian dollars being sold to buy foreign currency. A Canadian buying the services of a Japanese architect, for example, exchanges Canadian dollars for Japanese yen to pay the architect.

Currencies are traded in the global **foreign exchange market**. In the Canadian sector of this market, which is run by the chartered banks, Canadian dollars are exchanged for American dollars, Japanese yen, European euros, and other international currencies. The recent revolution in communications technology has made the foreign exchange market a truly global one, with currency prices internationally consistent and immediately available. For example, if the Canadian dollar is trading at a price of 80 American cents in Toronto, then the same price applies in London and Tokyo.

Recall from Chapter 11 that the exchange rate is the value of one nation's currency in terms of another currency, and it becomes the price at any location where the two currencies are being exchanged. There are many exchange rates for a certain currency. For example, at any given moment, one Canadian dollar may trade for 80 American cents, 130 Japanese yen, or 1.10 European euros. Because most of Canada's trade is with the United States, the price of the Canadian dollar is commonly related to American dollars. We will be using the example of Canadian and American dollars in the rest of the chapter, although the same principles apply to all currencies.

Two exchange rates can be used to compare any two currencies—for example, a Canadian dollar with its American counterpart. The first tells us how many American dollars it takes to buy one Canadian dollar—for example, one Canadian dollar may cost 80 American cents. The other way to express the exchange rate is to ask how many Canadian dollars are needed to purchase one American dollar. This amount can be calculated from the first exchange rate using the following formula:

$$\text{Canadian dollars to buy US\$1} = \frac{1}{\text{American dollars to buy CDN\$1}}$$

$$\text{CDN\$1.25} = \frac{1}{\text{US\$0.80}}$$

In other words, the second exchange rate—CDN$1.25 buys US$1—is the reciprocal of the first exchange rate.

Exchange Rates and Prices

One important application of exchange rates is to determine prices of products in terms of a foreign currency—either the American dollar price of a Canadian product, for example, or the Canadian dollar price of an American item.

Foreign prices of Canadian products are calculated by applying the exchange rate to the goods' Canadian dollar prices. For example, when a Canadian export with a Canadian price of $20 is sold in the United States, its American dollar price is found by multiplying its Canadian price by the exchange rate expressed as the number of American dollars it takes to buy one Canadian dollar. When the exchange rate has a value of US$0.80 for each Canadian dollar, the American price of this product is, therefore, US$16:

$$\text{American dollar price} = \text{Canadian dollar price} \times \text{American dollars to buy CDN\$1}$$
$$\text{US\$16.00} = \text{CDN\$20.00} \times \text{US\$0.80/CDN\$}$$

Canadian prices of foreign goods are calculated in reverse. As an example, an American product imported to Canada has an American price of $40. The import's Canadian dollar price is found by multiplying the American price by the exchange rate expressed as the number of Canadian dollars it takes to buy one American dollar. When the exchange rate has a value of CDN$1.25 for each American dollar, the item's Canadian price is CDN$50:

$$\text{Canadian dollar price} = \text{American dollar price} \times \text{Canadian dollars to buy US\$1}$$
$$\text{CDN\$50} = \text{US\$40} \times \text{CDN\$1.25/US\$}$$

Foreign Exchange Markets

To see how exchange rates are set, we must look at the demand for and supply of Canadian currency in foreign exchange markets. In doing so, we concentrate on the number of American dollars needed to purchase a Canadian dollar.

DEMAND FOR CANADIAN DOLLARS

demand for Canadian dollars: the relationship between the price of a Canadian dollar and the quantity demanded in exchange for another currency

The **demand for Canadian dollars** is the relationship between the price of a Canadian dollar and the quantity of Canadian dollars demanded in exchange for another currency during a given time period. The relationship can be expressed in a schedule and a curve. As Figure 15.4 shows, this relationship is inverse, so the curve has a negative slope. For example, a jump in the price of the Canadian dollar in terms of the American dollar reduces the quantity of Canadian dollars demanded.

Figure 15.4	A Foreign Exchange Market

Canadian Dollar Demand and Supply Schedules

Price of Cdn. Dollar (in $US)	Quantity of Cdn. Dollars Supplied	–	Quantity of Cdn. Dollars Demanded
	($ billions) (surplus (+) or shortage (–))		
↓ US$0.78	60 – 40 = +20 ↓		
US$0.76	**50 – 50 = 0**		
↑ US$0.75	45 – 55 = –10 ↑		

The demand and supply curves for the Canadian dollar determine its equilibrium value, which equals its exchange rate. If the price falls (to points c) below the equilibrium value (point b), a shortage of Canadian dollars results. Without government intervention, the forces of demand and supply push the price up to equilibrium (point b), causing the Canadian dollar to appreciate. A price above the equilibrium value (at points a) causes a surplus of Canadian dollars. Without government intervention, the Canadian dollar would depreciate, returning to its equilibrium value.

Canadian dollars are demanded on foreign exchange markets to finance foreign purchases of either Canadian exports or Canadian financial assets. Foreigners buying Canadian exports of goods and services exchange their own currencies for Canadian dollars in order to pay Canadian producers. Likewise, foreigners acquiring Canadian financial assets buy Canadian dollars to settle their purchases.

The negative slope of the demand curve is determined by the first of these two groups—foreign export buyers. A higher Canadian dollar means that Canadian goods and services have higher American prices. Suppose, for example, the exchange rate for Canadian dollars is US$0.75. As a result, a Canadian export with a price of CDN$2 originally has an American price of US$1.50 ($2 × $0.75). If the value of the Canadian dollar increases from US$0.75 to US$0.80, the American price of this export rises to US$1.60 ($2 × $0.80). Because American buyers find Canadian exports more expensive, they purchase fewer of them, decreasing both Canadian export receipts and the quantity of Canadian dollars demanded in exchange for American dollars.

SUPPLY OF CANADIAN DOLLARS

supply of Canadian dollars: the relationship between the price of a Canadian dollar and the quantity supplied in exchange for another currency

In contrast, the **supply of Canadian dollars** is the relationship between the price of the Canadian dollar and the quantity of Canadian dollars supplied in exchange for another currency during a given time period. Once again, the relationship can be expressed in a schedule or a curve. As Figure 15.4 shows, the relationship is direct, as is typical in supply relationships. A rise in the price of the Canadian dollar causes an increase in the quantity supplied of Canadian dollars.

Canadian dollars are supplied in foreign exchange markets for Canadian purchases of foreign products and financial assets. Canadians buying imported products or foreign financial assets sell Canadian dollars for another currency to complete their transactions.

The positive slope of the supply curve is determined by the first of these two groups—Canadian import buyers. For example, a higher Canadian dollar lowers domestic prices of imported goods and services from the United States. If the Canadian dollar rises from US$0.75 to US$0.80, the American dollar falls in terms of the Canadian dollar from CDN$1.33 ($1 ÷ $0.75) to CDN$1.25 ($1 ÷ $0.80). An American import that costs $3 in the United States, therefore, drops from CDN$4 ($3 × $1.33) to CDN$3.75 ($3 × $1.25). Canadians respond to these lower prices by purchasing more imports, increasing both Canadian import payments and the quantity of Canadian dollars supplied in exchange for American dollars.

MARKET EQUILIBRIUM

Recall that in competitive markets, the forces of demand and supply bring the market to an equilibrium point, where demand and supply intersect. The same is true of foreign exchange markets. So, when a government allows the value of its currency to vary, foreign exchange markets will move towards an equilibrium point where any discrepancy between amounts demanded and supplied is eliminated. Figure 15.4 provides a hypothetical example.

appreciate: to increase, as when a currency's price rises in comparison with the price of another currency

If (at points *c*) the Canadian dollar exchange rate is below its equilibrium price of US$0.76 (point *b*), the quantity demanded of Canadian dollars on this foreign exchange market is greater than the quantity supplied of Canadian dollars. This causes a $10 billion shortage of Canadian currency, as shown at the exchange rate of US$0.75 ($55 billion − $45 billion). When exchange rates are allowed to vary, the price of the Canadian dollar is forced up to its equilibrium value. In this case, when one currency's price increases against another, the increased currency is said to **appreciate**. The movement to equilibrium is very rapid because foreign exchange markets are highly competitive and involve large numbers of price-conscious buyers and sellers.

In contrast, if (at points *a*) the Canadian dollar is above its equilibrium price, the quantity supplied of Canadian dollars exceeds the quantity demanded on this foreign exchange market. The result is a $20 billion surplus of Canadian currency as shown at the exchange rate of US$0.78 ($60 billion – $40 billion). When exchange rates are allowed to vary, this excess soon pushes down the price of the Canadian dollar until it reaches its equilibrium value. In this case, the Canadian dollar is said to **depreciate**, compared with the American dollar. Again, the movement towards equilibrium happens very quickly.

depreciate: to decrease, as when a currency's price falls in comparison with the price of another currency

Note that both the preceding examples involve the variations in exchange rates that bring about changes in quantities demanded or supplied. In other words, the examples demonstrate movements *along* the Canadian dollar demand and supply curves.

Changes in Demand and Supply

Of course, other factors can cause the Canadian dollar demand and supply curves to *shift*. Demand and supply shifts in foreign exchange markets are related either to trade or to financial conditions. As a result of shifts in the curves, the equilibrium exchange rate changes. Four main factors affect the equilibrium value of the exchange rate: price differences, product demand, interest rates, and speculation.

PRICE DIFFERENCES

A country's price level may rise more rapidly than the price levels in other countries so that its own products become more expensive than foreign products. The left graph in Figure 15.5 illustrates a hypothetical example of what happens when Canada's rate of inflation outpaces inflation in the United States.

At any given exchange rate between the two currencies, increases in the prices of Canadian products mean that Americans will purchase fewer Canadian exports, reducing the amount of Canadian currency demanded on this foreign exchange market. This reduces the demand for Canadian dollars, shown as a shift in the demand curve for

Figure 15.5   **Exchange Rate Changes**

On the left graph, a decrease in demand, shown as the shift from D_0 to D_1, and an increase in supply, shown as the shift from S_0 to S_1, cause the Canadian dollar to depreciate from point *a* to point *b*. Conversely, as shown on the right graph, an increase in demand (from D_2 to D_3) and a decrease in supply (from S_2 to S_3) cause the Canadian dollar to appreciate from point *c* to point *d*.

Canadian dollars from D_0 to D_1. A lower American inflation rate also means that American products become cheaper relative to Canadian products. As a result, Canadian buyers purchase more American imports at any given exchange rate. This increases the supply of Canadian dollars, thereby shifting the supply curve from S_0 to S_1. As a result of these demand and supply changes, the Canadian dollar depreciates, or falls in value, from point *a* to point *b*.

PRODUCT DEMAND

The appeal of a country's products to prospective buyers can also affect exchange rates. Suppose, for example, the quality of Canadian products improves. As a result, the demand for Canadian products in both foreign and domestic markets increases. The result is illustrated on the right graph in Figure 15.5.

In this case, Americans increase their purchases of Canadian products, thereby shifting the demand curve for Canadian dollars from D_2 to D_3 in this foreign exchange market. Also, Canadians buy more domestic products and fewer American imports. This reduces the sale of Canadian dollars on this foreign exchange market and so shifts the supply curve to the left, from S_2 to S_3. Both trends cause the Canadian dollar to appreciate, or rise in value, from point *c* to point *d*.

INTEREST RATES

Suppose that the Bank of Canada implements expansionary monetary policy, causing Canadian interest rates to fall in comparison with corresponding American rates. As shown in Figure 15.5, on the left, this has implications for the Canadian dollar.

With the drop in the Canadian interest rate, Canadian bonds become less appealing to financial investors in both Canada and the United States. Fewer American purchases

THINKING ABOUT ECONOMICS

What factors prompt speculators to enter foreign exchange markets?

Speculators respond to three factors: interest rates, inflation rates, and the political climate. Because of the influence of interest rates on exchange rates, speculators pay particular attention to monetary policy. Any indication that the Bank of Canada is following contractionary policy, for example, leads speculators to forecast a rise in Canadian interest rates and a resulting increase in the value of the Canadian dollar. Speculation, therefore, hastens the Canadian dollar's appreciation in the foreign currency market. Speculators also act on the basis of expectations about inflation. For example, they may expect that the Canadian inflation rate will fall, compared with inflation rates in other countries. As a result, speculators expect a future rise in the Canadian dollar's value. This prediction again causes intervention in the foreign exchange market that immediately raises the value of the Canadian dollar. Finally, speculators pay attention to political factors—especially their possible impact on foreign-held debt. Suppose, for example, there is a risk that Canada will become politically unstable. Speculators will expect that instability to make Canadian bonds less attractive to foreign investors, thereby reducing the demand for Canadian dollars on the foreign exchange market. In anticipation of the possible fall in the Canadian dollar's value, speculators will sell Canadian dollars immediately, thus hastening the change they predict.

Question
How would speculators react to a tax cut in Canada that is expected to increase foreign-held Canadian debt?

of Canadian bonds mean that the demand for Canadian dollars decreases, thereby shifting the demand curve from D_0 to D_1. Meanwhile, Canadians also reduce their purchases of domestic bonds *and* are more likely to buy foreign financial assets. In order to buy the foreign financial assets, Canadians must sell additional Canadian dollars on foreign exchange markets. The result is an increase in the supply of Canadian dollars, shown as a shift to the right of the supply curve from S_0 to S_1. The movements in demand and supply both cause the Canadian dollar to depreciate.

SPECULATION

Some individuals, but more often financial institutions, buy and sell on foreign exchange markets simply in order to profit from short-run changes in currency values. The activities of these profit-seekers, known as **speculators**, affect the demand and supply of particular currencies and so lead to changes in exchange rates.

speculators: individuals or organizations that buy and sell currencies for profit

For example, if there are signs that the Canadian dollar will soon rise in value against the American dollar, speculators enter the market in such a way as to make this expectation a reality. Figure 15.5, on the right, shows the effects. Lured by potential profits, American speculators demand the currency that is expected to rise in value, so they purchase Canadian dollars by selling their holdings of American dollars. As a result, the demand curve for Canadian dollars shifts from D_2 to D_3. At the same time, Canadian speculators hold onto and perhaps buy more Canadian dollars rather than buying American dollars. As a result, the supply curve for Canadian dollars shifts from S_2 to S_3. As a result of both trends, the Canadian dollar appreciates and speculators make a tidy profit.

Brief Review

1. Exchange rates are prices of currencies in terms of other currencies. They are determined in global foreign exchange markets.

2. The demand for Canadian dollars is the relationship between the price of a Canadian dollar and the quantity of Canadian dollars demanded in exchange for another currency. The relationship is inverse, so, for example, an increase in price causes a decrease in quantity demanded. This is shown as a movement along the demand curve. Demand for Canadian dollars in foreign exchange markets is created by foreigners' purchases of Canadian exports and financial assets.

3. The supply of Canadian dollars is the relationship between the price of the Canadian dollar and the quantity of Canadian dollars supplied in exchange for another currency. The relationship is direct; so, for example, an increase in price causes an increase in quantity supplied. This is shown as a movement along the supply curve. Canadian dollars are supplied in foreign exchange markets for Canadian purchases of foreign products and financial assets.

4. When currency values are allowed to vary, a currency's exchange rate will move towards its equilibrium value, the point of intersection of the demand and supply curves for the currency.

5. Factors that shift the demand and supply curves for a particular currency, and so the equilibrium point as well, are price differences, product demand, interest rates, and speculation.

15.2 Practice Questions

1. For each of the following trends, outline the effect on the price of the Canadian dollar in terms of American dollars, taking into account shifts in both demand and supply.

   a. Canadian interest rates fall due to an expansionary monetary policy initiated by the Bank of Canada.

   b. Canada is viewed as a less attractive place to make financial investments by both Canadians and Americans.

   c. Canada's real output falls at the same time as real output in the United States is staying constant.

2. Using EconGraphKit (at www.mcgrawhill.ca/college/lovewell), show the shifts and demand and supply associated with the change in the price of the Canadian dollar in part a. of Question 1 above.

3 Outline how speculators would respond to the following events.

   a. The Bank of Canada increases the Canadian target overnight rate.

   b. There is an expectation that Canadian inflation rates will rise.

   c. Due to a new constitutional accord, there is a lower risk that Quebec will separate from Canada.

15.3 Exchange Rate Systems

flexible exchange rates: currency exchange rates that are allowed to move freely to their equilibrium levels; also called floating rates

Flexible Exchange Rates

Governments that allow the exchange rate of their currency to vary freely, as assumed in Figures 15.4 and 15.5, are following a system of **flexible exchange rates**, or floating rates, as they are sometimes known.

Flexible exchange rates offer one main advantage: market forces quickly eliminate shortages or surpluses so that inflows and outflows soon match each other. However, flexible rates also have an important disadvantage. Dramatic changes in exchange rates mean considerable risks for businesses involved in importing or exporting.

Consider, for example, a Canadian importer of American-made products. If the Canadian dollar depreciates suddenly, the price of the products is pushed up to the point that the products become too expensive for Canadian consumers, and quantity demanded decreases. Canadian exporters and their suppliers face similar uncertainty. Suppose, for example, the Canadian dollar jumps in value in relation to the American dollar. The exporter who exports Canadian products to the American market finds that they become too expensive for the American market, and quantity demanded decreases. Because of these fluctuations, incomes and employment in the import and export industries are harmed.

Fixed Exchange Rates

fixed exchange rates: currency exchange rates set or "pegged" to a certain value by each country's government

To avoid the uncertainty caused by flexible exchange rates, governments often intervene directly in foreign exchange markets. **Fixed exchange rates** offer the most striking alternative to floating rates. When a government establishes a fixed exchange rate, it sets or "pegs" the value of the country's currency at a certain price in terms of another currency.

IMPACT OF MARKET INTERVENTION

The effects of fixed exchange rates on a foreign exchange market are illustrated by the hypothetical example in Figure 15.6. This shows that whenever the government's target rate differs from the equilibrium level, either a balance-of-payments surplus or deficit is created.

Suppose the federal government sets a target exchange rate of 82 cents in American currency (at points *c*). Because this rate is below its equilibrium level of 84 cents (point *b*), it creates excess demand for Canadian dollars, with more sought than are available on the market. This means that the inflows represented on the current and capital and financial accounts, which are associated with buying Canadian dollars, exceed the outflows represented on these accounts, which are tied to sales of Canadian dollars. This shortage leads to a balance-of-payments surplus of CDN$20 billion.

To make up for the excess demand of Canadian currency in the foreign exchange market, the Bank of Canada intervenes by selling CDN$20 billion and purchasing American currency in return. In doing so, the Bank is able to curb any rise in the value of the Canadian dollar above the desired level of US$0.82.

Suppose, instead, the federal government set the target level of the Canadian dollar at 85 cents in American currency (points *a*), above the market equilibrium price (point *b*). As a result, a $10 billion surplus of Canadian dollars translates into a $10 billion balance-of-payments deficit. To prop up the Canadian dollar at this preferred rate of US$0.85, the Bank of Canada intervenes by buying CDN$10 billion and selling American currency in return. In this way, it eliminates the excess supply of Canadian dollars.

Figure 15.6   Fixed Exchange Rates

With fixed rates, the target value of the Canadian dollar can differ from the equilibrium determined by the market demand and supply curves. A target level above (at points *a*) the equilibrium value (point *b*) produces a balance of payments deficit. A target level below (at points *c*) the equilibrium value (point *b*) results in a balance-of-payments surplus.

Exchange Rate Policy

Sometimes governments use fixed exchange rates to affect domestic output and prices. To see how policy-makers can use exchange rate policy to different ends, let us consider the impact of low exchange rates, high exchange rates, and monetary policy.

LOW EXCHANGE RATES

A low target rate for the Canadian dollar, such as US$0.82 in Figure 15.5, makes Canadian exports cheap and imports of American products expensive. This policy stimulates export revenues and inhibits import spending, thereby increasing net exports. Recall from the discussion of aggregate demand and supply in Chapter 11 that a rise in net exports increases aggregate demand. Hence, lowering the exchange rate serves as expansionary policy. Both real output and employment are boosted, and any recessionary gap that exists is reduced.

However, there are several problems in setting a low exchange rate. First, there is the danger of inflation. This hazard is especially acute if the economy is near its potential output, when shifts in the aggregate demand curve primarily affect prices. Second, there is a chance that a country's trading partners may respond by reducing *their* exchange rates to maintain their own export markets. When this happens, currencies return to their original relative values, and the original policy achieves nothing.

Despite these risks, a policy of low exchange rates has sometimes been pursued with success. For example, Pacific Rim countries, such as Taiwan and South Korea, have in the past depressed the values of their currencies as a way of encouraging export-driven growth. Evidence of this strategy was found in their large holdings of foreign currency, which resulted from the balance-of-payments surpluses associated with a low exchange rate policy.

HIGH EXCHANGE RATES

Setting a high target for the Canadian dollar, such as US$0.85 in Figure 15.6, has the opposite effect: high exchange rates make imports cheaper and boost the prices of Canadian exports. Therefore, raising the exchange rate serves as contractionary policy by reducing net exports and decreasing aggregate demand. This puts downward pressure on inflation as well as on real output and employment.

Using a high exchange rate as an anti-inflationary tool has its problems, however. Not only is there a reduction in output and employment—especially in exporting industries—but also a reduction in the government's foreign currency holdings. Sooner or later, through continual balance-of-payments deficits, the holdings are depleted. In this situation, countries sometimes attempt to bolster their currency reserves by such measures as forcing citizens to sell their foreign currency to the government rather than allowing them to trade it privately. These laws produce underground foreign exchange markets, with prices set at equilibrium levels determined by demand and supply.

MONETARY POLICY AND EXCHANGE RATES

The Bank of Canada can use monetary policy to back its intervention in the foreign exchange market. Recall that interest rates and the price of the Canadian dollar move in the same direction. If the Bank wishes to raise the exchange rate without incurring a balance-of-payments deficit, it can force up interest rates using contractionary monetary policy. Conversely, an easy money policy of low interest rates can be applied to depreciate the exchange rate. In either case, the Bank of Canada influences the Canadian dollar by adjusting its equilibrium value.

Unfortunately, applying monetary policy in this way can complicate stabilization policy. If the Bank of Canada focuses its monetary policy excessively on maintaining a certain target exchange rate, it may end up worsening the business cycle. Therefore, the Bank must make sure its target value for the Canadian dollar allows the economy to move towards its potential output.

Evolution of Exchange Rate Systems

During the past century, there have been three major exchange rate systems used by industrialized countries: a fixed gold standard, a structure of adjustable fixed rates, and the widespread use of the managed float, which offers a middle ground between the extremes of fully flexible and fixed exchange rates.

THE GOLD STANDARD (1879–1934)

Except for a brief time connected with the financial turmoil caused by World War I, the international gold standard was in place for over five decades. With this system, each country set the value of its currency in terms of an amount of gold. (For example, the Canadian dollar traded for 23.22 grains of gold.) Because these standards were not adjustable, maintaining a constant exchange rate took precedence over stabilization policy. The gold standard finally broke down under the strains of the Great Depression of the 1930s as governments unsuccessfully attempted to stimulate their exports and domestic employment levels by depreciating their currencies.

THE BRETTON WOODS SYSTEM (1945–1971)

The disarray caused by exchange rate movements in the latter half of the 1930s led to the creation of the Bretton Woods system after World War II. (Bretton Woods is the name of the place in the United States where the conference to establish an international monetary system was held.) This system was based on adjustable fixed exchange rates. Governments set an official exchange rate for their currency until persistent surpluses or shortages in the foreign exchange market forced an adjustment. The currency then underwent a **devaluation** (reduction in value) when there were surpluses, or a **revaluation** (an increase in value) when there were shortages.

devaluation: a reduction in the value of a currency by the government that sets the exchange rate

revaluation: an increase in the value of a currency by the government that sets the exchange rate

The organization known as the International Monetary Fund (IMF) was also established at this time. Among other tasks, it promotes the stability of exchange rates through loans to countries that are running out of foreign currency reserves in order to stabilize their currencies.

From 1950 to 1962, the Canadian government chose to diverge from the international Bretton Woods system and adopted floating rates instead. Substantial inflows of foreign financial investment kept the value of the Canadian dollar high during these years. During most of this period, the Canadian dollar traded above the price of US$1.

Canada returned to a fixed exchange rate system from 1962 to 1970, pegging its dollar at a relatively low value of US$0.925. This action was prompted by speculators who were driving down the Canadian dollar's value. The Canadian experience in the 1960s points out an interesting problem with fixed exchange rates. With such a system, it is difficult for a country to shield itself from foreign inflation. In Canada's case, rising inflation experienced by the United States during this period was automatically "imported" to Canada as prices for American items sold in Canada increased.

MANAGED FLOAT (1971 TO THE PRESENT)

managed float: a flexible exchange rate system that sometimes involves short-term government intervention

The stability provided by the Bretton Woods system helped promote the high growth rates experienced by most countries in the post-war period. However, the system fell apart in 1971 when the United States—whose dollar had come to serve as an "international currency"—was forced to adopt a **managed float**. Under this system, the foreign value of a currency is allowed to vary over time, but the effects of short-run demand and supply movements in the foreign exchange market are sometimes lessened through government intervention. The move to a partially floating exchange rate provided the American government with the leeway needed to deal with imbalances in the foreign exchange market. By 1974, most other major economies had also switched away from fixed exchange rates.

Canada preceded most other countries in adopting a managed float in 1970. During the early 1970s, high prices for many of Canada's resource exports boosted the demand for Canadian currency. As a result, the Canadian dollar traded above US$1. Relatively rapid inflation in Canada during the late 1970s and early 1980s, however, caused the Canadian dollar to decline to an all-time annual low of US$0.72 by 1986. In the late 1980s and the first half of the 1990s, the dollar rose and then fell in response to interest rate adjustments by the Bank of Canada. It fell even further during the latter part of the 1990s and early 2000s, due in part to a slump in the prices of many of Canada's natural resource exports. The behaviour of the American price of the Canadian dollar in the last few decades is indicated in Figure 15.7.

Figure 15.7   Canadian Exchange Rates

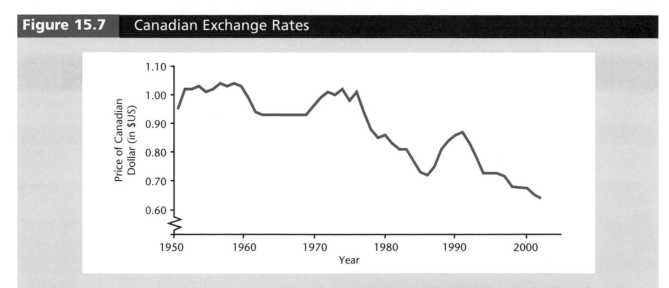

With floating rates, the Canadian dollar rose above US$1 in the 1950s. Between 1962 and 1970, it remained at its fixed value of US$0.925. With a managed float in place since 1970, the Canadian dollar has fluctuated widely.

Sources: Statistics Canada "Canadian Exchange Rates," adapted from the Statistics Canada publication "Canadian economic observer. Historical statistical supplement," 2001/02, Catalogue 11-210, Vol. 16, July 2002, p. 97, from the Statistics Canada CANSM II database http://cansim2.statcan.ca Table 176-0047 and from the Statistics Canada website http://www.statcan.ca/english/Pgdb/econ07.htm

THINKING ABOUT ECONOMICS

What are the trends in exchange rate systems?

Because of two factors—the uncertainty of fluctuating currency prices and multinational trade arrangements—some countries started moving back to pegged exchange rates in the 1990s. For example, various member nations of the European Union (EU), including Germany and France, synchronized their currencies through a system of adjustable fixed exchange rates. With the growing integration of national economies, these types of regional exchange rate arrangements will probably become more common. Many economists have predicted that the integration of national economies will bring about a single international currency.

Question
What are the main advantages and disadvantages of a single international currency?

Brief Review

1. While flexible exchange rates allow the foreign exchange market to correct imbalances automatically, this system can create instability in the domestic economy, especially for businesses involved in importing or exporting.

2. By fixing, or pegging, an exchange rate, a government can create balance-of-payments surpluses and deficits.

3. Governments can use exchange rate policy as a means of influencing output and price levels. A lower exchange rate fosters more domestic output and employment, while a higher exchange rate reduces inflation. Governments can also use monetary policy to influence exchange rates by adjusting interest rates.

4. Three main exchange rate systems have prevailed worldwide over the past century: the fixed gold standard, the Bretton Woods system of adjustable fixed rates, and the recent preference for the managed float.

15.3 Practice Questions

1. a. Assuming that the American dollar is the only foreign currency traded with the Canadian dollar, analyze the effects on the foreign exchange market when the Canadian government sets a target exchange rate of US$0.65 when the equilibrium value of the Canadian dollar would otherwise be $0.70.
   b. Would the "changes in official reserves" in Canada's balance of payments accounts be positive or negative? Explain.
   c. Using EconGraphKit (at www.mcgrawhill.ca/college/lovewell), show the effects on the foreign exchange market of the target exchange rate outlined in part a. above.

2. a. Summarize the main benefits and costs of a fixed exchange rate set below the equilibrium value of the Canadian dollar in terms of the American dollar.
   b. If, instead, the exchange rate is fixed above the equilibrium value of the Canadian dollar in terms of the American dollar, what are the main benefits and costs?

LASTWORD

In this chapter, we have examined what the balance-of-payments accounts reveal about the international aspects of the Canadian economy, and we have also seen how foreign exchange rates for national currencies, such as the Canadian dollar, are determined. In the next chapter, we extend this analysis by taking an in-depth look at foreign trade—the reasons why countries engage in trade, how governments sometimes seek to encourage or to block it, and why it is that in recent decades, there has been a move towards freer trade, both within certain regions and on a global scale.

Key Concepts

appreciate 364
balance-of-payments deficit 359
balance-of-payments surplus 359
balance of trade 357
capital account 357
capital and financial accounts deficit 359
capital and financial accounts surplus 359
change in official reserves 360

current account 355
current account deficit 357
current account surplus 357
demand for Canadian dollars 363
depreciate 365
devaluation 371
direct investment 358
financial account 357
fixed exchange rates 368

flexible exchange rates 368
foreign exchange market 362
managed float 372
merchandise balance of trade 355
portfolio investment 358
revaluation 371
speculators 367
supply of Canadian dollars 364

Questions

1. Outline the effects of the following situations on Canada's balance of trade:
    a. A boom in the American economy
    b. A rise in the value of the Canadian dollar in terms of American dollars
    c. An expansion of transnational corporations' production facilities in Canada
    d. A "made-in-Canada" recession

2. Despite the large negative balance on Canada's investment income account, in some recent years Canada's current account has shown a surplus and the capital and financial accounts have shown a deficit. Give one possible reason to explain this situation.

3. For each transaction below, identify where it appears on Canada's current account and whether it is classified as a receipt or payment:
    a. A Canadian furniture dealer buys an antique clock in France.
    b. A German bondholder is paid interest by the Canadian government.
    c. A Canadian shareholder receives dividends from a Mexican company.
    d. A Canadian spends her holidays in Switzerland.
    e. An Australian television network buys a weekly series from a Canadian program producer.

   f. A Canadian sends funds to relatives living in Somalia.

   g. An Israeli consumer buys paper stationery produced in Canada.

4. For each transaction below, identify where it appears in Canada's capital and financial accounts and whether it is classified as a receipt or payment.
   a. A British retailer opens a chain of stores in Canada.
   b. A Canadian buys 1000 IBM shares on the New York Stock Exchange.
   c. A Japanese investment company adds funds to its Canadian bank account.
   d. An American purchases a bond issued by a Canadian provincial government.
   e. A Canadian media company takes over a British newspaper.
   f. A Canadian mining firm opens a bank account in Chile.
   g. An Italian immigrant to Canada transfers funds to his Canadian bank account.

Delphi's Balance-of-Payments Accounts (Delphi $ millions)

	Receipts	Payments	Balance
Current Account			
Merchandise trade	183.4	323.6	_____
Trade in services	187.9	_____	+90.5
Investment income	192.3	157.9	_____
Transfers	_____	24.5	+32.3
Capital and Financial Accounts			
Capital Account	4.7	3.5	_____
Financial Account			
Portfolio investment	65.9	_____	−20.2
Direct investment	32.7	45.8	_____
Other financial investments	_____	15.2	+22.9

5. a. Copy and fill out the above table.
   b. What is Delphi's merchandise balance of trade? balance of trade?
   c. Calculate the surplus or deficit on Delphi's current account and the surplus or deficit on its capital and financial accounts.
   d. If the statistical discrepancy in Delphi's balance of payments accounts is +$4.5 million, is Delphi running a balance of payments surplus or deficit? Explain.
   e. Calculate the "change in official reserves" that appears in Delphi's balance of payments accounts. Is this figure positive or negative? Why?

6. Calculate the following:
   a. The American dollar price of an item priced at $520 in Canadian currency when the exchange rate is CDN$1 = US$0.81
   b. The Canadian dollar price of an item priced at $24 000 in American currency if the exchange rate is US$1 = CDN$1.22
   c. The American dollar price of an item priced at $3 in Canadian currency when the exchange rate is US$1 = CDN$1.25
   d. The Canadian dollar price of an item priced at $82 in American currency when the exchange rate is CDN $1 = US$0.80

Canadian Dollar Demand and Supply Schedules

Price of Cdn. Dollar (in $US)	Quantity of Cdn. Dollars Supplied	Quantity of Cdn. Dollars Demanded
	($ billions per year)	
0.81	75	35
0.80	65	45
0.79	55	55
0.78	45	65
0.77	35	75

7. a. Use the hypothetical data in the table above to draw demand and supply curves for the Canadian dollar in exchange for American dollars.
   b. With a flexible exchange rate, what will the value of the Canadian dollar be?
   c. If the Canadian government sets a target exchange rate of US$0.81, will a balance-of-payments surplus or deficit result? Calculate the "change in official reserves" that would appear in Canada's balance-of-payments accounts, presuming that the American dollar is the only foreign currency traded with the Canadian dollar.
   d. If instead the Canadian government sets a target exchange rate of US$0.78, will a balance of payments surplus or deficit result? Again calculate the "change in official reserves" that would appear in Canada's balance-of-payments accounts, again presuming that the American dollar is the only foreign currency traded with the Canadian dollar.

8. For each of the following trends, draw a demand and supply graph to show the effect on the price of the Canadian dollar in terms of American dollars:
   a. A contractionary monetary policy initiated by the Bank of Canada raises Canadian interest rates.
   b. Canada's real output rises at a time when real output in the United States is falling.
   c. Americans (but not Canadians) find Canada a more attractive place to make financial investments.
   d. Given Canada's aging population, more Canadian "snowbirds" travel to the United States each winter.

9. (Advanced Question)
   Given the close links between the Canadian and American economies, some commentators suggest that the Canadian dollar should be fixed against the American dollar. What would be the main advantages and disadvantages of this arrangement to Canadians?

10. (Policy Discussion Question)
   a. On the basis of the Bank of Canada site, *How Monetary Policy Works* (at http://www.bank-banque-canada.ca/english/monetary/index.htm), explain how an adjustment in the exchange rate fits into the chain of events that follows the Bank's increase in the target range for the overnight rate.
   b. Does this exchange rate adjustment counteract or reinforce the Bank's policy?
   c. On the basis of your answer to part b., is monetary policy likely to be more effective under a system of flexible exchange rates or fixed exchange rates?

http://www.bank-banque-canada.ca/english/monetary/index.htm

Internet Application Questions

http://cansim.epas.
utoronto.ca:5680/pwt/pw
t.html

http://www.statcan.ca/
english/Estat/licence.htm

1. Access the Penn World Tables (at http://cansim.epas.utoronto.ca:5680/pwt/pwt. html).
   a. Use the tables to retrieve data on Canada's exchange rate for the last five years for which data are available.
   b. Identify any trends shown by the data you have retrieved and discuss which Canadian groups are hurt and which are helped by the trends you have identified.

2. Access Statistics Canada's E-Stat site (at http://www.statcan.ca/english/Estat/ licence. htm).
   a. Using the information found in "Trade," generate a two-dimensional graph showing the (spot) exchange rate in Canadian dollars for the following currencies: the American dollar, the German mark, the French franc, and the British pound, since 1950.
   b. Which of these currencies has fallen against the Canadian dollar in this period? Which of these currencies have increased against the Canadian dollar?

Sharing Prosperity

Government's Role in an Age of Globalization and New Technologies

Leading Canadian economist and public policy specialist, Judith Maxwell, is the president of Canadian Policy Research Networks. In the following article, she offers her insights on the changing role of public policy given the challenges created by globalization and the rise of new technologies.

Globalization and new technologies unleash two contradictory forces—prosperity and polarization. Together they risk creating paralysis in public policy. How can we tame these forces for the public good?

Prosperity

Fortunes are being made by corporations and by some individuals. New knowledge-based businesses are born. At the same time, companies built and sustained by people over many years are now bought, sold, divided, and combined like spare parts for a car. The breathtaking speed of change leaves some long-time employees, and some communities, on the sidelines and slower moving companies in a state of high anxiety.

Polarization

The rising tide is not lifting all boats. Incomes from employment have been polarizing into good jobs and bad jobs for the past 25 years. Some people are simply not earning enough to support a family. Poverty has increased in the 1990s because it now takes 74 hours of work per week at the minimum wage to push a family above the poverty line.

Even the middle class is polarizing into high flyers with good jobs and those left behind. They may live in Canada but their expectations are set elsewhere. They say they need a level playing field—similar tax policies, tax rates, social policies, and regulatory structures to what they encounter in the United States or elsewhere.

Many others in the middle class are not flying so high, however. They are working hard, but their incomes have declined in the 1990s. At the same time, they see their access to public services diminish, even as they pay more taxes. Many other social programs are targeted to the poorest Canadians, meaning that this part of the middle class faces diminished well-being.

Countervailing Forces

But globalization and new technologies also create countervailing forces, interdependence and a quest for community. A borderless world creates interdependence. Countries, regions, provinces, and sectors are bound together by shared vulnerability to financial instability, global warming, and virulent new infections. These are not risks that can be managed by markets or by one government or institution acting alone. Working together, they have a chance. But working together requires trust, rules, standards, money, and highly qualified professional public servants.

Many citizens also experience a sense of helplessness in the face of globalization. They yearn for belonging and identity. They can achieve this in very positive ways by building communities of interest in their neighbourhood or through their professional or faith groups. Or, they may opt for negative routes, forming their own gangs, or tightening exclusive community ties and blaming others for their misfortune.

Judith Maxwell
Source: Judith Maxwell, from Lovewell and Lorimer. *Economics Today* (McGraw-Hill Ryerson, 1995) p. 393.

In their quest for community, citizens turn to the public sector to help rebuild community, to protect them against the excesses of polarization, and to defend national symbols of their identity. They expect governments to be sensitive to their quality of life. The polling evidence shows that they want governments to be guardians of the public interest.

But governments are fighting paralysis. They have spent 15 years fighting deficits and debt. Now they are under tremendous pressure to cut taxes, while renewing their commitment to social spending. When they want to take action, they face a society deeply divided on priorities. Their slow-moving decision-making makes them look like dinosaurs in a world where markets are transforming rapidly.

To break out of the paralysis, governments must actively take on the challenges of interdependence and community. Intelligent policy-making is needed here, that can:

- Balance short- and long-term goals, such as cutting taxes and strengthening social infrastructure, like education, health, and supports for children and families.

- Encourage community and business leaders to invest in shared public spaces, citizen participation, and building connections and trust within their communities.

- Mobilize all the players in society to invest in economic opportunities for those who are young and those who have been left behind.

- Design regulatory and governance structures (domestic and international) based on shared standards and guidelines.

Our challenge in a globalizing world is to recognize the role of the guardians of the public interest. Governments have acquired a bad name because of some of the excesses of the past 50 years. But it would be hard to think of another institution as the guardian of the public interest in the global, high-tech world we expect to see in the decades ahead. Markets do have their limits.

Therefore, we need to define our own bottom line about what determines quality of life and ensure that we have guardians with the skill and resources to manage the risks that lie ahead. We have to find a way to share this prosperity with all who contribute to it. This includes those who work hard, pay their taxes, and do the best they can for their families and their communities, not just the high flyers.

People elect governments and pay their taxes in order to share risk, to keep the peace, and to represent their interests in the wider world. All these roles continue to be important in the 21st century. Indeed, some may be more important than they have ever been for the survival and sustainability of life on earth.

Source: "All of Us Must Share in This New Prosperity," *Toronto Star* (January 9, 2000), p. A13.

1. Maxwell argues that the forces of globalization and the rise of new technologies have the potential to create paralysis for traditional forms of government policy. Give two examples of this problem.

2. Maxwell contends that national governments and other institutions must work together to deal with the social and economic strains caused by globalization and the rise of new technologies. What form do you think this cooperation should take to be made most effective?

CHAPTER 16

Foreign Trade

It is very odd that, enjoying one of the highest living standards in the world, Canadians in all walks of life should nevertheless believe that their economy is a frail, hothouse creation.

—John H. Dales, Canadian economic historian

Foreign trade is an everyday part of our lives. Consider, for example, what you are wearing or what you ate today. It is likely that many of these products come from outside Canada's borders. The role of exports in our lives is less obvious, but still significant, through the effect that export industries have on Canada's economic activity and employment. In this chapter, we will see why nations exchange goods and services and how governments influence foreign trade. We will also study how the trend towards freer trade is affecting Canada's economy and the well-being of individual Canadians.

LEARNING OBJECTIVES

In this chapter, you will:

1 learn about Canada's foreign trade, trade relationships, and trading patterns

2 analyze the case for trade, based on absolute and comparative advantage

3 examine the impact of trade protection and the arguments for and against it

4 learn about Canada's trade policies from its beginnings as a country and recent international trade arrangements

16.1 Canada's Foreign Trade

globalization: the trend of growing foreign trade and investment and the spread of international businesses and markets

LO 16.1

The Importance of Trade

The rapid growth of foreign trade and investment flows and the resulting spread of international businesses and markets are all part of a trend known as **globalization**. In recent decades, reductions in transportation costs have helped increase the worldwide importance of foreign trade. Between 1950 and 1997, for example, world trade grew almost three times as fast as world GDP. There has been an even more rapid increase in foreign investment flows. For example, global foreign direct investment has doubled from 1990 to 1997. Transactions in foreign exchange markets have soared and now total well over US$1 trillion a day. Since 1997, an economic crisis in Asia and a downturn in other parts of the industrialized world have reduced the pace of globalization—in particular the increase in trade flows. Whether this is a short-term problem, or one with longer-lasting implications, is difficult to judge.

But the effects of the globalization trend since the early 1950s are nonetheless profound. Because of these longer run changes, markets are no longer contained within national boundaries, and businesses are more likely to buy resources and sell products internationally. For example, a business with its headquarters in Canada may choose to borrow from Japanese savers, purchase German-made machinery, employ Mexican workers, and sell the bulk of its output in the United States. In both its resource markets and product markets, this Canadian company probably competes with businesses from all over the world.

THINKING ABOUT ECONOMICS

How has globalization been affected by the computer revolution?

Computing power is not the only product whose costs have undergone a precipitous decline over the past few decades. The costs of long-distance-communication have plunged at a similar rate. For example, the cost of a three-minute transatlantic telephone call in 1930 was about $500 in current Canadian dollars. It is now less than 30 cents for a regular phone hookup, and virtually zero if Internet-based phoning software is used. Such innovations have changed the way businesses are organized and have made global procurement and outsourcing more economically feasible than ever before—especially in the case of services that can be exchanged electronically. With ongoing technological improvements and a greater proportion of world economic activity tied to computer-related services, the globalization trend is bound to continue.

Question
What other major contemporary trends have helped encourage globalization?

Within this international trend, Canada has shown a heavy reliance on trade. Figure 16.1 compares the value of exports of various countries as a percentage of their GDP. Canada's exports have a value equal to 44 percent of its GDP, above the world average of 23 percent and considerably higher than the United States' 11 percent and Japan's 10 percent, whose large and diversified economies allow them to be less dependent on exports and imports. However, Canada's reliance on foreign trade is not so great as that of some small industrialized countries, such as Belgium (88 percent).

Figure 16.1   The Importance of Trade

(exports as a percentage of GDP, 2000)

	Percent
Belgium	88
Canada	44
Switzerland	42
Germany	33
France	29
United Kingdom	27
China	26
United States	11
Japan	10
World average	23

The exports of a small country, such as Belgium, are high in comparison to its level of GDP. In contrast, the exports of large countries, such as China and the United States, are lower as a proportion of overall economic activity. When compared with the world average of 23 percent, Canada's exports account for a fairly high proportion of its GDP.

Source: World Development Indicators 2002, International Bank for Reconstruction and Development/The World Bank. Table 4.9, "Structure of Demand,"   pp. 236–238.

Canada's Trading Partners

With whom is Canada trading? As Figure 16.2 demonstrates, the United States is Canada's principal trading partner. In 2002, 85 percent of Canada's merchandise exports went to the United States and 72 percent of its merchandise imports came from the United States. The remaining merchandise trade was shared among nations that are part of the European Union (a group of European nations we will discuss later in the chapter), Japan, other countries in the Organization for Economic Co-operation and Development (OECD) (which we will discuss in the next chapter), and all other nations.

Figure 16.2   Canada's Merchandise Trade by Region (2002)

	Merchandise Exports		Merchandise Imports	
	($ millions)			
United States	348 384	(85%)	254 688	(72%)
European Union (EU)	21 210	(5%)	36 144	(10%)
Japan	9 707	(2%)	11 736	(3%)
Other OECD countries	11 027	(3%)	19 481	(5%)
All others	20 359	(5%)	34 060	(10%)
Total	410 686	(100%)	356 109	(100%)

The bulk of Canada's merchandise trade is with the United States. The remaining merchandise trade is shared among the member countries of the European Union, Japan, other countries in the OECD, and all other nations.

Source: Statistics Canada "Canada's Merchandise Trade by Region (2002)," adapted from the Statistics Canada publication "Canadian economic observer." Catalogue 11-010, Vol. 16, No. 3, March 2003, pp. 31–32.

Canada's Trade Patterns

Canada's merchandise trade is made up of exports and imports of both natural resources and manufactured products. As Figure 16.3 shows, Canada's 2002 merchandise exports included almost equal portions of raw or processed natural resources (agricultural and fish products, energy products, forest products, and industrial goods, such as minerals and metals) and manufactured products (machines and equipment, automobile products, consumer goods, and other). In contrast, merchandise imports of manufactured goods are more than double that of natural resources. In total, Canada had merchandise exports of about $411 billion and merchandise imports of $356 billion.

However, this is not the whole picture. Canada trades in not only merchandise but also services. Of these—involving travel, transportation, and commercial and government services—Canada exported $56.2 billion but imported $62.8 billion in 2002.

Historically, Canada has been considered a significant exporter of natural resources. Recently, though, the proportion of natural resources in Canada's merchandise exports has decreased, while the proportion of manufactured goods has increased. For example, compared with the roughly equal proportions of manufactured and natural resource exports in 2002, just over a third of Canada's merchandise exports were manufactured goods in 1971. In the same period, the ratio of natural resources to manufactured goods in Canada's imports has varied only slightly, with manufactured goods expanding.

Within Canada's service trade, business services, such as insurance, management services, and research and development, have increased most quickly as a proportion of both imports and exports. Overall, Canada's trade in services has not grown as quickly as its merchandise trade. Between 1971 and 2002, service exports as a percentage of total exports fell from 15 to 13 percent, while service imports fell from 21 to 16 percent of total imports. These figures are surprising, given the recent growth in Canada's service sector. Between 1967 and 2002, for example, Canada's service sector grew from 55 to 69 percent of Canada's real GDP, while the goods sector fell from 45 to 31 percent. Employment growth in the service sector has been even more rapid. Service sector employment now represents over 70 percent of all jobs in the Canadian economy.

| **Figure 16.3** | Canada's Merchandise Trade by Type of Product (2002) |

	Merchandise Exports		Merchandise Imports	
		($ billions)		
Consumer Goods	17 341	(4%)	46 416	(13%)
Automobile Products	97 081	(24%)	81 446	(23%)
Machines and Equipment	94 718	(23%)	105 785	(30%)
Industrial Goods	69 435	(17%)	68 828	(19%)
Forest Products	36 650	(9%)	3 134	(1%)
Energy Products	50 419	(12%)	16 456	(5%)
Agriculture and Fish Products	30 542	(7%)	21 778	(6%)
Other	14 501	(4%)	12 266	(3%)

Agricultural and fish products, energy products, forest products, and industrial goods, such as minerals and metals, together accounted for about half of Canada's 2002 merchandise exports. Machines and equipment, automobile products, consumer goods, and other products made up the rest. In terms of merchandise imports, natural resources formed a third of the total, whereas manufactured goods formed about two-thirds.

Source: Statistics Canada, "Canada's Merchandise Trade by Type of Product (2002)," adapted from the Statistics Canada CANSIM II database http://cansim2.statcan.ca Tables 228-0001, 228-0002, and 228-0003.

THINKING ABOUT
ECONOMICS

Why has the rise of a service-based economy not been reflected in Canada's international trade?

One reason is that services are usually bought and sold within national borders. For example, in 1989 less than 10 percent of services produced in Canada were exported. In comparison, over a third of all Canadian-made goods were destined for foreign markets. Another reason for the apparent slow growth in service trade relates to measurement problems. Because services are intangible, foreign trade in these products often escapes detection, especially in the common case where services are traded within a single company. Furthermore, goods and services are often sold in "bundles," and it is the merchandise part of the bundle that is counted. For example, new computer software is usually exchanged in physical form and is, therefore, counted as a good rather than as a service. These problems make it difficult to collect trade statistics that adequately reflect the importance of services.

Question
Will the expansion of e-commerce make it more or less difficult to measure trade in services?

What Is Traded

In general, countries export the commodities they produce most efficiently and import those they would produce least efficiently. Whether or not a country can produce a particular product efficiently is determined by the country's resources, market size, climate, and sometimes by chance as well.

RESOURCES

A country's pool of resources is the main factor affecting what it exports and imports. For example, Canada has been endowed with plentiful and rich natural resources that have allowed it to be a major exporter of such products as paper, wheat, and natural gas. As well, Canada has developed its human resources and capital resources in such a way that it can export capital-intensive goods. In contrast, countries with less abundant natural resources, such as Belgium, tend to be major importers of unprocessed products, and countries with a huge pool of labour and relatively few capital resources, such as Bangladesh, tend to be major exporters of labour-intensive goods. For example, almost two-thirds of Bangladesh's exports consist of textiles and clothing, whose production tends to be labour-intensive.

MARKET SIZE

Recall that some products exhibit increasing returns to scale—that is, the cost of inputs per unit of output decreases as production increases. As a result, these products tend to be produced in markets where businesses can take advantage of increasing returns to scale. So, for example, cars tend to be produced in countries with large markets of car buyers rather than in small countries or in those where few people own cars.

CLIMATE

Climate plays a key role in determining where some goods are produced, especially agricultural products. While tropical fruit could be grown in Canada—in climate-controlled greenhouses, for example—it makes little sense to do so, since tropical fruit can be imported cheaply from countries that are internationally competitive in producing them.

16.2 The Case for Trade

LO 16.2

Gains from Trade

Having determined what Canada trades and with whom, the question of "Why trade?" still remains. International trade brings significant economic gains: it increases product variety for consumers, promotes competition in each country's markets, and adds to output by allowing countries to specialize in commodities in which they are internationally competitive.

PRODUCT VARIETY

When countries trade, the number of products available to consumers expands. Consider one category of products you purchase regularly—for example, clothing, CDs, or magazines. You will probably notice that many of your purchases were produced in other countries. Adding imports to domestic products gives you greater choice.

COMPETITION

International trade increases the number of businesses selling in a country's product markets. Added competition encourages all businesses to produce goods as efficiently as possible. This results in lower prices for consumers.

SPECIALIZATION

The most important gain from international trade comes from specialization. Without international trade, a country would have to produce everything its citizens need. With international trade, however, a country can use its resources to specialize in the products it makes most efficiently, allowing it to compete in the expanded market. The income from exporting the products that the country has made so efficiently can then pay for imported products that would be more expensive to make domestically. By increasing the output gained from various countries' resources, specialization raises world living standards. In the next sections, we will see how these gains from specialization can be quantified using two related economic concepts: absolute advantage and comparative advantage.

Absolute Advantage

Specialization is easiest to see in the case of two trading partners, each of whom is better than the other at one activity. Suppose a lawyer wants custom-made wooden furniture. At the same time a carpenter wants to prepare a will. As shown in Figure 16.4, the lawyer could build the furniture herself in 20 hours, or she could hire the carpenter to do the job in 5 hours. Similarly, the carpenter could prepare the will for himself in 10 hours or hire the lawyer to do it for him in 2 hours. If the two were to trade their products, each product would be produced in the most efficient way possible.

In the example, the lawyer and the carpenter each has an **absolute advantage**, that is, each trading partner is able to produce one product using fewer resources than would other producers. The resources—in this case, time—saved by trading partners

absolute advantage: the benefit enjoyed by a producer who can supply a certain quantity of an item more efficiently than can other producers

Figure 16.4   Gains from Trade Based on Absolute Advantage

	Time Spent Building Furniture	Time Spent Preparing a Will	Time Saved through Specialization
Lawyer	20 hours	2 hours	20 – 2 = 18 hours
Carpenter	5 hours	10 hours	10 – 5 = 5 hours

A carpenter can build furniture in less time than it would take a lawyer, while the lawyer can draw up a will in less time than it would take the carpenter. Each has an absolute advantage in one task. To use the resources most efficiently, the carpenter should specialize in building the furniture, while the lawyer should specialize in preparing the will.

specializing in what they each do most efficiently is summarized in the third column of Figure 16.4.

The same principle applies to countries that engage in trade. For example, Canada may be more efficient than Japan in producing wheat, while Japan is more efficient than Canada in producing stereos. Canadians should, therefore, specialize in wheat production, leaving the Japanese to concentrate on stereo production. Through trade, both Canada and Japan can use their economic resources to produce the greatest possible output of each commodity. As a result, living standards in both countries increase.

Comparative Advantage

Because of the varying strengths of countries, trade advantages are sometimes not so clear-cut as in the case of absolute advantage. Let us consider a hypothetical case. Both Canada and Mexico can produce paper and computers, but Canada has an absolute advantage over Mexico in both products. As shown in Figure 16.5, using equal resources, Canada can produce 12 tonnes of paper, compared with Mexico's 3 tonnes, or 12 computers to Mexico's 9.

For the sake of efficiency, it would seem that both paper products and computers should be produced in Canada. However, trade is a two-way street. So, each of the two trading partners must produce and trade a product. To determine what each trading partner should produce, they must determine the opportunity cost of each product, and then produce the product for which they have the lowest opportunity cost. The trading partner with the lowest opportunity cost for a given product has the

Figure 16.5   Gains from Trade Based on Comparative Advantage

	Hypothetical Output per Worker		Opportunity Cost	
	Paper	Computers	of 1 tonne of paper	of 1 computer
Canada	12 tonnes	12 computers	1.0 computer	1.0 tonnes paper
Mexico	3 tonnes	9 computers	3.0 computers	0.33 tonnes paper

Paper has a lower opportunity cost in Canada. Thus, Canadians have a comparative advantage in producing paper, while Mexicans have a comparative advantage in making computers. In other words, each has the lower opportunity cost of producing one product.

comparative advantage: the benefit enjoyed by a producer who can supply a certain item with a lower opportunity cost than can other producers

comparative advantage. This name reflects the fact that this benefit can be determined only after comparing opportunity costs in both countries.

In our example, the opportunity cost of producing 12 tonnes of paper in Canada is 12 computers, and the opportunity cost of 12 computers is 12 tonnes of paper. This gives a cost ratio of one to one between paper and computers so that the opportunity cost of 1 tonne of paper is 1 computer. In Mexico, the cost of producing 3 tonnes of paper is 9 computers, and the opportunity cost of producing 9 computers is 3 tonnes of paper. This gives a cost ratio of one to three between paper and computers in Mexico so that the opportunity cost of 1 tonne of paper is 3 computers and the opportunity cost of 1 computer is only 0.33 tonne of paper. Because paper has a lower opportunity cost in Canada than in Mexico, Canada has a comparative advantage in paper production. Conversely, since each computer has a lower opportunity cost in Mexico than in Canada, Mexico has a comparative advantage in computer production.

Given the comparative advantages in our hypothetical example, the opportunity costs would be lowest if Canada produced paper and Mexico produced computers. This conclusion follows the **law of comparative advantage**, which states that output is maximized when producers specialize in what they can make at a lower opportunity cost than can other producers.

law of comparative advantage: states that maximum output is achieved when producers specialize in what they can make at a lower opportunity cost than can other producers

Let us assume that there are twice as many workers in Mexico as in Canada. The gains from each country fully specializing in the product in which it has a comparative advantage are shown in Figure 16.6. If there is a total of 10 workers in Canada and 20 workers in Mexico, then before trade, each country may devote half its labour force to each product.

The combined paper output of both countries is therefore 90 tonnes—60 tonnes from Canada (5 workers × 12 tonnes per worker) and 30 tonnes from Mexico (10 workers × 3 tonnes per worker). At the same time, the combined computer production of both countries is 150 computers, with 60 from Canada (5 workers × 12 computers per worker) and 90 from Mexico (10 workers × 9 computers per worker).

When both countries specialize completely in the product in which they have a comparative advantage, Canada produces 120 tonnes of paper (10 workers × 12 tonnes per worker) and Mexico makes 180 computers (20 workers × 9 computers per worker). World paper production has, therefore, risen by 30 tonnes and world computer production by 30 computers. By specializing on the basis of comparative advantage, the two countries are, therefore, able to raise their total output of both items, with this added production being shared through trade.

Figure 16.6	**Total Gains from Specialization**			
	Before Trade		After Trade	
	Paper	Computers	Paper	Computers
Canada	60 tonnes	60 computers	120 tonnes	0 computers
Mexico	30 tonnes	90 computers	0 tonnes	180 computers
	90 tonnes	150 computers	120 tonnes	180 computers

Supposing that production in both Mexico and Canada were equally split between paper and computers before they began to trade, the combined countries would produce 90 tonnes of paper and 150 computers. By specializing through trade, combined production would rise to 120 tonnes of paper and 180 computers.

TERMS OF TRADE

terms of trade: the international price of one product in terms of another

The benefits of specialization are distributed between trading partners on the basis of the **terms of trade**, or the international price of one product in terms of another product. This price depends partly on the opportunity costs of the products in each country, since producers must get at least the opportunity cost that applies in domestic transactions if they are to engage in foreign trade.

Returning to our hypothetical example, recall that in Canada, tonnes of paper and units of computers have a cost ratio of one to one. In order to make trading with Mexico worthwhile, Canadian paper producers demand one or more computers for each unit of paper they sell to Mexico. At the same time, in Mexico the cost ratio of tonnes of paper and units of computers is one to three. To make trading with Canada worthwhile, Mexican computer producers demand 1 tonne of paper for every 3 or fewer computers they sell to Canada. As a result, the international price of one product in terms of the other must fall somewhere between these limits in order for the two countries to trade:

Limits to terms of trade   1 tonne of paper : 1 computer
1 tonne of paper : 3 computers

The actual terms of trade are then set by the international demand for each product. So, for example, when the demand for paper is high in both countries, the international price of paper in terms of computers will be close to the limit of 3 computers for 1 tonne of paper. If, instead, the demand for computers is high in both countries, the international price of computers will be pushed towards the limit of 1 computer for 1 tonne of paper.

Since Canadians export paper to purchase Mexican computers, they will be best off when paper has the highest possible international price in terms of computers—in other words, when 1 tonne of paper has its maximum value of 3 computers. In contrast, Mexicans are best off when the terms of trade have reached their lowest limit. In this case, each 1 tonne of paper imported by Mexicans has an international price of 1 computer, which is the minimum possible value for paper in terms of computers.

Brief Review

1. With the recent trend towards globalization, there has been substantial growth in foreign trade and investment and international businesses and markets.

2. In comparison with other countries, Canada depends extensively on international trade. Its most significant trading partner is the United States.

3. Canada's merchandise exports include almost equal portions of natural resources and manufactured products. In contrast, its merchandise imports of manufactured products are double that of natural resources. In addition to merchandise, Canada also has significant trade in services.

4. Canada's exports of natural resources are becoming less significant than they used to be. Since the early 1970s, manufactured goods have grown considerably as a proportion of merchandise exports and slightly as a proportion of merchandise imports. While the service sector has been growing in Canada, international trade in services has not grown as much as international trade in merchandise. This is because services tend to be bought and sold within national economies and because of problems in measuring service trade.

5. What specific products a country produces for trade depends on what it produces most efficiently. Three factors affect efficiency: resources, market size, and climate.

6. Trade among nations brings significant gains: product variety, increased competition, and specialization.

7. The gains of specialization can best be seen in the cases of absolute advantage and comparative advantage. The law of comparative advantage states that output is maximized when producers specialize in what they can make at a lower opportunity cost than can other producers.

8. The terms of trade are the international price of a product in terms of another product. The terms of trade are determined by both the opportunity costs of the products for the trading partners and the international demand for the products.

16.2 Practice Questions

Daily Output per Worker

	DVDs	DVD Players
Pisces	20	4
Aries	25	1

1. The table above shows how many DVDs or DVD players can be produced daily by one worker in Pisces and Aries.

   a. Which country is more efficient at producing DVDs? DVD players?
   b. On the basis of absolute advantage, which country should specialize in the production of each good? Explain.
   c. Identify the limits of the terms of trade for these two goods.

Daily Output per Worker

	Computer Monitors	TVs
Taurus	1	2
Virgo	2	6

2. The table above shows how many computer monitors or TVs can be produced daily by one worker in Taurus and Virgo.

   a. Which country is more efficient at producing computer monitors? TVs?
   b. What are the opportunity costs of the two goods in each country?
   c. On the basis of comparative advantage, which country should specialize in the production of each good? Explain.
   d. Identify the limits of the terms of trade for these two goods.

16.3 The Impact of Trade Protection

LO 16.3

Despite the benefits of international trade, countries often try to block imports or subsidize domestic industries. First, we will examine how governments intervene in international trade. Later, we will consider the arguments against trade that motivate such intervention.

Tariffs

To see the role that foreign trade plays in markets for a specific product, let us consider a hypothetical competitive market for bicycles in Canada. The left graph in Figure 16.7 shows the demand (D) and domestic supply curves (S_{d0}) for bicycles in the unlikely case where there is no foreign trade. Market equilibrium would occur at a price of $150 and a quantity of 90 000 (point c).

If international trade in bicycles existed and this trade were unrestricted, then Canadian consumers would have the opportunity to buy either domestic or imported bicycles. Assuming for our example that the cost of transporting the product is zero, Canadians would be able to purchase foreign-made bicycles for $100, which is the prevailing world price. Since Canadian consumers make up a small proportion of the world bicycle market, their purchases do not affect equilibrium in this market. Hence, an unlimited quantity supplied is available from foreign bicycle producers at $100, as shown by the horizontal line (S_{i0}) at this price.

As shown on the left in Figure 16.7, at a price of $100, Canadian consumers would demand 130 000 bicycles (point e). However, Canadian suppliers are only willing to supply 50 000 bicycles at this price (point a). The 80 000 difference between domestic supply (S_{d0}) and domestic demand (D) represents the quantity foreign producers could

| **Figure 16.7** | The Impact of Import Barriers |

Without trade, equilibrium price in the market for bicycles is at point c in the left graph. With unrestricted imports of bicycles priced at $100, consumers demand more bicycles (point e), but domestic producers will supply fewer bicycles (point a). Imports make up the difference. With a $25 tariff, the price rises to $125 (shown by S_{i1}), imports fall (points b to d), and the government gains extra revenue shown by the shaded rectangle.

With an import quota of 40 000 bicycles, as shown in the right graph, supply shifts from S_{d0} to S_1. Compared with the case of unrestricted trade, the change in price and the quantity of imports (from point g to point f) is identical to those resulting from tariffs, but now the shaded rectangle indicates extra revenue to foreign producers. This extra revenue from a higher price at least partially offsets the loss that is due to fewer sales.

sell in this market. As a result of the international trade, the price has fallen and a significant number of consumers are buying foreign-produced bicycles.

Governments may respond to such a situation by imposing a **tariff**, which is an excise tax on imported goods. Until recent years, tariffs were a major tool of trade protection in Canada as well as in many other countries, especially against foreign manufactured goods. In our example, if a $25 tariff is applied on foreign-made bicycles, Canadian consumers must pay an additional $25—or a total price of $125. The result of this price increase is again shown on the left in Figure 16.7. The supply of imported bicycles is now depicted by a horizontal line (S_{i1}) at a price of $125. At this price, Canadian consumers demand 110 000 bicycles (point *d*). Since Canadian suppliers are willing to supply 70 000 bicycles at this price (point *b*), the difference between domestic demand and domestic supply at this price is 40 000, which foreign producers supply.

When compared with the case of unrestricted trade, tariffs affect consumers and the government in opposite ways. Consumers pay a higher price ($125 instead of $100) and buy fewer bicycles (110 000 instead of 130 000) than they did before the tariff was introduced. However, the government benefits from the tariff through the additional tax revenue it is able to raise. With a $25 tariff per bicycle and 40 000 bicycles imported, the government's extra revenue is $1 million ($25 × 40 000). This is shown on the left graph by the area of the shaded rectangle, whose height represents the tariff per bicycle and whose width indicates the quantity of imports once the tariff is in place.

Domestic and foreign producers are also affected in opposite ways by the tariff. Canadian bicycle producers and their resource suppliers benefit because of the extra earnings tied to the increase in price from $100 to $125 and the rise in domestic production from 50 000 to 70 000 bicycles. Foreign bicycle producers, however, are harmed by the tariff. They face an unchanged after-tax price for each bicycle they sell ($100) while accepting a reduction in imports—from 80 000 to 40 000 bicycles.

Import Quotas

If tariffs are not an option, a government may use other trade restrictions, known as **non-tariff barriers (NTBs)**, to limit imports. Recently, these barriers have become more popular, since governments find it harder to levy tariffs because of international trade agreements.

The most common non-tariff barrier is an **import quota**, which is a set limit on the quantity of a good that can be imported in a certain year. Import quotas can work in two ways. A government can impose an import quota itself, or it can use the threat of trade restrictions to force foreign producers to set their own "voluntary" quotas, which are known as **voluntary export restraints (VERs)**. One well-known illustration of a voluntary export restraint involves Canada's imports of Japanese cars. In 1981, an agreement limiting annual Japanese exports of automobiles to Canada was worked out between the two countries. In 1986, when the agreement expired, Japanese automakers continued to limit their exports to Canada voluntarily to stop the Canadian government from taking other types of trade action.

More recent examples include agreements in 1998 and 1999 between the United States government and steel producers in Japan and South Korea to reduce US-bound exports. Because these agreements are now illegal under world trade law, they are now made informally, rather in being set out in writing.

Generally, foreign producers find import quotas preferable to tariffs. To see why, we return to our hypothetical example of the bicycle market in Figure 16.7. The impact of an import quota on this market is portrayed on the right graph, in which the domestic demand and supply curves, D and S_{d0}, as well as the prevailing world price, are identical to those on the left graph. As before, a situation of unrestricted trade (point *g*) leads to an original $100 price, with consumption exceeding domestic production by 80 000, which represents the initial amount of bicycles imported.

By imposing a maximum level of imports of 40 000, this number of bicycles is added to the domestic supply (S_{d0}) at every price, thereby giving the combined domestic and foreign supply curve S_1. Domestic demand (D) and the new supply (S_1) intersect at the new equilibrium price of $125 and quantity of 110 000 (point *f*). Again, production is split between domestic and foreign producers. Canadian businesses produce 70 000 bicycles, leaving 40 000 for foreign businesses, shown along the shaded area.

The policy's effect on consumers and domestic producers is the same as with a tariff. The results for the government and foreign producers are different, however. With an import quota, the government no longer receives tax revenue. Instead, the extra revenue indicated by the shaded rectangle on the graph on the right flows to foreign producers in the form of higher prices on the bicycles they still sell in Canada. This extra revenue partly counteracts the loss that foreign producers bear because of the lower quantity they supply in the Canadian market.

Domestic Regulations

Regulations in particular markets can make trade within them expensive for foreign producers, therefore acting as obstacles to trade. For example, Canada has certain licensing procedures and imposes relatively high safety and environmental standards. Also, rules controlling government purchases—known as government procurement policies—may require that whenever possible, domestic rather than foreign items should be bought by governments. If imports are successfully restricted through these practices, the results are the same as in the case of an import quota.

Export Subsidies

export subsidies: payments by a government to domestic exporters so that these exporters can reduce the prices they charge in foreign markets

Export subsidies are payments by a government to domestic exporters so that they can reduce the prices they charge in foreign markets. These programs are intended to raise the amount of exports, thus increasing output and employment in the domestic economy. Besides helping domestic exporters and foreign consumers, an export subsidy imposes a cost on foreign producers, who lose sales to the new low-priced competition, and on the exporting country's own taxpayers, who must foot the bill for the program. Such subsidies have been used by many countries, including Canada, and have been especially common in agricultural markets. Indeed, these programs were a major reason for low prices in global agricultural markets during the early 2000s.

The Case for Trade Protection

The gains in economic welfare associated with specialization and the law of comparative advantage are generally large enough to make a compelling case for free trade. Consequently, it is common for economists to oppose government policies that protect trade. Nonetheless, particular cases of trade protection can be defended with either economic or noneconomic arguments. We will look at each of these arguments in turn.

ECONOMIC ARGUMENTS

Five economic arguments can be applied to support various types of trade protection. According to these arguments, trade barriers help stimulate domestic employment, foster infant industries, improve a country's terms of trade, protect a country's environmental and safety standards, and shield domestic workers from imports produced with cheap foreign labour.

Domestic Employment

Because imports are a withdrawal from an economy's circular flow, they have a dampening effect on total spending and output. Thus, a reduction in the level of imports through trade barriers can potentially increase the level of economic activity in the country and provide more jobs for domestic workers.

This argument is legitimate only in certain circumstances, however. Because a strategy of import reduction causes foreign countries' exports to diminish, output and employment levels in these foreign nations will fall. Hence, the new domestic employment in the country imposing trade barriers comes at the expense of jobs elsewhere. The threat of foreign retaliation means that this policy can easily backfire—other nations may try to recapture some of their lost exports and jobs by imposing new trade barriers of their own. Such behaviour makes everyone worse off by limiting the opportunities for each country to specialize on the basis of comparative advantage.

Infant Industries

infant industry: a domestic industry that is young in comparison to its foreign competitors

An **infant industry** is made up of domestic producers that are young, compared with competitors in foreign countries. Because of their recent origin and small size, domestic producers are not able to take full advantage of increasing returns to scale. Until they are able to, according to supporters, lower-priced foreign imports must be blocked.

This type of protection is often used by countries whose prosperity is closely tied to just a few export products and where there is a wish to develop new industries in which there is no immediate comparative advantage.

But the argument for protecting infant industries is only valid if other countries do not retaliate with their own trade barriers. Even if retaliation does not occur, the argument is open to abuse. Once imposed, trade barriers in a given industry are difficult to eliminate. Industry groups—representing both business and labour—tend to fight any reduction in barriers, even after their industry has fully matured. And industries created in this fashion often represent an inefficient employment of resources. In the absence of international competition in protected markets, domestic consumers pay high prices for what may be substandard goods.

THINKING ABOUT ECONOMICS

In what industries is the infant industry argument currently relevant?

In recent years, the argument relating to infant industries has gained new importance in high-technology markets, such as the aircraft and semiconductor industries, where a few large businesses are able to take advantage of increasing returns to scale, and where the flourishing of one high-tech industry can act as a magnet for firms in other high-tech industries as well. Strategic trade policy is the use of tariffs and export subsidies to help domestic producers gain a foothold in these industries.

Question
What are some arguments that could be made for and against the use of strategic trade policy?

Terms of Trade

If a country's volume of trade is large enough to affect prices in a world product market, then it can use trade barriers to improve its terms of trade. For example, the United States could impose a tariff on its imports of Canadian lumber. This would decrease the global demand for lumber, pushing down lumber's international price. As a result, Americans would be able to acquire the same amount of Canadian lumber with a smaller quantity of American products. As long as Canada does not retaliate with its own trade barriers, the terms of trade move in the United States' favour.

Environmental and Safety Standards

In order to address spillover costs, in particular those related to the environment and safety, many governments impose standards that can be quite costly to certain businesses. However, standards vary. While some countries may regulate industry either to reduce or to compensate for spillover costs, other countries—especially those with low per capita GDP—may have very lax environmental and safety regulations to allow exporters there to reduce their expenses and product prices.

Critics of lax environmental standards suggest that without trade protection, increased globalization will be accompanied by an increase in environmental damage. Similarly, critics of lax safety standards believe that without trade protection, workers in all countries are hurt. Those in countries with low safety standards face increased risks of injury on the job, while those in countries with strict standards face a reduction in the demand for labour and, therefore, fewer available jobs.

According to critics of low environmental and safety standards, countries should maintain high standards and set up trade barriers against exports from countries with lower standards. They argue that without these two measures, businesses operating in countries with lax standards will continue to profit, other businesses will move their operations to such countries in order to gain a competitive edge, and spillover costs will increase internationally.

Cheap Foreign Labour

A related argument suggests that imports produced by cheap foreign labour need to be blocked from entering an industrialized country in order to protect the jobs of domestic workers. In its basic form, this argument is flawed because it ignores the key reason for the differences among wage rates in various countries. Workers in countries with a higher per capita GDP tend to earn more than workers elsewhere because of their higher productivity, as defined in Chapter 7. Workers in industrialized countries tend to be highly skilled and are employed along with larger amounts of capital per worker. Once average wages in various countries are compared with these different productivity levels, workers in industrialized nations still possess a comparative advantage over low-wage foreign labour in many types of production. Nonetheless, it is likely that certain groups of workers in industrialized countries—especially those in low-productivity sectors—will be hurt by increased trade with less-developed countries.

NONECONOMIC ARGUMENTS

The two remaining arguments in favour of trade barriers are based on noneconomic factors: national security and cultural sovereignty.

National Security

The oldest argument for trade barriers relates to national security. A country's citizens may wish to be self-sufficient in producing certain strategic commodities, such as basic food items and military equipment. If a war breaks out, supplies of these commodities will then be guaranteed. The way to ensure that domestic industries can develop in these sectors is to insulate them from foreign competition. This argument has been applied in such countries as Israel, where military threats to national security have been a major concern, but its relevance to Canada seems limited.

Cultural Sovereignty

Another noneconomic argument for certain types of trade protection relates to culture. Some countries, including Canada, have felt the need to protect and nurture their own cultural industries by, for example, restricting the imported content of radio and TV programming, limiting broadcast licences, subsidizing "home-grown" authors and visual artists, or purchasing only domestically produced textbooks. In one recent incident, in order to help the French movie industry withstand foreign competition—especially from Hollywood—France blocked American attempts to liberalize international trade in movies. However, critics suggest that in an age of satellite communications and the Internet, trade barriers relating to many cultural industries can no longer be enforced.

Brief Review

1. Governments may intervene in international markets through a variety of means, including tariffs, non-tariff barriers (import quotas, voluntary export restraints, and domestic regulations), and export subsidies.

2. Tariffs are excise taxes on imported goods. In contrast, import quotas and voluntary export restraints are limits on the quantity of a product that can be imported in a certain year. These barriers result in higher prices, lower consumption, fewer imports, and more domestic production of the item affected. With a tariff, governments gain extra tax revenue; with an import quota or voluntary export restraint, revenues from the resulting higher prices flow to the foreign producers, partly offsetting the effect of the decrease in sales.

3. Domestic regulations can present obstacles to trade. When successful, the results parallel the effects of an import quota.

4. Export subsidies are another form of trade intervention. In this case, governments make payments to domestic exporters so that exporters can lower the prices they charge in foreign markets. The results are lower sales of foreign products and higher domestic taxes.

5. The economic arguments in favour of trade barriers relate to domestic employment, infant industries, the terms of trade, environmental, and safety standards, and cheap foreign labour.

6. The noneconomic arguments in favour of trade barriers relate to maintaining national security and cultural sovereignty.

16.3 Practice Questions

1. Outline which groups in the economy are helped and which are harmed by a tariff on imports of a particular item sold in a perfectly competitive market.
2. Explain why foreign producers usually prefer an import quota rather than a tariff.

16.4 Trade Policies

Recall that Canada's most significant trading partner now and throughout much of its history is the United States. As a result, trade between the two countries has played an important role in determining Canadian trade policy.

Early Canadian Trade Policy

In 1854, British and American diplomats signed the Reciprocity Treaty, establishing favourable trade relationships between British North America and the United States. So, for the duration of this treaty, tariff rates were relatively low between the United States and what is now Canada.

This reciprocal trade relationship broke down in 1866 due to a number of political and economic factors. Thereafter, trade between Canada and the United States became increasingly restrictive. As portrayed in Figure 16.8, the average Canadian tariff rate as a percentage of total merchandise imports rose in the years after the Confederation.

THE NATIONAL POLICY

National Policy: a Canadian policy initiated in 1879 that included high Canadian tariffs on manufactured imports in order to stimulate a domestic manufacturing sector

In 1879, Canada's first prime minister, Sir John A. Macdonald, instituted a wide-ranging tariff policy based on the infant-industry argument for trade protection. The **National Policy** led to high tariffs on manufactured imports to stimulate the development of a domestic manufacturing sector. Without this policy, supporters argued, Canadian manufacturers would be swamped by low-priced American competition produced with the benefits of increasing returns to scale. Due to the National Policy, Canada's average tariff rate in the succeeding decades stayed above 15 percent. As a result, many American manufacturers chose to "jump the tariff wall" by setting up branch plants in Canada to allow them to continue selling in Canadian markets.

THE GREAT DEPRESSION

While Canada's tariffs gradually fell after World War I, the Great Depression sparked a new round of protectionism. Such a trend is common during economic downturns.

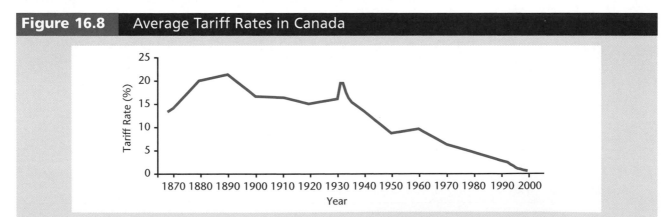

Figure 16.8   Average Tariff Rates in Canada

Since 1868, tariffs as a percentage of total merchandise imports have fallen from above 20 percent. The National Policy, which began in 1879, pushed up the average tariff rate. While the rate gradually fell from the early 1890s, it rose again during the Great Depression. Since the early 1930s, the rate has declined considerably due to the effects of various GATT and WTO agreements as well as regional agreements that Canada has entered.

Sources: Statistics Canada "Average Tariff Rates in Canada," adapted from the Statistics Canada publications "Canadian economics observer. Historical statistical supplement," 2001/02, Catalogue 11-210, Vol. 16, July 2002, p.5, "Historical Statistics of Canada," Catalogue 11-516, 1983, Series G473-487 and from the Statistics Canada CANSIM II database http://cansim2.statcan.ca Table 384-0007.

With falling output and employment, domestic producers see trade barriers as a way of maintaining their sales despite shrinking markets. In the early 1930s, governments in most industrialized countries raised tariffs—partly for domestic reasons and partly to retaliate against foreign trade barriers placed on their own exports. Not surprisingly, all countries were made worse off by this move because of the resulting decline in world trade.

Once the damaging effects of this protectionism became evident, Canada and the United States signed two trade-liberalizing agreements in the 1930s, reducing Canada's average tariff rate to below its pre-Depression level.

General Agreement on Tariffs and Trade

General Agreement on Tariffs and Trade (GATT): a multilateral trade agreement that lessened the degree of trade protection among member countries, including Canada

World Trade Organization (WTO): a multilateral trade organization that has replaced GATT

The liberalizing trend in global trade continued after World War II ended. Canada joined in this movement, partly because many of its manufacturing industries had matured sufficiently to be able to compete against imports without tariffs. In 1947, Canada was one of 22 nations that signed the **General Agreement on Tariffs and Trade (GATT)**, which until recently was the most important example of a "multilateral" trade agreement involving many countries. In 1995, GATT was replaced by the **World Trade Organization (WTO).** This organization, with over 120 members, continues GATT's task of lessening trade protection among member countries, including Canada.

The WTO is based on the principle that trade policies of member countries should treat all other members equally. Complaints by one country against the trade policies of another are subject to formal rules and judged by impartial panels. If a settlement cannot be reached through compromise, then the complainant country has recourse to limited forms of trade retaliation. In the past, GATT was the most important cause of liberalized global trade.

Through rounds of negotiation among GATT members, both tariff and non-tariff barriers were gradually reduced. The most important of these negotiations was the Kennedy Round, completed in 1967, which cut average tariffs by about a third, and the Tokyo Round, completed in 1979, which cut tariffs by another third. The result has been a marked reduction of tariffs—especially on manufactured products. Average tariffs for these products in industrialized countries, which were above 50 percent in the 1930s, have since fallen to below 5 percent.

The last GATT negotiations, which produced an agreement in 1993, caused GATT's replacement with the WTO. In addition, remaining tariffs on some manufactured products, such as prescription drugs and medical equipment, are being reduced, while trade in services, such as computer software, is being liberalized.

Previously protected agricultural products are also affected. Export subsidies to farmers are being cut, while import quotas on agricultural products are being gradually phased out. The agreement will have mixed effects on Canadian farmers. Because other countries must reduce their subsidies on grain exports, Canada's farmers will benefit from higher world prices for grain. At the same time, some Canadian farmers will be hurt. In the past, Canadian prices for eggs, poultry, and dairy products have been maintained above world levels through import quotas on these products. Because such quotas are now disallowed, the Canadian government has replaced them with tariffs—some at levels close to 300 percent, given the large difference between Canadian and world prices. Over time, the Canadian government is being forced to reduce these tariffs. The result is increased foreign imports.

Recent Trading Blocs

trading bloc: a relatively small number of countries involved in a trade agreement

A wish to pursue closer economic ties has led some groups of countries to liberalize trade among themselves. A **trading bloc** is a relatively small group of countries involved in a trade agreement. There are three types: free trade area, customs union, and common market. Each type involves increased integration of trade policies.

FREE TRADE AREA

free trade area: an area in which trade is tariff-free, although member countries are able to impose separate trade barriers on outside countries

Trade within a **free trade area** is tariff-free, although member countries are able to impose separate trade barriers on outside countries. A contemporary example of a free trade area is the North American Free Trade Agreement among Canada, the United States, and Mexico.

CUSTOMS UNION

customs union: a group of countries with common trade barriers with outside countries as well as a free trade area

A **customs union** is a stronger form of regional integration that includes not only free trade among member countries but also common trade barriers with the rest of the world. An example of an emerging customs union is Mercosur, which has four member countries, including Brazil and Argentina.

COMMON MARKET

common market: a group of countries with not only a free trade area and common trade barriers with outside countries but also free movement of labour and capital

European Union (EU): an expanding common market of European countries first formed in 1956, formerly known as the European Economic Community (EEC)

A **common market** is a customs union that allows for the free movement of labour and capital among member nations. The best-known example of an emerging common market is the previously mentioned **European Union (EU)**, formerly known as the European Economic Community (EEC), which was first formed in 1956 by six countries—Germany, France, Italy, the Netherlands, Belgium, and Luxembourg. Since then, the European Union has expanded to include a majority of countries in Europe. In 1992, a treaty was signed among member countries that sets them on a path to even closer economic and political integration. Once this process is completed, there will be freer movement of economic resources, standardized economic regulations, and probably a common currency throughout the EU.

Supporters of the EU suggest that the gains from past trade liberalization among members have helped boost recent living standards in West European countries. For example, a study on the effects of the EU's single market suggested that in its first six years it should reduce prices in member countries by 6 percent, increase real output by 4.5 percent, and create 2 million new jobs. Critics point out the loss of national sovereignty that has accompanied the EU's evolution and argue that European living standards would have risen with or without freer trade.

The Auto Pact

Auto Pact: the 1965 agreement establishing free trade in autos and auto parts between Canada and the United States; formerly known as the Canada–US Automotive Products Agreement

The Canada–US Automotive Products Agreement, or **Auto Pact**, of 1965 is an example of a free trade area in one class of products—autos and auto parts. Until 1965, high tariffs meant that Canada had an inefficient branch-plant auto industry with high prices for Canadian consumers. The pact eliminated tariffs on both sides of the border for the "Big Three" auto companies as long as their sales in North America had at least 50 percent North American content and their Canadian sales had 60 or more percent of their value added in Canada.

It also allowed them to escape a Canadian tariff on imports of autos from outside North America which other auto producers (such Japanese and European companies) must pay. The pact was beneficial for the three companies involved, allowing them to increase their efficiency. As costs and prices for Canadian-made autos fell, output and employment rose, aiding Canadian workers and the Canadian economy as a whole.

In 2000, a challenge against the Auto Pact by Japan and the European Union led to a decision by the World Trade Organization that Canada's implementation of the pact breaks international trade rules, since it unfairly favours the Big Three producers over their competitors. As the Canadian government responds to this decision, it is likely that the importance of the Auto Pact will be diminish or even disappear entirely in future years.

The Free Trade Agreement

Free Trade Agreement (FTA): the 1988 pact between Canada and the United States to form a free trade area

Like the Auto Pact, the Canada–US **Free Trade Agreement (FTA)** is an example of a "bilateral" free trade agreement, which involved two partners. Unlike the Auto Pact, the FTA included trade in virtually all products between the two countries. It was signed by Canada and the United States in 1988 and came into effect in 1989. Under the terms of the agreement, all remaining tariffs on trade between the two countries were phased out by 1998, and non-tariff barriers have been reduced. Services were also included, with a national treatment principle being adopted so that service industries in either country can compete in both national markets. Licensing procedures in the two countries have been standardized to help ease this liberalization of services. Canada's ability to screen foreign direct investment has been reduced, while non–North American car companies can trade autos and auto parts freely across the Canada–United States border if they meet a revised 50 percent North American manufacturing content rule. There is also greater access for American wine and liquor producers—and, more gradually, for American brewers—in the Canadian market. A continental market for energy has been created. While Canada may still limit its energy exports to the United States during a period of global shortages, Canadians will have to limit their own energy consumption by the same proportion. Of particular note, Canadian cultural policies are largely exempted from the agreement, allowing Canada to impose policies that affect the trade and ownership of its cultural industries. Finally, a dispute settlement procedure is in place so that when either country retaliates against the other's trade policies, the dispute is judged by an impartial panel using the trade legislation of the retaliating country.

As usual, supporters of free trade point out the economic benefits that have occurred from increased specialization and trade between the two countries. Canadian advocates of the agreement also suggest that it has reduced the risk of American protectionist measures directed against Canadian exports. Critics of the deal focus on the loss of political sovereignty for Canada, especially because of the restrictions placed on government attempts to screen foreign investment and restrict energy exports. While either country can end the agreement with six months' warning, the gradual strengthening of trade ties between the two countries has made it practically impossible for any Canadian government to do so. Critics also stress that Canadian jobs were lost in previously protected manufacturing industries as foreign companies closed their remaining branch plants so they could centralize their production and take advantage of increasing returns to scale. In the important auto industry, the phasing out of tariffs means that there are no longer penalties for companies that do not meet the Auto Pact guidelines, which critics say could work to the disadvantage of Canadian producers. Finally, in recent years critics point to the fact that the US has been willing to circumvent some panel rulings that go against American interests by reintroducing tariffs on certain goods and then using the delay in dispute resolution as an informal trade barrier. Such actions often reflect compromises by American presidential administrations to take account of protectionist-minded sentiments within Congress. However, it is argued, these actions nonetheless go against the spirit of the agreement.

EFFECTS OF THE FREE TRADE AGREEMENT

As expected, in the early years of the Free Trade Agreement Canada and the United States had greater trade flows. From 1989 to 1992, for example, Canadian merchandise exports in sectors liberalized by the agreement increased by 33 percent, while Canadian merchandise imports in the same sectors rose by 28 percent. The increase in Canada's exports was most pronounced in manufacturing industries, such as office and telecommunications equipment, as well as in resource-based industries, such as chemical products and paper. Meanwhile, Canada's merchandise imports grew most in such industries as processed food, clothing, and furniture. Since then, Canada's total exports to the United States have expanded by a further 182 percent by 2002, while American imports into Canada have risen by 131 percent. So far, the impartial dispute settlement procedure has often worked in Canada's favour, although the American government has shown a tendency to reintroduce trade complaints if a panel decision goes against its perceived interests.

There were also short-term adjustment costs associated with the agreement. The bulk of these costs fell on workers who lost their jobs in formerly protected industries. It is important to remember that other factors also caused unemployment to rise during the years immediately after the FTA took effect. The first was the continuing shift of Canadian jobs away from manufacturing and towards the service sector. Second, the agreement came into effect just before the start of a significant global recession. And, in the long run, trade theory suggests, jobs lost in declining industries hurt by free trade have been replaced by employment in expanding export industries—one more of the main reasons for the significant decline in Canada's unemployment rate during the latter part of the 1990s and early 2000s.

North American Free Trade Agreement (NAFTA): the 1993 pact among Canada, the United States, and Mexico to form a free trade area

The North American Free Trade Agreement

The **North American Free Trade Agreement (NAFTA)**, which was settled in 1993 and came into effect in 1994, is an illustration of a "trilateral" trade accord, which

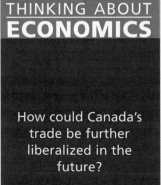

THINKING ABOUT ECONOMICS

How could Canada's trade be further liberalized in the future?

Canada signed bilateral trade agreements with Chile and Israel (both in 1996) and is participating in current WTO negotiations on agricultural trade and on services. It is also a member of the Asia-Pacific Economic Cooperation forum (APEC), whose goal is to liberalize trade with Asian countries, and it is involved in Pan-American talks, whose aim is to form a Free Trade Agreement of the Americas (FTAA) by 2005.

Some Canadians are also calling for the formation of a European-style common market with the United States, which would allow for the free movement of goods, services, and people across the Canada-US border. However, such a common market arrangement would be problematic from a political standpoint, given the reduction in national sovereignty that such a common market arrangement would cause.

Question
What are the main economic arguments for and against forming a common market with the US?

is among three countries. It extends most of the provisions of the Free Trade Agreement to include Mexico. If we consider only trade with this new partner, it seems that NAFTA will not have a significant impact on either Canada or Mexico because their trade relationship has never been significant. For example, in 2000 trade with Mexico made up under 1 percent of Canada's exports and 3 percent of its imports, and much of this trade was virtually tariff-free even before NAFTA.

However, critics of NAFTA suggest there are possible problems of including a country with a lower GDP per capita in the same free trade area as wealthier, more industrialized countries. They point to the loss of Canadian jobs that occur when businesses move to Mexico to take advantage of low-wage labour. Concern has also been expressed over Mexico's lax enforcement of labour and environmental standards. This last concern prompted the addition of two side-agreements to NAFTA. Under the side-agreements, two NAFTA members can set penalties on the third member if that country is not enforcing its labour and environmental laws. So far, these provisions have not been invoked, and it is difficult to judge the relevance of the criticisms made against NAFTA.

Brief Review

1. Until the 1860s, Canada had a favourable trade agreement with the United States with low tariff rates.

2. Canada became increasingly restrictive after 1866, particularly with the adoption of the National Policy in 1879. The National Policy raised tariffs to stimulate Canada's own manufacturing sector.

3. High tariff rates continued until after the Great Depression, at which point this approach to trade was reassessed.

4. The General Agreement on Tariffs and Trade (GATT) was a multilateral trade agreement created in 1947 and based on the principle that member countries should treat all other members equally. Until its replacement in 1995 by the World Trade Organization (WTO), GATT was a major force in liberalizing international trade.

5. Trading blocs, which are trade agreements among a small number of countries, take a variety of forms: free trade areas, customs unions, and common markets.

6. Trade within a free trade area is tariff-free, although member countries can impose separate trade barriers on outside countries. The Free Trade Agreement (FTA) and its extension, the North American Free Trade Agreement (NAFTA), are examples of free trade areas. Another example of such an area is the Auto Pact between Canada and the United States, which deals only with automobile products.

7. A customs union is an even stronger form of regional integration. Not only is the free trade area tariff-free, but members have common trade barriers with the rest of the world. An example is Mercosur.

8. A common market is a customs union that allows for the free movement of labour and capital. The European Union (EU) is an example of a common market. The EU is moving towards even closer economic and political integration.

16.4 Practice Questions

1. a. What were the main arguments used by those opposed to the Canada–US Free Trade Agreement (FTA) in the late 1980s?
    b. What were the main arguments used by the agreement's supporters?

2. a. What were the main arguments used by those supporting the extension of the FTA to include Mexico under the NAFTA agreement in the early 1990s?
    b. What were the main arguments used by those opposed to extending the FTA to include Mexico?

LASTWORD

This chapter has focused on foreign trade—the economic case for trade, the special cases in which trade protection can be defended, and the regional and global trade agreements that have arisen over the past few decades. We have seen that the main purpose behind the recent moves towards freer trade is its potential effect on real output. In the next chapter, we turn our attention to economic growth, and analyze its main determinants, both in a national context and from a broader global perspective. And we will also highlight some of the main arguments for and against economic growth as a central goal of public policy.

Key Concepts

absolute advantage 385
Auto Pact 398
common market 398
comparative advantage 387
customs union 398
European Union 398
export subsidies 392
Free Trade Agreement 399

free trade area 398
General Agreement on Tariffs and Trade 397
globalization 381
import quota 391
infant industry 393
law of comparative advantage 387
National Policy 396
non-tariff barriers 391

North American Free Trade Agreement 400
tariff 391
terms of trade 388
trading bloc 398
voluntary export restraints 391
World Trade Organization 397

Questions

1. Ada can prepare a tax return in 4 hours and paint a kitchen in 10 hours, while it takes Paulo 12 hours to prepare a tax return and 2 hours to paint a kitchen.
    a. Who is more efficient at preparing a tax return? at painting a kitchen?
    b. What are the opportunity costs for the two activities for Ada? for Paulo?
    c. Who should specialize in each activity? Why?

2. The table below shows how many computer games or radios can be produced daily by one worker in Atlantica and Pacifica.

| | Daily Output per Worker | |
	Computer Games	Radios
Atlantica	8	4
Pacifica	10	2

a. Which country is more efficient at producing computer games? radios?
b. On the basis of absolute advantage, which country should specialize in the production of each good? Explain.
c. Identify the limits of the terms of trade for these two goods.
d. Suppose there are 3 million workers in Atlantica and 4 million workers in Pacifica. Before trade, half of each country's labour force makes each good. Outline how specialization and trade lead to a gain in the two countries' total output of both goods.

3. The table below shows how many T-shirts or jeans can be made daily by one worker in Aquarius and Capricorn.

| | Daily Output per Worker | |
	T-Shirts	Jeans
Aquarius	40	4
Capricorn	30	2

a. Which country is more efficient at producing T-shirts? jeans?
b. What are the opportunity costs for each good in Aquarius? Capricorn?
c. On the basis of comparative advantage, which country should specialize in the production of each good? Explain.
d. Identify the limits of the terms of trade for these two goods.
e. Suppose there are 200 000 workers in Aquarius and 300 000 workers in Capricorn, and before trade, half of each country's labour force makes each good. Outline how specialization and trade lead to a gain in the total output of both goods.

4. Suppose that 1 CD player has an opportunity cost of 10 telephones in Canada and an opportunity cost of 5 telephones in Japan.
a. Identify the limits of terms of trade for these two goods and the factors that determine the exact international price of one good in terms of another.
b. What international price would be preferred by Canadians? by the Japanese? Explain each of your answers.

5. The table below shows hypothetical data for the Canadian market for watches, presuming this market is perfectly competitive.

Domestic Demand and Supply Schedules for Watches

Price ($)	Quantity Demanded (D_d) (millions per year)	Quantity Supplied (S_d) (millions per year)
80	1.4	1.8
70	1.6	1.6
60	1.8	1.4
50	2.0	1.2
40	2.2	1.0

a. Draw a graph showing the domestic demand and supply curves for watches. Identify the equilibrium point in the absence of foreign imports.
b. On your graph, show the effects of allowing unrestricted foreign imports of watches at a constant world price of $50.

c. Use your graph to explain how a $10 tariff on imported watches affects consumers, domestic producers, foreign producers, and the Canadian government.

d. On a separate graph, show how an import quota of 400 000 watches a year affects consumers, domestic producers, and foreign producers.

6. Explain how the requirement by the Canadian government that there be English and French labelling of products sometimes operates as an "invisible" non-tariff barrier and give a possible example.

7. Participants in so-called infant industries are like Peter Pan—they do not want their industry to be seen as "grown up." Why?

8. "Incorporating more countries within NAFTA is in Canada's best long-term interests." Discuss.

9. What are the special advantages and disadvantages of trade agreements between countries with significantly different levels of per capita GDP?

10. (Advanced Question)
In many cases, countries import and export the same products. For example, automobiles and auto parts are traded both ways across the Canada-US border. Why?

11. (Policy Discussion Question)
"Due to the effect on the Auto Pact, Canadian agricultural subsidies, as well as many other aspects of Canadian economic policy-making, Canada's decision to participate in the World Trade Organization, and its negotiations over further trade agreements, has been harmful to the Canadian economy." Discuss.

Internet Application Questions

http://www.wto.org/

http://www.statcan.ca/english/Pgdb/Economy/International/gblec02a.htm

http://www.statcan.ca/english/Estat/licence. htm

1. Access the web site of the World Trade Organization (at http://www.wto.org/). Use information at this site to explain the following principles of the WTO's multilateral trading system:
a. Most favoured nation (MFN) status
b. National treatment
c. Dumping
d. Plurilateral agreements

2. Use the most recent annual figures in Statistics Canada's *Imports and Exports of Goods Table* (at http://www.statcan.ca/english/Pgdb/Economy/International/gblec02a.htm) to update the statistics in Figure 16.2. With which countries or regions has Canada's trade become relatively more important since 1996?

3. Access Statistics Canada's E-Stat site (at http://www.statcan.ca/english/Estat/licence. htm).
a. Using the information found in "Trade," generate a two-dimensional graph showing monthly Canadian exports to the United States as a percentage of total Canadian exports (unadjusted raw data) since 1950.
b. What does your graph in part a. say about the importance of American ties for the Canadian economy since 1950?

Globalization: Myths, Facts, and Consequences

How significant is globalization in its effects on government policy-making? Many economists believe globalization's impact is revolutionary—with international borders tumbling, and national governments losing much of their policy-making power. But others disagree. In Canada, the best-known representative of this second group is well-known economist John Helliwell, who teaches at the University of British Columbia. The following are excerpts from his 2000 C.D. Howe lecture on globalization and its impact.

Commentators increasingly report that globalization has sharply diminished the importance of national borders, to the extent of leaving little scope for meaningful policies at the national level...The common perceptions about the extent of globalization are based much more on myth than fact. Distance and national borders have surprisingly large and continuing effects on the patterns of economic life, and these effects both permit and require a set of policy choices much different from what would be considered by anyone who thinks of the global economy as a seamless unit...

The Economic Separation of Nation-States

For most countries, foreign markets are, on average, much farther away than are domestic markets... For Canada and the United States, things are rather different, since Canada can be seen as the top row of an eleven-row rectangle with the United States represented by the lower ten rows. The top row also sags south in its populous middle, since more than half of the Canadian population lives south of the 49th parallel, nestled within in the heartland of North America. As a result, the average distance between Canadian provinces is almost exactly the same as the average distance between the provinces and 30 states...

If the border did not matter at all, then interprovincial trade flows (i.e., trade flows between provinces) would exactly match those between provinces and states. Thus, Ontario would trade ten times as much with California as it does with British Columbia, since California is more than ten times larger than British Colombia, while the two are both roughly the same distance from Ontario. Yet trade between Ontario and British Columbia is actually larger than that between Ontario and California... In 1996 the typical Canadian province traded twelve times as much with another Canadian province as with a US state of similar size and distance...

If domestic goods markets are much tighter than international ones, one expects to find the same thing true of capital markets. The commonly made assumption of perfect international mobility of capital requires the prevalence of a single global real interest rate, which, in turn, requires that prices move to maintain purchasing power parity between national currencies, an assumption that is rejected strongly by the results...

Why do national borders separate markets so strongly?...The costs of doing business depend on the extent of networks of association and trust. Recommendations carry more weight when they come from people who are known and trusted, and frequency of contact provides a natural flow of information that is useful in choosing future trade and investment partners...Distance separates markets and diminishes the frequency of casual contacts among traders, making it efficient for buyers, sellers, and investors to consider local options before proceeding farther afield. Exactly the same case can be made about national borders...Another possible reason for the large size of national border effects is the predominance of national currencies.

John F. Helliwell
Source: Courtesy of John Helliwell and the Institute for Research on Public Policy.

Globalization and Welfare

It is time to make at least a brave attempt to bring together a broader range of evidence on economic and social welfare. I consider separately here incomes, health, education and knowledge, and social capital. All are affected by globalization in complex ways, and all have dual roles

Incomes   Globalization, via increasing international trade and investment, is often charged with responsibility for growing income inequality within the United States and with losses of jobs and incomes among those with lesser skills...The relative importance of trade and skills-based technical change as sources of growing inequality of incomes is still not established. For the United States, the strongest point in favor of the skills-based technical change argument has been that the level and changes in trade are not large enough to have caused the changes in income distribution...

I am inclined to look for domestic causes and consequences of changes in inequality...That earnings inequality should have risen faster in the United States than in Canada is partly explained by...the ratio of earnings of university graduates relative to those of high school graduates [which] rose sharply in the United States and fell slightly in Canada during the 1980s and 1990s. (The increase in the supply of those with higher education has been greater in Canada than in the United States.)...Another reason for the rising inequality of earnings in the United States...[is] the drop in US unionization rates.

Health and Health Care   Good health is clearly valued for its own sake, as well as being both a cause and a consequence of economic progress...Seen in this general context, how do Canadian health and health care stack up?...The Canadian health care system is different mainly in relation to the United States. A cross-country survey of health care satisfaction in 1989 shows that, with one dramatic exception, countries with higher spending on health care also had higher satisfaction. The outlier was the United States, with health care spending far higher than in any other country but with a satisfaction rating much less than half of what it should have been, given the level of spending. If one excludes that country from the analysis, Canadian spending and satisfaction are at the top of the sample...As is the case for a wide range of policies and institutions, the answers and the preferred policies depend much more than is commonly believed on local preferences and choices.

Education and Knowledge   Education is frequently described as the only surefire insurance against being left behind in the decaying remains of the old economy. Rhetoric has leapt ahead of reality, but one cannot doubt that citizens with low skill levels face increasing disadvantages...Canada spends a somewhat larger fraction of GDP on education than do most other OECD countries: its total public and private spending on education is 7.2 percent of GDP... compared with 6.8 percent in the United States, and 6.3 percent for the OECD average...Although Canada has done more than most countries to increase the share of the labour force with education, the situation is much less rosy for knowledge production...Canadian provincial grants to support universities and their research has suffered relative to government support of higher education in other countries. For example, total government investment in higher education has grown much faster in the United States than in Canada over the past 20 years. These pressures lie behind some of the brain drain difficulties described earlier.

Social Capital

Social capital refers to the norms and networks possessed by individuals and their communities; its extent and nature are often measured by the number and strength of interpersonal contacts. The value of a community's stock of social capital is sometimes gauged by the extent to which individuals feel that other people can, in general, be trusted...Education is one means of building trust, it seems. Almost all studies of social capital find that individuals who have more education are more likely to be trusting and to participate more often in community life and organizations.

The Future for Canada

How should one assess the future for Canada? There is good news and bad news. The good news has two parts. First, despite many increases in the strength and depth of international linkages over the past 40 years, countries' internal economic and social structures remain much tighter than is commonly believed...

In fact, today's greater cohesiveness of national economies and societies is much more due to the strength of information and institutional networks that make it less costly for fellow citizens to deal with one another. Evidence that such pooling of activities in regional and national economies is not unduly costly and may, in fact, be advantageous is provided by the second piece of news: the fact that small countries remain as viable and vibrant as they were decades ago. Whether one looks at narrow economic measures, such as GDP per capita, broader social indicators, or even individual assessments of satisfaction, small economies continue to rank very well. Indeed, the small countries seem to do particularly well on broader measures of welfare.

Taken together, these two bits of evidence, if they can stand the tests of further research, suggest that globalization, to the extent it exists, does not pose a threat to the viability and independence of the smaller countries.

The bad news is that the good news is not more widely known and hence put to proper use.

Source: John Helliwell, *Globalization: Myths, Facts, and Consequences* (Toronto: C. D. Howe Institute, October 2000), pp. 1-5, 7-9, 11, 14, 16, 17, 19, 22, 24-27, 29, 30, 33-35, 39, 41.

1. Why, according to Helliwell, is the impact of globalization on the Canadian economy of only limited significance at the present time?

2. How does the existence of social capital in a certain country promote economic growth?

ADVANCING ECONOMIC THOUGHT

CHAPTER 17

Economic Growth

If we do not build economic growth that helps sustain communities, cultures, and families, the results will be harsh.

—Anita Roddick, English entrepreneur

The distinguishing feature of life in present-day Canada, compared with many other parts of the world, is the prosperity that most Canadians enjoy. Economic growth has transformed Canadian living standards in just a few generations, with real GDP per Canadian about five times higher in the 2000s than it was in the 1920s. Can this trend continue? Why are there such vast differences between rich countries, such as Canada, and poor countries? How can these differences be addressed? What are the implications of growth and development? These questions are explored in this final chapter.

LEARNING OBJECTIVES

In this chapter, you will:

1 learn about economic growth, its sources, and its impact

2 examine economic development, its dynamics, the vicious circle of poverty, and the strategies used to break the circle

17.1 Economic Growth

LO 17.1

As we saw in Chapter 11, economic growth can refer to either a change in a country's real GDP or a change in its per capita real GDP over a given time period.

Economic Growth and Its Impact

In terms of the aggregate demand–aggregate supply model outlined in Chapter 11, economic growth can be caused by a long-run increase in aggregate supply (which is accompanied by a rise in an economy's potential output) or by short-run changes in aggregate demand or aggregate supply.

Economic growth can also be portrayed using the production possibilities curve. In Chapter 1, we saw that this curve demonstrates the combination of outputs that an economy *can* produce, assuming constant economic resources and technology. Economic growth occurs either when there is an outward shift in the production possibilities curve (due to technological change or an increase in economic resources) or when there is movement towards the curve (in the case where the economy is inside the curve because all resources are not employed or used to their full capacity).

Consider the hypothetical economy illustrated in Figure 17.1. This economy produces consumer goods (hamburgers) and capital goods (lasers). Initially, its production is limited to the combinations of consumer goods and capital goods demonstrated by the curve PPC_0. The economy chooses to produce 40 hamburgers and 2 lasers (point *a*).

Because the curve represents all production combinations that are attainable, this hypothetical economy is producing the most it can, given its preferences for hamburgers and lasers. Only by increasing economic resources and/or improving the state of technology to use the resources more efficiently can production possibilities be increased. In Figure 17.1, the shift from PPC_0 to PPC_1 demonstrates an increase in production possibilities. Now, the economy is able to produce more of either good, and economic growth can take place.

Note that the production possibilities model highlights not only the limits of any economy but also the tradeoffs between various goods. Expanding our example in Figure 17.2, a country can choose to produce 40 hamburgers and 2 lasers (point *a*) on the left graph. Alternatively, it can choose to produce 100 hamburgers and 1 laser (point *c*) on the right graph.

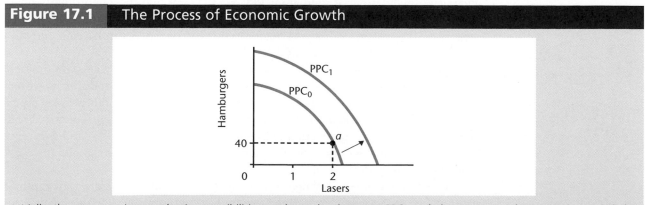

Figure 17.1   The Process of Economic Growth

Initially, the economy has production possibilities as shown by the curve PPC_0 and chooses to produce at point *a*. Only by increasing economic resources and/or improving the productivity of these resources can the economy grow. By doing so, the economy can expand the production possibilities from PPC_0 to PPC_1.

Figure 17.2   Production Options and Their Implications

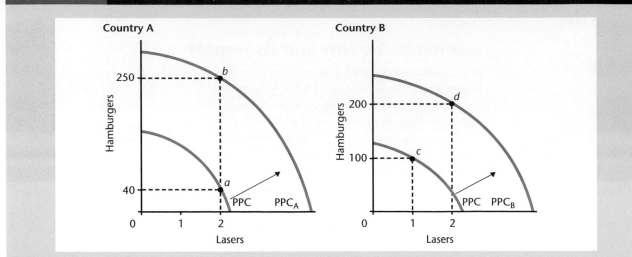

Suppose Countries A and B have the same initial production possibilities (PPC). However, Country A chooses point *a* on the left and Country B chooses point *c* on the right. Because Country A focuses more of its resources on producing a capital good (lasers) than does Country B, which focuses on a consumer good (hamburgers), Country A encourages greater growth. Within the same time period, Country A's production possibilities expand to PPC$_A$ so that it may choose point *b*. Country B's production possibilities expand less so, to PPC$_B$, so that it may choose point *d*.

Although a simplification, the two options demonstrate that economies can focus their resources on the production of consumer goods (hamburgers) or the production of capital goods (lasers). In contrast to consumer goods, which are simply consumed, capital goods can be used to produce more products. As such, capital goods are an investment in further production. Because of this, the choices that an economy makes between the production possibilities affect its future growth.

To demonstrate this, let us consider the hypothetical Countries A and B in Figure 17.2, which initially have identical production possibilities curves. By producing 40 hamburgers and 2 lasers (point *a* on the left graph), Country A adds to its economic resources, which, in turn, fuels economic growth and can mean that more of both consumer and capital goods will be produced in the future. As shown on the left, the production possibilities curve shifts from PPC to PPC$_A$. While the opportunity cost of focusing on capital goods is fewer consumer goods, production of both consumer and capital goods is enhanced in a year. So, for example, Country A can have an output of 250 hamburgers and 2 lasers (point *b*).

In contrast, Country B produces 100 hamburgers and 1 laser (point *c* on the right graph). Because of this choice, the country has more consumer goods for its citizens immediately. However, the opportunity cost of more consumer goods is fewer capital goods, which means that the economy grows considerably less than Country A's. As shown on the right, the production possibilities curve shifts—from PPC to PPC$_B$—but less so than Country A's curve. So, for example, Country B can have an output of 200 hamburgers and 2 lasers (point *d*).

By consuming fewer hamburgers in the first year, Country A's citizens have gained an advantage in the second year. If they wish, they can now consume more hamburgers and match the production of lasers in Country B. Moreover, Country A now starts from a position of even greater production possibilities as it seeks further economic growth in future years.

The benefits of a high-growth strategy multiply over time. To see why, imagine what happens if, instead of choosing point *b*, the citizens of Country A continue their emphasis on capital goods by again choosing a point on PPC$_A$ with fewer hamburgers and more lasers produced. The longer they follow this policy, the more their production possibilities curve expands and the greater is their future potential consumption, compared with consumption in Country B. With the passage of time, Country A reaps increasing benefits from high-growth strategy, while Country B's policy of favouring current over future consumption has an increasing opportunity cost in terms of sacrificed economic growth.

exponential growth: growth that is based on a percentage change and that builds on itself

rule of 72: states that the number of years it takes a variable to double can be estimated by dividing 72 by the variable's annual percentage growth rate

Even small differences in growth rates can have a major long-run effect on a country's prosperity and living standards. This is because economic growth, like population growth, builds on itself, thereby showing a pattern of **exponential growth**. To see the effects, we can use a handy mathematical rule, the **rule of 72**, which states that the number of years it takes a variable to double can be estimated by dividing 72 by the variable's annual percentage growth rate. A variable that grows exponentially at 4 percent a year, therefore, doubles its value in 18 years:

$$\text{Rule of 72: } \frac{\text{Number of years for}}{\text{variable to double}} = \frac{72}{\text{annual percentage growth rate}}$$

$$18 \text{ years} = \frac{72}{4\%}$$

Because of their long-term impact, small discrepancies in growth rates are treated seriously by economists and government policy-makers. Consider the hypothetical example in Figure 17.3. Both countries have a 1998 output of $100 billion but different growth rates (2 and 4 percent). After only 10 years, the difference between Country X's and Country Y's outputs is $26.12 billion.

Figure 17.3	GDP and Growth Rates	
	Real GDP in Country X **(2% annual growth** **in real GDP)**	**Real GDP in Country Y** **(4% annual growth** **in real GDP)**
1998	$100.00 billion	$100.00 billion
1999	102.00 billion	104.00 billion
2000	104.04 billion	108.16 billion
2001	106.12 billion	112.49 billion
2002	108.24 billion	116.99 billion
2003	110.41 billion	121.67 billion
2004	112.62 billion	126.53 billion
2005	114.87 billion	131.59 billion
2006	117.17 billion	136.86 billion
2007	119.51 billion	142.33 billion
2008	121.90 billion	148.02 billion

Two countries, X and Y, have the same initial GDP in 1998, but different growth rates. Because growth is exponential, Country X's GDP falls behind Country Y's by an increasing margin. For example, while Country X's GDP rises from $100 billion to $102 billion [($100 billion × 0.02) + $100 billion] to $104.04 billion [($102 billion × 0.02) + $102 billion], Country Y's rises from $100 billion to $104 billion [($100 billion × 0.04) + $100 billion] to 108.16 billion [($104 billion × 0.04) + $104 billion].

Sources of Economic Growth

The production possibilities model shows that the main causes of growth in an economy's total real output are the stock of economic resources and how productively these resources are used. One of the most important causes of growth in Canada's total output—accounting for an estimated 35 percent of the growth in Canada's real GDP between 1979 and 1997—has been the increase in the quantity of labour. Some of this increase is due to higher participation rates of women in the labour force. However, most of it arises from population growth, which now runs at just over 1 percent annually.

The long-term growth in Canada's living standards, as measured by per capita real output, is determined by the other main source of growth, labour productivity. Recall from Chapter 11 that labour productivity is the quantity of output produced per worker in a certain period of time.

Given the close association between changes in labour productivity and per capita real output, increases in Canadian labour productivity closely follow Canada's record of economic growth. There was a significant slowdown in Canadian productivity growth over recent decades. As shown in Figure 17.4, Canada's annual rate of productivity growth between 1989 and 2000 has surpassed only that of the United Kingdom among the big seven industrial economies (the first seven cited in the chart). Growth in labour productivity is dependent on the quantity of capital, technological progress, the quality of labour, efficiency in production, the quantity of natural resources, and social and political factors.

QUANTITY OF CAPITAL

As indicated by the production possibilities model, an economy's supply of capital resources plays a central role in enhancing economic growth. By saving a higher proportion of their disposable incomes, Canadians can increase investment and accelerate the accumulation of capital resources, which, in turn, fuel economic growth. On

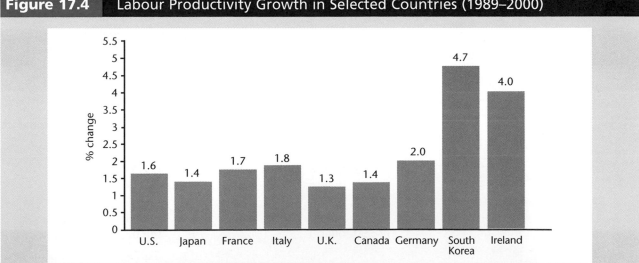

| Figure 17.4 | Labour Productivity Growth in Selected Countries (1989–2000) |

Over the long term, Canada's average annual growth in labour productivity, since 1989, at 1.4 percent has been less than in the other major industrialized economies, except for Japan and the UK.

Source: Pascal Petit "The Roots of the New Economy," in *International Productivity Monitor*, Spring 2002 (Ottawa: Centre for the Study of Living Standards), p. 40.

average, the rates of Canadian saving and investment as a proportion of GDP have been higher than in the United States but lower than in high-growth countries, such as Japan and Germany.

Nonetheless, increases in the quantity of capital goods in Canada were high enough to account for an estimated 40 percent of total growth in its real GDP between 1979 and 1997. Because capital inputs have risen more quickly than labour inputs in the Canadian economy, each Canadian worker is employed with a gradually increasing amount of capital. Since 1961, for example, it is estimated that the ratio of capital to labour in Canada has risen by over 80 percent.

TECHNOLOGICAL PROGRESS

technological progress: consists of scientific discoveries and their application, advances in production methods, and the development of new types of products

Technological progress is a broad term that encompasses scientific discoveries and their application, advances in production methods, and the development of new types of products. Technological progress—in all its forms—can cause economic growth. Over the long term, it plays an important role in increasing labour productivity, often by raising the quality of capital resources with which labour is employed.

research and development (R&D) expenditures: spending that is meant to accelerate the pace of technological progress

Some technological advances occur because of the ingenuity of individuals. Nonetheless, most technological progress is closely tied to **research and development (R&D) expenditures**, or spending whose purpose is to accelerate the pace of technological progress. Canadians have been relatively successful in taking advantage of international technological progress, but R&D expenditures by Canadian businesses have historically been relatively low compared with those of other countries. For example, R&D expenditures in 1999 represented 2.9 percent of GDP in Japan and 2.7 percent in the United States, but only 1.8 percent in Canada. It has been argued that because of a small national market, the potential benefits of R&D expenditures are lower in Canada than in other countries. To the extent that freer trade is creating larger product markets for Canadian businesses, however, this argument is no longer relevant. Predictably, Canadian R&D expenditures have shown an upward trend in recent years.

QUALITY OF LABOUR

The productivity of labour is tied not only to investment in capital goods but also to investment in human capital through education and training. Since the 1950s, a growing proportion of young people have been completing high school and then pursuing postsecondary education. While over 70 percent of those 15 years and older had finished high school in 1999, just over 20 percent of the comparable age group had done so in 1960. During the same period, the percentage of those between the ages of 18 and 24 years enrolled full-time in universities and community colleges increased from 10 to 34 percent. To the extent that these trends augment the quality of Canada's labour force, they are raising its productivity as well as the economy's rate of growth.

EFFICIENCY IN PRODUCTION

Economic growth is also influenced by changes in the efficiency of production through increasing returns to scale and the reallocation of resources among different sectors. Canadian businesses—especially those in manufacturing—have traditionally been unable to take full advantage of increasing returns to scale due to the small size of the Canadian market. Recent moves to freer trade are gradually removing this disadvantage, stimulating both labour productivity and the rate of economic growth. However, the shift of Canadian workers from the higher-productivity manufacturing sector to the lower-productivity service sector has, at least in the past, dampened the rate of economic growth.

QUANTITY OF NATURAL RESOURCES

Canada's rich supplies of natural resources have doubtless contributed to its past economic growth, as during the boom period of rapidly expanding western settlement between 1896 and 1914. During most periods, however, the stock of exploitable natural resources in a country remains constant so that their impact on economic growth is minimal—especially in the modern Canadian economy, which is no longer dominated by primary industries.

SOCIAL, POLITICAL, AND LEGAL FACTORS

There are a variety of social, political, and legal factors that can affect economic growth. Growth will be enhanced in a society that promotes competition, innovation, and entrepreneurship, and by social institutions geared towards enterprise and profit-making. In the political sphere, government regulations and taxes sometimes inhibit economic growth, especially through their impact on levels of saving and investment in the economy. Finally, a stable legal framework of property rights is an essential prerequisite to private investment and capital accumulation.

The Debate over Growth

Is economic growth necessarily desirable? There are arguments both for and against the emphasis placed on economic growth.

ARGUMENTS FOR ECONOMIC GROWTH

Supporters of economic growth point to three main advantages: its effect on living standards, the opportunities it provides for social improvements, and its psychological benefits.

THINKING ABOUT ECONOMICS

The growth in Canadian per capita incomes was lower between the mid-1970s and late 1990s than in previous decades. Why?

The main reason was lacklustre growth in labour productivity. Partly to blame for this poor productivity performance were Canada's low rates of investment and technological progress (due, in part, to contractionary government policies to combat inflation during much of this period) and the shift of workers from the manufacturing to the service sectors. In manufacturing, Canadian productivity growth continued to be high in certain "old economy" industries, such as textiles, clothing, leather goods, and furniture. But Canada's record in "new economy" manufacturing industries, such as those producing electrical and electronic machinery as well as industrial and commercial machinery, was less healthy. In the late 1990s and early 2000s, Canadian productivity growth rates began to improve, arguably due to the advances in information technology that have been occurring throughout industrialized economies. While this recent rise in productivity growth has not been as pronounced as in the United States, it has yet to be determined whether this improvement will be long-lasting.

Question
What have been the long-term consequences of Canada's relatively poor productivity performance in recent decades?

Living Standards

The main benefit of economic growth is its positive effect on living standards. With rising incomes and output, more wants can be satisfied, both for individuals and for society as a whole. Indeed, the main reason life for most Canadians today is more pleasant than for Canadians of three generations ago is due to the tremendous material benefits that economic growth has provided.

Social Improvements

Economic growth can be channelled not only into more consumption and investment by private households and businesses but also into higher government spending, allowing for greater expenditures in such areas as health, education, and the promotion of income equity. Such programs are easier to implement when they can be funded from the proceeds of growth rather than through reductions in existing incomes.

Supporters of growth point out that the supposed tradeoff between income equity and economic growth has often been broken in recent decades. In the period between 1965 and 1989, countries with high growth rates tended to have a *more* equal distribution of income than countries with low growth rates. For example, the ratio of income shares of the richest and poorest 20 percent of the population was just under 10 to 1 in Singapore, while the average annual growth rate in the country's per capita real GDP was 7 percent. In contrast, Brazil's ratio of richest to poorest income shares was almost 35 to 1, while its comparable growth rate was a much lower 4 percent.

Psychological Benefits

Some people suggest that there are intangible psychological benefits of economic growth as well. A growing economy helps create a mood of optimism and a sense of expanding opportunities.

ARGUMENTS AGAINST ECONOMIC GROWTH

Critics of the emphasis on economic growth point to its direct opportunity cost and to its indirect environmental and social costs.

Opportunity Cost of Growth

Economic growth has a direct opportunity cost, as indicated by the production possibilities model. To promote growth, a country must devote more of its scarce resources to investment in capital goods rather than to current consumption. While this cost is not an overwhelming one for a rich country, such as Canada, it is far more significant for citizens of poor countries as they choose an appropriate growth strategy.

Environmental Costs

One of the main indirect costs of economic growth is damage to the environment. Higher levels of economic activity lead to greater exploitation of the world's limited supply of natural resources as well as higher levels of pollution and waste. Supporters of growth suggest that environmental damage is the result of flaws in private markets rather than of economic growth itself. They also argue that, when moving from middle-income to high-income status, countries can actually improve their environmental performance, especially when moving from a manufacturing-based to a service-based economy. Proper government programs, these growth supporters contend, can create the conditions for sustainable growth in the future. Critics argue that the dynamics of growth tend to swamp the impact of government regulations and controls. Environmental damage cannot be corrected through tinkering with the market system, they say, but only by a shift in values to end the quest for never-ending increases in living standards.

Social Costs

The social costs of growth are related to the insecurity and risks that come with technological progress. While the general quality of life may be enhanced by technological advances, some resource suppliers will be hurt, and these individuals are often the members of society who are least able to adapt easily to change. At the same time, the pursuit of economic growth may not allow for traditional methods and lifestyles to be maintained. For some, the losses far outweigh any economic benefits.

Brief Review

1. Economic growth expands production possibilities, so this growth can be expressed as a shift to the right of the production possibilities curve. Such growth is caused by an increase in economic resources or by technological progress, which increases the efficiency of production.

2. An economy might choose to focus on producing consumer or capital goods. A high-growth strategy involves focusing production on capital goods at the expense of consumer goods in the short run.

3. Because economic growth is exponential growth, the rule of 72 applies. Even small differences in percentage rates of growth make a significant difference over time.

4. Population growth and labour productivity have been the sources of Canada's economic growth. In turn, labour productivity is determined by the quantity and quality of capital, technological progress, efficiency, and social and political factors.

5. Arguments for growth concern living standards, social improvements, and psychological benefits. Arguments against growth concern its direct opportunity cost and the indirect environmental and social costs.

17.1 Practice Questions

1. Calculate the following values with the aid of the rule of 72:
   a. the number of years it will take a country's population to double if the annual growth rate is 0.5 percent.
   b. the average annual rate of growth in per capita real GDP, if it takes this variable 27 years to double.
   c. the approximate number of times a country's capital stock will double in 25 years if the annual growth rate in the capital stock is 6 percent.

2. Using EconGraphKit (at www.mcgrawhill.ca/college/lovewell), show the difference in economic growth for two countries—Country C that focuses on producing capital goods and Country D that focuses on producing consumption goods.

3. a. What are the main determinants of the growth in labour productivity?
   b. What factor, in addition to labour productivity, helps determine the growth in real GDP?

17.2 Economic Development

LO 17.2

World Bank: an international lending institution known officially as the International Bank for Reconstruction and Development

high-income countries: countries with per capita incomes substantial enough to provide their citizens with widespread prosperity

middle-income countries: countries in which a sizable minority of the population no longer lives in acute poverty

low-income countries: the poorest countries in the world, as defined by per capita incomes

industrially advanced countries (IACs): countries that have a high degree of industrialization

newly industrializing countries (NICs): countries that recently have exhibited strong economic growth and rapid industrialization

less-developed countries (LDCs): countries with traditional mixed economies and low per capita incomes

The World's Rich and Poor

Most Canadians live in relative comfort. In contrast, one-fifth of the world's population—about 1.2 billion people who live mainly in Southeast Asia and sub-Saharan Africa (meaning African countries south of the Sahara desert)—must live on US$370 or less each year.

To consider the disparities between rich and poor countries, the **World Bank** (a key international lending institution whose official title is the International Bank for Reconstruction and Development) classifies nations into three groups based on their annual per capita GNP: high-income, middle-income, and low-income countries (Figure 17.5).

HIGH-INCOME COUNTRIES

High-income countries are nations with per capita incomes substantial enough to provide their citizens with widespread prosperity. In 2000, the World Bank classified as high-income countries those with a per capita GNP of US$9266 or more. All these nations have modern mixed economies based on capital-intensive production and the use of skilled labour. There are 52 countries in this "rich club" of nations.

MIDDLE-INCOME COUNTRIES

Middle-income countries are those in which a sizable minority of the population no longer lives in acute poverty. In 2000, this category was composed of nations with per capita GNP between US$756 and US$9265. Included are the former members of the Soviet Bloc—those countries in Eastern Europe and the former Soviet Union that until recently were command economies—as well as China and other countries primarily in Latin America, the Middle East, and the extreme northern and southern parts of Africa.

LOW-INCOME COUNTRIES

Finally, the **low-income countries** include the 66 poorest countries of the world. In 2000, this group included all nations with per capita GNP of US$755 or less. Along with India—the second most populous country in the world—this category includes countries in sub-Saharan Africa and some nations in Southeast Asia. These countries tend to have low levels of capital resources and use labour-intensive processes. Their economies tend to emphasize agriculture and other primary resource industries. Many of these countries share a history as colonies. In some cases, the national boundaries devised and the economies developed under colonialism have made the development of modern national economies difficult and often strife-ridden.

In addition to high-, middle-, and low-income countries, other terms are used to identify categories of countries with similar economies. For example, countries in Western Europe and North America (with the exception of Mexico), plus Japan, Australia, and New Zealand, are considered **industrially advanced countries (IACs)** because of their degree of industrialization. Hong Kong, Singapore, Thailand, Indonesia, South Korea, Malaysia, and Taiwan are sometimes called **newly industrializing countries (NICs)**— or, more colourfully, the "little dragons"—because of their strong economic growth and rapid industrialization during past decades. The term **less-developed countries (LDC)** is sometimes used to describe countries with traditional mixed economies and low per capita incomes.

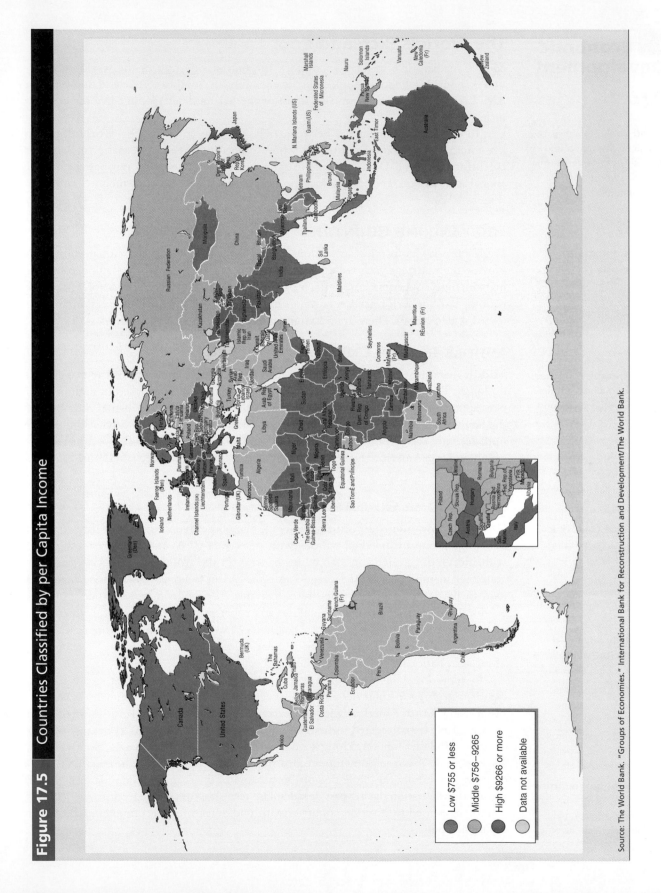

Figure 17.5   Countries Classified by per Capita Income

Low $755 or less

Middle $756–9265

High $9266 or more

Data not available

Source: The World Bank. "Groups of Economies." International Bank for Reconstruction and Development/The World Bank.

Points of Comparison

Figure 17.6 presents some points of comparison that together indicate the living standards in selected countries that are high-, middle-, and low-income.

PER CAPITA INCOME

The average per capita GNP for high-income countries is over US$27 600. In contrast, the corresponding figure for low-income countries is US$410, or just over $1 a day.

HEALTH AND SOCIAL INDICATORS

Not surprisingly, there are wide disparities in health and social indicators, such as life expectancy and infant mortality. While average male life expectancy in high-income countries is 78 years, it is 59 years in low-income countries and under 45 years in the poorest countries, such as Ethiopia. Similarly, less than 1 percent of women in

Figure 17.6	Indicators of Living Standards for Selected Countries (2000)						
	Per Capita GNP (2000)	Average Annual Growth Rate (%) (1990-2000)	Population (millions) (2000)	Life Expectancy at Birth (years)	Infant Mortality (per 1000 live births, 2000)	Adult Illiteracy (females%) (2000)	Commercial Energy Use per capita (kg of oil equivalent) (1999)
High-Income Countries							
1. Japan	35 620	1.3	127	81	4	...	4 070
2. U.S.	34 100	3.5	282	77	7	...	8 159
3. Sweden	27 140	1.9	9	80	3	...	5 769
4. Canada	21 130	2.9	31	79	5	...	7 929
All high-income countries	27 680	2.5	903	78	6	...	5 448
Middle-Income Countries							
5. Hungary	4 710	1.5	10	71	9	1	2 512
6. Mexico	5 070	3.1	98	73	29	10	1 543
7. Egypt	1 490	4.6	64	67	42	56	709
8. China	840	10.3	1 262	70	32	24	868
All middle-income countries	1 970	3.6	2 695	70	31	19	1 325
Low-Income Countries							
9. Azerbaijan	600	−6.3	8	72	13	...	1 575
10. Indonesia	570	4.2	210	66	41	18	658
11. India	450	6.0	1 016	63	69	55	482
12. Ethiopia	100	4.7	64	42	98	69	290
All low-income countries	410	3.2	2 460	59	76	47	567
World	5 170	2.7	6 057	66	54	...	1 671

While the average per capita GNP of high-income countries is almost 60 times that for low-income countries, the average growth rates per capita are greater in low-income countries than for high- and middle-income countries. Overall, life expectancy and energy consumption rise with per capita income, while infant mortality and adult illiteracy fall with per capita income.

Source: The International Bank for Reconstruction and Development/The World Bank. Table 1.1, "Size of the Economy," pp. 18–20, Table 4.1, "Growth of Output," pp. 204–206, Table 2.14, "Education Outcomes," pp. 8–10, Table 2.20, "Mortality," pp. 122–124, Table 3.7, "Production and Use." International Bank for Reconstruction and Development/The World Bank.

high-income countries are illiterate, compared with an average 47 percent in low-income countries.

ENERGY CONSUMPTION

The world's poor use less energy. Average per capita consumption in high-income countries is about 10 times that in low-income countries, with Canadians (who are among the highest per capita energy users in the world) each consuming almost 14 times what citizens of low-income countries consume.

THE GAP BETWEEN RICH AND POOR

When measured by increases in per capita income, recent average rates of economic growth in poorer countries have exceeded those in rich countries. Between 1950 and 1989, for example, the average annual growth rate of per capita incomes for all low-income and middle-income countries was 2.7 percent, compared with the 2.3 percent average for high-income countries.

However, there was a tremendous range of growth rates. Asian nations not included in the high-income category achieved an average growth rate of 3.6 percent in their per capita incomes between 1950 and 1989, largely due to the performance of Asia's "little dragons" and, more recently, China. In contrast, per capita incomes grew by only 1.2 percent, on average, in Latin American countries and by only 0.8 percent in sub-Saharan African countries.

Despite higher average growth rates in poor countries since 1950, per capita incomes in most of these countries have risen less quickly in dollar terms than in industrially advanced countries. This apparent paradox stems from the relative size of per capita incomes in each group of countries and the fact that growth is exponential. So, for example, a hypothetical country with a per capita income of $1000 growing at 6 percent annually adds $60 to this figure in one year. In contrast, a rich country like Canada with a $20 000 per capita income can add a much higher amount of $200 simply by growing at 1 percent a year.

The Dynamics of Development

economic development:
an increase in a country's per capita income that is accompanied by a general rise in living standards

Economic development is an increase in a country's per capita income that is accompanied by a rise in living standards for the bulk of its population. In other words, it requires both economic growth and a widespread improvement in living standards. For most economists and planners, economic development is desirable and is associated with a structural change from a traditional mixed economy to a modern mixed economy. However, not everyone embraces economic development or the modernization that accompanies it—especially those people who wish to maintain tradition and who oppose the upheaval caused by social and economic change. People who are concerned about the environmental effects of rapid industrialization may also oppose certain aspects of economic development.

vicious circle of poverty:
a cycle whereby low standards of living result in slow growth, thus keeping standards of living low in the future

Low-income countries face a daunting task in attempting to foster economic development. Many of these countries find themselves trapped in a **vicious circle of poverty**—a cycle whereby low standards of living lead to slow growth, thus keeping standards of living low in the future. As Figure 17.7 illustrates, low per capita incomes tend to cause both low investment and rapid population growth. These, in turn, perpetuate the focus on labour-intensive production, which restrains productivity, which dampens economic growth and keeps incomes low.

Figure 17.7   The Vicious Circle of Poverty

Low per capita income leads to rapid population growth and low investment, which, in turn, perpetuate the focus on labour-intensive production. This focus restrains productivity growth, which keeps incomes low.

LOW INVESTMENT

Low incomes mean that households must use most of their earnings for consumption. Thus, only a minor proportion of income is saved in most low-income countries, which makes the financing of investment projects difficult. Widespread poverty also means that product markets in most low-income countries are relatively small, reducing the opportunities for business to engage in profitable investment.

Economic and social conditions in most low-income countries constrain investment in other, more subtle ways as well. Traditions that do not encourage competition or profit-making, for example, can inhibit entrepreneurship.

RAPID POPULATION GROWTH

Not only are population levels in most low-income countries high relative to supplies of capital and natural resources, but current rates of population growth are increasing this discrepancy. Figure 17.8 outlines population levels in various parts of the world, along with estimates of how these levels will change in the coming decades. Among the poorer countries, those in Africa and the Middle East had the highest estimated growth rates between 1980 and 2000, while those in Europe and Central Asia had the lowest. With only one exception, these rates were higher than the expected average growth rates in high-income countries.

As these data suggest, low incomes and rapid population growth tend to go together. Low incomes tend to cause rapid population growth for several reasons. In particular, large families are seen as an economic necessity in low-income countries: given that poor families in these countries tend to have no income security nor pension, more children can provide more labour now to help the family and later to give the parents some security in old age. At the same time, the high infant mortality rates found in many low-income countries encourage greater birth rates. These factors, combined with little birth control (due to economic and social factors) and significant rates of female illiteracy (which reduce the opportunity cost of large families for parents), result in rapid population growth.

The combination of higher incomes and government-sponsored birth control programs is gradually reducing population growth in many low-income countries,

Figure 17.8	Global Population Trends				

	Population (millions)			Estimated Annual; Growth Rate (%)	
	1980	2000	2015 (estimated)	1980-2000	2000-2015
Low- and Middle-Income Countries	3640	5154	6154	1.7	1.2
Sub-Saharan Africa	382	659	881	2.7	1.9
East Asia and Pacific	1397	1855	2098	1.4	0.8
South Asia	901	1355	1682	2.0	1.4
Europe and Central Asia	426	474	479	0.5	0.1
Middle East and Northern Africa	174	295	389	2.6	1.8
Latin America and the Caribbean	360	516	625	1.8	1.3
High-Income Countries	790	903	948	0.7	0.3
World	4429	6057	7101	1.6	1.1

The world's population has increased at an average annual rate of 1.6 percent to 6.057 billion by the year 2000, then at an average annual rate of 1.1 percent to 7.101 billion by the year 2015. Most of this growth will take place in the low- and middle-income countries, with estimated average annual growth rates of 1.7 percent (years 1980 to 2000) and 1.2 percent (years 2000 to 2015) and the highest rates in Africa and the Middle East.

Source: The World Bank. Table 2.1, "Population Dynamics," p. 50. International Bank for Reconstruction and Development/The World Bank.

and this trend should continue, as shown in Figure 17.8. However, the projected increases in world population levels over the next few decades are still staggeringly high. The global population is expected to grow from 4.4 billion in 1980 to 7.1 billion by 2015, of which 6.2 billion will live in poorer countries.

LABOUR-INTENSIVE PRODUCTION

Low investment means that capital accumulates slowly, while rapid population growth leads to large increases in the supply of labour. Both factors are jointly responsible for creating large supplies of labour in relation to capital resources, thereby causing production in most low-income countries to be labour-intensive.

LOW PRODUCTIVITY GROWTH

Because of labour-intensive production, it is difficult for producers to make use of technological innovations or to achieve the high levels of capital often needed to take advantage of increasing returns to scale. Production remains less efficient, constraining growth in productivity. Without productivity growth, higher per capita incomes are impossible.

Strategies for Development

While difficult, it is possible to break the vicious circle of poverty, as the past success of the "little dragons" shows. Breaking the cycle involves three domestic strategies: ensuring a stable political and economic system, investing in resources, and controlling population growth. At the same time that low-income countries are using such domestic strategies, other higher-income countries can assist with two international strategies: trade liberalization and foreign aid.

POLITICAL AND ECONOMIC STABILITY

A stable political system and economy are preconditions for development, since political turmoil and wide swings in output and prices both inhibit saving and investment. One of the most important development tasks of governments in low-income countries, therefore, is to ensure a stable political system and a smoothly running economy. Frequent changes in the country's laws discourage business activity, as do "quick-fix" schemes by governments that involve public spending financed through persistent budget deficits or inflationary monetary policy. In some countries, such as China, economic development has been associated with political repression. However, some recent studies suggest that in general, economic development is enhanced if it is accompanied by political freedom and democracy. This is because a democratic political system tends to contribute to long-run political and economic stability.

INVESTING IN RESOURCES

For all low-income countries, government investment in human capital through education, health, and social programs is an important component of development. For example, greater education increases the supply of trained labour, which leads to long-term improvements in productivity. As a start, ensuring basic literacy through universal primary education enhances the opportunities for citizens to improve their own living standards.

Many governments in low-income countries also employ programs to stimulate investment in capital goods by trying to encourage the saving that is needed to finance this investment. In market economies, public policy-makers can impose taxes that promote private saving and discourage consumption. These savings can then be made available through financial markets to domestic businesses for investment. However, there is no guarantee that private saving will flow to domestic businesses. All too frequently, these savings leave the country. This problem, known as capital flight, is most acute in countries where internal conditions hinder the potential for profitable investment.

In command economies, the investment process is carried out by public authorities themselves, who channel government revenues to public enterprises for investment. Again, these programs have possible drawbacks, since public investment projects can be chosen for political reasons rather than for their potential economic benefits.

POPULATION CONTROL

Governments in low-income countries can use several approaches to limit population growth. One way is to introduce voluntary birth control programs, which operate by providing incentives for those who participate. Such programs have been used in many low-income countries with varying degrees of success. In India, for example, where such programs have been common for several decades, the annual rate of population growth between 1990 and 1999 remained at a relatively high 1.8 percent. A more stringent approach is illustrated by China's "one-child" policy, which imposes financial penalties on parents who have more than one child. This program has successfully reduced the country's annual rate of population growth between 1990 and 1999 to 1.1 percent. However, the success of this type of compulsory approach must be weighed against the loss of freedom for citizens to make their own decisions regarding family size.

Additional policies and programs can indirectly affect population growth. For example, governments can provide basic social services to the poor involving health care, nutrition, and primary education, as well as family planning. These—alongside other policies and programs that develop new markets, enhance employment opportunities, stimulate investment, generate higher incomes, and improve income distribution—tend to encourage smaller families. Although powerful, such policies and programs can be difficult to implement when they clash with traditions.

TRADE LIBERALIZATION

The export-driven growth of the "little dragons" shows that self-sustaining development in most low-income countries depends on making efficient use of their own resources, especially labour, to gain the benefits that flow from international trade. Therefore, one of the most important forms of assistance that industrially advanced countries can provide is to make their own markets more open to the exports of low-income countries—especially manufactured goods, which traditionally have often been subject to trade barriers. This causes short-run adjustment costs for higher-income countries, but economists generally believe that the long-term benefits to low-income countries of such freer trade—as well as to the higher-income countries themselves—far outweigh the costs.

FOREIGN AID

While liberalized trade has important long-term implications for international development, direct aid from higher-income countries is essential to breaking the vicious circle of poverty, especially for the poorest of the low-income countries. Most high-income countries run aid programs through their own national agencies; in Canada, government aid is administered by the Canadian International Development Agency (CIDA). A co-ordinated program of development assistance is also provided by two important international lending institutions: the International Monetary Fund (IMF) and the World Bank. While the IMF concentrates on short-term loans to governments, the World Bank uses its financial support from high-income countries to make loans to low-income countries for long-term investment projects that would otherwise not

The empirical record is mixed. According to a recent international study, foreign aid does increase income levels in countries that pursue economic policies conducive to stable growth—including low inflation, small budget deficits, openness to trade, strong rule of law, and a competent bureaucracy—with aid equivalent to 1 percent of the recipient country's GDP leading to a sustained increase of 0.5 percentage points in the country's annual rate of growth. But in countries with a different policy mix, there is no evidence that foreign aid raises living standards. So, while foreign aid may be a necessary condition to quicken the pace of economic development in low-income countries, it is by no means sufficient in doing so.

Question
What problems can occur in the second group of countries to minimize the impact of foreign aid contributions?

be funded. In particular, it focuses on basic health and education programs as well as on projects that provide such utilities as electrical power and running water. Nongovernmental organizations (NGOs) in high-income countries also provide aid. Recently, governments have begun to fund the work of several NGOs.

Despite the benefits that foreign aid programs can bring, certain programs have been criticized for being misdirected and badly implemented. Another criticism is that the aid is sometimes biased towards particular political aims or development paths, given for the political or commercial ends of the donor country, or designed to favour future markets. For example, in the past, donors tended to favour industry over agriculture and showed a bias towards large-scale projects rather than more basic, but essential, assistance to small-scale producers.

The IMF and the World Bank have been criticized for such large-scale bias. Also, both commonly require recipient countries to cut back on government spending, reduce their trade barriers, and promote competition within their domestic product markets before they can receive further loans. These organizations believe that these types of constraints are necessary to ensure that aid is effectively used. However, critics argue that these requirements often hurt the poorest groups within the low-income countries and represent interference in the internal affairs of independent nations.

Brief Review

1. Countries may be classified as high-income, middle-income, and low-income. At one extreme, high-income countries have modern mixed market economies based on capital-intensive production and the use of skilled labour. At the other extreme, low-income countries tend to have traditional mixed economies, use labour-intensive processes, and may have a history of colonialism.

2. Other classifications used are industrially advanced countries, newly industrializing countries, and less-developed countries.

3. While, on average, the economic growth rates of middle- and low-income countries are high, the gap between rich and poor countries continues to widen in dollar terms.

4. Economic development occurs when there is a rise in a country's per capita income accompanied by a general improvement in living standards. It is associated with a structural change from a traditional mixed to a modern mixed economy.

5. In the vicious circle of poverty, low incomes, low investment, and rapid population growth tend to perpetuate labour-intensive processes, which restrains productivity and economic growth and keeps incomes low.

6. Strategies for breaking the circle of poverty include domestic strategies (ensuring political and economic stability, investing in resources, and controlling population) and international strategies (liberalizing trade and foreign aid).

17.2 Practice Questions

1. Use the data in Figure 17.6 to answer the following questions.

   a. What proportion of the world's population lives in low-income countries? middle-income countries? high-income countries?

   b. What proportion of the world's total GNP is generated in low-income countries? middle-income countries? high-income countries?

   c. It is often said that 20 percent of the world's population gets 80 percent of the income. Based on your answers to parts a. and b. above, is this true? If not, how should the statement be amended?

2. a. Why do low investment and rapid population growth lead to a poverty trap in many low-income and middle-income countries?

   b. Name two policies that governments can use to lessen these obstacles to economic development.

LAST**WORD**

In this chapter, we have seen how the choices made by countries can significantly affect long-run living standards. Of vital importance is the split between the production of capital and consumption goods, which influences the extent to which a nation's production possibilities curve shifts outwards. But there are other factors as well—such as the pace of technological progress and the quality of a nation's labour force. To improve the growth in Canada's per capita incomes, which has lagged relative to other industrialized countries in recent decades, Canadians need to continue focusing on ways to encourage Canadian businesses to innovate. Low-income countries wishing to speed growth in their living standards face a different challenge—to break out of the vicious circle of poverty through an integrated set of development strategies.

Key Concepts

economic development 420

exponential growth 411

high-income countries 417

industrially advanced countries 417

less-developed countries 417

low-income countries 417

middle-income countries 417

newly industrializing countries 417

research and development expenditures 413

rule of 72 411

technological progress 413

vicious circle of poverty 420

World Bank 417

Questions

1. Binomia produces only milkshakes (a consumer good) and shovels (a capital good). With the aid of a graph, show the effects of each of the following trends on Binomia's production possibilities.
   a. Binomians decide to produce more shovels and fewer milkshakes.
   b. More economic resources become available in the Binomian economy.
   c. A technological innovation occurs in the production of shovels.

2. Calculate the following values with the aid of the rule of 72:
   a. The number of years it will take a country's real GDP to double if the annual growth rate of real GDP is 1.5 percent
   b. The average annual rate of inflation if the general price level doubles each 27 years
   c. The approximate number of times a country's population will double in a 100 years if the annual growth rate is 3 percent

3. In Ergonia, 8 million workers produce a real output of $500 billion in 2001 and the same number of workers produce $540 billion in 2002.
   a. Calculate Ergonia's labour productivity in each year.
   b. What is Ergonia's rate of productivity growth between 2001 and 2002?

4. Since 2000, the growth in Canada's per capita real GDP has been relatively high. What are some of the reasons for this impressive performance?

5. Summarize the main advantages of stable democratic government in fostering economic development. Are there any disadvantages associated with this form of government? Explain.

6. Outline the steps whereby a government investment strategy or program of population control can break the vicious circle of poverty in a low-income country.

7. "The greatest contribution industrially advanced countries can make to economic development in low-income countries is through trade liberalization rather than through foreign aid." Discuss.

8. (Advanced Question)
   a. Outline what you consider to be the three most likely sources of economic growth (defined in terms of real GDP) in the Canadian economy over the next decade.
   b. For each source of economic growth you have identified, give an example of a government policy that can promote its performance.

9. (Policy Discussion Question)
   a. Outline two possible policy changes that you think could help raise growth in Canada's labour productivity.
   b. In the case of each policy change mentioned in part a., outline why you believe it would stimulate productivity growth.

Internet Application Question

http://www.worldbank.org/

Access the web site of The World Bank Group (at http://www. worldbank.org/). Use the links at this site to summarize:
1. How the World Bank finances its spending
2. The interest rate and average maturity period of World Bank loans
3. The "graduation process" that determines which countries are eligible for loans

Nuala Beck
Source: Nuala Beck

SHIFTING GEARS

Nuala Beck and the New Economy

Why are economic changes becoming more rapid? And what are the signs of this rapid change? These are the questions that Canadian economist Nuala Beck asked herself when she saw the Canadian and world economies changing in ways that did not fit the old models and measures. In the following excerpt from her book Shifting Gears: Thriving in the New Economy, *Beck outlines how the current transformation of the Canadian economy is part of a long-term evolutionary process that will impact on future rates of economic growth.*

We really only need to turn the clock back about 150 years to see how we got where we are today.

By identifying three circles, each representing an economic movement that shaped the period from 1850 to the present, I had stumbled on a key to understanding the forward movement of our economy today. I've called these models the *commodity-processing*, or C Circle; the *mass-manufacturing*, or M Circle; and the *technology*, or T Circle. Each circle contains certain key, common elements; each makes sense of vast economic changes that otherwise don't fit into a sensible pattern; each is the natural extension of the one preceding. Specific industries, even the economies of entire nations, can be defined by their place inside these circles. And once that's determined, their future—and yours—can be foretold with a remarkable degree of precision.

After running my original musings through the gauntlet of hard economic analysis, it became clear that the key to each circle is a single, crucial ingredient whose abundant supply, at steadily falling prices, acts as a springboard, or catalyst, to levels of growth never before witnessed. In the commodity-processing era (the C Circle), it was cheap steel. In the succeeding mass-manufacturing era (M Circle), it was energy, specifically oil, whose discovery in vast quantities around the turn of the century fuelled the consumer-driven manufacturing boom that shifted the center of economic power to the United States from Britain.

Today, in the T (technology) Circle, the world is being driven by huge supplies of another product that was unknown outside the closely guarded doors of Texas Instruments and one or two other research laboratories thirty years ago—semiconductors, or microchips, so cheap and plentiful they can be stuck in watches to tell you when it's time to wake up. The technological leader in this circle is Japan, but America isn't nearly so far back as its internal and external critics like to think.

Besides those single, vital building blocks, each circle has other identifying traits.

- Every era has its *engines*—a handful of strategic industries that drive the entire economy and typically have risen rapidly out of humble origins. The roaring engines of the C Circle were steel, railways, textiles and coal. These were superseded in the mass-manufacturing era by autos, housing, machine tools and retailing. The T Circle, as you might guess, has been turbo-driven by computers and semiconductors, as well as telecommunications, instrumentation and the health and medical industry.

- Every era has its *virtuosos*—the innovative entrepreneurs, scientists and engineers who use existing technology merely as a stepping stone to new methods, processes and products, rather than endlessly reinventing the wheel.

- Every era can be defined by the *technology* these innovators develop. They spend their working lives looking for that better mousetrap, whether it's Henry Ford and his sturdy Model-T car or Jack Kilby and his microchips. (Ironically, Kilby, the Texas Instruments scientist who invented the first integrated circuit the size of a matchhead, never stopped using the slide rule that his pocket calculator made obsolete in 1971.) When they find it, the stage is set for the next explosive round of growth.

- Every era has its *technological pacesetters*, from Britain in the commodity-processing circle, to the United States and Germany in the manufacturing era, to Japan and the U.S. today. The key is the financial might needed to develop the better mousetraps.

- Every era has its own *management practices*. The C Circle, for example, saw the appearance of the first truly giant firms, cartels and trusts that weren't dependent on the whims of royalty or the vagaries of the trade winds. It was here that the foundation was laid for the first great industrial fortunes—a departure from the land- or merchant-based wealth of old.

- Every era has its *philosophers*, the gurus who spend most of their time formulating theories about an economy that no longer exists and may never have—except in their ideal universe.

- Every era has its *fast track*—the jobs that lead somewhere and provide the best chance of hitching dreams to reality in the workplace. In the M Circle, blue-collar workers achieved a level of prosperity beyond the wildest imaginings of previous generations. For the first time, factory laborers had the American dream within their grasp. Many acquired homes of their own, annual vacations, private transportation and other advantages that had long been the sole preserve of the rich.

Today, it's the workers in the new economy who have the best hope for a secure future. Individual computer or communication companies may come and go, but the worker with T Circle skills will still be better off than those being kicked off the assembly lines of the incredible shrinking auto industry and other outdated sectors. Seniority doesn't matter much when the company has sunk to the bottom of the lake. Everybody drowns, no matter what position they had in the boat!

- Every era has its *losers*—industries that were once a major economic force but are now more or less in permanent decline. Just ask the rail manufacturers or pig-iron producers.

- Every era has its *emerging industries*—fledgling sectors destined to carry the world into the next great period of growth, but still seeking a firm foothold. Once it was automobile manufacturing. Today, it's genetic engineering and artificial intelligence.

- Every era has its *roadblocks*, easily identifiable barriers that have to be overcome before the transition can be completed.

A natural limitation on the growth of the commodity-processing circle was the lack of standards—in everything from education and electricity to railroad tracks. In the manufacturing era, assembly-line technology overcame the severe restrictions on capacity caused by the old batch, or piecemeal, system of production, while rapid transportation removed the major roadblock to market access, and integration of design, production

ECONOMIC EVOLUTION

COMMODITY DRIVEN
Pig-Iron Production
Railroad Operating Income
Inner Tube Production
Coal and Coke Production
Textile Mill Production
Cotton Consumption

MANUFACTURING DRIVEN
Industrial Production
Capacity Utilization
Machine Tool Orders
Retail Sales
Housing Starts
Auto Sales

TECHNOLOGY DRIVEN
Computer Production
Semiconductor Production
Instrumentation Sales
High-Tech Trade Balance
Knowledge-Intensive Employment Growth
Medical Starts

ADVANCING ECONOMIC THOUGHT

and marketing shunted aside idea-strangling bureaucracies. The current technology-driven circle has developed through the application of electronics and miniaturization to largely remove the limitations of existing energy and materials. Without the magic of integrated circuits, computers would be way too unwieldy and far too expensive for ordinary mortals like you and me to ever make use of them.

- Every era *organizes work* in a particular way, linked to the needs and goals of society at the time, which is why change is doubly painful. Not only does the nature of the work change, so does the social structure that underpins it. The abolition of child labor and other worker reforms in the C Circle (when some industries were known as "slaughterhouses" for the high death rate of employees, some barely out of diapers) was, in its own time, as revolutionary a move as the organization of work along assembly lines in the M Circle and the later rise of middle management and the development of a professional class.

What doesn't (and can never) work is the grafting of old approaches and structures onto the new economy. That's why companies that have failed to make the successful leap from one circle to the next seem so unbelievably incompetent. Giants like General Motors once represented all the strengths and glories of the mass-manufacturing era. Yet today they are described in unflattering terms—"bloated," "groping," "slow" and "sloppy"—prisoners caged in their own past.

The startling fact of life in Canada is that 70 percent of Canadians are already employed in the new economy, which shows just how well we have adjusted.

It pays to be a supplier of the right materials, and although many Canadians don't realize it, their country is emerging as the principal provider of many of the commodities needed by the technology-driven economy. We are so wrapped up in our wintry view of our future that we don't realize how incredibly lucky—and smart—we've been over the years. It's no secret, for example, that nickel is *the* metal of the new economy, while copper is the dark horse, and Canada happens to be one of the world's principal sources of both.

As supreme hewers of wood, miners of metals and drawers of water, Canadians have been uniquely well placed to serve both the commodity-processing centers of mother Britain and the manufacturing dynamos of the neighboring giant to the south. In return, Canada has had one of the world's fastest-growing economies for decades. The bumpy ride that we're experiencing right now is caused simply by the shifting of gears as we move from supplying the stuff to the declining old economy. For people who aren't used to driving at high speeds, that's always a challenge.

Source
Abridged from *Shifting Gears: Thriving in the New Economy* by Nuala Beck. Copyright 1992 by Nuala Beck. Published by HarperCollins Publishers Ltd., pp. 19–24, 43–44.
Photo Source: Nuala Beck is the author of *Shifting Gears: Thriving in the New Economy* and *Excelerate: Growing in the New Economy* and is President of Nuala Beck & Associates Inc. The New Economy is the registered trademark of Nuala Beck & Associates Inc.

1. What are the three eras of economic development distinguished by Beck? Using the information in the article, as well as your own research, provide examples of (a) engines, (b) virtuosos, (c) characteristic technologies, (d) fast-track jobs, (e) losers, (f) emerging industries, and (g) roadblocks for each era.

2. Why, according to Nuala Beck, is Canada well-placed to benefit from the new economy?

GLOSSARY

ability to pay: the principle applied to taxation, whereby taxes vary in proportion to a taxpayer's financial resources

absolute advantage: the benefit enjoyed by a producer who can supply a certain quantity of an item more efficiently than can other producers

accounting-profit rate: a measure of a business's profitability, calculated as its accounting profit divided by owner's equity

aggregate demand: the relationship between the general price level and total spending in the economy

aggregate demand curve: the relationship between the general price level and total spending in the economy expressed on a graph

aggregate demand factors: variables that cause changes in total expenditures at all price levels

aggregate demand schedule: the relationship between the general price level and total spending in the economy expressed in a table

aggregate supply: the relationship between the general price level and real output produced in the economy

aggregate supply curve: the relationship between the general price level and real output expressed on a graph

aggregate supply factors: variables that change total output at all price levels

aggregate supply schedule: the relationship between the general price level and real output expressed in a table

annually balanced budget: the principle that government revenues and expenditures should balance each year

appreciate: to increase, as when a currency's price rises in comparison to the price of another currency

asset demand: the demand for money that is related to its use as a store of purchasing power

Auto Pact: the 1965 agreement establishing free trade in autos and auto parts between Canada and the United States; formerly known as the Canada–US Automotive Products Agreement

automatic stabilizers: built-in measures, such as taxation and transfer payment programs, that lessen the effects of the business cycle

average cost: the sum of average fixed cost and average variable cost at each quantity of output

average-cost pricing: the practice of setting price where it equals average cost

average fixed cost: the fixed cost per unit of output

average product: the quantity of output produced per worker

average revenue: a business's total revenue per unit of output

average variable cost: the variable cost per unit of output

balance-of-payments accounts: a summary of all transactions between Canadians and foreigners that involve exchanging Canadian dollars for other currencies

balance-of-payments deficit: a negative net balance on the balance-of-payments statement, demonstrating lower receipts than payments for the current and capital and financial accounts combined; balanced with changes in official reserves

balance-of-payments surplus: a positive net balance on the balance-of-payments statement, demonstrating greater receipts than payments for the current and capital and financial accounts combined; balanced with changes in official reserves

balance of trade: for both goods and services, receipts (inflows of Canadian dollars) less payments (outflows of Canadian dollars)

balanced budget: the situation where a government's expenditures and revenues are equal

bank rate: the interest rate CPA members are charged on advances from the Bank of Canada

barter: a system of trading one product for another

base year: the survey year used as a point of comparison in subsequent years

benefits received: the principle applied to taxation, whereby taxes are geared to the benefits each taxpayer gains from government activity

breakeven point: the profit-maximizing output where price (or average revenue) equals average cost

budget deficit: the situation where a government's expenditures exceed its revenues

budget surplus: the situation where a government's revenues exceed its expenditures

business: an enterprise that brings individuals, financial resources, and economic resources together to produce a good or service for economic gain

business cycle: the cycle of expansions and contractions in the economy

business's demand curve: the demand curve faced by an individual business, as opposed to an entire market

business's labour demand curve: a graph showing the possible combinations of workers demanded by a business at each possible wage

business's labour supply curve: a graph showing the possible combinations of workers supplied to a business at each possible wage

business's supply curve: a curve that shows the quantity of output supplied by a business at every possible price

Canada Savings Bonds: federal government bonds that have a set value throughout their term

capital account: the summary of transfers of ownership of savings and intangible assets

capital and financial accounts deficit: a negative net balance in the capital and financial accounts, demonstrating higher investments by Canadians in foreign markets than by foreigners in the Canadian economy

capital and financial accounts surplus: a positive net balance in the capital and financial accounts, demonstrating lower investments by Canadians in foreign markets than by foreigners in the Canadian economy

capital-intensive process: a production process that employs more capital and less labour

capital resources: the processed materials, equipment, and buildings used in production; also known as capital

capital stock: the total value of productive assets that provide a flow of revenue

cartel: a union of oligopolists who have a formal market-sharing agreement

cash reserves: funds kept on hand by deposit-takers to meet the needs of depositors withdrawing funds

ceteris paribus: the assumption that all other things remain the same

change in official reserves: use of the government's reserves of foreign currency to influence the international value of the Canadian dollar, as shown on the balance-of-payments statement

change in quantity demanded: the effect of a price change on quantity demanded

change in quantity supplied: the effect of a price change on quantity supplied

chartered banks: deposit-takers allowed by federal charter to offer a wide range of financial services

coincidence of wants: the situation where someone purchasing an item finds a seller who wants what the purchaser is offering in return

collateral: assets pledged by a borrower as security against a loan; these assets can be seized by the lender if the loan is not repaid

collusion: oligopolists acting together as if they are a monopoly

command economy: an economic system based on public ownership and central planning

common market: a group of countries with not only a free trade area and common trade barriers with outside countries, but also free movement of labour and capital

comparative advantage: the benefit enjoyed by a producer who can supply a certain item with a lower opportunity cost than can other producers

complementary products: products that are consumed together

complementary resources: resources that are used together

concentration ratio: the percentage of total sales revenue earned by the largest businesses in a market

constant-cost industry: an industry that is not a major user of any single resource

constant returns to scale: a situation in which a percentage increase in all inputs results in an equal percentage increase in output

consumer price index: a measure of price changes for a typical basket of consumer products

consumer sovereignty: the effect of consumer needs and wants on production decisions

contraction: a sustained fall in real output of an economy

contractionary fiscal policy: government policy that involves decreasing government purchases, increasing taxes, or both to restrain spending and output

contractionary monetary policy: a policy of decreasing the money supply and increasing interest rates to dampen the economy

contractionary policies: government policies designed to stabilize prices and reduce output

corporation: a company that has a legal status independent of its owners

cost-of-living adjustment clauses: provisions for income adjustments to accommodate changes in price levels, which are included in wage contracts

cost-push inflation: inflation that occurs as increased production costs decrease aggregate supply, which then pushes up prices

craft union: a labour union of workers in a particular occupation

credit card: a means of payment that provides instantly borrowed funds

credit risk: the assessed likelihood of a borrower not repaying a loan

cross-price elasticity: the responsiveness of a product's quantity demanded to a change in the price of another product

crowding-out effect: the effect of more government borrowing raising interest rates, which reduces or "crowds out" private investment spending

currency: paper money and coins

current account: the summary of all foreign transactions associated with current economic activity in Canada and involving Canadian dollars

current account deficit: a negative net balance in the current account resulting from lower receipts than payments for merchandise and nonmerchandise transactions

current account surplus: a positive net balance in the current account resulting from higher receipts than payments for merchandise and nonmerchandise transactions

customs union: a group of countries with common trade barriers with outside countries as well as a free trade area

cyclical unemployment: unemployment due to the ups and downs of economies and businesses

cyclically balanced budget: the principle that government revenues and expenditures should balance over the course of one business cycle

debit card: a means of payment that instantaneously transfers funds from buyer to seller

decision lag: the amount of time needed to formulate and implement an appropriate policy

decrease in aggregate demand: a decrease in total expenditures at all price levels

decrease in demand: a decrease in the quantity demanded of a product at all prices

decrease in supply: a decrease in the quantity supplied of a product at all prices

decreasing returns to scale: a situation in which a percentage increase in all inputs causes a smaller percentage increase in output

deflation: a general decrease in the level of prices

demand: the relationship between the various possible prices of a product and the quantities of that product consumers are willing to purchase

demand curve: a graph that expresses possible combinations of prices and quantities demanded of a product

demand deposits: accounts of funds to which depositors have immediate access

demand determinants: factors that can cause an increase or a decrease in a product's demand

demand for Canadian dollars: the relationship between the price of a Canadian dollar and the quantity demanded in exchange for another currency

demand-pull inflation: inflation that occurs as increased aggregate demand pulls up prices

demand schedule: a table that shows possible combinations of prices and quantities demanded of a product

dependent variable: the variable in a causal relationship that is affected by another variable

deposit-takers: institutions or businesses that accept funds provided by savers and lend these funds to borrowers

depreciate: to decrease, as when a currency's price falls in comparison to the price of another currency

depreciation: the decrease in value of durable real assets over time

depression: a particularly long and harsh period of reduced real output

desired reserves: minimum cash reserves that deposit-takers hold to satisfy anticipated withdrawal demands

devaluation: a reduction in the value of a currency by the government that sets the exchange rate

direct investment: financial investment (purchases of stocks) that gives the buyer of the financial assets a controlling interest in the institution issuing the assets

direct relationship: a relationship in which a change in the independent variable causes a change in the same direction of the dependent variable

discouraged workers: unemployed workers who have given up looking for work

discretionary policy: intentional government intervention in the economy, such as budgeted changes in spending or taxation

disposable income: household income minus personal taxes and other personal transfers to government

double-counting: the problem of adding to GDP the same item at different stages in its production

durable goods: goods that are consumed repeatedly over time

economic costs: a business's total explicit and implicit costs

economic development: an increase in a country's per capita income that is accompanied by a general rise in living standards

economic efficiency: employing scarce resources in such a way as to derive the highest benefit

economic growth: an increase in an economy's total output of goods and services

economic models: generalizations about or simplifications of economic reality; also known as laws, principles, or theories

economic problem: the problem of having unlimited wants, but limited resources with which to satisfy them

economic profit: the excess of a business's total revenue over its economic costs

economic resources: basic items that are used in all types of production, including natural, capital, and human resources

economic system: the organization of an economy, which represents a country's distinct set of social customs, political institutions, and economic practices

economics: the study of how to distribute scarce resources among alternative ends

elastic demand: demand for which a percentage change in a product's price causes a larger percentage change in quantity demanded

elastic supply: supply for which a percentage change in a product's price causes a larger percentage change in quantity supplied

entrepreneurship: initiative, risk-taking, and innovation necessary for production

entry barriers: economic or institutional obstacles to businesses entering an industry

European Union (EU): an expanding common market of European countries first formed in 1956, formerly known as the European Economic Community (EEC)

excess reserves: cash reserves that are in excess of desired reserves

exchange rate: the value of one nation's currency in terms of another currency

expansion: a sustained rise in real output of an economy

expansionary fiscal policy: government policy that involves increasing government purchases, decreasing taxes, or both to stimulate spending and output

expansionary monetary policy: a policy of increasing the money supply and reducing interest rates to stimulate the economy

expansionary policies: government policies designed to reduce unemployment and stimulate output

expenditure approach: a method of calculating Gross Domestic Product by adding together all spending in the economy

expenditure equation: the equation that states that GDP is the sum of personal consumption (C), gross investment (I), government purchases (G), and net exports (X – M)

explicit costs: payments made by a business to businesses or people outside of it

exponential growth: growth that is based on a percentage change and that builds on itself

export subsidies: payments by a government to domestic exporters so that these exporters can reduce the prices they charge in foreign markets

exports: foreign purchases of Canadian goods and services

fair rate of return: the maximum accounting-profit rate allowed for a regulated monopoly

final products: products that will not be processed further and will not be resold

financial account: the summary of all foreign transactions of financial assets involving Canadian dollars

fiscal policy: government stabilization policy that uses taxes and government purchases as its tools; budgetary policy

fiscal year: the 12-month period to which a budget applies

fixed costs: economic costs for inputs that remain fixed at all quantities of output

fixed exchange rates: currency exchange rates set or "pegged" to a certain value by each country's government

fixed incomes: nominal incomes that remain fixed at some dollar amount regardless of the rate of inflation

fixed inputs: inputs whose quantities cannot be adjusted in the short run

flexible exchange rates: currency exchange rates that are allowed to move freely to their equilibrium levels; also called floating rates

foreign currency deposits: accounts of funds held by Canadian residents that are valued in foreign currency

foreign exchange market: the global market in which national currencies are traded

foreign trade effect: with changes in the price level, expenditures on imports change in the same direction, while expenditures on exports change in the opposite direction

Free Trade Agreement (FTA): the 1988 pact between Canada and the United States to form a free trade area

free trade area: an area in which trade is tariff-free, although member countries are able to impose separate trade barriers on outside countries

frictional unemployment: unemployment due to being temporarily between jobs or looking for a first job

full employment: the highest reasonable expectation of employment for the economy as a whole

fully indexed incomes: nominal incomes that automatically increase by the rate of inflation

functional finance: the principle that government budgets should be geared to the yearly needs of the economy

GDP deflator: an indicator of price changes for all goods and services produced in the economy

GDP identity: Gross Domestic Product calculated as total income is identical to Gross Domestic Product calculated as total spending

General Agreement on Tariffs and Trade (GATT): a multilateral trade agreement that lessened the degree of trade protection among member countries, including Canada

globalization: the trend of growing foreign trade and investment and the spread of international businesses and markets

government purchases: current government spending on goods and services

Gross Domestic Product: the total dollar value at current prices of all final goods and services produced in Canada over a given period

gross investment: purchases of assets that are intended to produce revenue

Gross National Product: the total income acquired by Canadians both within Canada and elsewhere

high-income countries: countries with per capita incomes substantial enough to provide their citizens with widespread prosperity

human capital: the income-earning potential of a person's skills and knowledge

immediate run: the production period during which none of the resources required to make a product can be varied

impact lag: the amount of time between a policy's implementation and its having an effect on the economy

implicit costs: the owner's opportunity costs of being involved with a business

import quota: a set limit on the quantity of a good that can be imported in a given year

imports: Canadian purchases of goods and services from the rest of the world

income approach: a method of calculating Gross Domestic Product by adding together all incomes in the economy

income elasticity: the responsiveness of a product's quantity demanded to a change in average consumer income

increase in aggregate demand: an increase in total expenditures at all price levels

increase in demand: an increase in the quantity demanded of a product at all prices

increase in supply: an increase in the quantity supplied of a product at all prices

increasing-cost industry: an industry that is a major user of at least one resource

increasing returns to scale: a situation in which a percentage increase in all inputs causes a larger percentage increase in output

independent variable: the variable in a causal relationship that causes change in another variable

industrial concentration: market domination by one or a few large businesses

industrial union: a labour union of workers in a certain industry, no matter what their occupations

industrially advanced countries (IACs): countries that have a high degree of industrialization

inelastic demand: demand for which a percentage change in a product's price causes a smaller percentage change in quantity demanded

inelastic supply: supply for which a percentage change in a product's price causes a smaller percentage change in quantity supplied

infant industry: a domestic industry that is young in comparison to its foreign competitors

inferior products: products whose demand changes inversely with income

inflation: a rise in the general level of prices

inflation premium: a percentage built into a nominal interest rate to anticipate the rate of inflation for the loan period

inflationary gap: the amount by which equilibrium output exceeds potential output

injections: additions to an eco-nomy's income-spending stream

inputs: the resources used in production

interest: the payment to a lender by the borrower for use of money loaned

intermediate products: products that will be processed further or will be resold

inventories: stocks of unsold goods and materials

inverse relationship: a relationship in which a change in the independent variable causes a change in the opposite direction of the dependent variable

investment demand: the relationship between interest rates and investment

investment demand curve: the relationship between interest rates and investment expressed on a graph

investment demand schedule: the relationship between interest rates and investment expressed in a table

item weights: the proportions of each good in the total cost of the basket of consumer goods used to calculate CPI

kinked demand curve: a demand curve with two segments, one fairly flat and one steep, that is typical of rival oligopolists

labour: human effort employed directly in production

labour force: all people who either have a job or are actively seeking employment

labour force population: the population, with specific exclusions, from which Statistics Canada takes a random sample for the labour force survey

labour-intensive process: a production process that employs more labour and less capital

labour market demand curve: a graph showing the possible combinations of workers demanded in a certain labour market at each possible wage

labour market supply curve: a graph showing the possible combinations of workers supplying their labour in a certain labour market at each possible wage

law of comparative advantage: states that maximum output is achieved when producers specialize in what they can make at a lower opportunity cost than can other producers

law of demand: states that there is an inverse relationship between a product's quantity demanded and its price

law of diminishing marginal returns: at some point, as more units of a variable input are added to a fixed input, the marginal product will start to decrease

law of increasing opportunity costs: the concept that as more of one item is produced by an economy, the opportunity cost of additional units of that product rises

law of supply: states that there is a direct relationship between a product's quantity supplied and its price

less-developed countries (LDCs): countries with traditional mixed economies and low per capita incomes

liquidity: the ease with which an asset can be converted into a means of payment

long run: the production period during which all resources required to make a product can be varied, and businesses may either enter or leave the industry

long-run aggregate supply curve: the vertical AS curve at the potential output level

long-run average cost: the minimum short-run average cost at each possible level of output

long-run decrease in aggregate supply: a decrease in total and potential output at all price levels

long-run increase in aggregate supply: an increase in total and potential output at all price levels

Lorenz curve: a graph showing the cumulative distribution of income among a country's households

low-income countries: the poorest countries in the world, as defined by per capita incomes

M1: the narrowest definition of money, consisting of currency outside chartered banks and publicly held demand deposits at chartered banks

M2: a broader definition of money, consisting of M1 plus notice deposits, and personal term deposits at chartered banks

M2+: the definition of money consisting of M2 plus corresponding deposits at near banks and some other liquid assets

M3: the definition of money consisting of M2 plus nonpersonal term deposits and foreign currency deposits at chartered banks

macroeconomics: the branch of economics that takes a wide-ranging view of the economy, studying the behaviour of economic sectors

managed float: a flexible exchange rate system that sometimes involves short-term government intervention

marginal cost: the extra cost of producing an additional unit of output

marginal-cost pricing: the practice of setting price where it equals marginal cost

marginal product: the extra output produced by an additional worker

marginal productivity theory: the theory that businesses use resources on the basis of how much extra profit these resources provide

marginal propensity to consume: the effect on domestic consumption of a change in income

marginal propensity to withdraw: the effect on withdrawals—saving, imports, and taxes—of a change in income

marginal resource cost: the extra cost of each additional unit of a resource

marginal revenue: the extra total revenue earned from an additional unit of output

marginal revenue product: the change in total revenue associated with employing each new unit of a resource

market: a set of arrangements between buyers and sellers of a certain item

market demand: the sum of all consumers' quantity demanded for a product at each price

market economy: an economic system based on private ownership and the use of markets in economic decision-making

market equilibrium: the stable point at which demand and supply curves intersect

market power: a business's ability to affect the price of the product it sells

market share: a business's proportion of total market sales

market supply: the sum of all producers' quantity supplied at each price

means testing: a procedure whereby transfer payments vary according to a recipient's income

merchandise balance of trade: merchandise export receipts minus merchandise import payments

microeconomics: the branch of economics that focuses on the behaviour of individual participants in various markets

middle-income countries: countries in which a sizable minority of the population no longer lives in acute poverty

minimum-cost pricing: the practice of setting price where it equals minimum average cost

modern mixed economy: an economic system that combines aspects of a market economy and a command economy; production decisions are made both in private markets and by government

monetary policy: government stabilization policy that uses interest rates and the money supply as its tools

money demand: the amounts of money demanded at all possible interest rates

money demand curve: money demand expressed on a graph

money demand schedule: money demand expressed in a table

money multiplier: the value by which the amount of excess reserves is multiplied to give the maximum total change in money supply

money supply: a set amount of money in the economy, as determined by government decision-makers

money supply curve: money supply expressed on a graph

money supply schedule: money supply expressed in a table

monopolistic competition: a market structure characterized by many buyers and sellers of slightly different products and easy entry to, and exit from, the industry

monopoly: a market structure characterized by only one business supplying a product with no close substitutes and restricted entry to the industry

multiplier effect: the magnified impact of a spending change on aggregate demand

mutual interdependence: the relationship between oligopolists, in which the actions of each business affect the other businesses

national income accounts: accounts showing the levels of total income and spending in the Canadian economy

National Policy: a Canadian policy initiated in 1879 that included high Canadian tariffs on manufactured imports in order to stimulate a domestic manufacturing sector

natural monopoly: a market in which only one business is economically viable because of increasing returns to scale

natural resources: the resources from nature that are used in production, including land, raw materials, and natural processes

natural unemployment rate: the unemployment rate that defines full employment

near banks: deposit-takers that are not chartered and have more specialized services; mainly trust companies, mortgage loan companies, and credit unions

near money: all deposits not included in M1, plus some other highly liquid assets

negative unplanned investment: an unintended decrease in inventories; a shortage

net domestic income: the total income earned by households supplying resources in Canada

net exports: exports minus imports

net investment: gross investment minus depreciation

net tax revenues: taxes collected, minus transfers and subsidies

newly industrializing countries (NICs): countries that recently have exhibited strong economic growth and rapid industrialization

nominal GDP: Gross Domestic Product expressed in current dollars

nominal income: income expressed in current dollars

nominal interest rate: the interest rate expressed in money terms

nondurable goods: goods that are consumed just once

nonmarket activities: productive activities that take place outside the marketplace

nonprice competition: efforts to increase demand through product differentiation, advertising, or both

non-tariff barriers (NTBs): trade barriers other than tariffs that are used to restrict imports; include import quotas, voluntary export restraints, and domestic regulations

normal products: products whose demand changes directly with income

normal profit: the minimum return necessary for owners to keep funds and their entrepreneurial skills in their business

normative economics: the study of how the economy ought to operate

North American Free Trade Agreement (NAFTA): the 1993 pact among Canada, the United States, and Mexico to form a free trade area

notice deposits: accounts of funds for which deposit-takers may require notice before withdrawals can be made

oligopoly: a market structure characterized by only a few businesses offering standard or similar products and restricted entry to the industry

open market operations: the buying and selling of bonds by the Bank of Canada

opportunity cost: the utility that could have been gained by choosing an action's best alternative

output: the quantity of a good or service that results from production

overnight rate: the interest rate on overnight loans between chartered banks and other financial institutions

partially indexed incomes: nominal incomes that increase by less than the rate of inflation

participation rate: the percentage of the entire labour force population that makes up the labour force

partnership: an unincorporated business that is owned by two or more people

peak: the point in the business cycle at which real output is at its highest

per capita GDP: GDP per person, calculated as GDP divided by population

per capita real GDP: GDP per person, expressed in constant dollars from a given year

perfect competition: a market structure characterized by many buyers and sellers of a standard product and easy entry to and exit from the industry

perfectly elastic demand: demand for which a product's price remains constant regardless of quantity demanded

perfectly elastic supply: supply for which a product's price remains constant regardless of quantity supplied

perfectly inelastic demand: demand for which a product's quantity demanded remains constant regardless of price

perfectly inelastic supply: supply for which a product's quantity supplied remains constant regardless of price

personal consumption: household spending on goods and services

personal income: the income actually received by households

personal saving: funds saved by households

Phillips curve: a curve expressing the assumed fixed and predictable inverse relationship between unemployment and inflation

portfolio investment: financial investment (purchases of stocks and bonds) that does not

give the buyer a controlling interest in the institution issuing the assets

positive economics: the study of economic facts and why the economy operates as it does

positive unplanned investment: an unintended increase in inventories; a surplus

potential output: the real output, or Gross Domestic Product, associated with full employment

poverty: a situation in which a person's income is inadequate to provide the necessities of life

poverty line: an income level below which a household is classified as poor

predatory pricing: an unfair business practice of temporarily lowering prices to drive out competitors in an industry

price ceiling: a maximum price set below equilibrium

price elasticity of demand: the responsiveness of a product's quantity demanded to a change in its price

price elasticity of supply: the responsiveness of a product's quantity supplied to a change in price

price floor: a minimum price set above equilibrium

price leadership: an understanding among oligopolists that one business will initiate all price changes in the market and the others will follow by adjusting their prices and output accordingly

prime rate: the lowest possible interest rate charged by deposit-takers on loans to their best corporate customers

principal: the amount of a loan, excluding interest

product differentiation: efforts to make a product distinct from that of competitors

product markets: markets in which consumer, or final, products are traded

production: the process of transforming a set of resources into a good or service that has economic value

production possibilities curve: a graph that illustrates the possible output combinations for an economy

production possibilities schedule: a table that shows the possible output combinations for an economy

productive efficiency: making a given quantity of output at the lowest cost

profit-maximizing employment rule: a business should use a resource up to the point where

the resource's marginal revenue product equals its marginal resource cost

profit-maximizing output rule: produce at the level of output where marginal revenue and marginal cost intersect

progressive tax: a tax that increases as a proportion of income as income increases

proportional tax: a tax that remains constant as a proportion of income for all incomes

public debt: the total amount owed by the federal government as a result of its past borrowing

public debt charges: the amounts paid out each year by the federal government to cover the interest charges on its public debt

public good: a product whose benefits cannot be restricted to certain individuals

quantity demanded: the amount of a product consumers are willing to purchase at each price

quantity supplied: the amount of a product businesses are willing to supply at each price

real expenditures: total spending in an economy, adjusted for changes in the general price level

real GDP: GDP expressed in constant dollars from a given year

real income: income expressed in constant base-year dollars

real interest rate: the nominal interest rate minus the rate of inflation

real rate of return: constant-dollar extra profit provided by a project each year stated as a percentage of the project's initial cost

recession: a decline in real output that lasts for six months or more

recessionary gap: the amount by which equilibrium output falls short of potential output

recognition lag: the amount of time it takes policy-makers to realize that a policy is needed

regressive tax: a tax that decreases as a proportion of income as income increases

rent: the payment for use of a productive resource that is available only in a fixed amount

research and development (R&D) expenditures: spending that is meant to accelerate the pace of technological progress

reserve ratio: desired reserves expressed as a percentage of deposits or as a decimal

resource markets: markets in which economic resources are traded

retained earnings: profits kept by businesses for new investment

revaluation: an increase in the value of a currency by the government that sets the exchange rate

Rule of 72: states that the number of years it takes a variable to double can be estimated by dividing 72 by the variable's annual percentage growth rate

seasonal unemployment: unemployment due to the seasonal nature of some occupations and industries

self-interest motive: the assumption that people act to maximize their own welfare

seniority rights: the workplace privileges provided to workers who have the longest experience with their employer

short run: the production period during which at least one of the resources required to make a product cannot be varied

short-run decrease in aggregate supply: a decrease in total output at all price levels, with no change in potential output

short-run increase in aggregate supply: an increase in total output at all price levels, with no change in potential output

shortage: an excess of quantity demanded over quantity supplied

shutdown point: the level of output where price (or average revenue) equals minimum average variable cost

sole proprietorship: an unincorporated business that is owned by a single person

speculators: individuals or organizations that buy and sell currencies for profit

spending multiplier: the value by which an initial spending change is multiplied to give the total change in real output

spillover benefits: positive external effects of producing or consuming a product

spillover costs: negative external effects of producing or consuming a product

spillover effects: external effects of economic activity, which have an impact on outsiders who are not producing or consuming a product

stabilization policy: government policy designed to lessen the effects of the business cycle

stagflation: a combination of consistently low output (and so constant or expanding unemployment) and rising inflation

strategic trade policy: the use of such programs as export subsidies to help domestic producers enter potentially lucrative markets

structural unemployment: unemployment due to a mismatch between people and jobs

substitute products: products that can be consumed in place of one another

substitute resources: resources that can be used in place of one another without affecting output

supply: the relationship between the various possible prices of a product and the quantities of the product that businesses are willing to supply

supply curve: a graph that expresses possible combinations of prices and quantities supplied of a product

supply determinants: factors that can cause an increase or a decrease in a product's supply

supply of Canadian dollars: the relationship between the price of a Canadian dollar and the quantity supplied in exchange for another currency

supply schedule: a table that shows possible combinations of prices and quantities supplied of a product

surplus: an excess of quantity supplied over quantity demanded

tariff: an excise tax on imported goods

technological progress: consists of scientific discoveries and their application, advances in production methods, and the development of new types of products

term deposits: accounts of funds to which depositors have no access for a fixed period of time

terms of trade: the international price of one product in terms of another

total cost: the sum of all fixed and variable costs at each quantity of output

total product: the overall quantity of output produced with a given workforce

total revenue: the total income earned from a product, calculated by multiplying the product's price by its quantity demanded

trading bloc: a relatively small number of countries involved in a trade agreement

traditional economy: an economic system in which economic decisions are made on the basis of custom

traditional mixed economies: economic systems in which a traditional sector co-exists with modern sectors

transactions demand: the demand for money that is related to its use as a means of exchange

transfer payments: government payments to households or other levels of government

treasury bills: short-term federal government bonds that provide no interest but are sold at a discount

trough: the point in the business cycle at which real output is at its lowest

underemployment: the problem of workers being underutilized, either as part-time work-

ers or by working at jobs not appropriate to their skills or education

underground economy: all the market transactions that go unreported

unemployment rate: the percentage of a labour force that is involuntarily unemployed

unit-elastic demand: demand for which a percentage change in price causes an equal change in quantity demanded

unit of account: a pricing standard that allows all products to be valued consistently

universality: the principle applied to transfer payments, whereby benefits are provided to all, regardless of income

utility: the satisfaction gained from any action

value added: the extra worth of a product at each stage in its production; a concept used to avoid double-counting in calculating GDP

variable costs: economic costs for inputs that vary at each quantity of output

variable inputs: inputs whose quantities can be adjusted in the short run

variables: factors that have measurable values

velocity of money: the number of times, on average, that money is spent on final goods and services during a given year (a concept that is central to monetarism)

vicious circle of poverty: a cycle whereby low standards of living result in slow growth, thus keeping standards of living low in the future

voluntary export restraints (VERs): import quotas that are voluntarily put in place by the exporting country

wealth: ownership of financial assets, such as stocks and bonds, or real assets, such as buildings and land

wealth effect: with changes in the price level, the real value of households' financial assets changes, causing households to adjust their spending

welfare society: a society in which the government plays a major role in attempting to ensure the economic well-being of its citizens

withdrawals: deductions from an economy's income-spending stream

working to rule: the union tactic of members slowing down work by adhering strictly to their job descriptions

World Bank: an international lending institution known officially as the International Bank for Reconstruction and Development

World Trade Organization (WTO): a multilateral trade organization that has replaced GATT

Index